The Shaping of
Modern Psychology

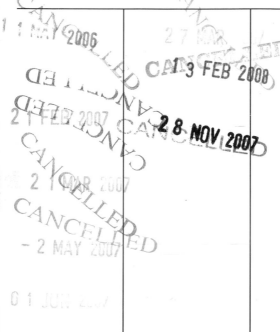

The Shaping of
Modern Psychology

L.S. Hearnshaw

Routledge
London and New York

First published in 1987 by
Routledge & Kegan Paul Ltd

Reprinted 1989
by Routledge
11 New Fetter Lane, London EC4P 4EE
29 West 35th Street, New York, NY 10001

Set in 10 on 11 point Times
by Columns of Reading
and printed in Great Britain
by T.J. Press (Padstow) Ltd
Padstow, Cornwall

British Library Cataloguing in Publication Data

Hearnshaw, L.S. (Leslie Spencer)
    The shaping of modern psychology
    1. Psychology, history
    I. Title
    150'.9

Library of Congress Cataloging in Publication Data

Hearnshaw, L.S. (Leslie Spencer)
    The shaping of modern psychology.
    Bibliography: p.
    Includes indexes.
    1. Psychology – History   I. Title. [DLNM:
    1. Psychology – history. BF 81 H436sb]
    BF81.H33   1986   150'.9   86-10115

ISBN 0-415-03903-7

Contents

Preface

The last quarter of a century has seen a remarkable growth of interest among psychologists in the history of their subject. Specialized journals have appeared; societies and groups devoted to the history of the behavioural sciences have been established; archives have been founded; and, particularly in America, there has been a spate of texts and monographs devoted to the history of psychology. If, as E.G. Boring maintained in the preface of his well-known *History of Experimental Psychology* (1929), historical sophistication is necessary for the working psychologist, this is all to the good. The very proliferation of historical studies and historical material, however, brings its own dangers. There is a risk of the subject being swamped in detail; of its becoming the preserve of specialists; of its turning into an inward-looking subdivision making very little impact by reason of its complexity and abstruseness on psychology as a whole. There is a need to correct these tendencies by means of synoptic surveys.

This book sets out to provide such a survey of the entire historical development of psychology from the dawn of civilization to the present day. It is not, and could not be, a detailed history. Many psychologists who have contributed significantly to the development of the subject receive no mention at all, particularly when it comes to the modern age. Not merely every chapter, but each section of every chapter, could easily be expanded into a separate volume. The mass of detail would then, however, be so great that the practising psychologist would simply put it aside and get on with his job, whether in research or application. The only way to provide a synoptic view is to eschew excessive detail and concentrate on the main influences that have shaped psychology in its development. I hope that extensive quotation from primary sources will awaken further interest, and that plentiful references to the literature will encourage psychologists, and not only psychologists, to take an interest in man's long struggle to understand his own mental make-up.

I myself became interested in the history of psychology in the early 1930s when I studied psychology at London University under Professors Francis Aveling and Charles Spearman, both of whom were mines of historical knowledge as well as having had first-hand contact with some of the founders of experimental psychology. To supplement the titbits of history scattered in various courses students were encouraged to read Gardner Murphy's *Historical Introduction to Modern Psychology* (1929), the first edition of which had just been published. I found this book more helpful than anything else in integrating the diverse and often conflicting data of psychology and in giving me a general conspectus of the subject, and when I came to teach psychology at the University of Liverpool, I introduced a full course on the history of psychology, which I believe many students found useful in providing general orientation.

The present book is based on a series of lectures which I gave at the University of Western Australia in 1976. It has been much revised, amplified and updated since then. I must thank Professor Aubrey Yates of that University for inviting me to give the course, and also various psychologists who have read and commented on draft chapters. Thanks are also due to the University of Liverpool, particularly to the University Library, and to Professor Dennis Bromley and the Department of Psychology for granting me office space in the department and the use of its facilities after my retirement from the staff. I am grateful to Professor Helio Carpintero, Editor of the Spanish journal *Revista de Historia de la Psicologia*, for permission to use the article on Francis Bacon which was published in his journal (1985.I) Finally I owe special thanks to my wife, Dr Gwenneth Hearnshaw, for her careful reading of my manuscript and proofs, and to my daughter, Carolyn Woollard, for comments on several chapters.

Chapter 1
Introduction

At the beginning of the nineteenth century the term 'psychology' was almost unknown in the English-speaking world. It was described by the philosopher-poet Coleridge as an 'insolens verbum' (an outlandish word), but nevertheless 'one of which our language stands in great need'.[1] Today it is commonplace. Nearly every university in the developed world provides instruction in psychology; psychologists are widely employed in many areas of public service, particularly health and education; and considerable sums of money are devoted to psychological research. At international gatherings of psychologists thousands of psychologists from sixty or more countries meet periodically to discuss a vast range of problems, both theoretical and applied. How has this rapid growth come about? Upon what foundations does it rest? What is the present state of psychology, and what are its prospects? It is to these questions that this book is addressed. It sets out to explore how modern psychology has been shaped by its history.

The relevance of history to a subject which professes to be scientific has often been questioned. The scientific revolution, which began in the sixteenth century and inaugurated the modern age, involved a widespread rejection of the classical and medieval past. According to Francis Bacon, 'science is to be sought from the light of nature, not from the darkness of antiquity. It matters not what has been done, our business is to see what can be done.'[2] The right road for the scientist is, in other words, not the study of history, but the active prosecution of research. His job is to create the future, not to cling to the past. Many psychologists from the time of Hobbes and Descartes onwards have echoed this sentiment. Wundt, the father of modern experimental psychology, proclaimed his intention of establishing psychology on new foundations, and in his massive textbook made few references to anyone prior to the nineteenth century.[3] The behaviourists, from their pioneer Watson to the contemporary Skinner have made it clear that they totally reject the historical past of psychology.[4] Prescientific views of human behaviour can, according to them, provide no help towards the creation of scientific psychology. Indeed for many psychologists their past history has come to seem irrelevant: the case for studying it must, therefore, be explicitly established.

It may first be worth observing that these rejections by psychologists of the views of their predecessors have never so far, in fact, been effective. Past concepts and past theories have persistently recrudesced; they have obstinately refused to die. Leibniz revived the 'philosophia perennis' that had earlier been cast aside; Brentano, a contemporary of Wundt, based his empirical psychology largely upon Aristotle; consciousness and the 'inner world', which the behaviourists banished, have once again crept back into psychology; and the faculties of the mind, whose death knell was sounded by Herbart at the beginning of the nineteenth century, have been restored to life by a leading philosopher of psychology of our own day.[5] So it would seem that there was more of value in the prescientific musings of the past than scientific purists have been prepared to admit, and perhaps it is still worth paying some attention to them.

But such recrudescences are not decisive. They may simply imply that psychology has imperfectly emerged from the prescientific to the scientific stage, that it is what Kuhn, the philosophic historian of science, has termed a 'proto-science'[6] The question involves deeper issues in the philosophy and history of science – issues which have been widely debated in the period since the Second World War. Is science a progressive enterprise, as Popper has proposed, slowly but surely building an edifice of truth, all the time approaching more closely to the real nature of things?[7] Or is it, according to Kuhn, subject to fashions and revolutions, one stage succeeding another without any continuity between them, and without logical development or convergence towards verisimilitude?[8] Or again is science, in Feyerabend's words, merely a 'fairy tale', with 'no greater authority than any other form of life', and no nearer the nature of things, in fact, than religion, myth, magic and witchcraft, which may indeed show greater insight than 'the most enlightened scientific doctrines'?[9] In any case, where does psychology stand in the scientific league? These are profound questions, which cannot be treated adequately in a short introductory chapter; but it is clearly necessary, before embarking on a historical study of psychology, to adopt some sort of standpoint towards them, as the meaning and relevance of the past is dependent on the answers given.

II

The rapid growth of psychology during the past hundred years together with its widespread application has rested on the assumption that psychology in the last half of the nineteenth century underwent a metamorphosis from speculative philosophy to scientific discipline. When this transition took place, science, and in particular the physical sciences, seemed to rest on solid foundations, and to constitute a continuously progressive enterprise converging towards an ever closer approximation to an understanding of the real nature of things. In the twentieth century, and particularly in the last few decades, there has been an erosion of this confidence. Not only has there been concern about the social effects of science, but doubts as to its objectivity. Even Popper, the champion of objective knowledge, has admitted that 'science does not rest upon solid bedrock. The bold structure of its theories rises, as it were, above a swamp. It is like a building erected on piles.'[10] The sociologists of knowledge go much further and maintain that all theories, even those of fundamental physics, are socially and historically relative, and based on nothing more than the consensus of the community of scientists. Such doubts, not surprisingly, have begun to undermine the confidence of at least some psychologists. If psychology is to progress they need answering.

One fact seems indisputable: scientific knowledge is extremely effective knowledge. As Bacon foresaw more than three centuries ago, it is capable of producing 'fruits'.[11] It cannot plausibly be maintained, as several contemporary philosophers of science have argued, that it rests on no more than 'the consensus of the scientific community',[12] which is something that might change when scientific and social fashions change. The consensus of the scientific community, however complete, could not on its own produce 'fruits' of the sort that science is capable of producing. Such 'fruits' can only spring from real insight, even if only partial insight, into the nature of things. Nuclear fission could not have been achieved unless the theories of the physicists had arrived at some measure of correspondence with the realities of atomic structure. Nor would genetic engineering have become a practical possibility without the cracking of the genetic code by Watson and Crick and their successors. Far from Feyerabend's contention that 'anything goes',[13] it rather appears that only that which is dead right 'goes'. No doubt science is dependent on social support and is coloured by social influences; no doubt there are subjective and personal elements in all knowledge, as Polanyi has maintained;[14] but the essential feature of science is that it rests upon methodological principles which enable it in the end to transcend the relative, the subjective and the conditioned, and to arrive at what Popper terms 'objective knowledge'.[15] The corpus of objective knowledge is a developing one, not perhaps in the simple nineteenth century sense, but as the outcome of 'the repeated overthrow of scientific theories and their replacement by better and more satisfactory ones'.[16] This does not imply, in Popper's view, scientific revolutions of the Kuhnian type, in which the past is expunged following a sort of 'conversion experience',[17] but a continuous critical examination of traditional views. Tradition is the necessary basis for future discovery; it constitutes the piles in the swamp. 'If you have nothing to alter and to change you can never get anywhere. . . . Human thought in general, and science in particular, are all products of human history.'[18] To discard the past is, therefore, to destroy the possibility of progress. No scientific revolution has, in fact, done this. There is always a continuity of development beneath the paradigmatic changes of scientific revolutions. As Hooykaas, the Dutch historian of science has pointed out, 'whatever the sixteenth and seventeenth centuries may have rejected of the ancient scientific heritage, they continued to use parts of it – logic, mathematics and experimentation'.[19] All ideas have their ancestry. That briefly is the justification for the study of the history of science. The special problems of psychology make the study of its history all the more pertinent.

III

It can hardly be denied that psychology is still in some ways a problematic science. It has not been as successful as was at one time hoped at disentangling itself from the swaddling clothes of philosophy. Problems relating to topics such as subjectivity, consciousness, intentionality, representation and voluntary activity obstinately refuse to disappear. Philosophical critiques of psychology from Kantian times onwards, instead of diminishing as psychologists attempted to establish their independence, have gathered in number and force.[20] Though the tougher-minded psychologists tend to dismiss them as irrelevant and to immerse themselves in their experimental investigations, it would be unwise not to take seriously the reasoned comments of able and often profound thinkers, particularly as a growing number of psychologists have come to have misgivings as to the road psychology has taken, and its adherence to a methodological orthodoxy derived from the physical sciences. The American psychologist, K.J. Gergen, recently wrote of 'the pervasive discontent with the outcome of traditional research pursuits', noted 'the generalized ferment in psychology', and listed a string of eminent psychologists bemoaning the state of their subject.[21]

A characteristic feature of recent years has been the search for alternative approaches to psychology, and a revival of views asserting the differing foundations, and consequently the differing methodologies, of the natural and the human sciences. These views can be traced back into the nineteenth century and indeed earlier, but were generally until comparatively recently resisted by psychologists, particularly those within the Anglo-Saxon tradition. Now they are beginning to capture an audience. Take, for instance, two contemporary examples: Gergen in America and Harré in England. Gergen claims that human beings show 'unlimited potential for variation. . . . So there appears little justification for the immense effort devoted to empirical substantiation of fundamental laws of human conduct. . . . The sociobehavioral sciences are essentially non-empirical.' And he concludes by proposing 'a metatheoretic basis for a unified alternative'.[22] In England Harré has somewhat similarly put forward an 'ethogenic alternative' to conventional psychology, based largely on ordinary language philosophy, the expressive aspect of human conduct, and the ability of human beings to follow rules and plans.[23]

These critiques and proposals cannot be dismissed offhand. They undoubtedly point to certain weaknesses in orthodox systems of psychology, particularly those of a behaviouristic kind. It must, moreover, be admitted that, judged by strictly pragmatic criteria, the success of psychology in practice has been a limited one. Confronted by the acid test of its power to change human behaviour, and to foretell outcomes, it has not got far, and before many obstinate problems, such as delinquency, drug addiction, obsessional behaviour, and violence, it remains largely impotent. That being so it would be unwise to preclude new initiatives, and to decry the value of unorthodox speculation. Nevertheless doubts arise as to the soundness of the initiatives of the Gergen-Harré school of thought. They have provided little hard evidence that their proposals are capable of producing 'fruits'; they are prone to undue verbalism and reliance on linguistic analysis; they have not demonstrated sufficiently cogently that there must be a methodological dichotomy between the natural and the human sciences; and finally their disillusionment with more orthodox approaches to psychology is unnecessarily severe. In spite of the problems with which it is confronted, psychology, as we shall see, has produced some 'fruits', and it has considerably clarified its subject matter.

At the heart of the difficulties relating to psychology lies the fact that psychology is an unusual science, in that in part it is unavoidably reflexive, that is to say that in psychologizing the mind is turning back upon itself. This inevitably creates special problems. There are two ways of dealing with this peculiarity, this element of uniqueness: it can be argued, on the one hand, that the subject matter of psychology is so special that the methods of the natural sciences are wholly inappropriate, and that entirely different approaches are needed; or, alternatively, it can be argued that scientific methodology has been conceived too narrowly, that it can be expanded, without abandoning the Popperian schema of conjecture and refutation, to cope with the special features of psychology. In line with this second view psychology requires what the French social psychologist, Moscovici, has termed a 'polythéisme méthodologique', that is an adherence to a diversity of methodological practices.[24] Perhaps the answer to the contemporary problems of psychology lies in boldness of imagination within the context of science, rather than in revolutionary despair in the garments of philosophy.

In this scenario the history of psychology has a threefold value. It is, firstly, a rich store of material, of problems and ideas. The past cannot usually provide answers; it cannot, as some historians have supposed, predict the future, nor does it contain a 'prophetic element';[25] but it is one source of questions and problems, and it is from questions and problems that scientific research derives its momentum. Secondly, history provides a sense of direction. It is easy for the working scientist to get bogged down with detail and routine, and to lose the larger perspective. History can enlarge the vision, enable him to stand back from his immediate task, and act as a safeguard against one-sidedness. Psychology, because it remains less surely founded than more advanced sciences, is still unduly subject to fads, fashions and extravagances. These are time-consuming and damaging. Speculation certainly must not be constrained, but to be valuable it needs grounding in tradition; and history is a storehouse of tradition. Finally a study of the history of psychology refutes the contention that the subject has not progressed. Half a century ago the eminent German psychologist William Stern made the claim that the picture of the human mind drawn by contemporary psychologists was incomparably richer than that of earlier ages.[26] Since Stern wrote the picture has been much further enriched. If today psychologists shiver in 'a winter of discontent', as Jerome Bruner maintains they do,[27] it must be because they have forgotten their history, have lost touch with the inspiration it provides, and are out of tune with the slow march of time. Hope for the future is closely linked with an appreciation of the past. There are good grounds, therefore, for looking at the way in which psychology has been shaped by its history, including its distant prehistory.

Chapter 2
Animistic beginnings

I

'The most ancient times', observed Bacon, 'are buried in oblivion and silence',[1] and this is certainly true of men's earliest speculations and beliefs concerning their own nature. The obscurity, however, is today not quite so dense as it was in Bacon's time. Some scraps of information about the prehistory of man during the three or so million years that he has been distinguishable from the anthropoid stock have emerged from excavations in Africa and elsewhere; while anthropological studies of still primitive and isolated peoples, even though they are several stages removed from human origins, have made possible tentative reconstructions of prehistoric man and his mode of life. From these gleanings a few crumbs of primeval psychology may be derived.

By the time he had become recognizably human man had already acquired a larger brain and an upright stance, and differentiated himself from other anthropoids by his taste for meat, a food preference which, it has been suggested, may have considerably affected both his biological and his cultural evolution.[2] For countless ages, before his first agricultural settlements were established in the river valleys of the Middle East around 10,000 BC, man lived in small tribal groups sustained by hunting and gathering. During this, by historical standards, immense span of time he spread across most of the globe and slowly laid the foundations for his subsequent cultural achievements. He acquired language; developed primitive tools; discovered the use of fire; began to bury his dead; and, towards the end of the prehistoric period some 50,000 years ago, began to express himself artistically in paintings, carvings and the making of ornaments. It has been suggested by Jung[3] that behind all these achievements was the coming of consciousness itself, and that this was in reality 'the most tremendous experience of primeval times'. In an eloquent and moving profession of faith Jung proclaims;

> I believe that, after thousands and millions of years, someone had to realise that this wonderful world of mountains and oceans, suns and moons, galaxies and nebulae, plants and animals, *exists*. From a low hill in the plains of East Africa I once watched the vast herds of wild animals grazing in soundless stillness, as they had done from time immemorial, touched only by the breath of a primeval world. I felt

7

then as if I were the first man, the first creature, to know that all this *is*. The entire world around me was still in its primeval state; it did not know that it *was*. And then, in that one moment in which I came to know, the world sprang into being; without that moment it would never have been. All Nature seeks this goal and finds it fulfilled in man, but only in the most highly-developed and most fully conscious man.

Beneath Jung's flights of fancy there is a hard core of fact. Animals are not conscious in the human sense. Human consciousness involves an integration of time, an awareness not merely of the present but of the past and the future, a grasp of enduring features that lie behind the passing moment.[4] This is what even intelligent animals like chimpanzees appear to lack, and it was considered by Köhler to be 'the chief difference between anthropoids and even the most primitive human beings'.[5] So Jung was in all probability right in regarding the coming of consciousness and the most momentous experience of primeval man. Certainly by the time he had achieved artistic expression man was actively conscious of the world around him; and by the time he had begun to bury his dead with provision for a hereafter, he was tacitly postulating a part of himself which survived death. In these experiences lie the seeds of a primitive psychology. For glimmerings of what this psychology might have been we must turn to anthropological evidence.

II

Among the best documented of the primitive peoples studied by anthropologists are the Australian aborigines.[6] Almost totally isolated from the rest of humanity for tens of thousands of years, when Australia was opened up for western European colonization at the end of the eighteenth century the aborigines were still living in a stone age culture, comparable technologically and in many respects culturally to those that prevailed during the ice ages, and it was only gradually as the white man spread over the continent that their ancient ways of life began to disappear. The first anthropologists caught them just in time while their culture remained intact. They still lived then, as they had always lived, in semi-nomadic tribes, averaging some five hundred individuals in number. They wandered over territories of varied size and subsisted by hunting and gathering. These aborigines constructed rough temporary shelters, but had no settled villages, no domesticated animals apart from tamed dingo dogs, relatively few material possessions, and little or no clothing. Each tribe had its own language and its own social structures, which were often complex and determined the relations of the sexes. Tools, baskets and weapons were carefully and skilfully devised, and the arts, particularly the decorative and pictorial, expertly practised. Underpinning the whole structure of life, social, economic and artistic, was an elaborate system of mythical ideas and beliefs, which expressed the essential unity of man and nature, the earth and all the creatures therein, and the solidarity of the present with the ancestral spirit beings of 'the eternal dreamtime'. The 'dreaming' permeated all aspects of aboriginal life, gave it meaning and endowed it with a deeply felt spiritual character. 'He who loses his dreaming is lost,' proclaimed aboriginal lore. 'The eternal dreamtime' integrated the world; but it was a unity of feeling, expressed in myth and ritual, rather than an articulated body of thought in which subject and object, spirit and matter were abstracted and distinguished. Reality was spiritual; spirit pervaded all time and space, endowing the world with life and meaning. The core of each person, his real self, belonged to the spiritual and sacred sphere; it came from a pre-existing world of spirits, descending from spirit ancestors, and it returned after death to its spirit home. But the spiritual and sacred were not divorced from the natural world and the material body. The material world was itself impregnated with spiritual qualities. Objects were sacred, and animal and plant species were spiritually linked with man through totemic cults. As Lévy-Bruhl observed, 'To the mind of the primitive there is existent and permeating on earth, in the air and on the water, in all the diverse forms assumed by persons and objects, one and the same essential reality; both one and multiple, both material and spiritual.'[7] This pervading quality was termed by the Melanesians 'Mana'.[8]

There is little psychology in the modern sense in these vague and mythically expressed ideas. Brett even denied that speculation about the supernatural soul made any significant contributions to western psychology.[9] Yet perhaps in coming to this conclusion Brett was wrong; while Jung was right in stressing the persistence of 'archaic thought forms imbued with ancestral or historical feelings, and beyond them the sense of indefiniteness, timelessness, oneness'.[10] William James certainly believed that primitive thought was far from dead.[11] It survives unquestionably in the occult cults of the contemporary world. But perhaps there is more to it than that; perhaps in its tacit denial of subject-object differentiation there was an essential and important core of truth, and possibly some of man's intellectual and practical strivings seek to restore the lost unity of primeval man's outlook.

III

Beliefs and practices comparable to those of the Australian aborigines prevailed, we may presume, for many millennia in prehistoric times, almost certainly at least as far back in time as the earliest burials. In his immense review of primitive thought Frazer noted 'the essential similarity with which under many superficial differences the human mind has elaborated its first crude philosophy of life'.[12] The philosophy was termed by Tylor, the father of British social anthropology, 'animism'.[13]

From the barely differentiated 'dreaming' of the aborigines' animism developed in three directions. In the supernatural sphere, which nevertheless exerted a potent influence on earth, a host of spiritual beings (gods, demons, devils, ghosts and so on) proliferated; in the world of nature animal souls, plant souls and object souls accounted for the way natural objects and living things functioned or behaved; and with regard to man himself spiritual potencies explained the vicissitudes of his experiences and the fluctuations of his behaviour and destiny. The very universality of these beliefs suggests that they must be based on universal features of human experience. Tylor himself attributed them to dreams and visions; Crawley attributed them to the workings of the imagination and memory.[14] Jung postulated 'archytypes' in the unconscious.

Whether these beliefs can be dignified with the title of 'philosophy' is perhaps open to question. But they do represent an 'effort after meaning',[15] and this 'effort after meaning' was equally a characteristic feature of primitive as of contemporary man. As soon as he became actively conscious man must inevitably have searched for meanings; he possessed by the time consciousness dawned an urge to symbolize; for he was, and is, as Cassirer maintained,[16] essentially an 'animal symbolicum', who needed to represent and explain, and, above all, in the uncertain world of primitive life, to account for the vicissitudes of his own experiences, for illness and fluctuations of vitality, the destructive passions of fear, rage and frenzy, the uncanny phenomena of sleep and dreams, the occasional flashes of inspiration, and the final mystery of death. He did this by postulating a soul, or souls, separable from the body, souls which came and went, which could journey in dreams away from the body, could lodge in other bodies and take possession of them, or could be taken possession of by alien souls, and which finally departed to a spirit world at death. The soul was conceived most often as a tenuous physical substance, such as wind or breath.

During the long primeval period of humanity the rate of change by historical standards was extremely slow. The technology of the paleolithic period hardly progressed for millennia, and systems of belief, we may suppose, were equally static. It is only when we come to the more advanced cultures of the neolithic period that we find signs of elaboration, for instance, to select one example from a multitude, in the spiritual and mental concepts of the New Zealand Maori.[17]

The New Zealand Maori were culturally and technologically considerably more advanced than the Australian aborigines. In the fourteenth century AD they had reached their new homeland from Polynesia by skilfully navigating their ocean-going canoes across thousands of miles of the South Pacific. They established permanent settlements with well-constructed and elaborately carved meeting houses and store houses; though still lacking flocks and herds and the use of metals, they tilled the soil, grew various crops, and practised weaving. They believed in a vast number of deities and spiritual beings dominated by the supreme deity, Io. Man inherited a portion of the divine nature (the *ira atua*), and this spark in man was sacred (*tapu*). It represented his true vitality, and was the source of his physical and moral welfare. It had above all things to be protected from pollution.

Once defiled its owner was rendered helpless, for the links between himself and the powers ruling the world were broken. Maori psychology was based, like that of the more primitive aborigines, on a deep feeling of unity between man and nature, between man and the powers of the spirit world, and between the individual and his fellow tribesmen.

The soul of man (the *wairua*), which departed from the body at death and during dreaming sleep, was not located in any particular organ. It was conceived as a tenuous material substance, which could actually be seen by persons possessed of second sight. After death its material elements were sloughed off, and it became a refined, immaterial, immortal spirit (the *awe*). The *wairua* was not the only spiritual principle. There was also a life principle (*mauri*) which could not leave the body, and which ceased to exist at death. Everything possessed a *mauri*, both living things and non-living. Then there was a principle of vitality (*hau*) which fluctuated according to the vigour of its owner, and flagged in sickness and old age. A distinction was made between thought (*hinegaro*), memory (*mahara*) and feelings (*ngakau*), and these were variously located in the heart, stomach and bowels. Psychological analysis went little further than this.

Indeed no significant psychological advances were made even in the much more complex civilizations that arose in the river valleys of the Middle East from 10,000 BC onwards.[18] The Egyptian *ka* (spiritual principle) was remarkably similar to the Maori *wairua*, and was central to the elaborate Egyptian cult of the dead, while the *bai* was a more tangible life principle. The heart was regarded as the seat of the intellect and the emotions, and the various sense organs were regarded as conveying their messages to the heart. The role of thought and speech as the ruling parts of the soul were recognized in an early medical text dating from the fourth millennium BC. In Mesopotamia and in Egypt these psychological ideas were backed up by what has been termed a 'chaotic polytheism'.

This was essentially the situation when European civilization dawned. Our earliest ideas of European psychology may be gleaned from the writings of Homer and Hesiod, which predated the intellectual revolution which began to change the face of European thought so profoundly in the sixth century BC. The soul ($\psi\upsilon\chi\eta$) was the principle of life and departed from the body at death. It was tenuously material, and identified most often with breath, from which the word derived. There was a distinction between intellectual function ($\nu o\tilde{\upsilon}\varsigma$ – mind) and emotions ($\theta\upsilon\mu\acute{o}\varsigma$ – desire, anger, courage). There was a general location of these functions in the middle parts of the body, the heart, the diaphragm ($\phi\varrho\acute{\eta}\nu$) and bowels. Not only was the terminology employed vague and shifting, but the distinction between functions and their localizations was imprecise and varying. There was as yet no systematically worked out psychology. As Onians,[19] who collated this early European material with meticulous thoroughness, observed, there was a close affinity between these vague conceptions and those of the Celtic, Slavic, Germanic and other Indo-European peoples, as well as those of the Egytians, Babylonians and Jews. It constituted the common matrix from which systematic psychology developed.

IV

In many ways animism in its primitive forms was a crude and credulous philosophy. It was wholly uncritical, it confused images and feelings with reality, and mere projections with the world outside, it was static and readily became superstitious, moreover when used magically to influence the course of events, to cure disease and promote the fertility of nature, it was largely ineffective.[20] Only deep-seated roots in human nature itself, and perhaps a central core of truth embedded in some of its vaguely formulated ideas, can account for its long endurance. For although the advance of science has gradually expelled animism from explanations of the physical, and more recently the biological, realm, animistic ideas are still prevalent, and the battle within psychology itself, in spite of a century of scientific endeavour and the spread of behaviourism, is far from settled. Hebb not so long ago[21] complained of the 'smell of animism' that still persisted in contemporary psychology, and since he wrote the smell has got stronger, not weaker.

Animism, of course, since primeval times has been enormously refined, particularly under the influence of high religions such as Judaism, Christianity and Buddhism, and by philosophic thinkers of idealistic persuasion. These developments will be touched on in later chapters. These refined forms of animism, central to religious belief, have exerted a powerful influence over even the most intelligent minds, and cruder vestiges (occultism, spiritualism, witchcraft, etc.) have survived and constantly recrudesced throughout the civilized era. Even professedly materialistic regimes have been unable to suppress animistic beliefs, and in western civilization some of the most eminent thinkers have unashamedly supported animism – in psychology, for example, Fechner, McDougall and Jung; while the recent growth of interest in consciousness, meditation and existential philosophies is strongly coloured by animistic ideas. The collapse of materialistic and mechanical explanations within the physical sciences has certainly helped to promote an animistic revival, and forced us to consider the possibility that within the luxuriant profusion of animistic ideas there may indeed be a central core of truth.

The philosopher Popper has recently put forward such a view, and summarized the significant psychological insights of primitive and prehistoric man.[22]

Death and its inevitability are discovered; the theory is accepted that states of sleep and of unconsciousness are related to death and that it is consciousness or spirit or mind which 'leaves' us at death. The doctrine of the reality, and therefore the materiality and substantiality of consciousness – of the soul or mind – is developed, and further the doctrine of the complexity of the soul or mind: desire, fear, anger, intellect, reason or insight are distinguished. Dream experience and states of divine inspiration and possession and other abnormal states are recognised, also involuntary and unconscious mental states (such as those of witches). The soul is regarded as the 'mover' of the living body, or as the principle of life. Also the problem of our lack of responsibility for unintentional acts or acts committed in abnormal states (of frenzy) is grasped. The problem of the position of the soul in the body is raised, and usually answered by the theory that it pervades the body, and is centred in the heart and lungs.

These insights were the starting point for the more systematic psychologies of the future, and were important as such. But even more important was the tacit recognition in these primitive forms of animism of the soul as an active agent, a principle of movement and feeling – a recognition that the visible body was not self-sufficient, but that there was something within man which accounted for his experiences and behaviour, and which bound him in sympathy not only with his fellow beings, but with nature and the supernatural. These insights have not always been accepted, indeed they have frequently in recent times been openly rejected by psychologists. Nevertheless they have played, and continue to play, a far from insignificant part in the shaping of psychology.

Chapter 3
Greek philosophers

I

Systematic psychology originated in Ancient Greece, and was an outcome of the revolutionary changes in modes of thinking which first clearly manifested themselves in the sixth century BC. The collapse of the earlier Mycenean civilization in the Aegean around 1150 BC was followed by a dark age lasting some three hundred years, during which the mainland of Greece was occupied by Dorian invaders, and the Asia Minor coast by Ionian settlers. By the eighth century a new civilization was beginning to emerge. A new alphabet, derived from Phoenicia but elaborated by the invention of vowels, formed the basis of a spreading literacy, the poets Homer and Hesiod provided the Greeks with a cultural identity, and the Olympic Games, first held in 776 BC, provided an institutional focus. More settled conditions, and technological improvements in metal working, pottery and other crafts, led to economic advances and a large growth of population, which was a main cause for promoting the establishment of Greek colonies throughout the Mediterranean basin. The Greeks were essentially seafarers and traders, living dangerously on the fringes, and under the shadow of, more powerful or more barbarous communities. This was the background of the astonishing flowering of the Greek genius, which occurred roughly between 600 and 300 BC and of which the creation of psychology was a part.[1]

This flowering of the Greek genius was characterized above all by the emergence of a new mode of thinking. Of course, men had engaged in thought before; they had solved technical problems, made plans, created things, and administered quite complex communities. But when not tied to immediately practical ends their thinking was mythical and imaginative.[2] They measured, but did not abstract from their measurements the axioms of arithmetic and geometry; they solved problems, but did not formulate the principles of logic; they believed, but did not critically analyse or question their beliefs Their curiosity as to the nature of the world and the meaning of life was satisfied by myths and theogonies. Their thinking was still at what Piaget has called the level of 'concrete operations'.[3] With the Greeks something different was born: abstract, critical, sceptical thinking, science of a theoretical kind, speculative philosophy and logic. The Greeks were the first men to attain to the level of Piaget's 'formal operations'.

14

What can explain this phenomenon? Why, after several thousands of years of urban civilization, did this sudden change in the manner of human thinking occur, a change which in the course of three hundred years totally transformed the intellectual environment? Probably many factors were involved, and it would be a mistake to lay too much stress on any one. The spread of literacy, facilitated by the new alphabet, was no doubt contributory. Goody has argued that it was the main explanation, and that 'writing, and more especially alphabetic literacy, made it possible to serialise discourse in a different kind of way by giving oral communication a semi-permanent form', which 'enabled man to stand back from his creation and examine it in a more abstract, generalised and rational way'.[4] Marxist theorists have argued that new modes of production and exchange rendered possible by the invention of coinage at the end of the seventh century BC were the basic reason. 'The old relations and ideas were dissolved and replaced by new relations and ideas, which being based on money, were abstract. This was the origin of philosophy.'[5] Both these explanations seem over-simple. As Dodds observed, 'the evolution of a culture is too complex a thing to be explained without residue in terms of any simple formula.'[6] The city states of ancient Greece were unusual institutions. They were small, self-governing communities, not dominated by centralized bureaucracies or priesthoods, and granting to their full citizens an exceptional degree of personal freedom and freedom of speech. Trading and navigation brought them into contact with a variety of different cultures, practices and beliefs, and encouraged individualism. In the colonies, in particular, colonists were compelled to make new starts and were to some extent released from old constraints – and it was on the fringes of the Greek world, in Asia Minor and Italy, that the new philosophies were born. The emergence of new modes of thinking must be attributed to a whole complex of novel and unique social circumstances.

The essence of the new mentality was critical doubt, the questioning of appearances and conventional beliefs, and the search for underlying reality. The philosophers commonly known as the Pre-Socratics, of whom the first was Thales of Miletus (c. 585 BC), gave what may seem odd answers to their questions[7] – water, air, or four basic elements (earth, air, fire and water), mind, numbers, the unbounded, the One, or a multiplicity of atoms were all proposed as basic reality. Some thinkers, like Heraclitus, doubted there was any permanent reality: all was flux, change and strife. As Bertrand Russell, however, has remarked[8] it is not the answers given, but the attempts that were made, that were important; and perhaps even more important was the critical argument, the conjectures and refutations, to which their theories gave rise.

The outcome of the intellectual mêlée was the emergence of two main lines of thought, materialistic and idealistic. These two lines of thought have divided thinkers ever since Greek times; they are mirrored in the ideological differences of the modern world, and, within psychology, in the opposing standpoints of the major contemporary schools. The first outcome of critical thinking was to shatter the consensus of more primitive cultures, to fracture what Dodds has called 'the inherited conglomerate'.[9] Critical thinking brought strife, controversy and what the Greeks termed στάσις (faction) in society; it also, of course, brought striking intellectual gains.

The basic divide between materialists and idealists was a product of starting point and method. Materialists began with simple material elements and reduced the complex to the simple; idealists began with the complex totality and regarded all else as derivative. This process of schismogenesis did not take place at once. The early Ionian materialists were not undilutedly materialistic; matter was tinged with spiritual properties and with a sort of divinity. As Aristotle noted, soul was for them 'diffused throughout the universe', or, as Thales put it, 'all things are full of gods.'[10] But as materialism gathered steam the gods got pushed into the background; chance and necessity reigned, and soul was reduced by atomists, like Leucippus and Democritus, to material particles of a mobile, spherical shape, and ceased to exist after death. These views obviously threatened very seriously the beliefs and traditions upon which social life rested, and according to Plato,[11] a century later, were largely to blame for the corruption of society.

Idealism, by contrast, defended traditional values, and gave priority to spiritual forces. As Plato put it, 'soul is one of the first existences, and prior to all bodies; and more than anything else is what governs all the modifications and changes of bodies.'[12] These views emerged in the Greek colonies of southern Italy, and were influenced by the reanimation of older modes of thought in the sixth century religious revival known as Orphism. The doctrines of Orphism, Cornford has noted, 'interpenetrate the whole mystical tradition of Greek philosophy, Pythagorianism, Platonism, Stoicism, Neoplatonism and Christianity.'[13] Orphism, which probably reached Greece from eastern sources, laid stress on the unity of life and the unity of God, on the double nature of man, the inferiority of body to soul, and on the need for purification and spiritual renewal. Mystical ideas of this sort would not, of course, have been a challenge to the materialists had they not been backed up by powerful arguments. And this is what the idealist philosophers provided. Pythagoras, the founder of mathematics, revealed a supersensible world of mathematical relations which could not be reduced to matter. The life-principle of the world, he argued, was a system of numbers. Harmony was a property of numbers; and harmony underlay both the beauty of art, and the health of body and soul. The Eleatic philosophers, Parmenides and Zeno, who followed, exposed with cogent logic the contradictions of the sensible world, and proved that the fabric of reality could not be broken into units, that only 'the One', the indivisible whole, could exist in the full and proper sense of the term.

It was in the course of these controversies that the seeds of what later became psychology were sown. Gradually the concept of the soul was crystallized and clarified. Its functions were defined, and its differences from body distinguished. The broad outlines of psychology as we know it today were sketched. It has been argued that in a very real sense the Greeks discovered the human mind.[14]

The way was prepared by the lyric and dramatic poets of ancient Greece. The Homeric conception of man activated by a variety of spiritual and bodily powers, and sometimes controlled by external agents, was gradually replaced by the realization that the individual actor was himself responsible for his behaviour. 'The human being', notes Snell, 'is made to stand apart from divine and earthly forces, and become himself the point where actions and achievements take their origin. His own passions and his own knowledge are the only determining factors.'[15] The way was paved for the philosophical and scientific reflection on the nature of the psyche, and the subject matter of psychology began to get focus and organization.

The soul ($\psi\upsilon\chi\acute{\eta}$), from being merely the breath or principle of life, and a diffuse presence in the universe, took over the properties of mind ($\nuo\hat{\upsilon}\varsigma$) and the passions ($\theta\upsilon\mu\acute{o}\varsigma$), which had previously been regarded as separate powers.[16] Its basic functions came to be regarded as movement and sensation. These were what distinguished the living animal from the non-living world. In both animals and men, the soul became conceived as essentially exercising sensori-motor properties.[17] Man, however, was distinguished from other animals by the additional power of reason. 'Man differs from the other animals because he alone has understanding, while the others perceive, but do not understand,' stated Alcmaeon, the first philosopher correctly to locate psychological functions in the brain.[18] It was even hinted by some thinkers, Anaximander for example, that man had evolved from lower forms, and he certainly retained many of the same driving passions in the irrational part of his soul. Soul became distinguished from body, though whether in itself substantial or immaterial remained a matter for argument. In its highest reaches the soul seemed to have affinity with the reason that ordered the universe. It was not merely the source and centre of human life, but, at least according to the idealists, transcendent, and participated in the divine. The materialists were more down to earth, and particularly concentrated on the consideration of sensation, for which they strove to provide materialistic explanations. If they could succeed in this a major obstacle to materialistic theories would be removed.

The crystallization of the concept of soul probably cannot be attributed to any one thinker. Burnet in a classic paper[19] argued that it was due to Socrates, but it is now more generally regarded as having emerged gradually during the sixth and fifth centuries BC. If any one person is to be singled out as the father of psychology, probably Heraclitus of Ephesus, who flourished at the turn of the two centuries, has the best claim.[20] Amidst the flux and change of the outer world the soul was for him the most real thing, and its most important attributes were thought and wisdom. 'I searched myself,' proclaimed Heraclitus, 'for truth lies within.'[21] As a result of his searching Heraclitus made a distinction between the private world of dreaming and illusion, and the public, common world of thought. 'Thinking is shared by all.'[22] By thinking man could come to terms with the universe, and its primary motivating forces, love and strife. For life is movement and change, and the clash of opposites: the soul was alive in so far as it shared in and mastered these conflicting forces. It could by taking thought escape from its isolation and participate in the universal process. If not the father of systematic psychology, it could be argued that Heraclitus was at least the ancestor of psychoanalysis. Psychology, without the name, had become a focal point of philosophic thought.

II

Psychological enquiry was further encouraged when in the latter half of the fifth century BC a significant shift occurred in the central interests of philosophers. The shift was attributed by Cicero, writing some centuries later, to Socrates. In Cicero's words, 'Socrates was the first to call philosophy down from the heavens and set her in the cities of men . . . and compel her to ask questions about life and morality and things good and evil.'[23] Man and his institutions, rather than the universe at large, became the focus of argumentation and enquiry, and this inevitably raised questions of psychology.

The priority of Socrates in bringing about this transition is, however, questionable, for he was preceded by a group of men, doubtfully perhaps termed philosophers, and more commonly known as Sophists.[24] These Sophists discussed human and social questions, matters of law, politics and morality; and they taught their followers how to get on in changing societies, where traditional values were increasingly in decay. Their attitude was sceptical and relativistic, and, as they taught for money, they tended to pander to the needs and weaknesses of their clients. Man was the measure of all things, and could, therefore, more or less shape his own destiny. There was no natural basis for morality; right and wrong were merely matters of convention; and conventions could change. The Sophists themselves may have been embryo practical psychologists, but they contributed very little to psychology as such, apart from raising questions which it required psychology to answer. This was a matter for their successors, Socrates, Plato and Aristotle.

Socrates himself (469-399 BC) was above all a catalyst.[25] He took on the Sophists on their own terms, outargued them, and undermined their pretensions. He insisted on clear thinking and the careful definition of terms.[26] Even if he was not responsible for the concept of the soul as it later became accepted, he was passionately concerned with its well-being, for its 'virtue', and he considered the care of the soul (θεραπεία ψυχῆς) to be man's most important task. For Socrates the soul was the essential man, and in his reflections on the soul he focused attention on the two great problems, the problem of knowledge, and the problem of conduct, from the consideration of which almost the whole of psychology has in fact derived.

Socrates prepared the way for his devoted follower, Plato. Though Plato never wrote a systematic treatise on psychology, he made enormous strides in assembling the necessary material for such a psychology, by providing a subtle analysis of the intellectual and emotional nature of man in the course of his discussion of moral, political, epistemological and metaphysical questions. We find for the first time in Plato much of the contents, and a good deal of the basic terminology, of psychology. His views, directly or indirectly, have profoundly influenced human thought throughout the ages. Though in the course of his long life (428-348 BC) Plato's views quite naturally developed,[27] and dialogues written at very different dates are not completely consistent, nevertheless the underlying theme of his philosophy remained constant: the shifting and changing world of sense is only a shadow of the truly real, invisible world of 'forms' and values. His psychology mirrors this basic tenet of his philosophy.[28]

Plato's major contributions to the development of psychology can conveniently be considered under five main headings:

(i)   he proposed a hierarchical model of the soul, which illuminates the whole field of psychology;
(ii)   in discussing the problem of conduct he sketched the first outline of an anatomy of motivation and the emotions;
(iii)   in treating the problem of knowledge he laid the foundations of cognitive psychology;
(iv)   he elaborated, even if he did not invent, the concept of mental health;
(v)   as a political theorist he insisted that account must be taken of the psychological differences between members of the community, and so he can be regarded as one of the first differential psychologists.

Three principal models of the soul are referred to in Plato's dialogues. One, the materialistic model, he rejects decisively, because it makes no sense of human behaviour, which is essentially goal-directed.[29] The second, dualistic model, on the other hand, which set the soul, immortal and rational, in opposition to the body with its appetites and emotions, found favour in his younger days. 'The body fills us with passions and desires and fears, and all sorts of fancies and foolishness.'[30] The job of the philosopher is, as far as possible, to free himself from its influences. But this model is later superseded by a third model, and the soul becomes a complex, hierarchically ordered entity.

At its lowest level, the soul is simply the principle of life.[31] At this level, Plato suggests in the *Philebus*,[32] there is no perception, no memory, and therefore no desire. Next comes the desiring level, the 'mortal' part, which contains the passions, affections and irrational sensations, and this part is itself arranged on two levels, the lower appetites and lusts, and the higher, or spirited, emotions.[33] Finally at the head of the hierarchy there is the 'immortal' part of the soul, rational, intelligent, and akin to the divine. This is not a dualistic model, but a multi-level model, in which soul and body are intermingled in various proportions. As such it is an important forerunner of later hierarchical models, even though these in modern times are depicted in evolutionary terms, while Plato's was not. The hierarchical model provides the essential key to Plato's psychology, and links to his metaphysical description of levels of reality, and his scheme for a hierarchically ordered society. It is an enormous advance on any previous theory of the soul, and begins to impose some order on the whole field of psychology.

In his treatment of motivation and the emotions, however, Plato is not consistently hierarchical. He was, in fact, attempting to do different things, and his various accounts are consequently somewhat confusing. Certainly in his later dialogues Plato conceives the whole soul as dynamic, each level possessing its own drives, and each its own source of pleasure. Thus in the *Laws* he speaks of 'wish, reflection, forethought, counsel, opinion, true and false, joy, grief, confidence, fear, hate, love and all the motions that are akin to these or are prime-working motions'.[34] A basic drive, like the Eros of the *Symposium*, operates at all levels of the hierarchy, and can be directed to sensuous objects or towards the most exalted levels of ideal beauty. Similarly pleasure occurs at every level of the hierarchy. Quite apart from the central place accorded to Eros there is a certain similarity between this hierarchical scheme and the Freudian trilogy of id, ego and superego.

The famous tripartite division of the soul in the *Republic*[35] on the other hand is not strictly hierarchical, since each component can take charge of the entire personality. It seems rather an attempt to depict the three main factors of temperament, and is remarkably similar to Sheldon's classification of cerebrotonic, somatotonic and viscerotonic components, which are blended in various proportions to give different personality types.[36] In Plato, too, the various components in different mixes give rise to distinct types of men, which are described towards the end of the *Republic*.[37]

In spite of this confusion of aims there are many interesting features in Plato's account of motivation and emotion. He acutely observed that the existence of psychic conflict necessitated the postulation of distinct emotional drives;[38] he noted the release of buried emotions in dreams;[39] he differentiated pleasure and pain from emotional drives, and provided a subtle analysis of their role in behaviour;[40] and he argued that cognitive factors, such as perception, memory, and foresight, were always to some extent intermixed with motivations, emotions and pleasures,[41] and that the latter, therefore, were not merely somatic in nature. So it is not going too far to assert that Plato provided the first rough sketch of man's emotional and conative life.

Plato was equally the father of the other main area of psychology, cognitive psychology. The doctrines of the Sophists and the atomists had undermined faith in objective knowledge. Knowledge was reduced to sensory perception and opinion, and sensory perception to the motion of material particles. It was to counter the scepticism and relativism that these views engendered that Plato turned to the consideration of the nature of knowledge.

All knowledge, argued Plato,[42] is directed towards objects. The objects of the various senses can be specified, and Plato discussed them in some detail, together with an account of their receptive organs, in the *Timaeus*[43] – an account, which in view of his almost complete lack of accurate physiological and physical knowledge, is at least ingenious. Knowledge, however, cannot be reduced to sense perception.[44] Sense perception is transitory, while some knowledge at least, for example mathematical knowledge, is enduring and certain. Knowledge consists not in sensations alone, for sensations can sometimes be misleading, but in the process of reasoning about them. And this involves memory, including innate memory, concept formation and logical analysis. 'The human being must understand a general conception formed by collecting into a unity by means of reason the many perceptions of the senses.'[45] And if knowledge is to be knowledge these unities must be objective; that is, have real and permanent existence outside the mind of the knower. Thus Plato arrived at his famous doctrine of 'Forms' – the eternal structures which order the world and which render knowledge possible. They are the main structures of the invisible world in which the contradictions of the visible world are resolved. This apparently high-flown doctrine of Plato is not in fact inimical to scientific knowledge, since it is grounded in order and rationality; rather it is its safeguard, whereas strict empiricism leads in the end to scepticism and doubt. It is worth noting that Plato was himself a considerable mathematician, and was deeply influenced by Pythagorean teaching. His views on knowledge have consequently commended themselves particularly to philosophers of a mathematical persuasion, such as Leibniz, Whitehead, Russell and Popper. Plato certainly opened up in a dramatic way many of the major problems of cognitive psychology, and his proposals, in their essential features, are highly pertinent even today.

Plato's concern with the problems of conduct was never merely abstract. The primary task of man was the care of his soul, the cultivation and training of his mind. The soul, like the body, could be diseased or healthy; so a constant preoccupation of Plato was with what is now called 'mental health'. 'The concept of mental health', writes Kenny, 'was Plato's invention.'[46] This is, perhaps, an exaggeration, for the Pythagoreans also seem to have been concerned with psychotherapy, but there is no doubt that Plato constantly reverts to this topic. Some diseases of the soul, he believed, were somatic in origin, due to physical causes and humours; sometimes heredity and upbringing were responsible – 'we must blame the begetters, more than the begotten, and the nurses more than the nurslings.'[47] Others were the result of internal conflict and 'rebellion within the soul'.[48] Ignorance was at times to blame, too, as well as lack of emotional control. By way of cure Plato did not believe in medication. This should be avoided if possible since 'by drugging diseases many and grave in place of few and slight are wont to occur'.[49] Since body and mind might both be involved in mental disorder, therapy should be psychosomatic. This meant gymnastic training for the body, and a twofold training of the mind – a training of the emotions through 'music', by which Plato meant the arts in general, and of the intellect through mathematics, science and philosophy.[50] The true philosopher regards life as a process of purification and assimilation to the divine.[51] There may be in the purified soul a sort of 'mania', but this is not the mania of disease, but a divine release from customary habits, an overmastering love of wisdom, beauty and goodness, in which the soul finds illumination and rest. There was in Plato a strong mystical element; and it is probable that it was in the ineffable mystical vision that he sought ultimately the health of the soul.

Nevertheless Plato was down to earth in his recognition of facts. He had no very exalted opinion of human nature in the mass, and only a few human beings, in his view, had the necessary endowments to reach the highest levels of development. He certainly regarded human endowments as basically innate. In the *Republic* in his myth of the metals in men,[52] in which he likens one group to gold, a second group to silver, and a third to iron and copper – a grouping which determined their place in society – Plato is clearly pointing to innate differences in ability and temperament. In the *Theaetetus*, when speaking of memory, which he likens to fixing impressions in wax, Plato notes that individuals differ in the receptivity of 'the wax in their souls'.[53] For each group to realize its potential there must be an appropriate education, and suitable surroundings are also necessary. So environment and training play their part, too, and this applies equally to women as to men. Plato's ideal polity depended essentially on the recognition of these individual differences, and the corresponding allocation of places in society. Together with the physician Hippocrates he can be regarded as the first differential psychologist.

The Academy of Plato, the institution which Plato founded and where he did his teaching, endured for nearly nine hundred years after his death, until finally closed by the Emperor Justinian in AD 529. By that time Plato's influence had spread far beyond the confines of the Academy, had given rise to a powerful school of Neo-Platonic thinkers, most important of whom was Plotinus, had moulded the outlook of educated Romans, like Cicero, and had penetrated the Christian Church in the teaching of the Christian Fathers, particularly St Augustine. Though Plato's writings in the original Greek were hardly known in western Europe in the Middle Ages, they survived in the Byzantine Empire and spread to the Islamic world, and they were available in part through Latin translations of Cicero and Boethius and through the summaries of later commentators. In the fifteenth century they emerged again on the western scene, were translated by the Florentine humanist, Ficino, and from then on increasingly influenced the mind of the west.[54] Plato has been, and remains, a main barrier against any wholly materialistic vision of the universe, against any purely behaviouristic psychology.

III

Plato's most illustrious pupil was Aristotle (384-322 BC), and it is to Aristotle that we owe the first systematic treatment of psychology.

Aristotle was, indeed, the great systematizer, who plotted the whole map of knowledge and laid down the principles of its construction. He defined the subject matter of the various sciences and disciplines, arranged their topics along rational principles, and formulated the logic upon which they rested. He was the first systematic scientific research worker, the first organizer of cooperative research and the first historian of science.[55] He touched most fields of knowledge apart from mathematics. Though profoundly influenced by his master Plato, Aristotle detached himself, as his thought developed, more and more from Platonic doctrines. Perhaps partly because he came from a medical family, and partly for temperamental reasons, he showed an increasing aversion to the mystical and idealistic aspects of Platonism, and an increasing concern for the accumulation of empirically established facts and for 'the scientific study of minutiae'.[56] Nevertheless there always remained some trace of its Platonic origins in his philosophy.

All these features are apparent in Aristotle's psychology,[57] the most enduring and influential system of psychology that has ever been put forward. He commenced his treatise, the *De Anima*, in a matter of fact way. 'Our aim is to investigate and ascertain the essential nature of the soul, and secondly to discover those properties which attach to it as accidents . . . we shall, therefore, be obliged to make enquiry into the question of method.'[58] His enquiries were guided, as usual, by a series of penetrating questions. His method was twofold, both inductive and deductive. He was an acute observer, and his psychological treatises are replete with observations, many of which have stood the test of time, but he was also an unrepentant theorist, who believed that 'wisdom deals with the first causes and principles of things'.[59]

His theories, however, were down to earth. 'The hallmark of Aristotle as a philosopher', states Guthrie, 'is a robust common sense, which refused to believe that this world was anything but fully real.'[60] His psychology was based accordingly not so much on metaphysics as on biology. The dualistic theory of the soul-body relationship, expounded by the early Plato, and adopted by Aristotle in his lost juvenile dialogue, the *Eudemus*,[61] was abandoned for a biological hylomorphism, which treated soul and body as dual aspects of the living organism. Psychology thus became an extension of biology, and vital and mental processes were regarded as lying on a common dimension. It was necessary, therefore, for the psychologist to consider the soul not only in man, but also in animals, and also, Aristotle believed, in plants. For there was a scale of souls, beginning with the merely nutritive soul of plants, followed by the sensitive soul of animals, and finally the rational soul of human beings. There was, indeed, no way of telling precisely where psychology began, for 'nature proceeds little by little from things lifeless to animal life in such a way that it is impossible to determine the exact line of demarcation.'[62] Aristotle's biology was far from merely academic. He was an admirable observer and classifier, who collected and dissected many species of animal. Darwin had a high regard for his biological attainments, in spite of the fact that most of his physiology was wrong, that he believed in vital principles, like the 'pneuma' which served as a sort of bond between soul and body, and that his standpoint was teleological and non-evolutionary.

In psychology Aristotle sharpened and clarified the hierarchical model of Plato's later dialogues, and proposed a theory of soul-body relations which resolved the conflict between the materialistic Ionians and the idealistic Italians. He was indeed the great integrator, with a foot in both camps: an Ionian coming from northern Greece by background, and an idealist trained by Plato by upbringing. His hylomorphic theory of soul-body relations has been described by one philosopher as still 'the best buy'.[63] For Aristotle soul and body were not two substances, but two aspects of the real living objects with which the world was populated. 'Substance is the composite of matter and form. Matter is potentiality; form is actuality or realisation. . . . The soul is the form of a natural body endowed with the capacity of life.'[64] Form and matter, soul and body, were correlative terms; neither could exist without the other. The soul was the perfect realization (ἐντελέχεια) of the material body and its inherent potentialities. There was, according to Aristotle, no ideal world of transcendent 'forms', but the real world in which we lived consisted of structured substances. This was realism, but not materialism, since structures (forms), potencies and purposes were as much a part of the composition of things as matter, motion and causal forces. Moreover it ruled out any simple reductionism, as proposed by the atomists of Greek times, or the behaviourists today, since potencies were as much to be reckoned with as actualities. Plans, purposes, aptitudes, attitudes, habits – all the underlying structures in fact that a behaviourist like Skinner dismisses[65] – find a perfectly legitimate place in Aristotelian psychology. Aristotle stuck firmly to the concrete reality of the whole man: 'it is better not to speak of the soul as feeling pity or as learning or thinking, but rather the man as doing this through the soul.'[66]

Within this hylomorphic framework soul manifested itself at various levels, of which Aristotle distinguished principally three – the nutritive, sensitive and rational. The lowest nutritive level is found in plants, where its functions are confined to nutrition and reproduction. At what point plants merge into animals Aristotle was uncertain. Some marine animals, like sponges and sea anemones, seemed to him to be transitional forms, possessing a low degree of sensation, but no power of movement.[67] Animals proper were endowed with sensitive souls, which implied sensori-motor capacities and corresponding desires. Man alone possessed the third, rational, level of soul. 'The animals other than man live by appearances and memories, and have little connected experience; but the human race lives also by art and reasonings.'[68]

Having defined the essential nature of the soul Aristotle proceeds to analyse its properties and powers. It is interesting to note that in his psychological treatises, the *De Anima* and the *Parva Naturalia* he is concerned almost wholly with cognitive and biological matters, and that he leaves man's conative and emotional life to his treatises on *Ethics* and *Rhetoric*. This division between the cognitive and conative sides of psychology, which has tended to persist throughout the modern period, and underlies the factions of today, goes back, therefore, long before the beginnings of experimental psychology to the time of Aristotle himself.

Aristotle distinguished a number of cognitive faculties – sensation, imagination, memory, practical reason and creative reason. He is, indeed, the fountainhead of faculty psychology, a type of psychology which, in spite of many attempts to kill it, refuses completely to die. Of the cognitive faculties he listed Aristotle devoted most space to sensation – about one-third of his *De Anima* and also the longest treatise in his *Parva Naturalia*, the *De Sensu*; it was also a subject of study by his successor in the school he founded, Theophrastus.[69] Though Aristotle's account of the senses is hampered by inaccurate physiology, erroneous physics and the absence of experimentation, it contains many shrewd observations and several features of interest. Sensations were for him not merely physical motions, although they always involved physical motion and transmission via a medium and sense organs. But they also involve the soul, which receives the form of the object without the matter; there is always in sensation an element of abstraction – Aristotle said abstraction of form from matter; today we should say of information from stimuli – and this abstraction is an active process. Aristotle distinguished five senses, and also postulated a 'common sense', which integrated data centrally, and which made it possible to compare information from the different senses and to appreciate 'common sensibles', such as magnitude and number, as well as being responsible for levels of awareness, sleep, waking and so on.[70] It was a powerful and important idea. Imagination (φαντασία) played a key role in Aristotle's cognitive psychology. It was the bridge between sensation and thought; at its simplest level tied to sensation, at its highest providing the necessary basis for thought processes. 'Imagination is impossible without sensation, and conceptual thought is impossible without imagination.'[71] Memory was a specialized form of imagination, to which Aristotle devoted a whole treatise, the *De Memoria*.[72] Memory was distinguished from pure imagination by correct judgment that the image had been encountered before, by an attitude of regarding the image as a copy, and by an awareness of elapsed time. Active recollection was distinguished from passive revival, and consideration was given to mnemonic techniques. Aristotle's treatment of memory was extremely full, and included a brief reference to the three principles of association,[73] as well as asking many penetrating questions. Dreams were also a function of imagination, and because during sleep masking was diminished, they were sometimes significant in their revelations, since 'the movements in sleep are often the starting points for the activities of the day.'[74] Nevertheless Aristotle regarded most prophetic dreams as the result of chance, and the fact that animals dream was an argument against their divine origin.

Aristotle's analysis of the rational level of the soul, and the thought processes that differentiate man from the rest of the animal kingdom, was the crown of his psychology, and, because it influenced western thinkers over a span of nearly two thousand years, the most important part of it. He rejected somatic explanations of thought, such as had been proposed by some of the Pre-Socratics since they could not account for error.[75] Thought involved formal properties, and, if it departed from these, fallacies in reasoning were the result.[76] Aristotle's study of these formal properties, his logic, dominated western thinking, at least until the time of Francis Bacon. Thought could be practical and concerned with the achievement of goals, or theoretical and concerned with knowledge. The concept of practical reason was an important recognition that intelligence played, or at least could play, a part in the ordinary affairs of life as an ordering and directing factor.[77] Indeed ethical conduct depended on its doing so.[78] Thinking involved two components, passive reason and active reason. Passive reason is assimilatory, synthesizing the data of sense and imagination; active reason abstracts, organizes and illuminates. 'It is unmixed, transcendent, passionless, of divine nature; it suffers no change, is not born; it has no bodily organ, enters the body from without, and is immortal. . . . It is a survival of the Platonic transcendentalism.'[79] At the highest level of intuitive thought the thinker and the objects of thought become one, and 'the soul is in a sense all reality.'[80] This conviction of Aristotle that ultimately the soul could not be wholly explained in empirical terms, but was a transcendent principle, a 'quintessence', provoked intense discussion in later ages. But it should not lead us to undervalue his detailed analysis of intellectual processes, and his epistemology which recognized the essential place of both sensation and thought in the generation of knowledge, and the varied manifestations of thought. The value of Aristotle's psychology, here as elsewhere, is the comprehensiveness of the vision that inspires it and its coverage of the whole range of subject matter from biological base to transcendent summit.

One problem on which Aristotle's views were not completely clear was the problem of self-awareness. The Greeks of the classical period, of course, had no term for 'consciousness' as we know it today. However in the *Parva Naturalia* Aristotle wrote, 'for when a person has a sensation we regard him as awake, and we believe that every waking person has sensation to a certain extent either of the external world or of internal processes.'[81] In the *Ethics* he asserts that the perception of our own existence is implied by our perception that we are sensing or thinking: 'He that hears perceives that he hears; and he that walks, perceives that he walks . . . but to perceive that we perceive or that we intellectually know is to perceive that we exist.'[82] So Aristotle appears to recognize the fact of self consciousness, though he has not singled it out for analysis or accorded it a central place in his system.

Aristotle did not make a sharp distinction between the cognitive and conative aspects of the soul. He recognized two main motive forces, desire (ὄϱεξις) and practical reason.[83] These, however, normally worked hand in hand.[84] The decision process (βούλησις) implied desire for an end; but ends were cognitively given through sensation, imagination or thought. So conation and cognition cooperated in action, though conflict could also occur when reason and appetite were opposed; this could happen in creatures endowed with a sense of time, in whom present urges and considerations of the future could clash.[85] Though Aristotle did not have a clear conception of will, he nevertheless made a distinction between voluntary and involuntary actions.[86] Action is voluntary when its origin is in the agent, and he is fully aware of what he is doing. Aristotle also recognized the power of choice[87] which he discussed at some length in connection with moral choice, and the possibility of volitional failure, which he termed 'incontinence' (ἀϰϱασια).[88] His account of the latter is an exceptionally interesting discussion of what we should now term 'neurosis', in which appetites distort and thwart reason. Though Aristotle's explanation is unduly intellectualistic his recognition of the problem is a landmark in psychology.

Aristotle's references to the emotions in the *De Anima* are surprisingly brief. For some reason he left his consideration of them to his *Rhetoric* when discussing the practical problems of persuasion. In this context he provided the most penetrating account of the emotions prior to Descartes and Spinoza.[89] He recognized three essential components of emotion. Firstly, there was always a somatic element. 'Courage, gentleness, fear, pity, audacity, also joy, love and hate, are all associated with the body.'[90] Secondly, emotions always involve a cognitive element, and this being so, they can be allied to reason, and need not necessarily conflict with it. Thus Aristotle defines fear 'as a pain or disturbance due to a mental picture of some destructive or painful evil in the future',[91] and such a fear may be perfectly rational and well-grounded. Thirdly, there is always an affective element in emotion. Emotions are defined as 'all those feelings that so change men as to affect their judgements, and are attended by pleasure or pain.'[92] This is a remarkably all-round account of the emotions, and it is accompanied by a recognition of the part played by emotional appeal in human affairs, and of the psychologically valuable cathartic effects of emotional arousal through the arts.[93]

With Aristotle psychology had acquired an identity, and achieved a basic conceptual framework. In this sense Aristotle was the father of systematic psychology, and his psychology was in due course to exercise an enormous influence in the west.[94] In the early Middle Ages Aristotle was known mainly for his logic, and through commentaries by Boethius and others. But after the capture of Constantinople by the Crusaders in AD 1204 his works became known in Europe, and the *De Anima* among others was translated into Latin. The Aristotelian commentaries of the great Islamic philosophers, Avicenna (eleventh century) and Averroës (twelfth century) also began to circulate. Roger Bacon dates the entry of Aristotelian philosophy into the Christian world to about AD 1230. Very soon a Christianized version of

Aristotle became the dominant philosophy in western Europe, and systematic expositions of Aristotle's psychology by Peter of Spain (c. AD 1250) and Thomas Aquinas (c. AD 1260) and others re-established psychology as a philosophical discipline. For nearly four hundred years Aristotelian psychology had no serious rivals, and even after its displacement by the new psychologies of the modern era, it continued to exert an influence, and indeed staged a revival in the late nineteenth century with Brentano and the school of catholic psychologists.[95]

IV

The death of Aristotle in 322 BC, following only a year after that of Alexander the Great, marked the end of an era. The Greek city states had lost their effective independence, and were absorbed first by the Macedonian, and then by the Roman Empire. Aristotle was the last of the ancient masters of all, or nearly all, knowledge. The sciences, centred in the new Greek city of Alexandria in Egypt, went their own way, and significant advances were made in mathematics, engineering, geography and astronomy.[96] The philosophers, of whom the new schools of Epicureans and Stoics were the most important, turned from the contemplation of the universe to the search for a way of life, for meaning in a world in which men had lost their bearings together with their political freedom. Their psychology was, like their philosophy, therefore practical rather than speculative, and its significance lies in the influence it had in the Roman world, and through Rome on the west, rather than in its breaking new ground.[97]

The two schools differed in their recipes for living. The Epicureans were materialistic, did not believe in the immortality of the soul, or the intervention of gods in the ordering of the universe, and recommended that men should make the best of their circumstances by freeing themselves from anxieties and grasping what happiness they could. The Stoics were rationalists, believed in the divine mind and the affinity of the human soul to it, and held that man's duty was to conform rigidly to the laws of divine reason, and to eradicate all weakness and all passion from his life. By the end of the pre-Christian era these two philosophies had spread to Rome, and both, particularly Stoicism, had gained a following among educated Romans. Their Latin adaptations were among the principal vehicles by which the philosophical ideas of the Greeks were transmitted to the west. Hence their importance in the shaping of psychology.

The Epicureans were represented above all by the magnificent poem on nature in six books by Lucretius, written about the middle of the first century BC.[98] Two of these books dealt with psychology, the third with the nature of the soul, and the fourth with the senses. In these books Lucretius expounded the materialistic theories of Democritus and Epicurus. The soul is part of the bodily organism, and is itself of a material nature, consisting of very small rounded particles. Mind is born, grows and ages with the body, has diseases like the body, suffers when the body suffers, is affected by material substances like wine and medicaments, experiences epileptic fits of bodily origin, is bound together with body in a common inheritance, and with the dissolution of the body itself ceases to exist. Lucretius' poem survived through only a single manuscript copy during the Dark Ages, and its influence was not widely felt until after the Renaissance and the printing of editions in the fifteenth and sixteenth centuries. It was not until the nineteenth century that its merits were fully appreciated.

Much more influential was Cicero (106-43 BC), the Roman orator and statesman, who in the last years of his life, after his retirement from active politics, devoted his time to the writing of philosophical works. 'If we were required to decide', writes one biographer of Cicero,[99] 'what ancient writings have most directly influenced the modern world, the award must probably be in favour of Plutarch's *Lives* and the philosophical writings of Cicero.' These philosophical works were absorbed by the Fathers of the Church, especially St Ambrose and St Augustine, and later by Montaigne, Erasmus and other Renaissance humanists. In particular Cicero's *Tusculan Disputations* written in 45 BC served as a source book of ancient psychology and psychotherapy. In Brett's words,

> However little claim Cicero may have to originality, he forms a landmark in the history of psychology; from him as from a perennial fountain have flowed the phrases of generations of later writers, and he exercised immeasurable influence on successive generations by simply coining the expressions that transmitted Greek notions to those who used Latin as their medium of communication.[100]

Cicero's own thinking was shaped primarily by Platonism and Stoicism. In the first book of the *Tusculan Disputations* he notes that there are many theories about the nature of the soul, but in the end he favours the general consensus that the soul is an immortal, spiritually self-moving principle. The soul possesses powers, particularly memory, creativity, active attention and wisdom, which material theories cannot properly explain. Although the lower parts show an affinity with the body (and this may account for the resemblance of children to their parents), the higher part of the soul is not of mortal origin. Indeed soul embodied is harder to understand than soul disembodied.

The remaining four books of the *Tusculan Disputations* are concerned with psychotherapy, and with the problems of coping with pain, distress, and various mental disorders. The need for psychotherapy (*animi medicina*),[101] he notes, was not so well established as the art of healing the body, and was even looked on with some suspicion. Yet the diseases of the mind were numerous and more pernicious than those of the body. Cicero argues strongly for regarding them as medical matters, which can be treated by a consideration of causes. Among these diseases Cicero distinguished insanity (*insania*), mental deficiency (*amentia*) and mental deterioration (*dementia*). The effect of these diseases could be deadly, and they could destroy the soul. Their origin, he believed, was psychological: even in a disorder like melancholia the mind was influenced not only by the black bile from which it takes its name, but by emotions like wrath, fear and pain. So their cure must be primarily psychological; and for Cicero this meant by will and conviction (*voluntate et judicio*).[102] Pain must be endured with fortitude; other disorders were largely the result of our own attitudes of mind, and our disregard of reason. 'For my part,' states Cicero, 'I think the whole train of reasoning which is concerned with disorder of the soul turns upon the one fact that all disorders are within our control, are all acts of judgement, are all voluntary.'[103] Our aim should be by means of philosophy to make ourselves 'safe, impregnable, fenced and fortified'[104] so that the afflictions of life cannot touch us. For this we need to be of outstanding intelligence, to have an enthusiasm for seeking truth, and a devotion to philosophical studies.[105] It was a doctrine that could never appeal to the multitude, and in the end it did not appeal even to the elite. It was indeed a doctrine which led to disillusionment, well expressed by Marcus Aurelius, the philosophic emperor of the second century AD in his *Meditations*.

> Of man's life, his time is a point, his existence a flux, his sensation clouded, his body's entire composition corruptible, his vital spirit an eddy of broth, his fortune hard to predict, his fame uncertain. Briefly all things of the body a river; all things of the spirit dream and delirium; his life a warfare and a sojourn in a strange land; his after-fame oblivion. What then can be his escort through life? One thing and one thing only, Philosophy.[106]

The multitude did not agree. They turned instead to Christianity and to oriental religions: only a minority of outstanding intelligence looked for a time to Neo-Platonic mysticism. Of these latter the most noteworthy was Plotinus, the last great philosophical figure of the ancient world of paganism.

Plotinus (AD 204-270) was born in Egypt of Roman parents, and was educated in the cosmopolitan environment of Alexandria, where Greek, Jewish and oriental influences intermingled. His acquaintance with eastern religions and philosophy was enhanced as a result of his participation in an unsuccessful military campaign in Persia, and this may have encouraged the mystical tendencies of his thought. His philosophy was derived primarily from Plato with Aristotelian admixtures, to which he added distinctive contributions of his own. He spent the latter part of his life as a teacher in Rome, and it was there that he composed his major work, the *Enneads*.[107] The hierarchical system of the universe which he there depicted differs in detail and in feeling from those of his predecessors, Plato and Aristotle. The 'One', which crowns the system, is not an intellectual principle, like Plato's 'Form of the Good', or Aristotle's divine 'nous'[108]: it is something 'ineffable . . . beyond all things . . . there is no name of it, because nothing can be asserted of it.'[109] 'Nor is it in place, or in time: but is by itself uniform, or rather without form, being prior to all form, to motion and to permanency.'[110] At a lower level, and derived from it, are Intellect (νοῦς) and the Forms, and at a lower hypostasis still stands soul, both the world soul and individual souls. 'There is one first soul, and many souls.'[111] Within the soul are three levels: 'one part always abides on high . . . another is conversant with sensibles . . . another has a subsistence in the middle of these.'[112] It is the lowest part of the soul that is concerned with the maintenance of bodily functions. At the foot of the hierarchy is matter. The important feature of the Plotinian hierarchy is its dynamic nature; each level is dynamically derived from the level above it, and ultimately from the 'One'; at each level there is a reverse upward striving towards assimilation with higher levels, and escape from the lower.

This is reflected in Plotinus' psychology, which is in many ways subtle and original, representing 'an important advance on the psychology of Plato and Aristotle'.[113] His views on the relationship of soul and body are nearer to Plato's than to Aristotle's. He rejects Aristotle's hylomorphic theory. The soul is for him a superior principle. 'We are not bodies, but souls resident in bodies.'[114] The soul is not itself material, nor the perfection (ἐντελέχεια) of the body. The body is merely annexed as an instrument to the soul.[115] Soul is separate from body, produces body, and inspires it with life. Moreover it integrates and coordinates. 'It is necessary, therefore, that the soul should be as it were a centre, that the senses should on all sides be extended to this, like lines from the circumference of a circle, and that a thing of this kind, which apprehends the perceptions of soul, should be truly one.'[116] So 'soul must be acknowledged to subsist with invariable sameness in its subject and essence.'[117] But the soul, though a unity, functions at various levels and manifests a variety of powers (δυνάμεις) or faculties. The faculties Plotinus distinguishes are basically Aristotelian, but there is a greater awareness of the inner world of consciousness (συναίσθησις) and of personal identity. Consciousness become explicity recognized. Brett, indeed, went so far as to assert that 'In Plotinus, for the first time in history, psychology becomes the science of the phenomenon of consciousness, conceived as self-consciousness.'[118] 'The intellect perceives intellectually, and sees that it sees intellectually,' says Plotinus.[119] Moreover there is a clearer distinction between sensation as a bodily process, and sense-perception involving interpretation and judgment. 'Plotinus holds', states Blumenthal,[120] 'that the soul's power of perception is directed not to the object, but rather to the impression produced in the "living being". When they reach the soul these "impressions" are already intelligibles (Enn. I.i.7).' There seems to be a distinction here between the inner and the outer world, which is foreign to early Greek psychology; and in Plotinus' conception of the 'We' (ἡμεῖς) there is an approach to the concept of individual personality which is again alien to Platonic and Aristotelian thought.

Though resident in a material body, the soul can purify itself even in this life, and liberate itself from sense and 'from all terrene concerns'.[121] The soul is by its very nature unbounded: 'with respect to souls, therefore, each is not that which it is, as if it were so much in quantity, through a foreign boundary; but it is as great as it wishes to be.'[122] The soul which has purified itself can, by a mode of intuitive knowledge superior to that of science, achieve ultimately to the perception of the 'One', a perception which is more than perception, but rather a form of union. This ecstatic mystical vision is the final goal, 'the flight of the alone to the alone'.

Greek thought began in Ionia with abstract analysis and with a shattering of the primordial feeling of unity bonding nature and man in 'an inherited conglomerate.' It ended with a mystical reunification. Plotinus both closes the book of Greek philosophy, and marks a new beginning. Though not a Christian he was '*anima naturaliter Christiana*', and his thinking influenced his Christian successors. It was through reading Plotinus in Latin translation that Augustine, just prior to his conversion, 'came to get a sight of the invisible things above',[123] and through Augustine the teaching of Plotinus was transmitted to the medieval world. The intellectual life of western man, and with it his psychology, was about to undergo a profound change. The warring philosophical schools closed their doors, and an age of faith, though not without its dissensions, began.

Chapter 4
Christian theologians

I

For a thousand years or more, from roughly AD 400 to AD 1450, the intellectual life of the west was dominated by Christian theology. Whatever views may be held as to the validity and as to the future of Christian doctrine, its influence in shaping the outlook of western man cannot be denied. As Thomas Carlyle put it, Christian theology was 'a great heaven-high unquestionability, encompassing and interpenetrating the whole of life'.[1] Even the rise of the physical sciences, as Hooykaas has recently shown,[2] depended a great deal upon the world picture of the theologians. Psychology, because of its intimate connection with the subject matter of religion, was even more deeply influenced. In an age when there was retrogression rather than advance in the physical and biological sciences, psychology, because of its religious affinities, was by no means completely stagnant, but significantly extended its range.

Central to Christian teaching was the value and importance of the individual soul. The soul was man's most valuable possession; 'For what shall it profit a man, if he shall gain the whole world, and lose his own soul.'[3] Moreover every individual was of significance in the Christian scheme of things, in which even the sparrows were counted, and the hairs of a man's head were numbered.[4] As one modern scholar put it, 'Everyone has a share, however ridiculously slight, in sustaining and changing the history of the universe.'[5] Greek thought was abstract and impersonal; Christian thought, on the contrary, was person-centred. Crowning the theological edifice was not supreme intellect as such, but the triune personality of God; and on earth there was at least the promise of an enduring community of persons constituting the Church. And because man was created in the image of God, there were depths and a uniqueness in the human person which transcended precise definition.[6]

Christianity was not primarily, however, a system of ideas; it was a way of life involving new modes of feeling, a quality of spirituality, and an awareness of the value of the non-intellectual sides of personality. The supreme Christian virtue was love, not Aristotelian detachment and high-mindedness. The new feelings and values soon began to express themselves in the arts – in the freshness and spontaneity, for example, of the Ravenna mosaics, in the Latin hymns of St Ambrose, and in the magnificent church of St Sophia in Constantinople, dedicated by the Emperor Justinian in the year 537. Not surprisingly a new dimension was added at the same time to psychology, a dimension first clearly expressed in the writings of St Augustine.

II

As far as the west was concerned the essentially new features in Christianity were of Jewish origin, and penetrated the Greco-Roman world partly through the contact between the Greek and Jewish cultures, particularly in the cosmopolitan city of Alexandria, and partly through the missionary endeavours of St Paul. Sandwiched between the powerful empires of the east and west, the Jewish people had managed to preserve a precarious independence, or semi-independence, for a few centuries before Jerusalem was destroyed in AD 71 and they were absorbed into the Roman state. During this period their unique religion was raised to a new height in the teaching of the Hebrew prophets, and formulated in the Torah. Their religion was unique in that their God, Jehovah, was wholly transcendent. He was not to be identified with the world of nature, of which He was the sole creator; He was not localized in any particular territory; nor was He representable by any graven image. He was a righteous God, whose wisdom commanded man's adoration. The world He had created was essentially good, and man himself was the crown of that creation, at least before sin had entered the world. Man's nature, therefore, was on a level above that of the animal kingdom, and his spirit (*ruah*), which the Hebrews distinguished from the vital principle (*nephesh*), linked man in a peculiar way to the divine, and to the unfolding of the divine purpose in history. The elevation and the uncompromising nature of their beliefs brought upon the Jews much odium. They were described by the Roman historian Tacitus as 'the vilest of peoples' (*taeterrima gens*),[7] and Cicero, who had come into contact with them during his governorship of Cilicia, regarded their religion as 'a barbarous superstition'.[8] Judaism itself was, no doubt, too exclusive and rigid a religion ever to have converted the world. But fused with Greek philosophical ideas, as well as liberated from many of its constricting features and universalized by Christianity, it gave rise to a much more appealing and potent faith.

The fusion between Jewish and Greek ideas was an outcome of the dispersal of the Jews over much of the Mediterranean basin and Middle East.[9] The largest of these Jewish colonies was in Alexandria, the city founded in 332 BC by Alexander the Great. About a third of Alexandria's population was Jewish, and it came before long to possess the largest conglomeration of Jews in its day. It also rapidly established itself as the leading Hellenic intellectual centre, and the Jewish residents, who become Greek-speaking and translated their scriptures into Greek, were not unnaturally influenced by Hellenistic speculation. The fusion between Jewish and Hellenistic thought was of seminal importance in the early formulation of Christian theology, and it was no accident that many of the first Fathers of the Christian Church (Clement, Origen and Athanasius, for example) were Alexandrians.

There were natural affinities, as well as substantial differences, between Jewish and Greek conceptions. It was not too difficult to marry the wisdom literature of the Jews with the λόγος concept of the Greeks, for λόγος in Greek meant both 'word' and 'reason'. But the transcendent God of the Jews was quite unlike anything in Greek religion or philosophy; world history, conceived by the Jews as commencing at a moment in time and guided by a divine plan, bore no resemblance to the cyclically repetitive chronology of the Greeks; and, as far as man was concerned, a contrite heart was of more value in Jehovah's eyes than any achievement of human reason. What the Hebrews added to the Jewish-Greek amalgam was, as Brett pointed out, 'the fire of passion and the impetuosity of faith'.[10] There was, he noted, a marked difference between the Hebraic and Greek temperaments, 'between the desire to feel strongly, to nourish lofty passion, and the desire to subdue passion by reason'.[11] It was the Hebrew component that, through the medium of Christianity, brought a new dimension into the psychology that had been systematized by the Greeks.

The first Christian theologian was St Paul, and it was St Paul who began the process of interpreting Jewish ideas to the European mind.[12] Born in Tarsus of orthodox Jewish parents, Saul, as he was known before his conversion, was from early life familiar with Greek and Roman thought. His father had acquired Roman citizenship, and the city of Tarsus was famous for its philosophers of the Stoic school. 'I am a debtor', St Paul claimed, both to the Greeks and to the barbarians.'[13] After his conversion to Christianity St Paul was thus well equipped to convey the Christian message to the pagan world, and to sow some of the seeds which were later to add new areas to psychology.

The new note was an introspective one, but it was saved from self-centredness by its emphasis on love and fellowship. The inner man (ὁ ἔσω ἄνθρωπος)[14] was the important side of the human being, linking him with things eternal, and the inner man was known primarily to the man himself. 'Who among men knoweth the things of a man save the spirit of man which is in him?'[15] The core of the inner man was his spirit (πνεῦμα), and this was distinct both from the soul (ψυχή) and from the body. Spirit, however, did not automatically rule, and another important feature of Pauline teaching was its stress on the conflict between the spirit and 'the flesh'. 'I delight in the law of God after the inward man, but I see a different law in my members, warring against the law of my mind.'[16] The solution of these conflicts could not be achieved solely by 'works' and individual effort. It required grace (χάρις), and the birth of a 'new man', who, thereby, became a fellow citizen with other believers and the departed saints. This conception of the fellowship of believers, and their unity in the community of the Church, where they were 'members one of another',[17] bound together in one body and one spirit, introduced the psychologically important concept of the ideal, universal society, transcending time and place, within which the individual was redeemed. The abstract world of Greek forms had been personalized and socialized.

It took some three centuries before Christianity converted the Roman world, and even longer before divergent heresies were eradicated and its intellectual implications fully grasped. Pagan ideas and practices, indeed, long survived beneath the surface of European life, and the eastern world, centred in Constantinople, went its own rather different way. With St Augustine, however, at the end of the fourth century and beginning of the fifth, the western Church achieved the distinctive formulation of its faith, and psychology a noteworthy enrichment of lasting importance.

III

'Augustine', wrote Reinhold Niebuhr, 'is the first Christian theologian to comprehend the full implications of the Christian doctrine of man.'[18] He has been described as 'the first modern man', and as 'the link between antiquity and the modern world'.[19] He was certainly the first great introspective psychologist in the western world. Born in AD 354 in North Africa of a Christian mother and a pagan father, Augustine was not, however, finally converted to Christianity until the age of thirty-three. Up till then he had been engaged on studies in rhetoric, first in Carthage, and then in Milan, with a view to preparing for a public career. In Carthage he came under the influence of the dualistic Persian religion of Manicheism, and in Milan he was drawn first to Neo-Platonism, and then to Christianity. After his conversion he returned to North Africa, was ordained, and in AD 395 was consecrated Bishop of the seaport town of Hippo. He remained there, living in a monastic community, administering his diocese, and writing the voluminous works which made him the most influential Christian thinker for at least eight centuries, not merely as a theologian, but as a philosopher, political theorist, moralist and psychologist. Even the sceptic Bertrand Russell considered that 'as a philosopher Augustine deserves a high place'.[20] As a psychologist he opened up new vistas, and is a supremely important figure.

Augustine's concern with psychology was both practical and theoretical. It was practical in that it sprang from the agonizing conflicts with which he was faced – conflicts between the worldly life in which he had been immersed and the demands of the Christian religion, conflicts between the collapsing classical world and the emerging 'City of God', and the tragic disparity which he observed between human potentialities and the miseries of so much earthly life, 'the host of cruel ills that afflicted man in this hell on earth'.[21] These conflicts were vividly described in his *Confessions*, the first autobiographical case study in the history of psychology. But his concern with psychology was wider than this; it was theoretically and theologically motivated, for Augustine believed that an analysis of the human mind could throw light on the nature of the Godhead, and that the mystery of the Trinity, of unity in diversity, could be illuminated by a study of the human personality.[22] For it was by looking inward that the most important truths were revealed. '*In interiore homine habitat veritas*'

(Truth dwells in the inner man).[23] So psychology for Augustine was a main key to reality.

The immediacy of conscious experience was, indeed, for him the starting point of all knowledge. 'So I will first ask you to start from the obvious, whether you yourself exist. Don't tell me that you are afraid of being mistaken in this question, since there would not even be any possibility of being mistaken if you did not exist.'[24] He returns to this theme again and again.[25] Consciousness of self was immediate and beyond all doubt, and quite different from the mediate knowledge of objects. So

> it could not possibly happen that the soul should think about what is itself in the same way that it thinks about what is not. . . . It thinks about fire, or air, or any other bodily matter . . . by means of imaginative pictures . . . but nothing is more present to it than itself; in the same way in fact that it thinks about itself living and remembering and understanding and willing.[26]

Augustine's descriptions of the stream of consciousness and of the depth of its recesses were quite unlike anything that had preceded him, and were his main contribution to psychology. Nevertheless he was also an acute observer of human nature from the outside, and his writings are replete with penetrating observations of persons at all stages of their development. He noted the jealousy of young infants from the sucking stage of life;[27] he described the gradual growth of awareness and the ability to communicate, which he attributed not to teaching, but rather to internal drives;[28] he observed the essentially concrete nature of children's thought processes;[29] he anticipated Freud not only in some of his views of infancy, but in regarding slips of the tongue as significantly revealing of inner conflicts,[30] and in attributing traits such as avarice to repressed sexuality: 'I have observed that, with certain people, when sexuality is repressed, avarice seems to grow in its place.'[31] His doctrine of *rationes seminales* (the hidden seeds that organize living forms) was an intuitive anticipation of genetic findings.[32]

Though Augustine was not a scientist, and though he regarded worldly knowledge as empty (*vana*), he was nevertheless a keen observer, and possessed a questioning sense of the mystery of things – and this applied particularly to the soul-body relationship. The soul he regarded as simple, indivisible and spiritual, the body as mortal and material. 'The manner in which spirits are united to bodies,' he mused, 'is altogether wonderful, and transcends the understanding of men'[33] – as indeed it still does! Though not extended in space, somehow, Augustine believed, the soul was resident throughout the body, and could act on the body, while not reciprocally acted upon in its turn. It was dynamic, and exercised force, but was not quantitative. Every movement of the soul in some degree affected the body. He wrote,

This is patent even to the senses, when the movements of the mind are vehement, as in grief, anger, and so forth. Hence we may conjecture that, when we are thinking, although no bodily effect would be discernible by us, there may be some such effect which would be discernible by beings with higher perceptive faculties. Therefore those first prints of its influence which the mind impresses on the body may perchance not only remain, but set up as it were a certain disposition.[34]

Indeed a most perceptive observation! Augustine had a remarkable insight into the complexity of quite ordinary psychological processes; thus when writing of the processes involved in reading a sentence, he distinguished three levels; the physical level involving the eyes, the psychological level involving the imaging of meaning, and the level of abstract intelligence. 'When we read "Thou shalt love thy neighbour as thyself", the letters are seen corporeally; the neighbour is thought of psychologically; and love is beheld intellectually.'[35]
Underlying these different levels was the fundamental distinction between time and eternity. The physical world existed in time: God is eternal and beyond time. Man's soul, though not in space, was in time, and his immediate experience was temporal[36] – the stream of consciousness as it was later termed. But man's destiny was eternal, and his spiritual progress involved an integration and transcendence of time.[37] Augustine was the first thinker to grasp the nature of psychological time. His account of time[38] was altogether more profound than that of his predecessors, and is a remarkable piece of psychological analysis. 'It is in thee, my mind, that I measure times,' he declared.[39] Instead of appealing to motion with its spatial associations he had recourse to the direct awareness of the flow of time in auditory rather than visual experience,[40] in the recitation, for example, of a psalm:

I am about to repeat a psalm that I know. Before I begin my expectation alone reaches itself over the whole; but so soon as I have once begun, how much so ever of it I shall take off into the past, over so much my memory also reaches: thus the life of this action of mine is extended both ways: into my memory, so far as concerns that part which I have repeated already, and into my expectation too in respect of what I am about to repeat now; but all this while is my marking faculty [attentio] present at hand, through which, that which is future, is conveyed over that it may become past: which how much the more diligently it is done over and over again, so much the more the expectation being shortened, is the memory enlarged; till the whole expectation be at length vanished quite away, when namely that whole action being ended, shall be absolutely passed into the memory. What is now done in this whole psalm, the same is done in every part of it, yea and in every syllable of it: the same order holds in a longer action, too, whereof perchance this psalm is but a part: this holds, too, throughout the course of man's life, the parts whereof be all the actions of the man: it holds also throughout the whole age of the sons of men, the parts whereof be the whole lives of men.[41]

This account of the subjective elements in time experience and its analysis into the three components of attention, expectation and memory, led Augustine naturally on to the consideration of memory.[42] Memory was the faculty that provided continuity amid the flux. In a sense 'the mind is memory itself'.[43] Augustine contemplated with wonder the scope and resources of memory. 'Great is the power of memory; a thing, O my God, to be amazed at, a very profound and infinite multiplicity; and this thing is the mind, and this thing am I.'[44] All psychological functioning depended upon memory; all the skills and habits that have been acquired; the grasping of the meaning of a sentence (for the beginning must be retained until the end is reached); the recognition of myself as a being continuing in time. Even the birds and mammals must have memory to enable them to find their nests and lairs. But how does memory work? How is material retrieved from its vast stores? 'Some things', noted Augustine, 'come out readily; other have to be fetched, as it were, from secret receptacles. Some things come out in a disordered rush, others in orderly sequences, and in correct classifications.'[45] Some things won't come out at all, and then there is forgetfulness. But when we remember again what we have forgotten, how do we know it as what was forgotten? In a sense, then, there must be a memory of forgetfulness to make this possible. 'When I remember forgetfulness, both memory and forgetfulness are present.'[46] There are few better accounts of the problems of memory than that given by Augustine until quite recent times.

Problems of time and memory merged naturally for Augustine into that of history, 'the whole age of the sons of men'.[47] He was indeed the first philosopher of history, the first to grasp the significance of the historical process which was implicitly in the scriptural account of creation and redemption. In his final masterpiece, the *Civitas Dei* (The City of God), written as barbarian hordes were sacking Rome, and civilization appeared on the point of collapse, Augustine expounded the Christian view of history and the meaning of what he elsewhere termed 'the close-woven sequence of the centuries'.[48] He saw more clearly than anyone prior to the eighteenth and nineteenth century philosophers of history that human behaviour could not be understood except in its historical context, that man was an historical being. History, contrary to the prevailing fatalism of the classical world, had a meaning, had a purpose, and unfolded according to a predestined plan.

To this plan the individual might, or might not, assent. He had freedom, something which was difficult to reconcile with God's omnipotence and his foreknowledge. Nevertheless man's gift of free choice was, according to Augustine, an essential feature of man's nature. In fact human beings '*nihil aliud quam voluntates sunt*' (the will is the basic core of the human being).[49] Augustine maintained that he had a direct awareness of volitional freedom. 'I knew as well I had a will, as that I had life; and when, therefore, I did either will or nill anything, I knew that there was the cause of my sin.'[50] Will was involved, moreover, even in cognitive acts, since they depended on attention, an '*intentio animi*', a direction of the mind.[51] Thus active looking preceded passive seeing. Because a man can control his attention, he is master of his first thoughts; by exercising will he can acquire discipline and control over them, given the grace of God. Nevertheless man's carnal nature wars against the spirit, and once on the downward path his will becomes enslaved by habit. 'From a perverted act of will desire had grown, and when desire is given satisfaction, habit is forged; and when habit passes unresisted, a compulsive urge sets in.'[52] An individual, therefore, was constrained by his past, and the grace of God was needed to save him. Here he disagreed with his contemporary, Pelagius, who held that man's salvation was in his power to achieve. Augustine's controversy with Pelagius occupied much of his time during his final years. Augustine was heavily conscious of human limitations, and of the problem of the divided will together with the torments of inner conflicts.

> The mind commands the body and it is presently obeyed; the mind commands itself and it is resisted. The mind gives the word commanding the hand to be moved; and such readiness is there, that the command is scarcely to be discerned from the execution. Yet the mind is mind, whereas the hand is body. The mind commands mind to will; it is the same, and yet it does not . . . but it willeth not entirely; therefore it doth neither command entirely.[53]

The trouble is that 'there are so many contrary natures in man, and these be wills resisting one another.'[54]

Yet standing as a unity above all these conflicting urges was the man himself – the individual person. Augustine has been described as the first personality theorist.[55]

> A man is not just a body, or just a soul, but a being made up of both a body and a soul . . . the soul is not the whole man, but the better part of a man; the body is not the whole, but the inferior part of a man. When both are joined together they have the name 'man'.[56]

It is impossible in a brief account to do justice to the richness of Augustine's psychological observations. He was a remarkable precursor of trends which later sprung in nineteenth and twentieth century thought from the existentialism of Kierkegaard. He had the same intense awareness of the human predicament as Kierkegaard, the same feelings of guilt and anxiety, the same penetrating insights into the nature of psychological processes, of both the potentialities and the limitations of human freedom, and the same distrust of abstract intellectualism. He introduced into psychology insights which only the most stubborn materialist can ignore.

IV

The long dark age which followed the final collapse of the Roman Empire in the west in AD 476 added nothing of significance to psychology. Men were concerned primarily with the salvation, rather than the understanding of their souls, and with preserving the relics of surviving knowledge, rather than creating new knowledge. The natural world as such ceased to arouse curiosity; the magical, the marvellous and the supernatural replaced it as foci of interest. Gradual and immensely important changes were taking place in western society, but it was not until the beginning of the second millennium that intellectual life began to revive. The learning of the ancient world had been conserved through three channels: through the monasteries that were established throughout Europe, through the Eastern Roman Empire, which lasted for a thousand years after the fall of Rome itself, and through the Moslem civilization which arose in the Middle East in the seventh century, and spread along the coast in North Africa as far as the southern half of Spain. Several of the early monks, like Cassiodorus (c.490-585) and Isidore of Seville (c.560-636) devoted themselves to making elaborate digests of such knowledge as had survived in Europe. Cassiodorus's *De Anima* provided a summary of classical and Christian views about the soul: Isidore's immense encyclopedia in twenty volumes, which has been described as 'one of the capital books of the Middle Ages',[57] covered the whole spectrum of ancient learning. But much had been lost and nothing was added to psychology. The much richer stores preserved in Constantinople and in the Arab world hardly began to penetrate to the west before the twelfth century. Although Charlemagne had close links with the Church in Jerusalem, it was not until the First Crusade in 1097 that large numbers of Europeans made contact with the east; and not until the occupation and despoliation of Constantinople during the Fourth Crusade in 1204 that Hellenic culture was brought into full purview of the western world. Perhaps even more important still was the re-introduction of the Aristotelian corpus through the medium of Arabic translations and the commentaries of great Arabic scholars such as Avicenna and Averroës. Meanwhile the rise of European universities in Salerno, Bologna, Paris, Oxford and elsewhere in the twelfth and thirteenth centuries provided a home for the revived learning – and eventually, in the course of some centuries, a home for a scientific psychology.

The culture of the new universities, however, was at first a literary, not a scientific culture. Ancient texts, Plato and Aristotle in philosophy, Galen in medicine, Justinian in legal studies, together, of course with the scriptures and the Church Fathers, constituted the substance, and verbal analysis and argumentation the methodology, of what is known as scholasticism. As Russell and many others have pointed out, the scholastic method suffered from severe disadvantages. 'The defects of the scholastic method are those that inevitably result from laying stress on "dialectic". These defects are; indifference to facts and science; belief in reasoning in matters which only observation can decide; and an undue emphasis on verbal distinctions and subtleties.'[58] Nevertheless scholasticism had an important and lasting effect in sharpening the terminology in which abstract issues were discussed, and in emphasizing the value of systematic and precise reasoning. 'The Middle Ages', observed Whitehead, 'formed one long training of the intellect of Western Europe in the sense of order. . . . The habit of definite and exact thought was implanted in the European mind by the long dominance of scholastic logic and scholastic divinity.'[59] And in psychology it bequeathed to the modern world a revived Aristotelianism, softened by Neo-Platonic influences and made conformable with Christian theology. There is no need in the present context to trace in detail the disputations of the scholastics from St Anselm in the eleventh century to William of Ockham in the fourteenth, though many of them discussed psychological topics, and some, like Roger Bacon and Robert Grosseteste in the thirteenth century, were interesting precursors of the scientific revolution to come. But two of the greatest figures did have a lasting impact on psychology, and require some mention, namely St Thomas Aquinas (1225-1274) and John Duns Scotus (c.1266-1308).

There are three main sources for St Thomas's psychology: the second book of the *Summa contra Gentiles* (the conspectus of Christian doctrine directed to Jews and infidels), parts of the first and second books of the *Summa Theologiae*, and his *Commentary on the De Anima of Aristotle*.[60] Though not perhaps a highly original thinker, St Thomas was assiduous, penetrating, and a master of systematization and clarification. His arguments were highly abstract, and only occasionally was there an appeal to concrete evidence, and never to experimentation. His masters were the scriptures and Aristotle, though he also quoted frequently from the Fathers of the Church, particularly Augustine. In psychology he indiscriminately brought the same sharp powers of analysis to questions of pertinence, as to questions which we should regard as totally unreal, for example speculation about the separated soul, the creation of the soul, the condition of the first man as regards his intellect, and the psychology of angels. Nevertheless he displayed a certain robust common sense as regards human nature, which rendered his philosophy of mind in its essentials not unfriendly to empirical psychology, and, in the words of Kenny, 'a structure which is fundamentally sounder than its more familiar rivals'.[61]

Following Aristotle, Aquinas regarded the soul as the form of the body. It must be incorporeal, otherwise it would be incapable of apprehending the forms of objects; at the same time it must subsist. It was, therefore, an incorporeal substance. The soul was unique to each individual, not, as Averroës and some other Arabs thought, part of a universal soul; and in spite of its diversity of functions it was a unity. 'In man the sensitive soul, the intellectual soul and the nutritive soul are numerically one soul.'[62] Within this unity Aquinas distinguished various faculties – rational, sensitive, appetitive, locomotive and vegetative – and these faculties formed a sort of hierarchy since 'the more simple and the more abstract a thing is, the nobler and higher it is in itself.'[63] Thus the intellect was the most noble faculty – a reversion, it would seem, away from Christian and towards Hellenic modes of thought. However, the intellect was not self-subsistent; it depended in human beings on sensory data, and was incapable of functioning apart from data from the senses. Though not an empiricist, there was a strongly empirical streak in Aquinas. Of the five exterior senses touch was the most fundamental, and Aquinas made the interesting but questionable observation that 'those who have the best sense of touch have the best intelligence'.[64] (It is interesting to note that Spearman in his first investigation into intelligence found that sensory discrimination, including tactile discrimination, correlated well with general intelligence.[65]) There was, Aquinas believed, no innate knowledge, except of certain basic first principles. 'It is impossible for our intellect to understand anything actually except by turning to the phantasms'[66] (i.e. to the impressions left by sense); and here interestingly enough he provides empirical evidence to support his contention, pointing to the loss of phantasms in mental disorder, disturbances of memory, the need for illustrative material in learning and teaching, and the impossibility of forming judgments while the senses are suspended. Sensory processes, however, were not themselves sufficient to produce knowledge. The intellect was always actively involved. In a pregnant statement Aquinas observed that 'the received is in the receiver according to the mode of the receiver'.[67] There was, therefore, an inevitably subjective aspect to knowledge as well as its objective side. In treating of intellect Aquinas followed Aristotle in distinguishing passive or potential, and active or actual intellect. The passive intellect consisted of the store of acquired knowledge; the active intellect, on the other hand, was 'the power to make things actually intelligible, by abstracting the species (i.e. the form) from the material conditions'.[68] Knowledge essentially consisted in the concordance of the form in the object and the form in the mind (the *esse intentionale* or intentional form). The concept of intentionality, or reference,* has been described by Kenny as 'one of the most interesting contributions ever made to the philosophical problems of the nature of thought',[70] and it was destined to play a considerable role in much later controversies. How the soul knows itself was another

---

* '*Intentio*', a term borrowed from Avicenna, played an important part in thirteenth century thought. The word literally means a 'stretching out', then 'a directing of the mind' towards something. Cicero (*Tusculan Disputations*, II.23.54) used the expression '*intentio animi*'. Perhaps the best English equivalent is 'reference', the term employed by Ogden and Richards in *The Meaning of Meaning* (1923). Cf. also Brentano, who re-introduced the term to western psychology: 'Every mental phenomenon is characterized by what the scholastics of the Middle Ages called the intentional (or mental) inexistence of an object, and what we might call, though not wholly unambiguously, reference to a content (*die Beziehung auf einer Inhalt*) or immanent objectivity.'[69]

problem touched on by Aquinas, and on which he made some pertinent observations. 'The intellect knows itself not by its essence but by its acts',[71] and to understand the human mind from its acts demanded 'a careful and subtle enquiry', i.e there was no immediate self-knowledge, apart from the fact that we had the bare knowledge of our existence.

The most important contributions of Aquinas to psychology, however, were perhaps his treatments of human action, emotion and disposition. In scope and clarity his account of these topics often went considerably beyond that of his master, Aristotle, and their value has only recently been properly recognized. Aquinas, unlike Aristotle, had a clearly formulated doctrine of will. 'Man is master of his actions because of his ability to deliberate about them; because his deliberating reason is balanced between opposites, it can dip to either.'[72] Though passion and physiological changes can sometimes defeat the will, in normal circumstances man can choose, can say 'yes' or 'no'. Aquinas went on to analyse the components of the voluntary act in detail,[73] distinguishing twelve phases, involving a constant interaction between intellect and volition, firstly in the establishment of an intention to act, and secondly in the actual execution of the intention. A contemporary commentator describes it as 'an original synthesis . . . the first in the history of philosophy to be devoted *ex professo* to the psychology of a typically human act'.[74]

In treating of emotions Aquinas largely followed Aristotle, but is interesting nevertheless. He did not share the theologico-ascetic rejection of emotion. In spite of the fact that the emotions could become disordered and tyrannical, he regarded their healthy development as 'one feature of human excellence'[75] and human life impoverished without emotional expression. His classification of the emotions into two main groups, affective (*concupiscibilis*) and spirited (*irascibilis*) was not perhaps very satisfactory in the way in which it was worked out; but it is noteworthy that he regarded love as the root of all the emotions. '*Amor enim est prima radix omnium passionum.*'[76] Aquinas recognized, too, that all emotions involved both a psychological and a somatic aspect, though the psychological side was primary. Emotions were essentially 'intentional', and there was thus more than a contingent relation between emotions and their objects. Most of these points had, of course, been made by Aristotle in his *Rhetoric*.

In dealing with dispositions (*habitus*), however, Aquinas was considerably more thorough than anything Aristotle had provided either in his *Ethics* or his *Categories*. The term '*habitus*' (disposition) was for Aquinas an 'omnibus' term embracing traits of character, acquired knowledge and beliefs, skills and even bodily characteristics. Dispositions were mainly acquired, and could be distinguished from natural powers in that they could be actualized in more ways than one: they depended, we should say today, mainly upon learning.

There is a certain natural condition which is appropriate to the human species, without which nothing can be a human being. . . .

But because the limits of this condition are fairly broad, it is possible for different degrees within these limits to be suited to different men according to their individual nature.[77]

There is clearly here in Aquinas the germ of a psychology of personality. As Kenny has observed,

The concept of disposition is an essential element in the characterization of peculiarly human behaviour and experience. . . . St Thomas has the merit of having grasped the importance of the concept and of having been the first great philosopher to attempt a full-scale analysis of it.[78]

The limitations of Aquinas's psychology are obvious. He was largely ignorant of physiology and biology; he paid little attention to development; he postulated an unbridgeable gap between man and animals, so much so that he regarded animals as incapable even of learning, unless trained by human beings;[79] and his methodology consisted largely of verbal analysis, with excessive reliance on literary sources. Nevertheless he produced a more comprehensive and a more systematic psychology even than Aristotle, and a conceptual framework which was capable of accommodating later findings quite beyond the range of his own vision.

His successor, Duns Scotus, was far less systematic or comprehensive. Of Scottish descent, and because of his ingenuity known to his contemporaries as 'Doctor Subtilis', Scotus is chiefly important for his doctrine of the will. His life was a short one, and he left no finished body of work comparable to the massive corpus of Aquinas, from whom he differed on a number of points of doctrine. Unlike Aquinas he maintained that the individual had, at least in principle, direct and immediate knowledge of his own mind, that there was a 'thisness' (*haecceitas*) in the individual which could be grasped. He held, too, that the faculties were not in reality distinct: '*non distinguiter inter se potentiae animae, nec ab essentia*'[80] (the powers of the soul cannot be distinguished among themselves, nor from the substance of the soul). So will and intellect, though distinguishable conceptually, were in fact inseparable aspects of one reality. 'For it is the substance of the soul itself which in all its diversity is the simple principle of its operations.'[81] But of these powers it was the will which, according to Duns Scotus, was really central and supreme. For the intellect was determined by the intelligible object; but the will was free from any internal or external compulsion. 'The will alone of all agencies maintains itself contingently to the production of opposite effects, all other causes being determined in their action to one result only.'[82] Or, as Scotus himself put it, '*voluntas autem sola habet indifferentiam ad contradictoria*', or again '*voluntas, in quantum est actus primus, libera est ad oppositos actus*'[83] (the will, in so far as it is an initiator, is free to act in contrary directions). The will, therefore, was totally free to accept or reject. It was free, indeed, to choose the ends of life, not merely the means to given ends, and was thus the source and origin of all moral values. Duns Scotus, therefore, granted to volition a much greater degree of freedom than Aquinas had allowed it, since for Aquinas 'the will must of necessity adhere to the last end which is happiness.'[84] For Scotus there was no such necessity. Harris writes,

> The importance of Scotus' psychology lies in the fact that he works out more systematically than had been done before the significance of the conception of will. . . . His insistence on the distinction between will and desire enables him to grapple more adequately with the psychological analysis of ethical problems, and leads to a deeper insight into the facts of moral experience than was displayed by any Christian thinker since the days of Augustine.[85]

The pioneer German historian of psychology Siebeck saw in his teaching the beginnings of the modern psychological outlook.[86]

V

The middle of the fourteenth century saw the commencement of the decline of scholasticism. By the sixteenth century, in spite of some fluctuating attempts at revival, the decline had become a rout. The schoolmen were accused of spinning 'cobwebs of learning, admirable for the fineness of the thread and work, but of no substance or profit'.[87] Scholasticism was rapidly being replaced by new modes of thought, and the scholastic psychology by new approaches to psychology. As Knowles wrote,

> The *philosophia perennis* had ceased to exist. . . . With the death of William of Ockham (1350) and his peers a great fabric of thought and an ancient outlook on philosophy as a single way of viewing the universe gradually disappeared, and gave place, after two centuries in which pure philosophy was in eclipse, to the new outlook and the varied ways of the modern world.[88]

Nevertheless the influence of medieval thinkers never completely disappeared, and, in due course, revived. Today their contributions to psychology are better appreciated than they were from the seventeenth to the nineteenth centuries. It is, indeed, only in fairly recent times that the full stature of Augustine has been rediscovered, perhaps partly because of his remarkable anticipations of a good many of the tenets of the existentialist movement, which sprang from the writings of Kierkegaard (1813-1855). Both alike were supremely great Christian psychologists.

Scholasticism itself has had its ups and downs. The Aristotelianism of Aquinas had a hard battle in its day against the earlier Augustinian modes of thought, and was for a time banned in the University of Paris. It had only a brief triumph before it was attacked by the Scotists and the nominalists led by William of Ockham. It was not until the late nineteenth century papal decree *Aeterni Patris* (1879) that Aquinas was made the official theologian of the Catholic Church. This led to an important revival of Thomism (Neo-Thomism), spearheaded in psychology first by Franz Brentano, whose *Psychology from an Empirical Standpoint* (1874)[89] has grown in influence in recent years, and then by Cardinal Mercier of Louvain, whose textbook of psychology which aimed at marrying Thomism and experimental psychology appeared in 1892. From these roots has sprung a movement which has given to modern psychology figures as important as Michotte (Belgium), Lindworsky (Prague), Gemelli (Italy), Aveling (England) and T.V. Moore (USA). Non-Catholics, too, have felt the influence of Neo-Thomism. Freud attended Brentano's lectures in Vienna, and it is possible that some of his ideas, for example the concept of cathexis, came to him from this source. Spearman was deeply read in, and frequently quoted, scholastic literature. Misiak and Staudt in their *Catholics in Psychology*[90] singled out three main Catholic contributions to psychology: first their focus on the whole man, on man as a person, secondly their opposition to reductionism and to the exclusion from psychology of man's higher faculties, intellectual and volitional, and thirdly, their opposition to extreme determinism. The revived interest in medieval thinkers is, therefore, not altogether difficult to explain.

Christianity, however, has always been more than scholasticism, and its influence more pervading than any system of philosophy. It brought about profound changes in attitudes, feelings and moral outlook – changes that were described at length in the classic work of the historian Lecky, *History of European Morals from Augustus to Charlemagne*.[91] Briefly these can be described as a new recognition of the sanctity of human life, a more vivid sense of the universal brotherhood of man, and in spite of St Paul, a changed attitude to women. Pagan society had a hard and brutal side to it; religion had very little to do with morals or compassion; and the philosophic creeds, which inculcated higher standards, were heavily intellectual in their appeal. The change in attitudes and feelings brought about by Christianity had a slow but steady effect in humanizing society, and led among other things to a much greater concern for the disabled and disadvantaged. There had, it is true, been charity in the form of largesse in the pagan world, but as Lecky pointed out, 'Christianity for the first time made charity a rudimentary virtue, giving it a leading place in the moral type.'[92] This led in the fourth century to the founding of the first public hospital in Rome by Fabiola, and the first asylum for lepers in Caesarea by St Basil, and much later – for the superstitious beliefs about the mentally disturbed were to persist for some time – to the establishment of asylums for the insane. Bedlam, indeed, in London, founded as a priory in 1247, was the first of such institutions. This concern for the sick and mentally disabled was in due course to have an enormously important impact on psychology, an impact whose roots were essentially Christian.

Together with these changes in moral feelings and attitudes, Christianity changed the intellectual climate of psychology in more ways than one. Personality, rather than intellect alone, became the distinguishing mark of man. The individual replaced the type as that which was most real. The individual was both free (hence the new emphasis on the will and on voluntary choice) and dependent (hence the emphasis on the objectivity of the moral law). He was, moreover, essentially a member of a brotherhood which had no territorial or other limitations, and he was immersed in a historical process which had direction and meaning. Academic psychology was slow to absorb these insights, but today they can no longer be ignored.

Chapter 5
The scientific revolution

I

In the three hundred and twenty-two years between the death of
Aquinas in 1274 and the birth of Descartes in 1596 there were,
according to one American historian of psychology, no 'great
psychologists'.[1] Nevertheless the new psychologies that emerged after
the end of this period were markedly different from that which
prevailed at the end of the thirteenth century, and they were shaped
not by 'great psychologists' so much as by radical transformations in
outlook, ideas and society. European man, in the striking phrase of
Butterfield, had donned 'a different kind of thinking cap'.[2]

The reasons for the breakdown of the medieval order, in spite of its
splendid visions and achievements, were no doubt many and complex.
The modern Renaissance was not, any more than the earlier Greek
Renaissance of the sixth century BC, the result of any one cause.
Economic, social and intellectual changes were equally involved.
These changes were not sudden. Medieval modes of thought persisted
well into the seventeenth century; by the end of that century, however,
they were merely vestigial. The closed world of medievalism had by
1687 been triumphantly replaced by the infinite universe of the modern
age.[3]

No doubt technological advances, and certain key inventions in
particular, played a part in the great transition. Gunpowder,
introduced into Europe in the fourteenth century, helped to undermine the feudal structure of society. The printing press invented by
Johann Guttenberg in the middle of the fifteenth century broke the
clerical monopoly of knowledge (it has been estimated that by the year
1500 at least nine million printed books existed in western Europe[4]).
The great navigational voyages, made possible by the introduction of
the magnetic compass, commencing with those of Henry the Navigator
early in the fifteenth century and leading to Columbus's discovery of
America in 1492 and Magellan's circumnavigation of the globe between
1519 and 1522, transformed the map of the world. Francis Bacon,
writing as the new age dawned, observed of printing, gunpowder and
the magnet that 'these three have changed the whole face and state of
things throughout the world'.[5]

Profound as these influences were, intellectual changes cannot be
attributed wholly to technological advances and their resulting social

and economic effects. By the middle of the fourteenth century strains and stresses were occurring within the philosophical and theological structure of medievalism. The unity of the intellectual and religious domains, the resplendent but closed cosmos of Dante and the majestic synthesis of Aquinas were beginning to fall apart. The sceptical intelligence of William of Ockham (c.1290-1349) demoted eternal essences to mere names, and by throwing doubt on anything not confirmed by the senses or directly founded on revelation drove a wedge between theology and philosophy; and this cleavage affected psychology, for Ockham held that nothing can be known about the immaterial soul, and that psychological knowledge was confined necessarily to the sensitive soul alone.[6] Beliefs of this kind helped at least indirectly to foster mysticism. Meister Eckhart, Saint Catherine of Siena, Jan van Ruysbroek and John Gerson all flourished during this period, turning inwards to immediate experience, and away from the arid intellectualism of the schools, while papal and monastic corruption led to dissident movements within the Church itself, and eventually in 1517 to the Protestant Reformation of Luther, and the subsequent proliferation of sects.

All this affected psychology in two principal ways: it led to increasingly strident attacks on Aristotle, and it led to novel conceptions of the nature of man. The very foundations of scholastic philosophy were thus gradually undermined. Increasing familiarity with the masterpieces of classical literature broadened men's minds and made them less and less willing to accept the constraints of scholastic dialectic. The Italian poet and humanist Petrarch (1304-1374), whose 'contributions to the forming of the modern mind can hardly be overestimated',[7] snarled at the 'stupid Aristotelians'. He wrote,

> Aristotle was a very great man, I know, but, as I have said, he was human. I know that much can be learned from his books, but I am convinced that outside of them much can be learned also; and I do not doubt that some men knew a great deal before Aristotle wrote. . . . I will only mention Homer, Hesiod, Pythagoras, Anaxagoras, Democritus, Diogenes, Solon and Socrates, and the prince of philosophers, Plato.[8]

Two centuries later, in 1536, the French logician Ramus went so far as to propose the thesis that 'everything that Aristotle states is false'.[9] In fact, of course, in spite of such attacks, Aristotelianism was still far from dead, and indeed revived in the sixteenth century, particularly in Padua, which had become the leading philosophical and scientific school in Europe. But it now had rivals in Platonism, humanism, and even, at times, a budding materialism, while individual thinkers went their own ways to produce the gentle scepticism of a Montaigne, the ribald libertarianism of a Rabelais, or the cynical realism of a Machiavelli. The arguments that arose led to no great progress in psychology; they concerned rather questions about the destiny and immortality of the soul than about its functioning. But thinkers like the

Italian Telesius (1509-1588), who held that the soul is influenced by material conditions and must have a material base, paved the way for subsequent empiricism, while Pomponazzi (1462-1524) even earlier had held that the soul was essentially mortal and inseparable from the body, though intellectually it could arise above mortality and 'in some fashion partake of immortality'.[10]

The breakdown of scholastic certainty opened the doors to less disciplined speculations about human nature; some exalted, like those of Pico della Mirandola, some condemnatory, like those of Martin Luther. In his famous oration *On The Dignity of Man*[11] Pico emphasized the universality of man, and his freedom from all restraints. His nature was coextensive with the universe.

> The nature of all the rest is defined and encompassed by laws prescribed by us; you, restrained by no limitation, of your own free will, in whose hand I have placed you, shall appoint your own nature. . . . We have made you neither celestial nor earthly, neither mortal nor immortal, so that freely choosing your own honour, as it were the moulder and maker of yourself, you may form yourself in what pattern you choose.[12]

Thus the Creator of his creation, man. By contrast Luther denigrated human nature. Man was a low and ignorant being, whose will was totally enslaved, and whose salvation depended not on his own merits but on God's grace. And Luther was prepared to defend his views 'even if the whole world had not only to be thrown into strife and confusion, but actually to return to total chaos and be reduced to nothingness'.[13] In these Renaissance views of man heights and depths of human irrationality were coming to the surface, forgotten areas which in the course of time were to extend the whole ambit of psychology.

The sanest and the greatest of the Renaissance humanists was the Dutchman Desiderius Erasmus (1466-1536). In opposition to Luther's 'on the bondage of the will'[14] he upheld 'the freedom of the will'.[15] In his classic *In Praise of Folly*[16] he poured scorn on the whole tribe of philosophers – 'They boast that they can see ideas, universals, separate forms, prime matters, quiddities, ecceities, things which are so insubstantial that I doubt if [the sharpest eye] could perceive them.'[17] 'Man's mind is far more susceptible to falsehood than to truth.'[18] He is endowed with 'more passion than reason – you could reckon the ration as twenty-four to one'.[19] Passions, however, were not necessarily bad; they could act 'like spears and goads as incentives to good deeds'.[20] Human beings, if they followed their natural instincts, could achieve perfection, could rise ultimately outside themselves, and enjoy 'some ineffable share in the supreme good'.[21] There was much here that could not be easily assimilated within the neat schematism of scholasticism, and which foreshadowed the empirical psychologies of the coming age. It was against this complex, shattered intellectual world that modern science began to manifest its first pregnant stirrings.

II

The use of the term 'science' in the sense that we understand it today dates only from the early eighteenth century, and the designation 'scientist' only from 1840. Science, however, is much older than the term, and much older than the modern world. It is, indeed, impossible to make a sharp distinction between scientific and everyday practical knowledge. Man, and even animals, have always had to acquire some knowledge about their environment. As crafts such as metallurgy, agriculture and medicine developed, so information about inorganic and organic nature inevitably accumulated, while both navigation and agriculture depended on the calendar, and this demanded a systematic recording of celestial phenomena. The early civilizations of the Middle East all acquired the rudiments of science, and all subsequent great civilizations have possessed some kind of scientific knowledge. Needham has shown the considerable achievements of Chinese science, and even suggested that its ideas influenced so eminent a western thinker as Leibniz.[22] The Hindus made important contributions to arithmetic and algebra.

Nevertheless it was the Greeks who laid the essential foundations of the scientific mentality, if by science we understand knowledge that is abstract, generalizable and based on principles, that is public and tested, and not esoteric, that is organized and coherent, open-ended and subject to correction, and, when possible, experimentally and mathematically grounded. The Greek achievements in science were admittedly limited, but men like Archimedes, Hipparchus and Eratosthenes were genuine scientists, and in Alexandria science was an organized activity. And Aristotle himself was no mean biologist. Greek scientific activity faded in Roman times, and virtually disappeared in medieval Europe from the fifth to the twelfth centuries AD, though it continued to flourish in the Islamic world. Sorokin's tables of scientific discoveries and technological inventions show a nadir between the fifth and ninth centuries.[23] There was, indeed, a positive hostility to scientific knowledge in Europe. 'We should rest content to be ignorant of the mysteries of the heavens and the earth,' asserted St Augustine.[24] The medieval mind, as described by Huizinga, was basically unscientific. It looked for symbolic resemblances rather than causal connections.

> In the minds of the Middle Ages every event, fictitious or historic, tends to crystallize, to become a parable, an example, a proof, in order to be applied as a standing instance of a general moral truth. . . . Inexactitude, credulity, levity, inconsistency are common features of mediaeval reasoning.[25]

To overcome these tendencies was an uphill task, and not surprisingly these characteristic modes of thought lasted until well after the Renaissance had dawned.

Yet there was a difference between medieval Europe and many

other civilizations dominated by prescientific thinking. Europe was the heir to the two great traditions of Greek philosophic thought and Judaic theology. Greek ideals of logic and rationality never wholly died out, and were revived in scholasticism, while the 'over-theoretical' propensity of the Greeks[26] was corrected by the Hebrew conception that the world was God's handiwork and deserved factual study as such. 'The new tinge in the modern mind', wrote Whitehead, 'is a vehement and passionate interest in the relation of general principles to irreducible and stubborn facts.'[27] In other words, it was the outcome of the fusion of Greek and Hebraic modes of thought. The trigger which initiated the scientific quest was no doubt the influx of Greek and Islamic scientific material in the thirteenth century. Sorokin's tables show from that time onwards a sharp and progressively accelerating rise in the output of scientific discoveries lasting right up to our own age. At first, as Butterfield pointed out,[28] experimentation was of an undisciplined nature, and science proper was for some time often inextricably mixed up with alchemy, astrology, and semi-mystical, hermetic ideas. It was not always easy to distinguish the scientist from the pseudo-scientist. Figures like Paracelsus and Bruno are hard to classify, and even the great Newton devoted large segments of his time and wrote upwards of a million words on matters such as alchemy.[29] Yet when we look at a fifteenth century giant like Leonardo da Vinci (1452-1519) we find many marks of the scientific mentality – his stress on the need for observation ('All sciences are vain and fall into errors that are not born of experience, mother of all certainty'[30]), his emphasis on quantification ('Whoever condemns the supreme certainty of mathematics feeds on confusion'[31]), and his belief in causal efficacy ('O marvellous, O stupendous necessity, thou with supreme reason compellest all effects to be the direct result of their causes; and by a supreme and irreducible law every natural action obeys thee by the shortest possible process'[32]).

It was not long after Leonardo's death that modern science ended its long gestation and celebrated its birthday. The year 1543 saw the publication of two famous books, the *De Revolutionibus Orbium Coelestium* of Copernicus and the *De Humani Corporis Fabrica* of Vesalius. In the following year appeared the Latin translation of the extant works of the Greek mathematician Archimedes, which laid down the foundations of theoretical mechanics, and a year later the *Ars Magna* of Cardano, a key work in the introduction of algebra into western Europe, marking, according to one historian of mathematics, 'the dividing line between mediaeval and modern thought'.[33] With the arrival of the heliocentric universe medievalism was doomed, and modern science launched on its momentous course; while Vesalius's anatomy of the human body opened the way for a new understanding first of the bodily, and then, consequentially, of the psychological functioning of man.

The heliocentric theory of Copernicus (1473-1543) was essentially a mathematical achievement, stimulated by the Neo-Platonic veneration for mathematics, and made possible by the revival of mathematics in

Europe. 'From the years 500 to 1400 there were no mathematicians of note in the whole Christian world.'[34] By the fifteenth century this state of affairs was gradually beginning to change. Translations of Euclid were printed in Venice in 1482 and 1505, and the Greek text was published in Basel in 1533. A Latin version of Ptolemy's *Almagest* appeared in Venice in 1515, and the Greek text in Basel in 1535. So Copernicus was equipped with the essential tools for his revolutionary theory, and as Burtt observed, 'the transformation to the new world-view was nothing but a mathematical reduction, under the renewed Platonism of the day, of a complex geometrical labyrinth into a beautifully simple and harmonious system.'[35] It took, of course, some time for the Copernican view, which dislodged the earth from the centre of creation, to replace the older view, and it was not until 1838 that the decisive verification of stellar parallax was recorded by the astronomer Bessell. Nevertheless the achievement of Copernicus unquestionably marked the arrival of a new age, and the whole imaginative backcloth of human existence was transformed. Early in the next century Copernican mathematics were allied by Kepler to the careful observations of Tycho Brahe to establish the fundamental laws of planetary motion. Tides were ascribed to lunar attraction, and principles of gravity enunciated. With Kepler came the recognition that theories must be in precise conformity with observations: 'without proper experiments', he asserted, 'I conclude nothing.'[36]

By the end of the sixteenth century these new scientific ideas were arousing growing interest, and small bands of enthusiasts were getting together to discuss them. Particularly noteworthy was the establishment of Gresham College in London. Sir Thomas Gresham, a wealthy London merchant who died in 1579, bequeathed in his will a sum of money to the Corporation of London for the establishment of a college in which seven professors, among them professors of astronomy and geometry, should deliver lectures. These lectures commenced in 1597, and until the foundation of the Royal Society served as an important meeting place for those interested in science. A little later even the universities began to open their doors to scientific enquiry. Savilian chairs of astronomy and geometry were founded in Oxford in 1619, and provision for a botanic garden agreed in 1621. Science was beginning to acquire a home and an organization. Then at the beginning of the seventeenth century emerged the prophet of its future role in the person of Francis Bacon, a man of exceptional vision, who 'took all knowledge for his province' and not only foresaw the impact that science would have on human affairs, but foresaw that psychology, the science of mind, would take its place among the sciences.

III

Francis Bacon (1561-1626) has always been a controversial figure. In his lifetime his reputation in public life was tarnished, and he was finally dismissed from the high office of Lord Chancellor on charges of corruption. As a philosopher he has often been adversely criticized, and more often ignored, while his positive contributions to science have usually been regarded as negligible and his methodological prescriptions as misguided. Nevertheless he was a man of extraordinary prophetic vision, who foresaw with astonishing clarity the role that science was destined to play in society. Though he may have underestimated the potential dangers springing from science,[37] he was certainly keenly aware of the benefits which power over nature would bring; he understood the essential basis for effective science and the need for organized research and the systematic collection of data, and he possessed a synoptic vision of the whole possible range of science and its applications. For these reasons his achievements have been regarded by one recent commentator as 'a major turning point in the history of the European mind'.[38] In the field of psychology his importance has generally been regarded as slight, and historians of psychology have accorded him small consideration. Brett was one of the few exceptions when he asserted that 'the ideas that he [Bacon] expressed ruled the progress of inductive or experimental psychology through all its development'.[39] The truth seems to be that though Bacon himself made few detailed contributions to general psychology as such, he saw more clearly than anyone of his time the need for, and the potentialities of, a psychology founded on empirical data, and capable of being applied to 'the relief of man's estate'.

Bacon, who entered Trinity College, Cambridge, at the astonishingly young age of twelve, was there subjected to the usual disciplines of dialectic, grammar and rhetoric,[40] and, although he acquired a deep dislike of the verbal logic-chopping of the dialecticians, he was, nevertheless, influenced by, and never entirely threw off, a good deal of its Aristotelian substructure. He still, even in his maturity, tended to think in terms of essential qualities and attributes rather than in functional and mathematical terms. His revolt was rather against the methodology and verbalism of the traditional schools than against their fundamental presuppositions. Bacon's really significant achievement was his grasp of the fact that scientifically based knowledge could become a source of man's mastery of nature, that it was the road 'to human utility and power',[41] that it enabled man to move from the passive imitation of nature to the active domination of nature. Scientific knowledge of an exact and fruitful kind was a novelty in Bacon's day, and still in a very rudimentary state; yet it seemed to him vastly superior in its potential to the three rival established forms of learning, which he labelled 'contentious learning', 'delicate learning' and 'fantastic learning'.[42] By 'contentious learning' Bacon referred to the logomachies of the scholastics; by 'delicate learning' to the rather spineless humanism of the Neo-Platonists; and by 'fantastic learning' to the esoteric mystifications of alchemists, hermeticists and magic-mongers. None of these three types of learning was capable of producing 'fruits'; and the test of sound knowledge was its fruitfulness. So Bacon set out on the ambitious attempt to provide 'a total reconstruction of sciences, arts, and all human knowledge raised upon proper foundations'.[43] Bacon had 'no entire or universal theory to propound'.[44] The proper foundations were not dogmatic, but method-ological. His aim was to lay the basis on which a progressive and growing body of scientific knowledge could be established. In advocating a fresh start he was not being merely iconoclastic. Indeed he asserted that he was 'zealous and affectionate to recede as little from antiquity either in terms or opinions as may stand with truth and the programme of knowledge',[45] and he held that in 'the wisdom of the ancients' (*Sapientia Veterum*, as one of his works was called)[46] there were often elements of truth. Nevertheless his programme was in many ways a radical one, and its implementation has largely shaped the modern world in which we live.

The core of Bacon's programme was his proposal for a new logic, a '*Novum Organum*', as he entitled one of his principal works,[47] to replace the Aristotelian logic of the schoolmen. Bacon's logic was basically an inductive logic. The essential starting point was the collection of facts; these facts must be arranged and classified in tables, and from these tables generalizations must be derived. This would ultimately enable the enquirer to arrive at a knowledge of causes, for scientific knowledge was essentially causal knowledge. By this Bacon meant a knowledge of efficient causes; final and formal causes he regarded as the proper concern not of science but of metaphysics. Bacon's proposals have often been criticized both for neglecting the role of hypotheses in scientific enquiry and for failing to appreciate the importance of the mathematical treatment of data. These criticisms are not entirely fair. Bacon did not dismiss, though he did not emphasize, the value of hypotheses. He did point out, however, that 'the fuller and more certain our anticipation is, the more direct and compendious our search';[48] and he did assert 'neither is it possible to discover the more remote and deeper parts of a science, if you stand upon the level of that same science, and ascend not to a higher science.'[49] Indeed, 'all true and fruitful natural philosophy hath a double scale or ladder, ascendant and descendant, ascending from experiments and the intervention of causes, and descending from causes to the invention of new experiments.'[50] And with regard to mathematics he did advocate that 'everything relating to both bodies and virtues in nature be set forth numbered, weighted, measured and defined . . . when exact proportions cannot be obtained, then we have recourse to indefinite estimates and comparatives,'[51] Bacon's principal weakness lay in the examples he chose to illustrate his method. The two detailed examples, the study of heat in the *Novum Organum*, and the study of whiteness in *Valerius Terminus*,[52] were of little scientific value, largely because his starting point, from a collection of qualitative properties, not from causal relations and measurements, was a mistaken one, and was soon overtaken by the advances in physics later in the century. Bacon failed, too, to appreciate some of the most significant scientific advances of his age, the Copernican theory, for example, and the contemporary work of Gilbert on magnetism. If not a model, his new logic was, however, an encouragement to empirical research and experimentation, and had something to do with the growing seventeenth century cultivation of science. Moreover Bacon did latch on to one extremely valuable logical principle, the 'vis instantiae negativae', the force of negative instances. As the logician von Wright observed, it was 'the immortal merit of Bacon to have fully appreciated this asymmetry in the logical structure of laws' – the fact, in other words, that a negative instance can disprove decisively, while an accumulation of positive instances cannot decisively prove.[53]

Besides advocating a new methodology Bacon was perhaps the first to propose the orderly and systematic prosecution of science, and to recommend its professionalization. In the utopian community of *New Atlantis*[54] scientific activity was concentrated in 'Salomon's House', a vast foundation equipped with all kinds of facilities for scientific research, zoos, health clinics, botanic gardens, laboratories, including visual, auditory and olfactory laboratories, and a 'house of deceits of the senses',[55] together with a team of specialized scientific workers, who consulted together in committee and planned new experiments under the guidance of top tier experts. Taken together with the orderly classification of knowledge set out earlier in *The Advancement of Learning* and the *De Dignitate et Augmentis Scientarum*[56] – a field in which he was a pioneer – Bacon's proposals must be regarded as a remarkable forecast of the way science was to develop over the coming centuries; and among the sciences that Bacon listed in his classifications were 'knowledges that respect the mind'.[57]

We must turn, then, to Bacon's psychology. The term 'psychology', though coined towards the end of the sixteenth century by the German savant Goclenius,[58] was not, of course, in general use until more than a century later even on the continent, and for considerably longer in Great Britain. Psychology was referred to by Bacon simply as 'knowledge of the mind', and to this he devoted a considerable portion of his *Advancement of Learning* and two books of the *De Augmentis*.[59] In his basic psychological conceptions Bacon mainly followed Aristotle and his scheme of faculties, but theological considerations, and possibly the influence of Ockham, led him to distinguish two parts of psychology, 'one that inquireth of the substance or nature of the soul, or mind, the other than inquireth of the faculties or functions thereof'.[60] Knowledge of the substance of the mind was beyond the scope of science, and a matter for theology; but human faculties and functions could be investigated by the same methods as the subject matter of other scientific disciplines. Of this latter, empirical, division of the subject there were two main subdivisions, the study of 'man segregate' (i.e. individual psychology) and of 'man congregate, or in society' (i.e. social psychology). In the study of the individual it was necessary first to consider 'human nature entire',[61] that is to say, body and mind together, and their interactions. Here Bacon was not considering the psycho-physical problem, for the simple reason that this problem did not clearly emerge until after Descartes. Influenced by the Italian thinker Telesius, to whom he frequently refers, Bacon was concerned rather with psychosomatic problems, with 'how far the humours and affects of the body do alter and work against the mind;

or again how and how far the passions and apprehensions of the mind do alter and work upon the body'.[62] He also noted the problem of 'the seats and domiciles which the several faculties of the mind do take and occupate in the corpus of the body'.[63] All these were far more pertinent questions than the sterile philosophical issues engendered by Cartesian dualism.

In the study of human faculties and functions Bacon advocated broadly the same methodology as in other fields of knowledge. He proposed 'a history and table of discovery for anger, fear, shame and the like, and again for the mental operations, composition and division, judgment and the rest',[64] though he recognized that some modification might be required to accord with 'the quality and condition of the subject of enquiry'.[65] In particular he suggested that explanations in terms of final causes, which were inadmissible in the physical sciences, were legitimate in the human sciences. Unfortunately Bacon did not go on to develop a general psychology on these lines. What he did do was to sketch in outline fields of enquiry which later became known as differential psychology, psychotherapy, and the psychopathology of thinking.

Bacon believed that it was of great practical importance 'to set down sound and true distributions and descriptions of the several characters and tempers of men, natures and dispositions'.[66] It was valuable to know 'what kind of wit and natures are most apt and proper for what sciences',[67] since 'there are minds which are proportioned to great matters and others to small . . . minds proportioned to intend many matters and others to few.'[68] At the time Bacon wrote, however, 'this kind of observation wandereth in words, but is not fixed in inquiry.'[69] To build up a sound knowledge it was necessary to consider differences resulting from sex, age, region, health, sickness and from external circumstances such as wealth and status. There was a need

> to procure good informations of particulars touching persons, their notions, their desires and ends . . . and not only of persons but of actions; what are on foot from time to time, and how they are conducted, favoured, opposed, and how they import and the like. For the knowledge of present actions is not only material in itself, but without it also the knowledge of persons is very erroneous.[70]

Bacon regarded this knowledge as important not only in vocational choice,[71] but also in the treatment of the mind when deranged.[72]

Psychotherapy, or the treatment of 'the diseases and infirmities of the mind',[73] was a matter of much concern to Bacon, who had, after all, a wide experience of public life in the law and politics, and extensive acquaintance with the aberrations of human nature. His famous *Essays* are a mine of shrewd observations and worldly wisdom. In practical affairs he regarded 'the management of the mind' as a matter having the first priority, 'for the remove of the impediments of the mind will sooner clear the passages of fortune, than the obtaining fortune will remove the impediments of the mind.'[74] There is a real need, therefore, for what he called 'The georgics of the mind', that is to say the husbandry or tillage of the mind, and this meant wise ordering and exercise, involving a consideration of individual differences, of the influence of environmental factors and of fluctuations of mood. In particular he prescribed a knowledge of affective dynamics, and a series of sensible rules for the acquiring and removing of habits – the desirability of limited goals, timing, attention to 'the good hours of the mind', the need for effort and the value of distractions.[75]

Of special interest to Bacon was the psychopathology of thinking. Here he was again a pioneer. Aristotle in his *De Sophisticis Elenchis* (Sophistical Refutations) had examined logical fallacies in thinking. Bacon in his famous theory of 'idols' was perhaps the first to grasp the importance, and to deal systematically with, psychological distortions of the thought process. By 'idols' Bacon meant the phantasms, delusions and prejudices to which the human mind is prone. 'The human understanding is like a false mirror, which receiving rays irregularly, distorts and discolours the nature of things by mingling its own nature with it.'[76] Some of these distortions are common to humanity, for example distortion by emotional factors (idols of the tribe). Others relate to individual biases (idols of the cave), for 'every individual in consequence of his education, interests and constitution is attended by a delusive power, his own familiar demon, which mocks his mind and troubles it with various unsubstantial spectres',[77] to verbal snares (the idols of the market place), 'those faulty meanings of words that cast their rays, or stamp their impression, in the mind itself',[78] and finally (the idols of the theatre) to the systems, or ideologies as we should term them today, that provide ready-made patterns of thought and thus obscure reality. These pathologies of thinking Bacon believed could be overcome by a strict adherence to a sound methodology. 'A new method must be found for quiet entry into minds choked and overgrown.'[79] Given sound methodology outstanding ability was not important. 'My system and method of research', declared Bacon, 'is of such a nature that it tends to equalise men's wits and capacities.'[80] No doubt Bacon placed too much faith in the virtues of strict methodology, and possessed an inadequate recognition of the deep-seated unconscious roots of human prejudice. All the same his account of the 'idols' was a remarkable first sketch of the psychopathology of thought.

Bacon's ideas for a soundly based empirical psychology, applicable to the cultivation and guidance of human nature and the correction of its diseases and infirmities, were too far in advance of his time to have an immediate impact. It was nearly three hundred years before his ideas began to be realized in the various fields of clinical and applied psychology. Equally some of his other prophetic visions, such as man's conquest of the air,[81] took some centuries before their realization. More immediate was his influence on some of the pioneers of British science who were responsible for founding the Royal Society later in the seventeenth century. 'Robert Hooke and Robert Boyle', writes Quinton, 'praised him without qualification and he became the patron saint or presiding genius of the Royal Society.'[82] The immediate road of advance in science, however, was not a Baconian one, and the next developments in psychology were due much less to Bacon than to the philosophers who succeeded him.

IV

It was Galileo Galilei (1564-1642) who above all others marked out the path that modern science was to follow, and who delivered the decisive death blows to Aristotelian physics and cosmology. Galileo first achieved fame by his employment of the newly invented telescope in astronomical observation, and in *Sidereus Nuncius* (1610) he described for the first time the mountains of the moon, the satellites of Jupiter, and numerous stars invisible to the naked eye. Bacon had recognized the need for 'instruments and machinery',[83] but it was Galileo who in fact inaugurated the instrumental phase of science. It was Galileo, too, who grasped the methodological principles that would actually transform the physical sciences. In *Il Saggiatore* (The Assayer) (1623) he proclaimed that 'the book of the universe . . . is written in mathematical language, and its characters are triangles, circles, and other geometrical figures, without which it is impossible to understand a single word'.[84] He advocated the use of the hypothetical-deductive method, and the experimental testing of hypotheses. He pointed out that the processes to be quantitatively assessed could be isolated and abstracted from the total situation, and handled abstractly by means of mathematics. In his famous *Dialogi sopra i due Massimi Sistemi del Mondo* (1632), which brought him into trouble with the Inquisition, he applied these principles to the comparison of the Ptolemaic and Copernican cosmologies and to an exposure of the errors of Aristotelianism; and in his final masterpiece, *Discorsi e Dimonstrazione matematiche intorno a due nuove Scienze* (1638), he expounded the essential principles of mechanics, including the law of falling bodies, the doctrine of forces and the theory of ballistics. 'We have developed', he wrote, 'a completely new science about a very ancient subject [i.e. motion].'[85] In so doing he completely demolished the superficially attractive Aristotelian doctrines that had prevailed for nearly two thousand years.[86] What Galileo had achieved was a replacement of the empirical generalizations of the Aristotelians with the concept of motion *per se*, mathematically expressed and abstracted from all constricting particular circumstances. He had ascended from the level of concrete generalization to the level of abstract postulation, and by rising to a higher level of thinking, greatly increased man's understanding and control of nature. The new doctrine of Galileo did not merely launch the physical sciences on their triumphant path, but incidentally had a profound effect on psychology. For in postulating a physical world ruled by mechanical law there was, as Galileo himself saw, no place for qualitative attributes. In *Il Saggiatore* he wrote, 'I think that these tastes, odours, colours, etc. on the side of the object in which they seem to exist are nothing else than mere names, but hold their residence solely in the sensitive body.'[87] So the psychological realm was set apart, a world of its own, in which attributes that physics had rejected resided in ghostly separation. A new era in psychology was thereby inaugurated, and a new set of problems raised.

These problems were compounded when physics became corpuscular, and psychology in imitation followed suit. In 1647 the French scientist, Gassendi, revived the atomic theory of Epicurus, and the idea was taken up by the son of a wealthy Irish peer Robert Boyle (1627-1691), who after extensive travels on the continent devoted himself to scientific experiments.[88] He was, perhaps, the most brilliant scientific experimenter of his age, famous for his work with air pumps and the formulation of the law usually known as Boyle's Law, and for his attacks on the doctrines of alchemy and early attempts to establish chemistry on a mechanical and atomistic basis. Though he did not arrive at the modern doctrine of chemical elements, and such works as *The Sceptical Chymist* (1662) and *The Origin of Forms and Qualities* (1666) he argued that the phenomena of nature were all derived from atoms in motion, and, following Galileo, he maintained that colours were not actually the property of bodies, but resulted from the modification of light. A keen Baconian, he was one of the founding members of, and a leading luminary in, the Royal Society. His importance to psychology, however, was primarily because of his contact with, and his influence on, John Locke. From 1654 to 1666 Boyle established himself in Oxford, which was then perhaps the chief centre of scientific activity in England. He had rooms and a laboratory in a house in the High Street, and employed Robert Hooke, famous later in his own right, as an assistant. It was here that John Locke, who had come up to Christ Church in 1652, made contact with him, and attached himself as an unofficial pupil, since Boyle had no established position in the university. Boyle became Locke's 'chief scientific mentor',[89] and from him Locke absorbed not only the corpuscular theory of matter, but also the distinction between primary and secondary qualities which Boyle had set out in *The Origins of Forms and Qualities* and the whole idea of empirical, analytical research. Locke remained in close touch with Boyle until the latter's death in 1691, and was an executor of his will. There was an extensive correspondence between the two men, who were both prominent members of the Royal Society. It was a relationship that was to exercise a lasting influence on the development of modern psychology.

The culminating achievement of seventeenth century science came in 1687 with the publication of Isaac Newton's *Principia*. Newton (1642-1726)[90] gathered together in one comprehensive, closely knit, mathematical system the whole range of physical phenomena, terrestrial and celestial, corpuscular and cosmological. His system was both simple (since 'Nature is pleased with simplicity and affects not the pomp of superfluous causes'[91] and universal (since it applied to the 'qualities of all bodies whatsoever'[92]). It was a self-sufficient mathematical system which ruled out the need for extraneous explanatory factors. 'What is not deduced from the phenomena is to be called a hypothesis, and hypotheses, whether metaphysical or physical, whether of occult qualities or mechanical, have no place in experimental philosophy.[93] There were, of course, presuppositions in the Newtonian system – the concepts of absolute time and absolute space, and the concepts of force and attraction were less straightforward than Newton supposed. But it was some time before the difficulties came to the fore, and for more than two centuries Newtonian mechanics dominated the world of science, and exercised a powerful influence on the whole intellectual landscape. The *Principia* moreover was not Newton's only achievement. He was also a brilliant experimentalist, and in his *Opticks* (1704) he described the experiments on the nature of light, carried out in the 1660s and 1670s, in which among other things he laid the foundations of the study of colour vision. In the final pages of the *Opticks* he set out in general terms his conception of the methodology of experimental science.

The immense and far-reaching consequences of the scientific revolution, which had its birth with Copernicus and which reached its maturity with Newton, were vividly described by Burtt in his *Metaphysical Foundations of Modern Physical Science* (1925):

> The gloriously romantic universe of Dante and Milton, that set no bounds to the imagination of Man, as it played over space and time, had now been swept away. Space was identified with the realm of geometry, time with the continuity of number. The world that people had thought themselves living in – a world rich with colour and sound, redolent with fragrance, filled with gladness, love and beauty, speaking everywhere of purposive harmony and creative ideas – was crowded now into the minute corners of the brains of scattered organic beings. The really important world outside was a world hard, cold, colourless, silent, dead; a world of mathematically compatible motions in mechanical regularity. The world of qualities perceived by man became just a curious and quite minor effect of the infinite machine beyond.[94]

A major mutation in the intellectual life of man had taken place. In the wake of the new physics it was inevitable that there should emerge new psychologies; for not only had the new physics given rise to a new methodology of unique authority, which was bound to exert a powerful attractive influence on the study of the human psyche, but by expelling mind and purpose from the physical world it forced upon psychologists the choice between, on the one hand, a materialistic assimilation to, or, on the other hand, a dualistic declaration of independence from, the domain of physics. The philosophical psychologies of the seventeenth and eighteenth centuries were attempts to come to terms with this dilemma.

Chapter 6
The philosophical renaissance

The philosophical renaissance of the seventeenth and eighteenth centuries was the direct outcome of the breakdown of the Aristotelian system and the revolutionary findings of the new physics. The rejection of the scholastic philosophy involved a corresponding rejection of scholastic psychology. So the philosophers of the period had to reconstruct psychology as part of their reconstruction of philosophy, and all were deeply concerned with problems crucial to the subsequent development of a science of mind. They raised new questions, proposed new answers, and were responsible for some of the controversies which have troubled psychologists ever since. In the disagreements of Hobbes and Descartes, or of Locke and Leibniz, we can trace the seeds of at least some contemporary disagreements.

I

Thomas Hobbes (1588-1679) has been termed 'the father of modern empirical psychology'.[1] It would be more accurate to describe him as the father of one important strand in modern empirical psychology, the reductionist, mechanistic strand which involves the attempt to assimilate psychology without remainder to the models of the physical sciences. Hobbes was the first prominent theorist 'to grasp the implications of the mechanical world view of Galilean science',[2] and the first to apply it uncompromisingly to the explanation of human nature and society. Most famous as a political theorist, and especially for his masterpiece, *Leviathan* (1651), he was at the same time a figure of enormous significance in the history of modern psychology.

Hobbes's aversion to Aristotle went back to his student days at Oxford, but it took another twenty years before he began to formulate his own philosophy. On leaving the university he was fortunate to obtain a tutorship to the son of William Cavendish, Earl of Devonshire, and for the greater part of his life he remained attached to this family. This gave him opportunities for travel, contacts with eminent persons, and the use of the Cavendish libraries at Chatsworth and Hardwicke. Hobbes became intimate with Bacon and Harvey, met many of the eminent thinkers of the continent, including Galileo, Descartes, Gassendi and Mersenne, and was involved in the philo-

63

sophical and scientific discussions of the period. Although interest in the earlier Greek materialists and atomists revived in the seventeenth century, there is no indication that Hobbes, good classical scholar as he was, owed anything to them. The two decisive events that influenced his outlook were his introduction to the writings of Galileo and his discovery of Euclid. Mersenne, with whose circle he associated when in France, had introduced Galileo into France, and Hobbes was later to write, 'Galileo in our time was the first that opened to us the gate of natural philosophy universal, which is the knowledge of the nature of motion.'[3] Euclid he discovered, also on a visit to France, in 1629, and the certainty and clarity of geometrical reasoning convinced him that this was the only way to arrive at truth. 'They that study natural philosophy study in vain except they begin in geometry.'[4] It was Hobbes's belief that by applying the methods and conclusions of the physical sciences to the problems of human nature and human society similar certainty could be achieved, and that the false ideas that had led to so much civil turmoil and confusion could be finally laid to rest. In this belief he was perhaps over-optimistic.

Hobbes first sketched his views in a short work which has become known as *The Little Treatise*, probably written soon after 1630. The manuscript was discovered in the British Museum by a German scholar, R. Tönnies, and published as an appendix to his edition of Hobbes's *Elements of Law* in 1889. In this treatise Hobbes already revealed an interest in applying mechanical principles to psychology. In the *Elements of Law* (1640) he outlined his psychological ideas more fully; the first book 'On Human Nature' was entirely devoted to psychology. His views on society and politics were set out in the *De Cive* (1642) and *Leviathan* (1651), and finally his general philosophy was expounded in the *De Corpore* (1655). Taken together his philosophical work covers the three great areas of knowledge, Corpus, Homo, Civis (the physical world, man and society), which he distinguished.[5]

Though written last the *De Corpore* is logically the basis of Hobbes's system. In it he reduced everything to bodies in motion. Bodies were 'the same with corporeal substance',[6] but not all bodies were observable. Indeed Hobbes relied in some of his most important theories on unobservables, '*materia subtilis*', too minute to be visible, and motions too slight to be detected. There was nothing apart from matter; 'substance incorporeal', i.e. soul, was an entirely meaningless expression.[7] All change was the result of motion, or, as Hobbes put it, 'all mutation is motion', and this included sensory and other psychological changes. Every change was thus externally caused; there was no inner principle of movement even in living things. The body, in fact, was just a complicated machine, and 'life is but a motion of the limbs . . . for what is the heart but a spring, and the nerves but so many strings, and the joints so many wheels, giving motion to the whole body.'[8]

In his early *Little Treatise* Hobbes applied the general principles of mechanics to the explanation of '*phantasmata*' (visual images) in the brain of the observer, and he made it clear in his later writings that he regarded it as the central problem in philosophy. There were, in fact, two crucial problems to which Hobbes had to provide answers, if he was to universalize his philosophical system based on mechanical principles – he had to explain knowledge, the representation of the world in sensation and thought, and he had to explain what appeared to be voluntary movement and the spontaneous action of human beings. On the face of it knowledge did not seem to be just movement, and voluntary action did not seem to be merely mechanical reaction. It was to these problems that Hobbes endeavoured to provide solutions in his psychology.

Hobbes's psychology, though materialistic and empirical in its conclusions, was deductive and rationalistic in its approach. Given matter and motion were the only realities, how could psychological properties be explained? Hobbes's conclusions were derived from, or at least intended to conform to, his premises; they were not established on the basis of observation. Men could, of course, observe the behaviour of their fellows; indeed they were also aware of their own thoughts and feelings, not as they actually occurred, but as a result of immediate memory; but such observation could not provide certain knowledge. It was certain knowledge that Hobbes was seeking, and that could only be derived, as the geometers derived it, deductively. Such was the knowledge that rulers required to govern their subjects, and, as the thoughts and passions of all men were marked by a basic similitude, the achievement of such knowledge was possible. This is what Hobbes set out to provide.

The first of the psychological problems that Hobbes confronted was the problem of knowledge, which using the Greek word he termed τὸ φαίνεσθαι (representation). 'Of all the phenomena or appearances which are near us, the most admirable is apparition itself, τὸ φαίνεσθαι, namely that some natural bodies have in themselves the patterns almost of all things, and others of none at all.'[9] All knowledge derives from sense; our 'phantasms', or sensory experiences, constantly change. 'There is always mutation in the sentient.'[10] But 'all mutation or alteration is motion'; sense, therefore, can be nothing else but motion. It is an internal motion of the sentient organism, propagated from the object, via a medium, to the sense organ and thereby the brain. This generates a reaction in the brain, a sort of rebound, which produces a phantasm or idea. Thus Hobbes defined sense as 'a phantasm, made by the reaction and endeavour outwards in the organ of sense, caused by an endeavour inwards from the object remaining for some time more or less'.[11] Secondary qualities, colours, sounds and so on, were not, therefore, part of the outside world, though what their exact status was Hobbes did not make clear.

The perseveration of the motions produced by sensory stimulation was the foundation of Hobbes's theory of cognition; it explained imagination, memory and thought, since 'the original of them all is that which we call sense.'[12] Imagination was simply 'decaying sense', and might be termed memory when its pastness was referred to. The flow of images, 'the train of imaginations', was generally guided by desire; but even the apparently wayward ranging of the mind, such as occurred in dreams, Hobbes suggested was not in fact merely random. The crucial factor distinguishing human from animal mentality was 'the most noble and profitable invention of speech'.[13] It was the use of words, names and other signs that made possible the addition and subtraction of ideas that constituted reasoning and thought. If truth was to be attained terms must be carefully defined and rightly ordered. Words could easily mislead; 'they are wise men's counters . . . but the money of fools.'[14] In particular Hobbes held that it was entirely erroneous to suppose that general names implied the existence of real universals, in the manner of Plato and the scholastics. For Hobbes thinking was not the intuition of universal essences, it was simply verbal behaviour, and this ultimately was just a form of motion.

The second great problem Hobbes had to tackle was the problem of volition – the apparent freedom and spontaneity of human behaviour. Here again Hobbes's proposals were revolutionary. He banished altogether the Aristotelian explanation in terms of ends, and the scholastic postulation of a special faculty of volition. 'A final cause has no place but in such things as have sense and will, and this also I shall prove hereafter to be an efficient cause.'[15] Volition, or voluntary movement, resulted from the small beginnings of motion, which Hobbes termed 'endeavour' (conatus). These were caused by the action of the imagination on the heart, and were either appetitive and pleasurable, or aversive and painful. All the passions, which Hobbes listed in detail, were derived from these basic tendencies. Will was simply 'the last appetite', that is the one that finally prevailed. It was not, therefore, a prerogative of man, but present 'no less in other living creatures'.[16] Freedom had no meaning except as the absence of external constraint. Man like every other animal was ultimately guided by his passions, and the central passion was the urge to dominate, 'the race to be first',[17] 'a perpetual and restless desire of power after power that ceaseth only in death', and never reaches a terminus.[18]

The psychology of Hobbes has striking limitations. It was a manifesto, rather than an empirically based science, a programme rather than a realization. Hobbes, indeed, was not truly a scientist, though his philosophy was derived from science. He himself made no significant contributions to scientific knowledge; he never experimented, and disparaged the experiments of others; his ideas about physics were often muddled, and his mathematics were shaky, even if he was considered good enough to tutor the youthful Charles II. He was quite rightly never elected to the Royal Society, and he was at loggerheads with its founding fathers. His knowledge of physiology was more or less confined to what he learned from his friend Harvey, and did not include any accurate knowledge of the workings of the sense organs and nervous system, though his psychology really demanded such a basis. When he came to pronounce on the social nature of man his ideas were mainly speculative, and the state of perpetual warfare, in which the life of man was 'solitary, poor, nasty, brutish and short'[19] not confirmed by empirical evidence. Finally on the philosophical plane he shirked the crucial difficulties to which his theories of cognition and volition gave rise.

Nevertheless Hobbes's psychological manifesto was enormously important as initiating a line of thought which has persisted to our time. It was reductionist in the sense that all explanation was reduced to the single level of physical motion. There was a complete abandonment of the ancient hierarchies. Not only were all psychological processes fundamentally alike, but all men were essentially equal; and indeed there was no basic difference between human beings and animals, apart from speech, and perhaps the human gift of curiosity. Nothing was real except matter and motion and the instant present.[20] Human behaviour was determined from without; there was no need to postulate final causes, ends and purposes. Behaviour was the result of sensory stimuli, initiating motions, which produced in their turn further movements in brain and heart, and ultimately led either to 'phantasms' or voluntary motions. In the last resort man was simply a machine to be explained wholly in naturalistic terms. It logically followed that there was no science of mind as such; and in his classification of the sciences Hobbes divided the subject matter of psychology among a number of separate sciences.[21] He would have agreed with Ryle in regarding it as 'a partly fortuitous federation of enquiries and techniques'.[22]

In the development of psychology Hobbes was much less immediately influential than his contemporary and rival, Descartes. His extremism aroused more antagonism than admiration. Nevertheless he inspired some materialistic followers in France and Germany; his views on 'conatus' (endeavour) interested Spinoza and Leibniz; and with advances in the life sciences in the nineteenth century reductionist and materialistic views gained a growing following. The Pavlovian and behaviourist movements were a natural outcome of these trends. On a much firmer basis of experimental evidence, and with greatly increased technical sophistication, large areas of twentieth century psychology show a close affinity with the presuppositions of Hobbes. He can, therefore, appropriately be regarded as the ancestor of one strand in modern psychology.

II

The influence of Descartes (1596-1650) on psychology was both more extensive than that of Hobbes and more malign – malign because, in spite of his contributions to particular areas, he directed psychology along a cul-de-sac from which it took more than two and a half centuries to extricate itself. Yet Descartes was a better philosopher, a better scientist, and a much better mathematician than Hobbes. His reflections were marked by freshness, honesty, and a large degree of open mindedness, his intellect was penetrating and clear, and he could expound his thoughts in a direct, simple and appealing style. In preserving God and the soul at the centre of his system he at least partly satisfied the conservatives, and in founding his physical philosophy on a material and mathematical basis he satisfied the emerging scientific community. The new knowledge could no longer be grafted on to the decaying Aristotelian system; it was necessary for philosophy to start again from first principles, and this is what Descartes did. 'As for the opinions which up to that time I had embraced, I thought that I could not do better than to resolve at once to sweep them wholly away, that I might be in a position to admit either others more correct, or even perhaps the same when they had undergone the scrutiny of reason.'[23]

Descartes's decision to begin again and to doubt everything in the search for certainties that it was impossible to doubt led him to conclude that ultimately he had to accept his own existence, and the existence of God. He wrote,

> Whilst I thus wished to think that all was false, it was absolutely necessary that I, who thus thought, should be somewhat; and as I observed that this truth, 'I think, hence I am' [*Cogito ergo sum*] was so certain, and if such evidence, that no ground of doubt, however extravagant, could be alleged by the sceptics capable of shaking it, I concluded that I might, without scruple, accept it as the first principle of the philosophy of which I was in search.[24]

As for God, 'the idea of God, which is found in us, demands God himself for its cause.'[25] Over and above these two basic certainties there were also indubitable mathematical truths, and, because God could not deceive, corporeal objects must exist, though as a result of the unreliability of the bodily senses, we could never arrive at firm conclusions about their nature.[26] The outcome of this line of argument was that 'the idea that I have of the human mind . . . is incomparably more distinct than the idea of any corporeal object'.[27]

However, the mind that Descartes intuited with such certainty was very different from the soul of Aristotle and the scholastics. It was not the 'form' of the body, or a principle of life; it was thinking, conscious substance. Mind had become equated simply with consciousness; and mind so conceived bore no resemblance to body, 'in respect that body from its nature is always divisible, and that mind is entirely indivisible'.[28] Hence, 'the mind, or soul, of man is entirely different from the body.'[29] In principle 'the mind can exist without the body, and the body without the mind.'[30] In this life, however, mind and body interacted, and they did this, Descartes believed, through the medium of the pineal gland, a small vestigial organ in the brain, which he selected because he thought that the integrating functions of mind could best be attributed to one of the few non-duplicated parts of the brain. Not only was this choice an unfortunate one, but the very idea of interaction between two totally distinct substances was fraught with difficulties. Nevertheless the two-world doctrine of Cartesian dualism became the commonly accepted creed of European thinkers.

There were fateful consequences for both physics and psychology in these theories of Descartes. Physics became emancipated from all occult and animistic influences, and the mechanical, mathematical viewpoint received a total vindication. Psychology, on the other hand, became split in two; there was the realm of pure consciousness, thought and will, totally divorced from corporeality and matter; and there was the mysterious area consisting of sensation, movement and emotion, where mind and body interacted. Man alone possessed consciousness and thought; all lower animals were merely machines. It was not that 'brutes have less reason than man, but that they have none at all'.[31] The most characteristic part of man was wholly non-biological, was wholly unrelated to anything else in the animal kingdom. It was this peculiarly human part that Descartes defined as thinking substance; for the essence of mind 'consists only in thinking'.[32] And a thinking thing is 'a thing that doubts, understands, affirms, denies, wills, refuses, imagines and also perceives'.[33] These various functions could be subsumed under the two main categories of understanding and will. Understanding involved 'ideas'; will involved volitions; while understanding and will jointly were involved in judgments. The term 'idea' Descartes defined not in the Platonic and Aristotelian way, but as 'that form of any thought by the immediate perception of which I am conscious of the same thought'[34] – an important transformation of the meaning of the term, which became, thereby, a key term in the new psychology. Ideas might be innate, adventitious (that is derived from experience), or factitious (that is purely human inventions). Innate ideas consisted, according to Descartes, of such things as mathematical truths and universal principles, such as the law of non-contradiction, and were essential ingredients of understanding.[35] Perceptions, on the other hand, derived from objects, but differed from mere sensations in that they always involved active mental judgments. 'I comprehend by the faculty of judgment alone which is in the mind, what I believed I saw with my eyes.'[36] In spite of these different functions mind was essentially indivisible (unlike bodily and other material substances), and hence the 'vis cognescens' (the power of knowing) was also ultimately simple, self-identical and absolute. 'It retains its single character in every field. One may call it "human or universal wisdom", or good sense [bona mens] or "the native light of reason"'.[37] In this way Descartes transmitted the concept of intelligence to the modern world.

These doctrines of Descartes in effect placed large, and perhaps the most important, areas of psychology beyond the reach of science, as he conceived it; for Descartes believed that science was necessarily quantitative and mathematical. Mind, on the contrary, in its essential nature could only be known intuitively, and, being indivisible, could not be analysed by the methods of science. This, however, did not apply to the mixed areas in which are located 'certain things of which we have an internal experience that ought not to be referred either to the mind of itself, or to the body alone, but to the close and intimate union between them'.[38] These could be subjected to scientific scrutiny, and it was to this region that Descartes made his most significant positive contributions to psychology. The mixed region contained three main types of phenomena: (i) sensation, (ii) movements, and (iii) appetites and emotions. Descartes was one of the first to propound a detailed account of the mechanisms of visual sensation,[39] and it has been said that 'he influenced all major theories from the seventeenth century to the present day'.[40] Though his account was necessarily largely speculative, because he lacked the required physical, chemical and physiological knowledge, there was much of interest in it. He made first-hand observations on the eyes of animals; he postulated a one-to-one correlation between sensations and brain events; and he recognized the necessary involvement of eye movements in providing essential information for judging distances. His account initiated the naturalistic investigation of visual processes. Nevertheless he finally insisted that it was 'the soul, not the eye, that does the seeing'.[41]

In the field of movement Descartes was the first to provide a clear account of reflex action, and although once again he lacked accurate physiological knowledge, the basic principles of the reflex, exemplified by the withdrawal of the foot from a heat source, was clearly set down.[42] Finally, in his last book, *Les Passions de l'âme* (1650), he laid the foundations for the scientific study of emotional life. Passions, or emotions, were essentially a product of the interaction of mind and body. They were caused by external stimuli which produced both psychic repercussions and physiological concomitants. Though passions had been linked with bodily humours from ancient times, and though Harvey had noted the influence of emotions on the heart, the attempt by Descartes to describe systematically the physiological basis of emotion inaugurated the modern study of the subject. We can even find anticipations of the James-Lange theory, in which flight precedes the experiencing of fear.[43] The Cartesian classification of the emotions was less successful. Rejecting the Thomistic division into irascible and concupiscible, Descartes proposed six primary emotions (admiration, love, hate, desire, joy and sadness), from which the remainder were compounded. His main concern in undertaking his work on the passions was a medical one.[44] He held that their proper control was necessary for the health of the mind.[45] Yet the passions 'sont toutes bonnes de leur nature'[46] and were biologically useful. It was uncontrolled emotion that exerted a deleterious influence. Passions, however, were not directly under control of the will, and could only be controlled by habit and training.

Descartes was an ambivalent figure, and his dualistic philosophy reflected his ambivalence. On the one hand he could not divorce himself from the principal tenets of the faith in which he had been brought up. He lacked the final courage of his convictions, and admitted that in the last resort 'I submit my opinions to the authority of the Church.'[47] On the other hand he equally could not doubt the clear and distinct conclusions of his own precise, mathematical mind. His psychology, like his philosophy, was torn asunder. On specific topics his progress towards a scientific psychology was notable, but on central issues his dualism retarded and constricted rather than advanced the subject. The psychosomatic unity of the Aristotelian model was shattered, and psychology was saddled with the impossible problems of mind-body interaction. Consciousness, rather than human personality in all its fullness, became the subject matter of psychological enquiry. Consciousness was identified with thinking, and thinking consisted of ideas, volitions and judgments. All mental processes could be regarded either as actions or passions, depending on whether they were, or were not, determined by the will. Instead of thoughts depending on, and deriving from, dispositions and structures, dispositions and structures were reduced to thoughts, since 'all the properties we discover in the mind are only diverse modes of thinking.'[48] The identification of mind with consciousness and clarity ruled out the possibility of unconscious *mental* processes. The human mind was thus divorced not only from its own deeper nature and its physiological substructure, but divorced from the rest of the animal kingdom. For between man and 'the brutes' there was no comparability. Thus psychology lost the biological roots with which Aristotle had endowed it, and became encapsulated in consciousness. In spite of these enormous drawbacks it was, nevertheless, the ideas of Descartes that largely shaped the development of psychology during the immediately succeeding centuries.

III

The most powerful of the early protests against Cartesian dualism came from Spinoza (1632-1677). The idea that two totally disparate substances could interact seemed to Spinoza absurd; it was, he said, 'a hypothesis more occult than any occult quality'.[49] Spinoza, however, was largely ignored in his lifetime, and it is only quite recently that his stature, and his importance in the history of psychology, have been recognized. There were several reasons for this neglect. Spinoza wrote in Latin at a time when Latin was rapidly being replaced by vernacular languages. His style was difficult and dense; and the geometrical method of exposition which he adopted in his principal work, the *Ethic* (1677), was unattractive. In the article on Spinoza in the *Dictionnaire historique et critique* (1695-1697) Bayle referred to the 'perplexities and impenetrable abstractions' of his philosophy. But perhaps even more damaging was the reputation Spinoza had gained for atheism. Even Hume wrote of 'this famous atheist' and 'his hideous hypothesis'.[50] So he was reviled and rejected without serious study. In fact, of course, Spinoza was not an atheist at all, and God held a central place in his philosophy; not, however, the personal and transcendent God of Judaism and Christianity, but a pantheistic and immanent Deity, more akin to the Hindu Brahman. And this is what upset both the Christian and Jewish communities. It was not until the late eighteenth century that these prejudices began to dissipate. Lessing introduced Spinoza's writings to the German philosopher Jacobi. In 1785 Jacobi published his *Letters on Spinoza*; and although he still regarded Spinozism as atheism, his analysis of Spinoza's doctrines interested German thinkers such as Goethe, Herder, Schelling and Hegel. Later in the nineteenth century Spinoza was to exert a considerable, though not publicly acknowledged, influence on Freud. In the English-speaking world recognition came a good deal later. There was no serious study of his philosophy until 1880, and no translation of his principal works until 1883.[51] In his history of psychology Gardner Murphy could still hold that Spinoza 'had strangely little influence upon psychologists'; he received only a passing reference in Watson's *The Great Psychologists*; and as late as 1971 Bernard could state that Spinoza's influence on the rise of scientific psychology was a neglected topic.[52] The fact is that many of Spinoza's ideas were far in advance of their time, and only in the twentieth century have they ceased to seem bizarre and unacceptable.

Spinoza was, of course, a Jew of Spanish origin. Born in Amsterdam, and educated in the Rabbinical school of that city, he was steeped in Hebrew literature and philosophy, including the mystical writings of the Kabbalah.[53] But his active mind soon strayed beyond the bounds of Jewish orthodoxy. He studied Latin and the scholastics, the new philosophies of Descartes and Hobbes, and became enthralled by the beauty and power of mathematics and the mathematical interpretation of nature. In 1656 he was excommunicated by the Jewish establishment, and for the rest of his days he led a life of seclusion and contemplation, supporting himself by the polishing of lenses. Because of the simplicity and dedication of his life he was considered by Bertrand Russell to be 'the noblest and the most lovable of the great philosophers'.[54] The significance of his philosophy for psychology is fourfold:

(i)   his double-aspect theory of mind-body relationship, which has interested several leading psychologists, and which three hundred years after his death seems less implausible than when originally put forward;
(ii) his ideas on determinism and the meaning of freedom;
(iii) his theory of '*conatus*', the essential dynamic drive which activates and sustains every mode or aspect of reality;
(iv) his account of the human emotions and their regulation.

Spinoza's theory of mind-body relations, though primarily a reaction against the difficulties of Cartesian dualism, was also a rejection of the stark, reductive materialism of Hobbes, and the categorial differentiation of Aristotle and the scholastics between soul as form and body as matter. For Spinoza mind and body were two aspects of a single underlying reality, a single substance. 'Substance thinking, and substance extended are one and the same substance, which is now comprehended under this attribute and now under that.'[55] This implied not only that all mental processes had material correlates, but also that all material entities were correspondingly mental. As Spinoza put it, 'everything is animate, though in different degrees.'[56] In a sense

Spinoza is propounding a form of panpsychism, but his theory differed from the older panpsychism of Thales, for example, who asserted that 'everything is full of gods' in being deterministically, not animistically, orientated. For Spinoza 'all things which come to pass, come to pass according to the eternal order and fixed laws of nature.'[57] There are obvious objections to a doctrine of the sort that Spinoza proposed, unless a distinction is made between organic entities, to which mental properties may not inconceivably be ascribed, and mere aggregates. He did not, however, make this distinction though he may perhaps have been moving towards it when he came to discuss 'in what manner a composite individual can be affected in many ways and yet retain its nature'.[58] All individual things in Spinoza's system were, of course, merely 'modes' of the one ultimate reality, God or Nature, which could be viewed either as thought or extension, mind or matter. So just as body was a dependent portion of the infinite natural world, the human mind was part of 'the infinite intellect of God'.[59] At a more mundane level the theory implied that 'the order and connection of ideas is the same as the order and connection of things';[60] that memories possessed a physical basis[61] and that when ideas were associated, there was a corresponding 'concatenation of the affections of the human body'.[62] For the same reason there were no mental faculties, such as will and intellect, only actions and passions manifesting themselves at various levels of psychosomatic complexity and perfection. Hierarchy was a significant feature of Spinoza's universe in both its aspects. 'Ideas, like objects themselves, differ from one another . . . one is more excellent, and contains more reality than another, just as the object of the idea is more excellent and contains more reality than another.'[63] Because there were degrees of reality or perfection, matter was not uniformly inert, but, at its higher levels, possessed as of yet unrecognised potentialities.[64] Spinoza's double-aspect doctrine in its broadest terms has commended itself to several eminent psychologists, and has found echoes in the psychological theories of Fechner and Wundt, in the isomorphism of the Gestalt psychologists, as well as the identity theory of certain philosophers of mind.[65] Reformulated in more modern terminology, in which extension becomes energy, and thought becomes information, it seems increasingly attractive, and is, in fact, attuned to various recent developments in physics.

Perhaps the strongest appeal of Spinoza to a scientific age lies in the dispassionate objectivity of his determinist approach to human nature. 'In nature there is nothing contingent, but all things are determined from the necessity of the divine nature to exist and act in a certain manner.'[66] There must, therefore, 'be one and the same method of understanding the nature of all things whatsoever, that is to say, by the universal laws and rules of nature.'[67] Human nature was no exception, and, therefore, Spinoza proposed 'to treat by a geometrical method the vices and follies of men', and 'consider human actions and appetites just as if I were considering lines, planes or bodies';[68] to view them, in other words, *sub specie aeternitatis*. So viewed, freedom, in the sense of free will, was seen to be a mere illusion. Man 'thinks himself free because he is conscious of his wishes, whilst at the same time he is ignorant of the causes by which he is led to wish and desire.'[69] 'All final causes are nothing but human fictions';[70] the will like all other things is determined by efficient causes. The only meaning that could be accorded to human liberty was the achievement of understanding and the acceptance of the inevitable.[71] So 'the wise man . . . is scarcely ever moved in his mind, but being conscious of a certain eternal necessity of himself, of God, and of things, never ceases to be, and always enjoys true peace of mind.'[72]

At first sight this seems a fatalistic doctrine; nevertheless Spinoza was not simply a mechanistic determinist. His doctrine of '*conatus*' ascribed to every mode, or entity, an essential drive (*conatus*), an inner source of energy and endeavour, which constituted its very being. Nothing was merely the passive plaything of external forces. 'Each thing, in so far as it is in itself, endeavours to persevere in its own being',[73] and 'the effort by which each thing endeavours to persevere in its own being is nothing but the actual essence of the thing itself.'[74] Unlike the endeavours of Hobbes, which were particular and reactive, the endeavour (*conatus*) of Spinoza was central and active. It was a universal principle applying to all finite entities. In human terms it could be described as appetite, or, when conscious, as desire. At its highest level it became 'the intellectual love of God'.[75] The intellect itself possessed a dynamic aspect, in so far as its ideas were 'adequate',[76] and could not be distinguished from will.[77] Though initially described as a principle of self-maintenance and inertia, comparable to a homeostatic regulator, there was in Spinoza's conception of '*conatus*' an implicit creative urge towards fuller reality and perfection, or what he termed a state of 'blessedness'.[78]

It was this doctrine that constituted the central core of Spinoza's treatment of the emotions, to which a large part of his *Ethic* was devoted. It is one of the most straightforward and satisfactory treatments of the subject ever formulated. The goal of the whole enterprise was a practical, therapeutic one, to attain 'a knowledge of the human mind and its highest happiness'.[79] There were just three fundamental components of emotional life; desire (the conscious aspect of *conatus*), joy (or pleasure) and sorrow (or pain). Joy was the passion 'by which the mind passes to greater perfection'.[80] There was a natural tendency for the mind to dwell on whatever enhanced its perfection, and to exclude whatever tended to diminish it, giving rise to love on the one hand and hatred on the other. 'Love is nothing but joy accompanied with the idea of an external cause, and hatred nothing but sorrow with the accompanying idea of an external cause.'[81] Although Spinoza listed and discussed nearly fifty different emotions, it was in fact impossible to compile a complete inventory since 'there are just as many kinds as there are kinds of objects by which we are affected',[82] and 'the affects can be combined in so many ways, and so many varieties can arise, that no limits can be assigned to their number'.[83] Not only do similar affects differ in different individuals, but 'the same man may be affected by one and the same object in different ways at different times.'[84] Affects might arise from association, from fortuitous and unnoticed incidents, from recollection of the past or projections into the future, and contrary associations could produce ambivalent, or, as Spinoza termed them, 'vacillating' affects, so that 'we shall at the same time hate the thing and love it.'[85] Spinoza backed up his analysis of emotional dynamics with many shrewd observations of affective behaviour.

Spinoza's primary motive in analysing human affects was a psychotherapeutic one. He was no puritan, and held that 'nothing but a gloomy and sad superstition forbids enjoyment'. Indeed 'the greater the joy by which we are affected, the greater the perfection to which we pass thereby, that is to say, the more do we necessarily partake of the divine nature.'[86] Nevertheless the passions were the source of conflict within the individual, and dissensions between individuals.[87] Ungoverned by intellect they led to human bondage. Affects, however, could not be directly controlled by the will. They could be removed by stronger affects, or by detaching the affect from the ideas that gave rise to it.[88] 'If we detach an emotion of the mind, or affect, from the thought of an external cause, and connect it with other thoughts, then the love and hatred towards the external cause and the fluctuations of the mind which arise from the affects will be destroyed.'[89] 'An affect which is a passion ceases to be a passion as soon as we form a clear and distinct idea of it.'[90] Men could be freed, therefore, and achieve 'blessedness' in so far as he possessed 'the power of arranging and connecting the affections of the body according to the order of the intellect';[91] and this required 'not a little practice and study'.[92] There were, of course, parallels to Spinoza's proposals in eastern systems, such as the Yoga Sutras of Patanjali, and striking similarities to psychoanalytic therapy.

The influence of Spinoza on Freud is perhaps his most important contribution to the shaping of psychology. Certain resemblances between the theories of the two men had been noted for some time, by Hamblin Smith, for example, in 1925; by Hampshire in his book on Spinoza (1951), and by Lou Andreas-Salomé in her *Freud Journal* (1964), where she described Spinoza as 'the philosopher of psycho-analysis'.[93] But it was doubtful whether the resemblances were more than coincidental, as Freud never refers to Spinoza in his published writings, and some commentators, for example Bidney, held that 'the differences between the metapsychology of Spinoza and Freud are far greater than their agreements'.[94] An entirely different light was thrown on the question when Hessing in 1977 published a previously unknown letter from Freud to L. Bichel, dated 28 June 1931, in which he wrote, 'My dependence on the teachings of Spinoza I do admit most willingly. I had no reason to mention his name directly, as I got my presumptions not from studying him, but from the atmosphere he created.'[95] In a subsequent letter to S. Hessing, dated 9 July 1932, Freud admitted that 'throughout my life I have shown an extraordinary rather shy esteem for the person as well as the thought of the great philosopher'.[96] The resemblances, therefore, that Hampshire and others had noted were not merely coincidental; Spinoza had a direct influence on the formation of Freud's views, and, in spite of certain differences, can be regarded as providing a sort of philosophical legitimization of psychoanalysis. Both systems are deterministic, both dynamic. The libido of Freud is not dissimilar to, though less all-embracing than, the '*conatus*' of Spinoza. The Freudian unconscious is foreshadowed in Spinoza's distinction between adequate and inadequate ideas and in his distinction between conscious desires and unconscious appetites. Spinoza's account of emotional dynamics is similar in many ways to Freud's, as Hampshire has pointed out.

> Desires and appetites are projected upon objects, as objects of love or hate, in accordance, first with the primary economic needs of the organism, as objects promoting or depressing its vitality, and secondly upon objects that are derivatively associated, through the complex mechanisms of memory, with increase or decrease of vitality. Following this conception of a person's undifferentiated energy of self-assertion, Spinoza's account of passive emotions, and of the laws of transference that govern them, is very close to Freud's mechanisms of projection, transference, displacement and identification in forming the objects of love and aggression.[97]

The way of release from emotional conflict is through intellectual insight or the reality principle, the replacement of confused 'id' functions by conscious, or, as Spinoza, would say, adequate 'ego' functions.

In regarding Spinoza's philosophy as a prop for psychoanalytic theory, it must not be forgotten that he was a seventeenth century philosopher, and that his views necessarily reflect the contemporary outlook and its limitations. No one at that period had a real appreciation of the relevance of time and evolution,[98] nor of the social dimension of human nature, nor of the objective correlates of mind. Insight into these features of human nature were later developments; but there is no insuperable reason why Spinoza's system of thought, while retaining its essential core, should not be modified to embrace them.

IV

Much more immediately influential than Spinoza's rather obscure metaphysical system was the homespun, common-sense philosophy of the contemporary English philosopher John Locke (1632-1704). His principal works went through several editions in his lifetime. His *Essay on Human Understanding* (1690) has been republished more times than any other modern philosophical classic, and translated into many other languages. Bertrand Russell has described Locke as 'the most influential, though by no means the most profound of modern philosophers'.[99] It was above all his tone of mind that commended him so widely. Calm, unpretentious, tolerant and reasonable, he dismissed all airy speculation, whether in philosophy, science or theology, and focused attention on the process of knowledge itself, on the questions of how knowledge was attained, and what were its necessary limitations. His outstanding qualities were his eye for the key issues, and his honesty in facing difficulties. His answers were often confused and prolix, but they were at least expressed in attractive and simple language, which the ordinary mortal could understand. Though not primarily a psychologist, he had more to do with shaping the course that modern psychology was to take than any other thinker. Much more than Bacon or Hobbes he was the fountainhead of the empirical tradition in psychology, which has not only dominated the Anglo-Saxon schools but also deeply influenced many continental thinkers, and eventually led to the foundation of experimental laboratories and the separation of psychology from philosophy.

There were, Locke believed, no short cuts to knowledge, no inner sources of illumination. Knowledge was derived from experience, from observation and reflection, and was 'a work of time, accurateness, attention and judgement'.[100] Much so-called knowledge was merely 'learned ignorance'.[101] 'We should not take doubtful systems for complete sciences, nor unintelligible notions for scientifical demonstrations. In the knowledge of bodies we must be content to glean what we can from particular experiments.'[102] Himself trained in medicine, Locke was above all impressed by the new 'experimental philosophy'. In 1668 he was elected a Fellow of the Royal Society only five years after its foundation, and thus came into contact with the most eminent scientists of his time. In particular he established close relationships with his old Oxford friend Robert Boyle, one of the leading experimentalists, and with Thomas Sydenham, the leading physician. His own philosophical outlook was largely shaped by their strongly empirical standpoint. Locke himself, however, was regarded by his scientific colleagues in the Royal Society as a sufficiently sound experimentalist to be appointed to a committee of eleven 'for considering and directing experiments,[103] and he expressed the conviction that real progress in knowledge was the result of progress in technology.[104] Hence Locke's famous statement that in the beginning the mind was empty of content, like 'white paper, void of all characters, without any ideas'.[105] If we wanted to know, we had to find out. The vast store of knowledge acquired by man had one source only, experience. In other words man had to learn. So quite naturally Locke thought childhood and education of paramount importance in the forming of the mind, and he followed the writing of his *Essay* with *Some Thoughts concerning Education* (1695), a pioneer work on educational theory. In it he noted that 'the little or almost insensible impressions on our tender infancies have very important and lasting consequences', and 'of all the men we meet with, nine parts of ten are what they are, good or evil, useful or not, by their education'.[106] In these observations Locke was already drawing some of the characteristic conclusions of empirical psychology.

Locke was motivated to embark on his enquiry into human knowledge because of his conviction that the troubles of the stormy years of civil warfare and ideological strife through which he had lived were the result of fanaticism, or 'enthusiasm' as he termed it, and that this evil was largely rooted in false philosophies and unsound pretensions to knowledge. He was opposed not only to the empty verbiage of the schoolmen, but also to the new philosophy of Descartes. It was, indeed, his acquaintance with the writings of Descartes which provoked him to philosophical reflection. 'He rejoiced in reading of these, because though he often differed in opinion from the writer, yet he found that what he said was very intelligible.'[107] In particular Locke was completely opposed to Descartes's theory of 'innate ideas', and when he came to write his *Essay on Human Understanding* he devoted the whole of the first book to countering this doctrine. His aim was to show 'how men, barely by the use of their natural faculties, may attain to all the knowledge they have, without any help of innate impressions; and may arrive at certainty, without any such original notions and principles'.[108] Locke did not go so far as to deny that human beings were endowed with native powers and inclinations; but he held that these could only be actualized and furnished by experience. Nor did he deny individual differences in capacity, and admitted that 'each man's mind has some peculiarity, as well as his face, that distinguishes him from all others: and there are possibly scarce two children who can be conducted by exactly the same method'.[109] These differences, however, did not invalidate Locke's thesis that all knowledge was derived from experience, and that human beings, in spite of their diversity, were fundamentally equal. As he said in his *Treatise of Civil Government* (1690), there is 'nothing more evident than that creatures of the same species and rank, promiscuously born to all the same advantages of nature and use of the same faculties, should also be equal one amongst another without subordination or subjection.'[110] In his emphasis on learning and experience rather than inheritance, and on equality rather than inequality, Locke was establishing the pattern of much subsequent empirical thinking.

One feature of Descartes's philosophy, however, Locke did accept, and that was his dualism. For all practical purposes he admitted a sharp distinction between the corporeal and the spiritual, between body and mind. He did not adopt Descartes's strange theory of how mind and body interacted;[111] he did not rule out in principle the possibility of thinking matter;[112] he adhered to the traditional doctrine of 'the great chain of being', and the hierarchically ordered universe with its implication of insensible gradations between animate and inanimate. But as an essential practical thinker his standpoint was dualistic. 'Natural philosophy,' he affirmed, 'being the knowledge of the principles, properties and operations of things as they are in themselves I imagine there are two parts of it, one comprehending spirits and their nature and qualities, and the other bodies.'[113] There were two spheres of reality, body and mind, and correspondingly two roads to knowledge – sensation, which provided knowledge of the external world, and reflection (or introspection as it later came to be termed), which provided knowledge of the internal world of mind or consciousness, for 'consciousness always accompanies thinking'.[114] This implied that the analysis of the mind could be carried out by introspective methods and that it was unnecessary, as far as cognitive psychology was concerned, 'to meddle with the physical consideration of the mind'.[115] This again established a tradition in psychology which was only slowly broken.

How then did Locke proceed in his introspective analysis of mind? Influenced largely by the corpuscular philosophy of his friend Boyle, and by the contintental thinker Gassendi, Locke looked first for the basic units of the mind, corresponding to the atomic corpuscles of the physicists. He found these in what Descartes had termed 'ideas'. Ideas were the building blocks of Locke's psychological system, and he defined them as 'whatsoever is the object of the understanding when a man thinks'.[116] The term 'idea' was an omnibus term, covering all forms of mental content, sensations, perceptions, thoughts, feelings, volitions, etc. Ideas initially were, according to Locke, simple and purely passive; some were provided by sensation, others by the internal sense which he termed reflection. Locke catalogued the principal simple ideas, and then went on to describe how the mind elaborated them by comparing, distinguishing, abstracting, uniting and so on, to form complex ideas 'to an almost infinite variety'.[117] In engaging in these processes the mind was no longer passive but active, and no longer confined to representing the real. Simple ideas, however, were both the essential foundation of all knowledge and at the same time 'the boundaries of our thoughts, beyond which the mind, whatever the effects it could make, is not able to advance one jot'.[118] Into the philosophical difficulties presented by Locke's theories we need not enter; they have been endlessly discussed by philosophers from his day to our own. It is their importance for psychology that must be stressed. Locke initiated the introspective analysis of mind that for over two hundred years remained the principal method of psychology. He coined the term 'the association of ideas';[119] and although he thought chance assocations a potent source of error, he regarded natural linkages and connections as the stuff of rational knowledge. In dissecting the way in which ideas of number, space, time, substance, relations and power, as well as psychological concepts, were derived, he established what has since been termed 'genetic epistemology'.[120] In doing so he laid down the main lines that psychology was to follow. Even those who disagreed with his answers accepted his definition of the questions; and his emphasis on cognitive problems left its stamp on academic psychology well into the twentieth century.

In two special areas Locke was also a pioneer. He provided 'the earliest systematic treatment of the problem of personal identity',[121] and in Book III of the *Essay* 'the first modern treatise devoted specifically to the philosophy of Language'.[122] On both these questions Locke's proposals no doubt present many problems. With regard to personal identity he recognized that the concept of 'spiritual substance' was devoid of precise content, so could not form the basis of our awareness of our own personal identities. His suggestion, however, that personal identity depended entirely on the continuity of consciousness is open to a good many objections, and indeed conflicts with his own statements as to the immediate intuitive knowledge that we have of ourselves.[123] Locke's importance once again, however, lies in his raising of the issues, rather than in the answer he provided. Similarly with regard to language, Locke recognized the vital role that language played both in communication among social beings and as an aid to thought. Words, however, were liable to abuse, and were full of imperfections. To be serviceable they must possess meaning, that is to say they must stand for ideas. But it is impossible that 'every particular thing should have a distinct particular name'. So 'words become general by being made the signs of general ideas',[124] and this is where the problems begin, for 'nominal essences' need not necessarily correspond with 'real essences'; they can be 'made very arbitrarily, made without patterns, or reference to real existence'.[125] In his observations on language, and the relation between words and ideas, Locke was in effect opening up a field of enquiry later to become known as psycholinguistics.

The real significance of Locke to psychology was not so much in what he achieved as in what he initiated. His actual achievements in psychology were slight. His detailed analysis of the intellectual life was neither very original nor very profound. Although he decried the old faculties, he still used the terminology of faculty psychology, and distinguished the two chief faculties of thinking and willing. He almost ignored man's emotional life, devoting a mere three pages of his six-hundred page *Essay* to 'modes of pleasure and pain'.[126] But his definition of the subject matter, and his prescriptions for the methodology of psychology, were highly influential, and he is not without justification regarded as the founding father of the empirical school of psychology, for although Hobbes preceded him, it was Locke rather than Hobbes who provided the starting point for further developments.

V

Locke's chief opponent as the eighteenth century dawned was the German philosopher G.W. Leibniz (1646-1716), a man of phenomenal gifts, whom Bertrand Russell has described as 'one of the supreme intellects of all time';[127] and of whom the American thinker John Dewey has written, 'There are but three or four names in the history of thought which can be placed by the side of Leibniz's.'[128] He was not only a logician, metaphysician and psychologist, but a creative mathematician of the first rank, a historian, lawyer, librarian and man of affairs. 'He was learned not merely in many things', said Du Bois Reymond, 'but so far as a man can be, in all and everything.'[129] He was the first of the great line of German philosophers who have so deeply influenced western thought over the last three centuries – and it must not be forgotten that, in spite of its strong Anglo-Saxon ingredients, modern psychology was actually born in Germany, and is inevitably coloured by its German origins and German philosophical parentage. Though the impact of Leibniz on the development of psychology was much less immediate than that of Locke – partly because the bulk of Leibniz's writings were not published until after his death – both his direct and indirect contributions to psychology were considerable, in particular his stress on the active nature of the mind, the role of innate powers, and the importance of unconscious processes.

Perhaps more than any of his contemporaries Leibniz was 'a spectator of all time and all existence'. In an age when it was fashionable to reject the past and to scorn the abstruse learning of the schoolmen, Leibniz, who was deeply versed in scholastic philosophy, maintained that the works of the scholastics 'sometimes contain substantial discussions'.[130] 'The opinions of the scholastic philosophers and theologians are much sounder than has been imagined, provided,' he added, 'that they are used appropriately and in their proper place.'[131] The son of a professor of philosophy at Leipzig, the precocious young Gottfried was early given the run of his father's library, and long before he entered the university at the age of fifteen had steeped himself not only in the philosophical writings of the ancient Greeks, the fathers of the Church, and the scholastics of the Middle Ages, but also in the esoteric writings of the hermetics and mystics.[132] At the same time he was sharply aware of the contemporary intellectual scene. He studied Bacon, Descartes and Hobbes, to whom he even wrote, though without getting a reply. He annotated Locke's *Essay* with meticulous care. Spinoza he personally met shortly before his death, having long discussions with him. While rejecting many of the central tenets of Spinoza's philosophy, Leibniz was certainly influenced by the *Ethic*, which he read prior to its publication. On a visit to Paris he met the leading mathematicians of the day, and, in spite of being largely self-taught, became the equal, if not the superior, in the mathematical field of his predecessor, Descartes. Though not a biologist he was nevertheless deeply interested in the progress of the biological sciences resulting from the development of the microscope. He was, in short, a master of knowledge, both past and contemporary.

But Leibniz did not merely absorb; he created, and, in his creative role, he has been described as 'the dawning consciousness of the modern world'.[133] He was, with Newton, the co-inventor of the calculus, and devised the notation which is now in general use; he constructed one of the first calculating machines; he was the father of modern symbolic logic, and envisaged the possibility of a universal science expressed in a universal symbolism; he grasped the importance of 'the study of degrees of probability', noted that 'it was still lacking, and that this is a serious shortcoming in our treatises on logic'.[134] In his views on the nature of matter, space and time, and his speculations on possible worlds he anticipated the modern age. In all that he undertook he strove for coherence, harmony and clarity. At the same time he was intensely practical. He showed a high degree of social concern, and belief in the application of science to social welfare. He founded, and became the first president of, the Berlin Academy of Science; he supervised the planning and construction of the first free-standing library building of the modern era; on behalf of his employer, the Duke of Brunswick, he often travelled abroad on diplomatic missions. His rare combination of theoretical power and practical effectiveness is well summed up in one of his favourite mottoes, '*In verbis claritas, in rebus usus*' ('Clarity in speaking and usefulness in action').

Recognition of Leibniz's philosophical stature was slow in establishing itself, particularly in the Anglo-Saxon world. This is partly because, as Bertrand Russell has noted, his system of philosophy had a certain 'fantastic' quality,[135] but more particularly because very little of his work was published by Leibniz in his lifetime, and a great deal of it was in the form of memoranda and correspondence, which was deposited in the library in Hanover, and only brought to light many years later. The definitive edition of his writings sponsored by the German Academy of Science has not yet been completed. Not until the beginning of the twentieth century did he become properly appreciated outside Germany as a result of the work of Dewey (1888), Latta (1898), Russell (1900), Couturat (1901), and others.[136]

Before turning to Leibniz's contributions to psychology, we must briefly look at the main tenets of his metaphysical speculations. Reality, according to Leibniz, consisted of an infinitely large system of individual entities, which he termed 'monads'. These monads were not material, but 'metaphysical points', or centres of activity (energy) and perception, each mirroring, from their individual standpoints, and in varying degrees, the entire universe. Though 'windowless', and activated solely from within, they kept in step because of a 'pre-established harmony'. Like the instruments of an orchestra they followed a prescribed score, and were governed by a conductor, the supreme monad, God, whose plan ensured that the world was 'the best of all possible worlds'; for even God was constrained by logical necessity. It is easy to miss the value of Leibniz's insights and to reject the whole system because of its more 'fantastic' features, its 'windowless' monads, and its 'pre-established harmony'. Indeed metaphysical speculation as such is unfashionable, and Leibniz was a quintessential metaphysician. Nevertheless Leibniz adumbrated some extremely fruitful ideas, which went some way to surmount the problems raised by Cartesian dualism, Spinozistic monism, and Newtonian mechanism. Leibniz was the first to argue that force was the essence of substance; that it was dynamic, not inert; and among the first, if not the first, to argue that mental powers could be unconscious. He stressed individuality as an ultimate feature of the world; no two monads could be completely identical. The ordered system of the cosmos was a hierarchical system in which monads were arranged according to the degree of clarity with which they mirrored the universe. Symbolization, representation, or information was important at every monadic level, even the simplest. Dominant monads were organisms, souls and spirits; and their ordering principle was not merely mechanical but logical and moral. Ultimately the world was a system of interlocking final causes, though within their proper limits mechanical explanations were 'well-founded' (*bene fundata*).[137]

It would be wrong for psychologists to dismiss this abstruse speculative system of Leibniz as a matter of no concern of theirs. Its implications for psychology are profound; and Leibniz himself wrote a psychological classic, the *Nouveaux Essais*, which has only recently become available in a satisfactory English translation, and which was not published in any language until half a century after his death. The complex nature of man was, indeed, for Leibniz a major problem. 'Now that we are conquerors of the world', he wrote, 'there assuredly remains an enemy within us; everything is clear to man, but man, the body to the mind, and the mind to itself. To drop the tragic style, and to speak more naturally, we are ignorant of the medicine of bodies and minds.'[138] His suggestion of the need for a '*medicina mentis*' directly inspired early work in psychiatry.[139]

The *Nouveaux Essais sur l'Entendement humain* (New Essays on Human Understanding) were a critical analysis of Locke's famous *Essay*. The work was written in French between 1703 and 1705, but its publication was suppressed by Leibniz on hearing of Locke's death in November 1704. It was first published in 1765, but no acceptable text appeared until the Berlin Academy edition of 1962, and no adequate English translation until 1981. The care with which Leibniz read and commented on Locke's book was in itself a recognition of his appreciation of Locke's enterprise. Nevertheless he disagreed fundamentally with several of Locke's doctrines. Above all, he insisted that knowledge cannot be derived solely from sensory experience. 'Our certainty would be small, or rather non-existent, if we had no foundation of simple ideas except one deriving from the senses . . . our certainty regarding universal and eternal truths is grounded in the ideas themselves, independently of the senses.'[140] Hence the famous adage, '*Nihil est in intellectu quod non fuerit in sensu . . . nisi intellectus ipse*.'[141] There is indeed 'a light born within us', an innate component upon which all our knowledge depends.[142] Locke's idea of the mind as a *tabula rasa*, devoid of content until the senses furnish it, was mistaken. The mind, insisted Leibniz, is structured from the beginning; just as the veins in the block of marble determine the way the sculptor chisels, so the structure of the mind partly determines the way knowledge grows. These innate structures are not themselves active ideas, but inclinations, dispositions, principles and instincts.[143]

> There are in us instinctive truths which are innate principles that we sense and that we approve, even though we have no proof of them . . . though we get one when we explain the instinct in question. This is how we employ the laws of inference, being guided by a confused knowledge of them, as if by instinct, though the logicians demonstrate the reasons for them; as mathematicians explain what we do unthinkingly when we walk or jump. . . . Setting

aside instincts, like the one which makes us pursue joy and flee sorrow, moral knowledge is innate in just the same way that arithmetic is, for it too depends upon demonstrations provided by the inner light.[144]

Leibniz clearly held, too, that there were innate differences between minds, as well as innate components common to all minds, though these inherent individual differences he did not regard as a barrier to achievement given adequate guidance.[145] Though there is no doubt that he overemphasized the innate components in knowledge, and even went so far as to state 'nothing enters naturally into our minds from without',[146] his stress on the active participation of the intellect itself in, and its contribution to, the knowledge process was extremely important, and almost certainly contained some validity. Not long after Leibniz's death Hume was to demonstrate that pushed to its logical conclusion the empiricism of Locke led finally to scepticism.

A principal reason for Locke's having denied the innate component in knowledge was, Leibniz held, that Locke, following Descartes, had identified mind with consciousness. To be in the understanding implied, for Locke, to be actually perceived.[147] Leibniz disagreed, and held, on the contrary, that there were degrees of perception, and that a great deal was in fact subliminal or unconscious.

There are hundreds of indications leading us to conclude that at every moment there is in us an infinity of perceptions unaccompanied by awareness or reflection; that is, alterations of the soul itself, of which we are unaware because these impressions are either too minute and too numerous, or else too unvarying, so that they are not sufficiently distinctive on their own. But when they are combined with others they do nevertheless have their effect, and make themselves felt, at least confusedly, within the whole.[148]

And he went on, 'insensible perceptions are as important to pneumatology [i.e. psychology in current terminology] as insensible corpuscles are to natural science.'[149]

The term 'perception' was, of course, used by Leibniz in a much broader connotation than it has now come to acquire. It was for him an omnibus term covering every kind of symbolic, representative or expressive process. 'Expression', he explained to his friend Arnauld, 'is common to all soul-principles. It is a genus of which natural perception, animal feeling and intellectual knowledge are species.'[150] According to Leibniz every monad in principle represented the whole universe. 'In a confused way they all strive after the infinite, the whole; but they are limited and differentiated through the degrees of their distinct perceptions.'[151] He distinguished three main degrees or levels of representation: the unconscious level of 'petites perceptions', the sensory level in which perception was more distinct and accompanied by memory, and the most advanced level which he termed 'apperception' and which involved self-conscious awareness and reflective knowledge.[152] In his postulation of unconscious processes Leibniz was a pioneer. There may have been suggestions of such processes in the writings of Malebranche and the Cambridge Platonists, but Leibniz was the first to develop the theory in any detail.[153] He proposed it partly on theoretical grounds and in conformity with the basic principle of continuity and insensibly graded transitions, and partly on the basis of quite acute observations of dreams, after-images, the process of awakening and so on. He held that minute unconscious perceptions could explain many peculiarities of external behaviour and internal feeling. 'When I take one way rather than another, it is often because of a series of tiny impressions of which I am not aware, but which make one movement slightly harder than another.'[154] States of desire and uneasiness could be accounted for in terms of 'minute sufferings of which we cannot be aware',[155] and well-being in terms of 'nature's accumulation of continual little triumphs'.[156] The unconscious preservation of past experiences also partly accounted for the identity of an individual's character. Unconscious processes thus played a highly significant role, according to Leibniz; and although there is no suggestion that they might also be used to explain mental pathology, Leibniz's theory was, as Russell observed, 'a very important advance'.[157]

Perhaps almost as significant was his emphasis on change. From the time Plato had confined the Heraclitan flux in a prison house of 'forms', European thought had been dominated by static concepts. Leibniz was one of the first European thinkers to move towards process concepts, to think in terms of constant change.[158] In the words of a modern commentator,

> At no two different moments of time can an individual substance
> have the same state, for if the state were exactly the same, the
> whole system of its contemporary substance states would have to be
> the same, and, therefore, moments of time being defined in terms of
> contemporary substance states, the moments of time would also be
> the same.[159]

In other words, without change there could be no such thing as time. Leibniz returned to the Heraclitan principle that 'all bodies are in constant flux like rivers.'[160] In psychological terms change revealed itself as appetition, and appetition as defined as 'the tendency to pass from one perception to another'.[161] Like perception, appetition manifested itself at various levels: the simplest level of unconscious impulse, the intermediate level of instinctive appetite or desire, and finally as self-conscious desire or will.[162] All three levels were present in man. Appetition always accompanied perception, since perceptions necessarily change; the present moment was, therefore, always pregnant with the future (appetition) as well as an inheritor of the past (memory). Temporality was a central feature of Leibniz's cosmos and of his psychology. And it is within this temporal context that he at least presaged the birth of evolutionary theory.

Perhaps at some time, or in some place, in the universe, he wrote, there are, or will be, species of animals more subject to change than those we now have here. Various cat-like animals, such as the lion, the tiger, and the lynx, may once have been of the same race, and may now amount to new subdivisions of the ancient cat species. Thus I keep returning to what I have said several times; that our determinations of physical species are provisional, and are adapted to what we know.[163]

In his emphasis on change Leibniz foreshadowed coming developments in eighteenth and nineteenth century thought.

Less successful was Leibniz's attempt to grapple with the mind-body problem. 'When I set myself to meditate upon the union of soul and body I was as it were drawn back into the deep sea'[164] was his frank admission. He fell back on the unsatisfying doctrine of pre-established harmony. Nevertheless by undermining the sharp Cartesian distinction between mind and matter, Leibniz did move some way towards simplifying the problem. When mind was no longer identified with consciousness, and matter was simply a 'well-founded' phenomenon, rather than a reality *per se*, the breach between matter and mind was significantly narrowed. The balance was tipped in Leibniz's system towards mind, rather than matter; monads were mind-like rather than material, and while thinking always required a material base, no purely mechanical contrivance could conceivably sense or think – or so Leibniz believed.[165]

It is only in the present century that Leibniz's full stature has become recognized. The definitive edition of his works is still incomplete more than two hundred and fifty years after his death. In spite of this handicap and the paucity of his published works his ideas penetrated German thought of the eighteenth and nineteenth centuries, and became the principal source of an approach to psychology which denied some of the fundamental presuppositions of the Lockean empirical school. If only because of his doctrine of unconscious processes, his role in the shaping of modern psychology is incontrovertible, and still far from spent.

VI

Though none of the great thinkers of the seventeenth century, whose views have been briefly outlined in this chapter, used the term 'psychology', they had, in fact, laid the foundations for the scientific study of the mind. Whether, like Hobbes, materialistic in their outlook, or, like Leibniz, inclined towards idealism, they all recognized that there was a special set of problems relating to mind, and they were all persuaded that the methods that were proving so fruitful in the study of the physical world could be, and must be, applied equally to these problems. For the scholastics who had preceded them Aristotle was the supreme authority; for the seventeenth century thinkers the authority was scientific method. With the exception of

Leibniz all these thinkers totally rejected scholasticism, and aimed at laying new foundations for philosophy and psychology. For psychology this brought losses as well as gains. The intimate relation of soul and body in the scholastic system was rudely shattered; the atomization of the mind into its constituent 'ideas' threatened the unity which the older doctrines had taken for granted; both the person and his persisting dispositions and faculties were in danger of getting lost in the mere flux of inner events; the ancient hierarchies were levelled; and final causes, with the goals and purposes they implied, in most systems other than Leibniz's, were cast away.[166] All this represented a real impoverishment of the psychology which had come down through scholasticism from the ancient world. Of course, the older psychology never completely died; Plato and Aristotle were still studied in the universities; the undercurrent of scholastic teaching never wholly disappeared, and the new psychologies had to borrow at least some of the terminology of the old. Above all Christianity still remained a potent influence in the western world, and its creed carried with it inescapable psychological implications. So the loss was not total.

On the other hand there were substantial gains, primarily methodological gains. Scholasticism had become unduly verbal, and its abstract superstructures lacked adequate observational and experimental foundations. The new psychologies were based on direct observation and analysis. True, they involved certain presuppositions: that mind could be equated with consciousness; that consciousness could be analysed into simple 'ideas'; that it was possible to find certain laws, such as the law of association, that could explain how complex states were built up from simple elements, and how trains of thoughts and actions were directed; and that the essential method for studying the mind was introspection. These presuppositions were to persist, in spite of some attempts to criticize them, right up to the early years of the twentieth century. Within this framework substantial advances were made – in the analysis of sensory and cognitive processes, in the description of emotional states, in the first rough account of reflex action, and in the raising of more complex problems, such as the problem of personal identity and the role of language in thinking. The singling out of the association of ideas as a basic explanatory principle may have been an undue simplification, but it was an enormously fruitful hypothesis, which initiated the study of human learning and habit formation. But the greatest gain of all was that psychology was on the move, and was no longer constricted within a rigid body of doctrine.

Of course, there were divergences of viewpoint and disagreements among the thinkers of the seventeenth century, and these disagreements, too, have persisted into our own times. There were disagreements as to the relation between body and mind, disagreements as to whether the structure of mind was to some extent innate, or wholly derived from experience, disagreements as to whether individual minds differed significantly from one another, or were fundamentally alike and equal, and disagreements as to whether all, or only some, mental processes were fully conscious. Broadly speaking there were two major schools of thought: the continental rationalists, of whom Leibniz may be regarded as the representative figure, and the British empiricists, represented by Locke. Their essential differences, doctrinal and methodological, have not yet been resolved.

In spite of these disagreements psychology was beginning to emerge as a separate, and important, discipline, perhaps mainly due to the influence of Locke. Though still to some extent entangled with epistemology, logic and ethics, with Locke psychology had shed a great deal of metaphysical lumber, and had launched itself as an empirical enquiry. The eighteenth century, the age of the Enlightenment, was to consolidate and enlarge the foundations laid in the seventeenth.

Chapter 7
Eighteenth century developments

I

The eighteenth century was a period of great significance in the development of psychology; it saw, on the one hand, the crystallization of the many suggestive new ideas of the seventeenth century philosophers into a separate *Wissenschaft*, or scientific discipline, with a recognized identifying label – psychology; and it saw, on the other hand, the beginning of protest movements against the imposition upon the study of the human mind of the methods and assumptions of the physical sciences. The guiding lights of the Age of Enlightenment, as the period is commonly termed, were the Englishmen Newton and Locke. They dominated the intellectual life not only of England, but to a great extent also of France and to a lesser extent of Germany, and the empirical approach of Locke was the major influence in the emerging discipline of psychology. Locke, however, never had the field to himself. He was challenged by Scottish philosophers of the 'common sense' school, by moralists and Platonists in England, and by rationalists in Germany. And all of these had a lasting influence on psychology. But perhaps even more important was the Romantic revolt, which began in the eighteenth century, against the whole ethos of the Enlightenment and the domination of reason, a revolt which involved 'a vast transformation of ideas, language, attitudes and ways of thinking', and which 'for two hundred years has deeply and decisively affected European life'[1] including, we may add, European psychology. This revolt was no doubt an outcome of the profound social changes which the eighteenth century brought about, involving the rapid decay of traditional values and ways of life, and the emergence of a new, largely secular society dominated by economic forces. Marx and Engels may have exaggerated in saying that there remained 'no other bond between man and man than naked self-interest and callous cash payments'.[2] Traditional ties and institutions did not vanish as completely as that; but the unequal growth of wealth resulting from colonial exploitation, changes in agriculture, and industrialization, together with the lifting of the medieval taboos on usury and the development of a capitalistic bourgeoisie, led to widespread social tensions and growing feelings of alienation, which in their turn gave rise to new psychological problems and new psychological reactions. The eighteenth century witnessed the birth of the modern world in all its complexity.

II

The empirically based associationist psychology which emerged during this epoch was an amplification and consolidation of the ideas of John Locke. Locke's ideas were developed by Berkeley and Hume, and consolidated into systematic form first by David Hartley, sometimes regarded as the founder of associationist psychology.[3] Associationist psychology accepted the dualistic doctrines of Descartes; as Hartley put it, 'Man consists of two parts, body and mind.'[4] Its aim was to analyse mind into its elements, and to discover the laws according to which these elements were compounded. Sensory elements were the basic stuff of knowledge; and pleasure and pain the controlling forces of conduct. There were no innate components of experience or behaviour. Apart from this broad framework of principles the associationists decried abstract systematization. Mind must be analysed step by step in the way that the physical scientists were gradually building up a model of the physical universe. As Newton proclaimed,

> To explain all nature is too difficult a task for any one man, or even for any one age. 'Tis much better to do a little with certainty and leave the rest for others that come after, than to explain all things by conjecture without making sure of anything; and there is no other way of doing anything with certainty than by drawing conclusions from experiments and phenomena.[5]

This has always been the creed of the empirical psychologist, and it is for their detailed analysis of particular problems that Berkeley and Hume, Locke's immediate successors, are of primary significance in the history of psychology.

George Berkeley (1685-1753), the Irish bishop, is important for his empirical theory of space perception, and for his doctrine of signs. His *Essay towards a New Theory of Vision* (1709), in which his doctrine of space was first propounded, has been described as 'one of the most brilliant psychological works that has ever been written'.[6] Naturally it did not give final answers, or resolve all the problems of space perception, but it laid the foundations for all subsequent accounts, from those of Helmholtz in the nineteenth century to those of Gibson, Gregory, Piaget, Held and others in the twentieth. According to Berkeley, 'we perceive distance, not immediately, but by mediation of a sign, which hath no likeness to it, or necessary connexion with it, but only suggests it from repeated experience.'[7] 'Distance of itself and immediately cannot be seen.'[8] Space Berkeley regarded as in its origin a tactile phenomenon, and only experienced visually as a result of signs or cues, such as ocular convergence and accommodation. Among the implications of this theory was the prediction that 'a man born blind, being made to see, would at first have no idea of distance by sight'.[9] This supposition had already been advanced by Molyneux, who in 1692 published the first English treatise on Optics, and had been noted by Locke.[10] In 1723, less than twenty years after Berkeley's *New Theory of Vision*, a London surgeon, William Chesselden, gave 'An Account of some Observations made by a young gentleman, who was born blind, or lost his sight so early, that he had no remembrance of ever having seen, and was couched between thirteen and fourteen years of age.'[11] According to Chesselden, this patient 'when he first saw was so far from making any judgment about distances, that he thought all objects whatever touch'd his eyes. . . . He knew not the shape of anything, nor any one thing from another, however different in shape or magnitude.'[12] Nor could he at first distinguish a cat from a dog. This remarkable case study, which has been described as 'the most celebrated case study in the history of science until the early case studies of Freud',[13] was generally regarded as confirming the essential validity of Berkeley's theory. More recent cases, of which there are a good many, and a mass of experimental evidence, suggest that the problem is decidedly more complex than Berkeley and his contemporaries thought.[14] Though space perception in man is clearly susceptible to modification by learning, there is probably also an innate component in it. The experiments of Held and his colleagues carried out a few years ago have shown in fact that the ability to see the world in three dimensions develops in infants at about the age of sixteen weeks, and develops very rapidly in the space of just over a month.[15] The complex processes whereby the child gradually acquires the adult conception of space have been studied in detail by Piaget.[16] Berkeley's original suggestions were, then, the starting point of a whole series of further investigations of considerable theoretical importance.

The other really interesting contribution of Berkeley to psychology is his theory of signs. In his *Treatise on the Principles of Human Knowledge* (1710) he put it thus: 'The connexion of ideas does not imply the relation of cause and effect, but only of a mark or sign with the thing signified. The fire which I see is not the cause of the pain I suffer upon my approaching it, but the mark that forewarns me of it.'[17] Such signs constitute a natural language, and the whole material world, as we know it, can be regarded as a system of sensible signs. Hobbes had attempted to explain sensation wholly in causal terms. Berkeley, on the contrary, regarded it as a form of communication based on a language of signs. It is interesting to note that Pavlov was later to insist that the sensory properties of objects were without any influence *per se*, and were important only as signals which gave rise to expectations. 'When a certain combination of stimuli, arising from the retina and ocular muscles, coincides several times with the tactile stimulus of a body of a certain size, this combination comes to play the role of a signal.'[18] The theory of signs and communication has, in the twentieth century, acquired a central place in scientific psychology. It can look back to Berkeley as a pioneer.

The philosophy of David Hume (1711-1776) was mainly critical and destructive. He envisaged a 'science of man' based on observation and experiment, but never personally achieved it, partly because he eschewed what he called 'all distant and high enquiries'.[19] The effect of his astringent and sceptical analysis was to undermine faith not only in religion and the powers of reason (which must always be a slave to the passions), but in the very basis of induction and scientific knowledge. 'The understanding when it acts alone', he proclaimed, 'and according to its most general principles entirely subverts itself, and leaves not the lowest degree of evidence in any proposition, either in philosophy or common life.'[20] In this flux of uncertainty our sole guides were blind feelings, instincts, habits and traditional prejudices. His psychology was sensory, associationistic and atomistic, his moral philosophy hedonistic and utilitarian. There was, in his view, no essential difference between the minds of men and those of animals.[21] For psychology his two most challenging conclusions were, firstly that it was impossible to discover any necessary connection between a cause and its effect, and secondly that the self was 'nothing but a bundle or collection of different perceptions, which succeed each other with inconceivable rapidity, and are in a perpetual flux and movement'.[22] These conclusions provoked the powerful response of Kantian philosophy, and in psychology they led later on to investigations on causation by Michotte and Piaget,[23] and continuing discussions on the self-concept from William James to the present day.[24]

Although David Hartley (1705-1757) disclaimed any pretence of being a 'system-maker',[25] Part I of his *Observations on Man* (1749) was the first book in modern times which bears some resemblance to a textbook of psychology as we know it today.[26] It was remarkable in several respects. Although a dualist Hartley upheld a strict parallelism between mind and body – between the sensations and ideas which made up mind, and the vibrations of the brain and nervous system which constituted its material base. As a practising physician Hartley was able to back up his theories with clinical observations. Though his physiology was to a considerable extent speculative Hartley was a forerunner of physiological psychology. He was moreover the first systematic associationist, who expounded associationism in the form of basic propositions and universalized them to cover sensory, motor, somatic, affective, volitional and higher cognitive functions. The basic law as applied to sensation he set out as follows:

> Any sensation A,B,C, etc. by being associated with one another a sufficient number of times, gets such a power over the corresponding ideas, a,b,c, etc. that any one of the sensations, A, when impressed alone, shall be able to excite in the mind, b.c. etc., the ideas of the rest. (Prop X.)[27]

Hartley's book was reprinted several times over the next sixty years, and his ideas were further propagated by the advocacy of Joseph Priestley.[28] It was the bible of James Mill, and, at a tender age, part of the educational pabulum of his son, John Stuart. It had, therefore, a lasting effect on the establishment of the associationist psychology which, in various forms, for so long dominated the Anglo-Saxon world. The classic, and purest, exposition of association principles was James Mill's *Analysis of the Phenomena of the Human Mind* (1829) – a dry and bloodless work, of the author of which it could be said, as his son said of Jeremy Bentham, 'all the more subtle workings both of the mind upon itself and of external things upon the mind, escaped him.'[29]

Empirical psychology was not confined to England. It penetrated into Germany and mingled with the native brands of philosophic thought. In France it manifested itself in more extreme forms, sensationalistic, materialistic and environmentalistic, than in the country of its origin. Condillac reduced all higher operations of the mind to transformed sensations; Le Mettrie reduced man to a mere machine; Cabanis proclaimed that 'the brain secretes thought as the liver secretes bile'; while Helvétius maintained that men were wholly the product of their environment, and infinitely malleable by education.[30] The massive Encyclopedia of Diderot and d'Alembert lent the stamp of its authority to a wholly naturalistic and deterministic theory of human nature. These views may have been extreme and over-simple; but they did something to consolidate and define the emerging science of psychology.

III

The empiricists, however, never had things all their own way. From the middle of the eighteenth century till well on into the nineteenth a group of Scottish philosophers headed by Thomas Reid (1710-1796) challenged a number of their basic presuppositions. The role of these Scotsmen in the shaping of psychology has often been underestimated. The common-sense views which they advocated were not very adventurous, and not very acutely argued. They were all long-winded and repetitive, and few modern readers can be bothered to wade through their prolix writings. They were important, however, in the influence they exerted on the early development of psychology in America, as well as on the continent of Europe. And Thomas Reid has the distinction of being the first academic teacher in the English-speaking world whose life, after some preliminary years as a minister of religion, was devoted very largely to the teaching of psychology. He was Professor of Philosophy at Aberdeen from 1752-1763, and from then until he retired in 1780 at Glasgow. His *Inquiry into the Human Mind* was published in 1764, and his two major works, *Essays on the Intellectual Powers of Man* and *Essays on the Active Powers of Man*, after his retirement in 1785 and 1788 respectively. All these works were largely concerned with psychology.

Reid objected to the sceptical and destructive views of his compatriot, Hume, and what he considered to be the absurd conclusions of Bishop Berkeley. Common-sense beliefs were 'older and of more authority than any principles of philosophy'.[31] So common-sense beliefs must serve as the starting point for any sound philosophy; and for Reid common sense implied belief in the existence of an objective material world with real secondary qualities (colours, smells, etc.), our direct awareness of this world, the identity of the self, and the existence of other persons. Such beliefs, though they may stick in the gullets of philosophers, are perhaps not a bad set of working principles for a psychologist. Within the framework of these assumptions Reid was empirical in his approach. He believed in careful observation, and even conducted simple experiments. He was, indeed, among the first to test some of his views experimentally. Where Locke and his followers had gone wrong was not in their empirical approach, but in their doctrine of 'ideas'. 'Ideas', according to Locke, were 'the objects of the understanding when a man thinks', and thus our knowledge of the external world was a mediated knowledge, mediated through 'ideas', which were a sort of screen between the mind and the outside world. And this Reid believed was the source of many of the absurd conclusions reached by Locke's successors. Reid was equally insistent that physiology had nothing useful to contribute to psychology. Hartley's book he described as 'this fallacious tract'.[32] His own aim was a straightforward, descriptive psychology, 'pneumatology' as he termed it, based on both observation and experiment, and avoiding both high-flown theory and undue simplification. This meant analysing the operations of the mind and laying bare its basic powers and faculties. Reid's psychology was essentially a faculty psychology, in which the major division was between powers of understanding or intellectual powers, and powers of will or active powers, embracing appetites, passions and affections as well as volitions. The methods of investigation which Reid recommended were threefold: (i) accurate reflection on the operations of our own mind, (ii) attention to the structure of language, and (iii) attention to the course of human action and conduct.[33] As has been noted, he was prepared occasionally to appeal to simple experiments. Thus when discussing the least noticeable interval of duration he 'found by some experiments that a man may beat seconds for one minute without erring one second in the whole sixty. . . . From this I think it follows that the sixtieth part of a second of time is discernible by the human mind.'[34]

He also carried out simple experiments on double vision,[35] examined more than twenty persons suffering from squints,[36] while delighting in the observation of animal behaviour.[37]

The main difference between Reid's 'common-sense' philosophy and the empiricism of Locke was that, whereas Locke regarded the human mind as empty and blank until passively provided with simple ideas from which all other mental furniture was derived, Reid held that it was equipped with both innate intuitions and innate instincts. 'All reasoning must be from first principles, and these are part of our constitution,' he maintained.[38] Moreover 'the mind is from its very nature a living and active being.'[39] It was necessary to remember, too, that man was an irrational animal for a considerable time before becoming rational,[40] that his higher powers only matured gradually, and this process was 'much aided by proper culture'.[41] Reid laid a considerable emphasis on 'the social operations of the mind',[42] and deplored the neglect of this aspect of 'pneumatology'. Reid's homespun psychology may not have been revolutionary or profound, but it was perhaps the most comprehensive descriptive treatment of the subject prior to the nineteenth century, and its influence on the development of the subject was considerable.

In Scotland Reid was followed by a number of pupils and disciples, of whom Dugald Stewart, Thomas Brown and William Hamilton were the most noteworthy. Thomas Brown incorporated elements of associationism into his system, and propounded the so-called secondary laws of association, which were a significant addition to associationist theory.[43] William Hamilton, the most learned British philosopher of his day, was the first to understand and embody Kantian teachings in his own thought, though still primarily dependent on Reid.[44] After Hamilton's death the Scottish school lost its special identity, but meanwhile it had migrated to America and there its influence continued. As Roback observed, 'Scottish philosophers and psychologists moulded the student mind in the United States and stimulated the teachers to write their texts in a similar vein.'[45] This influence had already been felt towards the end of the eighteenth century when John Witherspoon (1722-1794), President of the College of New Jersey, introduced works of Reid and of another Scottish philosopher, Beattie, in his lectures on moral philosophy. A further impetus was given to the Scottish influence in the next century, when James McCosh (1811-1894), a pupil of Hamilton, who had held a chair in Belfast and had written a book on *The Intuitions of the Mind* (1860), was in 1866 appointed to the Presidency of the College of New Jersey.[46] Not only was McCosh an able administrator, who upgraded the College into Princeton University, but he continued to propagate Scottish doctrines. He wrote on the emotions (1880), the motive powers (1887) and the cognitive powers (1886). He was largely responsible for the enormous impact of Scottish philosophy on the American academic establishment at the end of the nineteenth century. Among his ablest pupils was J. Mark Baldwin (1861-1934), who established the psychological laboratory at Princeton and founded the *Psychological Bulletin*.

The protest of the Scottish school was not the only protest against the tenets of Lockean psychology. Cambridge Platonists like John Norris stressed the importance of attention, and its active role;[47] and a group of eighteenth century moralists emphasized the place of instincts in human nature, and the particular place of social instincts in providing a basis for moral conduct. As Bishop Butler put it in the preface to his *Sermons*, 'Mankind has various instincts and principles of action, as brute creatures have; some leading most directly and immediately to the good of the community, and some most directly to private good.'[48] Shaftesbury in his *Inquiry concerning Virtue* (1699) had already referred to the natural impulse of sympathy, and this became a prominent feature of eighteenth century moral theory. Adam Smith, for example, opened his *Theory of Moral Sentiments* (1759) with a chapter on sympathy, and went on to maintain that human life was directed by and large 'by original and immediate instincts'.[49] Adam Smith, however, went further than simply postulating social instincts. He maintained that our self-knowledge was essentially social in nature. In Part III of his *Theory of Moral Sentiments* he wrote,

We can never survey our own sentiments and motives, we can never form any judgment concerning them, unless we remove ourselves, as it were from our natural station, and endeavour to view them as at a certain distance from us. But we can do this no other way than by endeavouring to view them with the eyes of other people, or as other people are likely to view them.[50]

Society provides a mirror through which we can see ourselves. It enables the ego, so to speak, to divide itself and become both subject and object.[51] Social instincts were not the only feature of human nature emphasized by moralists. Bishop Butler also asserted the claims of the superior faculty of conscience, which was also inbuilt in human nature, and ultimately possessed supreme authority. Perhaps, however, it was the moralists' doctrine of instincts that exerted the deepest influence on psychology. Allied with biological findings, it helped to shape the hormic psychologies and personality theory of the twentieth century.[52]

IV

While these developments were taking place in the British Isles and France, a rather different tradition, derived from Leibniz, was growing up in Germany. Even today German thought displays peculiarities and idiosyncrasies of its own, and these characteristics, just because psychology finally established its independence in Germany, have inevitably left their mark on its history. We have seen that Leibniz's theories for a variety of reasons were slow in penetrating outside Germany. In Germany itself they constituted the core of the philosophical tradition which grew up in the eighteenth century. This was largely due to the influence of Christian Wolff (1679-1754), whose philosophy came to hold almost undisputed sway in German universities until it was superseded by the Kantian revolution. Trained in mathematics and physics, Wolff quite early in his career made the acquaintance of Leibniz, and his own system of philosophy was, like that of Leibniz, essentially rationalistic. Wolff was an arch-systematizer, and aimed to set the brilliant, but somewhat disorganized, theories of Leibniz into disciplined shape. Eventually he settled in Marburg, where he became Chancellor of the University. His enormously prolific writings, recently reissued in sixteen German volumes and thirty-six Latin volumes,[53] cover a vast range of philosophy, law, economics, mathematics, theology and other topics, and include two volumes of psychology, written in Latin, and never translated into English, *Psychologia Empirica* (1732) and *Psychologia Rationalis* (1734). These psychological works are chiefly noteworthy because they canonized the term 'psychology' which had been coined in the late sixteenth century, but not widely adopted.[54] As a result of Wolff's advocacy it became common currency in Germany in the second half of the eighteenth century, and in the first half of the nineteenth spread to America and England. An agreed identifying label clearly does something towards the recognition and establishment of a discipline, and psychology has Wolff to thank for providing it with this. On other counts Wolff's psychology was not particularly notable. His empirical psychology was a conventional faculty psychology, in which the faculties of sensation, memory, imagination, attention, reasoning, will and so on were arranged in hierarchical order and discussed in somewhat abstract terms. In his rational psychology he reasoned from first principles about the simplicity, durability, modifiability and substantiality of the soul, much in the manner of a medieval scholastic. He borrowed a good deal from Leibniz including the doctrine of pre-established harmony between soul and body, and the doctrine of *'petites perceptions'*.[55]

Following the work of Wolff an abundance of psychological literature sprouted up in Germany in the eighteenth century, some of it empirically inclined, but most in the rationalist vein. In the 1780s there even appeared a journal, *Magazin für Seelenerfahrungs Kunde*, later renamed *Psychologisches Journal*. Perhaps the most significant feature of this German psychology was the growing emphasis on the creative aspects of the mind, on imagination and aesthetics.[56] The most striking figure was Johann Tetens (1736-1805) professor at Keil, and then in Copenhagen. His *Essays on Human Nature and its Development* (1776)[57] made some attempt to bridge the gap between empiricism and rationalism, but are primarily noteworthy for replacing the classical twofold division of mental powers, cognitive and orectic – a division which went back to Aristotle – with the threefold division, cognitive, conative and affective, i.e. understanding, volition and feeling.[58] Tetens argued that it was necessary to distinguish the *'actio immanens'*, which remains within ourselves, from the *'actio transiens'*, which passes beyond ourselves. This distinction was adopted by Kant, and constituted the basis for his trinity of Critiques. It became widely accepted, though not universally so, Brentano, for example, proposing a slightly different trichotomy.[59] The threefold division of Tetens seems, however, to gain some support from what is now known about the organization of the nervous system, affective states being closely linked to the functioning of the autonomic branch, while the other two psychological domains correspond to the sensory and motor branches of the central nervous system respectively.

With Immanuel Kant (1724-1804) we come to a much more formidable figure, whose 'Copernican revolution' marked a watershed in the history of western philosophy. Spending almost the whole of his life in Könisberg (now renamed Kaliningrad), where he was born, educated, and later became a professor, Kant was brought up in his university years on Wolffian philosophy and Newtonian physics, and his own critical philosophy may be regarded as an attempt to reconcile the rationalism of Wolff with the exact empirical science of Newton. Kant was not himself a psychologist, and opinions differ as to the influence his highly abstruse and difficult philosophy has had upon psychology. Some have regarded him as 'a disaster for psychology'.[60] On the other hand it has been claimed that 'more than any other philosopher of the eighteenth century Kant has profoundly influenced psychology since his time'.[61] Perhaps the truth is, as has recently been suggested, that 'Kant's heritage to psychology was a challenge'.[62] Kant's own attitude to the possibility of a science of psychology was, in fact, ambivalent, and the implications of his critical philosophy for psychology were contradictory. For various reasons Kant held that it was impossible to establish a science proper of the inner sense. Quantification he regarded as the mark of a true science, and the inner sense, he believed, could not be quantified. He also held that it could not be subjected to experimental analysis, since introspection was confined to one's own inner sense, and altered what it was observing.[63] So psychology could not be more than historical and descriptive, and, therefore, not a science in the true sense. Yet Kant also held that since all phenomena follow rules, 'the experience of our own faculties takes place according to rules'.[64] So he did not exclude 'a kind of physiology of the internal sense'[65] based on observation of the play of our thoughts and the natural laws of the thinking self. In his *Anthropology from a Pragmatical Point of View* (1798) he approached human nature from an empirical standpoint and discussed the functioning of the mind. There is, too, in fact a great deal that is of psychological importance in the abstruse reasoning of the Critiques.[66]

In his attempt to escape from the conflict between rationalism and empiricism, and from the blind alley into which Hume had precipitated the whole theory of knowledge, Kant proposed the view that in knowledge there are always, and of necessity, two components: intuitions (sense) and concepts (thought) – a view expressed succinctly in his well-known aphorism, 'Thoughts without contents are empty, intuitions without concepts are blind'.[67] Both empiricists, in attempting to derive knowledge from sensory elements, and rationalists, in attempting to derive it from reason, were mistaken. Again to quote Kant, 'Leibniz intellectualized phenomena, just as Locke sensualized the concepts of the understanding.'[68] Both were one-sided. All experience, that is to say the phenomenal world which constitutes our consciousness, is on the contrary a synthetic construction. Synthesis precedes any possible analysis, and this synthesis is inevitably constructed on an a priori framework, which renders the phenomenal world intelligible. This framework comprised the two pure forms of sensible intuition, space and time, corresponding to outer and inner sense respectively, and a set of a priori categories, one of which was the category of causation. So we inevitably envisage the world in spatio-temporal and causal terms. Human knowledge is confined to the phenomenal world, the synthetically constructed world which we experience. It cannot penetrate beyond the phenomenal veil to the 'noumenal' world of 'things in themselves'. So Kant both legitimized knowledge within the world of our experience and ruled out metaphysical knowledge of ultimate reality and the nature of the soul. Thus, argued Kant, 'the whole of rational psychology is impossible as transcending the powers of human reason.'[69] This at least cleared the air of a lot of profitless speculation!

Quite apart from this salutary conclusion there were a number of other important implications for psychology springing from Kant's doctrines. Firstly, the mind-matter dichotomy bequeathed by Descartes was transcended. According to Kant mind was implicated in what is knowable about matter; and matter implicated in what is knowable about mind. The distinction was not between mind and matter, but between a composite phenomenal world of experience and an unknowable 'noumenal' reality. This implied that there was inevitably a subjective element in our knowledge of the external world; but equally that it was impossible to study consciousness *per se* without considering its relation to the external world. It was a move towards the study of mind through its behaviour and its interactions with the environment.

Secondly, because conscious experience was essentially the result of a synthetic process it was always organized and unified. Kant abandoned the pure ego of rationalist psychology, but replaced it by what he called 'the transcendental unity of apperception'. 'No knowledge can take place in us . . . without the unity of consciousness which precedes the data of all intuitions, and without reference to which no representation of objects is possible.'[70] Kant, in other words, rejected the atomistic assumptions of the empiricists, and with it the central role of the association of ideas. As Kemp Smith put it in his *Commentary to Kant's Critique*, 'Ideas do not become associated merely by co-existing. They must occur together in a unitary consciousness. . . . Association is transcendentally grounded.'[71] That is the principle of association is grounded in the prior synthetic activity which alone renders consciousness possible. This was a move from a mechanistic to an organic view of mind.

Thirdly, Kant's doctrine, in limiting the domain of knowledge to the phenomenal world, at the same time legitimized other aspects of experience, in particular moral experience and aesthetic experience. These aspects were not necessarily excluded from reality merely because there was no place for them in a deterministic physical universe. The experience of moral freedom, and the intuitions of aesthetic value, were equally valid, as Kant went on to argue in his second and third Critiques, *The Critique of Practical Reason* (1788) and *The Critique of Judgment* (1790). In his own words, 'I had to remove knowledge, in order to make room for belief.'[72] This finally was a move towards an ego psychology in which values play their part.

These implications for psychology remain important even though Kantian philosophy is in some respects outmoded. Kant's conception of the a priori was constricted by the ideas of his own time and based on Newtonian physics with its postulates of absolute space and time, Euclidean geometry, and non-evolutionary biology. The strange worlds of modern physics and mathematics no longer fit the Kantian straitjacket. The essence of Kantian teaching, as far as psychology is concerned, can, however, be recast in modern terms. Several modern developments, including Kelly's personal contruct theory, have derived their inspiration from Kant, and Konrad Lorenz has pointed to an affinity between Kant and the ethological movement. As Lorenz wrote,

> The great and fundamentally new discovery of Kant was that human thought and perception have certain functional structures prior to every individual experience. . . . The a priori is due to hereditary differentiations of the central nervous system which have become characteristic of the species, producing hereditary dispositions to think in certain forms.[73]

So Kant is still relevant, quite apart from being the source of new movements in philosophy, which in their turn have helped to shape psychology, and quite apart from the fact that only thirty years after Kant's death there occurred in the work of Johannes Müller a marriage between physiology and psychology which was to lead to radical new developments which Kant did not foresee.

Before this happened, however, Kant's immediate successors were already questioning the negative side of Kant's attitude to psychology and justifying the claims of psychology to be a science.[74] Among these successors there was one figure of major significance, Johann F. Herbart (1776-1841), the father of scientific pedagogy, and the author of two textbooks of psychology, *Lehrbuch zur Psychologie* (1816) and *Psychologie als Wissenschaft* (1824-25).[75] As Boring pointed out,[76] Herbart did a great deal to give psychology status, and provide it with a mission of its own. Kant's attitude to psychology had been ambiguous. Herbart proclaimed it as a '*Wissenschaft*' (science), and even went on to propose mathematical treatment of psychological data, thus countering one of Kant's main arguments. He entirely abandoned the faculties of the Wolffians. 'The soul', he asserted, 'has no capacity nor faculty whatever either to receive or to produce anything.'[77] He replaced faculties with forces, the forces of ideas themselves. Ideas become forces when they resist each other in their striving to occupy the same conscious space. In this way there arises a dynamic interaction in which ideas blend, associate in 'apperception masses', and, when worsted in the contest, may be suppressed below the threshold of consciousness. Herbart's mathematical treatment of this dynamic process cannot be regarded as particularly successful, and has usually been ignored; but other aspects of his theories have borne fruit. Herbart shifted the attention of psychologists from faculties to contents. It was the actual building up of mental contents that was important in the process of development and education. Education was essentially a matter of grafting new information on to previously acquired 'apperception masses'.[78] The pupil could only be interested in what he already knew something about. Merely formal instruction was ineffective, because it never engaged the interest of the learner. These views of Herbart had a very great influence on education and educational theory in the nineteenth century. But they were of far more than just educational significance. His concept of a threshold, implicit in, and no doubt derived from, the doctrine of Leibniz, was a significant advance. The dynamic suppression of ideas below the threshold of consciousness, together with their capacity while suppressed to exert effects in consciousness, was a prelude to Freudian theory.

Indeed it is known that an Herbartian textbook was used in the *Gymnasium* which Freud attended, and that Meynert, under whom Freud worked in his early years, was Herbartianly orientated.[79] But between Herbart's death in 1841 and Freud's first major publication in 1895 a great deal happened in psychology, and Herbart's influence cannot be regarded as more than marginal.

V

We must turn back to the earlier years of the eighteenth century, and to another, and more extreme, revolt against the assumptions and conclusions of both empirical and rationalist psychologies, and indeed against the whole emerging scientific-technological ethos of the Enlightenment. This revolt was fed from two main sources: firstly from a group of thinkers who laid stress on history, and saw human nature as a product, neither of natural nor rational, but of historical forces; and secondly from the Romantic school of writers and artists, who gloried in the free creative imagination of man and his spontaneity of feeling in opposition to the rigid canons and rules of classicism. These were aspects of human nature to which both empirical and rationalist psychologies had accorded a subordinate place. The historico-romantic revolt, with its emphasis on time, process, creativity and spontaneity, introduced a new dimension into the awareness of western man and consequently a new dimension into his psychology.

The long-neglected prophet of the new outlook was the Neapolitan jurist and philosopher Giovanni Battista Vico (1688-1744). Not until the twentieth century has the full significance of his teaching been grasped. His chief work, *Principii d'una Scienza Nuova* (1725), was involved, difficult and fragmentary. It remained almost unknown until the French historian Michelet publicized it in 1824. In the English-speaking world it was even slower in gaining recognition. Robert Flint, the Scottish philosopher, wrote a monograph on Vico in 1884, but it was the advocacy of Oxford's Collingwood that finally established his importance, followed in our own day by the brilliant study of Isaiah Berlin.[80] There was no English translation of the *Scienza Nuova* until 1948.[81]

Vico's early works were on jurisprudence and the history of law, and it was through his study of different legal systems that he came to realize the importance of history and historical change. The *Scienze Nuova* universalized his ideas, and applied them to human culture and human nature generally. The central idea of his philosophy was the conviction that man and his institutions could not be explained in terms of the unchanging laws of the natural world. The whole endeavour of the Enlightenment – to create a science of man and society modelled on Newtonian lines – was mistaken. For, as Berlin succinctly put it, 'In history we are the actors; in the natural sciences mere spectators.'[82] There was, therefore, a radical difference between what later came to be termed the '*Geisteswissenschaften*' (human studies) and the '*Naturwissenschaften*' (natural sciences); their subject matter was different, and the methods of studying them must likewise differ. The interpretation of history required 'understanding' and imagination (*fantasia*), because history was concerned with the creative activities of man and his forms of self-expression in language, mythology, institutions and laws. These various forms of self-expression were organically related in patterns of culture, and as cultures changed and differentiated, so human nature changed. Whereas Voltaire believed that man, generally speaking, was always what he is now,[83] Vico replaced this static concept of an unchanging with that of a dynamically changing human nature. Man was in a sense his own creator, and possessed a certain freedom and autonomy. The revolutionary nature of Vico's insight has been summarized by Berlin as follows:

> The notion that there exist, eternal and unalterable truths, laws, rules of conduct which entail ends of life which any man might, in theory, have recognised at any time and in any place, and the discovery and pursuit of which is the sole sufficient goal of all human behaviour, is the central principle of the Enlightenment. Its rejection with its appeal for a far wider psychological interpretation marks a decisive turning point in the history of western thought.[84]

Though it was not until the second half of the nineteenth century that Vico's ideas began to percolate into psychology, his was not the only influence tending to undermine the ideas of the Enlightenment. The eighteenth century was marked by an increasing appreciation of history. Gibbon was only one among a growing band of historians. Man was beginning to discover his past, and to gain a wholly new awareness of time.[85] Explorers, navigators and colonizers were opening up the world, and revealing the diversity of human cultures. The French philosophical historian Montesquieu (1689-1755) absorbed these influences and in his *Esprit des Lois* (1743), which has been described as 'the greatest book of the French eighteenth century'[86] and which unlike Vico's book was attractively written, explored the diversity of human cultures and institutions. Turgot, the French statesman and economist (1727-1781), wrote on *The Historical Progress of the Human Mind* (1749). In Germany Johann Gottfried Herder (1744-1803), who had been a pupil of Kant in Königsberg, became one of the leaders of the historico-romantic revolt, and a very influential figure. In his *Ideas towards a Philosophy of History* (1784-91) he stressed the distinction between the natural sciences and the human studies, the organic conception of man and culture, the importance of 'belonging' or group membership, and the role of language in shaping human mentality. As Berlin writes,

> The extent of his influence has not always been recognised because it has entered too deeply into the texture of ordinary thinking. . . . As a social psychologist he rose above his generation; more clearly than any other writer, he conceived and cast light upon the crucially important social function of 'belonging'.[87]

In Great Britain Edmund Burke (1729-1797), pointing to the lessons of the French Revolution, laid a similar emphasis on the organic nature of human societies, the role of tradition, and the intricate and complex web of relationships underlying human association.[88] The violence of the French Revolution and the alarm it aroused brought history down from the closet to the marketplace. Human reason was seen to be a frail and vulnerable master, human passions fierce and destructive. Man's irrational nature could no longer be ignored, even by psychologists. The ideological cleavages, which long ago had wrecked the world of the Greek city states, rose to the surface again, and have bedevilled the human scene with their menacing controversies ever since, controversies from which psychology has not been able to disentangle itself, even though its true task is to transcend them and explain them.

The cataclysm of the French Revolution was heralded by rumblings in literature. These rumblings, indeed, were not confined to France, and represented a major shift in the attitudes of European man. The first stirrings of the Romantic movement, as it is generally termed, began to show themselves in England early in the eighteenth century. Addison wrote in the *Spectator* of 'The pleasures of imagination'; a generation later the poet Akenside wrote on the same theme in verse, while the imaginative novel was born with Samuel Richardson's *Pamela* (1740).[89] There were, of course, precedents and precursors for these stirrings extending back to medieval and classical times. Throughout history there have been storytellers, mystics and geniuses who have penetrated beyond the veil of conventionality. The Romantic movement of the late eighteenth and early nineteenth centuries, however, was not confined to a few individuals. It affected every aspect of life and thought, literature, art, philosophy, even dress and manners, and changed the basic '*Weltanschauung*' of western man. It both enlarged the subject matter of psychology and shifted its centre of gravity away from the cognitive surface to the inner depths and drives underlying human experience.

Oddly enough the seeds of the Romantic exaltation of the imagination were present in the down-to-earth reflections of the empiricists – in Hobbes's 'fancy', in Locke's active linking of simple ideas, and in Hume's elevation of feeling.[90] But it was left to the Germans to systematize them and to elevate them into the central principle of philosophy. Tetens was a key figure in the transition from rationalism to idealism, and in the endowment of the imagination with the central role accorded to it in the post-Kantian philosophy of men like Fichte and Schelling. In the end imagination became almost deified; it was the creative principle which linked man and nature, and unified the worlds of mind and matter in a transcendent vision.

There was, of course, a negative side to Romanticism. It was in part a movement of protest and escape from a world that was losing its simplicity and charm; from the 'dark satanic mills', and from 'the mind-forged manacles' of the scientific age;[91] from the greedy pursuit of wealth, the formality of education, and the dominance of reason.

All this was expressed in the poetry of William Blake (1757-1827) with its strange and powerful symbolism and its elaborate explorations of the inner world of the imagination, owing something to the Swedish mystic Swedenborg, but equally looking forward to the psychological analysis of Jung. In a sense this escapism was morbid, as Goethe perceived. 'The classical is healthy, the romantic sick,' he wrote.[92] His own Werther expressed something of the '*Weltschmerz*' and nihilism which became a feature of Romanticism in some of its manifestations. It went with a growing interest in the abnormal, the bizarre, the sadistic and the insane. The art of Goya, the poetry of Byron, and some of Beethoven's later music represented one side of the Romantic vision.

But there were more positive and healthy sides of Romanticism. The Romantics explored the deeper wells of human feeling, which a rationalist age had too long ignored; they exalted the imagination with its spontaneous creative power, and they worshipped individuality and variety. 'The heart is the key to the world and life', exclaimed Novalis, the German poet and novelist[93] while Shelley maintained that 'Reason is to the imagination as the instrument to the agent, as the body to the spirit, as the shadow to the substance.'[94] Reason imposed uniformity; the imagination was diverse and promoted individuality. 'One law for the lion and the ox is oppression,' said Blake. The imagination, on the contrary, was free and spontaneous, rich in variety, and the seed-bed of genius.[95] All this linked up with the historicism of Vico and Herder, and indeed the Romantics were strongly attracted to the past and its lost splendours. The Gothic revival, which was one aspect of the Romantic movement, attempted to recapture the glories of medieval Gothic architecture, and pre-Raphaelite painters the beauty of early Italian art. Chateaubriand in his *Génie du Christianism* (1802) lauded the magnificence of the Catholic liturgy and its symbolic significance, and heralded a religious reaction against the scepticism of the eighteenth century. Throughout western Europe there was a largely emotional revival of religious belief and practice. Above all Romanticism was marked by the glorification and divinization of nature, which reached its culmination in the poetry of Wordsworth. There was in this a strongly pantheistic streak, a yearning for the lost unity of man and nature, which marked the childhood, or so it was believed, both of the race and the individual.

Of all the figures of the Romantic movement perhaps the one of the greatest significance for psychology was Jean-Jacques Rousseau (1712-1778). He personified and expressed many of the urges which powered Romanticism. In spite of, or perhaps because of, his own emotional temperament and weakness of character, he possessed great psychological insight. His *Confessions*, published after his death, is one of the great psychological autobiographies. His insight into the developing mind of the child was unique in its day. In his early works, the *Discourse on the Arts and Science* (1749) and the *Discourse on Inequality* (1752), Rousseau railed against the corruption of the scientific and artistic world, and against the corruption and injustice of society, which he largely attributed to the evils of private property, and expressed a craving for a return to simpler, freer conditions, and communion with nature. The element of revolt and escape was strong in Rousseau. 'We are in search of love, happiness, innocence; the further we go from Paris the better,' he exclaimed in *Emile*,[96] psychologically his most important work, in which he laid down the principles of a natural education conforming to the development of the child and ultimately leading to socialization in a free democratic society. 'God makes all things good: man meddles with them and they become evil'[97] was his creed. The main cause of this was 'the crushing force of social conventions'. So we must break our bonds and get back to nature and the simplicity of natural life. 'Men are not made to be crowded together in ant-hills. . . . The more they are massed together the more corrupt they become.'[98] So Rousseau advocated maternal feeding of infants, bodily freedom, physical activity, contact with things, and only a very gradual approach to abstract studies. The child must be treated as a child, and the stages of his development respected. Of all man's faculties reason was the latest growth and should not be prematurely forced. In particular Rousseau was strongly against a too early religious indoctrination, and this brought him into conflict with the Church and enforced exile. Yet Rousseau was not a materialist, and far from irreligious. He worshipped the deeply felt spiritual aspect of nature, for we may take it that the famous 'Creed of the Savoyard priest' in *Emile* expounds his own views. There are two opposing principles in man, upwards to eternal truths, and downwards to the senses and passions. Man is in conflict with himself, but he 'is free to act, and as such as animated by immaterial substance.'[99] By the time adolescence is ending education proper, into religious, social and moral matters, must begin. This is, in a sense, a second birth. 'We are born, so to speak, twice over; born into existence, and born into life; born a human being, and born a man.'[100] Man's rebirth as a social being, however, does not mean the suppression, but the sublimation of passions, since 'only through passions can we win the mastery over passions.'[101] Nevertheless it involves a fundamental transformation of human nature. In his *Social Contract* (1762) Rousseau explained it thus:

The passing from the state of nature to that of civil society produces a remarkable change in man: it puts justice as a rule of conduct in place of instinct, and it gives his actions the moral quality they previously lacked. It is only then, when the voice of duty has taken the place of physical impulse, and right that of desire, that man, who has hitherto thought only of himself, finds himself compelled to act on other principles, and to consult his reason rather than his inclinations.[102]

In the free society based on consent which he envisaged Rousseau saw the possibility of achieving equality and justice. 'However unequal in strength and intelligence, men become equal by covenant and right.'[103]

Fundamentally, then, Rousseau saw education as a process of socialization, which respected at all stages the natural course of human development, but which in the end transformed the natural man into the moral being. His ideas have been the inspiration of most subsequent experiments in progressive education, and the fountainhead of systematic child study. 'I wish some trustworthy person would give us a treatise on the art of child study,' exclaimed Rousseau.[104] It is perhaps appropriate that the centre which has done most to meet this need in our time was named after him, the J.-J. Rousseau Institute in his native city of Geneva, where Piaget and other investigators have done so much to advance the study of the child mind.

VI

Although it is impossible to sum up the diverse movements of the eighteenth century thought in any single formula, and although at its close views on the nature of the human mind were even more divergent than they were at the beginning, as the nineteenth century dawned there was fairly widespread agreement at least on this: that there was a science of mind, and that this science was 'psychology'. In giving his support to this position John Stuart Mill in the section of his *System of Logic* (1843) entitled 'On the logic of the moral sciences'[105] expressed the enlightened view of his day. Psychology was not yet fully a science, but it was at least recognized as a possible science by the progressive thinkers of the time. This was above all the achievement of the eighteenth century.

The predominant trends of the period were empirical and based on the assumption that the methods of the psychologist must broadly conform to the methods that had proved so successful in establishing the magnificent Newtonian system of physics. But there was a divergence of views as to whether mental contents were wholly derived from experience, or whether there was also some innate component, innate principles of reason or common sense, according to Leibniz and the Scottish philosophers, or a priori categories according to Kant. Was the mind largely passive and moulded by experience, or was it active and creative? Was it built up from elements or mental atoms, or was it a differentiating whole? Were individuals essentially equal until shaped variously by circumstances, or were there differences from the start? Was man basically akin to the animals, or was he radically different? These were all issues which the eighteenth century bequeathed to its successors.

But it also bequeathed more radical doubts – doubts springing from Kantian philosophy as to the status of mind in the universe and the legitimacy of the simple mind-body dichotomy; and the doubts of the historico-Romantic school as to the applicability of scientific method to the study of human nature. These doubts have reverberated into the twentieth century, and have not been allayed by the advances in empirical psychology.

Moreover eighteenth century psychology was still floating in something of a vacuum. In spite of Hartley's endeavour it still had no firm links with the emerging biological sciences, and only very tentative links with the hardly existent social sciences. Psychology could not be firmly established into the scientific community until it had forged links with other scientific disciplines, and established its place in the house of science. This was what the nineteenth century and early years of the twentieth century brought about.

Chapter 8
The impact of the life sciences on psychology

I

Scientific psychology as we know it today is the offspring of the marriage of philosophy and the life sciences. All psychology prior to the nineteenth century lacked a foundation of sound biological knowledge. That does not mean to say that it was all entirely worthless, but it does mean that psychological speculation lacked a very important constraint. Many psychologists from Aristotle onwards had grasped the fact that psychology had roots in biology. Indeed Brett has expressed the view that more than a century before Aristotle 'Alcmaeon of Croton began the long history of the influence that a study of the human organism has had on theories of the soul.'[1] These studies, however, were handicapped by inadequate techniques for investigating organisms, and a lack of reliable knowledge. Even as late as the middle of the eighteenth century when Hartley attempted to propound a physiological psychology, the physiological basis of his observations was largely speculative.[2] Though the life sciences began to develop experimentally in the seventeenth century, it was not until the early nineteenth that they were sufficiently advanced to make much of an impact on psychology. Their development over the last two hundred years has been spectacular; indeed, it has been one of the greatest achievements in the whole history of human thought. The influence of this progress on psychology has steadily increased from the beginning of the nineteenth century up to the present day, and it will no doubt continue to be an important, though not an exclusive, influence in the future. We must briefly examine, therefore, some of the major developments in the life sciences of particular concern to psychology.

Until well into the eighteenth century, in spite of the revolution in the approach to the life sciences which began in the previous century, traditional views inherited from the ancient world were still largely prevalent. The system of living beings was a static system, in which each form of life held its appointed place in 'the great chain of being' ordained by the Creator. Life itself was explained in terms of an animating, vital principle, which differentiated it from non-living matter. The workings of the brain and nervous system had hardly begun to be understood, and even their basic structures were far from clearly delineated. Aristotle and Galen were still names to conjure with. Aristotle, of course, was no mean biologist. He made many first-hand observations, and pioneered the classification of living things. Nevertheless his physiology was largely erroneous, particularly with regard to the brain, and his approach to living organisms was fundamentally teleological and animistic. Galen's outlook was equally teleological, but his physiology was in many areas much sounder than that of Aristotle, and his authority in the medical world wider and more enduring. Born in Asia Minor about AD 130 he became the leading physician of the ancient world, and his immense corpus of medical writings formed the basis of medical education throughout the medieval period.[3] He has been described as the most influential physician who has ever lived. Based partly on his observation of brain and nerve injuries in the arena, partly on experiments with the dissection of animals, Galen arrived at a much fuller understanding of the functioning of the nervous system than any other ancient writer. He confirmed the finding of the Alexandrines, Herophilos and Erasistratos, that the brain was the seat of sensation and movement. Galen regarded all intellectual and volitional functions as located in the brain, but he still regarded the heart as the primary seat of the emotions. Though he began to grasp the integrative function of the nervous system, his account of how the nervous system worked was inevitably wide of the mark. He likened the nerves to hollow water pipes through which a subtle agent, the psychic pneuma, was transmitted. This pneuma was derived from the ventricles of the brain, which during the medieval period were often regarded as the main seat of psychic functioning, though this was probably not Galen's own view. His physiology was dominated by the doctrine of the four basic humours, from which the four temperaments were derived.

The authority of Galen was first seriously questioned by Vesalius in the middle of the sixteenth century. In the preface to his *De Humani Corporis Fabrica* he commented on the many errors and incorrect observations of Galen, and decried the slavish adherence of most of his contemporaries to Galen's teaching. The real revolution in the life sciences, however, began in the following century, with Harvey's discovery of the circulation of the blood, with Descartes's mechanistic theory of the functioning of the bodily organism, and with the development of the compound microscope by Hooke and van Leeuwenhoek, which provided biologists with their essential tool for exploring the intricacies of living matter. For the first time it became possible to envisage life not as a mysterious, extra-material power, but as explicable in terms of physical forces. Of course, the physical sciences of the day were almost totally unable to cope with the complexity of living processes, and it is not surprising that for a long time many biologists were still to advocate vital principles. In fact the debate between mechanism and vitalism[4] went on vigorously throughout the eighteenth and nineteenth centuries, and, in a somewhat modified form, persists to the present day in the argument between reducibility and emergence.[5] It is a debate which has been reflected in comparable terms within psychology.

This debate, however, did not prevent, and may even have stimulated, the accelerating progress of the life sciences. In three principal ways this progress has helped to shape the development of psychology: firstly, the complex constitution of living matter has gradually been revealed, and though this has not provided a full explanation of mind, it has thrown much light on the physical processes underlying mental activity; secondly, the doctrine of the evolution of life forms, including man and his mind, over large epochs of time, has demonstrated man's affinity to the animal kingdom, as well as his peculiarities, has underlined the need to study development, and has called attention to the importance of individual variability; thirdly, of particular moment to psychology have been the dramatic advances in knowledge about the brain and nervous system, and their modes of operation.

II

Before the construction of microscopes in the seventeenth century it was not possible for philosophers and physicians who reflected on the nature of life to do much more than indulge in speculation. It was as the result of his microscopic observations on thin slices of cork and other vegetable material that Robert Hooke in 1665 described them as made up of a 'great many little boxes', and coined the term 'cells'.[6] In 1839 the German biologists Schleiden and Schwann concluded that both plants and animals were entirely composed of cells, or the products of cells, and that cells have an individual life of their own within the organism as a whole. The nature of cells, however, was still very imperfectly understood. Schwann regarded them as liquid-filled cavities, and held that their membranes were the main functional parts. Not until the famous pronouncement of Rudolf Virchow, the founder of cellular pathology, in 1858 – 'omnis cellula e cellula' – was the origin of all cells through cell division recognized. The revelation of the complex internal structure of cells was dependent on improvements in the microscope (the achromatic microscope of the 1830s, the Zeiss microscope of 1878, and the electron microscope of 1931), and the introduction of methods of staining. Chromosomes were detected in 1870 and were named in 1888. The process of mitosis had been noted in 1878, but the connection between the chromosomes and heredity was not grasped until the early years of the twentieth century. By the 1860s the term 'protoplasm', coined in 1846 by a German botanist, had become generally adopted to denote the primary material of all living cells and tissues. The structure of protoplasm, however, could not be unravelled before the twentieth century development of biochemistry, and this was dependent on advances in the science of chemistry.

The science of chemistry is barely two hundred years old. For many centuries the study of materials had been the preserve of alchemy, which in its migration from Arabia to Europe had become mixed with 'much error and vanity', as Francis Bacon put it.[7] Yet, as Bacon also admitted, it had helped to promote experiments, and it was these experiments that eventually gave rise to chemistry. Initial progress, however, was fairly slow. Though Robert Boyle in 1661 had cast some doubt on the 'vulgar alchemists', and made some advance towards a theory of chemical elements, even so eminent a scientist as Newton was still deeply entangled in alchemical speculations. The tentative progress made by Boyle was, moreover, further blocked by the erroneous phlogiston theory of combustion propounded by G.E. Stahl in 1731, and not demolished, by Lavoisier, till 1783. Meanwhile some of the basic atmospheric constituents had been isolated: 'fixed air', or carbon dioxide, by Joseph Black in 1754, nitrogen by P. Rutherford in 1772, and oxygen by Joseph Priestley in 1774. The jigsaw of known chemical substances was put together by Lavoisier in his *Traité élémentaire de chimie* in 1789, and chemical nomenclature established on modern lines. Chemistry was now set on a rapidly expanding course, greatly aided by the atomic theory of John Dalton, first propounded in 1803. Before the eighteenth century had closed chemists were already beginning to look at living material in chemical terms. Early in the nineteenth century the great Swedish chemist Berzelius brought organic nature into atomic theory. In 1828 Wöhler prepared urea synthetically, thus showing that organic materials did not essentially involve living organisms, but could be regarded as ordinary chemical substances. By 1848 the role of carbon in all organic compounds was understood. In the same year the youthful Pasteur made the discovery that chemical molecules possessed three-dimensional shape, and that in certain substances there existed differently orientated forms, or isomers, which had biologically different properties. This was to prove a significant clue to the nature of living materials, an important class of which had been named 'proteins' in 1838. The physical and chemical properties of proteins were explored in the latter half of the nineteenth century, and units of amino acid detected. Early in the twentieth century the eminent German organic chemist Emil Fischer put forward the view that proteins were definite geometrical arrangements of amino acids. New techniques, such as X-ray crystallography, were to reveal the precise structure of protein molecules from 1940 onwards. Proteins exist in living organisms in a multitude of forms, many of them functioning as enzymes. Enzymes were discovered originally in connection with fermentation and their basically chemical nature was revealed in 1897. The metabolism of the cell, and all the essential processes of life, depend upon enzymes, thousands of which are present in the animal body, each performing a highly specific function. Proteins, however, were not the only chemical constituents of living material which chemists discovered in the nineteenth century. In 1869 the presence of nucleic acid was detected in cells, but its biological role was not suspected till much later, in the 1940s. Its structure, the famous double helix, was unravelled by Crick, Watson and Wilkins in 1953, and its unique function as a vehicle of genetic information explained. By the middle of the twentieth century life scientists had arrived at at least an outline picture of the structure and functioning of living material, as well as revealing the importance of special chemical substances, such as hormones and vitamins, in the working of organisms. Rather more than a century earlier Helmholtz, in formulating his celebrated principle of the conservation of energy,[8] had implied that somehow all the processes of life must be fitted into a physico-chemical framework. Now at last the nature of these processes was revealed. Vitalism of the old-fashioned kind was dead; there was no need to postulate a mysterious life principle. Nevertheless it was not a triumph for materialism of a purely mechanical kind, because a new, and highly important feature had been introduced – information – and this transformed the picture of the world. There was, moreover, one further outcome of the dramatic discoveries of the life scientists. They had demonstrated the essential kinship of all living forms: the structure of living material was identical in its main components from single-celled organisms to man. Even viruses consisted of the two basic components of protein and nucleic acid. How then did the vast variety of life forms in earth originate? That was the question the evolutionary biologists had been attempting to answer for just over a century.

III

Evolutionary ideas of a speculative kind had been aired prior to the nineteenth century. Leibniz, as we have seen, presaged the birth of evolutionary theory; Kant in an early work sketched a theory of cosmogenesis; Erasmus Darwin, grandfather of Charles, in his *Zoonomia* (1794) outlined a theory of evolution; and slightly earlier the eccentric Scottish peer, Lord Monboddo, a *bête noire* of Dr Johnson, in his voluminous work on language (1773) suggested that man was related to the orang-outang.[9] As the nineteenth century dawned the French botanist Lamarck propounded the theory that the species of today were descended from those of previous times, and that these changes had taken place through the transmission of acquired adaptations. These theories, however, were not generally accepted by biologists or the general public. Firstly, the available time since the creation of the world seemed too short for evolution to have been possible; secondly, the theory was supported by insufficient evidence to be really convincing; and thirdly such doctrines seemed, in the words of the theologian, William Paley, 'anti-scriptural and most debasing . . . standing in blasphemous contradiction to Biblical doctrine and narrative'.[10]

It was the geologists who provided the biologists with time. Instead of the few thousands of years calculated by the theologians, or the 75,000 years worked out by the naturalist, Buffon, in 1778, the geologist Charles Lyell, in his *Principles of Geology* (1830-33) wrote of 'an indefinite lapse of ages'. As Toulmin and Goodfield have pointed out,[11] the change of perspective brought about by the discovery of time has been one of the most profound in human history. Among other things it made the theory of evolution possible, and it is worth noting that Lyell's work on geology was one of the few books that Charles

Darwin took with him on the voyage of HMS Beagle. It was this famous voyage, which commenced in 1831 and circumnavigated the globe over a period of five years, that enabled Darwin to collect the essential factual information which stimulated him to formulate his theory of evolution. His notebooks show that he began to collect together his data on the species problem in July 1837 soon after his return to England. He jotted down a short summary of his theory in 1842, and wrote a longer sketch in 1844. But he withheld publication in the search for additional evidence, while at the same time working on various geological zoological and botanical themes. In 1858 his fellow naturalist A.R. Wallace, then in the East Indies, sent him a paper embodying almost identical ideas. The time had clearly come to publish. The joint reading of papers by Darwin and Wallace to the Linnean Society in July 1858 was followed in November 1859 by the publication of *The Origin of Species*. In arguing for the evolution of species over long periods of time by a process of natural selection, and by implying that man, too, was formed in this way, Darwin challenged the fundamental tenets of the old orthodoxies.

There is no need to enter into the details of Darwin's theory, or the evidence he marshalled in support of it. The members of a species varied from one another; there was a struggle for survival, for as the economist Malthus had demonstrated increasing populations tended to outrun resources; in the resulting competition the fittest survived, filling every available niche in all available ways; successful variations were transmitted through inheritance; and the process as a whole could be termed 'natural selection'. For the psychologist the important corollary was that mind, too, had evolved like every other piece of organic equipment; minds were subject to the laws of variation and inheritance; they were involved in the adaptations of organisms to their environments; they were subject to the process of trial and error; and just as bodies were the result of historical development and showed traces of their past, so minds revealed vestiges of earlier origins. Darwin himself was the first to apply these ideas to psychology. His notebooks on man were commenced in 1838. On 3 October 1838 he wrote, 'Experience shows that the problem of mind cannot be solved by attacking the citadel itself – the mind is a function of body – we must bring some *stable* foundation to argue from.'[12] The observation of human behaviour was for him a life-long interest. On his return to England and the birth of his first child he made an acute study of the development of his infant son;[13] in the *Descent of Man* (1871) he compared the mental powers of man and the lower animals, discussing such topics as instinct, curiosity, imitation, attention, memory, imagination, reasoning, sociability and sexuality. The conclusion he came to was 'the mental faculties of men and the lower animals do not differ in kind, though immensely in degree'.[14] Finally in *The Expression of the Emotions in Man and Animals* (1872), a book full of acute observation, Darwin was often able to account for emotional expressions as the vestiges of serviceable modes of behaviour, and to produce a considerable body of evidence to support the psychological kinship between man and the lower animals. All this constituted an enormously important approach to psychology. As the contemporary evolutionary philosopher Herbert Spencer put it, 'mind can be understood only by showing how mind is evolved.'[15] There was, however, one serious gap in the Darwinian theory; Darwin could give no satisfactory account of the origin of the variation on which his theory depended; his account of heredity was purely speculative, and, unknown to him, had already been shown to be erroneous.

The main missing link in Darwinian theory was provided by the Augustinian monk Gregor Mendel in 1865. In his monastery garden at Brno, in what is now Czechoslovakia, Mendel carried out his breeding experiments on peas which established the basic principles of genetics. He published his results in the local natural history journal, and sent a copy to Darwin.[16] Darwin, however, never read the article – his copy remained uncut. So the theory of particulate inheritance, the law of segregation and independent assortment, and the distinction between dominant and recessive characters remained unknown to him and to most of the rest of the world. For Mendel's paper did not emerge from obscurity until 1900, when three biological workers almost simultaneously publicized it. The subsequent progress of 'genetics', as it was termed by Bateson in 1905, has been dramatic. Chromosomes had already been discovered in 1870 and named in 1888. Johannsen coined the term 'gene' in 1909, identified 'genes' with Mendel's factors, and made the distinction between 'genotype' and 'phenotype'. In 1908 T.H. Morgan began his experiments on the fruit fly, *Drosphila*, and demonstrated that genes were physical units that could be mapped on chromosomes.[17] Some years previously the sex chromosomes had been identified. Mendelism, supplemented by the mutation theory of de Vries, provided the explanation of the variations which Darwinian evolution demanded. It could not be fully integrated with evolutionary theory, however, until the development of population genetics by R.A. Fisher and J.B.S. Haldane. The biometrical approach to heredity, derived from the work of Francis Galton and Karl Pearson, had contributed a statistical manner of treating population variability, but was regarded as incompatible with Mendelian particulate factors. Fisher reconciled the two approaches, by showing that the quantitative differences of the biometricians depended on gene differences at many loci, and that these could only be analysed through the study of populations.[18] Fisher's work vindicated the theory of natural selection. Recent developments in biochemical genetics have placed it on an even firmer basis. The discovery by H.J. Muller in 1922 that X-rays could cause mutations led him to postulate that genes existed as distinct chemical substances. In 1944 this substance was identified as deoxyribonucleic acid (DNA), and in 1953 the structure of DNA was revealed. Genetics had achieved firm foundations, and became the key life science.

Though Darwin's original views have had to be added to, and to some extent modified, the essential core of his theory has been substantially vindicated by subsequent workers in the biological sciences.[19] There are, of course, still unsolved problems in connection with evolution. How life originated in the first place is still not clearly understood, though it is now known that organic molecules exist in many parts of the universe. The possibility, however, of such complex structures as proteins and nucleic acids forming purely by chance, and then interacting reciprocally to constitute living cells, seems remote, though proposed by Monod in his theory of molecular ontogenesis.[20] The actual course of evolution on earth suggests what has been called 'punctuated equilibrium' (periods of rapid development followed by levelling off) rather than a smooth and continuous process. The evidence of cooperation and altruism in the behaviour of many species has given rise to the theory of 'inclusive fitness', which proposes that it is the group rather than the individual that is selected, and the theories of the sociobiologists. Moreover though there is ample evidence for natural selection, it has not been conclusively demonstrated that it is the only factor involved in evolution. Darwin himself never believed this; and various thinkers, including the philosopher Karl Popper, have suggested the presence of internal factors in evolutionary change.[21] In spite of uncertainties, however, the basic fact of evolution has been confirmed by a mass of evidence, palaeological, biological and biochemical.

The implications of evolutionary theory for psychology have been profound. However lofty the superstructure of human nature, its basis is biological. All organized systems have a historical dimension. As the French Nobel scientist François Jacob has observed, 'Living bodies are indissolubly bound up with time. In the living world no structure can be detached from its history.'[22] Life is a dynamic system: organisms are unstable entities, which continuously have to adapt to environmental change, preserving a moving and precarious equilibrium. Even if chance and trial and error are not the only factors involved in adaptation, they are certainly important factors. Mind as a part of nature has evolved as body has evolved, and must be studied genetically. These are among the conclusions which have helped to shape psychology over the past century. The input of these conclusions was not, of course, sudden; they percolated into psychology over a period of time. Prior and more immediate was the impact of neurophysiology, which began to advance steadily from the end of the eighteenth century. It was this above all that brought about the birth of scientific psychology.

IV

Scientific neurophysiology is almost entirely a creation of the last two hundred years. Galen on the basis of his animal dissections had described the brain and nervous system with some accuracy, but had no idea of their minute structures or mode of functioning. His fictitious vital and animal spirits persisted well into the modern period. When Thomas Willis (1621-75), the distinguished Oxford physician and neuroanatomist, wrote his celebrated *Anatomy of the Brain* in 1664 he still spoke in Galenic terms of a 'spirituous humour endued with very active particles which perpetually flow, though in a very small quantity, through the passages of the nerves from the brain and cerebel'.[23] In his pioneering study of physiological psychology *The Soul of Brutes* (1672), the processes of sensation were similarly described in terms of animal spirits. A century later the Swiss physiologist Albrecht von Haller (1708-77), who popularized the notions of the irritability and sensibility of nerves, still thought in terms of 'a liquor that comes from the brain, descends into the nerves, and flows out to the extreme parts of the body. . . . The same liquid being put in motion in an organ of sense, by a sensible body, transmits its motion upwards to the brain.'[24]

The half century that followed Galvani's discovery of animal electricity in 1780 laid the foundations for a transformation of the neurophysiological scene. Up to the middle of the eighteenth century 'electricity', as it became termed in 1736, was connected solely with frictional phenomena. In 1752 Benjamin Franklin conducted his famous experiments which identified lightning with these phenomena, and made the distinction between positive and negative electricity. Almost at the same time the Leyden jar was invented, acting as a condenser which enabled electrical energy to be stored. In 1785 Coulomb found a way of measuring electrical force. In 1795 Volta, inspired by Galvani's experiments on the twitching of frogs' legs, invented the first electric battery. These discoveries were to have momentous consequences, not least in leading to a progressive understanding of the nature of the nerve impulse, and a total demise of the ancient doctrine of animal spirits.

Equally important in the early years of the nineteenth century were advances in the anatomical understanding of the nervous system. In his *Idea of a New Anatomy of the Brain* (1811) Charles Bell of Edinburgh made the important distinction between sensory and motor nerves. 'Through the nerves of sense the sensorium receives impressions, but the will is expressed through the medium of the nerves of motion' was the way he put it.[25] The French physician Magendie repeated Bell's experiments in 1822, proving that in a spinal nerve the ventral route is motor, and the dorsal route sensory. It was this distinction that provided the essential basis for the understanding of reflex action. Three years previously, in 1819, Franz Gall's *Anatomie et physiologie du système nerveux en général, et du cerveau en particulier* was published. Gall (1758-1828), a German by birth, was a strange character, and, as the founder of the bogus system of phrenology, is often dismissed as a quack. He was, however, a capable anatomist who greatly improved the methods of dissecting the brain. He established the distinction between grey and white matter, mapped the pathways of the central nervous system, and described the decussation of the pyramidal tracts. His spurious phrenological theories of brain localization were soon disputed by Pierre Flourens (1794-1867), who on the basis of extirpation experiments carried out on pigeons put forward the view that there was no localization in the cerebral hemispheres.[26] Motor functions he located in the cerebellum, vital functions in the medulla. By the 1830s there was sufficient information about the brain, the nervous system and the sense organs for Johannes Müller (1801-1858), author of the law of specific nerve energies, to devote a considerable part of his *Handbook of Human Physiology*[27] to physiological psychology. Psychology, as far as certain topics were concerned, had been launched on a new, experimental, path.

In the present context it is only possible to sketch in the briefest outline some of the major landmarks in the subsequent development of neurophysiology that have had significance for the shaping of psychology.[28] The fine structure of the nervous system was elucidated following Schwann's discovery of the cellular composition of living matter. The connection between nerve cells and nerve fibres was established by von Kölliker in 1849. In 1873 the Italian histologist Golgi devised a silver impregnation method of staining nervous tissue which enabled him to plot nerve pathways in great detail. He still believed, however, that the nervous system formed a continuous network. This was disproved by the Spaniard Ramon y Cajal in 1889, when he showed that each nerve cell was a distinct entity, its prolongations approaching, but not touching those of other cells. The nerve cells and their fibres were termed 'neurons' by Waldeyer in 1891, and the minute gaps between the axons of one cell and the dendrites of adjoining cells termed 'synapses' by Sherrington in 1897. In his famous lectures on *The Integrative Action of the Nervous System*, published in 1906, Sherrington went on to show how the action of multitudinous independent neurons was coordinated through a balancing of excitatory and inhibitory impulses. The chemical factors involved in synaptic transmission began to be understood following Dale's discovery of acetylcholine in 1914, and since that time the microchemistry of nervous function has become a highly important field of enquiry, though it has also been discovered that at some synapses transmission is electrical, not chemical.[29]

Following Galvani's discovery of animal electricity there has been a steady development of electrophysiology. Du Bois Reymond in his *Tierische Elektricität* (1848) pioneered the systematic study of the electrical phenomena accompanying nervous activity, and discovered the difference of electrical potential between the cut and uninjured ends of an excised nerve. Shortly afterwards, in 1850, Helmholtz determined the speed of nerve impulses and showed that they were far slower than expected. In 1866 Bernstein described the nervous impulse as a wave of electrical negativity. Following Gotch's discovery of the refractory phase in 1899, it became clear that the nerve impulse was not continuous, but a series of pulses. This finding was elaborated by Adrian and Lucas in 1912, and the all-or-none principle was formulated. The membrane theory of nerve conduction was generally accepted by the 1920s. The ionic hypothesis of the nature of the impulse first proposed by Bernstein in 1902 was firmly established by Hodgkin and Katz in 1949. The electrical potentials of the brain itself, first detected by Caton in 1875, were rediscovered by Berger in 1924, and confirmed by Adrian in 1934. Since then the electro-encephalogram has become an important research tool.[30]

A major development in the macroscopic aspects of nervous function was the clarification of the nature of reflex activity. Reflexes had been proposed by various seventeenth and eighteenth century scientists – Descartes, Whytt, Unzer, Prochaska and others[31] – but it was Marshall Hall in 1833 who formulated the reflex concept as we know it today, and introduced the term 'reflex arc'.[32] The English physician T. Laycock argued in 1845 that the laws of reflex action also applied to the brain,[33] an idea taken up by the Russian physiologist I. Sechenov in his *Reflexes of the Brain* (1863), a book which greatly influenced Pavlov. In spite of being too simple an account of higher nervous activity these theories had an impact on psychology, particularly as they were contemporaneous with the growth of a much fuller understanding of the anatomy and functions of the spinal cord, and its sensory and motor routes, as well as of the relationship between the central and autonomic branches of the nervous system. Bichat in 1800 had divided the life of the organism into animal life and vegetative life (a distinction that, of course, Aristotle had made before), and proposed that the ganglia of the sympathetic nervous system were the organs of 'vegetative' life. In the 1850s Claude Bernard discovered the vasodilator and vasoconstrictor functions of the 'vegetative' nervous system, and went on to propound his famous theory of constancy of the internal environment, later termed by Cannon 'homeostasis'.[34] The structure of the 'vegetative' nervous system was elucidated by the Cambridge physiologist W.H. Gaskell between 1886 and 1889, and the term 'autonomic' coined in 1898 by another Cambridge physiologist, J.N. Langley, who also proposed the term 'parasympathetic' to connote the branch which acted in opposition to the sympathetic, adrenergic, branch. In 1928 W.B. Cannon in his book *Bodily Changes in Pain, Hunger, Fear and Rage* demonstrated the connection between the autonomic system and emotional states. This clarification of spinal and autonomic functioning has had a significant bearing on psychological theorizing.

Developments in the understanding of the brain itself have been no less striking, both with regard to its microscopic structure and to the localization of its functions. Cytoarchitechtonics did not begin until improvements in microscopes in the 1830s enabled cortical layers to be distinguished. Meynert in 1867 provided the first accurate description of the cell structure of the cortex, and in 1874 the Russian anatomist Betz discovered the pyramidal cells and described their motor function. Elaborate cytoarchitechtonic maps were drawn up by A.W. Campbell and K. Brodmann in the early years of the twentieth century. In recent years with new and more powerful techniques knowledge of the minute structures of the brain has been enormously advanced.[35] Similarly, partly through the employment of new techniques, and partly as a result of the study of brain injuries during times of war, ideas of cerebral localization have made striking progress. After the general rejection of the spurious localization theories of the phrenologists, the view of Flourens that the cerebral hemispheres constituted a homogeneous and uniform mass and that they did not possess motor functions prevailed until the 1860s. Then in 1861 the French physician Paul Broca concluded on the basis of clinical observations that lesions in a particular frontal convolution of the left hemisphere produced disturbance of articulated speech, and designated this area as a centre for motor speech. A decade later an area for speech comprehension was noted by Wernicke in the temporal gyrus of the left hemisphere. This led to a spate of rather wild localization proposals, which seemed to be in conflict with a good many reported cases where functions were gradually restored after injury. The resulting controversy between localizationists and anti-localizationists went on into the twentieth century. That the organization of the brain was more complex than the first simple ideas of the localizationists had allowed for had been grasped by the celebrated English neurologist Hughlings Jackson (1835-1911), working at the Queen Square Hospital in London.[36] Particularly on the basis of his studies of epileptic fits and of aphasia, he came to the conclusions firstly that there was a motor area of the cortex, secondly that localization within this area was not narrow, and thirdly that the brain was organized vertically in levels. Jackson recognized three main levels of nervous organization: the lowest, reflex level, that of the 'middle centres', and the highest voluntary level. The function of the highest level not only included the most complex coordinations, but also the control and inhibition of lower centres. When the highest centres were damaged there was a release of lower functions. In normal functioning the highest centres were 'protected' and partially insulated from the lower, while in cases of brain damage they were the first to suffer dissolution. Jackson also put forward the notion of a 'leading hemisphere', which as Zangwill has observed was 'the precursor of the modern concept of cerebral dominance'.[37] Jackson's postulation of a motor cortex was soon confirmed by Fritsch and Hitzig in 1870 and Ferrier in 1874 on the basis of experimental evidence, but his general doctrine of levels was not widely accepted until the twentieth century, and his *Selected Writings* were not available in book form until 1932. But as more has been learned about the functions of the sub-cortical areas of the brain – the thalamus, the corpus striatum, the cerebellum, the hypothalamus, the hippocampus and limbic area, the brain stem and the reticular formation – so the essential rightness of Jackson's views has become increasingly apparent. It is impossible in a brief space to do justice to the detailed knowledge we now have both of brain structure and brain function. But as a broad summary the conclusions of the Russian neuropsychologist A.R. Luria (1902-1977) are perhaps worth noting. He distinguished three principal functional units of the brain – a unit for regulating tone or waking, a unit for obtaining, processing and storing information, and a unit for programming, regulating and verifying mental activity. Each of these basic units is hierarchical in structure.[38]

V

The advances in the life sciences briefly outlined above were spread over two centuries. Their influence on psychology has been gradual and progressive, but profound. The 'offical theory', as Ryle has termed it,[39] of dualism became increasingly difficult to sustain. The bodily side of the mind-body equation had been radically changed, and the problem of their interrelationship demanded reconsideration. A whole host of new areas of psychological enquiry had been opened up. Scientific method had been vindicated and extended, and the prospects of a genuine science of mind greatly enhanced.

The life sciences had made it clear that living organisms were composed of ordinary chemical elements, organized in complex ways. They were self-sustaining entities, which while obeying physical laws were endowed with novel properties. Among these novel properties the French physician Bichat at the end of the eighteenth century singled out 'sensibility' and 'contractility'.[40] If this was the case there seemed no unbridgeable gap between mind and body, for Aristotle long ago had pointed out that sensation and movement were the fundamental marks of mind. As the life sciences advanced, more and more facts suggested the close interdependence of body and mind. By the middle of the nineteenth century it was increasingly obvious that psychology could not continue to ignore these facts. 'The time has come', wrote Alexander Bain, 'when the many striking discoveries of the physiologists relative to the nervous system should find a recognised place in the science of mind.'[41] Bain owed a great deal to the German school of experimental physiologists, and to Johannes Müller's *Handbook of Human Physiology*, which had been translated into English in 1842. As knowledge advanced it became apparent, in Claude Bernard's famous words, that 'the fixity of the internal milieu is the condition of the free life'; that mind, in other words, was completely dependent on the stability of the bodily environment, and that any disturbance, physical or chemical, could affect its workings.[42] But the influence was not one way. The striking manifestations of hypnosis, brought to public attention by Mesmer towards the end of the eighteenth century and studied intensively during the early half of the nineteenth, together with growing clinical evidence, made it hard to deny that the mind also had an influence on the functions of the body.[43] It seemed increasingly clear that mind and body were part of a single system. Later, in the 1920s and 1930s, the term 'psychosomatic' was introduced to express this unity.

In the light of these developments the mind-body problem needed re-thinking. The sharp dualism of Descartes, which had always been problematic, seemed increasingly unattractive, as animistic and vitalistic ideas were gradually eliminated from the life sciences. A powerful example had been set by the biologists, which psychologists were quite naturally tempted to follow. From a purely scientific standpoint reductionism seemed an attractive creed. 'The roots of psychology lie in the physiology of the nervous system, and what we call the operations of the mind are functions of the brain' was the way Thomas Huxley put it.[44] A century later Donald Hebb proclaimed, 'Modern psychology takes completely for granted that behaviour and neural function are perfectly correlated.'[45] This reductionist point of view, however, has not been universally accepted by psychologists, and not even by all neurophysiologists. Sherrington believed that there was an inalienable residue enshrined in the ancient concept of the soul, which could not be reduced to physiology,[46] and Eccles, too, in his *Neurophysiological Basis of Mind* propounded a dualistic theory.[47] There are, moreover, philosophical objections to reductionism of a materialistic kind. It is, as Popper pointed out, 'incompatible with the acceptance of the standards of critical argument',[48] in other words incompatible with the claims and status of knowledge itself. On the other hand the claim of idealist philosophers, particularly those of the Hegelian school, that 'the consciousness through which alone nature exists for us is neither natural nor the result of nature'[49] has held little attraction for most psychologists. Psychosomatic interaction, and the facts of evolution, seem too clearly to have been established. To some nineteenth century psychologists psychophysical parallelism appeared an attractive compromise. Bain in Great Britain and Wundt in Germany were both parallelists, and in the twentieth century the Gestalt psychologists held a comparable doctrine of 'isomorphism'.[50] The difficulties of parallelism, however, are profound. The intricate physico-chemical processes of organic functioning do not seem to be mirrored in any precise manner in the mental realm, nor do the qualitative aspects of psychological states appear to be paralleled in any meaningful way physiologically. Rather physiological states are vehicles of psychological states, but not identical, or parallel to them. In a somewhat similar way printed words are vehicles of meaning, though as purely physical entities completely meaningless. We seem to be dealing in fact with emergent properties, which are rooted in the physical, but cannot be reduced to it. The idea of emergence is not a novel one. Leibniz outlined a hierarchical organization of entities in which new capabilities come into play at the higher monadic levels.[51] J.S. Mill in his *Logic* spoke of 'the composition of causes', and the emergence of new properties and laws to generate altogether new phenomena. With the coming of evolution the doctrine took on new significance and acquired an extra dimension. It received support from philosophers like Bergson and S. Alexander,[52] and from psychologists like Lloyd Morgan, who popularized the term 'emergent evolution'. It agreed well with the dialectic doctrines of Marxism, and was accepted by Soviet psychologists.[53] Biological theorists did not wholly reject it.[54] Whether emergence involves mutations, or sudden jumps, as the doctrine in its earlier forms seemed to imply, or, on the other hand, 'a continuous transition of organic life from one development to another,' as Wolman's 'principles of monistic transitionism' proposes,[55] the theory seems to accord with the observed data better than any other rival theory, even if it cannot be regarded yet as wholly satisfying scientifically. Nevertheless, if it does not solve, it does perhaps clarify, the central issue of the mind-body relation. As the Medawars have said, 'The notion of emergence can be accepted as a straightforward recognition of the formal properties of a hierarchy such as that which is defined by the conventional sciences.'[56]

The development of the life sciences, however, has done more than re-define this central issue. Whole new areas of psychological enquiry have been opened up. First among these, and perhaps the most important, was physiological psychology. It was in this area that scientific psychology had its birth. Sensory and perceptual processes, motor reactions and reflexes, emotions and bodily needs, sleep and instinctive behaviour have become topics of intensive psychophysiological investigation, ever since the publication of the first edition of Wundt's *Physiologische Psychologie* in 1874. In recent years the more specialized area of neuropsychology, which deals especially with 'the higher cortical functions', has shown considerable progress, and the investigation of the influence of chemical factors, both natural and pharmaceutical, on behaviour has become a thriving area of study. The theory of evolution has promoted many new psychological disciplines, previously hardly developed at all. The scientific study of animal behaviour began with the comparative psychologists inspired by Darwin – G.J. Romanes, C. Lloyd Morgan and L.T. Hobhouse – and was followed by the experimental animal psychologists of the United States and later by the ethologists of the continent. The science of animal behaviour is now an important area of psychology with many implications for general psychology. The study of childhood was also inspired by Darwin, who himself contributed a valuable early study. W. Preyer in Germany, J. Sully in England and Stanley Hall in America laid the foundations of the systematic study of child psychology. Particularly as a result of the work of Jean Piaget child psychology has become an indispensable area of psychology. Many complex psychological problems can only be unravelled by treating them developmentally in the way that Piaget treated the whole problem of knowledge in his genetic epistemology. Finally mention must be made of differential psychology, psychogenetics, and the investigation of hereditary and environmental influences on psychological growth, achievement and breakdown. All these are ultimately derived from Darwin's work. Whole areas of contemporary psychology are biological, or biologically inspired.

But the life sciences have not only opened up new areas of psychology, they have, through their example, vindicated scientific method. The extension of scientific method to the realm of living organisms was a momentous one. It was more challenging to orthodoxy than the triumph of Newtonian physics. By the beginning of the nineteenth century it was clearly succeeding. Scientific method supported by new technologies was answering old problems, opening up new vistas, and providing new powers. Bacon's vision was in prospect of realization. Scientific method was triumphantly spreading its kingdom from the non-living to the living. Why not, then, to mind? The sixth book of J.S. Mill's *System of Logic* (1842), 'On the logic of the moral sciences', set forth the view that the study of man's mind and his institutions fell within the ambit of scientific method. The time was ripe for the birth of scientific psychology. This birth, however, took place not as Mill hoped and expected in his native land, but in the more highly developed university system of Germany.

Chapter 9
The beginnings of scientific psychology

I

Scientific psychology was born in the universities of nineteenth century Germany, and has since spread from there over the whole of the developed world. This birthplace was not accidental. Scientific psychology is a product of the modern university, and the modern university, with its dual emphasis on teaching and research, was first established in Germany. As the historian James Bryce observed a century ago, 'there is no people which has given so much thought and pains to the development of the university system as the Germans have done – none where they play so large a part in the national life.'[1] As a result of the fragmentation of the German nation into numerous kingdoms, duchies, bishoprics and self-governing cities, and the lack, before 1870, of any effective central government, there were far more universities in Germany than in other European countries. In the absence of either a unified state or a unified church universities became a leading vehicle of national culture. With the eighteenth century development of the faculty of philosophy, to supplement the traditional faculties of theology, law and medicine, arose the idea of a comprehensive and encyclopedic '*Wissenschaft*', embracing all knowledge, humanistic and scientific. The University of Göttingen, established in 1734, was the embodiment of this ideal, and the equally important ideal of '*Lehrfreiheit*', the freedom of the university teacher to go about his teaching and research without interference or constraint, and also the freedom of the student to study as the spirit moved him, and to attach himself to the teachers of his choice, at this university or that, where he could obtain the best instruction. This element of freedom was an enormously important factor in the rise of new disciplines like psychology. It was, however, the foundation of the University of Berlin in 1810 by Wilhelm von Humboldt that really established the pattern of the modern university. This coincided with the reform of elementary and secondary education by Baron von Stein, the abolition of serfdom and the caste system, and the extensive modernization of the Prussian state following its humiliating defeat by Napoleon after the battle of Jena in 1806. The pattern of excellence in teaching and research established in the University of Berlin spread rapidly to other German universities, and as state-supported institutions, whose professoriate was appointed and paid by the various governments of Germany, they received liberal grants for books and equipment. Well-furnished laboratories were soon set up for research in physics, chemistry, physiology and other scientific disciplines. As Flexner observed in his book on universities, 'no other country during the nineteenth century assembled equally eminent groups of scientists and scholars, provided them with equal facilities, or paid them equal deference.'[2] It was, then, no accident that scientific psychology first took root in Germany.

Not until the end of the nineteenth century did the academic institutions of other western countries begin to catch up with those of Germany. Indeed British universities received hardly any state support until the establishment of the University Grants Committee in 1919, and prior to the establishment of the PhD degree in the same year there was little training in research. The older universities, Oxford and Cambridge, were dominated by traditional disciplines; honour schools in the natural sciences were not set up till the 1850s and adequate laboratories not founded until the 1870s. New subjects of study often met with conservative opposition, and this applied particularly to psychology. When in 1877 James Ward and the logician Dr Venn made a move to promote experimental psychology as a distinct discipline in Cambridge, the University Senate turned it down on the grounds that it would 'insult religion by putting the human soul in a pair of scales'. There was no official teaching of experimental psychology in Oxford until 1936. In the United States the situation in the early 1870s was broadly similar. Not until the inauguration of Johns Hopkins University in 1876 did higher study and research on the German model become part of the pattern of American education. Under the early leadership of Stanley Hall, who was appointed to the staff in 1881,[3] Johns Hopkins soon became a pioneer in the development of American psychology. Similar developments rapidly followed in Harvard, Yale, Columbia, Princeton and other American universities, backed up by the founding of learned journals and learned societies. The necessary environment for the growth of a scientific psychology had spread from its motherland of Germany to the other side of the Atlantic with momentous consequences. The beginnings, however, were German.

As we noted in the last chapter, scientific psychology was the joint offspring of the older philosophical psychology and the newer experimental life sciences, in particular experimental physiology. German universities provided the initial meeting ground for this conjunction. The early part of the nineteenth century was a period of vigorous philosophical debate in Germany. The gigantic figure of Kant had raised philosophic discussion to a new level of sophistication; but his critical philosophy, while apparently solving some problems, had given rise to others, and the dichotomy between the phenomenal and noumenal worlds created as many puzzles as the mind-body dualism of Descartes. A powerful group of idealist thinkers, of whom Fichte, Schelling and Hegel were the most prominent, attempted to transcend the restrictions that Kant had imposed upon speculative thought, and for a time dominated German philosophy. Their metaphysical flights, and their non-scientific dogmatism, however, eventually alienated more sober thinkers, and after Hegel's death in 1831 the idealist school lost ground, though its influence never wholly died out. It came, however, under increasing attack. Feuerbach, who was highly regarded by both Marx and Engels, in his *Critique of the Hegelian Philosophy* (1839) accused it of being simply theology in disguise. In all these vigorously prosecuted metaphysical controversies the status of mind, and the possibility of a scientific psychology, played a prominent part. A stream of philosophical treatises on psychology, most of them now forgotten, poured out from German universities between 1830 and 1860. There was plenty of argument, but little in the way of firm conclusions. It was here that developments in physiology seemed to be opening up new possibilities, and at least in certain restricted areas of psychology, in particular sensory psychology, to be providing hard experimental answers. The first physiological laboratory was established in the University of Breslau, then part of Germany, by the physiologist J.E. Purkinje, known to psychologists mainly for his contribution to the study of vision. Other universities soon followed suit. In 1833 Johannes Müller was appointed professor of anatomy and physiology in the University of Berlin, and it was here that he produced his monumental *Handbuch der Physiologie des Menschen* (1833-40, English trans. 1842). Müller was a productive researcher in various fields, microanatomy, embryology, marine zoology, experimental physiology, and physiological psychology. He synthesized the physiological knowledge of his day. Most important was his work on sensation, in which psychological as well as purely physiological factors played a part, and his law of specific energies, which stated that each sensory nerve route, however stimulated, gave rise to one determinate kind of sensation only. He numbered many famous figures among his pupils, including the great Helmholtz. In Leipzig E.H. Weber carried out his pioneering investigations on the touch senses, published in his classic work, *Der Tastsinn und das Gemeingefühl* (On Touch and Common Sensibility, 1846).[4] In his researches he employed for the first time the method of 'just-noticeable differences', which can be regarded as the beginning of psychophysics and the quantitative approach to psychology, and formulated the law that detectable differences are a constant proportion of the magnitudes of the original stimuli. Among Weber's pupils at Leipzig was R.H. Lotze, and it was Lotze, trained in medicine but by inclination a philosopher, who combined the physiological and philosophical streams in his influential *Medizinische Psychologie, oder Psychologie der Seele* (1852).

The way had been prepared for the birth of a psychology that was quantitative as well as qualitative, experimental as well as introspective, organized, systematic, and with its own distinct identity. Between 1850 and 1879 three great figures in particular blazed the way. Fechner formulated the basic methods of quantitative psychophysics, Helmholtz systematized the experimental approach to problems of sensory perception, and measured the speed of nerve impulses, and Wundt organized the whole field of physiological psychology, related it to the larger domain of psychology in general, and gave psychology its institutional identity.

II

G.T. Fechner (1801-1887), a strange blend of physicist, philosopher, aesthetician, mystic and 'inadvertent' psychologist, did more than any other single individual, except perhaps Helmholtz, to change the course of academic psychology.[5] Working assiduously on a single restricted problem – the relation of stimulus and sensation – he introduced methodology, systematic experimentation, and the quantitative assessment of results. However disputable his assumptions and his conclusions, he inaugurated a new era in the study of mental processes. As Boring put it, 'Fechner's *Elemente der Psychophysik* of 1860 stands at the head of the new science of psychology.'[6] In the words of a more recent commentator, Fechner 'invented methods of psychological measurement based on statistical considerations which are the very foundations of present day experimental psychology.'[7] Though Fechner may have been deluded in imagining that he was laying the foundations of the 'exact science of the functional relation, or relations, of dependency between body and mind',[8] and that his psychophysical law would take on for the field of mind-body relations just as general and fundamental a meaning as the law of gravitation in the field of celestial mechanics,[9] nevertheless he proclaimed the need for psychology to have recourse to 'its own laboratory, its own apparatus, and its own methods',[10] and this was revolutionary. Occasional experiments, occasional measurement and occasional psychophysical proposals had been made before, but with Fechner they became systematized and worked out in detail.[11]

The *Element der Psychophysik* eventually appeared in 1860 after some ten years of assiduous work, following Fechner's premature retirement from the chair of physics at Leipzig, and a fairly protracted period of invalidism. Fechner, a parson's son, was deeply concerned with the advancing materialism of his day, and in opposition to the materialists he believed in the universal presence of the soul – he even wrote a book on the plant soul – and held that mind and body were two aspects, inner and outer, of one underlying reality. He set out to prove that this was so, experimentally and mathematically, by establishing a constant and lawful relation between them. This was the motivation of the work which he entitled 'psychophysics'. He commenced with what he called 'outer psychophysics', the relation between external stimuli and sensations, but he believed that the same principles could be applied to higher mental functions, too. 'Higher mental activity', he wrote, 'no less than sensory activity, the activity of the mind as a whole no less than in detail, is subject to quantitative determination.'[12] This, however, was an area he never got around to investigating, except in the area of aesthetics.[13]

The essential problem if mind was to be measured was to establish a scale of units, and a zero point from which measurements could commence. Mind could not be measured directly, but Fechner believed that he had found an appropriate indirect scale in the just noticeable differences (j.n.d.s) of E.H. Weber, who had established some years previously on the basis of experimental evidence that j.n.d.s in each sense domain bore a constant ratio to the basic stimulus magnitude. And as for the zero point, this could be taken as the absolute threshold, below which a stimulus was undetectable. The magnitude of any sensation could then be taken as the number of j.n.d.s above the zero point. To express this in numerical form and to establish the law relating the magnitudes of stimuli and of sensations, Fechner carried out a protracted series of experiments, lifting weights, estimating visual brightnesses, judging tactile and visual differences. Fechner recognized that psychological experimentation involved special difficulties, because results varied with conditions which could not be completely standardized, and that the results, therefore, must be treated statistically. Fechner's three psychophysical methods, which he termed the methods of j.n.d.s, the method of right and wrong cases, and the method of average error, were the first systematic experimental designs in psychology, and his application of the theory of probability to the evaluation of the numerical results was the beginning of psychological statistics.[14] Chapter 8 of the *Elemente*, in which Fechner discusses the methods of measuring sensitivity and the precautions needed in the use of these methods, is a classic in the history of psychology, and can be read with profit by the experimenter even today. The outcome of Fechner's protracted research was the formulation of his famous logarithmic law, which states that the magnitude of a sensation varies according to the logarithm of the stimulus.

Fechner's work was important not so much for what it established as for what it initiated. There were almost from the outset objections raised as to his procedures. He assumed the general validity of Weber's law; he assumed that j.n.d.s could be taken as equivalent units; and he assumed that thresholds could be regarded as zero points.[15] Brentano very early raised objections to the logarithmic law, and suggested an alternative, which he never backed up with experimental evidence, so that it was ignored until, many years later, provided with such support by the Swedish investigator Ekman.[16] William James scoffed at the whole enterprise, and denied that sensations could be treated as masses of units – 'our feeling of pink is surely not a portion of our feeling of scarlet.'[17]

The whole problem of the measurement of sensations has been endlessly discussed by psychologists for over a century without full agreement having been reached.[18] During the reign of behaviourism there were even doubts as to what psychophysics was all about. Nevertheless the logarithmic law was widely accepted as a useful generalization until the mid-twentieth century. It was applied in practical situations, such as the decibel scale for measuring sound intensity. Indeed the much older scale of stellar magnitudes devised by the Greek astronomer Hipparchus in the second century BC was approximately logarithmic, and since the introduction of photometric measurement has been adjusted to a logarithmic function. Physiological confirmation came from the work on the neural correlates of sensation by Adrian,[19] who found that the frequency of neural impulses increased as a logarithmic function of light intensity. Not until the 1950s did S.S. Stevens[20] produce clear evidence that in the estimation of loudness and of brightness the logarithmic function did not obtain, and proposed a power law which stated that in every sense modality the magnitude of a sensation is a direct power function of the stimulus.

Whatever the objections to Fechner's original proposals, the use of quantitative methods in psychology has proliferated, and a new psychophysics has arisen on the foundations of the older Fechnerian model. Direct scaling methods have led to a wide variety of applications of quantitative techniques to areas other than sensation;[21] and in the field of sensation new theories, such as the theory of neural quanta[22] and the theory of signal detection[23] have opened up new areas of investigation. Mathematical psychology has developed enormously, and has become a highly specialized area with its own highly technical journals.[24] All this ultimately derives from Fechner's initiative.

Problems, of course, remain. A leading expert in the field of mathematical psychology is modest about its achievements to date, and still has doubts as to its foundations, expressing 'the haunting fear that the existing mathematics is not, in fact, particularly suited to the problems of psychology'.[25] Apart from this two fundamental issues were involved in Fechnerian, and indeed all, psychophysics – the nature of measurement, and the status of sensations. There has been a great deal of discussion as to the nature of measurement both by physicists and psychologists, and gradually a less restricted view of measurement has prevailed, legitimizing forms of measurement more suited to the psychological domain than the scales commonly employed in physics.[26] The status of sensations raises two central problems; the relation of the sensory order to the external world, and its place within the psychological domain. With the demise of simple dualism Fechner's endeavour takes on a different complexion. Sensations are more like a form of language than something parallel to the physical, and the establishment of direct functional relations between stimuli and sensations becomes a doubtful exercise when complex transduction processes intervene. Moreover sensations cannot be totally divorced from their psychological environment. As Stern pointed out, 'all thresholds that we study by empirical science are subject not only to generic constitutional factors, but also to the special factors of personal set for the stimulus and the personal significance of the stimulus situation at the moment.'[27] Nevertheless in spite of these problems there can be no question that Fechner added a new dimension to psychology, and that what had hitherto been an essentially philosophical discipline became both quantitative and experimental. He is, therefore, one of the key figures in the history of modern psychology.

III

Hermann von Helmholtz (1821-1894), Fechner's slightly younger contemporary, was certainly another. One of the greatest scientists of the age, equally renowned as physicist, physiologist, mathematician and psychologist, he brought the whole armoury of science to bear upon one area of psychological investigation, that of sensory perception, and more than any other individual set the pattern for the development of an experimentally based psychology. Trained in medicine under Johannes Müller in Berlin, and after qualification working for five years as an army surgeon, he went on to hold professorial chairs successively in physiology, anatomy and physics at different German universities. Moreover he was a man of wide general culture, versed in several languages, and appreciative of both music and the visual arts. He attributed much of his success to the fact that he was not too narrowly specialized, and deplored the growing rift between the sciences and the humanities.[28] He was ideally equipped to launch psychology on a new path, even though he never himself claimed to be a psychologist. As Brett observed, Helmholtz's work constituted 'the real basis of experimental psychology'.[29]

Helmholtz, as a very young man, even before he attained his first academic post, shot suddenly to fame in 1847 with his address to the Berlin Physical Society 'On the conservation of force'.[30] This has been described as being, with the doctrine of evolution, one of the two great generalizations of nineteenth century science.[31] Though foreshadowed by various other scientists, Helmholtz's conception of a definite store of energy in the universe was more precisely formulated and backed up by experimental evidence. In particular Helmholtz demonstrated that the input and output of animal organisms were subject to the law of conservation, and, contrary to the tenets of vitalism, they must be regarded as parts of the natural order. In 1850, after he had moved from Berlin to Königsberg as professor of physiology, he successfully measured the speed of nervous impulses, first in the frog and then in man, and established the fact that these were not instantaneous, or almost instantaneous, as had previously been believed, but comparatively slow. This finding was soon to have a bearing on the astronomers' problem of 'the personal equation' in the precise timing of observations, and led to one of the major topics of enquiry in the early years of experimental psychology, that of reaction times.[32] It also clearly implied that mental processes, in that they involved causal sequences in time, were part of the physical world. It was in the course of this research that Helmholtz delivered his important lecture, 'On methods of measuring very small intervals of time, and their application to physiological purposes',[33] which was to have as significant an influence on experimental psychology as on physiology. In the same year he invented the opthalmoscope, a brilliantly simple device for examining the living retina of the eye, and his thoughts increasingly turned to the study of visual processes. His inaugural lecture in Königsberg in 1852 was 'On the Nature of Human

Perceptions'. The final result of these studies was his three-volume *Treatise on Physiological Optics*,[34] which William James, who was in some ways critical of Helmholtz's theories, nevertheless described as 'one of the four or five greatest monuments of human genius in the scientific line'.[35] The *Physiological Optics* was followed by an equally exhaustive treatment of the sense of hearing in *Sensations of Tone*.[36] With the appearance of these masterly treatises, to put it in Helmholtz's own words, 'the art of experimentation, which has become so important in natural science, found entrance into the hitherto inaccessible field of mental processes.'[37]

The treatises remain to this day shining examples of scientific methodology and thoroughness. Helmholtz approached the study of the senses with the precision of a scientific investigator. Every conclusion was confirmed by careful observation or experiment. 'The chief aim which I have had in view has been to verify all the fairly important facts by the evidence of my own eyes and my own experience.'[38] In his studies in mathematics and physics Helmholtz had learnt the importance of precision. In a letter to his father he wrote, 'we who approach natural science from the mathematical point of view are disciplined to a painful exactitude in the testing of facts and consequences, and compel each other to proceed by very short and safe steps in the hypotheses with which we endeavour to sound what is still an unexplored ocean.'[39] When necessary he used instrumental aids; he devised new apparatus, such as the opthalmoscope, the opthalmometer for measuring the curvature of the cornea, resonators for amplifying partial tones, and the tachistoscope; and he was also an adept at improvising equipment and constructing 'bits of apparatus for his optical experiments from his wife's reels and his children's bricks, with ends of wax tapers and scraps of string.'[40] He stressed the need for the scientist to possess manual skills. To this he added extraordinary powers of analytical observation; in fact, this hard-headed scientist was one of the most brilliant of psychological introspectionists, and there is little doubt that he, above all others, established the pattern of controlled introspection, which became a central feature of the first era of experimental psychology. Finally this expert experimenter and observer emphasized the need for a background of theory: 'the only successful experimenter in physical science is the man who has a thorough theoretical knowledge, and knows how to propose the right questions in accordance with this; while on the other hand, those only could profitably theorize who had a wide practical knowledge of experimental work.'[41] Helmholtz brought to his investigations not only a powerful theoretical mind, but a wide knowledge of the history of earlier work. Perhaps his most important contribution to psychology was his mastery of scientific methodology, and his recognition that this methodology was applicable to at least some of the problems of mind.

Helmholtz's psychological investigations were confined to the two major senses of vision and hearing. He regarded this area as of particular importance because 'the physiology of the senses is a border land in which the two great divisions of human knowledge, natural and mental science, encroach on one another's domain; in which problems arise which are important to both, and which only the combined labour of both can solve.'[42] He was indeed somewhat sceptical as to how far scientific method could be carried in 'mental science'. He spoke of 'a generic difference between the natural and moral sciences';[43] and he stated that 'in mental life the influences are so interwoven that any definite sequence can but seldom be demonstrated'.[44] Nevertheless he held that 'memory, experience, practice are also facts, the laws of which can be investigated';[45] and the future was to show that experimental methods could be applied far more extensively than he himself applied them. It was the methodological model that he established that was all-important.

His two treatises on vision and on hearing were the fruits of years of patient work, in which every aspect of these two senses, physical, physiological, psychological and aesthetic, was collated, examined and tested.[46] By means of acute and painstaking observation, and the use of ingenious equipment, Helmholtz revealed many new facets of sensory processes, some of which were commonly ignored, and some of which blended to create a total impression. 'Helmholtz's work on optics', commented James, 'is little more than a study of those visual sensations of which common men never become aware – blind spots, muscae volitantes, after-images, etc. . . . We notice only those sensations which are signs to us of things.'[47] In hearing these hardly noticed accompaniments, partial tones and combination tones were 'not, as hitherto thought, isolated phenomena of small importance, but, with a very few exceptions they determine the qualities of tone of almost all instruments.'[48] And Helmholtz went on to note that these phenomena 'can be made objects of analytical perception without any other help than a proper direction of attention',[49] thus setting the pattern of late nineteenth century experimental introspection. Many of his experiments were extremely simple and could be performed by anyone without elaborate equipment. To take one example: to illustrate contrast effects Helmholtz covered half a sheet of white paper with a piece of black paper, fixed his eye upon a point of the white part near the margin of the black, and after about a minute drew the black sheet away; whereupon the half of the white sheet then exposed appeared suddenly of the most brilliant brightness. These simple observations and experiments were made significant by their theoretical underpinning, and it is because of his theoretical proposals that Helmholtz's work is chiefly famous – his revival of Young's trichromatic colour theory, his resonance theory of hearing, and his general theory of perception – as well as for the richness of detail with which he described the physiology and the psychology of the senses.

Helmholtz's basic attitude to the study of human perception was empirical and Lockean. The metaphysical approach to the Hegelians he regarded as leading to 'a tissue of false conclusions',[50] and although he admired the critical Kantian doctrine of knowledge, he rejected Kant's a priori theory of spatial intuition. Perception, including the perception of space, was built up from experience. Sensations were merely symbols or signs for real relations of objects. Signs were not images or copies of what they stood for; the likeness of signs depended upon their systematic ordering or arrangement. We learn through experience, particularly through activity and movement in our early years, what these signs mean. So 'the tests we employ by voluntary movements of the body are of the greatest importance in strengthening our conviction of the correctness of the perception of our senses.'[51] Our basic interest in seeing and hearing is a practical one. We recognize objects and interpret sounds so that we may react appropriately to them. Thus the numerous optical defects of the visual apparatus (chromatic aberration, astigmatism, blind spots, venous shadows, etc.) are overlooked, and in spite of the mobility of the eyes a static world of objects is perceived. Perceptions which appear immediate and simple are in fact slowly acquired and complex. In his final contribution to the theory of perception, an article written in the last year of his life, he wrote,

> By frequent repetition of similar experiences we can attain the production and continual strengthening of a regularly recurring connection between two different perceptions, or ideas, for example between the sound of a word and visible or tactual perceptual images, which originally need not have any natural connection; and that when this has happened, we are no longer available to report in detail how we have arrived at this knowledge and on what individual observation it is based.[52]

A great many of our perceptual judgments thus depend on what Helmholtz termed 'unconscious inferences', and in the case of perceptual illusions these inferences mislead us. In the more recent words of Gregory, 'perceptions are like scientific hypotheses.'[53]

Helmholtz's work on the human senses of vision and hearing was an enormous advance over that of his predecessors, and was the foundation of all future work, as well as being the true beginning of experimental psychology. Barely a generation before, James Mill could write about sight and hearing in only the vaguest general terms,[54] and even Helmholtz's contemporary, Bain, who aimed to link psychology to physiology, could produce little hard data, and confined his observations on colour vision to one inadequate footnote.[55] Helmholtz transformed the scene. Not all his findings have been accepted. In particular psychologists influenced by the phenomenological tradition, Hering with regard to vision, and Stumpf with regard to hearing, pointed to features overlooked by Helmholtz, and proposed alternative theories. A century's additional work has naturally produced new findings unknown to Helmholtz. Still it remains true that in the field of sensory psychology Helmholtz laid the foundation on which all subsequent work rests, and the methods he employed to study the senses have spread to a large part of psychology.

IV

The 1850s constituted a watershed in the history of psychology. Up till then the study of the mind, if we exclude the clinical observations of the physicians, had been mainly philosophical. In 1842 J.S. Mill had proclaimed the possibility of a science of mind based on 'observation and experiment';[56] but it remained for the Germans Fechner and Helmholtz to take the first consistent steps in this direction. The separation, consolidation and institutionalization of this new approach to psychology was the result of the work of Wilhelm Wundt (1832-1920).[57] As early as 1862 Wundt had envisaged the possibility of an experimental psychology when he wrote, 'The importance which experimentation will eventually have in psychology has hardly been visualised to its full extent yet. We do have, surely, many noteworthy beginnings in the field of psychological investigations, but as a coherent science, experimental psychology still awaits its foundations.'[58] In 1874 he was to provide the foundations, proclaiming the fact in his classic *Grundzüge der physiologischen Psychologie*: 'Das Werk, das ich hiermit der Offentlichkeit übergebe, versuchten ein neues Gebiet der Wissenschaft abzugrenzen.' ('The book which I am now offering to the public attempts to define a new domain of science'.)[59] It is not, therefore, inappropriate to describe Wundt, in Boring's words, as 'the senior psychologist in the history of psychology',[60] since he was the first clearly to identify it as a distinct scientific discipline.

Wundt's essential importance lay in his consolidation and institutionalization of psychology. His own psychological system had few followers, and was, in fact, riddled with conflict, though not without some features of interest. Trained in medicine in the University of Tübingen, and spending a brief period in Berlin with Johannes Müller and Du Bois Reymond, Wundt worked for nearly twenty years in the University of Heidelberg, officially as a physiologist, though from 1860 onwards his interest increasingly turned to psychology. For a period he worked as an assistant to Helmholtz, who at the time held the Heidelberg chair in physiology, but he never seems to have established a close relationship with him. His first psychological publication was a treatise on sense perception in 1862, followed the next year by *Lectures on Human and Animal Psychology*,[61] and in 1873-4 by the first edition of the *Grundzüge der physiologischen Psychologie*. In 1875 Wundt was appointed professor of philosophy in Leipzig, and he remained in his chair at the university until 1917, three years before his death. The Psychological Institute, which he established in 1879,[62] rapidly became the focal point of the new experimental psychology, attracting students from many parts of the world. The year 1881 saw the first issue of the journal *Philosophischen Studien*, in which the findings of the Institute were published, and successive editions of the *Grundzüge* collated and organized the rapidly expanding data. This experimental activity, however, constituted only a small part of Wundt's prodigious labours. He took his duties as professor of philosophy seriously, and compiled works on logic, ethics and general philosophy; and, at the turn of the century, turned to a comprehensive study of human culture, language, myth and religion, which appeared in the twenty years before his death in a massive ten-volume *Völkerpsychologie*.[63]

There are considerable difficulties when it comes to assessing Wundt's psychology. The volume of his work was enormous; it was constantly being revised, expanded, and changed; and in psychology he worked assiduously for something like sixty years. Moreover there was a basic schism in Wundt's approach to psychology, two opposing strands which were never successfully reconciled. His philosophical inclinations were idealistic, and rooted in the mainstream of German philosophy; but he was trained in the life sciences at a time when the ideas of vitalism and '*Naturphilosophie*' were on the wane. This cleavage is apparent in his psychological system, and accounts for the divergent interpretations that have been given. Whereas Titchener and Boring and the older commentators stressed the empirical and scientific aspects of Wundt's work,[64] more recent studies have emphasized the idealistic and humanistic components.[65] There would seem to be an element of truth in both views, while each on its own is one-sided.

There is no doubt that Wundt regarded psychology as essentially the study of consciousness. He opened his *Lectures* (1863) by stating that 'Psychology has to investigate that which we call internal experience',[66] and he never deviated from this view. In his final publication on general psychology some fifty years later he wrote, 'the subject matter of psychology is the whole manifoldness of qualitative contents presented to our experience.'[67] The essential method of all psychology must, therefore, be 'unmittelbaren subjectiven Wahrnehmung der Bewusstseinsvorgänge oder Selbstbeobachtung' ('immediate subjective perception of the processes of consciousness, or introspection').[68] Introspection, however, needed to be disciplined by experimental control, and strictly managed, if it was to give reliable results. The aim of this experimentally controlled introspection was to discover the elements of consciousness, and the laws of their combination. In his last brief, but definitive, *Introduction to Psychology*, completed after the final revisions of the *Grundzüge* and the shorter *Grundriss*,[69] Wundt categorically stated, 'The whole task of psychology can be summed up in these two problems: (1) what are the elements of consciousness? (2) what combinations do the elements undergo, and what laws govern these combinations?'[70] It is, therefore, perhaps going too far to state, as one recent editor has done, that 'Wundt, contrary to the interpretations of Titchener and Boring, rejected the traditions of mental and individual atomism'.[71] To be sure the elements were fused and compounded in various ways, but the task of the psychologist was primarily an analytic one, and Wundt accordingly devoted nearly a third of his *Grundzüge* (over six hundred pages) to a consideration 'von den Elementen des Seelenlebens'[72] – and the two basic kinds of element he regarded as sensations and feelings. It is, however, incorrect to describe Wundt's psychology as simply 'content' psychology, as Boring does, because Wundt accorded much prominence to volitional processes. Perhaps influenced by Schopenhauer, he maintained that 'volitional activities are the type in terms of which all other psychological phenomena are to be construed.'[73] All the same he did not regard will acts as primary psychic elements; rather 'it [will] is to be considered an affective process',[74] reducible, therefore to feeling. Analysis into elements was certainly, therefore, a prominent feature of Wundt's psychology. But there were, also, synthetic processes, and synthesis produced compounds. These were of two kinds, associative fusions and apperceptive unities, and the fusions and unities might themselves be blended in various proportions. Wundt was emphatically not an associationist in the British mould; ideas were processes which fused rather than separate psychic entities which became linked. And more important than association, which was a passive affair, was the active process of apperception, the volitional ordering aspect of the mind, centred in inner acts of volition, or attention.[75]

Clearly in Wundt's psychology there were components from both the Lockean and Leibnizian traditions. Historians of psychology may have distorted Wundt's viewpoint beyond acceptable limits by ignoring the Leibnizian features;[76] but it is an equal distortion to ignore the empirical elements. For Wundt's *Grundzüge* contained not only a detailed account of the current knowledge about the brain, nervous system and sense organs, but a comprehensive review of empirical research, much of it carried out in his own laboratory, on the psychology of the senses, on psychophysical measurements, space perception, the time sense, feelings, attention and reaction times. Though centred on consciousness a great deal of this research was carried out objectively, meticulously, and within the tradition of the natural sciences. The schism, however, remained. Wundt stubbornly insisted that the psychical and the physical were two totally distinct realms, and that psychic causality and psychic laws were completely different from the causal laws of physics. He never satisfactorily reconciled the two realms. He spoke of 'the psychophysical unity of the individual', but he did not explain how, from his premises, such unity could be achieved. At times he seemed to be advocating psychophysical parallelism,[77] at others to deny that there could be any meaningful parallelism between what were essentially different orders. The fundamental dualism of his outlook found expression in his division of psychology into two distinct sciences, physiological psychology, and what he called '*Völkerpsychologie*' (cultural psychology). He believed that the higher and more complex functions of the human mind could not be examined experimentally by the methods of the natural sciences, but had to be studied through their historical manifestations in culture, language, myth and religion. Psychology was as much a humanistic discipline as a natural science. In Wundt's system there was no real bridge between the two.

The hesitations and ambivalence of Wundt undoubtedly militated against the wide acceptance of his psychology, and weakened his hold upon his students, though in a sense these hesitations were a recognition of the deep underlying philosophical problems involved in the study of the mind – problems which remain today and still give rise to conflicting 'models of man'. Very few of Wundt's students, however, were concerned with these issues, and for his American students in particular it was the experimental, natural science side of Wundt that appealed. When they returned to America they were inspired by Wundt to establish laboratories, but the topics upon which they researched, the methods they employed, and the doctrines they eventually came to hold increasingly diverged from those of Wundt, and they soon began to ignore the restrictions that Wundt had imposed upon experimentation. Nevertheless there are features in Wundt's psychology that remain of interest. His principle of 'creative resultants' was a recognition of the actively constructive aspects of mind and the place of emergent novelty, and his principle of 'the heterogony of ends' (the fact that all purposeful action involves not only intended, but also unintentional, consequences) implied the impossibility of predicting in all its details the outcome of human actions. Some of the topics that Wundt studied, but his successors neglected, have returned to favour. But more influential than any of his ideas, or his system as a whole, was the fact of his establishment of an experimental research institute in psychology. It was indeed a prime example of 'the heterogony of ends', for it led to consequences far wider than Wundt himself ever conceived, or indeed would have approved of – the blossoming of experimental psychology.

V

The growth of experimental psychology over the past century has by any standards been phenomenal. Not only has it developed as an experimental discipline, widening its scope, refining its methods, and establishing its institutional base, but it has fostered the growth of a variety of offshoots and applications. It has spread geographically over a large part of the civilized world,[78] and topically has come to embrace many areas of investigation outside the somewhat narrow confines of Wundt's experimental realm.[79] Whatever philosophical difficulties remain it is inconceivable that psychology could ever again become a wholly non-experimental discipline. Half a century ago Stern could assert 'that the picture that we now have of the human mind is incomparably richer than the inadequate scheme of Hume's or Herbart's days'.[80] Today, even if there have been no decisive breakthroughs, the picture is richer still. Judged by its fruits Wundt's initiative has paid off.

In the quarter century following the establishment of the Leipzig laboratory the psychological scene was rapidly transformed. Laboratories were founded in various parts of Germany, in the United States, France, Canada, Belgium, Holland, Austria, Great Britain, Argentina and Spain. Specialized journals followed in the path of Wundt's *Philosophischen Studien*: the *American Journal of Psychology* in 1887, the *Zeitschrift für Psychologie und Physiologie der Sinnesorgane* in 1890, the *Psychological Review* in 1894, *L'Année Psychologique* in 1895, the *British Journal of Psychology* and the *Journal de Psychologie normal et pathologique* in 1901, the *Revista di Psicologia* in 1905. Together with journals there came learned societies, the American Psychological Association in 1892, the British Psychological Society and the Société Française de Psychologie in 1901, and the Deutsche Gesellschaft für Psychologie in 1904. The first International Congress of Psychology was held in Paris in 1889, and similar congresses, ever growing in size, have been held periodically ever since apart from interruptions caused by global wars. By the beginning of the twentieth century psychology no longer consisted of the uncoordinated musings of philosophers; it had become a separately organized body of knowledge with its own methodologies and its own institutional base.

Up to the First World War the German-speaking world remained the principle centre of the new psychology.[81] Wundt himself did not retire until 1917 at the age of eighty-five. By then, however, his predominance and much of his influence had already begun to fade. Several of the most prominent psychologists in Germany had not been directly associated with Wundt, and even those who had did not always follow in his footsteps. As one German psychologist ruefully noted, 'Wundt attracted many pupils, but held only a few.'[82] Even Külpe (1862-1915), first a pupil and then an assistant of Wundt, after dedicating his own *Outline of Psychology* (1893) 'To my revered teacher, Wilhelm Wundt, in sincere gratitude and affection'[83] moved off to Würzburg in 1894 and began to branch out on his own, inspiring a prolonged series of introspective studies of the higher thought processes, of which Wundt strongly disapproved.[84] Prominent among those never associated with Wundt were Ebbinghaus, G.E. Müller and Stumpf. Ebbinghaus (1850-1909), after a wandering career in several German universities and abroad, settled in Berlin in 1880 and carried out his famous experiments on memory,[85] thus opening up a new field of experimentation, now of vast dimensions. In 1881 G.E. Müller (1850-1934) succeeded Lotze in the chair at Göttingen and built up an experimental department (specializing particularly in psychophysics, visual perception and memory) which before his retirement in 1921 had begun to rival the Leipzig department. Stumpf (1848-1936), who held the Berlin chair from 1894 to 1921, contributed notably to the psychology of hearing and the theory of music; but perhaps his chief claims to fame were, firstly, the welcome he gave to the philosophical ideas of his teacher, Brentano, who, trained for the Catholic priesthood, re-introduced Aristotelian and scholastic ideas into modern psychology; and, secondly, his fathering of the Gestalt psychologists, who largely dominated German psychology in the 1920s. Thus by the outbreak of the First World War several vigorous departments of experimental psychology were flourishing in Germany and pushing research into new areas which transcended the Wundtian confines.

Developments in the United States were even more dramatic. The original impetus for the transformation of psychology from a philosophical to a scientific discipline was Wundtian. Apart from William James most of the leaders in the first generation of American experimental psychologists were trained by, or associated with, Wundt – Stanley Hall, J. McK. Cattell, Scripture, Angell, Baldwin, Titchener, Witmer, Warren, Stratton and Judd, to mention only the most eminent. The first American laboratory was established by Hall at Johns Hopkins in 1883. By 1895 there were over two dozen psychological laboratories in the United States. At first the scope of their work was mainly Wundtian, and the earliest American manuals of experimental psychology, those by Sanford (1894), and Titchener (1901-5)[86] were modelled on Wundt's *Grundzüge* both in their thoroughness and in the narrowness of their coverage. American psychology was soon, however, to strike out on new paths, into new areas of experimentation, into applied fields of psychology, into differential comparative and developmental psychology, and to embrace new functional modes of thinking. With the advent of behaviourism in 1913,[87] it increasingly diverged from the Wundtian tradition, and after the First World War America began rapidly to overtake Germany as the leading psychological nation.

Even more significant than the geographical spread of the new psychology has been its gradual topical expansion to cover new areas of experimentation. Wundt had held firmly to the belief that experiment could only investigate those areas of mind 'which are directly accessible to physical influences . . . its outworks, the organs of sense and movement'.[88] So his experimental psychology was essentially a physiological psychology, which dealt with sensory and perceptual processes, attention, psychophysics, speed of reaction and so on. With ups and downs over the last century psychologists have continued to study these topics. Research on sensory and perceptual processes has always bulked large, and occupied a major place in the standard texts of experimental psychology.[89] With the application of new techniques and the introduction of new concepts, it has become a highly important and sophisticated area of research. The study of reaction times, which waned in the early years of the twentieth century, received new life with the application of information theory in the 1950s and 'is now again central to much of experimental psychology.'[90] Similarly the topic of attention, which almost faded from psychology in the first half of the twentieth century, became once again a matter of major interest following the work of Hebb, Broadbent, Sokolov and others.[91] All these traditional topics have been studied with vastly greater sophistication, with improved statistical and experimental designs, with advanced equipment, requiring expert technical assistance and often with computer control, and with a much fuller understanding of the physiological substructure of behavioural processes.

Equally striking has been the spread of experimentation to new topics and new areas.[92] Of these perhaps learning has been the most important. Beginning with Ebbinghaus's learning of nonsense syllables in the 1880s, it became in the twentieth century the focal point of experimental work, involving both human and animal subjects, and threatening to dominate the whole field of psychology. In the 1950s, however, the study of central cognitive processes, initiated by the Würzburg psychologists in the early years of the century, came back into favour, partly as a result of Piaget's studies of the development of children's thinking, and partly as a result of the work of Hebb, Bruner, Bartlett and others, together with the arrival of computers and the birth of artificial intelligence. Cognitive psychology and its related area of psycholinguistics has now become a major topic of experimental research. What Wundt regarded as matters falling wholly within the scope of 'Völkerpsychologie', to be investigated non-experimentally, have been incorporated, at least partially, into the field of experimental psychology. Again while Wundt was concerned directly only with the normal, adult, generalized human mind, and employed only trained subjects in his experiments, his successors have increasingly used animals, children, and pathological cases, and submitted their experimental subjects to unusual environments and unusual stresses. Moreover they have studied experimentally, and been interested in, both the range of individual and group variations and the effect of social situations. Thus experimental psychology has vastly extended its boundaries. There are, of course, still limits. Experimentation has, so far, not been able, and perhaps never will be able, to embrace either the creative heights or the emotional depths of human nature. There are still, and perhaps always will be, areas of psychology that transcend the domain of the exact sciences. Experimentation, however, is not the sole source of psychological data. Psychology in recent years has been partly shaped by influences from medicine, social studies and philosophy. But before we look at these influences, we must briefly mention some other developments of a scientific kind within psychology itself.

VI

The main component in the transmutation of psychology from a philosophical to a scientific discipline was, as we have just seen, the outcome of the marriage between philosophy and physiology in the universities of mid-nineteenth century Germany. There were, however, other significant components, one French and one British. The French component was closely allied to medicine, and emphasized the value of the natural experiments of pathology in providing information about both the abnormal and the normal processes of the mind, since 'disease is in fact experimentation of a subtle kind, instituted by nature herself.'[93] This approach will be touched on in the next chapter in the broader context of medical influences. The British component derived from Darwinian theory, and led, on the one hand, to the pioneering work of Francis Galton and the scientific study of individual differences, and, on the other hand, to comparative psychology and the study of animal behaviour. The primary impact of Galton's work was in the fields of differential and applied psychology. The work of the comparative psychologists, however, before long began to influence general psychology, particularly through the work of Lloyd Morgan.

Early movements towards a more scientifically based psychology in Great Britain foundered because they lacked an experimental base.[94] Alexander Bain (1818-1903) attempted to link psychology to the new findings of the physiology of the brain and nervous system, but never himself carried out any experimental work. Similarly Herbert Spencer (1820-1903) propounded an evolutionary psychology, but was content with an abstract exposition of his views backed up with merely generalized observations. W.B. Carpenter (1813-1885) derived material from physiology and medicine, but not from the laboratory. It remained for Darwin himself and the post-Darwinian comparative psychologists, Spalding, Lubbock, Romanes and, above all, Lloyd Morgan, to introduce experimentation to the study of animal behaviour, and it remained for American psychologists to incorporate the results of their work into general psychology. The link figure in this development was Lloyd Morgan.

Lloyd Morgan (1852-1936) has been unduly neglected in the standard histories of psychology.[95] He has become identified with his 'canon' and with little else. In fact, in the decade from 1890 to 1900 he was one of the most significant and progressive figures in psychology, and his influence on the behaviouristic revolution that followed was considerable. Encouraged by Thomas Huxley the young Morgan abandoned mining and metallurgy for biology, and it was through Huxley that he first acquired an interest in animal behaviour. After five years teaching in South Africa he was appointed in 1884 to the chair of geology and zoology at Bristol, where he remained until 1919. His most important psychological work was carried out in Bristol, and appeared in four notable books, *Animal Life and Intelligence* (1890), *Introduction to Comparative Psychology* (1894), *Habit and Instinct* (1896) and *Animal Behaviour* (1900). In the mid-1890s Morgan visited the United States and lectured in Boston, Chicago and New York. His Lowell lectures in Boston in 1896 were heard by the young American E.L. Thorndike, who largely through listening to Morgan was stimulated to begin his own work on animal learning.

Lloyd Morgan's contributions to psychology can be considered under three main headings: methodological, conceptual and theoretical. His methodological contributions are the best known, and his 'canon' is generally recognized as a landmark, though it is not so often observed that Wundt had in fact proposed a somewhat similar maxim some years earlier.[96] The 'canon' that Lloyd Morgan formulated ran as follows: 'In no case may we interpret an action as the outcome of the exercise of a higher psychical faculty, if it can be interpreted as the exercise of one which stands lower in the psychological scale.'[97] A scientific psychology must, in other words, look for the simplest tenable explanations. It must work, too, with data obtained under strictly controlled conditions. 'Problems will have to be settled not by any number of anecdotes, but by carefully conducted experimental observations, carried out as far as possible under nicely controlled conditions.'[98] Also, as Thorpe has noted, Morgan stressed the need both for the precise operational definition of terms, and for the replication of experiments.[99]

Lloyd Morgan's conceptual contributions have been much less frequently recognized. He is, in fact, a main source of some of the key concepts of behaviouristic learning theory.[100] At the same time, in his recognition of the role of instinct he made contributions to what later came to be named 'ethology'. Though Morgan himself was not a behaviourist, and always accorded a role to consciousness even at the animal level, he was largely responsible for giving the term 'behaviour' a central place in psychology. It was not in general use as a psychological term at the beginning of the twentieth century. Thorndike used it incidentally in 1898 in his monograph on *Animal Intelligence*.[101] But Lloyd Morgan in his *Animal Behaviour* (1900) first used it systematically as a central concept in psychology. 'The term in all cases indicates and draws attention to the reaction of that which we speak of as behaving in response to certain surrounding conditions or circumstances which evoke the behaviour.'[102] In his account of animal learning Lloyd Morgan writes of 'the conditioning effects of the environment'[103] some years before Pavlov had begun work on conditioned reflexes; he spoke of the basic mechanism of 'trial and error' before it was taken up by Thorndike, and of the 'reinforcement' of successful modes of response and the 'inhibition' of the unsuccessful, before these concepts entered the vocabulary of behaviourism. Morgan had also clearly grasped the importance of homeostatic principles when he noted that 'a tendency to pass to a condition of more stable equilibrium runs through the whole gamut of animal behaviour'.[104] Thus many of the basic concepts of behaviouristic learning theory are to be found in Lloyd Morgan's writings, and Lloyd Morgan backed up this conceptual apparatus with a good deal of experimental work carried out for the most part under fairly natural, though controlled, conditions. He was critical of the artificiality of Thorndike's puzzle boxes, though he agreed with many of Thorndike's conclusions.

The field of animal learning, however, was only one side of Lloyd Morgan's work on animal behaviour. He observed that there were 'two opposing schools of psychology . . . the empiricists, who are apt to regard psychological genesis as wholly a matter of the conditioning effects of the environment . . . and the apperceptionists who insist on the central importance of selective synthesis in psychology'.[105] Lloyd Morgan's system embraced both views. Environmental conditioning could explain some behaviour, but it was not the whole story. Working mainly with birds Lloyd Morgan noted, and experimentally confirmed, numerous examples of instinctive behaviour, and such behaviour, he held, was connected with innate structures and central coordinations.[106] As Thorpe observed in his appreciative account of Morgan's work, 'Lloyd Morgan's contribution was indeed so outstanding as to warrant our considering him as one of the founding fathers of both comparative psychology and ethology.'[107]

We cannot leave Lloyd Morgan without noting some of his theoretical contributions, particularly with regard to the role of consciousness, and to the theory of emergent evolution. He conceived consciousness as being essentially concerned with 'control'. Behaviour lacking consciousness was marked by automatism; on the other hand

> control of motor activities involves, and must always involve, a loop-line, in the course of which there are developed certain centres, called control centres, whose function it is either to augment or to inhibit the lower coordinating centres of the automatic mechanism. Associated with the control centres of the loop-line there are sensory centres, the functional activity of which is conscious, or is associated with consciousness.[108]

Conscious experience and its mental products consisted, Morgan thought, of 'constructs'; and he postulated three main levels of such constructs, which he was later to term percipient, perceptive and reflective.[109] In accordance with his 'canon' he held that there was no good evidence that animals ever attain to the reflective level. But he did consider that there was a basic similarity of aim in constructs of different levels, in that all gave rise to expectations, and 'the activities of organisms are moulded in accordance with these expectations'.[110] In this way consciousness enters into the control of behaviour. The various strands of Lloyd Morgan's theoretical system were brought together in his theory of 'emergent evolution',[111] of which, though not the originator, he was certainly a principal advocate. It was a theory which to a large extent avoided the difficulties of dualism, the simplifications of reductive materialism and the improbabilities of idealism.

Lloyd Morgan's work, which deserves to be more widely appreciated, contributed significantly to the development of twentieth century scientific psychology, supplementing and broadening the base of Wundtian experimentalism. Unfortunately Morgan never succeeded in getting a chair of comparative psychology with its attached experimental station established in England, and it was left to the Americans to fuse together the two streams, German experimentalism and Morgan's work on behaviour. The way had been prepared by the publication in 1890 of William James's exciting *Principles of Psychology*.

VII

The role of William James (1842-1910) in the development of scientific psychology was a peculiar one. Unlike Fechner, Helmholtz, Wundt or Lloyd Morgan he was not himself an experimental scientist. Indeed James very early admitted his own temperamental unfitness for laboratory work,[112] and this was combined with a positive dislike of mathematics and logical analysis.[113] So in some ways he was very ill-equipped for appreciating, or contributing to, the new movement in psychology. On the other hand he was an intuitive genius of amazingly wide sympathies, trained in medicine, well-versed in the life sciences, and alive to the literary, artistic and philosophical trends of his day. In every science there are two main ingredients – contents and methodology. James was weak in methodology, but he had an intuitive grasp of the richness and range of psychology's potential contents exceeded by few other psychologists. On his visit to Germany in 1868 he realized that a new phase had opened up in the development of psychology. 'It seems to me that perhaps the time has come', he wrote in a letter, 'for psychology to begin to be a science',[114] and he firmly believed that such a psychology must be rooted in biology, though he never acquiesced in the reduction of the richness of lived experience to the abstract formulations of a deterministic and mechanistic scientific ideology. In psychology he was a transitional figure, but a transitional figure of enormous importance, whose wide-ranging ideas could not be confined within the preoccupations and limitations of the early experimentalists. So while absorbing a good deal of what was happening around him in psychology, together with the treasures of the past, his restless mind was constantly looking towards the future.

William James owed much to his unusual family background and his unusual education.[115] The family was gifted, highly verbal, and endowed with ample worldly means, as William's grandfather, who had emigrated to America from Ireland at the end of the eighteenth century, had accumulated one of the largest fortunes of the day. This enabled the James family to travel extensively, and from 1855 to 1860 most of their time was spent wandering around Europe, William and his equally talented brother Henry being schooled and tutored in England, France, Switzerland and Germany. As a result William became fluent in both French and German, and early acquainted with continental, as well as English, thought and literature. This was of enormous value to him when he later became interested in psychology. Equally valuable was his own psychological make-up, comprising both what Perry, his biographer, has termed his 'morbid' and his 'benign' traits.[116] On the 'morbid' side his neurasthenia and instability gave him a direct sympathy with 'the sick soul' and its psychopathic manifestations. He himself suffered not merely from 'insomnia, digestive disorders, eye troubles, weakness of the back and sometimes deep depression of spirits'[117] but occasionally from 'a horrible fear of my own existence'.[118] For some years in the 1870s he was incapable of working, and even after he had come to terms with his own nature, he was easily exhausted. The compensating 'benign' traits included his immense vivacity, his refined sensibility, and his great gifts of sociability. He had an enormous liking for people, particularly unusual and slightly odd people; he could establish rapport with human beings of a totally different make-up from himself; and he had a natural understanding of human nature. As his friend the philosopher C.S. Pierce observed 'he was even greater in the practice than the theory of psychology.'[119] Partly as a result of these social gifts he made contact, and often established warm friendships with, many of the leading psychological and philosophical figures of his day. His voluminous correspondence with them provides a lively commentary both on the personalities and on the issues of the period.[120] There was, therefore, a great deal to compensate for the total lack of James's education of any formal training in either psychology or philosophy. As he himself admitted, 'the first lecture in psychology that I ever heard was the first I ever gave.'[121] The only formal training James had was in the biological sciences and medicine, but one cannot read far in his *Principles of Psychology* without recognizing that he had, in fact, mastered most of the relevant psychological, physiological, and philosophical literature, and indeed his heavily annotated copies of the classics of this literature indicate the great care and thoroughness with which James had read them.

James qualified in medicine in 1869.[122] It was five years before he obtained his first teaching post in physiology at Harvard. In the interval he experienced a long neurotic breakdown, from which he was extricated after reading the writings of the French philosopher Renouvier, and accepting his bracing doctrine of free will. For some years after his appointment at Harvard his teaching was largely on comparative anatomy and physiology of the vertebrates, but he soon began to show an interest in physiological psychology. He announced a graduate course on the relations between physiology and psychology in 1875, and introduced experimental demonstrations the following year. In 1878 the course was transferred to the philosophy department, and in 1885 James was appointed professor of philosophy. Meanwhile in 1878 he had signed a contract with Holt, the publisher, to write a textbook of psychology. This was the origin of his *Principles of Psychology* which appeared, after much travail, twelve years later in 1890. It is perhaps the best-known, and most readable, of all textbooks of psychology, and nearly a century after its original publication it still retains its vitality.[123]

The value of the *Principles* lies in James's combination of massive scholarship with a radical and questioning approach and brilliant powers of exposition. James's wanderings on the continent had given him a first-hand knowledge of what was going on in the new German laboratories, and he had met many of the leading figures in Germany, England and France. He had soaked himself in the relevant literature, scientific and philosophical, in the main European languages. But he refused to identify himself with any of the prevailing schools of thought. He was equally critical of the sensationalist-associationist-materialist approach of the empiricists, and the spiritualist assumptions of the idealists. The hypothesis of the soul, he maintained in one of his well-known aphorisms, 'explains nothing and guarantees nothing.'[124] On the other hand he considered associationism to be 'tainted with one huge error',[125] that of mental atomism. His psychology rested on two main planks: firstly biology, and secondly what he termed 'radical empiricism', by which he meant the acceptance of the full richness and variety of experience. The ultimate '*Weltanschauung*', he said, is one 'of maximum subjective as well as objective richness'.[126] Firstly, however, biology: 'the way to a deeper understanding of the order of our ideas,' he maintained, 'lies in the direction of cerebral physiology.'[127] The most fundamental doctrine of cerebral physiology was the doctrine of reflex action, and this implied that the outcome of all nervous and cerebral functioning was a motor discharge. In other words, 'perception and thinking are only there for behaviour's sake.'[128] This was an enormously important shift from the analysis of consciousness to the study of behaviour, and James devoted a fair portion of his textbook to the consideration of various types of action, instinctive, habitual and voluntary. He went some way towards explaining mental events in physiological terms; thus memory was explained in terms of 'brain-paths',[129] and in the well-known theory of emotion, named the James-Lange theory (because of its almost simultaneous promulgation by James and the Danish physiologist, Lange) the physiological changes were prior to the experienced emotion.[130]

In spite of his emphasis on action, behaviour and the physiological aspects of mind, James did not become, and never could have become, a behaviourist. He believed in internal structures – 'the mind is filled with necessary and eternal relations' was how he put it[131] – he believed in free will, the ultimate power of decision, the 'fiat' of the will[132] and the ability of the individual to transcend circumstances,[133] and he believed in consciousness, not as an entity, but as an organic function, 'an organ added for the sake of steering a nervous system grown too complex to regulate itself'.[134] Thus introspective observation remained for him a primary method,[135] and it was through introspection that he arrived at one of his most characteristic doctrines, that of 'the stream of thought',[136] the idea of a continually moving and ultimately unanalysable continuum, within which could be distinguished clear 'substantive' parts and vaguer 'transitive' parts.[137] James laid a great deal of stress on 'the re-instatement of the vague to its proper place in mental life',[138] and the importance of the fringes of consciousness. And though doubtful as to what the self was he felt introspectively sure that 'every thought is part of a personal consciousness'.[139] But it was a complex affair, the self; there were 'as many different social selves as there are distinct groups of persons about whose opinion he cares',[140] and beyond these an active element, a spiritual self, 'with which we have direct physical acquaintance'.[141]

All this went a good deal beyond the experimental psychology of the German laboratories, and indeed James's attitude to German experimentalism was distinctly ambivalent. Initially he was intensely interested in it; he went out of his way to visit its leaders, Helmholtz and Wundt, he began to stage experimental demonstrations even before Wundt had established his Leipzig Institute, he built up a first-rate laboratory in his own department at Harvard,[142] and when no longer prepared to direct it himself he imported a leading German experimentalist, Hugo Münsterberg, to do the job. Yet before long he became deeply disillusioned with the outcome of experimentation. In 1899 he wrote in a letter to Stumpf, 'the thought of psycho-physical experimentation and altogether of brass-instrument and algebraic-formula psychology fills me with horror.'[143] He thought that 'the proper psychological outcome [of Fechner's psychophysics] was just nothing',[144] and as for Wundt, he poured scorn on his pretensions and described him as 'a Napoleon without genius and with no central idea'.[145] In the conclusion of his *Briefer Course* (1892) he wrote,

> When, then, we talk of psychology as a natural science we must not assume that that means a sort of psychology that stands on solid ground. It means just the reverse; it means a psychology particularly fragile, and into which that waters of metaphysical criticism leak at every joint, a psychology all of whose elementary assumptions and data must be reconsidered in wider connections and translated into other terms. . . . This is no science, it is only the hope of a science.[146]

This did not imply that James had abandoned hope; it meant that 'the natural science assumptions that psychologists had adopted must be regarded as provisional and reversible things.'[147] The future lay in new ideas and new data, and James was always on the look-out for such data and such ideas. He looked for them particularly in the fields of abnormal psychology, psychical research and supernormal achievements. Towards the end of his life James put it thus:

> The clinical conceptions, though they may be vaguer than the analytic ones, are certainly more adequate, give the concreter picture of the way the whole mind works, and are of far more urgent practical importance. So the 'physician's attitude', the 'functional psychology', is usually the thing most worthy of general study to-day.[148]

He had earlier expressed the opinion that the discovery in the 1880s of the unconscious direction of activity in certain situations was 'the most important step forward in psychology',[149] and he told Stumpf that he thought Janet's work on hysteria was worth more than all exact laboratory measurements.[150] In 1896 he referred to the possible usefulness of Freudian discoveries in the relief of hysterical conditions,[151] and after attending the Clark University conference on psychoanalysis in 1909, at which Freud delivered his Five Lectures upon *Psycho-Analysis*, James commented,

> I hope that Freud and his pupils will push their ideas to their utmost limits, so that we may learn what they are. They can't fail to throw light on human nature; but I confess that he made on me personally the impression of a man obsessed with fixed ideas. I can make nothing in my own case with his dream theories, and obviously 'symbolism' is a most dangerous method.[152]

Long before this James had made use of clinical case studies in his *Principles of Psychology*, and this is partly what made the book of such great human interest. His Gifford Lectures on *The Varieties of*

Religious Experience (1902) have been described as a study in clinical psychology, embracing as they did both the pathological manifestations of 'the sick soul' and 'the divided self', the phenomena of religious conversion, and 'the enormous diversities which the spiritual lives of different men exhibit'.[153]

In all this James was looking away from the closed world of the nineteenth century laboratories to the twentieth century and its wider concerns – to the impact of new ideas from medicine and the social sciences, to the rise of applied and differential psychology, and to new open-ended philosophies. The dominant interest of the last two decades of James's life was indeed philosophical.[154] He was unusual among philosophers in preferring muddle to tidy order, heresies to orthodoxies, the 'cash value' of practical results to abstract speculative truth. 'Reality, life, experience, concreteness, immediacy, use what term you will, exceeds our logic, overflows and surrounds it.'[155] Psychologists have not always heeded James's message; but James certainly not only made psychology seem a profoundly interesting subject, he also paved the way for a variety of new developments.

Chapter 10
Medical influences

I

It seems at first sight surprising that prior to the nineteenth century medical influences played so small a part in the shaping of psychology. Critical discussion on the nature of the soul and scientific medicine had a common origin in the Greek cities of Asia Minor. Aristotle came from a medical background, and in the Moslem world, which carried on the tradition of ancient thought after the collapse of Rome, leading philosophers, like Avicenna, were also practitioners of medicine. Plato in ancient times, Moses Maimonides in the Middle Ages, and Spinoza more recently adumbrated concepts of mental health and had some grasp of the nature of mental conflict. But their psychotherapeutic insights had comparatively little effect on the mainstream of philosophical psychology. Medicine and psychology went their separate ways. For this there were perhaps two main reasons. Firstly the viewpoint of the philosophers was a static viewpoint in which the central core of the human soul – call it divine reason, spirit, or conscious mind – stood above and apart from the material world. The breakdown of madness was conceived, therefore, as due to intrusions from without, either material intrusions caused by humoral imbalance, or supernatural intrusions caused by celestial or demonic influences. Hence the term 'alienist', which persisted as a designations of the psychiatrist well into the nineteenth century. It was taken for granted, therefore, that the phenomena of mental breakdown could throw no light either on the essential nature of the soul or its functioning. Secondly, moreover, what the doctors could offer to psychology was very limited. From the time of Hippocrates they could provide a rough classification of mental illnesses, but they possessed little precise understanding of the bodily organism, and still less of the material basis of mind, and they had nothing much to offer by way of treatment for mental disorders. So psychologists found little to interest them in medical writings. Indeed psychology contributed more to medicine than medicine to psychology.

The growth of the scientific spirit, and particularly the development of the life sciences, in the seventeenth and eighteenth centuries laid the foundations for change. Before the middle of the nineteenth century medical findings were beginning to make an impact on psychology; by the beginning of the twentieth they had become a major influence.

149

Several factors were involved in this development, quite apart from the general social and intellectual changes to which writers like Foucault and Ellenberger[1] have drawn attention. There was progress in the field of psychiatry itself. Gradually the study of mental disorders became recognized as a special field of study to be furthered by observational and scientific methods. When Robert Burton wrote his famous and often reprinted psychiatric compendium *The Anatomy of Melancholy* in 1621, he could still number among the causes of melancholy, God, devils, witches, magicians and the stars. William Battie's *A Treatise on Madness* (1758), written just over a century after Burton, was a very different kind of work, founded on long observation of the insane in the London hospital, St Luke's, which Battie established and directed. It was a systematic attempt 'to discover the causes, effects and cure of madness'.[2]

> Battie, it has been stated, initiated a new era in psychiatry in a number of ways. As the first physician of repute with a scientific background . . . who made insanity his whole time work he raised the 'mad business' to a respectable medical speciality. . . . He became the first teacher in psychiatry in England, if not the world, and created opportunities for studying the insane unencumbered by centuries old traditions.[3]

Battie's example led to the building of other hospitals for the mentally deranged, and paved the way for the work of Pinel and Tuke, and the psychotherapeutic 'moral' treatment of the nineteenth century. The foundations had been laid for a more scientific and humane psychiatry, which psychologists could no longer ignore.[4]

Two other important influences of a more general nature finally brought about the breakdown of the barriers separating medicine and psychology, namely the discovery of the unconscious mind and the theory of evolution. As long as mind was identified with consciousness, as it was identified by Descartes and his successors, the 'alien' forces responsible for mental breakdown could not be located within the mind itself; they had to be regarded either as material or as supernatural. One school of thought, from the time of Thomas Willis (1621-1675) onwards, emphasized the physical basis of mental disorders, and this viewpoint is still very prevalent; others, impressed by the power of the human imagination, stressed the psychological factors involved in breakdown, and for them the unconscious mind proved a useful ally. 'The idea of unconscious mental processes', wrote L.L. Whyte, 'was in many of its aspects, conceivable around 1700, topical around 1800, and became effective around 1900.'[5] Intuitively grasped by imaginative writers, the idea entered philosophy with the seventeenth century Cambridge Platonists in England, and Leibniz in Germany, and began to flower among the romantic, idealistic thinkers of nineteenth century Germany. But what brought it decisively within the ambit of medicine was the arrival of Mesmerism towards the end of the eighteenth century. The phenomena which Franz Mesmer (1734-

1815) produced in his seances were not entirely novel. The priest-doctors of primitive tribes, the shamans of the east, and strange figures like Paracelsus, and the Irishman Greatraks, in the west, knew how to produce in their different ways rather similar effects. But Mesmer formulated scientifically testable propositions by linking the phenomena with the manifestations of 'a universally distributed and continuous fluid . . . of an incomparably rarefied nature', and 'with properties similar to those of a magnet', and by maintaining that 'this principle can cure nervous disorders directly and other disorders indirectly'.[6] The French Academy of Sciences in 1784 put Mesmer's claims to the test and found his physical hypotheses wanting. There was, they concluded, no such thing as 'animal magnetism', no rarefied fluid. His curative results were essentially the result of the imagination of his patients. Cures, however, there certainly were, and Mesmer, in spite of his showmanship, was the primary source in modern times not only of what was shortly after called 'hypnosis', but of all schools of psychotherapy. Moreover it was through hypnosis that the influence of unconscious factors on behaviour became clearly demonstrated, and the doctrine of the unconscious mind ceased to be merely a philosophical abstraction.

The other major influence furthering the rapport between medicine and psychology was the theory of evolution, which brought mind into the natural world as a factor in the adaptation of organisms to their environment. Failure to adapt and maladjustment were capable of throwing as much, or even more, light on the fundamental processes involved as did the perfect functioning of the well-adapted organism. They were capable of revealing the dynamic processes involved in the struggle for survival. Development was seen no longer as divinely pre-ordained, but the result of a complex interaction of genetic and environmental forces which could go wrong at any stage. Though this did not in itself provide an answer to psychiatric problems, it put them in a new setting, and opened the way for a new dynamic approach to psychology. Moreover it forced psychologists to think in terms of the historical dimension, to see the adult as the product of the child, and the civilized man against the background of the primitive. The aberrations of the deranged mind, which at one time seemed outrageous and bizarre, took on a new and pertinent meaning of enormous interest to psychologists. When Freud arrived on the scene at the end of the nineteenth century, medicine and psychology had very definitely come together.

II

There was, however, one exception to the general neglect by psychology of medical findings, one lasting contribution of ancient medicine of which note must be taken, namely, the doctrine of temperaments. Early thinkers such as Anaximander, Alcmaeon and Empedocles had regarded health as a matter of balancing opposites, and had propounded the theory of four basic elements (earth, air, fire and water) and four basic qualities (hot, cold, moist, dry). Hippocrates in his treatise on 'The nature of man'[7] extended the doctrine to physiology by defining four 'humours' or fluid substances (blood, phlegm, yellow bile and black bile) present in the human body. On the mixture (κρᾶσις) of these humours the moral and physical character-istics of human beings depended and, to some extent, the diseases to which they were subject.[8] Galen amplified the doctrine, and described four basic temperaments (sanguine, choleric, melancholic and phleg-matic) and five mixed forms.[9] The doctrine of the four temperaments persisted through the Middle Ages into the modern world.[10] It was accepted by Kant in his *Anthropology*, by Herbart in his *Textbook of Psychology*, and even by Wundt in his *Physiological Psychology*.[11] Perhaps more surprising still Pavlov concluded from his conditioning experiments on dogs that there were just four basic temperaments, and though he proposed a new explanation in terms of excitation and inhibition, he adopted the ancient terminology to denote them. 'The old view', he asserted, 'is essentially correct.'[12]

More commonly, however, the ancient doctrine has been modified, extended and enriched by twentieth century workers, Jung, Kretschmer, Sheldon and others;[13] they have introduced their own idiosyncratic terminologies, and buttressed their conclusions with clinical data and precise measurements of physique. Others have sought confirmation for temperamental differences in statistical and factorial studies.[14] In spite of these developments there is a continuity between ancient and modern theories, and the doctrine of temperament, originating in medicine, has been incorporated into modern differential psychology, and become part of the theory of personality.

III

The first major psychologist fully to integrate philosophical, exper-imental and medical psychology was William James, and the excitement that his work aroused was largely due to this. His achievement, however, was the outcome of nearly a century's work by others, beginning tentatively in Great Britain early in the nineteenth century, and then taken up by French psychologists. In Germany, although psychology and psychiatry were both highly developed, there was less interaction between them, perhaps because each discipline had rather early acquired its own identity.

Dugald Stewart (1753-1828), professor of moral philosophy at Edinburgh, was, it would seem, 'the first philosopher who recognised the scientific potential of mesmerism'.[15] He regarded the phenomena produced by Mesmer as 'inestimable data for extending our knowledge of the laws which regulate the connection between the human mind and our bodily organization'.[16] Though Stewart's lectures were not published until 1827, it is probable that, as he retired from his chair in 1809, these observations were made in the first decade of the century. The rapprochement between medicine and psychology was furthered from the side of medicine by the Edinburgh physician John

Abercrombie, whose *Inquiries concerning the Intellectual Powers* (1830) included a good deal of clinical data, and from the side of philosophy by William Hamilton, the most learned of Scottish philosophers, who held that 'in madness, in fever, in somnambulism and other abnormal states the mind betrays capacities and extensive systems of knowledge of which it was at other times wholly unconscious', and used this as evidence for the existence of an unconscious region of the mind.[17] After the introduction of Mesmerism to England in 1828, and its use shortly afterwards in surgery by the eminent surgeon John Elliotson, hypnotism, as it was first termed by James Braid of Manchester, became for a time extremely popular.[18] Braid to some extent demystified it by treating it as a state of the cerebrospinal centres comparable to sleep, and it became of great interest to the new school of British physiological psychologists, among whom W.B. Carpenter (1813-1885) and T. Laycock (1812-1876) were the most prominent representatives.[19] Both wrote systematic treatises on psychology, and both supported what they termed 'unconscious cerebration'. Though they quarrelled between themselves about priorities, they essentially agreed that 'the scientific study of the various forms of abnormal activity is probably the most promising field of psychological enquiry'.[20] Henry Maudsley (1835-1918), the psychiatrist after whom the Maudsley Hospital in London is named, made an even more ambitious attempt 'to bring the manifold instructive instances presented by the unsound mind to bear upon the obscure problems of mental science'.[21] Unfortunately in Great Britain at that time there was no organized study of psychology as a separate discipline in any university, and departments of philosophy were increasingly falling under the domination of idealist influences opposed to empirical psychology. So the insights of these pioneers did not immediately take root.[22]

In the German-speaking world, in spite of the fact that Hegel in his *Philosophie des Geistes* (1830) devoted considerable space to a consideration of animal magnetism and insanity, medical findings made remarkably little impact on psychologists, devoted as they were to the study of the generalized normal mind, quantitatively, physiologically and experimentally. True, Lotze in his *Medizinische Psychologie* (1852) introduced some pathological data in the final part of his work,[23] but, though he had some training in medicine, his interests were essentially philosophical. Wundt, too, briefly discussed the anomalies of consciousness (hallucination, sleep, dreams, hypnosis) in his *Physiologischen Psychologie*, and contributed a paper on 'Hypnotismus und Suggestion' to his journal.[24] None of the leading figures in German psychology, however, regarded the data of psychopathology as an important key to the understanding of the workings of the human mind.

It was left to French psychologists to further the rapprochement between psychology and psychopathology, and because of the influence that their work exerted on William James, for example, and on Freud, it is of historical importance. The ground had been prepared for these French developments by a succession of eminent psychiatrists, P. Pinel (1745-1826), J. Esquirol (1772-1840) and J. Moreau de Tours (1804-1884), who had placed France in the forefront of psychiatric progress. Then came the revival of hypnotism. This started when the country physician A. Liébeault (1823-1904) settled in Nancy in 1864, and, using hypnosis and suggestion, produced many remarkable cures. Disdaining publicity and showmanship, and at first ignored by the medical profession, he eventually came to the notice of H. Bernheim (1840-1919), an able professor of medicine at the University of Nancy. Bernheim was converted and made Liébeault's work known to the world. In Paris a rival school under J.M. Charcot (1835-1893), neurologist at the Salpêtrière mental hospital, claimed, in opposition to the Nancy physicians, that the hypnotic state was an hysterical phenomenon, and could be invoked only in hysterical patients. In his demonstrations Charcot purported to prove that hysterical symptoms, such as paralysis and anaesthesia, could be both produced and abolished by psychological techniques, and that hysteria, therefore, was essentially a psychological disturbance.[25]

This work soon began to interest philosophers and psychologists, and the 'natural experiments' of psychopathology came to be regarded as a primary source of psychological insight. H. Taine (1828-1893), a teacher of philosophy, man of letters and historian, was the first to incorporate data from abnormal psychology to help to explain the workings of the human intellect.[26] Well versed in both French and British thought, he not only made use of case material from the Salpêtrière and other pathological data, but also material from British associationism, and from medical writers like Abercrombie, Braid, Carpenter and Tuke. The real founder, however, of the French school of psychology was T. Ribot (1839-1903), who in 1888 was appointed professor of experimental psychology at the Collège de France. In his first book, *La Psychologie anglaise contemporaine*,[27] he already noted the importance of what he called 'psychological teratology' (i.e. the study of anomalies and 'monsters' in the psychological order), and he went on to write a series of works on diseases of memory, will and personality. 'Disease', he held, 'becomes a subtle instrument of analysis: it makes experiment impossible by any other method,'[28] since 'in seeing how the ego is dissolved we discover how it is made.'[29] Neither introspection nor experimentation on normal subjects could provide similar data since 'personality is not a momentary event but a history.'[30] There were limitations in Ribot's work, because he himself was not medically trained, and he had to rely on second-hand case material, and though he held a chair of experimental psychology, he did not himself experiment. But he wrote well, and exerted a considerable influence both in France and in America, where his works (including his later works on the affects and imagination) were translated and achieved wide popularity.[31]

His younger contemporary A. Binet (1857-1911), too, best known for his work on intelligence and as one of the founders of 'la psychologie individuelle' (differential psychology), also commenced his career in the field of psychopathology.[32] A self-made psychologist, who never qualified either in medicine or philosophy, he attached himself to Charcot at the Salpêtrière, and worked for some time on 'animal magnetism', as he still termed it,[33] with the psychiatrist C. Féré. Although he later became disillusioned with Charcot's methods, he continued to write on hypnotism and to employ hypnotism in his experimental researches on reasoning.[34] He regarded this approach as important, since 'classical psychology . . . represents the side of the mind that is in the light, without taking note that there exists also the side in the shadows'.[35] When later he turned his attention to problems of intelligence, he collaborated closely with the psychiatrist T. Simon in the examination of subnormal children. He was, as Claparède said at the time of Binet's death, a psychologist of 'original versatility and fecund genius'[36] and his work was largely inspired from medical sources.

The tradition established under Ribot was continued at the Sorbonne by G. Dumas (1866-1946), a medically qualified psychologist who is best known for his editorship of the seven-volume *Nouveau Traité de Psychologie* (1930-1949), in which considerable emphasis was laid on the affective side of life and its disturbances, and by the psychiatrist, P. Janet (1859-1947), who succeeded Ribot at the Collège de France in 1902. Janet is an interesting figure, who paved the way for, but was eventually almost completely eclipsed by, Sigmund Freud. A nephew of the philosopher Paul Janet, and himself trained in the subject, Janet, while teaching philosophy at Le Havre, became interested in hypnotism, and carried out a series of hypnotic experiments with the subject Léonic, a classic case of multiple personality. His description of this case, and other cases, in *L'Automatisme psychologique* (1889), it has been said, 'stands at the threshold of all modern dynamic psychology.'[37] It preceded Freud's first papers on psychotherapy by several years, and was all the more remarkable because at the time Janet had no medical training. He went on to qualify in medicine, worked for a time in Charcot's laboratory, and was appointed to a chair of experimental psychology in 1898. He was, however, never really an experimental psychologist. Indeed he held that the mathematical and physiological approaches of the experimentalists had turned them away from their proper subject matter. 'Accurate study of the details of behaviour, of the need to love and be loved, of jealousy, of timidity, etc. . . . which in former days were regarded as minor accessories, as literary adjuncts of true psychology, have now come to be regarded as the very core of a truly useful and practical psychology,'[38] and these details could be provided, he believed, only through clinical experience. It was in this field that Janet worked for the rest of his life. He was an admirable clinician, who held that 'clinical observation and description of characteristic types are more useful than systematised theories'.[39] Hence his own theorizing was fairly modest, and centred on an economic model of mental energies, which set out to 'make it possible to budget the income and expenditure of a mind just as to-day we budget the income and expenditure of a commercial concern'.[40] He was critical of psychoanalysis, which he regarded as essentially a speculative system of philosophy rather than a branch of medical science.[41] How much influence his early work had on Freud is a matter of some dispute. Freud reacted coolly to Janet's criticisms, and came to deny that psychoanalysis owed anything to Janet's prior work.[42] In Ellenberger's view, however, this disclaimer went too far, particularly as earlier, in 1909, Freud had admitted to having followed Janet's example in attempting to penetrate into the psychic processes of hysteria.[43] What is certain is that Freud quite early on not only introduced new methods of treatment, but a new theoretical approach. As Freud said,

> The differences between our theory and that of Janet is that we do not derive the psychic fission from a congenital lack of capacity on the part of the mental apparatus to synthesize its experiences, but we explain it dynamically by the conflict of opposing forces, we recognise in it a native striving of each mental complex against the other.[44]

Undoubtedly it was the powerful theorizing of Freud that finally threw psychology and medicine irrevocably together. This conjunction, however, was the outcome of a century-long *rapprochement*, in which French pioneers played a leading role.

IV

Nearly half a century after his death Sigmund Freud (1856-1939) remains a controversial figure. Scientific purists still maintain that psychoanalysis, the system of theory and therapy that Freud created, is nothing more than 'a stupendous intellectual confidence trick',[45] and his descriptions of psychic structure mere 'Homeric myths'.[46] Many psychologists share this scepticism and distrust, dismissing Freud, whatever his literary and imaginative gifts, as a bogus scientist.[47] Yet, in sharp contrast to these views, we are told that psychoanalysis is 'perhaps the most important body of thought committed to paper in the twentieth century',[48] and the most powerful of all influences that have shaped contemporary psychology.[49] We are confronted once again with the old divide between subject matter and methodology, between those who stress the rich content of psychological material, and those who stress the strict requirements of scientific methodology. For the former Freud is a great figure, for the latter he is seriously wanting. It is necessary, of course, to distinguish influence from validity. Doctrines can be influential without at the same time being valid; they can raise significant questions and arouse strong emotions, without having provided convincing answers or satisfied the requirements of logic. Whatever the validity of psychoanalytic theory, there can be little doubt that by enlarging its subject matter it has changed the face of psychology.

For the lasting achievement of Freud was to have brought

psychologists face to face with the whole range of human problems, with the central questions that had been treated by great thinkers, artists and writers from ancient times, but had been almost excluded from the arid abstractions of the academic schools – with problems of love and hate, of happiness and misery; with the turmoil of social discontent and violence, as well as the trifling errors and slips of everyday existence; with the towering edifices of religious belief as well as the petty, but tragic, tensions of family life. Freud could certainly have said, in the words of the Roman poet, 'humani nihil a me alienum puto.'[50] Every aspect of human nature, from the most bestial to the most sublime, found a place in Freudian psychology. The minutest details of behaviour were regarded as significant and parts of 'the sacred text'.[51] There were no barriers any longer between the normal and the abnormal. Mankind suffered from a universal neurosis. Everyone dreamed; and 'the dream is a pathological product, the first member of the class.'[52] So psychoanalysis, which started off as a system of therapy, 'ceased to be a purely medical subject.'[53] It became a general system of psychology with theoretical implications of great importance. Above all it restored the hierarchical model, which Plato had established, but the dualistic and materialistic systems of modern times had destroyed, and placed this in an evolutionary, developmental setting. First there was the 'id', the biological base with its instinctive drives; then the 'primary processes' of the psyche, the primitive fantasy stages of mental development; followed by the 'secondary', more rational processes of the 'ego'; and finally the socially shaped 'superego'. In the complex personality of man all these levels coexisted, not, however, in peace, but in frequent conflict. Freud was deeply influenced by Darwin and the concept of life as involving a dynamic process of struggle.[54] He conceived man's inner life as a field of warring forces just as much as the world of outer nature. And just as the natural world could only be explained in terms of its history and development through time, so human personality could only be explained in the light of the childhood both of the race and of the individual himself. Freud, well versed both in the humanities and in the sciences of life, made the most ambitious attempt yet tried to fuse these two streams together, and this is why he remains important, even if the scientific validity of some of his theories is open to question. The weakness of Freud was that he never established a satisfactory methodology to validate his insights. The hermeneutic skills on which he relied were never adequately formulated, and indeed he made unjustified and mistaken claims to have established psychology 'upon foundations similar to those of any other science, such as physics'.[55] In claiming this Freud fooled himself as well as many of his followers. The reasons for his controversial status are, therefore, not far to seek.

The magnetic attraction which Freud has nevertheless exerted on many thinkers and writers of the twentieth century was partly due to the fact that his system of psychology, however unique and original in its final synthesis, was in fact derived, as several recent commentators have noted,[56] from a good many tributary sources of late nineteenth

century thought. Classically educated and an excellent linguist, Freud
was early acquainted with many of the masterpieces of European
literature, ancient and modern. Also, as a Jew he inherited the rich
tradition of Jewish thought. On this foundation was superimposed the
study of medicine and the life sciences. For some years Freud was
engaged in research, some of it distinguished, in physiology, cerebral
anatomy, neurology and pharmacology. The Vienna school of
medicine, where he studied and carried out his research, was
dominated then by Helmholtzian ideas, and was as advanced as any in
the world. Here Freud came under the influence of such eminent
teachers and colleagues as Brücke, Meynert and Exner. His lifelong
adherence to the deterministic, scientific *Weltanschauung*, his early
attempt in 'project for a scientific psychology'[57] to expound his
psychological ideas in physiological terms, and his continued belief that
'all our provisional ideas in psychology will some day be based on an
organic substructure'[58] were a consequence of this background
training. Moreover, as Freud observed in his autobiography[59] the
theories of Darwin strongly attracted him while still a schoolboy, and
they remained a foundation stone of his psychoanalytic system.[60]
Among other things Darwin had demonstrated that 'instincts are as
important as corporeal structures for the welfare of each species',[61]
and among the most powerful of the instincts, of course, was the sex
instinct. Freud was not the discoverer of the importance of sex in
human life. The late nineteenth century saw a flowering of sexology,
the scientific and clinical study of sexual functioning. The first edition
of Kraft-Ebbing's *Psychopathia Sexualis* appeared in 1886, Binet's
studies of fetishism in 1887,[62] Moll's *Perversions of the Sex Instinct* in
1891 and the first volume of Havelock Ellis's *Studies in the Psychology
of Sex* in 1897. Sex was becoming a much discussed subject before
Freud's *Three Essays on the Theory of Sexuality* appeared in 1905.
Nor, as we have seen, was Freud the first psychotherapist. He was
preceded by several members of the French school, and did not take
up psychotherapeutic work till after studying under Charcot, nor begin
publishing any of his case studies until after he had visited Liébeault
and Bernheim in Nancy. The psychoanalytic system which eventually
emerged was the product of a good many contemporary scientific and
medical ingredients.

But this was not all; for Freud was never simply a scientist. Indeed
he went so far as to admit that he was 'not really a man of science
[but] . . . a conquistador, an adventurer'.[63] However averse he
professed to be towards philosophy, he possessed the speculative drive
of a philosopher, and parts of his 'metapsychology' bear a striking
resemblance to the systems of other influential nineteenth century
thinkers, particularly those of Schopenhauer and Nietzsche. Freud
always seemed reluctant to admit having been influenced by philosophy,
declaring indeed, that he had a 'constitutional incapacity' for it,[64] but
his professions of disinterest were not entirely convincing. As a student
he attended lectures by the philosopher Brentano for several
sessions;[65] as a young man he translated essays of J.S. Mill, including

one on Plato;[66] he later admitted a lifelong attraction towards Spinoza;[67] and though he professed not to have been acquainted with the writings of Schopenhauer and Nietzsche, 'in point of fact,' writes Sulloway, 'both Schopenhauer's and Nietzsche's ideas were so widely discussed within late nineteenth century intellectual circles that Freud could not possibly have escaped a reasonably general education in their doctrines.'[68] Moreover Freud did quote both writers in his *Interpretation of Dreams* in 1900. The romantic and irrationalist currents of German thought were, we may conclude, among the ingredients of psychoanalysis.

Academic psychology as such, on the other hand, contributed comparatively little to Freud's system. He was, writes his biographer Ernest Jones, 'ill-informed in the field of contemporary psychology'.[69] Two psychologists only, Herbart and Fechner, seemed to influence him to any extent. While still at school he had read an Herbartian text, and it has been suggested that the idea of repression may have been derived from this source.[70] Certainly he borrowed from Fechner, admitting that he 'followed that thinker upon many important points'.[71] His borrowings, however, were conceptual, not methodological. The experimental and quantitative approach was fundamentally alien to the Freudian endeavour, and his early 'Project for a scientific psychology'[72] was derived from a combination of neurophysiological concepts with those of pre-experimental introspective psychology.

The term 'psychoanalysis' was first employed by Freud in 1896.[73] By that time many of the key ideas that he had absorbed over the previous quarter of a century had been fused together in a new and powerful synthesis; he had commenced the self-analysis which served both to contribute material and to strengthen his convictions; and he had worked out the new techniques of free association and dream analysis, which formed the core of his psychotherapeutic methods. As a way of probing the unconscious, free association was an innovation on the part of Freud. It has been suggested that the technique may have been derived from an essay on creative writing by the author, L. Börne, with whose work Freud was familiar.[74] In fact the diagnostic power of free associations had been noted some years previously by Francis Galton in his 'Psychometric experiments', but there is nothing to indicate that Freud had read Galton's article, which strikingly anticipated the findings of psychoanalysis. Galton had observed the way in which freely wandering associations revealed the hidden depths of the mind and brought back 'many bygone incidents, which I never suspected to have formed part of my stock of thoughts'.[75] 'They lay bare the foundations of a man's thoughts with curious distinctness, and exhibit his mental anatomy with more vividness and truth than he would probably care to publish to the world.'[76] This is precisely what Freud discovered after he had abandoned hypnotic therapy, on the ground that it failed to face up to the two crucial problems of resistance and transference – the blockages against recall and the reactivation in the analytic situation of early interfamilial emotions.

Psychoanalytic therapy, which rested on total honesty, aimed to handle these two basic problems, and to bring about a permanent alteration in the patient's mental economy. Its efficacy is, of course, still a much debated question, but it is worth noting that Freud himself was never 'a therapeutic enthusiast',[77] and in the last years of his life expressed doubts as to its general effectiveness.[78] His primary interest was always not therapeutic but theoretical, and the high value which he placed upon his work on dreams was essentially because of its contribution to theory.

'The theory of dreams', wrote Freud, 'occupies a special place in the history of psychoanalysis.'[79] 'It contains . . . the most valuable of all the discoveries it has been my good fortune to make.'[80] Dreams, of course, had been a matter of interest to philosophers from the time of Aristotle onwards, and there was a considerable flowering of literature on the subject in the nineteenth century. Freud was familiar with this literature, and devoted nearly a quarter of his *Interpretation of Dreams* (1900) to a study of it. Many of the ideas which found a place in his own theory were derived from his predecessors,[81] and once again it was in his cogent synthesis that Freud's main achievement lay. The great importance of dreams, according to Freud, was due to the entry they gave to the repressed primary areas of the mind, the 'imperishable' primitive regions,[82] the contents of which emerged not only in dreams, but in neurotic and psychotic disturbances. Freud's central hypothesis was that there were 'no indifferent dream stimuli'.[83] Dreams were motivated, were the expression of wishes; they had, therefore, a meaning which could be discovered. The meaning was not, however, immediately apparent, because the 'manifest' content of the dream did not directly reveal the 'latent' content. The dream 'censorship' and the processes of 'dream work' introduced disguises, condensations and distortions. Dreams, therefore, had to be interpreted, and this could be done partly by getting the dreamer to associate around the dream content, and partly by a translation of certain commonly employed dream symbols, using analogies from folklore and mythology in support. Dreams generally had several layers of meaning, the deepest stratum, Freud believed, deriving from the experiences of infancy, often from the first three years of life, and possessing sexual significance.

Many of Freud's propositions about dreams seem to contain at least an element of truth. Dream material is certainly not merely a chance evocation of psychic content elicited at random by physiological and somatic stimuli. The content of dreams is psychically biased. Calvin Hall, analysing a large sample of dreams, noted the concentration of dreaming on personal, intimate, emotional and conflictual data, and an absence of technical and professional subject matter.[84] Jung, too, observed that 'a series of dreams was not a senseless string of incoherent and isolated happenings but . . . the successive steps in a planned and orderly process of development'.[85] In this determination of subject matter motivational factors would seem to play a part, as Freudian theory requires, judging from studies of children's dreams[86] and the dreams of native peoples.[87] There is evidence, too, lending some support for Freud's theory of dream symbolism,[88] and to the concept of a more primitive, symbolic mode of thinking. Piaget, for example, has pointed out that dream symbols are closely allied to other forms of symbolism, such as the ludic symbolism of children's play.[89] It is not far-fetched, therefore, to regard dreams as part of 'an archaic world of vast emotions and imperfect thoughts, the study of which may acquaint us with the primitive stages of the development of mental life'.[90] Dreams are, as Freud saw, of psychological significance, and, because they plumb inaccessible regions of the mind, a valuable aid to psychodiagnosis.

In two respects Freud's theory of dreams was inadequate. He had no knowledge of the profound physiological changes that accompany dreaming, changes that were only discovered from the 1950s onwards, and he formulated no satisfactory canons of interpreting dream content. In 1953 Aserinsky and Kleitman reported that there were two types of sleep, paradoxical or rapid eye movement (REM) sleep and orthodox sleep.[91] REM sleep occupies up to a quarter of sleeping time in adults, occurring at intervals of roughly ninety minutes, and it is during these phases that dreaming takes place. Many physiological changes accompany REM sleep, including changes in the electrical rhythms of the brain, changes in the blood flow to the sexual organs, changes in muscle tone, heart rate and breathing. These phenomena occur not only in man, but in all species of mammals,[92] and presumably, therefore, must have some evolutionary value. Whether in animals paradoxical sleep is accompanied by dreams is impossible to prove, but it would seem that the function of dreams is not merely psychological, and to safeguard sleep, as Freud suggested, but in part at least biological.

The unsatisfactoriness of Freud's canons of dream interpretation is a more serious weakness of his theories. 'The accumulation of many exactly similar instances affords us the required certainty,' asserted Freud.[93] This, is, of course, a logical fallacy, as it does not rule out systematic bias; and when he goes so far as to state that 'anything in a dream may mean its opposite',[94] any hope of falsification seems to have vanished; and a theory is not scientific unless open to falsification. Freud may have had, almost certainly did have, profound insights, but he did not buttress them with convincing scientific proof.

Nevertheless *The Interpretation of Dreams* remains a masterpiece, and in its final chapter Freud summarized for the first time the basic principles of psychoanalytic theory: the concept of psychic reality ('a special form of existence, which must not be confounded with material reality'[95]); the doctrine of the unconscious and psychic locality; the idea of regression; the distinction between primary and secondary processes; the nature of repression; the motivational aspects of the mind; and the importance of the past in the explanation of the present. It was on these foundations that the theoretical additions of the remaining forty years of Freud's life were erected. The developments were in three main areas: the doctrine of instincts; the classification of psychic structure; and the elaboration of the various mechanisms of defence.

The Freudian doctrine of instincts went through a number of mutations, and was marked to the end by a certain tentativeness. In his autobiography Freud noted the speculative and provisional nature of his final theory, in which he postulated two main instinctive drives, Eros or the libido, and 'the death instinct'.[96] The libido, of course, had been a feature of psychoanalysis from the beginning. In his essay on anxiety neurosis, written in 1895,[97] Freud attributed anxiety to a deflection of sexual libido, and he later defined libido as 'the energy . . . of those instincts which have to do with all that may be comprised under the word "love"'.[98] Sex, in this broad sense of the term, was present in infancy and the early years of life, and it was made up of various component parts, oral, anal and genital, which in the perversions had not normally blended.[99] Central to sexual development in Freud's theory was the 'Oedipus complex' (the emotional relationships of the child to its parents), and he maintained that this was 'the nuclear complex of every neurosis'.[100] No doubt the Freudian emphasis on sexuality was an important and enlightening contribution to psychology, opening up a topic which academic psychology had often ignored, but in the face of more recent evidence[101] it appears unduly dogmatic and rigid in its prescriptions.

The 'death instinct' was a later addition, and even more controversial. It was introduced in *Beyond the Pleasure Principle* in 1920 to explain the phenomena of 'repetition compulsions' and the traumatic neuroses. It was a complex idea, involving a homeostatic tendency to restore equilibrium, ultimately the equilibrium of inanimate existence, and an aggressive, destructive element, directed primarily against the self, but capable of being directed outwards.[102] It was a somewhat muddled conception, of romantic rather than biological origin, and rejected by many even of Freud's closest followers. Nevertheless Sulloway sees it as an important part of the Freudian system,[103] introducing a balance between evolution (progression) and involution (regression); and it provided some sort of place for man's aggressive tendencies. 'It really seems', wrote Freud, 'as though it is necessary for us to destroy some other thing or person in order not to destroy ourselves.'[104] He had no illusions about the goodness of human nature! Even the apostate Jung had to admit that 'all that gush about man's innate goodness . . . was blown to the winds by Freud'.[105]

Freud's theory of instincts, recognized by him to be merely tentative, received some indirect confirmatory support from the work of the animal ethologists. An analysis of man's romantic fantasies, as projected into his creative products and art forms, suggests, too, that sex and aggression obsessively occupy his thoughts. Love and hate, those 'mythical entities, magnificent in their indefiniteness'[106] certainly must play a major part in any realistic description of human nature, and in recognizing their central role Freud was doing little more than reviving in modern dress the ancient insights of the poets and philosophers of Greece.

In the years immediately following the publication of *Beyond the*

Pleasure Principle Freud introduced his new structural model of the mind, his threefold division of ego, id and superego.[107] The model was, in fact, nothing more than a recognition that man's psychological make-up comprised biological, personal and social components. What was special about Freud's construction was the weakness of the personal ego system, which represented 'what we call reason and sanity'.[108] For the Freudian ego was controlled by 'three tyrannical masters . . . the external world, the superego and the id',[109] and was 'essentially passive'[110] in the face of these forces, the id representing 'the dark inaccessible part of our personality'[111], its biological urges, and the superego, through the power of conscience, the severity of social constraints. In Freud's philosophy 'a return from the over-estimation of the property of consciousness is the indispensable preliminary to any genuine insight into the course of psychic events.'[112] No doubt Freud's dethronement of the ego was a valuable correction to the classical rationalistic and voluntaristic pictures of the mind, but many of his psychoanalytic successors believe that he went too far in making the ego merely a passive plaything of unconscious forces, a conflict-riven entity which was concerned primarily with the defence of its precarious status.[113]

The concept of defence, and the various mechanisms involved in the defence of the ego, came in the end to play a central role in Freudian theory. He had used the term 'defence processes' in an early paper,[114] and then dropped it, only to revive it again as 'a general designation for all the techniques which the ego makes use of in conflicts which may lead to a neurosis'.[115] These included repression, but also other mechanisms such as displacement, rationalization, negation, projection, reaction formation and sublimation. Many of these mechanisms, which were described systematically by his daughter, Anna Freud, in *The Ego and Mechanisms of Defence* (1936), have been confirmed experimentally,[116] and they probably constitute the most substantial factual contribution of psychoanalysis to general psychology.

Freud, however, did not restrict psychoanalysis to the exploration of the individual psyche, and went on to apply its findings to the explanation of social phenomena, religion, art, anthropology and the general problems of civilized societies.[117] His approach was diametrically opposed to that of his predecessor, Karl Marx. Whereas Marx held that the psyche of man was determined by, and a reflection of, social forces, Freud held precisely the contrary, that the phenomena of society were projections of man's psyche. He regarded religion as the expression of his obsessional neuroses, art, of his fantasies, and the strange rites and practices of primitive man, his totems and taboos, as the outcome of the same forces that produced neuroses in his civilized successors. Freud did not deny that the social nature of man. He would not have agreed with Rieff that 'psychoanalysis is the doctrine of the private man defending himself against public encroachment'.[118] Rather he recognized that 'in the individual's mental life someone else is invariably involved . . . from the very first individual psychology is at the same time social psychology.'[119] What he doubted was the primacy of society and the so-called social instinct, and he considered it a delusion to hope with Marxists and revolutionaries that human nature could be altered by social reform. Revolutionary enthusiasm he regarded as a neurotic manifestation; only the gradual overlordship of reason could save civilization.[120] No doubt in its incursions into territory already occupied by students of religion, art, anthropology and sociology, psychoanalysis was sometimes rash in its pronouncements, and lay itself open to the charge of meddling in matters it did not fully understand. The psychohistory of cultural phenomena is even more methodologically suspect than the psychoanalysis of individuals.[121] No one, however, who lived through the events of the 1930s, and suffered from them as Freud himself did, can doubt that political and social life may be dominated by bizarre and horrible fantasies, by demonic forces released from man's unconscious depths. Freud was unquestionably right, up to a point, in seeking psychological explanations of social phenomena. The problem that confronted him was essentially that of finding an appropriate methodology, and in this he was far from successful.

There is no question that Freud himself believed in principle in scientific method, nor equally that he regarded psychoanalysis as adhering to the methods of science. 'Scientific work', he maintained, 'is the only road which can lead us to a knowledge of reality',[122] and 'the intellect and mind are objects for scientific research in exactly the same way as non-human things.'[123] Though the psychoanalyst could not experiment in the manner in which the physicist could,[124] the way theories were derived from observations was essentially similar in its underlying logic in both physics and psychology.[125] In spite, however, of these professions of faith what Freud actually did in his analytic sessions was not at all like what the natural scientists did. As Farrell has pointed out, the 'logic [of psychoanalysis] is very different from that of an advanced natural science.'[126] Psychoanalysis is based on interpretation, on the reading of meanings, generally hidden meanings derived from the verbal utterances of those being analysed. It involves as Freud noted in the first of his *Introductory Lectures*,

> an exchange of words between the patient and the physician. The patient talks, talks of his past experiences and present impressions, complains, and expresses his wishes and emotions. The physician listens, attempts to direct the patient's thought processes, reminds him, forces his attention in certain directions, gives him explanations, and observes the reactions of understanding or denial thus invoked.[127]

This dubiously objective procedure is clearly a '*geisteswissenschaftlich*', not a '*naturwissenschaftlich*' technique, and interestingly enough the parallel example that Freud provided in the lecture quoted was to the work of the historian in sifting and interpreting evidence. Yet Freud went on professing to adhere to the strict methods of the natural sciences. The first to point to this anomaly in Freudianism was the

Russian critic Voloshinov, in 1927.[128] It has now become a central tenet of Lacan and the French school of analysts. Freud's essential weakness was that, wrongly identifying himself with the natural scientists, he failed to explicate and justify the hermeneutic techniques that he was in fact employing. As Paul Ricoeur, the French philosopher, has observed, 'psychoanalysis has never quite succeeded in stating how its assertions are justified, how its interpretations are authenticated, how its theory is verified.'[129]

Freud nevertheless was a powerful thinker, and eager to discipline the wilder speculations of his often unbalanced followers. Discipline was not built into psychoanalysis itself; it had to be imposed, imposed by Freud's personal authority and his autocratic control of the movement. Psychoanalysis, therefore, soon came to present the anachronistic appearance of a 'school', isolated from related disciplines, and maintaining the purity of its creed in an authoritarian manner. No one who had not been analysed could properly appreciate its validity; every practitioner had to undergo a training analysis; psychoanalysis was 'a unit from which elements cannot be broken off at the caprice of who ever comes along'.[130] These are not the marks of a scientific enterprise; and for this reason psychoanalysis, in spite of the profound impact that it has made, has never been fully accepted by the psychological community.

V

The immensely rich contents of Freudian psychology together with its unsure methodological foundations inevitably led to chequered consequences. The lack of strict logical canons of proof opened the way for a diversity of interpretations, and a splintering of the psychodynamic movement into various factions, coloured by the philosophical outlooks, social viewpoints, and personalities of their leading figures, while the scientifically minded psychologist, fascinated but critical, watched ambivalently from the sidelines.

The fissiparous tendencies of the psychoanalytic movement surfaced very early. In 1902 Freud had begun to collect around himself a small band of followers. Alfred Adler (1870-1937) was a founder member of the group, and the first to defect, in 1911.[131] Gaining his early experience in the field of social and industrial medicine and an ardent socialist in his political outlook, Adler before long came to object on the one hand to what he regarded as the excessive Freudian emphasis on sex, and on the other to the neglect of the place of domination and subordination in human relationships. The primary drive in his view was the impulse to dominate, and the primary root of neurosis the inferiority complex. Though his system became termed 'individual psychology', its main stress was on the importance of 'social interest'. 'Social interest is the true and inevitable compensation for all the natural weakness of individual human beings,'[132] he wrote, and the principal task of therapy was to strengthen this interest. Though Adler worked largely on a common-sense level, and was far from an acute or profound thinker, some of his concepts have penetrated psychological thinking, and helped to promote the social approach to mental hygiene.[133]

Only two years after Adler's defection came the more serious defection of C.G. Jung (1875-1961). Jung became the favourite follower of Freud, had been elected first president of the International Psychoanalytic Association, and had been appointed editor of their *Jahrbuch*. Commencing his career at the Berghölzli psychiatric hospital near Zurich under E. Bleuler, Jung had carried out distinguished work on schizophrenia and on word associations[134] before he became interested in, and made contact with, Freud. The collaboration between them was for six years a close one,[135] but ideologically they were always, in fact, poles apart. The son of a Swiss pastor, Jung was from the beginning an anti-materialist and believer in the reality of the soul. Among his earliest published works were papers on the limits of the exact sciences, and on occult phenomena.[136] Religion was his dominating concern, and he believed that 'God speaks chiefly through dreams and visions'.[137] So, whereas for Freud the unconscious was 'a dump for moral refuse',[138] for Jung it was the source of spiritual illumination. 'The irrational cannot and must not be extirpated. The gods cannot and must not die.'[139] In accordance with these views Jung found that, at any rate among patients in the second half of life, psychological problems were always in essence religious problems. In view of these ideological differences it was perhaps surprising that the association between Freud and Jung lasted as long as it did. In spite of the strongly mystical strain in his outlook, and his flirtations with alchemy, oriental cults and occultism, Jung nevertheless made several valuable contributions to psychology: his technique of word association, the concept of 'complexes', and his distinction between extraversion and introversion. And although his doctrine of 'archetypes' (the inherited ancestral symbolic constructions surviving from primitive times) may be suspect, the parallels he drew between dream symbolism and the mystical symbols of ancient cults raise intriguing problems.

As psychoanalysis spread round the developed countries of the globe its fissiparous tendencies continued, and it took on different colourings in different lands. Although the official Freudians adhering to the International Psychoanalytic Association, founded in 1910, continued to grow in numbers, and indeed increased more than tenfold in the half century between 1925 and 1975, rival psychotherapies increased even faster. This was particularly the case in America, where innumerable conflicts have split the psychoanalytic movement,[140] fostered by the individualistic and anti-authoritarian streak in the American make-up. Eccentric analysts like O. Rank, T. Reik and W. Reich found a home there; socially orientated therapists like Karen Horney, E. Fromm and H.S. Sullivan acquired a sympathetic following; and many Americans preferred the watered-down therapeutic systems of 'counselling psychology' and 'client-centred therapy' to the bleak creed of pure psychoanalysis. In Great Britain, the country in which

Freud spent the last year of his life, and where his daughter, Anna, continued to work, similar splits occurred between the orthodox Freudians, the followers of Melanie Klein, who pushed back the analytic process to the early months of the infant's life, the 'object relations' school of W.R.D. Fairbairn and H. Guntrip, who objected to Freud's doctrine of instincts, and the Bowlby school with its emphasis on the relations of mother and child and the effects of maternal deprivation. In Great Britain too, there emerged a considerable number of eclectic psychotherapists, who accepted some of, but not all, the Freudian findings. Nor in France was the psychoanalytic movement immune from dissension. J. Lacan, their most eminent analyst, was expelled from the International Psychoanalytic Association in 1963 both for his heterodox methods of therapy and his heterodox views. Throughout Europe, and then in America too, philosophical influences derived from phenomenology and existentialism began to make themselves felt, led by men such as K. Jaspers in Germany, L. Binswanger and M. Boss in Switzerland, R.D. Laing in Great Britain, and Rollo May in America. Reuben Fine, the historian of psychoanalysis, was not overstating the situation when he wrote of its 'incurable inner conflicts, so similar in many ways to the inner conflicts that psychoanalysts find in their patients'.[141]

These 'innumerable conflicts' among the post-Freudian psychodynamic schools were a direct and inevitable consequence of their leaky methodological framework, which exposed them to all the gusts of ideological fashion. In the midst of this confusion it has even been suggested by Szasz that the very concept of mental illness is a myth, and that the medical model used in treating disturbances of human behaviour is a wholly inappropriate one. 'Psychiatrists are not concerned with mental illness and their treatments. In actual practice they deal with personal, social and ethical problems of living.'[142] No doubt Szasz has pointed to a major problem; but the remedy he suggests is worse than the disease, for in effect he is denying the biological foundations of human nature and reasserting the fatal dichotomy of body and mind. If one thing has become clear in the post-Freudian era it is surely that body and mind cannot be divorced, that mental processes are rooted in organic functions, and organic functions in their turn are influenced by processes taking place in the mind. The *rapprochement* between body and mind that Freud brought about cannot be reversed. In spite of the methodological weaknesses of Freudianism, in more ways than one it inaugurated a new era in psychology.

For largely as a result of Freud's work psychology could no longer be regarded as confined to the introspective study of consciousness, as it had been regarded by most academic psychologists up to the end of the nineteenth century; it became inevitably the study of the total personality, rooted in biology, developing over time, and shaped by interpersonal and social relations. The clinic became as essential a venue for psychological research as the laboratory. The barrier between psychology and medicine had been broken down, and this had wider long-term consequences than simply the incorporation of psychoanalytic concepts. Forced to study real-life problems, psychology was on the way to becoming not merely an academic study but a profession. The interaction between psychology and medicine became two-way and manifold. Many lines of enquiry became of equal significance to both disciplines; for example, investigation into the electrical activity of the brain, the effect of drugs, brain chemistry, the sequelae of stress, and the influence of emotion on bodily functioning. Psychology, too, began to contribute significantly to medical practice and research through its methodological sophistication, its techniques of assessment and evaluation, and its incursions into the field of behavioural medicine. A fruitful partnership thus sprung up between the psychiatrist and the clinical psychologist.

The impact of medicine on general psychology in the first third of the twentieth century can be gauged by contrasting texts published at the turn of the century with those published a generation later. In Great Britain, in the early editions of G.F. Stout's *Manual of Psychology*, the most widely used text (1st edition 1898, 3rd edition 1913, 5th edition 1938), there is hardly a trace of medical influence, apart from a brief reference to blind deaf-mutes like Laura Bridgman and Helen Keller, and a very short section on the pathology of self-consciousness. By contrast R.H. Thouless's *Social Psychology* (1st edition 1925, 2nd edition entitled *General and Social Psychology* 1937) includes extensive references to abnormal psychology and psycho-analysis, and its whole approach has been coloured as much by psychodynamic concepts as by the older academic psychology. A similar development is apparent in American texts, as can be seen by comparing standard works like Titchener's *Outline of Psychology*, originally published in 1896 but reprinted many times during the first decade of this century, or Angell's *Psychology* (1904), with Woodworth's *Psychology: A Study of Mental Life*, which even in the first edition (1921) took cognisance of psychoanalysis and admitted that 'though his theories are open to criticism Freud has made important contributions to the study of personality'.[143] As Woodworth had observed some years previously in his *Dynamic Psychology* (1918), 'abnormal mental conditions offer a great mass of facts for observation, and the need of taking account of these facts in any adequate treatment of mental life, has been one of the forces driving psychology to the scientific attitude.'[144]

The first decade of the twentieth century saw many changes in psychology, but among the most important was the influx of entirely new sources of information. Of these the medical were perhaps the most significant, but as the advice of Jung to the students of the human mind indicated, they were not the only sources:

> The man, therefore, who would learn the human mind will gain
> almost nothing from experimental psychology. Far better for him to
> put away his academic gown, to say good-bye to the study, and to
> wander with human heart through the world. There, in the horrors

of the prison, the asylum and the hospital, in the drinking shops, brothels and gambling hells, in the salons of the elegant, in the exchanges, socialist meetings, churches, religious revivals and sectarian ecstasies, through love and hate, through experience of passion in every form in his own body he would reap richer stores of knowledge than text-books a foot thick could give him. . . . For between what science calls psychology and what practical needs of daily life demand from 'psychology' there is a great gulf fixed.[145]

This is, of course, a romantic view of the situation, though Jung's dismissive attitude towards experimental psychology was partly justified by the type of experimentation then being carried out in German laboratories. Today his strictures would be much less applicable. The unreal concentration of psychology on the field of consciousness has been broken down by more influences than one. Among these influences the *rapprochement* between psychology and medicine was the most far-reaching, but next in importance were developments in social psychology and in related social sciences, to the examination of which we must now turn.

Chapter 11
The social dimension

I

It is broadly true that, with few exceptions, prior to the end of the nineteenth century the psychologies of the philosophers and the early scientific psychologists were psychologies of the individual mind and that they ignored the social dimension of human nature, or regarded it as merely derivative. Aristotle, of course, had recognized the political or, as we should rather say, the social make-up of man. He asserted,

> Man is by nature a political animal. The state is by nature clearly prior to the family and the individual, since the whole is of necessity prior to the part. . . . The proof that the state is a creation of nature and prior to the individual is that the individual, when isolated, is not self-sufficing; and, therefore, he is like a part in relation to the whole.[1]

But when he wrote his *De Anima* Aristotle made no mention of the community, and the essentially individualistic treatment of the soul which he inaugurated persisted for more than two thousand years. In the course of time this individualistic tendency was strengthened by a succession of social and ideological changes. The collapse of the Greek city-states, by depriving the majority of citizens of any say in the running of their communities, promoted philosophic doctrines of withdrawal and resignation. Each man became sufficient unto himself, and had to find his own consolation either in private happiness, cynicism, or stoic acceptance. Christianity, in spite of its emphasis on the brotherhood of man, enhanced the sense of individuality, because, as the theologian Reinhold Niebuhr has observed,

> according to the Christian faith, the human spirit in its freedom is finally bound only by the will of God, and the secret of its heart is only fully known and judged by the divine wisdom. This means that human life has an ultimate religious warrant far transcending the custom of tribes, natural rules of conduct, and all general and abstract norms of behaviour.[2]

On the breakdown of the medieval order the emphasis on the individual became even stronger as the bourgeois gradually threw back the authority of the Church and state, and asserted their rights to freedom of conscience, liberty of action, and the inalienable ownership of private property.

It was against this background that the fathers of modern psychology formulated their theories. The natural condition of man, according to Locke, was 'a state of perfect freedom to order their actions, and dispose of their persons and possessions as they think fit, without asking leave or depending on the will of any other man'.[3] Nearly two centuries later J.S. Mill was expressing much the same viewpoint when he wrote, 'the only part of the conduct of anyone for which he is answerable to society is that which concerns others. In the part which merely concerns himself his independence is, of right, absolute. Over himself, over his own body and mind, the individual is sovereign.'[4] So when, in his *System of Logic* Mill turned to consider what he termed 'The Logic of the Moral Sciences' it was not surprising that he propounded the view that 'human beings in society have no properties but those which are derived from, and may be resolved into the laws of the nature of individual man'.[5] Such a viewpoint seemed to accord not only with the general principles of natural science, which had achieved its successes by atomistic reductionism, but also with the only developed social science of the day – economics – which was based on the doctrine of individual self-interest and *laissez-faire*.

True the stark view of Hobbes that naturally 'every man is enemy to every man'[6] was modified by his eighteenth century successors, who recognized the role of social instincts. Shaftesbury spoke of 'the social passion', Butler of 'the natural principle of benevolence', Hume and Adam Smith of the instinct of sympathy.[7] According to Hume, 'we must renounce the theory which accounts for every moral sentiment by the principle of self-love. We must adopt a more public affection, and allow that the interests of society are not, even on their own account, entirely indifferent to us.'[8] Darwinian theories of instinct, and observations on the gregarious propensities of at any rate some animal species, appeared to lend support to the view that the basis of man's social life was an innate social instinct, or cluster of instincts. This was the view for example of McDougall, whose *Introduction to Social Psychology* (1908) was, together with Ross's *Social Psychology*, the first to bear this designation. In spite of its title McDougall's psychology was still basically individualistic, and according to him man is 'born as a creature in which the non-moral and purely egoistic tendencies are so much stronger than any altruistic tendencies'.[9]

These views of human nature have been gradually modified, at first slowly and almost imperceptibly during the nineteenth century, and then rapidly in the twentieth, by three developments: the rise of a socialist philosophy of man, the fieldwork of social anthropologists, and the growth of sociology. Together these developments have forced psychologists into a recognition of the social dimension of human nature, forced them to become, at least to some extent, social psychologists.

II

The term 'socialist' is a modern one, coined in the nineteenth century, first apparently by members of the London Cooperative Society around 1827.[10] It was adopted by Robert Owen, the industrial reformer, and by various French social reformers, and by the end of the century had become the label for a growing body of political and economic thought. This would have been of no direct relevance to the shaping of psychology had socialistic theories not also involved a new philosophy of man, a new conception of the relation of man to society. For this new philosophy Karl Marx was primarily responsible.

Karl Marx (1818-1883), of course, was not a psychologist, nor was he greatly interested in psychological problems as such. The influence of his speculations on the evolution of modern psychology has been questioned.[11] For a variety of reasons his key psychological ideas were slow in making an impact, and for a long time only did so indirectly. Indeed the stature of Marx as a thinker, rather than as a revolutionary agitator, has only been fully recognized in the west since about 1960. Born in the city of Trier, the third child of a Jewish lawyer, Karl Marx was intellectually gifted, and received a first-rate education in philosophy and law at the universities of Bonn and Berlin, eventually gaining his doctorate with a thesis on 'The differences between the Democritean and Epicurean philosophy of nature'. Shortly after graduating he plunged into political journalism and revolutionary activity, and this eventually led to his exile, first to France, and then to England, where he spent the larger part of his life from 1849 till his death in 1883. Once he had found his mission Marx devoted himself to it with total dedication and fanatical energy. In spite of banishment in a foreign land, social isolation, poverty, squalor and ill-health, his achievement, though unfinished and in many ways flawed, was immense, and his ability to see through appearances made up for a certain uncompromising narrowness of vision. His close friend Frederick Engels, on whose support and assistance he had relied for the last forty years of his life, pronounced him, in his funeral oration, as having been in his day 'the greatest living thinker'.

> Just as Darwin discovered the law of development of organic nature, so Marx discovered the law of development of human history: the simple fact, hitherto concealed by an overgrowth of ideology, that mankind must first of all eat, drink, have shelter and clothing, before it can pursue politics, science, art, religion, etc.[12]

Nearly a hundred years later Isaiah Berlin could still maintain that Marxism 'remains the most powerful among the intellectual forces which are to-day permanently transforming the ways in which men act and think'.[13]

The philosophy of Marx, however original in its final synthesis, was derived from a number of sources. Apart from the British economists, whose influence was confined to his economic doctrines, the most important of these sources were Hegelianism, the ideas of the early socialists, and the materialistic teachings of the German philosopher Feuerbach. Marx moved to the University of Berlin in October 1836, nearly five years after the death of Hegel at the end of 1831. Hegelianism was still a predominant force in the intellectual life of the university, and Marx, though before long decisively rejecting Hegel's idealism, was permanently influenced by a number of his key ideas, in particular Hegel's concept of historical development, his recognition of the social aspects of the human mind, and his grasp of the dialectics of change, the necessary conflict involved in all development, the interdependence of creation and destruction. Hegel's *Philosophie des Geistes* (Philosophy of Mind, 1830) was too abstract a work in general to have much direct influence on psychology at a time when it was turning towards empirical studies, but as Brett observed, 'The "objective mind" of Hegel's system is the true architect of all theories which pass beyond the individualism of earlier schools and see in mind a reality which is not separated from other minds, as one body is separated from another.'[14] What has been termed Hegel's 'situated subjectivity'[15] was certainly a main source of Marx's own theories. The essential difference between Marx and Hegel, though this difference has perhaps been exaggerated,[16] was that for Hegel the world was an expression of spirit (*Geist*) and the dialectic process of change essentially a logical one, whereas for Marx consciousness was merely a 'reflection' of the world, and the motive power of change was essentially material, being tied to the mundane realities of economics and the class structure of society. The common ground between them was a belief that the processes of historical change and development could be understood. This is what the early socialists, St Simon, Fourier and Proudhon in France and Robert Owen in Britain, with their somewhat Utopian ideas, had lacked – a sense of the logic of history. So though Marx agreed with many of their criticisms of existing society, he was often scornful of their Utopianism and the lack of logical rigour in their thinking. Feuerbach, too, the German materialist philosopher, whose attacks on religious ideology and whose grasp of the social nature of man strongly appealed to Marx, was nevertheless criticized for his failure to understand the interactions between man and nature, and man's creative work in this interaction. In his pithy 'Theses on Feuerbach', which were written in 1845, but not published until 1888, Marx made his momentous declaration, 'Philosophers have only *interpreted* the world in various ways; the point is to *change* it.'[17]

From these various ingredients Marx derived a powerful and original synthesis. The nature of man at any given place or time was rooted in history, and shaped by the social circumstances, in particular the hard facts of economic reality, which prevailed at the time. Because history changed, and because circumstances changed, there was no unchanging human nature. 'The phantoms formed in the human brain are necessarily sublimates of their material life process.'[18] Thus 'the essence of man is no abstraction inherent in each separate individual.

In its reality it is the ensemble of social relations.'[19] The ultimately determining factors in any society were the methods of production upon which its material life was based, and from which its structure and institutions, particularly the class structure and division of labour, were derived. Human society was, of course, man-made; but it was made blindly, under the influence of forces men did not understand, and hence could not control. This blind development involved the warping and stunting of human nature, its 'alienation',[20] in an environment which denied most members, at any rate in capitalist societies, the opportunity to develop what Marx called their 'species characteristics', that is their essentially human characteristics as free, creative beings. In order to bring an end to the ills and exploitation of existing societies two things were necessary: firstly, an understanding of the laws of historical development – and Marx thought that he had achieved this – and secondly, 'the forceable overthrow of all existing social conditions',[21] an outcome which he believed to be inevitable.

Although Marx never developed a psychology of his own, embedded in his doctrine of historical materialism there were at least two implications of profound psychological importance: firstly, that human nature could not be understood simply by looking inwards or by any kind of purely psychological analysis, and secondly, that human nature was not unchanging, but historically and socially conditioned. Though neither of these doctrines was wholly original, Marx gave them a novel and distinctive slant.

In a sense the theory that human nature could not be understood simply by looking inwards goes back to Plato, and the Platonic doctrine of 'participation' (μετάληψις) discussed in the *Parmenides*,[22] where Socrates argues that 'ideas' cannot be just 'in the mind'. So Plato postulated what Popper has since termed 'a third world of intelligibles or ideas in the objective sense'.[23] For Plato this was a static world of 'eternal objects'. Hegel transformed this static Platonic world by introducing the idea of process and development. 'Objective mind' became part of the expression of the eternal, but self-developing universal spirit.[24] Marx's crucial achievement was to give Hegel's 'objective mind' a material, social embodiment, which was not merely derivative, but essential. 'In direct contrast to German philosophy which descends from heaven to earth, here we ascend from earth to heaven.'[25] The ideas with which human minds were stocked were a 'reflection' of the social realities in which they were immersed. Since minds were social products, there was, therefore, necessarily a social dimension to psychology.

Societies, however, were historical phenomena, immersed in time and change. So human nature inevitably changed as the social milieu changed. Marx, of course, was not the first to think in terms of historical flux. Leibniz, Vico, Herder and Hegel had all propounded dynamic philosophies of change, but Marx was the first to propose a material dynamics of social transformation, and to link mutations of human psychology to mutations in technology and economic organization. In order to exist men had to work. Indeed the majority of mankind spent the bulk of their waking life working. How they worked, how their labour was organized, was, therefore, necessarily the most important determining factor in their lives, and had a decisive influence on their psychological make-up. The psychological stunting, or 'alienation', which so many human beings experienced, was a direct result of the inhuman division of labour that prevailed in existing societies. For Marx this psychological malaise was a direct function of social conditions, and could only be remedied by a revolutionary change in society. This, he believed, would necessarily come about, as history was governed by inescapable laws.

Though never expounded systematically in a developed form, these theories of Marx, in spite of their vagueness and one-sidedness, gave a new dimension to psychology, bringing it face to face with concrete social realities. There are, of course, serious objections to Marxism in its purest, unadulterated form. It concentrates too much on the relatively short historic period of human development. Mankind has had a long prehistory, and an even longer animal past, and Marx, who constantly and rightly stressed the differences between men and the rest of the animal kingdom, largely ignored the more primitive elements in human nature, and naively believed that when society had changed and existing social institutions had 'withered away', together with the bourgeois family and private property, men would blossom creatively in perfect harmony and liberty.[26] Marx undoubtedly underestimated the irrational components of human nature. Freud's observations in this regard are worthy of note:

> The strength of Marxism lies . . . in its sagacious indication of the decisive influence which the economic circumstances of men have upon their intellectual, ethical and artistic attitudes. A number of connections and implications were thus uncovered which had previously been almost totally overlooked. But it cannot be assumed that economic motives are the only ones that determine the behaviour of human beings in society. . . . It is altogether incomprehensible, how psychological facts can be overlooked when what is in question are the reactions of living human beings.

So Freud concludes, 'we shall still have to struggle for an incalculable time with the difficulties which the untameable character of human nature presents to every kind of social community.'[27]

Marx, then, was one-sided; he was also vague, in that he never explained clearly what he meant when he wrote, 'the ideal is nothing other than the material world reflected in the human mind.'[28] There were, in fact, contradictions between the idea of consciousness as simply a reflection and the idea of man as a free, creative agent, capable of decisions, and capable of understanding the laws of his own development. And Marx held both views. The doctrine of social determinism is, as Popper pointed out,[29] logically self-defeating. Nevertheless even if Marx did not provide a full and satisfactory solution to the problems of the relation between mind and society, or explain in detail how society shapes the individual, and how in his turn the individual can act freely and creatively in a social milieu, he certainly raised new questions, and by doing so significantly influenced the future development of psychology.

There were a number of reasons why the impact of Marx on western psychology was slow, and at first mainly indirect. Marx was not a psychologist, and his writings were not regarded as having psychological relevance; his advocacy of violence alienated sober opinion, and branded him as an agitator; and, finally, many of his more significant psychological observations were in works either not published, or not readily available, till many years after his death. The full texts of *The German Ideology* (1845) and his *Economico-philosophical Manuscripts* (1844) were first published in 1932, and the English translation of the latter was not available until 1963. The *Grundrisse der Kritik der politischen Ökonomie* (1859) was first published in Moscow in 1939, and an English translation was not available until 1964. It was in these early writings that Marx's most significant philosophical doctrines were adumbrated. So it was not surprising that Marxism was slow in making an impact on psychology.[30] It did so in the west mainly indirectly through its influence on sociology, and through the general change in the climate of opinion which took place in the late nineteenth and early twentieth centuries, a change which the jurist A.V. Dicey documented with regard to England in his *Law and Opinion in England* (1905). In America the changing climate was much slower in manifesting itself.

It was, of course, in Russia, which became a professedly Marxist society in October 1917, that Marx not unnaturally made his greatest impact. As a result of the earlier work of Sechenov, Pavlov and Bekhterev, the way had already been prepared for a materialist approach to psychology. By the early years of the century Russian revolutionaries had already absorbed a good deal of Marx's teaching. Lenin's philosophical work, *Materialism and Empirio-Criticism* (1909) was based on the Marxian doctrine of 'reflection'.[31] After the revolution, in the early 1920s, Soviet psychology became increasingly Marxist in outlook, and in 1936 Marxism was officially proclaimed as 'the ultimate criterion of the truth or falsehood of psychological investigations'.[32] In listing the essential characteristics of Soviet psychology B.G. Ananiev of Leningrad in 1948 mentioned six basic premises: psychological monism, the theory of reflection, the materialist determination of consciousness and activity, the principle of contradiction in development, the unity of consciousness and activity, and the class and historical character of psychic processes.[33] Most of these are of Marxist origin. Not all Soviet psychology has in fact slavishly followed this model, but the work of perhaps the two most eminent Soviet psychologists, L.S. Vygotsky (1896-1934) and A.R. Luria (1902-1977) was significantly influenced by, and significantly added to, Marxian ideas.

The work of Vygotsky has only fairly recently become known in the west. He was a brilliant young innovator who unfortunately died very young. His seminal *Thought and Language* was not translated into English until 1962, and a selection of his early papers did not become available in translation until 1978.[34] According to his American editor, M. Cole, Vygotsky was 'the first modern psychologist to suggest the mechanism by which culture becomes part of each person's nature'.[35] In particular he studied the processes involved in the internalization of social speech, and showed how this affected not only higher psychological functions, but every form of psychological activity, including perception, attention and memory. Thus 'the internalization of socially rooted and historically developed activities is the distinguishing feature of human psychology'.[36] Human mental functioning, therefore, could only be understood as a social process to be studied not so much experimentally, though Vygotsky did experiment, as developmentally.

Vygotsky's pupil, the equally brilliant Luria, carried on and developed his work. Particularly important in this connection was Luria's early work on cognitive development, carried out in Uzbekistan around 1930, when the primitive preliterate culture of the area was being rapidly restructured.[37] Agriculture was being collectivized, the urban population being educated, and women were being emancipated. Luria made a comparison between the psychological functioning of villagers in remote areas still untouched by change and that of the newly educated and urbanized. He tested and documented the way their minds worked, showing how perceptual processes, thinking, reasoning and self-awareness were all qualitatively changed. It was a significant confirmation of the validity of at least one of the central hypotheses of Marxism. The value of this Russian work has recently become recognized in the west, and has added its weight to the conclusions based on the fieldwork of social anthropologists, at whose contribution we must now briefly glance.

III

The term 'social anthropology' was first proposed by Sir James Frazer, the British classicist and anthropologist, in the inaugural lecture he delivered in Liverpool in May 1908.[38] But the subject was in fact born in the mid-nineteenth century after a gestation period of several centuries.[39] The great navigational voyages from the fifteenth century onwards brought European man into contact with an ever-growing variety of human races and cultures, far more alien and far more 'savage' than anything previously known. Sailors and traders, missionaries and colonists, brought back many varying tales, some giving highly coloured accounts of 'the beastly devices of the heathen', and some of the innocence and happiness of natural men. Literary and philosophical circles in Europe were fascinated by these tales.[40] Towards the end of the eighteenth century several French and Scottish savants had begun to collate and systematize this data.[41] In 1799 a Société des Observations de l'Homme was established in Paris, and in 1839 London followed with an Ethnological Society.[42]

The centre of interest in these early ventures tended to be on physical characteristics, racial differences, linguistics and technology. The middle of the century saw new developments: the rise of 'folk psychology' (*Völkerpsychologie*) in Germany, and the theory of evolution in England. 'Folk psychology' had Herbartian and Hegelian roots, and emphasized the concept of 'the racial mind' which could be investigated through the study of mythology, language, art, customs and economics. In 1860 Lazarus and Steinthal founded a *Zeitschrift für Völkerpsychologie und Sprachwissenschaft*. It formed a background to Wundt's *Völkerpsychologie* (10 volumes, 1900-20), and had some influence on the work of Franz Boas, who, though born in Germany, was to become a leading figure in the rise of American anthropology. More important still, however, was the theory of evolution, with its emphasis both on development and on variation, since it seemed to imply that anthropology might be able to throw light on human origins, and that 'savages', far from being merely degenerate specimens of humanity, were simply survivals of earlier, more primitive, stages of human society. The first systematic anthropologists, Herbert Spencer, E.B. Tylor and James Frazer in England and J.H. Morgan in America, adopted an evolutionary approach to the study of human cultures. As Tylor (1832-1917), the real founder of British anthropology, put it, 'the various grades [of civilization] may be regarded as stages of development of evolution, each the outcome of previous history, and about to do its proper part in shaping the history of the future,'[43] and among the values of anthropological study was the tracing of 'survivals' of earlier practices and beliefs in the fabric of more advanced societies. These early anthropologists were essentially academics, relying largely on the accounts of travellers and missionaries for their data. Frazer, for example whose massive *Golden Bough* (12 volumes, 1890-1915)[44] constituted an encyclopedia of primitive beliefs and customs, had never travelled out of Europe, and had no first-hand acquaintance with most of the cultures he was dealing with. A new phase in the development of anthropology commenced with the inauguration of systematic field studies at the close of the nineteenth century. Among the earliest and most important of these were the studies of *The Native Tribes of Central Australia* by Spencer and Gillen,[45] and the study of American Indians, particularly the Kwakiutl of the north-west coast, by Boas.[46] By the 1920s, as a result of the work of Malinowski and Radcliffe-Brown based in Britain,[47] and that of Ruth Benedict, Margaret Mead and others in America,[48] fieldwork had not only become an essential basis for anthropology but, through the richness and complexity of the cultural phenomena it was bringing to light, was undermining simplistic theories of evolutionary development. Particularly in Great Britain anthropology became for a time markedly anti-historical and anti-psychological, and this led to a certain divergence between British and American anthropologists. In the absence of a clear-cut evolutionary framework anthropologists tended to split into various schools, some stressing a functional approach and looking for the utility value of cultural practices and beliefs, others stressing social structures, particularly kinship structures, and their influence in determining behaviour.[49] The promising collaboration between psychologists and anthropologists which seemed to be emerging early in the twentieth century with the work of Rivers and his colleagues in Great Britain,[50] and the culture-pattern theories in America, experienced a temporary decline. The disciplines drifted apart, partly as a result of the aloofness and introversion of the anthropologists, and partly because of the doubts among psychologists about the methodological soundness of at least some anthropological work. Recently, however, there has again emerged a recognition of 'the complementarity of psychology and anthropology',[51] and of the contribution that anthropological material can make to psychology, particularly in the social field.

Social anthropology, broadly speaking, has had two main aims. Firstly, it has aimed at documenting the practices and beliefs, the codes of behaviour and ways of thinking, of those human groups least touched and contaminated by the spread of western civilization. These groups, mostly small and isolated, in Australasia, South America and parts of Africa, South-east Asia and Oceania, were generally illiterate and technologically primitive. They are, of course, a rapidly disappearing species, and probably the most important anthropological work in this area has already been done, so that anthropologists are now turning to the study of more complex societies and to problems of cultural contact and change. The relevance of the anthropological data so collected to the psychologists was grasped by Herbert Spencer in the very early days of anthropology, only a couple of years after the appearance of Tylor's *Primitive Culture* (1871). 'For every society,' wrote Spencer, 'and for each stage in its evolution, there is an appropriate mode of feeling and thinking . . . the average opinion in any age and country is a function of the social structure of that age and country.'[52] Spencer's conclusion was slow in impressing itself on psychologists, and not everyone today would agree with his precise wording, but his emphasis on the social component of psychology was unquestionably perceptive.

The second aim of social anthropology has been to uncover some kind of patterning and meaning underlying the confusing variety of primitive practice and belief. With the rejection of simple evolutionary models, this search has tended to concentrate on structural universals. In particular this has been the aim of the French school of anthropologists led by Claude Lévi-Strauss.[53] If correct, the structural model is of considerable interest to psychologists because it professes to be uncovering basic properties of the human mind of which cultural institutions are the concrete external projections or manifestations. As Lévi-Strauss himself put it, anthropological study provides a way of distinguishing 'what is primordial, and what is artificial in man's present nature'.[54] It enables the psychologist, in other words, to escape from the parochialism which confuses the peculiarities of western man with the universal properties of human nature.

By the 1920s the fieldwork data of the social anthropologists began to interact with the emerging discipline of personalistics, or the psychology of personality, to produce the influential culture-pattern theory. From the earliest days the concept of 'culture' had been central to anthropology. *Primitive Culture* was the title of Tylor's pioneering work, and in it he defined culture as 'that complex whole which includes knowledge, belief, art, morals, law, custom and other capabilities and habits acquired by man as a member of society'.[55] Unfortunately the characteristic of 'wholeness' was ignored by encyclopedists like Frazer, and it was left to the culture-pattern theorists to re-emphasize it. As Ruth Benedict put it, 'a culture, like an individual, is a more or less consistent pattern of thought and action',[56] and the pattern of a culture greatly affected the personality structure of the individual members. Ruth Benedict illustrated her thesis from three diverse cultures: the Zuni Indians of New Mexico (formal and polite), the Dobu of New Guinea (lawless, cruel and treacherous), and the Kwakiutl of the Pacific coast of North America (megalomanic and paranoid). Her work, together with that of anthropologists like Malinowski and Mead, had a powerful influence on the development of social psychology.[57] Mead, on the basis of her work in Samoa, New Guinea and Bali, came to the conclusion that 'human nature is almost unbelieveably malleable, responding accurately and contrastingly to contrasting cultural traditions'.[58] Even 'male and female personality are socially produced',[59] and 'many of the phenomena of human nature in our society, which we treat as biologically determined, are really socially determined.'[60] Thus she suggested on the basis of her Samoan studies that the stresses associated with adolescence among western youth were socially conditioned.[61] This led her to enquire into the nature of the socialization process, the ways in which the norms and attitudes of a culture were transmitted, and in particular the predominant role of child-rearing practices.

However, it was not only personality as a structured whole that showed the influence of cultural factors; specific psychological functions were likewise affected. This has been shown to apply to perception,[62] memory,[63] and learning and thinking,[64] and there is now a growing body of evidence from cross-cultural research, covering most areas of psychology.[65] The 'cultural walls within which an individual can operate', to use Margaret Mead's phrase,[66] exert a powerful influence on all his psychological functions, and tenaciously resist change.

Beneath these cultural variations, however, there are uniformities. These were noted even by the earliest anthropologists. Tylor in his very first work observed that 'gesture language is essentially one and the same in all times and in all countries'.[67] He went on to assert that the beliefs of primitive peoples showed universal animistic features.[68] Frazer, too, commented on 'the essential similarity with which under many superficial differences the human mind has elaborated its first crude philosophy of life'.[69] It has been noted, too, that the millions of figures depicted in cave art all over the world show remarkable similarities. The fundamental 'psychic unity of mankind' had been postulated by the German anthropologist P.W.H. Bastian in 1860, even before Tylor.[70] The theme has been taken up in our own time by the Frenchman Lévi-Strauss, who carried out adventurous journeys in the late 1930s in the remoter regions of Brazil.[71] Lévi-Strauss protested against indiscriminate data collecting, which seemed to him to be the vice of the field anthropologist. 'We have been behaving like amateur botanists, haphazardly picking up heterogeneous specimens,'[72] and 'feverishly piling up information without any clear idea of what it meant, or above all of the hypotheses which it should have helped to test.'[73] The need, according to Lévi-Strauss, was to look for the underlying structural universals, of which kinship relations, myths, religious ideas, and social and linguistic practices were exemplifications. He regarded these structures as the work of the unconscious mind which imposed forms upon contents. In spite of an impressive amount of evidence in support of his thesis – he has analysed, for example, the structure of some eight hundred myths[74] – Lévi-Strauss has not convinced the majority of his anthropological colleagues, especially those of the Anglo-Saxon world. Even his English admirer, Edmund Leach, has accused him of ignoring negative instances which do not fit in with his schemes.[75] It is only fair, however, to recognize the enormous difficulty of the enterprise that Lévi-Strauss undertook, and the boldness and power of his structuralist vision. In some ways his work is a throwback to earlier patterns of anthropologizing, in its recognition of the need to explain in general terms, in the valuation it places on comparative studies, and in its recognition of the importance of history. For the structures Lévi-Strauss proposed were both 'synchronic' and 'diachronic', the terms being borrowed from linguistics.[76] 'Synchronic' structures were currently extant, 'diachronic' involved the temporal dimension and required recourse to history for their discrimination. This might seem to have made room in Lévi-Strauss's system for evolutionary development, but he rejects simple schemes of evolutionary progress on the ground that they involve arbitrary value judgments: 'With an unlimited choice of criteria an unlimited number of evolutionary systems could be constructed. . . . The Eskimo, while excellent technicians, are poor sociologists; the reverse is true of the natives of Australia.'[77] 'The various choices cannot be compared with one another; they are all equally valid.'[78] Again, 'a primitive people is not a backward or retarded people; indeed it may possess, in one realm or another, a genius for invention, or action, that leaves the achievement of civilized people far behind.'[79]

In thus rejecting evolutionary models Lévi-Strauss would seem to be in tune with the majority opinion of contemporary anthropologists. As far back as 1911 Boas ventured to maintain that 'there is no fundamental difference in the ways of thinking of primitive and civilized man'.[80] Indeed 'the mental attitude of individuals who develop the beliefs of a tribe is exactly like that of the civilized philosopher'![81] In his studies of witchcraft among the Azande of the Sudan the British anthropologist Evans-Pritchard emphasized the reasonableness and intellectual consistence of their ideas.[82] The earlier view of Frazer, who regarded primitive beliefs as a 'melancholy record of human error and folly',[83] has been discarded, and the former popularity of Lévy-Bruhl's theories of the prelogical nature of primitive mentality[84] has sharply waned. If there are differences in the way members of primitive communities think, these differences are regarded as the results of situational and environmental factors, which evoke different cognitive strategies. As Michael Cole put it, on the basis of his studies on 'The Cultural Context of Learning and Thinking',[85]

> it is not the case that the non-educated African is incapable of concept-based thinking nor that he never combines sub-instances to obtain a general solution to a problem. Instead we had to conclude that the situation in which he applies general concept based modes of solution are different, and perhaps more restricted than the situations in which his educated mate will apply such conditions.[86]

These views, however, are not entirely convincing. The simple evolutionary model may have been too crude; it may have ignored the rich diversity of cultural forms, overestimated the virtues of civilization and undervalued the achievements of primitive man. Nevertheless the idea of developmental stages is not wholly mistaken. It may involve value judgments; but value judgments are unavoidable when dealing with the higher reaches of human nature. The subtlety and power of an Einstein's thinking – which depended, of course, on a strong supporting cultural tradition maturing over many generations – cannot seriously be compared with the fantasies of an Azande witch-doctor. The developmental model elaborated by Heinz Werner more than a generation ago,[87] and recently revived by Hallpike along Piagetian lines,[88] has much evidence to support it. Even Cole had to admit that there were differences, large differences, in attainments and learning capacity between his West African Kpelle tribesfolk and members of more developed cultures.[89] These differences need not be regarded necessarily as innate and unalterable; indeed as Luria showed in Uzbekistan, when social conditions change, mentality may change correspondingly. Confusions and controversies of this sort have arisen from the lack of an adequate theory of the relation between the individual mind and society, and the importance of social anthropology is that it provides a great deal of material contributory towards such a theory, supplementing the more general contribution of sociology itself.

IV

Sociology as a systematic, theoretical discipline was an even later arrival on the intellectual scene than psychology, and it has been torn by even deeper dissensions. Like psychology it had its predecessors – in moral and political philosophy, in jurisprudence and in economics.

But the study of human society was not designated 'sociology' till 1830, when the French philosopher Auguste Comte (1798-1857) coined the term. His massive six-volume *Cours de philosophie positive*, which appeared between 1830 and 1842, covered the whole range of knowledge, and for a time exerted a considerable influence on progressive thinkers, Comte even being regarded by some of his contemporaries as 'the greatest thinker of modern times'.[90] His sociology, however, and his dogmatic pronouncements on social statics and social dynamics, made no great impression on psychologists, perhaps partly because there was no room in Comte's scheme of things for a science of mind based on introspection (all that could not be explained sociologically about behaviour could be explained, he thought, physiologically), but more especially because Comte's sociology lacked a firm basis of empirical observation.

Much the same applied to the other founding father of sociology, Herbert Spencer (1820-1903). Inspired by the embryological work of the German biologist von Baer, and by evolutionary theories, Spencer formulated a sociology modelled on biological lines. His first work on society, *Social Statics* (1851), which he maintained was wholly uninfluenced by the prior work of Comte,[91] compared the social to the biological organism. Each was subject in its development to a similar progression from homogeneity to heterogeneity. The comparisons were further elaborated in Spencer's huge *Principles of Sociology* (3 volumes, 1876-96), in which detailed parallels were drawn between the functions of society and those of the organism, each having sustaining, distributing and regulating functions. A great deal of Spencer's sociology was in fact armchair anthropology and a vast collection of material about primitive man, and the domestic, ceremonial and institutional aspects of society. As an individualist Spencer maintained that 'there is no way of coming to a true theory of society but by enquiring into the nature of the component individuals'.[92] Nevertheless he also recognized that 'the control exercised by the aggregate over its units tends to mould their activities and sentiments and ideas into congruity with social requirements'.[93] Though Spencer was very influential in his day, particularly in the United States, which he visited in 1882, a pronounced reaction against his somewhat pretentious system-making set in well before his death. Only recently has there been a mild revival of interest in some of his ideas.[94]

Three main factors began to transform sociology at the end of the nineteenth century: firstly, the empirically based theories of the pioneer continental sociologists, secondly, the accumulation of factual data about society resulting from official reports and systematic social surveys, and thirdly, the secularization and professionalization of charitable work.

The investigations of Emile Durkheim (1858-1917), who has been described as 'the first sociologist who conceived and constructed the framework within which sociology as a viable science can operate',[95] were decisive in the influence they had on psychology. After Durkheim it was no longer possible to deny that human behaviour could only be explained by taking social forces into account, and that these forces formed a constituent part of an individual's personality. Durkheim, professor in succession at Bordeaux and at the Sorbonne, and founder in 1895 of *L'Année sociologique*, in which many of the researches of his school were published, brought sociology down to earth by insisting that it must deal with particular restricted questions by empirical methods, and that it must deal with social facts, not in terms of psychology or biology, but in their own right. 'The determining cause of a social fact', he maintained, 'should be sought among the social facts preceding it, and not among the states of the individual consciousness.'[96] In his first book, *The Division of Labour in Society* (1893), Durkheim showed how in complex communities the division of labour could become forced and artificial, so that essential bonds between individuals and the group were snapped, and a state of '*anomie*' (perhaps best described as 'rootlessness') resulted, leading to pathological symptoms in society and in affected individuals. In this condition there was a breakdown of recognized and accepted norms to regulate behaviour. What Durkheim had demonstrated was that the maladjustment of individuals was often best explained in social rather than psychological terms. This came out even more clearly in his most famous work, *Suicide* (1897). Collecting a mass of statistical evidence Durkheim showed that suicide rates tended to be constant within a community, but varied between communities. There were significant differences for example, between Catholic and Protestant communities. What seemed an essentially individual act was clearly influenced by social factors. In Durkheim's words, 'Suicide varies inversely with the degree of integration of the social groups of which the individual forms a part. . . . It is society which fashions us in its image, fills us with religious, political and moral beliefs that control our actions.'[97] In the last major work before his death, *The Elementary Forms of the Religious Life* (1912), Durkheim defended the thesis that religion was essentially a social phenomenon, representing the moral ascendancy of society over the individual. Indeed not only our religious beliefs, but all knowledge and accomplishments are socially shaped.

> We speak a language we did not make; we use instruments we did not invent; we invoke rights that we did not found; a treasury of knowledge is transmitted to each generation that it did not gather itself. It is to society that we owe these various benefits of civilization. . . . A man is a man only because he is civilized.[98]

Durkheim has often been criticized for hypostasizing society, for postulating a social consciousness over and above that of individuals, and he certainly held that collective tendencies ('*représentations collectives*') have an existence of their own, and exerted forces as real as cosmic forces. Nevertheless his influence has been profound. Durkheim's sociology, converging with Freudian theories of the superego and Piagetian studies of the development of moral judgments,[99] has gradually led to an appreciation of the central importance in the formation of personality of the processes of socialization and the internalization of the cultural world. The individual must clearly be conceived as a social being. The social dimension of his make-up could no longer be ignored, or regarded as of secondary importance, as it had been by many psychologists.

The other great figure in the development of European sociology was the German Max Weber (1864-1920). Best known for his book on *The Protestant Ethic and the Spirit of Capitalism* (1904), in which he expounded the influence of ideas and ideals on economic life in opposition to Marxian materialism, and for his description of the part played by charismatic leaders in changing the course of history, his primary importance was probably the methodological and conceptual basis he provided for sociology. It is for this reason that he has been regarded as 'the most important European social theorist of the twentieth century'.[100] At the end of the nineteenth century the German philosophers Windelband and Dilthey had maintained that there were two quite distinct realms of knowledge, that of the natural sciences (*Naturwissenschaften*) and that of human studies (*Geisteswissenschaften*), the former based on causal analysis and the latter on 'understanding' and 'interpretation' – a division which seemed to debar sociology and a good deal of psychology from the domain of science. Weber accepted the existence of a difference between the two realms, but denied that this implied an essential difference in methodology. Human behaviour was just as lawful as events in the natural world. Though in a sense free, it was not arbitrary. It required, however, a different set of concepts from those employed in dealing with the natural world, and a recognition that meanings, ends and values play a part in human life. Though the social investigator must himself be detached and uncommitted, and in that sense 'value-free', he could not ignore the part that values play in directing human activity.

The most important, and still imperfectly recognized, contribution of Weber to psychology was his concept of action. At a time when psychology was beginning to be dominated by behaviouristic doctrines based on the mechanisms of learning, Weber was putting forward an alternative, voluntaristic theory. Only since the decline of behaviourism has the full significance of this alternative become recognized. 'We shall call "action" [*Handeln*], wrote Weber, any human attitude of activity [*Verhalten*] – no matter whether involving external or internal acts, failure to act, or passive acquiescence – if, and in so far as, the actor or actors associate a subjective meaning [*Sinn*] with it.'[101] And social action, which constitutes the basic subject matter of sociology, is 'such action as according to its subjective meaning to the actor, or actors, involves the attitudes and actions of others and is oriented to them in its course.'[102] Weber did not go so far as to hold that all human action was fully rational; he recognized that some actions were 'affectually' oriented, and some purely habitual. Nevertheless much behaviour was '*zweckrational*' (rationally oriented and goal-directed), involving a calculation of means and an awareness of goal values, and action in this sense must constitute the foundation of a science of man.

Weber was by no means a mere theorist, and made many historical and empirical studies of religion, ideology, law, urbanization and bureaucracy. Perhaps of particular interest to psychologists, especially occupational psychologists, was his far-sighted monograph on the selection and adaptation of workers of major industrial enterprises, first published in 1908, and only recently fully translated into English.[103] It would have saved industrial psychologists in Anglo-Saxon countries a good many mistakes in the early days if Weber's appreciation of the social factors involved in industrial enterprises had been properly recognized.

As H.S. Hughes pointed out in his book *Consciousness and Society* (1974), there was a massive re-orientation of European social thought in the period between 1890 and 1930. Many thinkers contributed to this re-orientation – Dilthey, Croce, Bergson, James, Pareto and others – but perhaps as important as any was Max Weber. For as Hughes remarks, 'Alone among his contemporaries Weber was able to bridge the gap between positivism and idealism,'[104] and thus go some way to heal the breach which has bedevilled European thought from Greek times onwards.

This re-orientation of social thought was slow in making itself felt in Great Britain. Translations of the European sociological classics did not make an appearance, with few exceptions, for many years after their original publication. British social thought was dominated by other influences, philosophical, political, economic and anthropological. The first professor of sociology appointed at the London School of Economics (founded in 1895) was L.T. Hobhouse, and he was influenced mainly by Comte, Mill and Spencer, and very little by contemporary continental thinkers. His successor, M. Ginsberg, was broader in his sympathies;[105] nevertheless it is true to say that there was very little appreciation of continental sociology in Great Britain prior to the Second World War. The change began with the arrival of Karl Mannheim (1893-1947) at the London School of Economics. Mannheim was a Hungarian Jew, born in Budapest, who fled to Germany after the collapse of Béla Kun's short-lived communist regime in 1919. At Heidelberg he came under the influence of Max Weber, and subsequently was appointed to the chair of sociology at Frankfurt. On Hitler's accession to power in 1933 Mannheim had again to uproot himself, this time crossing to England, where he spent the remaining years of his life. It was not until the translation of *Ideology and Utopia* in 1936 and *Man and Society* in 1940 that he began to have an impact on British thought. The latter book was particularly powerful. Its central theme was 'the problem of how psychological, intellectual and moral developments are related to the social process',[106] and it was an eloquent plea for a new psychology more closely linked to the social sciences and recognizing the social aspect of every psychological phenomenon. Mannheim was quick to appreciate the attitudes of the new and very different cultural milieu in which he was working, and his book was a valuable synthesis of continental and

Anglo-Saxon modes of thought, and it contained a long and useful classified bibliography, which opened the eyes of British thinkers to unknown riches. Not until after the war did Mannheim's work begin to bear fruit, becoming one of the major stimuli for the post-war development of sociology and social psychology in this country.[107]

Sociology took much earlier root in the United States. Spencer went down better there than in his native land, and several textbooks of sociology, inspired in part by Spencer, appeared between 1895 and 1905.[108] In 1895 *The American Journal of Sociology* was founded, and in 1905 the American Sociological Society established. Then in 1906 W.G. Sumner's *Folkways* introduced a concept of 'mores', 'a vast system of usages covering the whole of life'.[109] A few years previously, in 1902, C.H. Cooley's *Human Nature and the Social Order* developed the concept of primary groups, and introduced his well-known metaphor of 'the looking-glass ego', based on the idea that 'the "I" of common speech has a meaning which includes some sort of reference to other persons'.[110] The new century saw, too, a spate of empirical enquiries, not all of them very meaningful, but the best of them, such as Thomas and Znaniecki's study of the Polish peasant, Park's studies of city life and the Lynds' detailed dissection of 'Middletown',[111] making valuable contributions to sociology. By the Second World War American sociology had reached maturity. As a recent commentator has observed,

> Sociology was made a reasonably unified and coherent subject by the Americans, who welded together very diverse streams; the heritage of Spencer, much modified and criticized; the great tradition of empirical research on urban, racial and social problem areas, begun by Park, Thomas, and their disciples in Chicago; the native social psychology of Cooley and Mead, which later fused insights of Durkheim and Freud, to produce the first really satisfactory theory relating individual and society; the absorption of much material from Pareto, Weber and other continental sociologists, and from British social anthropologists, by Parsons, Merton, Homans and others. By the 1940s all this was being synthesized into a mainstream theory to which most on-going research was related.[112]

The key theorist in this synthesis was Talcott Parsons, who was responsible, too, for bringing psychology and sociology into much closer relations.

Talcott Parsons (1902-1979) introduced continental sociology to America, and became the leading sociological theorist of his time. After graduating in biology and philosophy he crossed to Europe to study at the London School of Economics under Malinowski, the anthropologist, and Hobhouse, the sociologist, and then moved to Heidelberg, where Max Weber's influence was still dominant. This proved to be the decisive turning point in his development, and when he returned to America to an appointment at Harvard, where he remained for the rest of his life, he gradually constructed an elaborate theoretical system of sociology, derived essentially from the work of Weber and other continental thinkers.

Parsons was above all a theorist – a 'grand theorist' according to some of his critics – whose aim was to look at society as a whole, and analyse its basic structures and essential modes of functioning. In the introduction to his first book he defended the need for theory, not to replace but to guide empirical work, and contrasted his approach with that of his behaviouristic contemporaries with their piecemeal empirical methodology.[113] Covering a period of fifty years Parsons's theories naturally developed and became more elaborate. Three main periods can be distinguished:[114] in the first, he formulated the basic principles of the voluntaristic theory of action, which he derived mainly from Weber; in the second, he shifted the theoretical level from the analysis of the structure of social action to the structuralist-functionalist analysis of the social system; and in the third and final stage he introduced informational and cybernetic models to describe hierarchy of control, and a neo-evolutionist model of social change.

According to Parsons the actions which constitute the basic fabric of society are intrinsically rational, goal-directed, and normatively controlled. In his first major work, *The Structure of Social Action* (1937), Parsons discussed in detail the work of his continental predecessors, and expounded the methodological and theoretical implications of action theory, contrasting it with utilitarian and positivist rivals. After the war, in *The Social System* (1951) he analysed the emergent properties of the ordered structures of society, its norms, roles, institutions and culture, which though they exist relatively independently of any variations in the personality structure of its members, are not imposed on, but by a process of socialization became integratively incorporated into, their personalities. The basic task of sociology was to explain how social order comes about, and how social structures control social functioning. In his final period, represented by *Social Systems and the Evolution of Action Theory* (1977), Parsons distinguished four levels – the organism, personality, the social system, and the cultural system – regarding each as a step in the hierarchy of cybernetic control with a constant flow of energy and information within and between the systems. In this period of his theorizing Parsons recognized both the process of evolution, and the facts of social change and conflict, whereas previously his emphasis seemed to have been on social stability and order. This brief summary does not do justice to the intricacies and elaborate details of the Parsonian theory, and presents only its bare bones.

Perhaps it is not surprising that Parsons's system provoked criticism, and even a certain amount of ridicule. C. Wright Mills in particular pilloried his 'grand theory' for its abstract verbosity. The 555 pages of *The Social System* were, he asserted, fifty per cent verbiage, and could be reduced to 150 pages of straightforward English, when it would become obvious that it was mostly just well-known textbook material.[115] More seriously Parson's theory has been accused of leading to few practical results,[116] and of ignoring the basic factor of power, and resulting conflicts within the social order.[117] None of these criticisms is entirely fair. Parsons's theory was unquestionably abstract, but abstract theories are valuable as an exercise in rigorous and systematic thinking, and undoubtedly this is what a lot of empirical sociological work has lacked. Theories are only dangerous if they are rigid and unchanging, and held dogmatically. This was never the case with the Parsonian model, which changed over time, and which there is no reason to believe could not be further modified and extended,

For psychology Parsons is important for two main reasons. Firstly, he developed and formalized the Weberian action theory, and the concepts of norm, role, and socialization. Since the decline of behaviourism action theory has become increasingly popular among psychologists, though they do not always recognize its sources.[118] Secondly Parsons helped both theoretically and practically to forge links between sociology and psychology: theoretically by his hierarchical scheme of action systems – organic, personal, social and cultural – and suggestions as to how these systems might interact, and practically by the large part he played after the Second World War in the establishment of the Department of Social Relations at Harvard, a department which united sociologists, anthropologists, psychologists and personality theorists, and included such well-known figures as G.W. Allport, H.A. Murray and C. Kluckhohn, besides Parsons himself. The department remained in existence for nearly a quarter of a century, but never managed to attract the more experimentally and behaviouristically inclined psychologists, in spite of the recommendation of a high-level committee that there should be no such split among psychologists.[119] Parsons himself was always a leading figure in the department and underwent psychoanalysis in order better to appreciate the contribution of psychiatrists and clinical psychologists. He published a number of articles in the journal *Psychiatry* on the relations between psychoanalysis and personality, and on the part played by social situations on the development of personality.[120] Although, since his death, the popularity of Parsonian theory has declined, the *rapprochement* he affected between sociology and certain areas of psychology has persisted and indeed strengthened, and at least some psychological theorizing has moved in a Parsonian direction.

Largely independently of these theoretical developments taking place in sociology went the gradual accumulation of accurate factual data about society, particularly about its problem areas, and the growth of practical social work to deal with these problems. This down-to-earth material, and these mundane activities, provided the stuffing needed to humanize the high flights of theory, and forcibly depict to psychologists and others the realities of social living. Systematic surveys of human society were not, of course, entirely new. Indeed they could be said to go back to the end of the seventeenth century. King's studies of the population of England and Wales threw much light on the social structure of the time, estimating, for example, that about a third of the inhabitants of the country were unable to support themselves without some charitable assistance, or were living in a state of vagrancy.[121] Comprehensive censuses of the modern type began in America in 1790, and in Great Britain in 1801, and began to provide some information of psychological interest. For example, the British census of 1871 endeavoured to collect information on the number of non-institutionalized mental defective persons living at home.[122] With the growth of urbanization from the end of the eighteenth century conditions in the rapidly expanding towns aroused increasing concern. The appalling urban squalor in and around Manchester was vividly described by J.P. Kay-Shuttleworth,[123] and also by Frederick Engels, Marx's friend. 'In the working-men's dwellings of Manchester,' wrote Engels, 'no cleanliness, no convenience, and consequently no comfortable family life is possible: in such dwellings only a physically degenerate race, robbed of all humanity, degraded, reduced morally and physically to bestiality, could feel comfortable and at home.'[124] Many of these conclusions were later confirmed by the reports of official commissions on the health of towns and the state of factories, and in spite of legalisation and reforms designed to remedy these evils, later surveys still revealed wide deprivation. Thus the detailed surveys by C. Booth of London life and labour at the end of the nineteenth century,[125] and B.S. Rowntree's studies in York at the beginning of the twentieth,[126] showed that poverty was still prevalent. In America the work particularly of the Chicago school of sociologists produced comparable findings. These surveys were an important complement to theoretical sociology. Their aim was different: 'A survey', stated Park, 'is never research – it is explorative; it seeks to define problems rather than to test hypotheses.'[127] These surveys revealed clearly that within communities there were vast differences in conditions and ways of life, both reflecting and moulding differences in psychological make-up.

The existence of social distress has always been obvious in a general way, and charitable endeavours, particularly those fostered by the churches and religious bodies, have attempted to alleviate deprivation and suffering. In England the Poor Law Amendment Act of 1834 centralized and institutionalized the relief of destitution, but did not do away, by any means, with the continued need for private charity. In 1869 the Charity Organization Society was founded, and this eventually led to the training and education of the voluntary social workers who carried out its work in the field, and to the first training courses for social workers at the London School of Economics.[128] In the United States the American Social Science Association, set up in 1865, promoted rather similar developments. In the twentieth century social work gradually became a recognized and organized profession, or group of professions, based on the concept of social casework. The principles of social casework were first clearly formulated by the American social worker Mary Richmond, in her *Social Diagnosis* (1917). Regarding social casework as just as important to the social worker as medical diagnosis to the physician, she set out the details required for a full social history: but even more important, she helped to change the ethos of the social worker, discarding the concept of the 'poor' as one of economic connotation. In its place steps the 'client' conceived as a person (or family) whose character, physical condition or circumstances, or a combination of these, have made him incapable of full self-maintenance in his social setting. The problem, then, is one of character and environment: or more accurately it is psychological, physical and sociological. The economic distress of the client is only one possible symptom of his inadequacy.[129]

Particularly important for psychology was the use of social workers in the treatment of problem children and of psychiatric patients. Both of these uses originated in America. Social workers were part of the team in the Child Juvenile Psychopathic Institute set up in Chicago by W. Healy in 1909; and psychiatric social work owes its origin and its name to May Jarrett, who in 1913 became Director of Social Service at the Psychopathic Hospital in Boston. Similar movements followed in the 1920s in Britain.

With these developments in sociological theory and sociological investigation on the one hand, and in social case work on the other, psychologists, by the early years of the twentieth century, were confronted with a mass of data which forced them to accord recognition to the social dimension of psychology, and to cultivate the new field of social psychology.

V

The birth of social psychology was foreshadowed by William James in 1890, when he wrote of the 'social self':

A man's social self is the recognition he gets from his mates. We are not only gregarious animals, liking to be in the sight of our fellows, but we have an innate propensity to get ourselves noticed, and noticed favourably by our kind. . . . Properly speaking a man has as many social selves as there are individuals who recognize him and carry an image of him in their mind.[130]

The first texts entitled *Social Psychology*, those by the American sociologist E.A. Ross and by the British psychologist William McDougall, appeared together in 1908. Both books proved enormously popular, Ross's achieving twenty-two reprints and McDougall's twenty-three.[131] According to Ross,

Social psychology studies the psychic planes and currents that come into existence among men in consequence of their association. It seeks to understand and to account for those uniformities in feeling, belief, or volition – and hence action – which are due to the interaction of human beings, i.e. to social causes.[132]

By 'planes' Ross was referring to the constant uniformities of social life, and by 'currents' to temporary waves of fashion. His principle explanatory concept was that of imitation, which he borrowed largely from the French philosopher Tarde, while his methodology was mainly descriptive and anecdotal. McDougall's standpoint was somewhat different, although he, too, upheld the important part played in social life by imitation. Impressed by his anthropological experiences in the Torres Straits and Borneo, McDougall came to recognize 'the extent to which the adult human mind is the product of the moulding influences exerted by the social environment'[133] – but he held that the social environment was itself shaped essentially by the primary tendencies, or instincts, with which human beings were endowed. His approach to social psychology was, therefore, in the last resort biological and individualistic.

In the three-quarters of a century that have followed these pioneering texts, social psychologists have been searching for adequate theoretical concepts and appropriate methodologies for their discipline.[134] A decisive turning point came in the 1920s when the instinct concept was largely rejected, and social psychology was re-directed into behaviouristic and experimental channels by F.H. Allport.[135] 'Social behaviour comprises the stimulations and reactions arising between the individual and the social portion of his environment,'[136] and the social psychologist was primarily concerned with 'the influence of one individual upon another'.[137] Such influences could be studied experimentally, and since Allport held that group phenomena could be reduced to the mechanisms of individual behaviour in a social environment, social psychology could become an essentially experimental discipline. In America this is largely what happened. In 1931 the Murphys were already able to write a text on *Experimental Social Psychology*,[138] though admittedly they took the term 'experimental' rather broadly to embrace most objectively acquired data. The percentage of experimental studies in *The Journal of Personality and Social Psychology* grew from thirty per cent in 1949 to eighty-seven per cent in 1969.[139] Europe was slower in following the experimental trail, but in 1963 a European Society for Experimental Social Psychology was established. This experimental impetus inevitably tended to inhibit theorizing. The only serious American attempt at a theoretical analysis of the foundations of social psychology, G.H. Mead's *Mind, Self and Society From the Standpoint of a Social Behaviorist* (1934), was a difficult and abstract work, which made comparatively little immediate impact, though it has since been coming into its own. In these lectures, not published till after his death in 1931, Mead, who had studied in Berlin and been influenced by German thought, endeavoured to show the essentially social nature of mind and self, and explain how gradually through childhood play and games, and the use of language, the idea of 'the generalized other' arose, and generated the idea of the self. Thus for Mead, 'it is absurd to look at the mind simply from the standpoint of the individual human organism, for although it has its focus there, it is essentially a social phenomenon; even its biological functions are primarily social.'[140] Even though

Mead's theory was far from satisfactory, in that it failed to make sufficient room for individual differences in personality, at least some of which seem to be of genetic and biochemical origin, nevertheless it was an attempt to provide social psychology with a general framework of theory. And this is what social psychology has conspicuously lacked. There have been many partial theories, but no deep general theory:– theories of social learning (Miller and Dollard), field theories inspired by Gestalt concepts (Lewin), balance theory (Heider), the theory of cognitive dissonance (Festinger), attitude theories (Thomas and Znaniecki, Newcomb), role theories (Woodworth), etc.[141] Such theories, though influential in their day, were limited in their scope and subject to changes in fashion, with the result that social psychology has tended to present 'a non-cumulative character', and to consist of 'a series of successive starts of jerks'.[142]

Similarly there has been a search for an appropriate methodology, with a growing emphasis, particularly in America, on laboratory experiments with small groups. Such experiments have often been criticized for their artificiality. The traditional experiment takes no account, according to some critics, of the meanings assigned to the experimental situation by the participants.[143] In an endeavour to achieve verisimilitude experimenters have not infrequently had recourse to deception, when they have come under even more severe objections.[144] But in spite of these criticisms the spate of experimental work continues. It has, of course, been supplemented by other approaches, by attitude measurement, by statistically analysed survey data, by the content analysis of verbal material, by systematic observation and by other methods.[145] Perhaps, however, the main need is not for methodological refinement so much as for theoretical background and conceptual clarification. 'Like all behavioural science,' wrote G.W. Allport half a century ago, 'social psychology rests ultimately on broad metatheories concerning the nature of man and the nature of society.'[146] The lack of such theory does not mean that all the empirical work of the last half century has been wasted; it has, however, led to its somewhat inchoate and unsatisfactory shape, and has exposed it to increasing attack. There is accordingly a new move on both sides of the Atlantic towards what has been termed 'a transformation in social knowledge',[147] and a radical revision of the whole foundation of social psychology. Looking towards the future the French social psychologist Moscovici predicts 'un polythéisme méthodologique', a mixing of experimental with other approaches, and closer links with neighbouring disciplines.[148]

In this transitional situation it is helpful to make a clear distinction between two radically different groups of problem which have become incorporated into social psychology, and which have often been confused: firstly, the influence of others on the behaviour of the individual, and secondly, the socialization of the individual, his acquisition of the culture into which he has been born with its traditions, norms, beliefs and skills. The first of these groups springs from, and is related to, the Anglo-Saxon empirical tradition, the second derives largely from the German tradition of 'objective mind' and *Völkerpsychologie*. Each of these groups of problem requires a different approach, and both are important areas of social psychological investigation.

The study of the behaviour of individuals in social contexts, that is in the presence of other persons, can be carried out both experimentally and observationally in an empirical framework. As far back as 1897 Triplett discovered the dynamogenic influence of competition.[149] Cyclists could ride twenty per cent faster when paced, and children, provided they were not subjected to undue pressure, usually carried out routine tasks more quickly in groups. By 1924 F.H. Allport could report numerous experiments on the topic of social facilitation. Clearly a simple social situation can be conceived, as Allport conceived it, in stimulus-response terms. The members of a group communicate with each other. Signs are emitted, signs are perceived, and responses made accordingly. Such signs may be verbal, or non-verbal taking the form of gestures, among which may be classed vocal gestures, or what have been termed the 'paralinguistic' features of language.[150] The communication process, both linguistic and non-linguistic, has become an intense and fruitful field of research,[151] and as communication can be regarded from one viewpoint as involving a set of acquired skills in perceiving and performing, the way has been opened for training in social techniques. As Argyle has pointed out, 'social skills can probably be learnt in ways similar to those found successful in the learning of motor skills.'[152] One cannot help feeling that Aristotle, the author of the *Rhetoric*, would have approved of this development! A social group, however, is more than a set of individuals communicating with one another. It constitutes, as Lewin observed half a century ago,[153] a dynamic field of influences, depending on various factors, such as the composition, size, context and other features of the group, all factors which can be studied experimentally. In small groups structures soon begin to form, dominance-submission patterns emerge together with group leaders, roles are acquired, and norms and attitudes established.[154] There is a strong tendency towards group conformity.[155] These processes, too, have been experimentally investigated. In larger groups the phenomena of mass, or crowd, behaviour have intrigued psychologists for several generations;[156] it was, indeed, the earliest type of social behaviour to arouse speculation. Ordinary social behaviour, too, has come under minute observational scrutiny, particularly by Goffman, who looked at social behaviour as largely a 'theatrical performance', aimed at 'impression management'[157] – a somewhat cynical approach which overemphasized 'the froth and efflorescence of life',[158] and unduly discounted underlying sincerities. We can confidently say that, as a result of the work of two generations of social psychologists, the intimate nature of social interaction is beginning to be better understood.

The second group of problems raises much deeper questions, in that it involves the relationship between the individual and the larger society. The Polish-born psychologist Henri Tajfel made a useful distinction between the microscopic and macroscopic approaches to social psychology.[159] Experimental social psychology necessarily deals almost wholly with microscopic, or small-scale situations, as the manipulation of larger communities is in all but exceptional circumstances out of the question. This means that experimentation cannot tackle many of the urgent social problems of the day, such as those which gave rise to the brutalities of the Second World War, from which Tajfel himself suffered, or the acute social problems of contemporary urban communities. So Tajfel insisted that 'social psychology can and must include in its theoretical and research preoccupations a direct concern with the relationship between psychological functioning and the large-scale social processes and events which shape this functioning and are shaped by it'.[160] These preoccupations, of course, are not the exclusive concern of the psychologist, and from the psychological standpoint perhaps the basic issue is how the individual becomes socialized and acquires the traditions and values of his cultural milieu, and when socialization fails, what accounts for these failures. It has become increasingly recognized in recent years that behaviour is controlled not simply by stimuli from the environment, but by plans or programmes. As Lashley observed, trains of behaviour are serially ordered, and this ordering is centrally organized.[161] In lower organisms the programming is predominantly genetic, to some extent modified by individual learning. In man the programming is largely cultural. In the terminology of Dawkins human behaviour is directed not only by genes, but by new replicators of cultural origin, which he called 'memes'.[162] Not only is a great deal of the individual's information store culturally derived, but his motivations are culturally fashioned, and his skilled performances culturally transmitted. Social programming continues throughout life, but predominantly it takes place during childhood and adolescence, and the processes of socialization have been studied not only by social, but also by child and educational psychologists.[163] A significant early work in this area was Piaget's *The Moral Judgment of the Child* (1932), in which he traced the development of the child's grasp of rules, such as those involved in playing games, and the gradual appreciation of moral concepts like truthfulness and justice. Piaget particularly emphasized the part played in the acquisition of moral concepts by interaction with other children in social situations. These studies have stimulated much further work, some of it critical of Piaget, into moral learning and development.[164] Particularly valuable has been the work of Soviet psychologists, who have emphasized the relation of school instruction to the psychological and social development of the child.[165]

One of the great difficulties of this area of research is that it is necessarily inter-disciplinary. Social programmes, or 'memes', though man-made cannot be reduced to psychological terms, but transcend the realm of the individual mind. It is for the linguist to unravel and explicate the structure and principles of language, for the philosopher to formulate the principles of logic or the principles of justice, whereas the job of the psychologist is to study how, and to what extent, the individual in the course of his development acquires these principles, and what circumstances militate against his doing so. This confronts the psychologist with a gargantuan task, for not only is there the huge range of abilities and interests among individuals, but an enormous richness and complexity in the cultural heritage confronting them. Particularly in the vast urban communities of the developed world the quantity of social stimulation and cultural input is often overwhelming in its impact, as well as most uneven in its spread, leading as Tinbergen and others have pointed out to widespread dis-adaptation.[166] The phenomena of deviance, delinquency, crime, vandalism, racial tension, prejudice, mental pathology and 'anomie' in contemporary urban communities have indeed provided much of the raw material for some of the most valuable work by social psychologists.[167] It is probably in connection with these applied problems, provided they can be approached against a theoretical rather than an ad hoc background, that future progress is likely to be made. For as we shall see in the next chapter, applications often stimulate theoretical developments. Meanwhile we can affirm that, whatever the shortcomings of contemporary social psychology, it has been established beyond question that the social dimension is one of the most important dimensions of human nature. This is a significant advance, which is predominantly an achievement of the last hundred years.

Chapter 12
Application, specialization and fragmentation

I

The character of twentieth century psychology differs markedly from that of all previous centuries, largely as a result of fundamental changes in its institutional setting. These changes have been brought about above all through the application of psychology to the solution of practical problems. By providing a career structure for psychologists, this has led to a steady growth in their numbers, to a rapid expansion of university departments of psychology, and to a substantial increase in research funds, which were indeed at the beginning of the century minute. Psychology has ceased to be an esoteric pursuit of a select few, and has become a sizeable profession with all the paraphernalia of professionalism. Growth of this sort has led inevitably to specialization within psychology, necessitated by the sheer quantity and diversity of subject matter attracting the attention of psychologists, and to their increasing technological sophistication. Further fragmentation of the subject has been caused by ideological and cultural differences, due partly to the variety of roads of entry into psychology, which have exacerbated the philosophical divide of earlier ages. By the middle of the century it was hard not to agree with the philosopher Ryle, who advocated the 'abandonment of the notion that "psychology" is the name of a unitary inquiry or tree of inquiries', and maintained that the term could more appropriately be used 'to denote a partly fortuitous federation of inquiries and techniques'.[1] This was echoed by one British psychologist who wrote a book entitled *Psychological Sciences*.[2] We must look, therefore, first at the applications which brought these changes about, secondly at the specialization and fragmentation that has taken place in psychology, and finally at how psychologists have responded to this threat to the unity of their subject.

II

The term 'applied psychology' can be taken in two different ways. On the one hand it may refer to the application in some real-life situation of the findings of pure laboratory experimentation undertaken in the first place with no practical end in view. For example, the finding of the experimentalists that the time actually spent on learning is reduced when practice is spaced rather than massed can be applied to the learning of school work or the acquisition of industrial skills. Applicable findings of this sort resulting from laboratory experimentation are now quite considerable in number.[3] However, because the whole setting, both social and material, is as a rule highly relevant to psychological functioning, there are limitations to the direct application of laboratory findings to the complexities of real life, and 'applied psychology' needs defining more broadly to mean the application to the study of practical problems of the methods of psychological enquiry. As the human factor is involved in all but totally automated processes, the capacities, needs and limitations of human beings, as well as the range and variety of their individual make-up, become matters of concern. The scope of applied psychology is, therefore, potentially nearly as wide as human life itself.

It was, however, in the field of education that applied psychology began. Several nineteenth century psychologists – Spencer, Bain, Ward and Sully in Great Britain, Stanley Hall in America and Meumann in Germany – had recognized the potential relevance of their subject to education,[4] but it was not until towards the end of the century that practical applications actually began. These took two forms, the development of 'mental tests', and what was termed 'experimental pedagogy'. The first psychological tests were devised by Galton in 1882 in his investigation of individual differences; they were developed and christened 'mental tests' by J.M. Cattell in 1890 in his efforts to determine the intelligence of college students; and used by Ebbinghaus with schoolchildren in Breslau in 1897. The first really effective scale for the measurement of scholastic intelligence was that devised by Binet and Simon in 1905.[5] Psychological tests of educable capacity have been used extensively since then both on a group basis and for individual diagnosis, and, in spite of justifiable criticisms for exaggerated claims and occasional misuse, are likely to continue to be employed, since the measurement of human performance and the estimation of human potential under standardized conditions is for many purposes essential in highly organized communities, where exacting requirements of technical and professional expertise are demanded. The other field of application, 'experimental pedagogy' was the father of today's educational research, in which psychologists play a considerable part. Stanley Hall in America and E. Meumann in Germany were the pioneers. Both founded journals, Hall the *Pedagogical Seminary* in 1891 to promote the study of child development and progressive education, and Meumann the *Zeitschrift für experimentelle Pädagogik* in 1905. Apart from investigating child development, experimental pedagogy studied methods of teaching and learning, problems of fatigue and mental work, the organization of classes, and problems relating to special topics such as reading, writing, language learning and arithmetic.[6] In recent years many of these topics have been crystallized under the rubric 'instructional psychology' and have formed close links with research in cognitive processes in general.[7]

The next field of application was industry, where Hugo Münsterberg, the German psychologist who was invited to Harvard by William James, first systematically outlined its scope in 1912.[8] Münsterberg laid great stress on the investigation of individual differences: 'The study of individual differences,' he wrote, 'is not applied psychology, but it is the presupposition without which applied psychology would have remained a phantom.'[9] He divided the field of industrial psychology into three main areas: firstly, the selection of the best possible man for the job through the use of psychological tests and vocational guidance, secondly, the provision of the best possible conditions of work, including suitable training methods, and thirdly, the selling of the products of work by effective advertising and display. In each of these areas Münsterberg provided experimental results to support his claims for the value of psychological research. Since his day industrial psychology, or as it is now often termed 'occupational psychology', has not only developed in all the areas he described, but widened its scope to embrace the social and organizational aspects of work, to consider in much greater depth the problems of motivation and job satisfaction, and to investigate the intricate relations between men and the machines they operate and control.[10] With the growing cost and complexity of this machinery the last topic has become of extra importance, and a speciality, now commonly known as 'ergonomics', has developed to study the problems involved. The Ergonomics Research Society was founded in England in 1949 by psychologists, physiologists and engineers to work in the first instance on problems of equipment and apparatus design, a topic which had become prominent in the Second World War in all the main combatant nations.[11] The term 'ergonomics' was coined by a British psychologist, H. Murrell. There is now an International Ergonomics Association, and similar societies throughout Europe, Asia, Australia and the Americas. The Soviet Union, too, actively sponsors the subject,[12] for the problems of industrial society are not, as is sometimes claimed, a result of the capitalist organization of industry, but for the most part universal problems arising from modern methods of industrial production.

The third major branch of applied psychology is the clinical branch, where the psychologist is usually associated with medical and social workers in studying individual cases where there is some problem of adjustment, medical or social. The distinguished German psychiatrist Kraepelin, who, as a student of Wundt, was familiar with experimental psychology, carried out a number of psychological experiments on mental patients, which he reported in 1895.[13] In 1896 Lightner Witmer established a psychological clinic at the University of Pennsylvania, and first used the term 'clinical psychology'. William Healy, a medical man who was interested in problems of delinquency and founded the Chicago Juvenile Psychopathic Institute in 1909, set the collaborative pattern of physician, psychologist and social worker which has become general.[14] Since those early days clinical psychology has long ceased to be mainly concerned with children, though child guidance is still an important area, and since the development of behaviour therapy, has ceased to be primarily concerned with assessment and diagnosis, and has become deeply involved in treatment and counselling.[15] Clinical psychology is now in many countries the largest branch of applied psychology.[16]

A fourth old established field of applied psychology is concerned with crime, delinquency and legal psychology. To some extent this overlaps with clinical psychology, but there is now a speciality, sometimes termed 'forensic psychology', which deals with a variety of legal matters.[17] Indeed this was one of the earliest applications of psychology. Stern's work on the psychology of testimony (*Aussage*) was published in 1902, and Münsterberg's *On the Witness Stand* in 1908. It is an area in which German psychologists continue to show a pre-eminence.[18] However, in spite of the conservatism of the legal profession, it is beginning to expand in Anglo-Saxon countries. The first *Annual Review* chapter on 'Psychology and Law' appeared in 1976. The British Psychological Society started a Division of Criminological and Legal Psychology in 1976 and the American Psychological Association its Psychology and Law Division in 1981.[19] The employment of psychologists in prisons is now common practice, where they are engaged not only in assessing individual cases but also in evaluating regimes and running therapeutic groups.[20] Among other problems falling within the scope of forensic psychology the problem of person identification has been exciting growing interest,[21] and lie detection, which was pioneered by the Austrian psychologist Benussi as far back as 1914, has become a lively subject of research and controversy.[22]

Advances in the application of psychology were greatly stimulated by the problems raised by the First and Second World Wars. During the First World War psychological tests were employed on a mass scale by the American Army in 1917; psychologists were called in to assist medical men in assessing and treating war neuroses, then termed 'shell shock' cases; investigations by psychologists and physiologists into the incidence of fatigue and accidents in munitions factories were the first substantial studies in the field of industrial psychology; and in a small way experimental psychologists were roped in to study special problems such as the selection of hydrophone operators for submarine detection.[23] This all helped to establish the claims of applied psychology, and led to its continuation on a still small, but nevertheless significant, scale.[24]

In the Second World War the employment of psychologists was immediate, and much more extensive. In addition to the massive psychological testing programmes in the main combatant forces, and the development of complex and refined selection procedures,[25] the psychiatric disabilities of war became a subject of intensive research, which did a great deal to promote the development of clinical psychology after the war;[26] social psychology was advanced by large-scale attitude studies carried out by the American Army;[27] and above all the employment of experimental psychologists to study problems of man-machine interactions, training methods, stress and so on, led to a significant transformation of the conceptual framework of psychology.[28] In fact the subsequent development of psychology has been shaped to a considerable extent by the work carried out by psychologists during the Second World War.

Since the war psychologists have been involved in an ever wider range of practical problems concerning, for example, traffic accidents, road design, telecommunication, environmental planning, escape from fires, football violence, the impact of disasters, and even such relatively trivial matters as the human aspects of leisure travel. Indeed as one applied psychologist observes, 'there is hardly an area of human experience which is not touched,'[29] and the periodical congresses of the International Association of Applied Psychology, which was founded by the distinguished Swiss psychologist Claparède in 1920,[30] embrace more and more areas of application at its successive meetings, while the traditional fields, educational, occupational and clinical, continue to expand.

Not surprisingly this growth of applied psychology has not been unchallenged by theorists and experimentalists ensconced in their universities and research institutes, and often critical of the lack of methodological rigour and absence of solid theoretical foundations in much applied work. Real-life problems are often messy; variables cannot be precisely controlled, and part of the problem may well be the definition of the problem itself. So the work of the applied psychologist must often aim not at the perfect, but at the least bad solution, which is nevertheless better than no solution at all. The long history of medicine from its empirical beginnings and quack remedies to its present scientific level ought to encourage a tolerant attitude towards the efforts of applied psychologists in the endeavour to deal with even more difficult problems than those that confronted medicine. As Cronbach noted more than a quarter of a century ago,[31] there has been an unfortunate tendency for psychologists to split into two camps, the pure experimentalists, and the psychometricians and applied psychologists, each group going its own uncomprehending way. Such a split, if it persisted, would be unfortunate, because a sound psychology requires a marriage of methodology and content, of theory and practice, and while experimenters can set an example of rigorous methodology, the applied psychologists are often much better at locating fruitful problems and avoiding the narrow scholasticism of the laboratory purist. Moreover applied psychologists are all the time increasing their methodological sophistication. As Münsterberg noted, applied psychology was in the first instance made possible by the invention of tests for quantifying individual differences. The early methods were necessarily crude, but Galton, who devised the first tests, also did a good deal to lay the foundations of the statistical techniques needed to assess the results of tests, in particular by means of his correlation coefficient.[32] Statistical techniques have greatly advanced since Galton's day. Measures of significance, analysis of variance, experimental design, factor analysis and multidimensional scaling are just some of the achievements of the present century which provide at least some support for the work of applied psychologists[33] They are admittedly not enough without theoretical underpinning, but theory emerges gradually from the applications of psychology. Indeed, as already noted, the work of applied psychologists has contributed much to, and to a considerable extent shaped, the conceptual development of psychology since the Second World War.

III

'Psychology has benefited more than is often recognised by symbiotic interactions between basic and applied science,' observed Neil Miller.[34] Perhaps the chief of these benefits has been the conceptual enrichment of psychology as a result both of the resuscitation of several old concepts discarded through the reductionist zeal of academic psychologists and the introduction of several fruitful new concepts. Intelligence, personality, vigilance, decision, skill and stress – to select some of the more important – are all concepts that have been brought to the fore and rescued from neglect as a result of applied work. The first two of these concepts are central to differential psychology, which Binet and Henri in their classic paper of 1895 had noted was then in 'an embryonic state';[35] they have since become, as a result of practical demands, important topics in general psychology.

The concept of intelligence is an ancient concept, which had its origins in the faculty psychology of Aristotle. 'Understanding' (διανοία) was one of the powers (δυνάμεις) of the soul, and in Latin this became 'intelligentia'. 'Intelligentia est, per quam animus ea perspicit quae sunt,' wrote Cicero ('Intelligence is the power which enables the mind to comprehend reality').[36] The medieval scholastics adopted, refined and extended the apparatus and terminology of ancient philosophy, and intellect and intelligence became central concepts of their systems. We have already noted that the rejection of the scholastic philosophy during the Renaissance involved a corresponding rejection of scholastic psychology.[37] In their devotion to new physical models the empirical psychologists of the modern age progressively discarded the notions of faculties and powers which underlay the concept of intelligence. The rejection started with Hobbes, and was implicit, though more ambivalent, in Locke. By the nineteenth century it had become psychological orthodoxy. Herbart in 1806 called the tune when he stated that the soul had 'no capacity nor faculty whatever either to receive or to produce anything'.[38] And at the end of the century the British theoretical psychologist G.F. Stout was saying much the same thing when he maintained that 'such words as potentiality, faculty, susceptibility, are mere marks for our ignorance'.[39] Though he wrote of 'noetic synthesis' the term 'intelligence' occurs neither in Stout's *Analytic Psychology* nor in his later *Manual*.[40] Together with this rejection of faculties, and consequently of intelligence, went a disinterest in individual differences. 'Psychology as a science', stated Sully in 1884, 'has to do with general facts and traits of mind. It takes no account of individual peculiarities.'[41] In ignoring topics such as intelligence, and deriding the study of individual differences, Wundt, the founding father of modern scientific psychology, was merely reflecting the general tendencies of his time. Fortunately, though some experimentalists are still disdainful of differential psychology, not all psychologists have followed Wundt's example. Two forces led psychology back to revive the ancient concept of intelligence: firstly, evolutionary biology, and secondly, the practical needs of highly organized, educated and increasingly urbanized industrial societies.[42]

For the evolutionists, beginning with Spencer, intelligence was both an outcome of, and a factor in, evolutionary development. Aptitudes and capacities, including intelligence, were functionally formed organizations which had become structuralized because they were advantageous, and were hereditarily transmitted. It was Galton's idea to attempt the measurement of these aptitudes in man, and to apply the notion of statistical distribution within a population to mental faculties.[43] This was the origin of the intelligence testing movement. But its further development was the result of practical demands, primarily within the field of education, but also for assistance in assessing mental deficiency, in vocational placement and selection, and in the military sphere. The important outcomes of the testing movement were, firstly, to confirm in an irrefutable way the considerable range of human capacities,[44] and secondly, to demonstrate both the ubiquitous positive correlation among virtually all tests of mental ability of whatever sort, and also the correlation of measures of intelligence with a considerable range of educational, vocational and social phenomena. It was on the basis of these positive correlations that Spearman propounded his well-known theory of the general ability factor, or 'g', which is commonly identified with intelligence. Not all psychologists, of course, have accepted the 'g' theory, but it has recently been defended by Jensen,[45] and it is in conformity with a hierarchical view of psychological structure acceptable on other grounds, particularly when group factors, which Spearman at first discounted, are admitted together with 'g', as is now universally the case. The nature of 'g' is another question, and as Jensen himself pointed out, we still have no adequate theory.[46] Spearman at least made suggestions in his equation of 'g' with mental energy and his theory of 'noegenesis';[47] most intelligence testers, however, have been content to accept the vague eclectic ideas of Binet, and made no attempt to define intelligence with precision.[48] Thus though the technology of intelligence testing, with its sophisticated methods of test construction and standardization, has advanced substantially, its theoretical basis has remained obscure. There are, however, promising signs of closer links with cognitive psychology, information processing and work on artificial intelligence.[49] A good, deal, too, is now known about the genetic and environmental factors influencing intelligence,[50] and, as a result of Piaget's work, about its development during childhood. Ageing studies have also thrown light on changes in intellectual functioning in later life.[51] Applied psychology has, therefore, rescued from neglect, and opened up for scientific exploration, a highly relevant and theoretically important topic.

The same is true with regard to the correlative concept of 'personality'. The psychology of personality in an organized form goes back only to the 1930s, but once again its roots lie much deeper. The term 'personality' was not, of course, in its origins a psychological one; it was dramatic, theological, legal and grammatical. The concept of the soul was the unifying concept of psychology in the early stages of its development. Individual differences were subsumed under the heading of 'character', a Greek word denoting a distinguishing mark. Theophrastus, the successor of Aristotle, was the first recorded characterologist,[52] but characterology became a literary pursuit, and was not integrated with psychology at all until the nineteenth century, and then only marginally.[53] J.S. Mill noted the deficiency in 1843 when he observed that 'mankind have not one universal character, but there exist universal laws of the formation of character' capable of constituting a science which he suggested should be termed 'ethology'.[54] However, judiciously ignoring the efforts of the phrenologists, he affirmed that 'ethology is still to be created'.[55] Though an attempt was made by the British psychologist Shand to realize Mill's proposal in a rather abstract way,[56] it was the development of medical, clinical and vocational psychology that finally brought the concept of personality to the fore. The French led the way. Ribot's *Les Maladies de la personnalité* appeared in 1885. In 1892 Janet in his *L'Etat mental des hystériques* wrote of 'the all-embracing idea of personality. . . . It is the notion of my body, of my capacities, of my name, my social position, of the part I play in the world: it is an ensemble of moral, political, religious thoughts, etc.'[57] Anglo-Saxon writers followed early in the twentieth century. In 1906 Moreton Prince discussed the phenomena of multiple personality in his *The Dissociation of the Personality*,[58] and in the same year F.W.H. Myers in *Human Personality and its Survival of Bodily Death* dealt with both the abnormal and paranormal sides of personality. The first general book on the psychology of personality in English was that by R.G. Gordon, a British physician, who was influenced by psychoanalytic developments.[59] In his preface he asked, 'why should a practising physician write on personality?', and went on to say, 'the answer may be that personality is essentially a practical entity and not a theoretical composition.'[60] The 1930s saw an increasing flow of works on the subject. Lewin's *Dynamic Theory of Personality* (1935) was among the first, but the work which put personality on the psychological map was undoubtedly G.W. Allport's *Personality* which appeared in 1937. By proposing a theory based on traits, and by relating personality to general psychology, Allport brought personality decidedly into the ambit of psychology. 'Personality', according to him, 'is the dynamic organization within the individual of those psychophysical systems that determine his unique adjustments to his environment.'[61] Allport's work was followed the year after by another Harvard product, H.A. Murray's *Explorations in Personality*, based on a clinical and experimental study of fifty men of college age by members of the Harvard Psychological Clinic. Murray went further than Allport in one respect in that he proposed that 'personalities constitute the subject matter of psychology, the life history of a single man being the unit with which this discipline has to deal',[62] and he introduced a number of new diagnostic procedures, the best known being the Thematic Apperception Test.[63] This test in particular has been widely used, but on the other hand his neologistic terminology and catalogue of needs has not found general acceptance. The field of personality was magisterially surveyed just after the war by Gardner Murphy in his *Personality: A Biosocial Approach to its Origins and Structure* (1947).

The Second World War did much to promote personality study. It was to show its practical value both in the assessment of officer material and in the study of war neuroses. War Office Selection Boards were set up in Great Britain in 1942, and by the end of the war some hundred thousand applicants for officer rank had been psychologically examined.[64] In America rather similar procedures were introduced, proving equally successful.[65] On both sides of the Atlantic new methods of assessing personality were devised, particular use being made of situational tests to supplement the projective and verbal methods previously in vogue. It was during the war, too, that factor analytic methods were first applied on a significant scale to personality variables. Spearman had recognized that what he called 'oretic factors' might be discovered,[66] and several members of his school carried out small-scale analyses, including Burt, whose analysis of temperamental types was based on a sample of twelve women only.[67] By contrast the factor analytic study carried out by Eysenck during the war was based on seven hundred patients at the Mill Hill Emergency Hospital, and led to the description of two main axes, the neuroticism axis and the introvert-extrovert axis.[68] Even more elaborate statistical analyses, made possible by the arrival of computers, have since been carried out by R.B. Cattell, who has located sixteen basic personality factors, and devised a series of tests, questionnaires and ratings aimed at assessing them.[69] Though Cattell's 16PF Test, as it is termed, has been widely used, it is hard not to feel that the elaborate multivariate analysis has been imposed on somewhat flimsy empirical foundations. In spite of methodological and conceptual refinements, methods of assessing personality are still distinctly less reliable than measures of intelligence and other aptitudes, and the theoretical basis of personality study is still far from agreed. In this context clinical and qualitative methods of collecting data still have a great deal to offer. As Bromley has pointed out, 'the study of individual cases in psychology and social work is grounded in common sense and ordinary language,'[70] and this being so, clinical studies can lead to a significant body of knowledge about personal adjustment if systematicaly analysed. Some forty years ago Murphy concluded his study of personality by affirming that 'we shall rectify mistakes not primarily by minor readjustment of the lines of the argument, but by recognition of the fundamental limitations of the whole present system of conceptions'.[71] Some, but certainly not all these limitations have since been overcome, and, though problems remain, personality has undoubtedly emerged as a central topic not only in differential, but also in general psychology, and undoubtedly the work of applied psychologists has been the spur to this development.

IV

The application of psychology in the Second World War brought other problems to the fore. The war of 1939-1945 presented a very different aspect technologically from that of 1914-1918, and the vastly increased complexity of machines of all kinds made entirely new demands on their human operators. Hence psychologists turned their attention to matters such as vigilance, decision-making, skills and stress, all topics which have become of importance subsequently.

Vigilance problems arose early in the war, particularly as a result of the invention of radar, which required the continuous scanning of screens by human observers. Radar operator fatigue and lapses of vigilance became a serious practical issue, and as Broadbent later commented, 'vigilance problems have forced us to acknowledge again the importance of attention.'[72] Attention is another very ancient concept, which had gradually faded from psychology by the 1930s. It held a prominent place in the psychology of Augustine, and later of the scholastics. It was kept alive in the rationalist psychologies of the continent, but, as James observed, 'attention has received hardly any notice from psychologists of the English empirical school. . . . In the pages of such writers as Locke, Hartley, the Mills and Spencer the word hardly occurs.'[73] It re-appeared for a time in the work of psychologists like Ward and Stout, who were in revolt against associationism,[74] but rapidly lost ground as the twentieth century dawned. Although Titchener wrote a book about it in 1909, the concept had evaporated into feelings and tensions with just a dash of sensory clarity.[75] The behaviourists, who were soon to arrive on the scene, totally discarded it together with all the paraphernalia of consciousness. In standard textbooks of the mid-century, such as that by Boring, Langfeld and Weld,[76] it received hardly a mention. Though the problem of attention had arisen in connection with inspection processes in industry in the 1930s,[77] it was the exigencies of war that brought it back urgently in connection with monitoring tasks and the need for vigilance.

The term 'vigilance' was first employed by the neurologist Henry Head to describe the state of the nervous system conducive to speedy and adequate responses.[78] It was adopted by Mackworth, the Cambridge psychologist, in his wartime studies of visual and auditory monitoring, and defined by him as 'a state of readiness to detect and respond to certain specified small changes occurring at random time intervals in the environment'.[79] It led to an active programme of research into problems such as the division of attention, the effects of expectancy and set, of knowledge of results and motivation, and of environmental variables, together with matters such as the influence of speed of information transmission, and rate of recovery after responding to signals. This work continued vigorously after the war, particularly important being the investigations of Broadbent and Cherry on selective listening to speech, which led Broadbent to propose some far-reaching theories on the nature of attention.[80] In both Europe and America it remains a lively area of experimental study, and of periodical symposia.[81] From the 1950s onwards the study of vigilance and attention received strong reinforcement from neuro-physiology. The relations between the brain stem reticular formation and the activation of the electroencephalogram, discovered by Moruzzi and Magoun in 1949,[82] and the work on the orienting reflex by the Russian psychologist Sokolov,[83] have provided a psychological basis for the concepts of vigilance and attention, and made them even more acceptable to 'tough-minded' psychologists.

The problem of vigilance led on naturally to that of decision-making. In tasks involving vigilance the observer had to decide what were and what were not relevant signals. Signals could be contaminated by 'noise', and it was not merely a matter of their being observed and rising above the threshold, but of the observer deciding whether or not a signal was genuine. Eventually this led to the formulation of what was termed 'signal detection theory',[84] which was in turn linked to the wider theory of decision-making. This has brought back into psychology the ancient concepts of decision and choice, concepts first explicitly used by Aristotle, who pointed out that, when confronted by situations marked by uncertainty, we had first to deliberate and weigh the situations up, and then to decide,[85] – a process that was not simply an intellectual one.[86] The matter was discussed at length by the scholastics,[87] but was progressively banished by their empirically minded successors, only occasionally flickering back on to the psychological scene. James, for example, talked about decisions in a non-technical way, and distinguished five types;[88] but once again by mid-century they had vanished from psychology, and decision-making characteristically received no mention in the standard texts of the time.

The high stakes and the complexity of the circumstances involved in modern warfare, however, brought the whole question of decision once more to the fore, not only in connection with signal detection, but within the wider field of operational research.[89] It was soon recognized that decision-making in the face of uncertainty had in fact been treated by mathematicians in connection with gambling, gaming, speculation and business enterprise, and that it had links with the theory of probability, and in particular with the ideas of J. Bernouilli and Bayes in the seventeenth century.[90] A landmark in the resurrection of this earlier work was the appearance in 1947 of von Neumann and Morgenstern's *The Theory of Games and Economic Behavior*. The year 1954 saw its psychological enfranchisement with the publication of articles by Tanner and Swets on signal detection, by Edwards on 'The theory of decision making', and of Savage's book *The Foundation of Statistics*.[91] The theory of decision-making has since become a technical but important branch of mathematical psychology.[92]

Vigilance and decision involved the resurrection and experimental investigation of ancient concepts under the pressure of practical needs. Skill and stress, on the other hand, were psychologically new concepts, of which there is no mention in the psychological literature prior to the twentieth century. Skills began to be studied experimentally in an industrial context in the late 1890s and the 1900s. Bryan and Harter investigated the learning of telegraphic language, Book the acquisition of skill in typewriting, Lahy in France and Viteles in America the problem of driving skills.[93] Skills became an accepted topic within the field of industrial psychology, and an increasing number of books on the subject appeared in the 1930s.[94] In general skill was treated as a special aspect of learning and habit formation. Bryan and Harter, for example, described the expert telegraphist as having acquired a hierarchy of habits, involving overlapping higher units. There is, of course, a learned aspect of skills, but when confronted by the much more complex skills demanded by pilots and others in the Second World War, psychologists were forced to recognize that this was not the whole story. This was first clearly enunciated by F.C. Bartlett in his paper to the Royal Society in 1943 on 'Fatigue following highly skilled work'.[95] He argued that skills were not just repetitive actions, but rather flexible adjustments depending a great deal on central control and precise timing. It was these factors which were upset with the onset of fatigue. Intensive investigations were carried out in Cambridge on pilot error, using a specially designed cockpit invented by K.J.W. Craik, who went on to propose a 'Theory of the human operator in control systems', in which he conceived the operator as an engineering system behaving basically as an intermittent correction servo.[96] The arrival of cybernetics and information theory in the late 1940s lent further support to this line of approach.[97] Researches on skill continued after the war both in Britain and America, and the concept of skill extended from the manual to the mental sphere, so that thinking itself became regarded as a form of skill.[98] Skill, therefore, had evolved into a central concept in psychology, basic to an understanding of human activities and performances of all kinds. Welford in his analysis of the nature of skill referred to reception processes, the role of past experience and learning, central translation processes, the effect side, the serial aspect of skill, feedback, the formation of higher units, and the role of short-term memory.[99] As Broadbent wrote,

> The picture of skilled performance is one of complex interaction between man and environment. Continuously the skilled man must select the correct cues from the environment, taking decisions upon them which may possibly involve prediction of the future, and initiate sequences of responses whose progress is controlled by feed-back, either through the original decision-making mechanism, or through lower order loops.[100]

The study of vigilance, decision-making and skill led quite naturally on to the study of stress. All were high-level performances liable to disruption under adverse conditions, in other words under conditions of stress. Some of the problems connected with stress had been studied round the turn of the century under the heading of 'fatigue'. Laboratory studies by Mosso, Kraepelin and others had quantified declines of performance following continuous work.[101] The matter became of practical importance in the munitions factories of the 1914-1918 war, and investigations into industrial fatigue continued after the war.[102] But the wider concept of stress was not clearly formulated until 1926 when a Prague medical student, H. Selye, introduced it. Later, moving to Canada, Selye has continued to write on the topic for half a century, defining what he termed the 'general adaptation syndrome' as 'the sum of all non-specific reactions of the body, which ensue upon long continued exposure to stress'.[103] These reactions include nervous and endocrine changes taking place in a series of stages and ending in a condition of exhaustion. Stress may be brought about by a large variety of factors, physical, physiological, psychological and social. The problem of stress was brought into prominence by the exacting demands met in the Second World War. Mackworth in his researches on human performance conducted investigations into the effect of various environmental stresses on vigilance tasks.[104] In particular the stresses to which aircrew were subjected were intensively studied. It became clear that the concept of fatigue was insufficient to explain the observed symptoms, and that the disturbances were more widespread and deep-seated.[105] All sorts of factors played a part in causing psychological disorders in flying personnel – anticipation, uncertainty, inactivity, adverse weather, extreme cold, lack of sleep, poor morale, domestic worries and leadership deficiencies, as well as individual differences in temperament.[106] Research on stress has continued actively since the war in many fields, medical, experimental and social. The treatment of stress by pharmacological means has advanced considerably, and older techniques of meditation and relaxation have been revived, often supplemented by newer methods of biofeedback.[107] Experimentation by laboratory psychologists has gone on, particularly notable being Broadbent's work on the effects of stress on decision-making.[108] The topic, too, has become an important one in social psychology, since environmental stresses resulting from crowding, lack of privacy, organizational pressures and so on have been shown to be related to violence, crime and mental breakdown.[109]

General psychology has clearly been enriched in a diversity of ways by its symbiotic interaction with applications. The secondary consequences resulting from the subsequent growth of psychology have been equally marked.

V

Specialization within psychology has perhaps been the most important long-term secondary consequence of the growth in the number of psychologists. This growth, primarily the outcome of the spread of psychology into applied fields, has no doubt been a major, though not the only cause of specialization. Since the beginning of the century the number of psychologists in technically advanced countries has increased dramatically. The British Psychological Society was founded in 1901 with thirteen members. There were just under a hundred members at the close of the First World War. In the 1980s its membership had risen to some 10,000. Similarly in the United States the American Psychological Association, founded in 1892, has grown from a few hundred to over 50,000 members. Quantitatively, if not always qualitatively, the published output of psychologists has correspondingly increased. When Psychological Abstracts was established in 1927 it contained, in the first year of its publication, 2,730 abstracts culled from 267 journals. A quarter of a century later the number of abstracts had risen to 7,297 and the number of journals to 467. Half a century later, in 1977, there were 27,003 abstracts from a list of nearly 700 journals. When confronted with this massive output psychologists had of necessity to select and specialize. Their divergent interests were recognized by the sectionalization of their professional societies. The American Psychological Association was reorganized in 1946, and eighteen divisions established to cater for the various specialisms within psychology. By 1982 the number of divisions had risen to forty-two. In the British Psychological Society medical and educational sections were set up as early as 1919, and by 1983 the Society had formed five divisions and nine sections. Communication between these diverse groups has become increasingly difficult to maintain. Psychologists meet at annual conventions, they still have their common organizations and institutions, and the *Annual Review of Psychology*, founded in 1950, bravely endeavours to cover the whole field of psychology, though even here the sub-fields have increased in the course of the years from eighteen to over sixty. But the fissiparous forces show no signs of diminishing, and as the editorial in the 1970 *Annual Review* observed, 'more and more frequently authors assigned a broad area feel that they can cover only a particular sub-area in it.'[110] Sheer volume of output is, of course, by no means the only barrier keeping specialist groups apart. Each area inevitably becomes technologically and methodologically more complex and sophisticated, requiring longer and longer training for its mastery, and making intercommunication between areas increasingly difficult. In addition to these barriers there is the basic dichotomy between psychologists, mainly applied psychologists, whose interests focus on humanistic problems, such as the relief of stress and maladjustment, and the laboratory psychologists, whose interest is primarily scientific and concerned with elucidating the nature and functioning of mental processes and behaviour.

It is obviously impossible to survey, even in outline, the numerous contemporary specialisms within psychology. As examples two important, but diverse fields may serve to illustrate trends – the fields of visual perception, and child, or developmental, psychology.

The study of visual perception, according to one reviewer, has now grown to such an extent as to become 'an independent discipline in its own right, investigated by specialists in many fields'.[111] Yet vision is man's leading sense, and in the words of the eminent French psychologist Pièron, 'la sensation est le guide de vie'[112] – a sentiment echoed more recently by the American psychologist Geldard, who states in his book, *The Human Senses*, 'The high road to the understanding of human nature is by way of appreciation of man's senses and of the fundamental role they play in the attainment of knowledge and the regulation of behaviour.'[113] The study of visual perception is, therefore, on the one hand, so complex as to have become virtually an independent discipline, while, on the other hand, it is a necessary and integral part of psychology. Empirically minded philosophical psychologists of the seventeenth and eighteenth centuries gave it a prominent place in their systems, and for the early experimentalists it became a central topic of study. One of Wundt's first pieces of work was on sense perception,[114] and in the final edition of his *Grundzüge* visual perception occupies about one-sixth of the whole three-volume work.[115] The problem raised by the growing complexity of the study of vision is not a new one. Boring, in his *Sensation and Perception in the History of Experimental Psychology* (1942) already observed that 'the subject of visual sensation seemed to me so vast and complicated that only a specialist might undertake to assess its discoveries and abstract its history'.[116] Indeed as far back as 1896 the second edition of Helmholtz's *Physiological Optics* contained no fewer than 7,833 titles in its bibliography![117]

One of the difficulties of research into vision is that it is necessarily interdisciplinary, involving physics, physiology and biochemistry as well as psychology, and all these areas have become more complex. The psychologist who devotes himself to the study of vision has not only to have a grasp of increasingly sophisticated psychophysical methodology, but a good understanding of the other relevant disciplines and the dramatic advances resulting from the probing of the activity of single neurons at all levels of the visual system, as well as the biochemical investigations of photosensitive pigments, and the engineering problems of information-gathering systems. The amount of material in all areas related to vision is now immense. Nine of the twenty-four volumes of the massive *Handbook of Sensory Physiology* (1971-78) are devoted to visual processes.[118] Davson's treatise on *The Eye* (1961-74) now runs to six volumes.[119] Yet Marr's recent book *Vision* (1982) not only shows that psychology has a vital contribution to make to the study of vision, but that the study of vision has a vital contribution to make to psychology.[120] Marr has gone far to demonstrate that an elucidation of the retinal and nervous mechanisms and structures involved in vision is insufficient in itself to explain visual phenomena. 'There must exist an additional level of understanding at which the character of the information-processing tasks carried out during perception are analyzed and understood.'[121] In spite of the findings of the neurophysiologists that 'each single neuron can perform a much more complex and subtle task than had previously been thought',[122] there is nevertheless a representative process, taking place in stages and at different levels, which must be studied by psychologists. What Marr has done has been to uncover some of the complexities of visual functioning at the psychological, information-processing level – a striking advance over the interesting, but theoretically more naive, work of the earlier Gestalt school.

To turn to the other chosen example, child or developmental psychology arose about the same time as experimental psychology with the publication of Preyer's *Die Seele des Kindes* in 1882, and was promoted at the end of the century by Hall in America and Sully in England.[123] Largely as a result of its direct relevance to practical problems of child adjustment and education, it has grown enormously since then. In the early 1930s Murchison edited the first comprehensive *Handbook of Child Psychology*.[124] In the second edition of nearly one thousand pages he noted 'the great expansion of the field'.[125] In the 1940s Murchison was replaced by Carmichael's *Manual of Child Psychology* of about equal length.[126] In 1970 it was revised by Mussen, and now ran to two volumes and 2,391 pages; and this again was replaced in 1983 by a new *Handbook of Child Psychology* in four volumes amounting to 3,819 pages, representing a fourfold growth in size in the half century since the publication of Murchison's compendium.[127] As Mussen, Conger and Kagan note in the fifth edition of their standard manual on *Child Development and Personality*,[128] 'research in child development has continued to expand at an impressive rate. Our knowledge in established areas has broadened and deepened, and many new areas of enquiry have emerged,' and it is marked by 'a new level of sophistication and complexity'.[129] Not only has the long series of studies of cognitive development carried out by Piaget over a span of sixty years led to voluminous research and discussion, but there has been mounting concentration on the linguistic development of children and on the processes of socialization.

What has happened in these two cases of vision and of child development is exemplary of what has happened throughout psychology. Psychology has become a cluster of complex specialisms from which new specialisms are constantly budding. But this does not represent the only fissiparous tendency in psychology. There is in addition the ideological fragmentation represented by the various 'schools' of psychology.

VI

There have always been splits and divergencies of viewpoints among psychologists. Even during the Middle Ages an overriding Christian orthodoxy could not entirely prevent disagreements and disputations. The rise of modern science accentuated the cleavage between empiricists and rationalists, materialists and idealists. The fragmentation of psychology into a variety of 'schools' was still further intensified during the first half of the twentieth century following Wundt's claim to have established the subject on an entirely new and scientific basis.

Wundt's system, if it can be called a system, was, as we have seen, riddled with conflicts. Moreover it was never widely accepted as an adequate basis for psychology either in England or in France, and in Germany there was from the start philosophical dissent from men such as Brentano, Dilthey and Nietzsche. In America, in spite of Titchener's attempts, Wundtian psychology never really took root, and the most notable of Wundt's American pupils, Hall, Cattell, Baldwin, Angell and Witmer, drifted off into very un-Wundtian lines of work. So from the beginning the seeds of dissension were present. Some schools of psychology, like the psychoanalytic, had never taken much notice of Wundt, but had simply gone their own way; others positively revolted against the presuppositions and the methods of the Wundtians, and particularly against the narrow travesty of Wundtianism represented in America by Titchener.

There have been several different enumerations of the schools that were a dominant feature of the psychological scene in the first half of the twentieth century. Murchison, who started the listing of schools in his *Psychologies of 1925* and *Psychologies of 1930*, described ten or eleven schools; Woodworth in 1931 gave six; and Heidbredder in 1933 seven.[130] Attempts have been made to rationalize these classifications. Griffiths, for example, recognized two major groupings, the behavioural-functional and the mental-analytic.[131] Wolman opted for three large groups: the behaviouristic, the psychoanalytic and the personalistic-gestalt.[132] Coan has proposed a description of the different schools in terms of basic factors, and listed six bipolar factors, which seem, however, somewhat to overlap.[133] No entirely watertight classification of schools is possible, nor can all individual psychologists be neatly pigeon-holed, but a description in terms of two bipolar factors is perhaps the best working scheme. The first factor then is analytic vs. wholistic, and the second functional-dynamic vs. structuralist-static. This gives four main groupings: (i) structural-analytic, (ii) structural-wholistic, (iii) functional-wholistic, and (iv) functional-analytic. These divergent schools have often been described[134] and a detailed account will not be attempted here. However a survey of the recent past would be incomplete without at least an outline of the fragmentation that prevailed in psychology in the first half of the century.

The structuralist-analytic group took two main forms, the Titchenerian analysis of consciousness and Spearman's factor-analysis. E.B. Titchener (1867-1927), an Englishman, who after an Oxford education studied under Wundt, and then migrated to America and established himself at Cornell, was the dominant figure in the structuralist-analytic type of psychology based on introspection. Boring, one of his pupils, spoke of his 'militant spirit' and 'magnificent personality',[135] but these were not sufficient to gain victory for the pedantically arid psychology he attempted to promote.[136] It was, indeed, as has recently been pointed out, a distorted travesty of Wundtianism.[137] It confined psychology to the study of the generalized, human, adult, normal mind, it scorned applications, it objected to the consideration of function and meaning in the study of mental life, and it insisted that psychology should concern itself in the first instance exclusively with the introspective analysis of conscious states, and with the way that the two basic elements of consciousness, sensation and feeling, combined in a sort of mental chemistry. As Titchener himself put it, 'The primary aim of the experimental psychologist is to analyse the structure of mind and to ravel out the elementary processes from the tangle of consciousness.'[138] All other tasks must wait until this basic job had been accomplished. Such a psychology, it soon became apparent, was a sterile dead end, and by the 1920s it was practically dead. Boring's *The Physical Dimensions of Consciousness* (1933), coming from a former supporter, dealt the final blow.[139]

A much more fruitful type of structuralist-analytic psychology was that of the factor-analytic school deriving from the work of C.E. Spearman (1863-1945). Spearman, like Titchener, was a pupil of Wundt, but he largely abandoned the Wundtian methods for quantitative measures of performance. His aim was to describe the structure of the mind, not in terms of the vaguely defined 'faculties' of the past, but in terms of precisely derived 'factors'.[140] Spearman's own fairly simple 'two-factor' model of a common 'general' factor (g), usually equated with general intelligence, and numerous 'specific' factors (s) has been superseded by more complex models, and factor analysis has subsequently been incorporated as a useful exploratory technique into the general body of psychology. In England it dominated the London school of psychology till the middle of the century, led by Burt after Spearman's retirement, and in the wider field of personality by Eysenck.[141] In America elaborate factorial schemes were proposed by Thurstone, Guilford, W. Stephenson and R. Cattell, the two latter being pupils of Spearman.[142] Spearman himself was by no means exclusively or narrowly a factorist. In addition to his two-factor theory he proposed a set of subsidiary laws, including what he called the law of 'noegenesis' (creative mind), but these were, in fact, little more than descriptive generalizations, and made little impact.[143]

Contemporaneously with these movements in America and England a strong protest against Wundtianism arose in Germany with the group of psychologists that came to be known as the 'Gestalt psychologists'. Their protest was primarily against the analysis of consciousness into elements, but it became equally a protest against the analysis of behaviour in terms of reflexes. The Gestalt school originated, after various premonitory rumbles, in the experiments of Max Wertheimer (1880-1943) on apparent movement (the so-called phi-phenomenon),[144] and led to a good deal of valuable experimental work on the organizational aspects of perception, and the formulation of laws, such as that of figure-ground, closure, '*Pragnanz*' (good form) and so on.[145] The fundamental formula of Gestalt theory, according to Wertheimer, was, 'There are wholes the behaviour of which is not determined by that of their individual elements, but where the part processes are themselves determined by the intrinsic nature of the whole.'[146] The Gestalt approach was extended into areas such as learning, memory and thinking by Köhler, Koffka and Wertheimer himself, and into the field of action, personality and social psychology by Lewin and his followers.[147] The rise of Hitler led to the rapid demise of the Gestalt school in Germany, the migration of its leading figures to America, and its ultimate decline. In spite of the experiments it inspired it was marred by serious theoretical weaknesses. It was too easy to proclaim that organized wholes (*Gestalten*) were the primordial data of experience, which could be explained simply as the immediate outcome of field forces, and it led to the ignoring of most of the complex processes of integration and learning involved in even the simplest experiences or actions. It led, too, to a denial of the importance of evolutionary development in explaining mind and behaviour, and a claim that 'no forces or elementary processes occur in organisms which do not also occur in physics and chemistry'.[148] It also committed itself to an untenable doctrine of 'isomorphism', a precise dynamic parallelism between phenomenal and cerebral organization. The valuable demonstrations of the Gestaltists in the field of perception can be interpreted in other ways.

The various functionally oriented schools of psychology were rooted in Darwinian biology, in the growing interest in animal behaviour, and the desire for a psychology that could be applied to human problems. The functionalist movement took root in America in the 1890s with the work of William James, Dewey and Angell.[149] In America it soon became absorbed in behaviourism. In England it took a rather different form under the leadership of William McDougall (1871-1938), a form commonly termed 'hormic psychology'.[150] Like the Gestaltists, McDougall was opposed to atomistic reductionism, but his inspiration was biological rather than physical, and his emphasis was on drive and function rather than on configurational structures. There was a natural affinity between his system and the psychodynamic schools derived from Freud, though McDougall rejected a number of the specific doctrines and the exclusiveness of the psychoanalysts. But like Freud he maintained that 'what we call personality or character is a highly complex product of a long integrative process, a process which may go wrong and may be largely undone at any stage'.[151] In his stress on personality and character as the ultimate integration through the medium of the self-regarding sentiment, McDougall was wholistic; in his stress on the instinctive springs of all human action and on purposive direction he was functional in his approach to psychology. He was opposed equally to the narrow introspective structuralism of Wundt and his followers and to the mechanistic approach of the behaviourists. Both these schools, he believed, 'in striving to become branches of natural science, conceived necessarily as physical science, have lost touch with human life.'[152] McDougall, who had had wide experience not only as an experimental psychologist but also as an anthropologist and a psychotherapist, was certainly in touch with life. But he was more a prophet than a scientist, and there were inadequate empirical foundations for his theories. His intuitions, however, were not always mistaken, and on a sounder basis, are coming back into favour.[153] But in the 1920s and 1930s hormic psychology, particularly in America, became almost wholly eclipsed by behaviourism.

Behaviourism represented the most extreme protest not only against Wundt, but against all traditional psychology. It inaugurated what has undoubtedly been the most powerful and the most characteristic psychological school, or group of schools, of the twentieth century, at any rate among academic psychologists. It was a thoroughgoing attempt to align psychology wholly with the natural sciences, to deny the validity of introspection, and, in its radical forms, to discard the concept of mind completely. It differed from earlier materialistic attempts, such as that of Hobbes, by providing at least some experimental support for its theories. The behaviourist movement was precipitated by the rise of animal psychology in the closing years of the nineteenth century. Animals could not introspect, and inferences about animal consciousness were clearly precarious, though writers like Margaret Washburn attempted to justify them.[154] There were obvious advantages in adopting Lloyd Morgan's proposal and talking instead about animal 'behaviour'. Neither Lloyd Morgan nor his American follower Thorndike, however, were radical behaviourists, and both continued to use mentalistic terms. It was J.B. Watson (1878-1958) who in 1913 launched the new movement. 'Psychology as the behaviorist views it,' he declared, 'is a purely objective, experimental branch of natural science. Its theoretical goal is the prediction and control of behavior. Introspection forms no essential part of its methods.'[155] All mentalistic terms were, therefore, to be eliminated, and replaced by stimulus-response connections and habit formation. Psychology, Watson maintained, had 'made a false start under Wundt . . . because it did not bury its past.'[156] But far more lumber was to go than mere introspective terminology. 'There is no such thing as an inheritance of capacity, talent, temperament, mental constitution and characteristics. These things depend on training that goes on mainly in the cradle.'[157] And in what is sometimes termed 'muscle-twitch' psychology, thinking was reduced merely to movements of the vocal chords.[158] Watson was neither experimentally very sophisticated nor philosophically very literate, but he was possessed of a missionary zeal, and was attuned to a growing mood of disillusion with the introspective approach. Fortunately for him his cause was soon to be furthered by the far more exacting experimental work of Pavlov.[159] I.P. Pavlov (1849-1936), the Russian physiologist who won a Nobel Prize for his work on gastric secretions, had noted that these secretions could, in the course of an experimental programme, be produced by 'psychic' causes, and decided to investigate these 'psychic secretions' in purely objective ways.[160] Psychological explanations seemed to him to be merely vacuous. This led to over thirty years of experimentation on what he came to term 'conditioned reflexes'. Though he mistakenly believed that conditioning was invariably dependent on the cerebral hemispheres, and though his views on the workings of the brain were largely erroneous, Pavlov achieved results of great importance for psychology. He showed that simple forms of acquired behaviour could be studied objectively and under precise experimental control; he discovered a number of significant facts about the mechanisms involved in behavioural processes such as active inhibition, spontaneous recovery, disinhibition, extinction, generalization, positive and negative induction; and he showed that conditioned reflexes could be used for investigating on objective lines an animal's powers of sensory discrimination, for producing 'experimental neuroses', and for assessing difference in temperamental make-up. In this way the study of one type of behaviour, widely present in the animal kingdom, had been placed on a firm experimental basis. Unfortunately Pavlov went on to generalize his results, to speak loosely of reflexes such as 'the reflex of purpose', and 'the reflex of freedom'[161] and to expand the reflex theory to the functioning of the higher cortical areas and the language system, which he termed 'the second signalling system'.[162] Meanwhile his work had become known in the west. Pavlov himself had lectured on conditioned reflexes at the Charing Cross Medical School in London as early as 1906, and he addressed the International Congress of Physiologists at Gröningen in 1913. Watson, who up to 1915 had made no mention of conditioned reflexes, but merely of habits, wrote on 'The place of conditioned reflexes in psychology' in the following year.[163] But not until the translation of Pavlov's *Conditioned Reflexes* in 1927, and his *Lectures on Conditioned Reflexes* in 1928,[164] did Pavlov's work become adequately available to English-speaking readers. He had a profound effect on the subsequent development of the behaviourist movement, and on the various theories of learning that dominated American psychology for the next quarter of a century. Hull based his behaviour system primarily on Pavlov's work, and Skinner, though he went his own way, was impressed on reading the translation of *Conditioned Reflexes*.

The immense mid-century concentration of interest on the topic of learning which followed the discovery of Pavlov's work focused on the divergent viewpoints expressed in three very different books: E.C. Tolman's *Purposive Behavior in Animals and Man* (1932), B.F. Skinner's *The Behavior of Organisms* (1938), and C.L. Hull's *Principles of Behavior* (1943). The last of these three books made the most immediate, but least permanent, impact. Hull (1884-1952), an engineer by training, took Newton's *Principia* as a model, and endeavoured to construct a deductive theory of behaviour. A theory, he wrote, is 'a systematic deductive derivation of secondary principles of observable phenomena from a relatively small number of primary principles or postulates, much as secondary principles or theories of geometry are ultimately derived . . . from a few original definitions and primary principles called axioms'.[165] Hull's behaviour system ultimately consisted of sixteen postulates and fifteen corollaries.[166] From these some one hundred and eighty theoretical statements were derived, of which, Hull claimed, two-thirds had been experimentally tested with animal subjects, and for the most part validated. In spite of Hull's ingenuity, and the vast amount of experimental work that he inspired, his attempt was premature, if not wholly mistaken. The empirical data of psychology, even within the restricted field of learning, were not ready for formalization along hypothetical-deductive lines; and as Koch was later to show there were, in fact, many logical inconsistencies and weaknesses in Hull's somewhat pretentious formulations.[167]

The purposive behaviourism of E.C. Tolman (1886-1959), which seemed, in contrast to Hull's tight system, much less rigorously scientific, has, as it turned out, stood the test of time rather better. Behaviouristic in its methodology, it was mentalistic in its conclusions, allowing for 'intervening variables deduced from experimental evidence, such as cognitions, expectations, purposes and belief-value matrices.'[168] Nevertheless Tolman shared in the over-optimism of the other early behaviourists, and held the view that the study of the behaviour of rats at a choice point in a maze could serve as the basis of everything important in psychology.[169] Like all the behaviourists Tolman minimized species differences, and seemed to assume that unified laws of behaviour applied throughout the animal kingdom. Rats were easier to control experimentally and more docile than men; therefore, he argued, let's study rats.

The most enduring and fruitful behaviourist system has proved to be that of B.F. Skinner (born 1903). Skinner is a radical behaviourist who totally rejects anything remotely suggesting mentality. Organisms act upon the environment, and respond to the environment, but no mental processes are involved. Behaviour is completely shaped by environmental pressures, which serve as positive or negative reinforcers, and it can therefore be controlled by appropriate reinforcement schedules. Working with rats and pigeons, Skinner has convincingly shown that animals can be trained to do just about anything within the limits imposed by their anatomical make-up. 'Operant conditioning shapes behaviour as a sculptor shapes a lump of clay,' he said.[170] Operant behaviour, unlike respondent behaviour, is 'emitted rather than elicited'[171] (i.e. there is no prior environmental stimulus as in Pavlovian conditioning), but once emitted it can be shaped by contingencies of reinforcement. Thus 'the consequences of behavior may feed back into the organism. When they do so, they may change the probability that the behavior which produced them will occur again.'[172] Skinner holds that it is not necessary to postulate any other underlying change. There is nothing corresponding to storage of information or to memory, no copies of the environment or 'cognitive maps', to use Tolman's term. Nor is any hedonistic satisfaction involved, as was implied in Thorndike's law of effect. An act which has been learned is simply an act which is more likely to be repeated. The environment selects acts which make for survival; survival for Skinner appears as the only criterion. The same force operates in the realm of biology. The role of the environment in behaviour, according to Skinner, is similar to that in natural selection, though on a very different time scale. 'The environment not only prods or lashes, it selects. . . . Behavior is shaped and maintained by its consequences.'[173] The traditional views which held that human beings have minds, that they are to some extent autonomous and responsible, that they make plans, have feelings, and possess talents and character, are all simply erroneous, and the traditional ways of influencing human behaviour by education and punishment equally mistaken. Skinner claims to have seen beyond the mirages of freedom and dignity.[174]

Not surprisingly Skinner rejects almost the whole past history of psychology. His *Science and Human Behavior* (1953) significantly contains no references and no bibliography. He is in the fullest sense of the words an 'original' – a quixotic original, not without a beguiling quality. Within the limits of the rigidly controlled experimental situations and the insulated Skinner boxes with which he works he has undoubtedly produced convincing results, and he has pioneered extremely useful applications to human behaviour in the form of programmed learning and behaviour therapy, a form of therapy now practised on a large scale by psychologists. 'Within behavior modification,' observes one historian of the movement, 'no single conceptual and experimental approach has generated the breadth of applications that operant conditioning has.'[175] There is no doubt, then, of Skinner's lasting importance. Nevertheless a large part of Skinner's psychology is an extrapolation beyond experimental proof. Just because some behaviour under tightly controlled conditions can be shaped and explained on Skinnerian lines, it does not logically follow that all behaviour can be so explained. Skinner's extrapolations to the verbal behaviour of human beings are largely speculative, are backed up by very limited experimental support, and are opposed by most linguists.[176] The extensions of his system to cover human social behaviour, culture, morals, law and religion are simply Utopian,[177] and indeed his romantic fable *Walden Two* demonstrated that there is a naive Utopian streak in Skinner's make-up.[178] But this is not the only unsatisfactory feature of Skinner's psychology. His 'empty organism' doctrine, and his rejection of physiological explanations for behavioural phenomena, can only be regarded as bizarre. 'A science of behavior', he asserts, 'has its own facts. . . . No physiological fact has told us anything about behavior that we did not know already.'[179] When the deficiency of a single chemical element, such as iodine, can profoundly influence the functioning of the organism and change its behaviour radically, the Skinnerian position is obviously untenable and absurd. Indeed the very idea that behaviour is a subject matter in its own right, with its own self-contained orderliness and lawfulness, is certainly a mistaken one, as is Skinner's total rejection of the inner world. There is no adequate explanation by Skinner as to why organisms should 'emit' behaviour at all, and nothing to account for the human capacity to process information at a high level of complexity, evaluate and decide. It is, in short, an intensely limited psychology that he has proposed, however powerful within the strict limits of its validity.

Indeed the most striking feature of all the major schools which flourished in the first half of the twentieth century was their restriction in the scope of psychology. The Titchenerian structuralists concentrated on the introspective analysis of consciousness, the Spearman school on abilities, the Gestaltists on perception, the hormic school on instincts and emotions, and the behaviourists on learning. Within the areas of their concentration they all produced results of value, but in attempting to extrapolate their findings to other areas and build up exclusive systems they went astray. There was too often an emphasis on particular methodological approaches, and a denial of the value of alternative methods. None of the schools really came to terms with the richness, diversity and complexity of psychological phenomena. Underlying these differences in content and methodology were philosophical differences. The structuralists tended to be Lockean empiricists and the Gestaltists phenomenologists, while the behaviourists soon came under the dominant influence of the Vienna school of logical positivism which flourished in the second quarter of the century. In the form of 'operationism', the theory that any concept to be scientific must be tied down to specific operations, either observational or mathematical, logical positivism enjoyed increasing popularity, particularly among the behaviourist fraternities, who agreed with Carnap's basic thesis that 'every sentence of psychology may be formulated in physical language'.[180] It was a proclamation that subjectivism must be totally expelled from psychology. What, however, the fragmentation of psychology into schools had clearly demonstrated was that, in spite of the strident declarations by psychologists of their rejection of their philosophical parentage, the ancestral bonds had not in fact been severed. After the decline of the schools in the 1950s the basic philosophical differences between psychologists, their contradictory 'models of man', still persisted.[181]

VII

In response to the fragmentation of their subject into specialisms and schools, psychologists who were neither dedicated adherents to a particular viewpoint nor specialists totally immersed in their speciality divided into three loose groupings. The first group resignedly accepted the diversity of psychology, and opted for an eclectic 'middle of the road' position, some hoping for an ultimate *rapprochement*, others abandoning any hope of a unified psychology. A second group proposed a methodological rather than a substantive unity, while a third looked to an underlying theoretical unity beyond the fragmentations and specializations.

It was Woodworth who, in his *Contemporary Schools of Psychology*, first used the phrase 'the middle of the road'.[182] He pointed out that 'only a minority of psychologists had become adherents of any of the schools',[183] and that the majority were prepared to accept the positive findings from them all, while discounting their negative pronouncements. This was the general solution adopted by the writers of textbooks, at any rate American textbooks, which were unashamedly eclectic and rarely adopted any overall systematic position.[184] Some psychologists piously hoped for an ultimate *rapprochement* between the factions,[185] some even maintained that already in the 1930s 'rapprochements are becoming visible'.[186] Others, however, were less optimistic. Beloff, for instance, stated that 'as soon as one attempts to say what psychology is about, it becomes clear one is dealing not with a single unified science, but with a collection of more or less loosely affiliated disciplines each with its own peculiar concepts and laws, its own methods and techniques'.[187] Koch, reviewing the state of psychology in mid-century, saw a 'rich and disorderly matrix', a state of 'contentual and methodological pluralism', and maintained that there was 'no question of tongues blending into a single narrative'.[188] His collaborators reviewed thirty-four 'systematic formulations' of substantial influence in mid-century psychology. In effect this group, when confronted with the diversity within psychology, either tacitly or overtly abandoned the idea of any overall unity.

The attempt to unify psychology on a methodological basis, characteristic of behaviourism, was typified by Egon Brunswik (1903-1955), an Austrian psychologist who moved to the United States and worked with Tolman. Brunswik was influenced by the Vienna school of logical positivism and the theories of the philosophers Neurath and Carnap as to the basic methodological unity of all the sciences. He contributed to Neurath's *International Encyclopedia of Unified Science* a volume on *The Conceptual Framework of Psychology*.[189] He argued for a distinctive discipline of psychology within the broad unitary framework of science in general aimed at studying the molar features of behaviour along probabilistic lines. The nature of the subject matter of psychology made a strictly nomothetic approach inappropriate. Instead, he maintained, 'we must propose the statistical approach as an ultimate norm for psychology as a whole.'[190] Within this probabilistic framework the job of the psychologist was to establish the statistical regularities of behaviour. Brunswik envisaged his 'probabilistic func-tionalism' as reconciling the viewpoints of the various psychological schools. But it still left him open to the charge levelled by Zener, that the term 'behaviour' itself only possessed a spurious unity.[191] Moreover by emphasizing methodology it tended to restrict psychology to those problems that could be fitted within a rather narrowly conceived methodological straitjacket, and had, as Koch pointed out, 'a long-term restrictive impact on problem selection'.[192]

The third group of psychologists, a small band, were not discouraged by the baffling diversity of psychology, and looked for a unitary theoretical framework, some for at least a partial framework, a few, bolder and perhaps more visionary, for an all-embracing 'synoptic view'. Razran may be taken as an example of the first sub-group, Stern of the second.

Gregory Razran (born 1901), whose *Mind in Evolution* was published in 1971, but who had worked for forty years on conditioning and learning, was for a number of reasons an exceptionally interesting figure. He possessed a first-rate knowledge of Russian and Russian psychology, matched by only a very few other Western psychologists; he made the doctrine of evolution central to his thought, observing that American psychology in particular had lost almost all commerce with evolution as a result of the combined influences of neo-behaviourism and Gestalt psychology;[193] and insisting that 'the man-ape divide is very special',[194] he observed that 'time-based biography rather than space-bonded contemporaneity is the domicile of man's mind'.[195] These are all important preliminaries to the unification of psychological theory. Confining himself to learning and cognitive functioning, and in this sense, as he admitted in the final pages of his book[196] proposing only a partial system, Razran proposed a scheme of eleven developmental levels, covering all stages of mental evolution from the simplest organisms to man. These eleven levels could be ordered in four 'super-levels': (i) primitive non-associative learning (habituation and sensitization); (ii) simple associative learning or conditioning (aversive inhibitory conditioning, classical conditioning and operant conditioning); (iii) configural learning (perceptual learning, relational learning and the apprehension of objects); and (iv) symboling (concept formation, planning and willing). A vast amount of experimental work, both Russian and western, was described in support of this scheme, and its theoretical and practical implications were discussed. It is a scheme which transcends, and goes far to reconcile at least some of the divergent 'schools'.

Even more ambitious and comprehensive was the personalistic psychology of William Stern (1871-1938).[197] In the preface to his final work, *General Psychology from the Personalistic Standpoint*, Stern proclaimed the need for a 'synoptic view' of the whole field of psychology:

> No science can progress without projecting from time to time a total picture of its field, including methods and data, points of view and theories. Present day psychology urgently requires a synoptic view of this sort, considering the chaotic outcome of specialization and divergence in the psychological work of a generation. We have had many distinctive psychologies: elementaristic psychology and Gestalt psychology, *verstenhende* psychology, and analyzing psychology; topological and operationistic psychology, purposive and mechanistic psychology; psychologies of the unconscious, of consciousness, of behaviour, etc. – but no inclusive general psychology. It is the function of the present book to give a new foundation of the general psychology of the human individual.[198]

Stern was well qualified, perhaps better qualified than any other psychologist of his time, for accomplishing this task. Born and brought up in Berlin, he graduated from the university under Ebbinghaus and Stumpf. His early work was experimental and connected with the perception of change.[199] In connection with this work he devised his '*Tonvariator*' for investigating changes in auditory perception, a piece of apparatus widely used in psychological laboratories prior to the introduction of electronic equipment. From 1897 to 1916 he taught in Breslau, then part of Germany, and from 1916 to 1933 at the new University of Hamburg.[200] He was immensely productive, and his investigations covered many areas of psychology – the psychology of individual differences, the psychology of testimony, child study, and applied psychology.[201] In the course of his work on differential psychology he proposed the IQ index; he was the first director of the Institut für angewandte Psychologie (applied psychology) in Berlin, a founder of the *Zeitschrift für angewandte Psychologie*, and when he moved to Hamburg he founded and directed the Hamburg Institute. His treatise on children's language development (*Die Kindersprache*) became a classic; and he produced a large philosophical work in three volumes, *Person und Sache*.[202] In 1933 Stern, being a Jew, was forced to leave Germany, and after a brief sojourn in Holland migrated to America, where he spent the final years of his life at Duke University. In America he made few converts to his personalistic system. It was then the heyday of the behaviourist movement; American psychologists shied away from anything that smacked of metaphysics, and there was a smack of the metaphysical and Germanic in Stern's personalism. The only notable American psychologist to recognize the significance of Stern's work was Gordon Allport.[203] After the war his name was hardly ever mentioned except in connection with the Intelligence Quotient, and occasionally the '*Aussage*' experiment. Yet looking back his most inspiring achievement, and certainly the one he himself would have valued most, was his 'synoptic view', his personalistic psychology.

Stern fully accepted the importance of the findings and procedures of 'exact' psychology: his aim was to place them in context in a sound theoretical framework, which also recognized the valuable features contained in the naive, artistic and philosophical psychologies of the past. Two main requirements had to be met if this aim was to be realized: firstly, the method of interpretation must be personalistic, and embrace both the naturalistic and the cultural aspects of the person, and secondly, it must be 'polysymptomatic', that is capable of dealing with every variety and level of psychological data.[204]

The core of Stern's psychology lay in his concept of the 'person-world' relation and it was this relationship that, according to him, provided the basic plan of all mental functioning. His definition of 'person' ran as follows: 'The person is a living whole, individual, unique, striving towards goals, self-contained and yet open to the world around him: he is capable of having experience.'[205] In the person-world relation there were two directions of activity: 'the one is centripetal (world-person), the other is centrifugal (person-world). In the first case the person is receptive and responsive in entering the world, in the second he is seeking and giving.'[206] And then Stern continues,

These principles put into the shade the impoverished 'reaction' theories, which view all that transpires in the person, even mental activity, solely as processes of response to environmental stimuli. While such a conception may be efficacious to a considerable extent in zoology (although even here it is insufficient by itself) it is at all events wholly inadequate for human beings. Those specifically human modes of living that are accompanied in large measure by experience are certainly never consummated through mere responses; under them, on the contrary, the person has in his own right a determinative effect upon the world; his relations with the world are extended and multiplied by reason of his spontaneous activities. The world is the point of attack, the raw material for these spontaneous actions, though it also proceeds to offer resistance, and to set limits, so that spontaneous action is integrated with reaction, and is thereby made specific. The sovereignty of pure creativity is quite as impracticable a principle as passive acquiescence to the world; in reality there is simply endless oscillation between spontaneity and reactivity. The personal world is at all times both the destiny and the product of the person.[207]

Within the person-world relationship Stern recognized a hierarchy of levels which he called 'modalities'. He distinguished three main levels which he set out in the following table:

Modalities of Life

	Person	World
I	Vitality	Biosphere
II	Experience	World of objects
	(*Erleben*)	
III	Introception	World of values[208]

Introception was defined as the coalescence of the world of objective values with the substance of the person. Stern insisted that at the human level values must be given a place in psychology, though their full treatment was a matter for philosophy. Stern's recognition of the hierarchical principle of levels, and of what the philosopher Popper has called 'the third world', which must be actively assimilated and re-created in each individual, constitutes a central feature of his psychology, and one of its main merits.[209] It contains, however, many other valuable elements, such as its acceptance of the concept of dispositions as lasting structural aspects of personality, its recognition of the central significance of the time dimension in the person-world relation, its principle of '*unitas multiplex*', of diversity within the unity of the person, as well as its detailed treatment not only of sense-perception, memory, thought and imagination, but of striving, action, attention, willing and feeling, all within the framework of the person-world relationship. Stern managed to combine in a remarkable way descriptive richness and theoretical strength and unity.

A good deal of water has flowed under the bridges since 1935 when the *Allgemeine Psychologie* was published in German – advances in the understanding of the neurophysiological and biochemical bases of behaviour, and the great deal of work on sensory and perceptual processes, memory, learning, operational conditioning, skills, vigilance, developmental psychology, ethology, language acquisition and development, together with new concepts connected with cybernetics and information-processing, and the rise of computers and computer models. In matters of detail Stern's *General Psychology* is dated, in much the same way as James's *Principles* are dated. There is little doubt, however, that Stern would have welcomed these newer developments. He was an extremely open-minded psychologist who never hesitated to incorporate the latest findings into his system. The synoptic scheme he proposed is broad and flexible enough to assimilate the advances of the last half century; it recognizes the natural psychosomatic unity of the individual person, the *'unitas multiplex'* that demands both synthesis and analysis; and it possesses a special contemporary importance in so far as it is one of the most thoroughly worked out attempts to reconcile and transcend the philosophical dichotomy which since the demise of the schools still troubles psychology. It is to this dichotomy, and to some of the recent philosophical critiques of psychology, to which we must now turn our attention.

Chapter 13
Philosophical critiques

I

Up to the year 1879 psychology, in spite of the scientific trimmings which it had begun to acquire, was still regarded basically as a branch of philosophy, and, in the English-speaking world at least, the reverse proposition, that philosophy was dependent on psychological foundations, was equally generally held. The journal *Mind*, which first appeared in 1876, and which claimed to be 'the first English journal devoted to psychology and philosophy',[1] though it referred to the 'need to procure a discussion as to the scientific standing of psychology', nevertheless maintained that the subjects were inextricably linked, and that psychology could never be fully assimilated to the natural sciences.

Only three years later, in 1879, Wundt institutionalized psychology's independence, and in the same year the philosopher Frege produced the first system of formal logic, insisting that logic was not to be 'infected with psychology', as it often had been.[2] The denunciation of 'psychologism', the confusion of philosophical and psychological questions, by Bradley in England, for example, and Husserl in Germany,[3] became standard among philosophers of most schools. It seemed that not only did psychologists want to be free of psychology, but philosophers reciprocally to be free of psychology. So when the *British Journal of Psychology* was established in 1904, the editors, Ward and Rivers, no longer fudged the issue, and stated in their editorial, 'Psychology which till recently was known among us chiefly as Mental Philosophy, and was mainly concerned with problems of a more or less speculative and transcendental character, has now at length attained the position of a positive science.'[4] In Germany, though Wundt himself remained ambivalent, his pupils were not. For instance, Ziehen, writing in 1895, proclaimed,

> The psychology which I shall present to you is not that old psychology which sought to investigate psychical phenomena in a more or less speculative way. That psychology has been abandoned by those whose method of thought is that of the natural sciences, and empirical psychology has justly taken its place.[5]

During the first half of the twentieth century the majority of psychologists would have assented to this pronouncement. Why then, we must ask, in the second half, have the margins between psychology and philosophy again become blurred? Why has psychology become increasingly infected with philosophical doubts? Why has there emerged a reinvigorated philosophy of mind?

Three main reasons may perhaps be singled out for this development. Firstly, there have been, since 1900, enormous changes in the scientific background, which neither psychology nor philosophy could ignore; secondly, as the twentieth century has run its course, both the pretensions and the philosophical naivety of psychologists have tended to increase, making them increasingly vulnerable to philosophical critiques; and thirdly, revolutionary new movements in philosophy could not avoid reactivating the philosophy of mind in ways directly relevant to psychology. We must, therefore, examine these three factors.

Psychology hitched itself to the scientific wagon at a time when science seemed established on solid and permanent foundations. Newtonian physics still prevailed, and developments in technology derived from science – telecommunications, electric power, internal combustion engines, industrial chemistry, the conquest of the air, to mention just a few – were naturally regarded as a confirmation of the claims of science. By 1900 this impressive edifice rather suddenly began to crack, initiating a second scientific revolution, perhaps even more momentous than that of the sixteenth century. In the words of a theoretical physicist, 'With an impeccable sense of timing the first major crack in the edifice of classical physics became apparent in 1900. Its discoverers were the English theoretical physicists, Rayleigh and Jeans. They were concerned with black box radiation.'[6] Their observations stimulated Planck to propose his quantum doctrine, 'arguably the great cultural achievement of our century'.[7] A few years later, in 1905, Einstein formulated his theory of special relativity, and in 1911 Rutherford discovered that atoms were not the ultimate particles of which matter was composed, and 'the nuclear atom dealt the coup de grâce to classical physics.'[8] The new world of subatomic particles which followed – the world of baryons, mesons, leptons and quarks, of matter and anti-matter, of 'spin', 'strangeness' and 'charm' – was significantly unlike the world of everyday experience.[9] Quite different principles were needed to explain it, while the shift from atoms to quarks involved a change of scale of at least ten million times. Equally amazing was the vastness of the cosmos revealed by twentieth century astronomers. In 1922 Spencer Jones, later to become Astronomer Royal, estimated the diameter of the universe to be perhaps 300,000 light years, and the spiral nebulae, he thought, were probably about 25,000 light years away.[10] The present estimate of the scale of the visible universe is at least 600 million light years, and within this immense space the number of galaxies has been estimated at ten billion, and the number of stars in each galaxy approaching a hundred billion.[11] The physics which served as a model for late nineteenth century psychology has been almost totally transformed.

Yet psychologists, up to at least the middle of the present century, continued slavishly to adhere to it. The human mind is, of course, adapted primarily to dealing with a middle-scale world, and for practical purposes the psychologist must consider its adjustment to this world. But the middle-scale world has now almost vanished between the infinitely small and the infinitely large. Within it no stable basis for theory remains, and beyond it common-sense generalizations no longer apply. No wonder that psychological theory and psychological methodology needed re-thinking; no wonder that philosophy began to intrude again! There has indeed been what the theologian Tillich termed a 'shaking of the foundations'.[12] Together with profound social, artistic and cultural changes it has inevitably affected the whole intellectual cosmos.

Psychologists, particularly the new breed of twentieth century academic psychologists, were remarkably slow to respond to these challenges. Many of them were more interested in experimentation on rats and other animals, where old-fashioned methodology could be applied, than in considering the difficult problems of human psychology. They ignored, or brushed aside, the criticisms philosophers were making, and indeed had been making since the early days of experimental psychology. Even in the 1880s the German philosopher Dilthey had maintained that psychology had taken a wrong road in claiming to be a natural science; it was rather a 'Geisteswissenschaft' (human study) allied to history, and based on an 'understanding' and interpretation of expressions. 'What man is, he learns not by rummaging about in himself, nor yet by psychological experiments, but by means of history.'[13] Nearly a century after Dilthey wrote these words, they are still not without their influence, and interest in Dilthey's 'hermeneutics' has markedly increased. Dilthey, however, was not alone in his attacks. In France, Bergson, in his Essai sur les données immédiates de la conscience (1888), criticized the analytic procedures of psychologists, maintaining that the temporal flux of inner experience could not be dissected in the manner of spatial entities. He advocated instead reliance on 'intuition', which he regarded as 'a kind of intellectual ascultation, to feel the throbbings of the soul'. Such 'intuition', he believed, 'attains the absolute'.[14] Not surprisingly psychologists, excited by their new laboratories and scientific methodology, were not impressed by these critiques. Philosophers, however, continued to snipe. Collingwood, in Oxford, went so far as to describe psychology, the whole of psychology, as 'the fashionable scientific fraud of the age';[15] Wittgenstein, more temperately, simply convicted it of 'conceptual confusion'.[16] Until the 1950s psychologists just ignored these criticisms. However, psychology was becoming increasingly vulnerable to philosophical objections. The early generations of scientific psychologists usually had some training in philosophy. Philosophy and psychology were often taught together in universities, and there remained for some time a sprinkling of psychologists competent in both subjects. By the middle of the century this had become much rarer, and the majority of psychologists had become philosophically distinctly naive. At the same time their pretensions had increased. Not content with experimental work on topics such as perception, memory, learning and reaction times, they began to study experimentally such complex areas as thinking, motivation and personality, which Wundt had discreetly bypassed. It was not difficult for philosophers trained in logic and analysis to pick out confusions, in the way, for example, that Peters exposed the muddles underlying the much-used psychological concept of 'drive'.[17] These critiques were fortified by the revived philosophy of mind following the appearance of Ryle's *The Concept of Mind* in 1949 and Wittgenstein's *Philosophical Investigations* in 1953. In 1957 publication commenced of a series of 'Studies in Philosophical Psychology' in Great Britain,[18] and in 1963 the American Psychological Association created a Division of Philosophical Psychology (Division 24). By the 1960s psychologists could no longer ignore philosophical critiques: the philosophy of mind had by then become a thriving branch of philosophy.

It was, of course, primarily the revolutionary new growths in philosophy during the present century that nourished this psychological offshoot. By the end of the previous century philosophy appeared to have lost its impetus, and to have lapsed into satisfaction with refurbishing old doctrines in the form of neo-idealism, neo-Kantianism and neo-materialism. The one philosophic voice to shatter the calm was that of Nietzsche (1844-1900). Nietzsche was in many ways the precursor, the philosophic John the Baptist, of the new age. The French philosopher Foucault held that Nietzsche marked the threshold beyond which contemporary philosophy could begin thinking again. For Nietzsche, in effect, questioned the whole tradition of western philosophy, the concepts of truth and of morals, as well as the religious flavour with which it was often infected. His thinking was aphoristic rather than logical, his philosophy symptomatic of the dawning crisis in European culture, rather than intellectually convincing. But his astringent debunking of accepted value systems certainly cleared the air, and forced philosophers to meet his challenges. 'Nietzsche's importance', wrote the psychiatrist-philosopher Jaspers, 'lies in his loosening function. His exciting force, which leads the human being to the authentic problems and to himself, does not instruct the reader, but awakens him.'[19] Indeed he awakened both philosophers and psychologists, and it is noteworthy that Freud held that Nietzsche 'had a more penetrating knowledge of himself than any other man who ever lived or was ever likely to live'.[20]

In the face of Nietzsche's demand for a 'revaluation of all values' philosophers had to search for some basis of certainty, and they did this along two divergent roads, firstly by way of logic and linguistic analysis, and secondly by a direct recourse to immediate experience. Eventually both these movements were to have an influence on psychology, and their divergent prescriptions must be regarded as a root cause of the opposing 'models of man' that prevail among contemporary psychologists. Both philosophical schools, moreover, have contributed to the revived philosophy of mind. It would be inappropriate to give more than a brief, and inevitably inadequate, outline of these philosophical developments in a survey of this nature, but as important trends in psychology during the past half-century have been shaped by them, a cursory account, at least, is necessary.

II

The first group of philosophers may broadly be regarded as empiricists and reductionists. They looked to formal logic, scientific methodology and linguistic analysis for the foundations of certainty, or at least for the greatest attainable degree of probability, because they tended to insist on the necessary limitations both in the scope and the conclusiveness of empirical knowledge. On the one hand there were the rigorous formal-analytic features of logic, on the other the more provisional empirical-synthetic characteristics of factual knowledge. It was the development of formal logic that demarcated these philosophers from the older empirical schools. Logic in the nineteenth century witnessed a remarkable resurrection. The foundations of symbolic logic, which had been foreshadowed by Leibniz, were laid down by Boole, de Morgan and Peirce, and the construction of formal deductive systems by Frege and Peano, before Russell and Whitehead in *Principia Mathematica* (1910-13) propounded a complete axiomatic system for both logic and mathematics, which they treated as basically identical.[21] Here assuredly was something that possessed both clarity and certainty, though twenty years later Gödel was to cast doubt on its finality. But how was formal logic to be related to empirical knowledge? This was the question which the Vienna school of logical positivists, which congregated around Schlick in 1922, attempted to answer, by blending the positivist philosophy of Mach with the logic of Russell and Whitehead.[22] Sharply demarcating the tautological and essentially formal statements of logic from the meaningful statements of scientific discourse, they maintained that the validity of the latter was determined by the method of their verification based on observation or 'protocol' statements. Anything that could not be so verified was nonsense, or merely meaningless emotional expression. There were a number of important corollaries to these contentions. Clearly the 'protocol' statements, and the concepts which they contained, must themselves be testable. This meant that they must refer to physical events which could be publicly observed or repeated, and precisely defined in operational terms. Vague concepts based on unspecified operations, or on no operations at all, were scientifically indefensible. The implication of this principle was clearly that statements reporting private or inner experiences were unacceptable unless they could be translated into physical language and be operationally defined. This necessarily involved a careful analysis of the meaning of terms and led to a stress on the importance of linguistic analysis. As a leading member of the Vienna group put it, 'Philosophy is to be replaced by the logic of science – that is to say by the logical analysis of the concepts and sentences of the sciences, for the logic of science is nothing other than the logical syntax of the language of science.'[23] Such linguistic analysis became one of the main tools of the philosophers of mind from the 1950s onwards. Two further corollaries followed from the logical positivist position: firstly, as logic demanded formal systems, all sciences, as well as being validated by observation statements, had to be logically coherent, and this implied hypothetico-deductive methodologies; secondly, the methodology of science was mandatory for all empirical enquiries, and hence all sciences were essentially one. If there was to be a science of psychology at all, it could only be expressed in behaviouristic terms. *The International Encyclopedia of Unified Science*, which was published in America after several of the leading logical positivists had migrated there to escape the Nazis, was an important outcome of the belief in the unity of all the sciences, and contained several monographs of direct relevance to psychology.[24]

From the 1930s onwards logical positivism had a profound impact on psychology, particularly in America. The behaviourists naturally regarded it as a powerful ally, and all the principal behaviourists of the second generation, including Tolman, Hull and Skinner, acknowledged allegiance to it, Tolman and Skinner to operational definitions, and Hull to hypothetico-deductive systematization. In his article on 'Psychology and the science of science'[25] the psychophysicist S.S. Stevens wrote in 1939, 'Science seeks to generate confirmable propositions by fitting a formal system of symbols (language, mathematics, logic) to empirical observations: the propositions of science have empirical significance when their truth can be demonstrated by a set of concrete operations.'[26] This was the creed of a generation of behaviouristic psychologists, and it was marked by an adherence to 'operationism' and to hypothetico-deductive methodology, by faith in quantification and as a result an examination of problems of measurement in psychology, and more generally by an emphasis on methodological rigour.

The creed of 'operationism' was formally enunciated by the Harvard mathematician P.W. Bridgman in his *Logic of Modern Physics* (1927). He went even further than the Vienna positivists in maintaining that concepts must actually be defined, not in terms of their properties, but in terms of the operations by which they were made known. In his own words, 'the concept is synonymous with the corresponding set of operations.'[27] When the operations differ, as for instance when time is measured by different techniques, the concepts of time so arrived at also differ. Applied to psychology this meant, for example, that intelligence measured by different kinds of test was not the same intelligence. For a time operationism had a considerable vogue in psychology. Stevens, in the article already quoted, supported it, as did C.C. Pratt in an influential book, *The Logic of Modern Psychology* (1939). And in 1945 Skinner asserted that behaviourism was 'nothing more than a thoroughgoing operational analysis of traditional mental-istic concepts'.[28] There were, however, many objections to operationism as a necessary method of defining concepts.[29] It had some value in curbing the tendency of some psychologists to indulge in empty verbiage, but taken literally it unduly restricted speculation, and speculation is one of the essential ingredients of scientific activity. It is not so much how concepts are generated and defined as how they are validated that matters, and the two processes are not necessarily the same.

The recognition of the part played by hypotheses in science, though not a novel one, was strengthened by the appearance of Popper's *Logik der Forschung* in 1934. 'A scientist', wrote Popper, 'whether theorist or experimenter, puts forward statements, or systems of statements, and tests them step by step. In the field of the empirical sciences, more particularly, he constructs hypotheses, or systems of theories, and tests them against experience by observation and experiment.'[30] Popper, though a Viennese by birth and acquainted with several members of the Vienna Circle, was never himself one of the group. His views on the role of hypotheses were not, however, incompatible with the positivists' position. They agreed, moreover, on the importance of verifiability, or, as Popper preferred, falsifiability. It was not long before psychologists began to recognize the importance of hypothetico-deductive thinking. Not many went as far as Hull in proposing comprehensive systems. Rather they tended to agree with Pratt, who held that 'at the present time numerous small hypotheses in the various fields of psychological enquiry are probably more profitable than any attempt to work out large theories intended to cover everything'.[31] Hypothesis testing soon became the accepted creed of experimentally minded psychologists, and Eysenck in 1952 gave expression to it when he affirmed that

what is needed in psychology, as in any other science, is greater understanding of and more extensive use of, the hypothetico-deductive method, in which a clear, unambiguous hypothesis is stated, deductions, preferably of a quantitative kind, are made, and experiments performed to verify or disprove the hypothesis.[32]

The correlative of hypothesis-formation was hypothesis-testing, and as psychological data were often complex, this inevitably raised problems of measurement, probability and statistics. From the time of Fechner onwards statistics had become an essential feature of experimental psychology. The renewed interest in methodology arising from the impact of logical positivism led to a searching analysis of the nature of psychological measurement and experimental design in psychology. The statistical work of R.A. Fisher, originally directed at biologists, was taken up by psychologists, and his doctrine of the 'null hypothesis' became gospel. 'Every experiment', wrote Fisher, 'may be said to exist only in order to give the facts a chance of disproving the null hypothesis'[33] (i.e. the hypothesis that the measures obtained from two samples treated differently, do not differ in fact, or only differ by an amount small enough to be the result of chance, the result of the experiment, therefore, being non-significant). Particularly influential on the topic of measurement in general was the chapter by Stevens, which opened his *Handbook of Experimental Psychology* in 1951.[34] Since then elaborations in measuring techniques and discussions on the nature of measurement have proliferated.

In fact, the one permanent result of the logical positivist movement has been the steady concern of psychologists with questions of methodology. Most issues of the *Annual Review of Psychology* in recent years have contained two or three chapters on research methodology, each reviewing a hundred or more bibliographical listings. This is obviously an important development, since psychology's claim to scientific status must rest on its adherence to scientific methodology. But there is an underlying assumption in a great deal of this work, the assumption namely of the unity of science, as proposed by the Vienna school. This necessarily implies a physicalist model of the mind, such as that powerfully argued by Feigl, a former member of the Vienna group.[35] This model denies psychology any special sort of content. It is this model that has increasingly come under challenge. As Koch pointed out some twenty years ago, 'perhaps the most decisive indictment of [this] position is its long-term restrictive impact on problem selection . . . and problem treatment.'[36] What, in fact, had happened was that psychologists, under the influence of logical positivism, elevated consideration for method above consideration for content. By contrast the opposing philosophical school, as we shall see, elevated content above method. They pointed to several significant areas of psychology, which had been pushed out by the naturalistally minded; but their methodology, if it existed at all, was at least questionable. It is their viewpoint which must now be examined.

III

Today this rival philosophical school is commonly referred to as the phenomenological-existentialist. It is necessary to plunge briefly into the often murky and turgid waters of this stream of philosophy for two reasons: firstly, because its fountainhead is a very distant one, going back to St Augustine and beyond, and not only does it have links with certain kinds of idealism, but affinities to mystical traditions and various eastern philosophies; and secondly, because it is, together with Marxism and neo-Marxism, a main source of the turbulence which has surfaced in psychology during recent years. The revival of this ancient tradition in the nineteenth century is generally attributed to the strange figure of the Danish religious thinker Kierkegaard (1813-1855). Kierkegaard was slow to influence the intellectual life of the west, partly because he wrote in Danish, and partly because he was in many ways an oddity, who stood outside the main movements of the time. Not until the 1930s and 1940s did English translations of his works begin to appear, and his importance become appreciated.[37] He has recently been described more than once as the greatest Christian psychologist. The core of Kierkegaard's standpoint was his emphasis on the primacy of lived experience – 'existence', as he termed it – which was more authoritative than all the abstractions of the philosophers. Neither rational speculation in the manner of the Hegelians nor natural science could give us the answers we wanted; these could come only from self-knowledge attained through the inward realization of each individual's potential. Such realization depended on choice, and the basic tenet of Kierkegaard was man's freedom to choose when confronted with the 'Either-Or'.[38] Man must choose, must move forward from lower stages of sensual life to the moral and spiritual orders, and this involved 'qualitative leaps'. Because of the enormous responsibilities involved in these crucial decisions mankind is plagued with anxiety, or dread – existential anxiety. Such anxiety Kierkegaard described as 'the dizziness of freedom', and it had a positive side, 'a serving spirit, tormenting everything finite and petty away'.[39] In the twentieth century these ideas of Kierkegaard not only began to make an impact on psychology and psychiatry, but began to link up with another philosophical movement, the phenomenological.

Although the main source of phenomenology was the German philosopher Husserl, it is generally agreed that Husserl's teacher Brentano was responsible for reviving perhaps its central concept of 'intentionality'. Brentano (1838-1911) was a Catholic priest who later became a professor of philosophy, first in Würzburg and then in Vienna, where Freud as well as Husserl attended his lectures. His first book was on the psychology of Aristotle, but the work by which he is remembered is his *Psychology from an Empirical Standpoint* (1874).[40] In this book Brentano did not completely move to the phenomenological position, because he still regarded psychology as 'the crowning pinnacle' of knowledge, and the phenomenologists came to reject this 'psychologism'. But he did centre his system on 'phenomena revealed by inner perception',[41] and he did clearly distinguish such inner perception from introspection as commonly understood. For he held that there was an essential difference between inner and outer perception, because the physical and the mental worlds were totally distinct. They represented 'two great classes of phenomena'[42] – on the one hand 'that which is presented', and on the other 'the act of presentation'. And then Brentano went on, 'Every mental phenomenon is characterised by what the Scholastics of the Middle Ages called the intentional (or mental) inexistence of an object . . . reference to a content, direction towards an object . . . or immanent objectivity.'[43] No physical phenomenon exhibits anything similar to this property of 'intentionality', this duality of act and content. Brentano's doctrine of 'intentionality' provoked much discussion among philosophers regarding the status of the objects of mental acts, but it unquestionably pointed to an essential characteristic of mind, which associationist psychologies had almost completely overlooked, and it has become a central topic not only in phenomenology but also in the philosophies of mind which have followed.

Phenomenology proper begins with Husserl (1859-1938), one of the most influential of twentieth century philosophers on the continent of Europe. For those brought up in Anglo-Saxon traditions he is not an easy philosopher to understand, or to come to terms with, as he is deeply imbued with the rationalism of continental thought, and writes, moreover, in a 'forbidding style'.[44] Husserl was a Moravian Jew by birth, but was later baptised as a Lutheran. He had a broad scientific and philosophical education, studying mathematics, physics, astronomy, philosophy and psychology at the Universities of Leipzig, Berlin and Vienna. It was Brentano who converted him to philosophy. His psychological teacher was Stumpf of Berlin, a keen admirer of Brentano's 'act' psychology.[45] At the age of twenty-eight he was appointed professor of philosophy at Halle, moving on to Göttingen and Freiburg, where he was eventually stripped of his professorship by the Nazis. Husserl was enormously impressed, as a great many philosophers of an idealist persuasion have been impressed, with the beauty and certainty of mathematics, and his first book was on the philosophy of arithmetic. His aim was to lay the foundations of a philosophy which should be as rigorous and certain as mathematics, and he believed that this could be achieved by intuiting the a priori features of experience itself. Just as mathematics deals not with actual objects but with abstract quantities and mathematical essences, so philosophy must deal not with the 'facticity' of phenomena (which is the province of psychology) but with their transcendental foundations. To arrive at these transcendental foundations involved a process which Husserl called 'bracketing' (*epoché*), a sort of suspension of judgment and response. It meant beginning, in Husserl's words, 'with total poverty and destruction',[46] by removing oneself from active engagement and all presuppositions, and adopting the standpoint of the transcendental observer.

> The phenomenological epoché eliminates as worldly facts from my field of judgement both the reality of the objective world in general, and the sciences of the world. Consequently there exists no 'I', and there are no psychic actors, that is psychic phenomena in the psychological sense. To myself I do not exist as a human being.[47]

These were obviously very strange doctrines, smacking of Nirvana and eastern mysticism rather than the traditions of western thought. And indeed when he insisted that philosophical activity must be presuppositionless, and return to naked experience, Husserl was, in fact, rejecting the whole history of philosophy, as well as the whole corpus of scientific knowledge. In the quest for certainty he did not hesitate to destroy the heritage of civilization. In doing so he constantly inveighed against the errors of naturalism and the scientific outlook.[48] There was in his view no objective world independent of consciousness; consciousness was world-constitutive. When consciousness was examined phenomenologically 'intentionality' was seen to be its essence. When through the process of 'bracketing' consciousness was stripped of its contingent characteristics it was revealed simply as a beam of 'intentionality' directed towards content. But content was not external. There was no outside to the transcendental ego, and hence no dualism. Act and content, *'noesis'* and *'noemata'*, though they must be distinguished, were only aspects of the phenomenological totality.[49] The 'eidetic science' which Husserl erected on these foundations was far from friendly to the experimental psychology of his time, and he maintained that there was a 'need for a reform of modern psychology in its entirety'.[50] On the positive side, however, were his subtle descriptions of phenomenological content, developed still further by his French follower, Merleau-Ponty,[51] his enrichment of the concept of 'intentionality'; and the doctrine of transcendental subjectivity, the ultimate core and ground of experience. These contributed something of value to psychology.

Heidegger (1889-1976), the philosopher who succeeded Husserl at Freiburg, was an even more obscure and iconoclastic thinker than Husserl himself, and on the continent his influence eclipsed even that of his predecessor. His vast output (the collected edition of his works runs to fifty-seven volumes!) has been described, even by one of his admirers, as 'a thicket of impenetrable verbiage'.[52] Obscure statements about 'the Nothing' were pilloried by the logical positivist Carnap as 'meaningless word sequences'.[53] Nevertheless even such a hard-headed philosopher as Ryle described him as 'a thinker of real importance',[54] and Hannah Arendt exclaimed in her panegyric on 'Heidegger at eighty' that with him 'thinking has come to life again'.[55] His power as a lecturer and his magnetic personality became legendary, and young Germans flocked to hear him. Only his temporary support for the Nazi movement, when he was Rector of Freiburg University, cast a cloud upon his reputation.

Heidegger turned to philosophy at a very early age after reading a dissertation of Brentano's on the meaning of 'Being' according to Aristotle. Other major influences were Nietzsche, upon whom Heidegger later wrote voluminously, and Husserl. He came to differ from Husserl in emphasizing not 'transcendental subjectivity' as the ultimate ground, but 'Being' itself. 'Being' was the centre, not man.[56] To attain 'Being' it was necessary to penetrate beyond the whole paraphernalia of civilization, beyond everyday experience, beyond scientific knowledge and the seductions of technology, even beyond logic. 'The idea of logic itself disintegrates in the turbulence of a more original questioning.'[57] Heidegger even seemed to envisage an end of philosophy in mystical experience and oneness with 'Being'. Man had become alienated from 'Being'; he had fallen into a state of *'Seinsvergessenheit'* (forgetfulness of 'Being'), become 'homeless', and divorced from truth. Truth was not a matter of logic and correct propositions; it was a matter of 'unconcealment', 'a disclosure of Being through which openness essentially unfolds'.[58] When 'Being' reveals itself directly in this way, it manifests itself as temporal flux. Ontology is rooted in time. We do not live 'in time', rather we 'live time'.[59] This revealing of 'Being' to itself is an exclusively human property. Animals have no world, are not aware of the world. Only man has a world, and thus has a special status. 'Man', proclaimed Heidegger, 'is the shepherd of Being;'[60] his 'language is the house of Being.'[61] Man has

'*Dasein*' (Being-in-the-world, or conscious Being). This being 'is farther than all beings, and is yet nearer to Man than every being.'[62] It is 'Being held out into Nothing'.[63] These were indeed even stranger doctrines than those of Husserl! But the heart of Heidegger's thought is really simple: it is an immense mystical nostalgia, a search for the '*Urphänomen*' (the primal beginnings), a move away from the complexity of civilization, with its science, its destructive technology, its artificiality and divisive tensions, back to the primitive oneness of earth and sky, gods and man.[64]

If we ask what, if anything, the phenomenological-existentialist movement has contributed to psychology, it must be admitted that, in spite of its markedly unscientific stance, it has enriched the subject. It has called psychologists back to first-hand experience, with its immediacy, complexity and authenticity. It has emphasized the need for 'as naive and full a description of direct experience as possible'.[65] This has led to much more subtle accounts of perceptual phenomena, for example by Katz, Michotte and Merleau-Ponty.[66] It has underlined the crucial nature of choice and decision processes, stressed the importance of the time dimension in human experience, and given new meaning to the concept of lived space and the phenomenal environment.[67] The philosophy of phenomenology-existentialism is the basis of a quite important psychiatric school, represented by Jaspers, Bingswanger, Boss, Frankl, Laing and May among others,[68] and it has at least contributed to the fabric of the new movement which in the introductory chapter was referred to as 'the Gergen-Harré school', marked by its attacks on traditional psychology and support for an 'alternative metatheory'.[69] The weakness of the phenomenological-existentialist approach is its reliance on intuition, its lack of any acceptable criterion for validating intuitions, and in general its failure to provide a scientifically plausible methodology.

IV

About the middle of the present century the two streams of philosophy outlined in the previous sections began to mingle in a revived philosophy of mind. The philosophy of mind, which had formerly been a central concern of philosophers, had been pushed from the centre of the stage by the rebirth of logic and the coming of phenomenology. It never wholly faded away; there was still a trickle of books in this area in the first half of the century, for example, Russell's *Analysis of Mind* (1921), Broad's *The Mind and its Place in Nature* (1925), and C.I. Lewis's *Mind and the World Order* (1929). But they were of marginal, rather than focal, interest to philosophers. The picture changed with the publication of Ryle's *The Concept of Mind* (1949) and Wittgenstein's *Philosophical Investigations* (1953). Both Ryle and Wittgenstein combined features from each of the philosophic streams, and the new philosophies of mind that followed endeavoured to merge the rigorous thinking of the analytic schools with the phenomenologists' feeling for everyday experience.

Ryle (1900-1976) was one of the most influential Oxford philosophers of recent times, and his *The Concept of Mind* has been described as one of the most important books on philosophy published this century. Ryle was influenced as a student much less by the moribund Oxford philosophy of his time than by Russell and Wittgenstein on the one hand and by the continental phenomenologists on the other. In the late 1920s he was already lecturing on Brentano and Husserl, and soon after the publication of Heidegger's *Sein und Zeit* he contributed a lengthy review of the book in *Mind*.[70] Though himself adhering to neither philosophical school he was well placed to appreciate what each had to offer.

The aim of *The Concept of Mind* was to analyse what we already know, as part of our everyday knowledge, about what are commonly called minds, and to demonstrate that this does not imply either a mind inhabiting a body, 'a ghost in the machine', or a mechanistic or materialistic doctrine of mind. The mistake of the dualist view was the mistake of supposing that the existence of mental processes implied a substantial mind. This Ryle described as a 'category mistake'. It was rather like the absurdity of treating fire and water as comparable elements in the manner of the ancients, an absurdity revealed by the impossibility of talking about a pound of water and a pound of fire! Ryle's method was to expose such muddles by means of a logical analysis of mental-conduct concepts. In the course of his book he examined concepts like will, emotion, disposition, self-knowledge, sensation, imagination and intellect. Broadly his conclusions were behaviouristic. 'When we describe people as exercising qualities of mind,' he wrote, 'we are not referring to occult episodes of which their overt acts and utterances are effects; we are referring to these overt acts and utterances themselves.'[71] But this did not imply a mechanistic or reductionist viewpoint. 'Man need not be degraded to a machine by being denied to be a ghost in a machine, He might after all be a sort of animal, namely a higher animal. There has even yet to be ventured the hazardous leap to the hypothesis that perhaps he is a man.'[72] Ryle made little use of technical psychology in his book; his aim instead was 'to rectify the logical geography of the knowledge we already possess'.[73] Like most philosophers he tended to take everyday experience too much at its face value, and to underestimate the elaborate development and processing involved in such experience. Nor is his rejection of 'internal' events really convincing. To say that imaging occurs, but that there are no imaged objects, is hardly a satisfactory account of imaginary processes.[74] Nevertheless Ryle's provocative book was a powerful stimulus to discussion.

Wittgenstein (1889-1951), another major twentieth century philosopher, had an unusual career. Born into a wealthy Austrian family, he went first to Berlin, and then to Manchester, to study engineering, and carried out research in aeronautics. In 1912 he moved to Cambridge to pursue logic and mathematics with Bertrand Russell. After the war, in which he served in the Austrian army, he temporarily abandoned philosophy and devoted himself to architecture and elementary school teaching, but came back to Cambridge in 1929, and was eventually elected to a philosophical chair. He was responsible for publishing only two important, but scrappy, books, the *Tractatus Logico-Philosophicus* (1922), and, appearing just after his death, *Philosophical Investigations* (1953). He left, however, voluminous notes, many of which have since come out in book form. He was a man with an unusual, intolerant but magnetic personality, who cast a sort of spell upon many of those who came into contact with him. His two books represent two phases of his thought. The *Tractatus* had affinities with the Vienna school of positivists. Its aim was to plot the limits of language, and to determine the dividing line between sense and nonsense. *Philosophical Investigations*, on the other hand, was closer to existentialism. Wittgenstein opened the book with a quotation from St Augustine, and he was known to have expressed his admiration for the saint as well as for Kierkegaard.[75] The major topic of concern, however, was still language, and mankind's 'language games', rather than experience of 'Being' as such. As one commentator writes,

> It is Wittgenstein's later doctrine that outside human thought and speech there are no independent, objective points of support, and meaning and necessity are presented only in linguistic practices which embody them . . . what really gives these practices their stability is that we agree in the interpretation of the rules.[76]

Wittgenstein's investigations involved an intense focusing on the meaning and usage of words – words like 'perception', 'understanding' and 'remembering'. 'In order to see more clearly,' he wrote, 'we must focus on the details of what goes on; must look at them from close to.'[77] Subjected to this kind of self-hypnotizing gaze the meaning of words seemed to evaporate. 'When you ask what "remembering" consists of, no answer comes.'[78] So we are simply left with the everyday usage of words, and 'philosophy only states what everyone admits.'[79] 'Since everything lies open, there is nothing to explain.'[80] It is all simple and familiar. There are no philosophical problems, and consequently no scientific problems relating to mind. To regard seeing, hearing, thinking, feeling and willing as possible topics of scientific investigation is a mistake.[81] Inevitably, therefore, Wittgenstein regarded psychology as 'barren' and marked by 'conceptual confusion'.[82] Mental states were for him 'queer' (*merkwürdig*) and to think about them produced a feeling of 'slight giddiness'.[83] The reason for this, Wittgenstein suggested, was that public criteria are needed to discuss mental phenomena; there can be no description of events which are private. To regard mental phenomena as inner or private 'leaves us floundering in a quagmire'.[84] So instead of looking inside we should be looking outside, at contexts, and at everyday linguistic usages. Clearly these views, like Ryle's, were in some ways allied to behaviourism, but they also had an affinity with existentialism in their stress on ordinary experience. Parallels have been drawn between the teachings of Heidegger and those of the latter Wittgenstein.[85] Both were unfriendly to the claims and pretensions of science. Both men, and Ryle too, emphasized the everyday, Wittgenstein everyday linguistic usage, Heidegger our 'throwness' into the everyday being of the world. In both there was more than a streak of mysticism. Wittgenstein concluded his *Tractatus* with the words, 'What we cannot speak about we must consign to silence',[86] or in other words to 'the ineffable'; and Heidegger saw the task of thinking proper as beginning where philosophy ended.[87]

Following these two seminal works the philosophy of mind has burgeoned. Much of it has not unnaturally been a reactivation and a fresh consideration of older problems employing the new tools of logical and linguistic analysis. New tools, however, have not sufficed, it seems, to bring about new consensus. Philosophical disagreements are as conspicuous as they have been since the birth of philosophy. The mind-body problem has not been resolved; some philosophers such as Feigl, Armstrong and Smart profess physicalist views; others like Popper favour a form of mentalism.[88] The status of consciousness is still a matter of contention. There is no agreement as to whether teleological explanations are tenable or not. Taylor in his book *The Explanation of Behaviour* (1964) supports teleology; Davidson, on the other hand, asserts that causal explanations are necessary, since 'cause is the cement of the universe, a picture that would otherwise disintegrate into a dyptych of the mental and the physical.'[89] Personal identity remains an open question. For Wittgenstein 'there is no such thing as a subject that thinks or sustains ideas.'[90] The subject is merely the limit of the world. Just as the eye cannot see itself, so the subject cannot grasp itself. It is nothing but a limit. But for Strawson the concept of the person is primitive, and logically prior even to that of individual consciousness.[91] And as to freedom there is no agreement between those, like some existentialists, who hold that man's freedom is total, and those who hold that we have no freedom at all. The philosophy of mind, for all its technical sophistication, presents a chaotic picture.

From this chaos of conflicting views, however, at least three positive and promising features have begun to emerge: a clarified analysis of intentionality, a tentative theory of action, and a rudimentary methodology of hermeneutics. Intentionality, it is now generally agreed, is the conceptually critical characteristic of mind.[92] It is, as Searle puts it in his recent book *Intentionality* (1983), 'a ground floor property of the mind';[93] it is part of the very structure of behaviour, and a psychology that ignores it, as many schools of psychology have, is doomed to sterility. Searle begins by defining it as 'that property of many mental states and events by which they are directed at or about objects and states of affairs in the world'.[94] Not all mental states are intentional, for some emotional states, like nervousness, elation and diffuse anxiety are undirected and floating. Nor is intentionality identical with being conscious, or with linguistic coding. Language is derived from intentionality, not vice versa, and meaning Searle treats as 'a special development of more primitive forms of intentionality'.[95]

Intentions do not function atomistically, but as part of a 'network of intentional states',[96] and against a 'pre-intentional' background, 'a set of non-representative mental capacities that enable all representing to take place . . . a set of skills, stances, assumptions and presupposing practices and habits'.[97] Searle's account of intentionality is based on a healthy realism, and a naturalistic approach which is likely to appeal to many psychologists. At the same time he believes that 'mental states are as real as any other biological phenomena'.[98] The mind-body problem, on the other hand, he dismisses as no more a genuine problem than 'the stomach-digestion problem'.[99] 'Mental states', he writes, 'are both *caused by* the operations of the brain, and *realized in* the structure of the brain.'[100] With Searle's impressive book the philosophy of mind has made a notable advance, which psychologists can welcome.

The second promising development is in the analysis of the concept of action. In a lecture on 'Human Action and Psychological Research', delivered in 1971, the British psychologist Borger contrasted 'the continuing philosophical interest in action' with 'the almost total absence of even the relevant terms from the psychological literature'.[101] The concept of action played a central role in the older psychology of scholasticism and its derivatives,[102] but it got lost in the associationist-behaviourist epoch that followed. It was revived by the sociologists of the Weber school,[103] but has only recently begun once again to interest psychologists, largely as a result of the discussions of the philosophers of mind.[104] These discussions have brought out various distinctive features of action, a mode of behaving which though possessing biological roots and a physiological base, manifests a number of novel and specifically human characteristics. Among the most important of these characteristics are the following: action implies an agent; and action normally possesses meaning, and involves at least a tacit decision process; it is generally, though not invariably, intentional at least with regard to its principal aim; it is commonly goal-directed, and more often than not structured according to conventions and rules; at the same time it is nearly always expressive, or at least imbued with expressive characteristics, and therefore reflects the actor's personality. The majority of human actions take place in a social context, and this social context is an integral part of any action. Action cannot be understood apart from the time dimension, and this means a consideration, on the one hand, of the history both of the social group and of the individual, and, on the other, the expected future towards which the action is directed. Quite clearly a topic of central importance has been revived through the philosophical treatment of the concept of action.

Thirdly, there is hermeneutics, which promises to provide a much-needed methodology for those parts of psychology which do not readily fit into the model derived from the physical sciences, in particular for the area of social action. Hermeneutics has a long history. Plato used the term ἑρμηνεία (interpretation) in discussing the nature of definition,[105] and Aristotle wrote a treatise 'On

Interpretation' which dealt with matters relating to symbols.[106] In modern times it came to be understood as 'the theory of the operations of understanding in their relation to the understanding of texts',[107] particularly classical texts and scriptural texts. The German religious philosopher Schleiermacher first formulated its basic principles as a unitary discipline, distinguishing links with grammar and linguistics on the one side, and with psychology and logic on the other.[108] Later in the nineteenth century, Dilthey widened its scope to embrace all cultural manifestations and the whole domain of human history. All human disciplines involved problems of the understanding and the interpretation of evidence. So according to Dilthey a large area of psychology, too, fell within the scope of what he called 'human studies' (*Geisteswissenschaften*).[109] These prescriptions of Dilthey, however, were not on the whole well received by psychologists, who objected to the romantic overtones of the concept of 'understanding' with its emphasis on intuition and empathy. As Holt put it, 'The methodology of verification, the hypothesis-testing phase of scientific work, involves well-developed rules and consensually established procedures, and intuition and empathy have no place in it.'[110] It is such objections which the newer critical hermeneutics is attempting to surmount. Ricoeur in France, Gadamer in Germany, Hirsch and Palmer in America, and Thompson in England are among its protagonists.[111] The new hermeneutics is marked by a shift from the psychological to the objective basis of interpretation, an examination of the logic of guessing, of weighing up evidence, and of establishing criteria of validity. There is in Ricoeur's view no essential opposition between 'understanding' and interpretation carried out by critical methods, and explanation in the usual scientific sense.[112] Of course, not everyone agrees that hermeneutic methods can achieve the kind of objectivity which science requires. Gergen has noted the problems involved in behavioural identification, that is in the describing of behaviour, before the process of interpretation can take place, and also the elements of social relativity that seem difficult to overcome when interpreting.[113] But we must remember that all science is provisional, not absolute and final. Objectivity is only its target. The methodology of science is always critical, a matter of conjectures and refutations, and critical hermeneutics seems to be aiming in this direction, and hence to be a valuable development and worthwhile extension of scientific methodology.

V

How much have these philosophical critiques contributed to the shaping of psychology? Are the critiques themselves open to criticism? To what extent has the scientific standing of psychology been undermined? These are the questions we must attempt, however cursorily, to answer.

That philosophers have made worthwhile contributions both to the methodology and to the contents of psychology has, perhaps, already become apparent. Psychologists are much more conscious of methodological problems than they were at the beginning of the century. In fact, for a period between the 1930s and the 1950s they became over-solicitous and too narrow in their methodological orthodoxy. Hence the developments in hermeneutics, sketched in the previous section, must be regarded as a promising liberalization of the methodological creed, and a move towards the necessary tailoring of methods to content. The content of psychology has also, as we have seen, been enlarged by a revival of older concepts that had been abandoned in the heyday of empiricism. The concepts of intentionality and action are likely to become central features of all future psychologies. In addition to these contributions to the methodology and to the content of psychology, there is a third important outcome of philosophical discussions, namely the demonstration of the necessary limits of all knowledge, and the inevitability of metaphysics, not as a form of knowledge, but as an imaginative and speculative complement to knowledge. Gödel's proof of the impossibility of establishing the sufficiency and non-contradiction of a theory on its own level, and by its own methods, was a decisive turning point in logic. Even the tight formal systems of mathematics were not self-subsistent. Much less can any empirical science provide its own foundations. As Hayek, the economist, pointed out in his book *The Sensory Order*, applying Gödel's argument to psychology, 'no explaining agent can ever explain its own operations. . . . Mind must remain for ever a realm of its own which we can know only through experiencing it.'[114] Perhaps this is what the phenomenologists and the existentialists were really getting at amidst their clouded verbosity. The 'transcendental ego' and 'Being', or something of that sort, is a necessary ultimate postulate.[115] But this still leaves open vast territories within the field of mind and behaviour for empirical enquiry.

Philosophical critiques, however, did not result only in positive contributions to psychology. The critics were commonly disparaging towards the scientific approach, and often did not hesitate to imply that philosophers of mind had something better to offer. Their offerings, however, when examined, frequently seem remarkably naive. The belief, repeated by Ryle, Wittgenstein, Heidegger and others, that we already know all we need to know about the human mind, that everything is clear and open to view, that all we need is to dispel 'category mistakes' in talking about mental matters and exorcise the 'bewitchment' of our intelligence, can only be described as 'the philosophers' illusion'. It is a sterile belief, devoid of any spark of curiosity, and completely at variance with the facts. Even the simplest mental event, whether on the stimulus side or on the response side, is highly complex, resting on a substructure of many layers, and involving a developmental process both phylogenetic and ontogenetic. Piaget has argued powerfully against the illusions of philosophy, while admitting its insights, in his book, *Insights and Illusions of Philosophy*.[116] When minds so often malfunction, and when we still know so little as to how to heal them and put them right, it seems extraordinary to maintain, as

Wittgenstein did, that 'everything lies open to view, and there is nothing to explain'.[117]

But there are other weaknesses displayed by the philosophers of mind, apart from their naive belief in the sacredness of the given. They place undue reliance on linguistic analysis. It is no more possible to unravel the workings of the mind by the analysis of 'mental-conduct' terms than to construct a botany by examining popular plant names. Science is concerned with events and matters of fact, not with words, and whatever the place of linguistic analysis, and it has a role to play, it cannot be a substitute for scientific observation and experiment. Nor can observation be equated with intuition. Intuitions profess to be self-validating; observations need confirming and checking. As Piaget has noted, there is an essential difference between the reliance on speculation by the philosophers, and the insistence on verification by the scientific fraternity. As the American philosopher Quine has pointed out, all intuitive knowledge depends on a system of background assumptions and is open to revision.[118] It cannot be accorded the status which some philosophers have accorded it. Philosophy, therefore, cannot solve problems intuitively. 'It raises problems,' observed Piaget, 'but does not solve them,' while science solves some problems, but at the same time raises new ones.[119] As a consequence science is an open-ended, forward-moving endeavour. Its results are cumulative, in spite of paradigm changes; and over large areas there is a high measure of agreement among scientists, contrasting markedly with the disagreements of philosophers. Philosophers have argued at cross-purposes for thousands of years without settling their differences. Darwin hit the nail on the head when he wrote in his 'N' notebook in 1838,

> The study of metaphysics, as they have always been studied, appears to me like puzzling at astronomy without mechanics. Experience shows that the problem of mind cannot be solved by attacking the citadel itself. The mind is a function of body. We must bring some stable foundation to argue from.[120]

It is, then, primarily upon the scientific approach that the future of psychology is likely to depend. Philosophy with its critiques may assist in various ways, but how far it can assist depends largely on a higher degree of scientific sympathy and sophistication among philosophers. Fortunately not all philosophers are as hostile to science as Wittgenstein, Heidegger and some of the philosophers of mind. Russell and Whitehead in the past generation, Popper, Feigl and Quine in the older generation of contemporaries, and Searle and Dennett among the newcomers, to mention a few of the more prominent names, have all shown, or show, sympathy with science. Quine has consistently argued that scientific theories, even of the most abstruse kind, are based on the same foundations as ordinary everyday knowledge.[121] The formal testing of scientific hypotheses is not different in principle form the practical testing of everyday know-how. To reject science is, therefore, by implication to reject ordinary common sense. What is needed in psychology is not the overthrow of the scientific approach, but an extension of scientific methodology through creative and imaginative leaps to conquer new territory. That is why the attempt by Rychlak to show that scientific methodology is 'consonant with humanistic theoretical formulations' is a valuable one.[122]

Undoubtedly the attacks on scientific psychology that have occurred in recent times are linked to a more general, ideologically inspired, movement against science. This movement is in part the result of understandable fear of some of the outcomes of scientific research; in part, in times of rapid and disturbing social change, an atavistic longing for a simpler, idealized past, or an utopian faith in a visionary future. We need constantly to remind ourselves of the central role that science, and the technology derived from it, have played in 'The Ascent of Man', as Bronowski entitled his stimulating panegyric to the place of science in civilization. In Bronowski's words, 'We are a scientific civilization; that means a civilization in which knowledge and its integrity are crucial.'[123] If our ascent is to continue, we cannot dispense with science. We must look, therefore, not primarily to philosophy, but to the new vistas that are already opening out within scientific psychology itself, if we are to gauge how psychology is shaping today.

Chapter 14
New vistas I

I

'It is a daunting task to attempt to sketch the new vistas that have been opening out in psychology since 1950. Judged by quantity alone it is safe to surmise that the published output of psychologists has, during these years, considerably exceeded that produced in the whole previous history of the subject from the time of the Greeks onwards. Psychology has penetrated into every niche of its subject area, pure and applied. New problems are constantly emerging to exercise the attention of psychologists; new techniques of investigation and data handling are being devised; and, in response to novel social demands, new areas of application are being marked out – organization psychology to deal with the human aspects of streamlined organizations, environmental psychology in answer to environmental degradation, the psychology of women to reflect the new feminism, and sports psychology the intensification of competitive sports. There are only two ways of canalizing the flood of literature that has been generated by these developments, one subjective and one semi-objective. Subjectively a writer who has lived, worked and attended numerous conferences throughout this period can have recourse to his memories and global impressions; or, rather more objectively, he can consult the successive volumes of the *Annual Review of Psychology*,[1] which commenced publication in 1950, and which set out to provide annual surveys of developments seen through the eyes of specialist contributors. Neither of these sources is finally satisfactory. No one individual can have read more than a fraction even of the output highly rated by reviewers, nor, because of growing specialization, understood large segments of it. The *Annual Review* to some extent surmounts these difficulties, though even its specialized contributors frequently complain that the volume of publications assigned to them is too great to cope with. Moreover *Annual Review* chapters are not immune from regional and temporal limitations – regional limitations, because ninety per cent of the contributors and all the editors have been American, and of the remaining ten per cent, two-thirds have been from members of English-speaking countries; and temporal limitations, because long-term trends cannot be brought out in summaries covering mainly from one to four years. The historian of the recent past is hampered by the lack of perspective which only time can bequeath.

Of course, by no means all this vast psychological output is significant. There is much trivial work in psychology, and much downright poor work. Contributors to the *Annual Review* constantly complain of the quality of the publications they have to cover, though not many are as scathing as Tulving and Madison, who held that 'at least some writers, faced with the decision of whether to publish or perish, should seriously have considered the latter alternative'.[2] Reviewing work on memory and verbal learning during the years 1967-69 these authors considered that only ten per cent of publications were worthwhile. Psychology, however, is not unique in this respect. Any mainstream activity, and psychology has become a mainstream activity in the contemporary developed world, manifests this qualitative spread. Creative geniuses are always surrounded by a host of humdrum practitioners. The great artists of the Renaissance were accompanied by hundreds of second and third-rate painters, Shakespeare by many inferior playwrights and versifiers, the Einsteins and Rutherfords by thousands of 'normal' scientists. Psychologists need not be unduly worried by a slush of inferior work. It does, however, create difficulties for the historian writing before time has carried out its beneficent sifting. There are, moreover, special problems in psychology, resulting from the lack of an agreed theoretical matrix. This makes it harder to distinguish valuable trends from passing fads, and increases the tendency for the subject to sprawl and to pile up accumulations of not very significant detail. The historian must of necessity select, and his selection cannot avoid a measure of arbitrariness and subjectivity.

New vistas may emerge either as a result of new ways of looking at old problems, or as a result of the genesis of new problems. Both ways have been operative in psychology. Sensory processes, perception, memory, learning and motivation, to mention some of the central topics of traditional psychology, have remained focal areas of investigation. Sensory processes, such as vision, have, as we have already seen,[3] become highly specialized and highly technical fields of enquiry, in which considerable progress has been achieved. Exceptionally interesting has been the recent work on pain, where there have been marked advances since the gate-control theory of Melzack and Wall was propounded in 1965,[4] and the discovery by Hughes in 1975 of the existence within the medial brain stem of mechanisms of pain inhibition and the isolation of endorphins or endogenous opiates.[5] A new journal, *Pain*, established in 1975 signalled this forward movement. In the field of perception generally new vistas have opened up as a result of neurophysiological developments and computer modelling. New techniques of investigating cellular activity in the brain, such as those employed by Hubel and Wiesel,[6] have thrown light on the transformation of visual signals through various stages, while attempts to copy visual processing by means of computers have emphasized the complexity of even the simplest act of perception. The richness of the information available in the perceptually given has been brought out vividly by Gibson,[7] but on the whole the balance of evidence seems to support a more active view of perception, such as that proposed by

Gregory in his *Mind in Science* (1981),[8] in which he treats perceptions as essentially similar to scientific hypotheses. According to him the signals arising from sensory systems are first read according to codes to provide data, and these data are then used to generate perceptual hypotheses, which are the actual percepts. The whole field of perceptual investigation has been, and still is, as one annual reviewer notes, in a 'state of ferment'.[9]

This is equally true of memory, which is rightly regarded as one of the key problems of psychology. It has fascinated psychologists from the time of Aristotle and St Augustine onwards, and now seems to be yielding new secrets.[10] Together with 'increasing awareness of the complexity of the problem', Baddeley (1976) noted 'genuine cumulative progress in the study of human memory'.[11] The information-processing approach to memory has yielded important data particularly with regard to coding. The simple two-stage distinction between short-term and long-term memory has given way to a more flexible theory of processing levels (Craik and Lockhart).[12] Distinctions have been drawn between different types of memory, in particular between semantic and episodic memory (Tulving).[13] And 'the search for the engram', as Lashley[14] termed it, continues. Hormones and other chemical factors are now known to be implicated in memory; parts of the brain, such as the hippocampus, known to be involved in the establishment and storage of memory have been located; and there is clear evidence of microstructural changes at synaptic junctions when learning occurs.[15] The engram, however, still eludes discovery.

The topic of motivation, which became a key area in the dynamic psychologies which flourished at the beginning of the century, has been dislodged from its central position by the information-processing models of recent times. Nevertheless it has still been an area of considerable activity, as well as some confusion, as reflected in the annual symposia on motivation which have been held from 1953 onwards in Nebraska.[16] There has been a clash of theories, homeostatic theories, drive theories, arousal theories, cognitive theories, self-actualization theories, and so on. Madsen (1968) distinguished no fewer than twenty motivational theories.[17] Perhaps the most significant progress has been made in the exploration of the physiological bases of drives such as hunger, thirst, sex and maternal behaviour,[18] and in connection with the experiments on self-stimulation through electrodes implanted in the brain initiated by Olds and Milner in 1954.[19] But interesting work has also been carried out on levels of aspiration, achievement motivation, curiosity, aggression and anxiety.[20] What seems to be lacking is any general theory of motivation, or any satisfactory synoptic view of the topic as a whole. The topic, however, is of such theoretical and practical importance that it must obviously return to the centre of the field.

More dramatic, and possibly more far-reaching in their consequences, are developments in psychology evoked by technological developments outside psychology – by developments such as the conquest of space, the great increase in the speed and quality of communications, the deciphering of the genetic code, and above all by the rise and spread of computers. These developments have already substantially shaped psychology, and have opened up vast new possibilities. The first man-made satellite was launched by the Russians in October 1957. In April 1961 Yuri Gagarin became the first man to leave the confines of the earth. In July 1969 American astronauts landed on the moon. The consequences of these achievements for psychology are potentially momentous: man for the first time has been removed from the natural environment in which all his evolution has taken place and was freed from gravity, from the diurnal succession of light and dark, and from spatial points of reference. A whole host of new problems, both theoretical and applied, were forced upon psychologists. The intimate interlocking of human nature and its natural environment became apparent, and hence environmental psychology became a matter of urgent enquiry. Special problems of biological rhythms in relation to diurnal cycles, to vestibular functions in relation to gravity, and, more generally, to the maintenance of normal functioning when removed from many of the props of normal existence – all these demanded the attention of psychologists and other scientists. Indeed without their aid survival in space would not have been possible.[21] Somewhat similar were the problems raised by the more mundane improvements of communications of all sorts that have eventuated since the Second World War – rapid air travel, the instantaneous and worldwide transmission of information, visual and auditory, and the mass communication of broadcasting and television, that have turned the world into a 'global village'. The role of biological clocks is implicated in the phenomenon of 'jet lag';[22] information technology has raised issues of enormous interest to psychology;[23] and the influence of mass communication on attitudes and behaviour has become a burning issue.[24] No less important for psychology was the discovery of the double helical structure of DNA by Watson and Crick in July 1953, and the subsequent cracking of the genetic code. Firstly this led to a new surge in the field of psychogenetics, which we shall briefly examine in a subsequent section; secondly it underlines the central role of codes and programs in the control and development of behaviour generally. Finally, and perhaps most important of all, was the rise and rapid spread of computers. The first automatic calculating machine was conceived by Charles Babbage, a Cambridge mathematician, in 1832. But it was not until 1946 that the first electronic computer, ENIAC (Electrical Numerical Integrator and Calculator) was constructed in America. The development and spread of several generations of vastly improved computers is now common knowledge. They have had a revolutionary effect on many aspects of practical life and scientific research, and their influence in psychology has been as profound as in any other branch of knowledge. For not only have computers enabled psychologists to handle the complex data which their science produces with new effectiveness, but they have provided them with unique means of modelling mental processes. If not mind-like in the full sense of the word, computers at least carry out functions which can be described as mental.[25]

The new vistas which have been opened up from within psychology and from outside sources have been rapidly transforming the subject. There has been a marked retreat from mechanistic, stimulus-response, reductionist theories, a return to central processing, and a recognition of the active and creative aspects of mind. Landmarks in this reorientation were the appearances of Hebb's *The Organization of Behavior* in 1949, and Miller, Galanter and Pribram's *Plans and the Structure of Behavior* in 1960. For Hebb the key problem of psychology was 'the problem of thought; some sort of process that is not fully controlled by environmental stimulation, and yet cooperates closely with that stimulation'.[26] The emphasis was once more firmly placed on autonomous central activities. Hebb's stimulating book opened up many of the new vistas that now confront psychologists. The transition from cognition to behaviour through the medium of 'plans' was the main theme of Miller, Galanter and Pribram's equally significant book. A 'plan' is for an organism essentially the same as a program for a computer, in that it controls the order in which sequences are performed.[27] The impact of these books was much enhanced by the fact that both were written by behaviouristically inclined psychologists essentially antipathetic to animistic thinking. They served, however, as an encouragement to humanistically orientated contemporaries, to men like Maslow, who emphasized the higher reaches of human nature,[28] and Kelly with his theory of personal constructs and stress on man's conceptual freedom,[29] and they built bridges to the work of continental psychologists like Piaget. All this was accompanied by a gradual methodological liberalization. In this connection the recent work of Meehl, another hard-headed scientist, is notable. In an article which has been described as 'the single most important theoretical and methodological article in the psychological literature in recent years',[30] Meehl writes, 'I believe that the universal reliance on merely refuting the null hypothesis as the standard method for corroborating substantive theories in the soft areas is a terrible mistake, is basically unsound, poor scientific strategy, and one of the worst things that ever happened in the history of psychology.'[31] The liberalization of methodology may have opened the gates to some rather dubious 'alternative' psychologies, but these are probably less deleterious than the constipation that resulted from the restrictive regime of positivistic puritanism.

The new vistas facing psychologists are the combined effect of this methodological liberalization, and the restoration of lost content, together with scientific and technological progress in areas outside psychology. Every aspect of psychology, pure and applied, has been affected by these changes. In a brief couple of chapters much must be overlooked, and attention confined to mainstream psychology. New vistas in developmental, social and applied psychology, which have been touched on in previous chapters, cannot be treated further. Attention must be confined to two main areas in which progress has been of most general significance – the biological, and what may be termed the cognitive-phenomenological. Within these two broad groupings several sub-topics may be distinguished: the chemical, neurophysiological, psychogenetic and ethological in one group, and information-processing, artificial intelligence, psycholinguistics, cognitive development, consciousness and values in the other. Inevitably there is an element of arbitrariness in such a selection, but perhaps there would be fairly wide agreement that these are among the most significant developments in the years since 1950.

II

In the field of the life sciences there have unquestionably been spectacular advances during the present century, and particularly since the Second World War. These advances are still continuing at a remarkable rate, and their effects on psychology, which have already been considerable, are likely to become even more far-reaching, opening up new vistas and generating new interdisciplinary specialisms. Of particular relevance to psychology are the advances that have taken place in biochemistry, neurophysiology, genetics and ethology, and I shall confine my attention to these. The roots of all these disciplines, of course, go back into the nineteenth century and even earlier, but new techniques, new instrumentation, and new concepts have led to striking breakthroughs. Beneath the fabulous diversity of life a remarkable underlying unity has become apparent, and certain very general concepts, such as homeostasis and information, have acquired a wide relevance. But progress has also brought a recognition of the immense complexity of life and all its manifestations. As Eccles observed in considering the brain, we are confronted with 'a level of complexity immeasurably greater than anything else that has ever been discovered elsewhere in the universe or created in computer technology'[32] There is a long way to go before the functions of organisms, particularly the higher organisms, are fully understood, and there is no likelihood in the foreseeable future of psychology being swallowed up by neurophysiology, as Hubel, the neurologist, thinks it one day may be.[33] Indeed there are strong arguments against any such reductionism. A hierarchy of levels seems to be the pattern of reality, and this implies correspondingly hierarchical levels of scientific activity. Mental processes and behaviour are dependent on, but not determined by, their biological base. Their framework is set biologically, and their manifestations are modulated biologically. In human beings, changes of mood, differences between individuals, and breakdowns can often be explained, sometimes wholly, sometimes partially, in biochemical, genetic or neurophysiological terms, but under normal conditions of equilibrium what Claude Bernard termed 'the free life' is possible, and then behaviour transcends the purely biological level. This is the standpoint from which the new vistas opened up by the life sciences must be viewed.

One of the most notable developments in twentieth century science has been the rise of biochemistry.[34] That life was a physico-chemical system had become clear by the middle 1800s. Liebig's *Animal*

Chemistry appeared in 1842. The psychiatrist Maudsley, in his *Physiology and Pathology of Mind* (1867), already recognized that brain functioning was dependent on chemical factors, and suggested that insanity might be the result of chemical disturbances. Shortly afterwards Thudichum further developed this theme.[35] But biochemistry as a specialism did not really get under way until enzymes were isolated by Buchner in 1897. It is indeed essentially a twentieth century science. In Great Britain the *Biochemical Journal* dates only from 1907, and the Biochemical Society from 1910. The science has progressed with the development of techniques for investigating the extremely complex molecules which make up the substance of living bodies and their cells, the enzymes, nucleotides, hormones and neurotransmitters upon which integrated organic functioning depends. Both theoretical and practical advances, moreover, have sprung from the development of pharmacological products that modify vital processes. All this has led to a much deeper understanding of the nature of life, and, of special relevance to psychology, the operation of the nervous system and the brain. The equilibrium of all living organisms is maintained by a continuous process of metabolism; there is constant activity, constant utilization of energy, and constant renewal, involving both input and output of materials. Any shortage of vital substances leads sooner or later to malfunctioning, and this applies not only to basic elements like oxygen and glucose, but also to trace elements and important compounds termed vitamins. Deficiency in the supply of any of these vital materials can affect mental functioning and behaviour. The dependence of mental efficiency on oxygen concentration, and on levels of carbonic acid and of glucose, has long been known.[36] The influence of dietary deficiencies on maturation and behaviour has been the subject of detailed studies during the last thirty years, and a speciality termed 'psychodietetics' has emerged.[37] Also in an increasingly polluted environment the effect of toxic substances (e.g. atmospheric contaminants, industrial solvents, insecticides in foodstuffs) on the nervous system and mental functioning has become a matter of concern.[38] Metabolic disturbances can result in mental deficiency, a striking example being the disorder known as phenylketonuria.[39] But the most important recent developments, as far as psychology is concerned, have been those relating to neurotransmitters, hormones and drugs.

The first demonstration of the chemical transmission of nerve impulses at synaptic junctions was obtained by Loewi in 1921.[40] The chemical substance involved was identified by Dale in 1936 as acetylcholine,[41] and the elaborate processes involved in the release and breakdown of acetylcholine have since been studied in detail. Many other neurotransmitters have subsequently been identified, the most important being the catecholamines (noradrenaline, adrenaline and dopamine), serotonin, and the inhibiting substance commonly termed GABA (gamma-aminobutyric acid).[42] With the publication of Eccles's lectures *The Neurophysiological Basis of Mind* in 1953, this whole topic was seen to be of direct relevance to psychologists, and later work, particularly in the area of brain biochemistry, has confirmed its importance. Disturbances in motor behaviour and emotion, mood changes and certain psychiatric syndromes have all been shown to be linked to abnormalities in neurotransmitters. The motor disabilities of Parkinson's disease, for example, are the result of dopamine deficiencies in areas of the mid-brain. Catecholamines control, or modulate, many autonomic functions, and affect emotional balance.[43] There is a good deal of evidence to suggest that at least one of the factors involved in schizophrenia is an excess production of dopamine. Not only are schizophrenic symptoms relieved by drugs which are antagonistic to dopamine, they are to some extent mimicked by catecholamine releasers such as amphetamine.[44]

The study of hormones and their relation to behaviour is another important twentieth century development. Hormones were so named in 1905 by the British physiologist E.H. Starling, consolidating earlier observations, and biochemists became interested in analysing the products of the various endocrine glands. The relevance of this work to psychology, and the light it seemed to throw on temperament, became apparent in the 1920s, and for a time there was a somewhat sensational popularization of what were termed 'the glands of destiny'.[45] A more scientific approach was initiated by Cannon's *Bodily Changes in Pain, Hunger, Fear and Rage*,[46] and in the mid-1920s accounts of the endocrines began to appear in the standard psychological textbooks. In the 1950s it became clear that hormones were an even more important regulator of behaviour than had previously been suspected by the main body of psychologists. There was a close affinity between some of the neurotransmitters and some of the endocrines, and there was a close relationship between the master gland, the pituitary, and one of the chief regulating systems of the brain, the hypothalamus. Beach's *Hormones and Behavior* (1948) and Harris's *Neural Control of the Pituitary Gland* (1955) marked the beginning of a new era of what came to be termed 'psychoneuroendocrinology'.[47] Hormones are of particular significance in the control of sexual and aggresive behaviour; they are involved in stress, depression, and possibly various forms of mental disorder; and it is suggested that they are concerned with memory functions.[48] Their influence on brain development and functioning is considerable, and 'psychoneuroendocrinology' is now a growing specialism, as recent surveys in the *Annual Review of Psychology* have demonstrated.[49] A new journal, *Hormones and Behavior*, commenced publication in 1969.

A closely linked area is that of psychopharmacology, the study of the effect of drugs on behaviour. The use of drugs is, of course, very ancient, but the elucidation of their chemical structures, their mass manufacture, and the understanding of their modes of operation are fairly recent. Their importance is threefold: firstly, because of their many therapeutic properties; secondly, because of the problems presented by addiction, which has spread widely since 1950, as a result of social alienation, the growth of subcultures in large urban communities, and commercial exploitation; and thirdly as a research tool. Though the psychiatrist Kraepelin may be regarded as the founder of psychopharmacology, it was not until 1953 that the subject really began to take off.[50] It was in that year that reserpine (an old Indian herbal remedy) and chlorpromazine were introduced into clinical practice. In the following year Aldous Huxley's *The Doors of Perception*, in which he described the mind-enlarging influence of the drug mescaline, popularized the taking of hallucogens, and their use spread widely. LSD (lysergic acid diethylamide) first synthesized in 1938, but not adopted for its psychedelic properties until the 1950s, heroin (an opium derivative first introduced in 1898), and the milder cannabis, known from ancient times, all became nagging social problems and the subject of official enquiries.[51] Though addiction is a matter of legitimate concern, psychopharmacology is primarily interested in the clinical and research aspects of drugs. Because of their widespread clinical use the pharmaceutical companies have been busy creating new products. Those of special interest to the psychologist are the tranquillizers, sedatives, stimulants and anti-depressants used in the treatment of neuroses, psychoses and milder forms of emotional upset. Scientifically the principal area of interest is to determine the mode of operation of drugs, in particular their relation to neurotransmitter substances and hormones, and their effects on both the central and autonomic nervous systems. They have widespread effects on emotion and motivation, on learning and memory, and on personality generally.[52] There are significant individual differences in reactions to drugs, some of which appear to be of genetic origin.[53] The research psychopharmacologist makes extensive use of animals for research purposes. This involves quite tricky problems in the precise assessment of behavioural changes, and also raises questions as to the legitimacy of extrapolating from animals to man.[54] Psychopharmacology has been the subject of several *Annual Review* surveys from 1960 onwards.

III

Between the chemically centred topics discussed above and the broader field of neurophysiology there is no sharp dividing line. The one deals with the intricate details of neural and cerebral working, the other embraces mass functions and effects. Once again progress has depended considerably upon the introduction of new techniques, such as the staining method invented by Nauta in the 1950s, which has enabled brain pathways to be mapped in great detail, upon developments of the electroencephalograph, particularly the technique of evoked potentials, and upon the employment of microelectrodes.[55] Even so the immense complexity of the human brain ensures that progress can only be slow. Nevertheless our knowledge is certainly more advanced than it was in 1940. The war itself, of course, with its crop of brain injuries, was one factor in the advance. What is now more clearly than ever apparent is that the brain is not only well structured and programmed, but also, even in adult humans, quite plastic and capable of new growth. The conditions promoting growth, both during early development and after injury, have become a topic of great practical and scientific interest.

Of central importance to psychology is the much fuller knowledge of brain organization that has been acquired since 1950. A striking advance was the discovery of the role of the reticular activating system in the brain stem and basal diencephalon by Moruzzi and Magoun in 1949.[56] Stimulation of this system produced marked changes in EEG rhythms and in behaviour, and was shown to be related to the induction and maintenance of the waking state. This has thrown light on the basis of sleep, and also on the physiological basis of alertness and consciousness generally. These observations of Moruzzi and Magoun not only form 'a major landmark in neurophysiology'[57] but a major advance in neuropsychology. Equally significant has been the elucidation of the functions of the hypothalamus and limbic system in the subcortical areas of the brain. The hypothalamus is a control centre for the balance of the internal environment, and involved in the regulation of bodily functions and emotional life. In fact the whole area from the hypothalamus to the hippocampus, amygdala and neighbouring areas has been termed by the neurologist Papez 'the circuit of emotion'. This so-called 'limbic system' has also been shown to have a role in filtering input to the cortex, and in the establishment of memories. Luria summarized the matter thus:

> The deep zones of the brain, neighbouring on the reticular
> formation of the upper part of the brain stem, and including the
> limbic structure, are directly concerned not only with the
> maintenance of optimal cortical tone, but also with the creation of
> the necessary conditions for retention of traces of direct experience.[58]

At the cortical level perhaps the split-hemisphere work initiated by Sperry is of special note. The work began in the 1950s on animal brains. It was discovered that visual discrimination trained to one hemisphere of a cat's brain could not be performed by the other, when connecting fibres between the hemispheres were cut.[59] In the 1960s dissections were carried out on human patients suffering from epilepsy. The operation relieved epileptic symptoms, and did not cause major intellectual disturbance. But it became apparent that there was an assymmetry of cerebral functioning, and a degree of specialization between the hemispheres, speech functions being normally located in the left hemisphere, and spatial and musical functions in the right.[60] Subsequent experimental work with intact human brains using special techniques, such as divided visual fields and dichotic listening, has tended to confirm the findings on operated subjects.[61] The linking of different aptitudes with different areas of the brain is of particular interest to the psychologist, as it confirms and strengthens some of his psychometric findings.

These advances have led to a rapid growth of what is now termed 'neuropsychology', a specialism which embraces both the experimental investigation of brain-behaviour relationships and also the clinical application of psychological methods to the assessment and rehabilitation of brain-damaged patients. The functions of the brain in processing information, evaluating and selecting, programming and control, are gradually becoming better understood, and this is of enormous significance to psychology.[62]

IV

We have already noted some of the steps which during the first half of the present century turned genetics into the key science of life.[63] Since 1950 progress in this branch of biology has been rapid and remarkable. The chemical structure of DNA, the universal genetic material of all forms of life, has been elucidated; a great deal is now known about the complex processes by which genes produce proteins and control development; the genetic code has been deciphered; and the switching on and off of genes is beginning to be understood.[64] No wonder that genetics has been having an increasing influence on the outlook of psychologists, and that a new speciality, psychogenetics, has been born.

It was Calvin Hall in 1951 who observed that 'a real genetics of behavior promises to emerge . . . an interdisciplinary science of psychogenetics'.[65] Though Hall recognized the potential of psychogenetics as 'a prerequisite for the development of a dynamic psychology',[66] his approach was a cautious and limited one. He held that studies must be confined to animal species upon which controlled breeding experiments could be carried out, and in his article he restricted himself to discussing selective breeding and strain differences. He made no mention at all of population studies or human genetics. The real birth of the subject was the publication of Fuller and Thompson's *Behavior Genetics* in 1960.[67] Their approach was far more comprehensive than that of Hall, embracing both ·animal breeding experiments and population genetics, and giving consideration to a whole range of studies on human intellectual abilities, personality and temperament, as well as on behavioural abnormalities. They mapped out for the first time the potential scope of the subject. Since the appearance of their book psychogenetics has grown enormously. Between 1960 and 1982 the *Annual Review* has devoted six surveys to it, and in one of these surveys the authors noted 'an accelerating growth that is matched by few psychological specialities'.[68]

Like most new developments, roots and origins can be traced back into earlier years. The psychogenetics that finally emerged in 1960 was an amalgam from a variety of sources. Selective breeding experiments with animals in relation to various behavioural traits had been carried out in the 1930s. Calvin Hall had studied emotionality in rodents, using defecation and urination as measures of emotional disturbance; others had experimented on activity levels and maze-learning ability. Differences between strains in liability to seizures, in aggressiveness and in tameability had been measured.[69] With human populations

Newman, Freeman and Holzinger had begun the collection of data on separated twins; Burks and Freeman had independently undertaken the collection of data on foster children. Both types of investigation were done with a view to determining the influence of heredity on abilities and personality.[70] That genetic factors played a part in a good many forms of subnormality and abnormality had been recognized for a long time.[71] Rather later, in 1956, in an article which became famous, if not notorious, Burt applied the multifactorial theory of inheritance, based on Fisher's quantitative method, to the analysis of intellectual differences, an application in which, as Jensen observed, Burt was 'outstandingly ahead of all others of his time'.[72] In the same year, perhaps most important of all, the chromosome number of man was determined precisely as a result of methodological improvements in cytological preparations, the number being not, as previously supposed, forty-eight, but forty-six, consisting of forty-four autosomes and two sex chromosomes.[73] This was followed by the discovery of various chromosome anomalies responsible for significant psychological consequences. Down's syndrome (mongolism) was found to result from an additional autosome, or sometimes the translocation of part of an autosome; and various sexual anomalies were found to be due to extra, or deficient, sex chromosomes, the anomalies at least sometimes being accompanied by psychological aberrations.[74] These were some of the ingredients which Fuller and Thompson merged into the speciality, psychogenetics.

Since 1960 psychogenetics has grown greatly in volume, methodological sophistication and range. Its importance for general psychology lies in the light it can throw on two key problems – the origins of human variability, and the existence, if any, of biological universals built into human nature and responsible for essential characteristics and constraints. To consider human variability first: it is generally agreed that variability is the result of both genetic and environmental forces, and that this applies both to abilities such as general intelligence and to many basic personality traits. The combined influence of genetic and environmental factors is not easy to disentangle owing to their great complexity, but quantitative genetics is making an inroad into the problem,[75] and it is a matter of practical importance to know the answers, as social policy and remedial programs depend to some extent on them. Evidence from various sources all points to a sizeable genetic component in intelligence; there are sex differences, basically genetic in origin, in some special aptitudes, such as spatial and verbal ability; while personality traits, such as neuroticism and extraversion, appear to some extent to be inherited tendencies.[76] A good deal of research has also been carried out on the genetics of schizophrenia, manic-depressive psychosis, criminality, alcoholism and other behaviour disorders.[77] For various reasons these research findings, suggesting often quite significant genetic influences, sparked off a great deal of controversy; but the event which triggered the major explosion was Jensen's 1969 article, 'How much can we boost IQ and scholastic achievement?'.[78] It was in this article that Jensen maintained that the generally lower IQs of American Negroes were predominantly of genetic origin. In spite of virulent attacks on this position Jensen has stubbornly maintained his ground.[79] His arguments were ably presented, but he probably underestimated the complexity of the problem and the difficulties of coming to even tentative conclusions from present evidence. Psychogeneticists have since become rather more prudent, and the controversies are now fortunately less heated, though still far from resolved. The environmentalist lobby, too, has been somewhat sobered by the manifestly disappointing results obtained by the optimistic educational enrichment programs of the 1960s, such as Head Start in America and the Educational Priority Areas experiment in England.[80] No doubt early experience is important in development, but it is not easy to institutionalize the subtle social and environmental forces involved.[81] A second edition of Fuller and Thompson's book in 1978 documented some of these developments, which at the latest *Annual Review* survey notes, are now marked by increased caution and sophistication.[82]

The problem of the biological constants of human nature is a related and equally controversial matter. The evidence springs partly from cross-cultural comparisons, and partly from animal studies, particularly comparisons between man and other members of the primate group. The ethologist Tinbergen has argued that man presents certain 'environment-resistant' traits, almost invariable between cultures, and revealing 'the deeper structure, the ancient roots of human behaviour'.[83] The theme has been taken up by E.O. Wilson and the sociobiologists. In his recent book *Human Nature* (1978), Wilson lists characteristics that have been recorded in every culture known to history and also points to various similarities between human and chimpanzee social behaviour.[84] His conclusion is that 'we are biological and our soul cannot fly free . . . the genes hold culture on a leash. The leash is very long, but values will be constrained in accordance with their effects on the human gene pool.'[85] Wilson's conclusions are not unlike those of Dawkins, whose book *The Selfish Gene* (1976) proposed the provocative doctrine that 'we are survival machines – robot vehicles blindly programmed to preserve selfish molecules known as genes'.[86] True, Dawkins modified the harshness of his thesis by postulating 'memes' (units of cultural transmission), by his admission that man's evolution was not explained by genes alone, and by suggesting that man's capacity for conscious foresight enabled him to rebel against the tyranny of selfish replicators.[87] But in his subsequent work, *The Extended Phenotype* (1982), Dawkins maintained that not only the organism's phenotypic characteristics, but also the artifacts it constructs and the environmental changes it engineers, are genetically controlled and can be regarded as an 'extended phenotype'.[88] Genes, therefore, remain the ultimate controllers of our destiny. It remains to be determined how far the sociobiologists are correct, or whether cultural factors and the 'conscious foresight' which Dawkins admits can to some extent enable man to transcend and transmute his biological heritage. The elucidation of these important issues is among the vistas being opened up by the advance of psychogenetics. The more fully genetic mechanisms are understood, the more hope there is of some control being brought to bear on genetic variations with a prospect ultimately of ameliorating, or even eliminating, those of a deleterious nature. The successful treatment of phenylketonuria, a genetically transmitted metabolic failure, exemplifies the fruits of understanding.[89]

V

The fourth important area of biological science we must briefly consider is ethology, 'the comparative study of the natural behaviour of animal species' to quote the definition of a leading practitioner.[90] It was described in the mid-1960s by Julian Huxley as 'that rapidly growing branch of science which is destined to provide a strong foundation for the science of human behavioural psychology'.[91] Perhaps we should qualify Huxley's observation by saying 'one of the foundations', for psychology is not likely to be totally reduced to biology.

Ethology, though it began to cohere as a distinct discipline on the continent of Europe in the 1930s, has its roots in the earlier work of naturalists and evolutionary biologists. In his recent account of *The Origins and Rise of Ethology*[92] Thorpe has traced its beginnings from the Cambridge biologist, John Ray, in the seventeenth century, through a line of French, British, American and European observers of animal behaviour. The key figures in its eventual crystallization were the Austrian Konrad Lorenz, who in the 1930s published a number of papers on instinct, which, according to Thorpe, 'established the bounds of the discipline of ethology, and largely determined the future course of ethological investigation for some twenty years',[93] and the Dutchman Niko Tinbergen, who after the war settled in England. Together with Lorenz's immensely readable popular book, *King Solomon's Ring*, Tinbergen's *The Study of Instinct* did much to introduce ethology to the English-speaking world in the early 1950s.[94] Already, before the outbreak of the Second World War, specialized journals for ethological research had begun to appear.[95]

The importance of ethology lay both in its methodology and in its conceptual system. The ethologists did not deny the value of experimentation, beloved by comparative psychologists of the American school, but they insisted on the necessity of prior observation of animal behaviour in its natural context. Through a long course of evolution animal species had become adapted to particular ecological niches, and experiments in which they were abstracted from these niches were largely meaningless. So the ethologists were primarily observers, and then, when they experimented, designed their experiments on appropriately naturalistic lines. Conceptually they emphasized the rich diversity of animal life and behaviour, but underlying this diversity they saw basic patterns of inherited instinct, marked by fixed action patterns and innate releasing mechanisms. Instincts could be divided into hierarchically ordered segments from the appetitive to the consummatory; these had arisen from, and could be modified by, Darwinian processes of natural selection, and were often transmuted in the course of time to serve as social signals. As Lorenz demonstrated in the case of the Anatinae (geese and ducks), behavioural characters could be used in taxonomy equally with morphological traits.[96] These generalizations were backed up by a mass of precise observations of animal behaviour from insects and fishes to birds and mammals, and tested frequently by simple, but ingenious, experiments.[97] Not all animal behaviour, of course, could be explained in terms of instinct; learning also played a part; but here again the ethologists tended to stress the role of maturation and sensitive, or critical, periods during which learning most readily took place. One of the striking early results of Lorenz was his demonstration of 'imprinting' in young birds, i.e. the response of following almost any moving object, as they would a parent bird, provided that the object was presented during the first few hours or days of life.[98] Somewhat later Thorpe was to present fascinating evidence on the combined influences of internal (genetic) and external (learned) factors in the development of bird song.[99]

The reaction of psychologists to this early work of the ethologists was a mixed one. In Europe, including Great Britain, the ground had been prepared, and the reaction was in general welcoming. In America there was a strongly entrenched rival tradition of comparative psychology, and for at least a decade after ethology emerged into general view, the reaction was dismissive. Under the influence first of Thorndike and then of the behaviourists animal psychologists in America concentrated largely on problems of learning, usually in artificial laboratory situations (mazes, puzzle boxes, etc.) and with a few docile species. The concept of instinct had been almost wholly abandoned, and species differences were largely disregarded.[100] The emphasis was not on naturalistic observation, but on experimental methodology, quantification of results, and the precise control of variables. The methodological looseness and conceptual vagueness of the ethologists came, therefore, under their heavy criticism.[101] In general the work of the ethologists was just ignored. It is significant, for example, that in a standard American textbook of comparative psychology published in 1951 there was, apart from one minor reference, no mention of any ethological research.[102] Among American psychologists the only two prominent figures sympathetic to ethology were Lashley and Beach.

This gap, however, was slowly bridged, and by 1976 the *Annual Review* could report that the synthesis between ethology and comparative psychology was essentially complete.[103] Probably the work of the British ethologists Thorpe and Hinde had a great deal to do with this reconciliation. In 1956 Thorpe published his scholarly work *Learning and Instinct in Animals*, in which he aimed to 'point out to psychologists and learning theorists, and to zoologists and physiologists how dependent each should be on the work of the other'.[104] This was followed ten years later by Hinde's *Animal Behaviour: A Synthesis of Ethology and Comparative Psychology*.[105] Thus the richness of content of ethology has been successfully married to the psychologist's methodological emphasis, and as a result a more powerful science of animal behaviour is beginning to emerge. This received the general recognition of the scientific community when, in 1973, Lorenz, Tinbergen and von Frisch (famous for his work on the language of bees[106]) were jointly awarded a Nobel Prize.

Apart from a vast increase in the quantity of work on animal behaviour in the last quarter of a century, there has been a marked growth in its sophistication. The rather crude earlier models of instinct have been discarded, though the importance of fixed, or rather modal, action patterns is still emphasized.[107] It is significant that in Hinde's recent survey of ethology the term instinct is not used at all.[108] The interaction of innate and environmental influences is now generally recognized even in stereotyped behaviour, and though the search for the neurophysiological bases of fixed action patterns has not been abandoned, the simplistic isomorphic concepts held by some pioneer ethologists have been.[109] At the same time ethology has branched out in new directions, particularly in the field of social ethology (Crook) and animal communication (Hinde *et al.*).[110]

Of special interest to psychologists has been the work on members of the primate group, an area in which, as the *Annual Review* noted in 1964, 'research is mushrooming at an unbelievable pace.'[111] The growth of interest was signalled by the founding of a *Journal of Primatology* in 1958, and a meeting of the first annual Primatology Research Conference in Oregon in 1962. By that date seven primate research centres had been established in America, and a well-known centre was already operating in Japan. Of course, here again some work on primates had commenced much earlier. In Russia Ladygina-Kots began her studies as far back as 1913, when she founded a laboratory in Moscow. She published a detailed study in 1935 on the raising of a young chimpanzee in her home, and in 1959 a report on tool-using by chimpanzees, to mention only the most notable items in a lifetime's work.[112] In the west fieldwork on primates began with the researches of Yerkes, Bingham, Nissen, Carpenter and Zuckerman in the 1920s and 1930s;[113] while Köhler's experimental work on *The Mentality of Apes* concentrated particularly on the use of implements and on insight in problem-solving.[114] The impact of ethology has encouraged the observation of primate behaviour in its natural settings. Particularly valuable for the light they have thrown on the social relations and mode of life of primates have been the long-term field studies of Jane van Lawick-Goodall and Dian Fossey on chimpanzees and mountain gorillas respectively.[115] Observations on tool-using, on social cooperation and on modes of communication under natural conditions have been supplemented by an increasing amount of experimental work, the best known among which are probably the attempts by Gardner and by Premack to teach chimpanzees to use sign language.[116] These attempts have been successful up to a point, though that point falls a good deal short of the spontaneous linguistic achievements of the human race.

Though the work of ethologists is fascinating for its own sake and for the light it throws on the diversity and intricacy of animal behaviour, the question remains of its relevance to human psychology. Answers to this question, as might be expected, differ widely. There is a commonly held view, which goes back at least to Locke, that human nature is basically 'void of all characters',[117] and, therefore, wholly shaped either by environmental circumstances or by its own free decisions. A motley band of behaviourists, sociologists and existentialists, though they share little else in common, have shared this preconception. It has recently been restated by Harré, who maintains that biology can tell us very little about human social behaviour, as this consists almost wholly of a florid, non-biological superstructure.[118] By contrast the philosopher Mary Midgley, in her *Beast and Man*, writes, 'we are not just rather like animals: we *are* animals. Our differences from other species may be striking, but comparisons with them have always been, and must be crucial to our view of ourselves.'[119] The pioneer ethologists themselves certainly believed that their work was relevant to man. Lorenz held that it could help to illuminate man's frequently irrational behaviour,[120] and Tinbergen concluded his book on instinct with a section on the ethological study of man.[121] Hinde in his recent survey has a long section on 'Ethology and Human Social Sciences', in which though he observes that 'direct parallels between animal and human behaviour are rarely appropriate', he considers a number of directions in which ethology has illuminated human psychology.[122] Particularly notable is Bowlby's work on attachment, mother-child relationships and psychopathology, largely inspired by ethology, and a growing volume of work on non-verbal communication in man.[123] Another interesting development is Crook's endeavour to link ethology with some of the more complex aspects of the human personality.[124]

There is, in fact, no case for dogmatically taking sides in this controversy. Man is a bio-social organism; both biology and culture are relevant to the investigation of his psychology. It remains for research to determine the complex relationships and interactions between these two sets of variables. As Freud clearly saw, disharmony between the two major elements of human nature is a prime source of the tensions and discontents to which civilized man is prone. The topic is, therefore, one of central significance. What the recent advances in the biological sciences have demonstrated is that the biological components provide crucial information on a good many aspects of human behaviour, and particularly on divergences from normal functioning. The working of the human organism is dependent on its chemistry, constrained by the structure of its nervous system and genetic composition, and in many respects comparable to that of other members of the mammalian kingdom, particularly the primates to which mankind is intimately related. This does not mean that the biological imperialism of the sociobiologists is justified.[125] There are a number of special and unique features about mankind which transcend any reasonable definition of biology – his language, his enhanced manual skills, his powers of abstract and creative thought, and the complex social and cultural superstructures established on these foundations. It is to the recent investigations into these crucial features that we must now proceed, for these investigations, too, have opened up new vistas.

Chapter 15
New vistas II

I

It has become increasingly clear that in the years immediately following the Second World War a new age, the age of information technology, had its birth. We have already begun to experience some of the profound social consequences of these technological developments; the intellectual consequences have been equally far-reaching. For between 1946 and 1950 not only was the first electronic computer (ENIAC) brought into operation, but with Wiener's *Cybernetics* (1948), and Shannon and Weaver's *Mathematical Theory of Communication* (1949)[1] the new disciplines of cybernetics and information theory were first systematically formulated, and they have had a deep influence on intellectual life generally and on the shaping of contemporary psychology in particular. It may be going too far to regard the Second World War as a 'boundary between history and pre-history' in psychology,[2] for most of the problems in psychology are old problems, and new ideas and techniques have their roots in the past. In a book entitled *The Nature of Explanation* (1943), which foreshadowed at least some of the ideas of the information revolution, Kenneth Craik, the brilliant young British psychologist who was tragically killed in an accident in 1945 at the age of thirty-one, propounded his 'hypothesis on the nature of thought' within the framework of ancient philosophical problems.[3] Craik's hypothesis, in brief, was 'that thought models, or parallels, reality – that its essential feature is not "the mind", "the self", "sense-data" nor propositions, but symbolism, and that this symbolism is largely of the same kind as that which is familiar to us in mechanical devices which aid thought and calculation'.[4] In this prescient statement Craik had formulated a key doctrine of cybernetics and information theory. The new technologies, which had already begun to emerge, meant that this hypothesis was no longer merely speculative, but could be practically tested and realized.

The term 'cybernetics' was coined, and the discipline defined, by the distinguished American mathematician Norbert Wiener (1894-1964), who after graduating in America studied with Bertrand Russell in Cambridge. His book *Cybernetics* was subtitled *Control and Communication in the Animal and Machine*, and it was Wiener's conviction that the same general principles could be applied to explaining the functioning of self-regulating machinery and living organisms. In both there was regulation by feedback, and control through the communication of information. Implied in these regulatory processes was the idea of goal or 'purpose'. This might either be the steady homeostatic state of the machine or organism itself in relation to its environment, or it might be the hitting of a changing external target, as in the case of a self-guiding missile. In either case the achievement of the goal could be explained in mechanical terms, given that there was a system capable of receiving, storing and utilizing information and monitoring the course of events. Earlier mechanistic theories had been caged in the doctrine of energy and its conservation. The concept of information brought in the ideas of organization, negative entropy and continuity through time. Clearly this was an enormous advance in understanding the functioning of organisms, replacing both the older mechanistic theories and the wholistic doctrines associated with organismic and Gestalt viewpoints, with an analytical theory of organization and direction, and making way for investigations into the processes involved. Wiener himself was a visionary thinker who foresaw far-reaching consequences and applications resulting from cybernetics, not only in biology, but in psychology and the social sciences.[5] His ideas were soon to be taken up by leading figures in all these disciplines, for example, by Monod and Jacob in biology, by Piaget in psychology, and Parsons in sociology.[6]

The relevance of cybernetics to psychology was soon demonstrated both experimentally and through the construction of mechanical contraptions simulating various aspects of behaviour. A particularly striking experimental illustration of the importance of feedback was the demonstration of the disruptive distortion of speech brought about by delay in a subject's hearing of his own voice.[7] Early simulations of behaviour were those of Ross Ashby and Grey Walter in Great Britain. Ashby's 'homeostat' was a device that not only maintained a stable steady state, but could adjust to changed circumstances, a property which he termed 'ultrastability'.[8] In his *Introduction to Cybernetics* (1956) Ashby put forward the view that cybernetics provided 'a single vocabulary and a single set of concepts suitable for representing the most diverse types of system',[9] thus aligning it with the General Systems Theory of von Bertalannfy.[10] Grey Walter constructed a cybernetic 'tortoise' which could home on to a light target, avoiding obstacles, and when meeting other 'tortoises' engaging in a sort of 'social' behaviour.[11] These were among the first of numerous artifacts showing behavioural properties, and, with the development of computers, becoming capable of playing games and solving problems.[12] The topic of robotics has now become a leading technological, as well as philosophical, problem.[13]

Basic to cybernetics was the concept of information and its transmission in the form of messages. In the century preceding the outbreak of the Second World War there had been a dramatic increase in man's ability to communicate over vast distances. Telegraphic communication and the binary Morse Code went back to the 1830s, the telephone to the 1870s, wireless communication to the 1890s, and television to the late 1920s. But the mathematical theory of communication was not fully formulated until the appearance of Shannon and Weaver's book in 1949.[14] The pressure on communication systems during the war was intense. The need to transmit the maximum possible information in coded form through channels of limited capacity was among the factors instigating Shannon's mathematical treatment of the problem. Some earlier work of R.V.L. Hartley in the 1920s had paved the way.[15] Information was seen as essentially dependent on a choice between alternatives. If the alternatives were few, the amount of information provided by a message was minimal; it increased as the alternatives increased. The simplest situation was that of a binary choice between two equally likely alternatives, and Shannon took this as his unit of information, namely 'one bit'. From this starting point the quantity of information contained in messages was assessed logarithmically on a binary base. In practice most messages contained a good deal of what Shannon termed 'redundancy', that is surplus information. This particularly applied to language, printed English being about seventy-five per cent redundant. The letter 'u', for example, after the letter 'q' is completely redundant from the informational point of view, as it invariably follows. Nevertheless because of 'noise', or interference, in communication channels a certain amount of redundancy has been shown to be advantageous.

Information theory was an abstract, mathematical theory, but its relevance to psychology soon became apparent. The brain could be regarded as an information store and processor, the nervous system as a complex communication network, and the whole system as a control mechanism with defined capacities. George Miller of Harvard University was the first psychologist to respond to the challenge of the new ideas. His pioneer article on the subject appeared in 1949,[16] but it was not until his article 'What is information measurement?' appeared in the *American Psychologist* in 1953, and his famous discussion on 'the magical number seven' in 1956,[17] that information theory began to capture the allegiance of a growing band of psychologists. In the English Cambridge, too, the theory early gained favour. Hick applied it to the interpretation of the results of choice-reaction experiments, and it was basic to the work of Broadbent on hearing.[18] In 1959 Attneave in America summarized the results of the applications of information theory to psychology over a considerable range of problems.[19] Particularly important was the work of Newell and Simon on human problem solving in 1958, which they later claimed to be 'the first explicit and deliberate exposition of the position known as information processing psychology'.[20] It has now become a dominant approach to, at any rate, the cognitive side of psychology, particularly to perception, pattern recognition, memory, thinking and decision procedures.[21] The attempt to model mental processes, whether by computer programs or robotically, has compelled psychologists to recognize the intricacy of the processing that must take place in the brain to account for the transformation of incoming information and the outcomes, behavioural and phenomenological, actually achieved. An early example of this recognition was Grey Walter's conditioned reflex analogue, CORA, the construction of which forced him to admit 'the number and complexity [of the operations involved in the provision] of a conditioning connection between two circuits'.[22] The conditioned reflex, far from being the basic unit of behaviour, involved at least seven essential steps from chance to meaning, all of which had somehow to be provided equally by the mechanical analogue and by the nervous system of an animal. For this alone cybernetics and information theory has proved of immense importance to psychology. It disproves decisively, for example, the view put forward by the philosopher Searle, when he maintained that there is no intermediate processing level between experience and neurophysiology.[23]

The importance of information theory, however, goes much further than simply providing a demonstration of complexity. It has rescued psychology from its fixation on the externals of behaviour, on stimuli and responses, and restored its rightful subject matter, the internal mechanisms involved in the processing of information, decision making and control, the traditional properties of mind. It has revivified the cognitive side of psychology, which had withered in the early years of experimentalism, and re-established the value of verbal reports of cognitive processes.[24] It has focused attention on symbolism, codes, programs and structures, on choice in the face of uncertainty; and it has re-emphasized the importance of the temporal, historical dimension of behaviour and experience. Above all the concept of information itself is of central significance, for as Wiener observed in his seminal book, 'Information is information, not matter or energy. No materialism which does not admit this can survive at the present day.'[25] Psychology had been turned, perhaps permanently, from the Lockean mode, which had dominated during the associationist-behaviourist eras, to a Leibnizian mode of thought.

It is the conceptual, rather than the mathematical, side of information theory that is likely to be the most lasting for psychology. Not that the quantitative approach is without value. When precise measurements can be made of information content the results constitute a confirmation of basic theory. But the complexity of human situations generally precludes precise measurements, and in any case information has a semantic as well as a mathematical connotation. This was pointed out very early by the British communication scientist D.M. Mackay, who emphasized the need to distinguish the 'logon' content and the 'metron' content of messages (i.e. the meaningful and the quantitative).[26] A good deal of experimental work had demonstrated that semantic meaning was as important as information content in the quantitative sense in determining outcomes, for example in memorizing and recognition tasks.[27] The difference between quantitative information and semantic information is clearly brought out by considering the phrase in Hamlet's soliloquy, 'To be or not to be'. From a quantitative point of view this provides no information at all, as these are the only possible alternatives, and everyone already knows this. But the phrase is nevertheless loaded with profound overtones of meaning. As David Marr saw in his studies of vision, to explain perception it is necessary to postulate, over and above the successive stages of information processing, a set of 'internal representations which capture this information'.[28] We are back again at an internal world of representations, a mental world of symbolism and intentions, which to some extent matches and reflects the external world, but which in its imaginative supplementation of that world extends creatively, and sometimes dangerously, into many other 'possible worlds'.

II

Of all the changes associated with information technology the development of the computer has been the most dramatic. It is, as one British expert observed, a change 'faster by orders of magnitude than anything that has happened before'.[29] The full implications of the computerization of society are impossible to forecast. We can only note that the major scientific revolutions of the past have been preluded by advances in the informational field – the Greek revolution by the introduction of alphabetic scripts, the seventeenth century revolution by printed books. The computer shows every sign of being even more far-reaching in its effects. In psychology particularly its influence is likely to be profound, since for the psychologist the computer is more than a tool or a toy; it is to some extent a model of the mind, throwing light on its very workings. For in spite of differences in texture computers are mind-like in their structure; they have inputs and outputs, memory stores and programs, logic and control units. They not only open up fascinating vistas of research, but raise fundamental problems for the psychologist.

The development of computers rests on two foundations, on technology and logic. Charles Babbage in the nineteenth century had with his 'analytical engine' grasped many of the basic ideas, but was defeated from realizing them by technical difficulties.[30] The development first of relays and thermionic valves, then of transistors, silicon chips and very large-scale integration has made the progress of computers possible, and led to vast increases in their speed and power.[31] Other technical advances, following von Neumann's crucial invention of the stored program in 1946, have given the computer almost limitless flexibility. Equally important have been advances in logic and programming. In 1936 the British mathematician A.M. Turing in a key paper formulated the principles of a hypothetical universal computing machine capable of modifying its instructions and solving any problem that could be precisely stated.[32] After working highly successfully on enemy code breaking during the war he went on to write on computing machinery and intelligence, prophesying that by the end of the century 'one will be able to speak to machines thinking without expecting to be contradicted'.[33] Already in 1949, a year before

Turing's article, E.C. Berkeley, in a remarkable book, *Giant Brains*, had concluded with a chapter on 'The Future: Machines that think and what they might do for men'.[34] The ideas of Turing needed translation into hardware before they could be realized. This was made possible by Shannon's design of circuitry on the basis of Boole's binary logic as formalized by Whitehead and Russell.[35] This link between logic and computers was a vital stage in their development. Of hardly less practical importance than these developments in logic and theory have been the changes in the programming of computers. Early methods of programming were tedious and complex. With FORTRAN in 1956 high-level languages appeared on the scene, and in recent years languages like LISP, specially designed to mould cognitive and other psychological processes have proved of special interest to psychologists. Undoubtedly these latest developments have landed computers into the very centre of the psychological scene.

The use of computers in departments of psychology has been rapidly rising during the last quarter of a century. At the time of writing all departments of psychology in British universities are computerized.[36] The average number of microcomputers per department is nineteen; in addition there are commonly 'dedicated' (i.e. special purpose) machines, time-sharing systems, word processors, and access to external computing facilities. The majority of psychology students learn something about the programming and use of computers and this is, of course, backed up by the fact that nearly all schools and a quarter of all homes now own their own machines. There are three major uses of computers in psychology: firstly, for basic data processing, enabling psychologists to carry out more ambitious experiments, with more subjects and more variables, and to deal with much more complex situations; secondly, for the on-line control of experiments, bringing much greater precision both to input and in analysis of output; and thirdly, for the computer modelling of psychological processes and the testing of theoretical proposals.[37]

It is the last of these three areas that is of the greatest interest. The weakness of psychological theories has often been the vagueness of their verbal formulations. To model a theory on a computer forces the psychologist to state his theory precisely. 'The computer program', writes Longuet-Higgins of the Theoretical Psychology Unit in Edinburgh, 'offers us the possibility of formulating adequately sophisticated theories of cognition. It sets new standards in the formulation of models of cognitive processes, these models being open to direct and immediate test.'[38] Margaret Boden, more succinctly, spoke of 'the double discipline of explicitness and testing'.[39] Cognitive theories, like those of Hebb and Piaget, have already been sharpened by these disciplines,[40] and we have previously noted how Grey Walter with his CORA machine was able to unpack the concept of the conditioned reflex.

Computer simulation has reached out into many areas of psychology – visual processing, skills in work and games, problem-solving, language, and even personality and its disturbances. Perhaps the most significant outcome of these excursions is the recognition which they have forced on psychologists of the enormous complexity of human mental processes. No theories in psychology which do not recognize this complexity are any longer tenable. None the less, significant achievements have been recorded in the field of simulation, some of them quite striking. Visual processing has been one of the most intensively studied areas, as it is basic to the construction of 'intelligent' robots. To get a computer to 'see' is no easy matter.[41] In the words of Donald Michie,

> the problem of making a computer see what is going on around it is inextricably linked with such problems as dealing with unreliable information, making hypotheses and testing them, making plans of action, using knowledge about the state of the world and its laws, integrating fragments of information to produce a coherent whole and learning complex relationships.[42]

Far from being a simple photographic-like recording, vision involves an elaborate constructive and interpretative process. What a human being does apparently without effort depends in fact upon numerous operations, the details of which he is wholly unaware. In spite of these complexities the new generation of robot machines is beginning to acquire perceptual skills, computers which can recognize human faces seen from unfamiliar angles have been devised,[43] and the psychology of vision has been much enriched in the process.

The competence of computers in game playing and problem solving has been equally striking. Samuel in 1959 contrived a draughts (or checkers) program that could beat even expert players,[44] and chess-playing programs (which are necessarily of enormous complexity, as the number of possible combinations of chess moves is said to exceed the number of atoms in the universe!) can beat even quite talented amateurs, though they succumb to grandmasters. The analysis of chess playing was undertaken by Newell and Simon, among others, in their work on human information processing and problem solving generally.[45] This has been one of the most important of simulation projects. With their General Problem Solver Newell and Simon have been successful in programming a computer to prove a considerable number of the theorems in *Principia Mathematica*, to crack arithmetical codes, and solve simple problems in symbolic logic.[46] The greatest difficulties have arisen in attempts to program computers to understand and use human language, man's unique gift. It has proved so far impossible, in spite of strenuous efforts, to translate from one language to another with idiomatic naturalness.[47] Nevertheless some limited progress has been made. By the 1960s computers could answer questions in English on a wide range of topics, though the answers were fairly stereotyped. Problems arise from the immense flexibility and subtlety of language. It is not enough to provide computers with dictionaries; much more than this they need to be rendered linguistically competent, with a 'knowledge' of the universe of discouse, an 'understanding' of grammatical rules, and logical skills in interpretation. The most successful program, commonly known as SHIRDLU, was developed by Winograd in the early 1970s. Within the very limited universe of building blocks arranged in a restricted area the computer did appear to 'understand' instructions, and to be capable of carrying out appropriate actions.[48] More ambitious programs attempting to simulate the verbal exchanges involved in a Freudian analysis and Rogerian psychotherapy have had only very limited success.[49]

The progress that has been made in computer simulation, though not as great as at one time hoped, has nevertheless fired workers in the field known as 'artificial intelligence'. Intense research in this area is now in progress in America, Japan, Great Britain and on the continent of Europe, and hopes are rising that Turing's dream of an intelligent machine may ultimately be realized. There have been and are, however, many sceptics. Von Neumann himself, the architect of the modern computer, pointed to essential differences between computers and brains.[50] In Great Britain in 1973 the Science Research Council commissioned a distinguished Cambridge mathematician, Sir James Lighthill, to report on 'artificial intelligence', and he was so dismissive that official support in this country dried up for some years.[51] Only when, in 1981, the Japanese established an Institute for New Generation Computer Technology did the tune change, and the Alvey Commission persuaded the British Government to support a five-year project with considerable funds. Europe followed with its 'Esprit' project in 1984, and America has never ceased researching in advanced computer design, largely for military reasons.

The progress in the field of computing over the last forty years has been so remarkable that it would be surprising if all this was suddenly to stop. There seems reason to suppose that a 'fifth generation' of computers will eventually be born, and that these will be more flexible and more 'talented' than existing machines, in short, more mind-like. But doubts of a fundamental nature are voiced, particularly by philosophers. A.J. Ayer, for example, finds it difficult to 'allow machines an inner life, to credit them with feeling and emotion, to treat them as moral agents'.[52] In his Reith lectures Searle argued powerfully that computer programs, however sophisticated, in that they are entirely formal structures, cannot possibly possess the semantic and meaningful properties characteristic of minds.[53] Intentionality is the mark of mind, and it is this which is lacking in machines. Others, however, dispute this pessimistic conclusion. Margaret Boden, in her book on artificial intelligence, which has been described as 'a classic',[54] maintained, in spite of some reservations, that computer models do display intentionality, and that it is not inappropriate to speak of purposes, plans, hypotheses and inferences. In fact she went so far as to state that the real significance of intelligent machines was that they served as a counteraction to the dehumanizing influences of crude materialism.[55] If machines are indeed so human, we need not fear if humans in their turn are just complex machines!

In these debates it is important to distinguish the logical from the psychological aspects of the matter. Artificial intelligence aims at a logical simulation of intelligent mental processes; it cannot simulate them psychologically. Human psychology is rooted in biology; it is a produce of a long evolutionary history; it is stamped by individuality; it is motivated by powerful drives of individual and racial survival; and it is steered very largely by feelings, by loves, by hates and by fears. There is none of all this in a computer. Indeed there is no more intentionality in a computer program than there is in the printed pages of a book. A machine cannot think, any more than a book can remember. The meaning of the words on a printed page are bestowed by minds; they have only a delegated intentionality. True, the computer, unlike the book, is dynamic, it involves processes in time, and is not merely the static record of the results of thought. It can provide answers to problems that the unaided human mind cannot provide. But this does not imply intentionality. A simple calculating machine can give answers that no human being can immediately give; but no one has suggested that it 'thinks'. Nor does a computer 'think' in the full sense of the word, even though it can pass a Turing test and momentarily fool an interlocutor.[56]

The danger of excessive claims for artificial intelligence is that they may obscure the real value of computers for psychology. As a tool they have already proved their worth, and they have demonstrated their capacity for modelling at least some features of minds. It seems certain that they will continue to be fruitfully used for this and other purposes. There is, however, a debit side to the matter. Computer bewitchment threatens to eclipse an appreciation of the biological and historical depths of human nature. As Bolter has argued in *Turing's Man*, an impressive study of the impact of computers on western culture, the image of man generated by computer technology is not that of the whole man; it is an image which has lost 'the Faustian concern with depth', and its goal is 'to demonstrate that man is all surface, that there is nothing dark or mysterious in the human condition'.[57] The influence of the computer, and of information technology generally, on psychology has been to shift the balance of the subject to the cognitive pole. It is to this characteristic trend of the psychology of recent times that we must now turn our attention

III

Cognitive psychology is both the newest and the oldest strand in the history of the subject. From the time of Plato and Aristotle onwards up till the seventeenth century the supremacy of reason (νοῦς) was not seriously questioned, and the analysis of cognitive faculties constituted the central topic of psychology. There was, according to Thomas Aquinas, an ordered hierarchy in the soul of man, and the powers of the intellect were the crown and source of this order.[58] Over a period of three centuries, from 1650 onwards, this belief was steadily eroded. The intellect was emasculated by the associationists, subordinated to instincts and passions by biologically orientated dynamic psychologists, rejected as a possible topic of experimental and introspective study by Wundt, and finally dealt a nearly mortal blow by twentieth century behaviourists. 'What the psychologists have hitherto called thought', declared Watson, 'is nothing but talking to ourselves.'[59] So thinking, as Bruner has observed, ceased to be 'a mainstream topic in psychology'; it was 'too mentalistic, too subjective, too shifty'.[60] It never, of course, passed completely out of view. A small band of Catholic psychologists kept the scholastic faith alive;[61] Külpe and his Würzburg followers breached the Wundtian taboos and attacked thinking introspectively;[62] the Gestaltists, dissatisfied with mechanical learning theories, found traces of 'insight' even in animals and children;[63] and there was, in the 1920s and 1930s a rather desultory sprinkling of experimental studies on concept formation and reasoning.[64] But as Humphrey lamented in his historical review, 'fifty years of work has not brought us very far.'[65]

Humphrey's book *Thinking* (1951) was among the first faint signs of a revival. Several books on thought processes appeared about then, for example Rapaport's *The Organization and Pathology of Thought* (1951) and Vinacke's *Psychology of Thinking* (1952); while Stevens's *Handbook of Experimental Psychology*, also published in 1951, included a brief chapter on 'Cognitive Processes' by Leeper, which, in spite of its slightness, at least recognized the existence of the subject.[66] But there was no indication yet of any sudden blossoming of cognitive psychology; there was no theoretical initiative, no recognition of the relevance of information processing concepts and computers. Even Woodworth and Schlosberg in their 1954 text looked back to the past rather than forward to the future.[67] The faint signs of revival seemed to spring from a discontent with learning theory rather than from any new positive inspiration. As late as 1960 it was still necessary for Hebb, in his presidential address to the American Psychological Association, to campaign for a new revolution. 'Let us,' he urged, 'press on with serious, persistent, and if necessary daring exploration of the thought processes by all available means.'[68]

It was above all the arrival of computers, backed by the disciplines of cybernetics and information theory, that brought about the decisive change in outlook. It had obviously become quixotic to grant machines mind-like properties, and to deny these properties to the minds that had constructed the machines. If it was necessary to speak of control processes, rules, programs, strategies and so on in connection with machines, clearly it was not out of order to employ similar concepts with regard to minds. To quote Bruner again: 'You cannot conceive of managing a complex world of information without a workable concept of mind.'[69] So mind returned, and with it cognitive psychology. Though Bruner himself dates the birth of cognitive science precisely to September 1956, when a symposium on information theory was held at the Massachusetts Institute of Technology, bringing together experimental psychology, linguistics and computer simulation,[70] in fact acceptance of cognitive psychology was a gradual one, as an analysis of the contents of the *Annual Review of Psychology* indicates. In 1953 the *Annual Review* devoted just two pages to 'thinking' in its survey of learning, noting that 'research in this area continues to move at an appallingly slow pace'.[71] In 1955 an 'increased interest' in problem solving and thinking was reported;[72] in 1959 'an accelerated interest' and the beginnings of a solid experimental literature.[73] In spite of this rise of interest progress to the 1961 reviewer appeared small.[74] Not until 1966 did a full-scale survey of 'Cognitive Functions' appear in the *Annual Review*.[75] By 1972 it was possible to write of a 'resurgence' of cognitive psychology,[76] and in 1975, shortly after three new journals devoted to cognition had been established, the mind was 'really back in style'.[77] In the fifteen years between 1955 and 1970 cognitive science had gradually become a dominant movement in psychology.

This revival of interest generated an extensive and rapidly growing experimental literature, which it is impossible to review here in detail.[78] It covered concept formation, reasoning and problem solving (with a particular emphasis on types of error, blockages and difficulties), and differences in cognitive styles and strategies. Fruitful analogies between thinking and other skills were drawn, for example by Bartlett,[79] and analyses of particular skills, such as those of the expert chess master,[80] brought out various important aspects of intellectual functioning, such as planning and the complexity of the hierarchical system of problems and sub-problems involved. An interesting and significant chapter in this resurgence was the returning popularity of imagery.[81] Above all a growing feature of the new cognitive psychology was the precision of formulation required by the demand for the computer simulation of cognitive processes. From 1960 onwards this became more and more common, greatly increasing the power and exactness of theorizing.

Let us, in default of a detailed review, examine a few selected landmarks in the advance of cognitive psychology. The selection of these landmarks is necessarily a somewhat dubious procedure, and can hardly claim representativeness. But since it would require a large volume to be reasonably comprehensive, selection of some sort is obligatory. With due hesitation, therefore, I pick what I regard as seven key works.

(1) If any one book can be said to have marked the rebirth of cognitive psychology perhaps *The Study of Thinking* (1956) by Bruner, Goodnow and Austin has the best claim to have done so.[82] For one thing it was extremely readable, which not many of its successors have been; it combined, moreover, carefully controlled experimental situations with many observations from practical life; and it broke new ground with its emphasis on coding, strategies, and general tendencies in information-getting and information-using behaviour. It was the first fruit of the Cognition Project which Bruner set up at Harvard in 1952, and which eventually became incorporated in the Center for Cognitive Studies at that university.[83] Bruner later shifted the focus of his interest to matters related to cognitive growth and the development of children's language functions. Though his lively and exploring mind never rested happily in a too narrow definition of cognitive science, his early contribution was of pioneering importance.

(2) E.B. Hunt's *Concept Learning*, which appeared six years later in 1962, was more tightly linked to information processing, symbolic logic, set theory and computing.[84] Hunt himself regarded his work as an elaboration of Hovland's earlier, path-breaking 'communication analysis of concept learning'.[85] He summed up his position by stating that 'concept learning can be thought of as a technique for solving an induction problem in symbolic logic through the use of information-processing routines'.[86] Such learning had to be regarded as a decision-making process, and could not be explained in stimulus-response terms. Hunt's work was a further step in the demise of learning theory models of thinking, which he regarded as unsatisfactory even when mediation processes were included, and it marked progress towards greater precision in the formulation of cognitive systems.

(3) The year 1967 saw the publication of Neisser's *Cognitive Psychology*. It was preluded four years previously by his article on 'The multiplicity of thought',[87] in which he underlined the need to distinguish multiple, or parallel, and sequential processes involved in thinking. 'Human thinking', he maintained, 'is a multiple activity . . . a number of more or less independent trains of thought usually coexist. Ordinarily, however, there is a 'main sequence' in progress. . . . The concurrent operations are not conscious, because consciousness is intrinsically single. . . . The main sequence usually has control of motor activity.'[88] This standpoint was developed in *Cognitive Psychology* with a lot of experimental evidence from the fields of visual and auditory cognition. Seeing and hearing were treated as constructive processes, marked by two stages: a primary, fast, crude, wholistic, parallel stage, and a secondary, deliberate, attentive, detailed, sequential stage. In a final, rather sketchy section Neisser suggested that the higher processes of remembering and thinking could be treated on analogous lines. He also concluded that it was necessary to postulate a separate, executive processor, comparable to the computer's 'executive routine'.[89] Nine years later Neisser followed his earlier book with a shorter, more ruminative, essay, *Cognition and Reality* (1976), in which he expressed some disillusion with the narrowness of cognitive psychology, and its tendency to focus on laboratory situations rather than looking outward on the world beyond. He seemed impressed, perhaps unduly, with Gibson's work on perception, and revived the concept of 'schemata' to reconcile information processing and 'information pick-up'.[90] 'Pick-up', however, is a reversion to vagueness; if it explains why perceptions are usually accurate (and there are other possible explanations for this), it fails to explain why in certain circumstances they are not.

(4) Newell and Simon's *Human Problem Solving* (1972), which became practically the Bible of information processors, summed up more than fifteen years of work based on the sequential processing of their General Problem Solver.[91] This work was highly significant in the development of the newer cognitive psychology in general, and artificial intelligence in particular. In their 1972 book Newell and Simon considered three special areas in detail, cryptarithmetic (in

which arithmetical problems are presented in code), problems in symbolic logic, and chess-playing programs. They concluded with a general theory of human problem solving in which they listed the main characteristics of the information system that carries out the processing, and the nature of the various task environments in which the processes operated and the extent to which the environments affected the internal structure of the processing system itself. They ended modestly by admitting that little was in fact known about how new programs were constructed in real life to cope with new tasks. Nevertheless their book was a powerful card in the information processor's hand.

(5)   A more sceptical view was provided somewhat later by Fodor's *The Modularity of Mind* (1983). In his distinction between 'modular' and 'central' processing Fodor aimed at making faculty psychology once more respectable. It was, in his view, necessary to postulate many fundamentally different kinds of psychological mechanisms to explain the facts of mental life, in particular specific modular input systems which were informationally 'encapsulated' (i.e. largely screened from each other and from central processes). This applied, above all, to the main perceptual systems and to language mechanisms. He supported his thesis with a good deal of evidence and experimental data. By contrast the non-modular central system, which exploited the information that input systems provided, was so global and unstructured that Fodor was doubtful whether it could be captured scientifically. Not only did he conclude pessimistically that 'cognitive science hasn't even started',[92] but he seemed to throw doubts on its very possibility, for 'the more global a cognitive process, the less anybody understands it.'[93]

(6)   This pessimistic conclusion was tacitly contradicted by Johnson-Laird's *Mental Models* (1983) which appeared almost simultaneously. Johnson-Laird plunged unhesitatingly into an analysis of the central processes of reasoning, both syllogistic and inductive, explaining them in terms of mental models that were computable, finite and representative. His account of syllogistic reasoning was particularly thorough, and went a long way to account for the difficulties subjects experience in coping with various modes of syllogism as revealed by extensive experimental evidence.[94] Cognition, he maintained 'appears to be comprehensible.'[95] It cannot be grasped introspectively, but it can be simulated on computers. And he went so far as to claim that 'in so far as there can be a science of mind, it will almost certainly be restricted to accounts that can be formulated as computer programs'.[96] He concluded by suggesting that consciousness, 'the most puzzling of all phenomena of mental life'[97] could be explained as a means of overriding deadlocks and pathological interactions among subordinate levels of cognitive organization. He also denied that it was necessary to postulate an 'innate mental logic', for 'there can be reasoning without logic',[98] a reasoning achieved it would seem by a mere inspection of models. There may be difficulties in this particular point of view, but in the detail of its theoretical exposition, as well as its rich experimental back-up *Mental Models* taken as a whole was an impressive addition to the literature of cognition.

(7) Equally impressive was its American counterpart, J.R. Anderson's *The Architecture of Cognition* (1983), which was again based on a computer simulation and supported by a mass of experimental evidence. Anderson, in contradiction to Fodor, advocated 'a unitary system of higher-level cognition', a system he termed ACT (Adaptive Control of Thought), operative over all aspects of mental life, and embracing both 'declarative knowledge' (knowledge about) and 'procedural knowledge' (knowing how, i.e. skills).[99] The striking feature of Anderson's proposal was its ability to integrate theoretical analysis and experimental evidence over the whole range of cognitive psychology. It probably ordered a larger area of cognitive functioning than any previously published system.

It is not easy in the midstream of a powerful movement to sum up its achievements so far. Though there is now a widespread and very general agreement that the information-processing model of cognition is the appropriate model, there are disagreements on matters of important detail – on the generality-modularity issue, on the relation of psychological processing to logic and on the status of language functions. But in spite of disagreements there is little doubt that substantial progress has been made. It is only necessary to compare a work like Titchener's *Experimental Psychology of the Thought Processes*, written near the beginning of the century (1909), with its reduction of thought to sensory-imaginal patterns, and Anderson's recent *Architecture of Cognition* to recognize that there has been enormous advance in cogency and verisimilitude. Nevertheless there are limitations, even dangers, in the computerization of thought. Psychology has suffered more than once in its recent history from the dominance of methodology over content. Psychophysics in the nineteenth century, behaviourism in the early twentieth, and now computer modelling, have all been attempts to achieve scientific precision, and all these movements have tended to impoverish the database of psychology. Far from all human thinking consisting of problem solving or being reducible simply to logic, a great deal is expressive, symbolic, and agonistically motivated. Much thinking is extremely weird, and computers have not yet captured this weirdness. Nor have the cognitive scientists we have considered, apart from Bruner, given enough attention to the social components of thinking. They have tended to ignore the enormous cognitive capital of society, Popper's 'Third World', and the ways in which it is assimilated by, and in which it affects the thinking of, the individual person. Finally cognitive science has saddled itself with an untenable dualism – the dualism of 'hardware' and 'software'. 'Psychology', wrote Neisser, 'deals with the organization of information, not with its representation in organic tissue.'[100] The analogy with the computer, however, here breaks down. In the computer 'hardware' and 'software' do not influence each other; in the organism they do. There is constant psychosomatic interaction. Neisser was right in another context when he concluded his *Cognitive Psychology* by remarking that 'the study of cognition is only one fraction of psychology, and it cannot stand alone'.[101] Cognitive psychology is not the whole of psychology, nor is computer modelling the whole of cognitive psychology. There are two other important streams of influence that have broadened the field, Piaget's genetic epistemology and psycholinguistics.

IV

Jean Piaget (1896-1980) is unquestionably one of the outstanding figures of twentieth century psychology. His influence over the past quarter of a century has steadily grown, and he has generated an enormous volume of critical comment and research throughout the world. In spite of many reservations that have been expressed as to certain features of his theories, his stature as a giant of psychology is now recognized even by his critics. No one since Freud has had so marked an influence on the subject. Although Piaget commenced writing on psychological topics in 1920, it was not till about 1960 that his influence was widely felt, at any rate in Anglo-Saxon countries. Before that, comment in Great Britain was mostly fairly critical, and in America his theoretical position and methodological approach were dismissed as incompatible with the prevailing tenets of behaviourism. In some ways Piaget has been his own worst enemy. He has been a compulsive and untidy writer, often abstract and obscure, and endlessly repetitive. The solid worth of his achievement has to be laboriously extracted. However, by 1960 the climate for recognition had become more favourable. Behaviourism was on the wane, cognitive psychology was beginning to gain favour, and Piaget no longer appeared to be so alienated from the dominant '*Zeitgeist*'. Peel and Lovell in England and Flavell in the United States brought his work into wider notice among psychologists and educationists.[102] In 1969 the American Psychological Association accorded him its Distinguished Scientific Award, and in the early 1970s a Piaget Society was established in USA to promote discussion of his doctrines.[103] In England the National Foundation for Educational Research has been responsible for publishing an eight-volume survey of research derived from Piagetian principles, the product of the massive Piaget industry that has steadily grown over the last quarter of a century.[104] By 1970 no one could afford to ignore Piaget.

Like several other leading figures in twentieth century psychology (William James, Freud and Pavlov, for example), Piaget had no systematic training as a psychologist. His primary interest was in biology; his first publications from the age of eleven onwards were in that subject, and his doctorate, awarded in 1918, was for a thesis on the molluscs of the Valais area of Switzerland. In his autobiographical study Piaget has recounted how his interests widened to embrace philosophy, psychology, sociology and the history of scientific thought generally; how he was initiated into psychological research first in Zurich and then in Paris; and how, through the influence of his compatriot, the psychologist Claparède, he was given his first psychological post at the J.-J. Rousseau Institute in Geneva.[105] From then onwards his progress was unstoppable, and more than fifty years' work produced a massive monument of published research. His psychological output falls into four main periods, which, though overlapping to some extent, form a rough succession. In the first period, in the 1920s and early 1930s, his system was loose, his methodology mainly clinical, and his primary emphasis on the differences between the 'egocentric' thinking of the child and the socialized thinking of the adolescent.[106] The second period involved intense observational and experimental investigations into his own three children, from the hour of birth up to the emergence of formal thinking about the age of eleven. In the course of these minute and detailed studies his system became more articulate, and took on the form it was to retain throughout.[107] In the third period, which followed in the 1940s and 1950s, Piaget and his collaborators, who now began to flock around him, moved on to a series of experimental investigations of special topics: the development of the concepts of number, time, movement, space and geometry, the growth of logic, and the ripening of perceptual processes.[108] In spite of a certain looseness of methodology, the combination of theoretical insight and experimental ingenuity made this phase, together with phase two, perhaps the core of Piaget's achievement. In the final period Piaget milled over his findings, and discussed their philosophical and scientific implications.[109] He did not stop writing until the year of his death, and since then at the Centre d'Epistémologie Génétique, which he founded in 1955, his pupil and former collaborator Bärbel Inhelder has perpetuated the tradition of his work.

A consistent aim guided the whole of Piaget's career, the aim of creating 'a biology of knowledge', of reconciling the world of nature and the world of ideals, and of harmonizing the rival philosophies of empiricism and rationalism. Psychology he conceived as holding the master position in the whole system of science and hence the route by which these reconciliations could be achieved.[110] Piaget was, in one aspect of his make-up, an idealist. An early prose poem, written when he was still in his teens, was entitled 'The Mission of the Idea'.[111] Among the philosophers he studied were the continental rationalists and Kant, by whom he was deeply influenced. Like Kant he was strongly averse to pure empiricism and 'the myth of the sensory origin of knowledge'.[112] There was, however, a second side to his make-up, the scientific, and he regarded this as 'a protection against the demon of philosophy'.[113] In particular he was influenced by evolutionary thinkers, especially by Spencer from whom he acquired the key idea of 'equilibration',[114] and by Baldwin, from whom he derived several concepts, including the term 'genetic epistemology', though as James Russell has recently pointed out, Piaget's system diverges from Baldwin's in important respects.[115]

The term that best represents Piaget's position is probably 'constructivism'. The title of one of his most important books was *The Child's Construction of Reality*, in which he set out 'to understand how the budding intelligence constructs the external world',[116] the world of permanent objects in a spatial universe, regulated in time and obeying the principle of causality. This world of objects, according to him, is not innately given, but constructed little by little, in a series of stages, the three principal ones being the sensory-motor stage (from birth to about eighteen months), the stage of symbolic and preconceptual thought (up to about four years) and of intuitive thought (from four to seven years), and finally the period of concrete operations (up to about eleven) and formal operations (over eleven). Between these various stages there is both continuity and discontinuity – continuity in the basic processes involved, and discontinuity in the structures resulting. The basic fact about knowledge is that 'human knowledge is essentially active. To know is to assimilate reality into systems of transformations.'[117] Knowledge derives from activity, never from sensation alone. Sensory information is always assimilated into the ongoing activity of the organism; this may set up a disequilibrium, whereupon an adaptive transformation takes place and a process of accommodation which results in a restoration of equilibrium. From the beginning of life until knowledge ceases to grow, if it ever does, these same basic processes – assimilation, accommodation and equilibration – are involved. But the structures that result change radically from the sensory-motor schemata of early life, to the preconceptual groupings and symbolic representations of the second stage, involving a process of interiorization, and finally to the decentralized and reversible formal structures of operational intelligence, which are organized by what Piaget calls a 'psycho-logic', an embodied logic, as distinct from the wholly abstract logic of the logicians.[118] None of these structures, at any stage of development, must be conceived statically, but always as active dynamic operations. There are two important implications of this scheme of stages: firstly, all human beings, whatever their cultural background, must proceed along the same pathway even if they fail to reach the same terminal point, and secondly, there are qualitative, not merely quantitative, differences between minds at different stages of development.

There is no doubt that these proposals of Piaget were enormously stimulating and provocative. They raised many new questions about the genesis of knowledge, and explored the complexities involved in even the most ordinary cognitive achievements of the child. Nevertheless Piaget has been widely criticized even by his admirers. As Boden has pointed out, critics censure his methodology, question his data, and often reject his theoretical proposals.[119] Criticisms of his methodology are perhaps the least important. Piaget was by training and inclination a naturalist, an observer, who did not trouble unduly with the niceties of sampling and statistical treatment. He was more interested in problems than methods, and for a preliminary exploration of new territory there is a lot to be said for his fairly free approach. When his experiments have been repeated with tighter controls, his results have more often than not been confirmed at least in general outline.

Criticisms that attack Piaget's data are more serious. Numerous critics have obtained results which seem to show that children can think logically much earlier than Piaget believed they could. Susan Isaacs in the 1930s, Valentine in the 1940s, and now Bryant and Margaret Donaldson, all discovered evidence of precocious logical thinking.[120] Donaldson asserts that 'by the time they come to school all normal children can show skill as thinkers and language-users to a degree which must compel respect, so long as they are dealing with "real life" meaningful situations'.[121] Bryant attributes children's failures to reason correctly to memory failures rather than to a deficiency in logical capacity. The issue is partly one of the dating of stages, and Piaget's dating has frequently been attacked. To be fair to him, he was not as rigid as he was sometimes made out to be. He admitted uneven development, and what he termed *'décalage'* (displacement).[122] So his stages should not be taken as more than fairly rough descriptive terms.

Most serious of all are the attacks on his theoretical proposals. His constructivism has been attacked by realistically inclined philosophers, his 'psycho-logic' by logicians and cognitive scientists, and the 'surplus baggage' and imprecision of his conceptual apparatus by psychologists, while his views on evolution run counter to neo-Darwinian orthodoxy.[123] On more specific points he has been criticized for underplaying innate and maturational factors in human cognition, for understressing the social components in knowledge, for unduly neglecting language and the part it plays in mental life, and for almost wholly omitting to consider the motivational element in knowledge formation. Piaget's constructivism virtually rules out innate factors other than the reflex equipment of the neonate. All else is the result of interaction and the processes of assimilation and accommodation. To attribute so much to learning is very doubtful, and there is a good deal of evidence to disprove it. As Russell pertinently observed in his very penetrating critique, 'the human infant is left an awful lot to do by himself.'[124] Moreover it involves a considerable break between mankind and the rest of the animal kingdom, where innate mechanisms are well established. It is indeed odd that Piaget, the biologist, who held so firmly to the principle of continuity in human development, should assert the total psychological discontinuity between animals and humans, when he said of man, 'a new cognitive evolution begins, and it begins all over again from zero, since the inner apparatus of instinct has gone.'[125]

The question of the social component in knowledge is more debatable. Piaget's attitude to sociology was somewhat equivocal. He certainly paid lip service to it, but the burden of his explanation was individualistic, and he criticized Durkheim for regarding the individual as 'an empty box to be filled in by society'.[126] Nevertheless there are plenty of references to social factors in Piaget's writings. 'The interactions between psychology and sociology are clear,' he said, 'since man is a social being, and since society modifies, develops and perhaps creates out of nothing certain mental mechanisms.'[127] Again, 'human knowledge has a collective as well as an individual nature.'[128]

And he concluded his *The Psychology of Intelligence* with a chapter on 'Social factors in intellectual development'.[129] In spite of these avowals, however, in the last resort Piaget must be regarded as an individualist; for, though assisted and accompanied by both socialization and verbalization, cognitive development was in its essence an internal evolutionary process.

On the question of language Piaget disagreed with those theorists who claimed language to be a special innately grounded and maturing function. Rather he maintained that it was a competence that developed subsequent to, and was derived from, the same processes as other cognitive attainments. Cognitive development was not dependent on language; on the contrary language was dependent on cognitive development. In a famous debate with Chomsky neither protagonist was able to convince the other. In a review of the differences of the two positions Beilin concluded that 'it is time for Piagetians to rethink their position on language, and instead of relegating it to a position secondary to activity, to see language activity as a dynamic and necessary force in intellectual and social development'.[130] The Piagetians responded by claiming that 'it is quite wrong to assert . . . that Piaget leaves language completely outside his considerations', and by bringing evidence to support the view that language is not the source of the logical development of thought.[131] Once again the issue seems to be one of emphasis and priority.

Finally there is Piaget's neglect of the motivational and affective factors that maintain, and frequently distort and block, cognitive processes. Though he admitted that 'every action involves an energetic or affective aspect' as well as 'a structural or cognitive aspect',[132] in fact he paid little, if any, attention to the former. There is, however, as Berlyne observed, much evidence that 'affective processes have a special role in helping a new form of learned behaviour to establish itself'.[133] It is these factors of goal striving, the will to learn, and its associated feelings and values that Piaget neglects. According to Piagetian theory cognitive development provided its own dynamics. 'The assimilation principle', commented Russell, 'was supposed to remove the need for determination by interests,'[134] and he contrasted Piagetian theory with the earlier genetic epistemology of Baldwin, who accorded a large role in cognitive development to interest, reality, feeling and belief.[135] Russell was surely right in calling attention to this weakness in the Piagetian system; and certainly when it comes to the consideration of the pathology of thinking, Piaget is of little assistance in explaining either the hold of Bacon's 'Idols', the strange delusions of the paranoic, or the biased fanaticisms that grip an uncomfortable proportion of the human race.

Yet in spite of these various criticisms there is widespread agreement that Piaget is among the great psychologists of this century. The breadth of his knowledge, the fundamental nature and the novelty of the questions he raised, the freshness and penetration of his observations, the ingenuity of many of his experiments, together with the massive persistence of his endeavours which covered some sixty years, all render his achievement remarkable. His advocacy of the developmental approach to the unravelling of complex psychological problems was powerful and important. He has, as one of his critics commented, 'opened so many doors to the future';[136] and the memory of his endearing personality will long remain in the minds of those who were fortunate enough to know him.

V

When Piaget commenced his investigations into children's thinking in the 1920s language was not generally regarded as a central topic in psychology, and the standard texts did not accord it much space. When he died in 1980 'psycholinguistics' had exploded into a major area of investigation and controversy. By 1967, in fact, the volume of work had already become so great that a specialized *Language and Language Behavior Abstracts* was needed to keep track of the profusion. As a leading psycholinguist was to observe, 'ours has been an age of intense, almost morbid, interest in language.'[137] Of the importance of language to the psychologist there can be no doubt. It impinges on almost every aspect of psychology – developmental, social, logical, experimental and theoretical; and to add to the complexity it overlaps many other disciplines – neurology, audiology, phonology, linguistics, communication theory, anthropology, sociology and philosophy, to list but the more important. Though in its modern forms the study of language goes back only about two hundred years, its origins can be traced back to the beginnings of European thought, and to understand recent developments it is necessary to look back very briefly into this earlier history.

The Greek word λόγος (logos) originally meant the outward expression, the word, and this is the sense in which it was used by the Greek poets Homer and Hesiod. The Pre-Socratic philosophers of the sixth century BC enlarged its scope to embrace the power of the mind that is manifest in speech, the power of reason, and λόγος became a constitutive principle of the soul, and even the universe itself. It almost seemed as if the study of language might become the clue to the unravelling of the ultimate mysteries; but in spite of an early attempt by Plato to examine language in his dialogue *Cratylus*, it was the connotation of λόγος as 'reason' that was to dominate philosophy. This domination persisted throughout the medieval period up to the eighteenth century, while the study of language as such became the province of grammarians and rhetoricians.[138] When philosophy revived in the seventeenth century, in spite of the fact that Descartes had based his differentiation between man and 'brutes' partly on the lack of language in animals,[139] philosophers were more concerned with the abuse and misuse of words than with the fundamental problems of language. According to Locke, 'words interpose themselves so much between our understanding and the truth,'[140] and it was to overcome these problems that Leibniz proposed his calculus-like ideal language. Against this background it was not surprising that when psychology began to emerge as a separate discipline in the eighteenth century language was not accorded a central role. Thomas Reid in the opening words of his *Essays on the Intellectual Powers of Man* expressed the common view: 'There is no greater impediment to the advancement of knowledge than the ambiguity of words.'[141] It was almost as though language was regarded as grit in the mental machinery rather than as an essential adjunct of intellectual functioning.

The eighteenth century, however, also saw two important developments which ultimately led to a fundamental reassessment of the role of language and its place in human history. Firstly, there was the emphasis placed by the romanticists on the creative and expressive aspects of language. Here Vico was a pioneer, when he asserted that 'minds are formed by the character of language, not language by the minds of those who speak it'.[142] According to Isaiah Berlin, Vico was 'the first to grasp the seminal and revolutionary truth that linguistic forms are one of the keys to the minds of those who use words, and indeed the entire mental, social and cultural life of societies.'[143] Later in the century the German philosopher Herder took up this theme, and in recent times Cassirer, Langer and Polanyi have been prominent in their emphasis on the expressive and cultural aspects of language as a key to the understanding of human mentality.[144] For, as Cassirer put it, 'man lives in a symbolic universe . . . instead of defining man as an "animal rationale" we should define him as an "animal symbolicum"'.[145] It was a return to the vision of the Pre-Socratics!

The second key development was the rise of the comparative study of languages, which led to the absorption of grammar into the wider discipline of linguistics. In 1786 an English judge in Calcutta, Sir William Jones, who had an extensive knowledge of oriental languages, grasped the affinity between Sanskrit, the ancient language of India, and the languages of the west. The insight of Jones was taken up and developed by a succession of comparative philologists in Germany. About the 1850s philology widened to embrace questions of grammar and the structure of language, and by the early twentieth century linguistics was consolidated by the Swiss linguist de Saussure into a formal discipline in which '*langue*' (language) and '*parole*' (speech), as well as 'synchronic' (structural) and 'diachronic' (historical) aspects were distinguished, and the general structure of linguistic systems clarified.[146] Linguistics, its adherents began to claim, had 'at last cast off its chains, and gone far on the way to becoming an exact empirical science'.[147] Meanwhile the subject had been greatly enriched by the anthropological study of the huge range of native languages, several thousands of them, still spoken by the 'savage' races of the world. In particular the study of American Indian languages was largely responsible for the development of linguistics in the United States, and constituted the basis for the formal, structural linguistics of Bloomfield and his school, which dominated the field in the early part of the century, at the same time proclaiming the 'autonomy' of the subject.[148] If the psychologists were not particularly interested in language, it was even more true that the linguists rejected any contamination by psychology.

In spite of this discouragement a tentative *rapprochement* between the two disciplines began in the 1860s, only to wither after a rather stunted growth by the 1920s. Blumenthal has recently resurrected this early, almost forgotten, chapter of psycholinguistics, or '*Sprachwissenschaft*' as it was then termed, in his valuable historical study, *Language and Psychology* (1970). Ever since the time of Herder interest had been growing in Germany in the cultural aspects of language, and in 1860 two German Herbartians, M. Lazarus and H. Steinhal, founded the *Zeitschrift für Völkerpsychologie und Sprachwissenschaft* (Journal of Racial Psychology and Linguistic Science). Language, mythology, religion, art, customs and economics were regarded as clues to the 'racial mind' and to the diverse forms of social life, manners and beliefs which humanity manifested. The importance of the work of Lazarus and Steinthal was that it was the first serious attempt to bridge the gap between the new science of linguistics and psychology. It also constituted the soil from which eventually sprung Wundt's massive *Völkerpsychologie*, the first two volumes of which were devoted to language (*Die Sprache*). Blumenthal in his book draws a comparison between the earlier '*Sprachpsychologie*' of Wundt and the new psycholinguistics of the 1950s.[149] But there was no direct connection between the two. Wundt's interest in language was perpetuated by the Austrian psychologist Karl Bühler, who wrote extensively on the psychology of language, but who died in America in 1963 without making a great impact on mainstream psychology.[150] In 1920, with the death of Wundt, the tides of psychology had already turned in other directions, in Europe to Gestalt psychology and psychoanalysis, in America to behaviourism. As Blumenthal notes, the aspect of language most frequently investigated by psychologists was the acquisition of language by children.[151] Darwinian theories about the origin of language had stimulated studies of linguistic development, and a series of notable investigations were carried out from 1880 onwards by Preyer, Meumann, Sully and the Sterns, as well as several French workers.[152] This, however, was a specialized field, and throughout the first half of the twentieth century psychologists in general devoted little of their consideration to language. 'With the rise of conditioning studies and the use of laboratory animals,' observes Blumenthal, 'attention to natural languages declined.'[153] Even before that, however, language had almost disappeared from the horizons of psychologists. James in his *Principles* (1890) devotes a mere two or three pages to its consideration, and Sully in his *Human Mind* (1893) one page, a brief appendix, and a few scattered observations. Language, it seems, was already regarded as a superficial manifestation of underlying psychological forces, and behaviourism simply strengthened this trend.

There were several reasons for the revival of interest in the subject in the early 1950s. Firstly, philosophers from the 1930s onwards had been laying increasing stress on language, and on linguistic analysis as a path to the understanding of mind.[154] Secondly, information theory had emphasized the importance of codes in communication, and language was obviously the most generally used communicative code.[155] And thirdly, behaviourist psychologists themselves were being forced to recognize that human behaviour could not be adequately explained without giving special consideration to verbal activity, to what Pavlov had termed 'the second signalling system'. 'Speech', wrote Pavlov, 'constitutes a second signalling system of reality which is peculiarly ours, being the signal of the first signals. . . . It is precisely speech which has made us human.'[156] Russian psychologists grasped this truth rather earlier than psychologists in the west,[157] where perhaps the first clear sign of renewed interest in language was the brilliant article by Lashley on 'The problem of serial order in behavior' in 1951,[158] in which he observed that 'language presents in its most striking form the integrative functions that are characteristic of the cerebral cortex, and that reach their highest development in human thought processes. . . . The problems raised by the organization of language seem to me to be characteristic of almost all other cerebral activity.' Two years later Lashley's article was followed by the long chapter on 'Language behavior' in Osgood's *Experimental Psychology*.[159] Osgood was a behaviourist by inclination, and he insisted on the need to study language and meaning by objective methods. However he rejected the crude early behaviourism of Watson, and, influenced by the philosophical writing on language of Charles Morris,[160] proposed a 'mediation' hypothesis of verbal behaviour, the mediating reaction 'being some fractional part of the total behaviour elicited by the object, and producing distinctive self-stimulation that mediates responses'.[161] Following Osgood there have been several diverse attempts to capture language within some sort of behaviouristic framework, the most notable being those of Skinner in his *Verbal Behavior* (1957) and O.H. Mowrer in his *Learning Theory and the Symbolic Processes* (1960).[162]

In 1957, however, a new star, which was destined rapidly to eclipse the behaviourists, suddenly appeared in the sky – Noam Chomsky and his *Syntactic Structures*. This work, the first of many,[163] revolutionized the study of language, led to a surge of psycholinguistics, and, in the course of time, had a profound effect on psychological theory in general. It is to Chomsky, therefore, that we must now turn. Noam Chomsky (born 1928) was the son of a distinguished Hebrew scholar, and it was from his father that he early acquired an interest in languages. At the university he studied linguistics, mathematics and philosophy, coming under the influence of modern theories of logic and the foundations of mathematics. His approach to the study of languages has been highly formal and mathematical, and he has been aptly described by Beloff as possessing 'a brilliant, but essentially medieval mind, somehow strayed into the computer age'.[164] In spite, however, of his non-experimental approach, his influence on psychology has been considerable, ever since his critical review of Skinner's *Verbal Behavior* dealt a devastating and indeed almost mortal blow to behaviourist ideology. In its place Chomsky adumbrated a psychology of language that was essentially cognitive and mentalistic, derived in large part from Descartes, and that like Descartes's work postulated a total gulf between animal and human communication systems.[165]

There were three main reasons why Chomsky believed that learning theories were incapable of explaining language behaviour. Firstly, these theories could not account for the rapidity and sureness of children's language acquisition. 'The knowledge of language', he wrote, 'is acquired on the basis of degenerate and restricted data . . . it is to a large extent independent of intelligence, and of wide variations in individual experience.'[166] It could not, therefore, conceivably be explained in terms of the imitative and reinforcement mechanisms that learning theorists postulated. Secondly, underlying all languages there were universal principles of grammar, phonetics, semantics and syntax, and these could only, he believed, be explained in terms of innate 'competence', which manifested itself in a variety of more or less adequate linguistic 'performances'. 'All languages, as it were, were cut from the same pattern', and beneath the vagaries of 'surface structure' there was an underlying 'deep structure' of grammatical universals.[167] Thirdly, there is the creative productivity revealed in language, the fact that an endless number of new sentences can be generated by the speaker. It would, calculated the psycholinguist George Miller, take a thousand times the estimated age of the earth to utter all the admissible twenty-word sentences in English![168] Yet all this potentially vast array is rule-governed, in particular by syntactic rules and a flexible system of transformational grammar, capable of modulating linguistic expressions to all sorts of purposes and with all sorts of nuances. Lashley had shown in his article on serial order that sentence generation could not be explained stochastically in terms of chain reflexes, but required the postulation of central cortical control.[169] This controlling centre was, according to Chomsky, an innate language faculty, or in Miller's phrase, 'some kind of language engine'.[170] These views of Chomsky created a powerful impression, because they were argued with great cogency, and backed up by a formidable mastery of logic and mathematics, which compelled respect.[171]

We must now look briefly at their influence on psychology. Chomsky is not a psychologist, and he has been critical not only of behaviourism but of a great deal of contemporary psychology, which he regards as having saddled itself with irrelevant and restrictive methodological requirements, thereby dooming itself to triviality.[172] Nevertheless he regards the study of language as 'a branch of human theoretical psychology',[173] and indeed 'central to the study of human nature'.[174] For 'the structure of language can truly serve as a mirror of mind'[175] and throw light on the main conceptual lacuna in psychological theory, namely the notion of 'competence'. In effect Chomsky has returned to the Aristotelian and scholastic concept of potentiality (faculty, power, capacity), and what he has done is to buttress this ancient concept with an impressive and robust mathematically based filling of transformational grammar. He has presented psychology, in the area of human language, with an alternative to behaviourism, an alternative which, unlike the various 'humanistic' psychologies, is not verbal and vague, but as strict and precise as behaviourism itself. This is obviously an important development, and it has led to a rapid growth of interest in psycholinguistics.

It is impossible to do more than sketch the main outlines of this speciality, which has grown prodigiously over the last thirty years. Chomsky himself was essentially a theorist, but the interest in language which he has generated, and the problems he has raised, have spawned progeny in many directions. Lennenberg has explored the biological foundations of language;[176] George Miller was the first of many experimental psychologists to test psycholinguistic theories experimentally, studying problems of speech perception, speech production and the influence of semantics and meaning;[177] there has been renewed, and intense, interest in the language acquisition of young children;[178] in the non-verbal communication of both animals and humans;[179] and strenuous efforts by several investigtaors to teach chimpanzees to use language.[180] Over and above all this there has been work in sociolinguistics, cross-cultural studies of language development, investigations into bilingualism, and into the various disorders of language.[181] The study of language and verbal behaviour generally has become a major, and increasingly technical, psychological speciality.

Much, of course, in psycholinguistics, and especially in Chomskian psycholinguistics, still remains controversial. We may note four main counts upon which Chomsky's views have been challenged. Firstly, the total disjunction which he postulates between human and animal communication conflicts with the central idea of evolution, and is based on the misconception that continuity and discontinuity are irreconcilable. Both are, in fact, characteristic of evolutionary processes, where there is both a discontinuity between species and a great deal of continuity.[182] All novelty is based in part on what has gone before. Popper, who studied in Vienna under Bühler, has rightly pointed out in his observations on language that some functions of language are shared in animal and human communication, and others arc not.[183] Secondly, Chomsky underestimates the role of learning in language acquisition. There is considerable evidence that 'an adequate psychology of language', to quote one pair of investigators, 'must take account not only of the creative aspects of language, but also of the important role played by contextual factors'.[184] Thirdly, Chomsky overstresses what has been termed by Fodor the 'modularity' of linguistic competence, that is its character as a cognitive system which is 'domain specific' and autonomous.[185] While there is clear evidence supporting a degree of speciality for language behaviour, it must be recognized that both phylogenetically and ontogenetically language is not the beginning of human mentality. There is evidence that language was probably quite a late acquisition of the human race, and that Neanderthal man may not have had the vocal apparatus needed for developing speech.[186] And as Piaget has shown, linguistic performances rest on, and are, he believed, assimilated to a well-established basis of prior sensori-motor learning. Indeed Plato pointed out in the earliest of all treatises on language that things may be learned without the employment of names.[187] The strategies of language acquisition are not, as Chomsky suggests, totally divorced from learning in general. Finally, in his stress on the formal properties of grammar, Chomsky constantly underplays the role of semantics and meaning, and also the pragmatic functions of language as a means of expression and communication. The formal study of grammar needs supplementing by the study of the expressive functions of language in the manner of Vico and Cassirer, and the communicative functions of language in the speech acts of everyday life.[188] So while recognizing the stimulating character of Chomsky's provocative views, and their immense value in bringing language back into the ambit of psychological consideration, we must insist that language be viewed in a broader framework than the rigid formalism of his transformational system. In the broader framework it is likely to remain a major area of psychological research, and possibly the realm of symbolism may be extended to include even consciousness itself.

VI

The revival of interest in consciousness, after its methodological ostracism and its replacement by 'behavioural science', has been one of the more surprising outcomes of the cognitive revolution. In 1950 consciousness seemed almost to have vanished from the psychological scene. Hebb in advocating the objective study of thinking was hoping at the same time to get rid of the 'last smell of animism'.[189] The outcome was the opposite of his expectations. At the Laurentian Conference on 'Brain Mechanisms and Consciousness' held in Canada in 1953 – a select conference which Hebb himself attended, but which was dominated by physiologists – 'the great sphynx, the phenomena of consciousness' was the central topic of discussion.[190] The conference had been summoned to consider, in particular, the chance observation of Moruzzi and Magoun in 1949 that the electrical excitation of the reticular formation of the brain stem induced changes in the EEG which appeared to be identical with those observed in awaking from sleep or alerting to attention.[191] It became apparent that consciousness was an active process, rooted in physiological events which could be scientifically recorded. It took psychologists some time to come to terms with this turn-about. It was reinforced a few years later by the observations on sensory deprivation from Hebb's own laboratory.[192] In conditions of reduced sensory input strange changes in consciousness progressively occurred, and with the advances in space and submarine exploration these findings became of considerable practical importance. It is noteworthy that at the First International Symposium on Submarine and Space Medicine held in America in 1958 the topic of discussion was 'Environmental Effects on Consciousness'.[193] By 1960 consciousness was beginning to edge back into psychology. In the 1970s and 1980s there was a spate of conferences on the subject, and from 1976 onwards a number of important seminars at Harvard.[194] In 1980 there was a sufficient volume of work to justify a separate *Annual Review* survey.[195] On both sides of the Atlantic consciousness had become a live issue.

For two hundred and fifty years after Descartes had demarcated the conscious mind, with its immediate and certain knowledge of itself, from the material world,[196] the study of consciousness had been regarded almost universally as the essential subject matter of psychology, and introspection as its essential method. Psychology was concerned, in Reid's words, with 'that immediate knowledge which we have of all the present operations of the mind'.[197] Towards the end of the nineteenth century doubts began to creep in. Developments in child and animal psychology derived from evolutionary theory could not depend on introspective analysis, and even in adult human beings there was increasing evidence of unconscious functioning which could not be observed introspectively. Quite early in the new century matters rapidly came to a head. In 1904 James boldly declared that 'the hour is ripe for it [consciousness] to be openly and universally discarded',[198] though he still maintained it could be treated as a function. In the previous year the British philosopher G.E. Moore had remarked that 'the moment we try to fix our attention on consciousness and see *what* distinctly it is, it seems to vanish: it seems as if we had before us a mere emptiness'.[199] Introspective psychology struggled on, in an emasculated state, for a few more decades, but by the late 1930s, under the combined onslaughts of behaviourist psychologists and logical positivist philosophers, it had virtually vanished from the Anglo-Saxon scene, though in the somewhat different guise of phenomenology it maintained a hold in Europe. The methodologists, however, were quite insistent. 'There is no objective indication of the presence of consciousness that could withstand scrutiny', and 'concepts become scientific when they are anchored in physical observation.'[200] It followed, therefore, that consciousness had no place in a scientific psychology. Few psychologists in mid-century could have anticipated the extraordinary changes that have since taken place.

We have already noted some of the physiological and practical factors that led to a revival of the study of consciousness in the 1950s. To these must be added the sudden upsurge of interest in hallucinatory drugs that followed the publication of Aldous Huxley's *The Doors of Perception* in 1954. Altered states of consciousness induced pharmacologically were clearly topics that could not be ignored, and they linked up to a revival of interest both in hypnotic phenomena and in the techniques of meditation which had long been practised in the Orient.[201] Moreover the fantasies accompanying psychedelic states brought up once again the whole question of imagery, which had faded with the demise of introspective psychology. The economist Boulding's book on *The Image* (1956) was favourably regarded by Miller, Galanter and Pribram in 1960,[202] and from the time of Holt's article on imagery in 1964[203] there has been a steady increase in research in this area. In the last few years it has become a lively topic of discussion, with many links with cognitive psychology, abnormal psychology, developmental psychology and the study of consciousness, from which the study of imagery is inseparable. By the 1970s these various strands were beginning to be woven together, and books like Ornstein's *The Psychology of Consciousness* (1970) and Tart's *States of Consciousness* (1975)[204] began to appear. Hilgard's article on 'Consciousness in Contemporary Psychology' in the *Annual Review* for 1980 was the final recognition that consciousness was back on stage. With it came the return of introspection. 'In the last few years,' noted, surprisingly, one of Skinner's PhD students, 'we have seen a major release from inhibition, and the appearance in the experimental literature on a large scale of studies reporting the introspections of subjects.'[205] Introspection and neurophysiology, instead of being regarded as antagonistic, have come to be seen rather as partners in a joint enterprise.[206] Of course, these developments have raised many problems, both methodological and philosophical, but before we glance at these, we must take note of the interesting *rapprochement* that has now sprung up between western and oriental psychologies, a *rapprochement* that has a direct bearing on the psychology of conscious states.

Oriental psychology is as old as, or even older than, psychology in the west. It goes back to the Hindu Upanishads, some of which date back to 800 BC. But there was little direct contact between the civilizations of the east and those of the European west before the fourth century BC. The lack of maritime communications, and the barrier of the empires of the Middle East, effectively isolated Orient and Occident. In 325 BC, however, Alexander the Great, in the course of his conquests, reached the Indus valley and the Indian Ocean, and the road to the east was opened up. Eastern influences began to penetrate the western world, particularly through the Greek cities established in Asia Minor and Egypt. It has been suggested that Plotinus may have come into contact with the teachings of the Hindu sages;[207] but soon after his death barriers sprang up again. Christian theology was not friendly to contamination by gnosticism and other alien faiths, and it had its own brand of mysticism from at least the times of Augustine and the Pseudo-Dionysius.[208] It was not until the nineteenth century that oriental influences began to make themselves felt once more. By that time the British East India Company was firmly established in India; the Opium Wars of the 1840s and 1850s opened up China to the west; Commander Perry broke down the walls around Japan in 1854; and, as a last chapter in the saga of western penetration, the Younghusband expedition of 1904 bludgeoned its way into the fastness of Tibet with its rich tradition of Yoga. Schopenhauer (1788-1860) was the first major western philosopher to be influenced by Hindu thought.[209] By the end of the century many of the oriental scriptures were available in translation as a result of the organizing efforts of F. Max Müller, the Anglo-German orientalist who settled in Oxford and edited the fifty-one volumes of *The Sacred Books of the East*.[210] Some of the results of the opening of the doors were far from scientific, and indeed an invitation to occultism. Madame Blavatsky's

Theosophical movement, founded in 1875, was an example of this. But it also led to a more critical interest in oriental thought by some psychologists. In 1912 Brett found it worthwhile to include a chapter on 'The idea of the soul in some eastern writings' in his *History of Psychology*.[211] After the First World War interest grew, perhaps as a result of the sceptical questioning of western values which the war provoked. Count Keyserling's *Travel Diary of a Philosopher*, based on extensive travels in the east just prior to the war, was published just after its termination, and proved an enormous popular success in introducing eastern ideas to the west.[212] Indian thinkers themselves began to produce works for western consumption, for example the poet Rabindranath Tagore and the philosopher Radhakrishnan,[213] while in the west Jung was the most prominent of the psychological fraternity to immerse himself in eastern writings, though he warned westerners against a blind adherence to eastern cults: 'Yoga in Mayfair or Fifth Avenue, or in any place which is on the telephone, is a spiritual fake.'[214] A particularly interesting work dated from between the wars was Geraldine Coster's *Yoga and Western Psychology* (1934). This contained a complete translation of the Yoga Sutras of Patanjali (second century AD), a detailed commentary, and a comparison between the techniques of Yoga and psychoanalysis. Just after the Second World War the Indian philosopher Akhilananda, who for some years had taught at the Ramakrishna Vedanta Centers in Rhode Island and Boston, published his *Hindu Psychology: Its Meaning for the West* (1947), which contained an introduction by G.W. Allport. In the 1950s the writings of the Japanese Suzuki popularized the teachings and methods of Zen Buddhism.[215]

So by the 1960s the ground had been well prepared for the consideration of eastern systems by western psychologists. For several reasons these systems began then to be regarded more favourably than they had been. The inadequacies of behaviourism revealed gaps in the edifice of western psychology; altered states of consciousness, a central theme of oriental psychologies, had been shown to have physiological correlates, and meditation, properly conducted, to have therapeutically useful results; while the growing alienation of many from a world increasingly dominated by technology and violence fostered the cult of oriental inwardness. The so-called 'transpersonal psychologies' grew, therefore, in favour. These psychologies have been fully expounded elsewhere, and are too large a subject to detail here.[216] Not all the assumptions upon which they are grounded are capable of scientific verification, and they are all prone to occult and gnostic contamination,[217] but the altered states of consciousness which they explore and describe with much elaboration, and the rigorous personal disciplines which they impose, are matters that can profitably be studied by psychologists.

Nevertheless there are reasons for holding with Jung that the west, while learning what it can from the east, should not sell its soul and renounce its own heritage. The aim of all oriental systems is 'one-pointedness', the mystical condition 'when all mental processes are transcended'.[218] Suzuki, the Zen Buddhist, quite clearly states that 'Zen advises us to reverse the direction science is pursuing if we are really to get acquainted with the Self'.[219] 'Silence, absorption, eternal peace', not knowledge in the western sense, is the goal of eastern disciplines and meditation.[220] Eastern systems are essentially non-progressive. There is no basic difference between the Yogic teachings of the Bhagavad-Gita (c. AD 200) and those of contemporary Yogis.[221] Nor are the complex conceptual systems of oriental thinkers subjected to experimental testing other than through personal experience. So while there are interesting parallels between the psychologies of the Orient and the revived psychology of consciousness in the west, there are differences in background and in methodology which cannot be overlooked.

Along what lines, then, are western psychologists attempting to come to terms with consciousness within the framework of scientific psychology? It seems clear that consciousness is not a basic, but an emergent, feature of mind. It rests upon a complex foundation of information processing, only the results of which may become conscious. As Lashley put it in his contribution to the Laurentian Symposium, 'there is never an awareness of the integrative activity of the brain while it is in progress. . . . In every case that of which we are aware is an organized structure; the organizing is never experienced.'[222] The functions of consciousness are essentially two – integration and control. In James's words, written before he discarded the concept, 'consciousness [is] an organ added for the sake of steering a nervous system grown too complex to regulate itself.'[223] In particular, consciousness is concerned with temporal integration.[224] All behaviour involves some kind of retention of past experience and anticipation of future outcomes. Consciousness makes possible temporal integration at a higher level, with clearer recall of the past in its particularity, and the facilitation of planned outcomes. Moreover it can integrate the information involved in these operations with information from within – with feelings, wishes and values. Consciousness, however, is not merely integrative; it serves as a central control system. In Sperry's words, it 'causes rather than correlates';[225] it is linked to action and the preparation for action, and, as Freud put it, has 'control over the approaches to motility'.[226] The origins of consciousness as we find it in man is a matter of speculation. Jaynes's theory, that it only came into being about three thousand years ago, seems distinctly unplausible.[227] Human language is certainly much older than that, as written records date back to the late fourth millennium BC, and it is difficult to believe that the artists of the magnificent Lascaux cave paintings, which are much older still, were not fully conscious of what they were doing. As Crook observed in his stimulating and erudite work on The Evolution of Human Consciousness (1980), human consciousness has probably grown slowly through several phases, and has developed in conjunction with social organization, and the roles and rules involved in social behaviour.[228] Piaget's work on the development of consciousness in children supports such a viewpoint, and it is, of course, in line with

Vygotsky's even earlier theories.[229] How far animals are conscious is another and more difficult question. Physiological correlates of different states of consciousness have been found in most mammals, but it is not easy to answer the whimsical question of the philosopher Nagel, 'What is it like to be a bat?'[230] Nevertheless it is not unreasonable to postulate that human consciousness has emerged from simpler, and more restricted, forms of consciousness at the animal level.

Within an information-processing framework consciousness is best regarded as a form of language, something which represents events in the world and within the organism itself in coded form. Bishop Berkeley was on the right lines when he suggested that visual experience was 'a natural language'.[231] We need not, however, confine his theory to vision. It can be applied equally to all the senses; and we need not conceive the language of consciousness as directly 'instituted by the Author of Nature',[232] but rather as a product of evolution, genetically transmitted in its fundamental structure, and tested through action to fit the world outside. There is no question of representations remaining in the mind, or, as Wittgenstein has it, 'in the box'.[233] Consciousness is not just contemplative, but linked from the beginning to action. It is this which gives it its essential attribute of intentionality, and at the same time explains its selectivity and restrictiveness. In integrating and focusing information, consciousness also excludes and rejects; and it is this aspect of consciousness which leads to that stunting and maladjustment that the analytic techniques of the west and the meditative techniques of the east have been designed to remedy. Consciousness, in short, is a unique kind of representational symbolism, a product of the creative activity of the organism; it is an eiconic symbolism capable of integrating informational input and capable of controlling the paths to motility.

If this is what consciousness is – a form of language – there must also be an interpreter and executive agent, or, in other words, in human beings, a self. 'An organism', wrote Bartlett in his book on *Remembering*, has somehow to acquire the capacity to turn round upon its own schemata, and to construct them afresh; it is what gives consciousness its most prominent function. I wish I knew how it was done.'[234] How it is done is still a baffling problem. The nature of the self, or ego, is the deepest mystery of psychology. There seem to be three possible types of answer. Either there must be a 'transcendental' ego, as Kant and the phenomenologists have proposed, or there must be an emergent ego, a secondary creation of the consciousness-forming processes themselves, involving, as Hoffstadter suggests, 'an exquisite closed loop of causality',[235] or both these answers may be valid, and, as James maintained, we must postulate both an 'empirical self' and a 'spiritual self', and possibly sub-classes of self as well.[236] For the time being psychologists do well to leave these problems for philosophers to puzzle out. They have enough to do with exploring the vistas which the resurrection of consciousness has opened up, and the role of the self in integration and control.

VII

The changes that have taken place in psychology since the middle of this century have been dramatic and momentous, opening up exciting prospects for the future. Lost content and structures have been replaced into the vacuum of the empty organism, consciousness and thought have been brought back to the centre of the stage, an understanding of the chemical and neurological foundations of mind has been much enhanced, and the methodological straitjackets which restricted the growth of psychology have been loosened. There has been a steady advance in sophistication and knowledge, not only in the biological and cognitive areas briefly examined in this and the previous chapter, but in many other areas of psychology. Perhaps the most promising feature of these developments is that they have been grounded on theoretical concepts and technological advances more fundamental than at any previous stage of psychology's history. The concept of information as an abstract entity, the concepts of 'programs' and cybernetic control, the huge surge forward of computer technology, together with many conceptual and technical advances in the biological realm, have provided psychology with new and powerful equipment, more closely matched than ever before to its subject matter. Psychology has indeed become a focal point in scientific enquiry and technological progress, and is at last beginning to emerge into scientific adulthood.

These are striking positive achievements. But the history of psychology prescribes caution. Psychologists have too often been over-optimistic in the past. Locke, Wundt, Freud, Watson – all of them in their day seemed to be inaugurating new eras, only to be scaled down subsequently to size. In the light of history there is a dangerous one-sidedness in the informational revolution in psychology, an excessive concentration on the cognitive aspects of human nature, and, as Bolter observed in *Turing's Man*,[237] a neglect of inner depths. The aseptic logic of information technology is far removed from the fanaticisms, anxieties, devotions, enthusiasm, and at times the mindless abandon that characterizes a good deal of human behaviour. In the very early days of European psychology Plato, who in spite of his scientific ignorance often saw things clearly and whole, likened the soul of man to a charioteer driving a two-horse vehicle.[238] The charioteer was reason (νοῦς), the horses the drives and passions. Recently psychology has been concentrating on the charioteer, and relegating the horses to the background. But as Aristotle remarked, striking the same Platonic note, διανοία αὐτὴ οὐθεν κινεῖ (intellect itself moves nothing).[239] There must also be ὄρεξις (motivation). The Apollonian aspects of man must be complemented by the Dionysian in any rounded and adequate psychology.[240] The realms of feeling, motivation and value are as vital to an understanding of human nature as the realm of cognitive processing, and though not entirely neglected in contemporary psychology, they are theoretically anaemic, and indeed less well developed than in the noonday of hormic psychology or of the psychoanalytic schools. Psychology badly needs a corrective synoptic vision of the sort provided half a century ago by Stern, who recognized three principal modalities of mind:- the biological foundation, the modality of cognition and control, and the third modality of ends and values.[241] The demise of 'grand theory' has left a gap in the contents of psychology; Stern's third modality is largely missing.

Once again the deficiencies of psychologists seem on the point of correction from outside psychology itself, by physiologists, biologists and philosophers. Two eminent physiologists, Eccles and Sperry, have both recently stressed values as the principal determinants of human behaviour. In Eccles's judgment, 'the guidance of a consciously planned life by some value system more than anything else sets man apart from animals.'[242] And Sperry asserts that 'the factor of human values stands out as a universal determinant of all human decisions and actions'.[243] Among biologists Thorpe and J.Z. Young have been striking similar notes,[244] while particularly notable among philosophical contributions is the work of Susanne Langer *Mind: An Essay in Human Feeling*, in which she defends the thesis that 'feeling is the starting point of a philosophy of mind'.[245]

There is, in fact, a whole dimension of mind, rooted in feeling, culminating in value, and intimately bound up with motivation, that cognitive psychology is tending to ignore. In Langer's view feeling, combining as it does sensibility, emotivity and activity, is the primitive matrix from which all aspects of mind emerge, and which remains at the core of mentality right up to the highest level. It is this core which is the hardest to capture scientifically, and which Langer believes is best approached at the human level through the arts, since 'art is the objectification of feeling'.[246] Certainly a picture like Picasso's 'Guernica' objectifies and expresses the horrors of war. The main criticism of such attempts as have been made in recent times by psychologists in this area is their disjointed nature and lack of theoretical ballast. We know a bit more about the neurological basis of feelings and their relation to the limbic area of the brain. But the topic of motivation in general, as we saw in the last chapter, is marked by a clash of theories and considerable confusion, and values have been treated, if at all, either as an adjunct to decision theory, an aspect of socialization, or a variable in differential psychology.[247] There has been almost nothing in the way of a '*Wertphilosophie*' to back up these rather desultory efforts, as there was with Stern's *General Psychology*.[248]

How, then, are we to conceive this domain – the feeling-value domain? Contemporary philosophers, with exceptions like Langer, can give us little help. They are too much at odds with each other, and, as Popper has scathingly observed, 'so much of the talk about values is just hot air'.[249] We can hardly do better than look back to Spinoza, who held that the core of each existing thing was a '*conatus*', an endeavour to persevere in its being. To this '*conatus*' were attached two basic feelings, joy and sorrow, joy accompanying a movement of greater perfection and sorrow to less perfection.[250] The complex emotional and motivational life of man was developed from this basis, and constituted the foundation of value judgments. 'Each person according to his affect judges a thing to be good or evil, useful or useless.'[251] This Spinozistic scheme links together feeling and value, and embraces the two essential dimensions of value, conservative and creative – the urge on the one hand to preserve, and on the other to reach out to novelty and greater perfection and ultimately to attain 'blessedness'.[252] Today we can amplify this scheme into a hierarchical system of feelings and values, distinguishing four main levels, the biological, the personal, the social and the transcendental, each with their associated levels of feelings and values. The relation between these levels remains a matter of argument. There is agreement among biologists like J.Z. Young and philosophers like Popper that 'values enter the world with life',[253] and in a primitive form go back to the beginnings of living organisms. All living involves some sort of choice. But there is disagreement as to the weighting of these levels in man. In his book on *The Biological Origins of Human Values*, Pugh designates biological values as primary.[254] Sperry, on the other hand, holds that cognitive values at the ideological level, that is the highest transcendental level, carry the greatest weight.[255] Perhaps Maslow's proposal of a hierarchy of values with varying prepotency is the most realistic solution. Maslow, it is worth noting, was one of the small band of 'third force' psychologists who in mid-century took values seriously. 'The state of being without a system of values is psychopathogenic,' he maintained. 'The human being needs a framework of values, a philosophy of life, religion, or religion-surrogate to live by and understand by.'[256]

We cannot foresee at this juncture how this undoubted gap in contemporary psychology is going to be filled. Scientific advance depends on detailed and precise work and on technological progress. But it also demands speculative boldness, fruitful hypotheses, and imaginative leaps which reach beyond the problems of the present to unifying solutions in the future. It is this combination of imagination and meticulous persistence that made a scientist like Einstein great. 'The greatness of Einstein', wrote his fellow physicist, Infeld, 'lies in his tremendous imagination, in the unbelievable obstinacy with which he pursues his problems. Originality is the most essential factor in important scientific work. It is intuition which leads to unexplored regions.'[257] Psychology, too, needs a speculative, imaginative component. It needs to look beyond the immediate problems of the laboratory, the clinic and the social milieu. It would do well not to forget the insights of its historical past, but neither should it be afraid of a speculative 'metapsychology'.

Chapter 16
Metapsychology

I

Psychology as we find it today has been shaped by many influences – philosophical, theological, scientific, medical, sociological and, behind all these 'the massive central core of human thinking which has no history'.[1] It has become an immensely complex and rich subject. What it has not yet found is an agreed theoretical framework.

We have already noted that in reviewing the state of psychology in mid-century Koch saw only a 'disorderly matrix' and a state of 'contextual and methodological pluralism', and that he envisaged no hope of 'tongues blending into a single narrative'.[2] In 1970 at the First Banff Conference on Theoretical Psychology, the theme of which was 'Toward Unification in Psychology', the outcome was again pessimistic. Krech, in summing up, spoke of 'a mélange of sciences, technologies, professions, arts, epistemologies and philosophies – many of them but distantly related to each other – all called "psychology"'.[3] Perhaps the splintering of psychology is somewhat less marked now than it was a quarter of a century ago, but there are still competing 'models of man', still calls for radical transformations of psychology, its total reshaping. The central problem, as Wittgenstein saw, is the bypassing of problems and methods. 'In psychology', he wrote, 'there are experimental methods and *conceptual confusion*. . . . The existence of experimental methods makes us think we have the means of solving the problems which trouble us, though problems and methods pass one another by.'[4] The nineteenth century attempt to align psychology to the natural sciences involved the gradual domination of restrictive, and sometimes inappropriate, methodologies and the progressive elimination of content, culminating in the radical behaviourism and operationism of the mid-twentieth century, when almost all the traditional subject matter of psychology had been thrown overboard. Since the 1960s much of this jettisoned cargo has been retrieved. Cognitive processes, innate structures, imagery, consciousness, competences and dispositions have been restored to respectability. But unification is still but a dream. To dream, however, is not an unscientific activity, unless dreams are mistaken for contemporary reality. Metapsychological dreaming has a vital part to play in the progress of psychology. A speculative optimism is not out of place. We need to look forward in the future to a unified theoretical framework.

From the beginnings of European thought there has been a remarkable consensus among the most eminent philosophers of science on the importance of the speculative component in knowledge. At the dawn of western thought the father of psychology, Heraclitus of Ephesos, is reported to have said, 'He who does not expect will not find out the unexpected, for it is trackless and unexplored';[5] 'much detailed learning [πολυμαθίη] on its own', he added, 'does not lead to understanding.'[6] At the commencement of the modern age, Bacon, the advocate of empirical science, complained that

> men have abandoned universality, or *philosophia prima*, which cannot but cease and stop all progression. For no perfect discovery can be made upon a flat or level: neither is it possible to discover the more remote and deeper parts of any science, if you stand but upon the level of the same science, and ascend not to a higher science.[7]

In our own day Popper has proclaimed that 'bold ideas, unjustified anticipation, and speculative thought, are our only means for interpreting nature; our only organon, our only instrument for grasping her. And we must hazard them to win our prize.'[8] Finally, Freud tuned in with these great thinkers when he wrote, 'without metapsychological speculation and theorizing – I had almost said 'phantasying' – we shall not get another step forward.'[9] So the upshot is clear – psychology needs metapsychological complementation, provided this is regarded strictly as heuristic superstructure and not as established knowledge.

The term 'metapsychology' was, it would seem, coined by Freud himself. Its first recorded use was in 1896 in a letter to his friend Fliess, its first published appearance five years later in *The Psychopathology of Everyday Life*.[10] Subsequently Freud planned to write a treatise on metapsychology, but this never materialized and only certain chapters appeared in article form. The term came to mean a comprehensive overview of psychology, embracing all aspects of the subject.[11] It is such a synoptic view that psychology urgently requires to reconcile its differences and discipline its vagaries. This is a vast and difficult task and only a sketchy outline, based on indications from the history of the subject, can be attempted here.

II

As Stern proposed half a century ago, the 'person' is the basic unifying concept which a synoptic psychology requires.[12] Only the *unitas multiplex*', the complex unity, of the person can embrace the whole field of psychological enquiry in both its theoretical and applied forms. The concept of personality is, of course, a problematic one. Since the time of Locke the very nature of personal identity has become a matter of controversy. The 'person', the 'self', disappeared in Hume, and was elevated to the transcendental realms by Kant. But for the psychologist, with his feet on the ground, there are strong attractions in accepting the philosopher Strawson's doctrine of the 'person' as a fundamental feature of the world we actually live in; and it tunes in with the views of those biologists like Jacob who see the need for an ultimate integrating factor, a higher 'integron', to explain the logic of living systems.[13]

In line with these views the person must be conceived hierarchically as involving a series of levels – biological, psychological and trans-personal – corresponding roughly to the three basic aspects of reality – energy, information and value. All three levels are of vital importance to the psychologist, since there is interaction between levels, and the person cannot be properly conceived except as a psycho-somatico-ideological unit. At the basic level the human being is a biological organism, and as such is bound by biological constraints and shaped by biological forces. The ignoring of these biological roots by revisionists who treat the human person as shaped almost completely by culture, not nature, and by existentialists who accord mankind unlimited freedom, flies in the face of a mass of evidence. On the other hand psychology cannot, as some have proposed, simply be reduced to biology and the physico-chemical level. The realm of representations, feelings and directed actions is an essential core feature of psychology, which recent history suggests cannot sensibly be jettisoned or reduced. Finally there is the transpersonal region, socially derived and transmitted, which Popper has termed 'the third world', 'the world of objective contents of thoughts, especially scientific and poetic thoughts and works of art',[14] to which we must add values and ideals. 'It is', wrote Popper, 'impossible to understand the human mind and the human self without understanding the third world.'[15] By processes which Stern termed 'introception' these third world entities become incorporated into the person.[16] The only type of psychology to come to terms with this tripartite hierarchy of levels is a personalistic psychology on Sternian lines. This is not only theoretically the most fruitful, as alone envisaging the unity of the entire field of psychology, but practically the most valuable in recognizing the realities and complexities of everyday life.

A hierarchical scheme of levels is, of course, an ancient idea, going back to Greek thinkers. The essentially modern note derives from the historico-evolutionary insights of the last two and a half centuries. These various levels have emerged over time. Human personality is a late development grounded in a long process of biological and cultural evolution, Hegel was one of the first thinkers to grasp the implications of this developmental process, though he was thinking in cultural rather than biological terms. 'The life of the world', he wrote in his *Philosophy of History*, 'is a totality of levels, which on the one hand exist side by side, but which, on the other, appear transitorily one after another. The moments which the mind seems to have left behind actually exist in it at the present time in full depth.'[17] Darwin widened the setting to embrace the whole process of biological evolution, and since Darwin's time various thinkers, Lloyd Morgan, Bergson and

S. Alexander among others, have expounded the doctrine of emergent evolution. The central thesis of emergence was succinctly stated by Samuel Alexander in his Gifford lectures, *Space, Time and Deity*. 'The higher quality emerges from the lower level of existence and has its roots therein, but it emerges therefrom, and it does not belong to that lower level, but constitutes its possessor a new order of existent with its special laws of behaviour.'[18] The doctrine has aroused much controversy, and excited the ire of reductionist zealots, as well as the criticism of committed dualists; but it has been blessed by philosophers of science like Broad, Popper and Nagel, by biological theorists like Woodger and Beckner, by hard-headed scientists like Medawar, and by psychologists, both Soviet and western, of whom Piaget may be taken as an exemplar. Piaget wrote,

> Since the higher cannot be reduced to the lower, except by destroying the higher or prematurely enriching the lower, the developmental explanation can only consist in showing how, at each new stage, the mechanism provided by the factors already in existence makes for an equilibrium which is still incomplete, and the balancing process itself leads to the next level.[19]

This unfortunately is still a somewhat vague description of the emergent process, hardly less vague than Wundt's doctrine of 'creative resultants'. The creation and emergence of new modes of being and functioning so far defies precise explanation. Looked at in the large and retrospectively they seem to involve a certain rationale: but looked at in detail and contemporaneously there appear to be inexplicable quantum jumps, or, in Marxian terminology, 'dialectical leaps'. We seem to be confronted with an extra dimension of reality, with which the natural sciences have not as yet come to terms. Nevertheless, in spite of its provisional, descriptive nature, emergence theory provides the best working hypothesis for psychology. It is, as Nagel said, 'a wise strategy of research' for the biological and human sciences.[20]

We conclude, therefore, with Stern that the person, conceived hierarchically and developmentally, is the unifying concept that psychology requires to provide the framework for the detailed research upon which its progress depends. Such a framework is needed to provide direction and to warn against the wasteful cul-de-sacs down which psychology has too often strayed. Naturally for progress to materialize the framework must be filled in with creative ideas and appropriate methodologies. It is in connection with methodology that most of the controversies of the past century have arisen. Methodology is unquestionably a crucial factor in science, and to be a science psychology must adhere to acceptable canons of scientific discipline. But as Beveridge pointed out in his stimulating book on scientific research, there is a large element of art involved in the practice of science, and treatises on logic and scientific method 'will be of little help.'[21] Creative scientists in general don't get worked up about methodology; they get on with their jobs. By contrast psychologists during the present century have too often been obsessionally neurotic on questions of scientific method, and unduly restrictive in their demands. They have ignored the advice of William James when he asserted that 'at a certain stage in the development of every science a degree of vagueness is what best consists with fertility'.[22] A hierarchy of levels requires as a correlative a certain methodological diversity and tolerance, what Moscovici termed a *'polythéisme méthodologique'*,[23] embracing at one end precise quantitative techniques and at the other shading off into the weighing of evidence and the hermeneutical interpretation of meanings. The essential characteristics of a science are carefulness in collecting information, honest attempts to check, verify or falsify explanatory hypotheses, the weighing up of probabilities in the light of all relevant facts, and caution in arriving at conclusions. The most appropriate model for the psychologist, at any rate at the present stage of the development of the subject, is not the precision of the mathematical physicist but the looser methodology of a biologist like Darwin, whose transformation of biology was brought about largely by careful naturalistic observation, unbounded patience, and a strong desire 'to group all facts under some general laws'.[24]

There are weighty reasons for believing that psychology can never become a precise science, capable of exact predictions and perfect control. The Skinnerian ideal is a mirage. There is too much 'elbow room' (in the philosopher Dennett's terminology[25]) in the world we live in, where chance as well as necessity holds sway, and the subtle swarm of influences that affect the human brain at any given moment defy precise determination. Moreover man's creative potential adds to the uncertainty and unpredictability. On the other hand there *are* regularities in human behaviour. Personalities, in spite of their individuality, fall into recognizable patterns and types. There is no good evidence to believe with revisionists like Gergen that human beings show 'unlimited potential for variation'.[26] This is to overlook the constraints within which all variations take place. The ethologists are surely right in claiming that man presents many 'environment-resistant traits', and many common characteristics deeper than any cultural variations. Hume in his *Enquiry* had already noted that human nature everywhere remains basically the same in its principles and operations, and that this made a science of man a practical proposition.[27] Provided that they recognize the complexities and the limitations of their programme, there is no reason why psychologists should not have confidence in the future of their science, no reason why they should not establish what Bacon termed a 'georgics of the mind',[28] a practically useful psychology which can provide some understanding of the way that human competences and dispositions are formed, operate and at times break down.

III

The metapsychologist cannot confine himself, however, to a practically useful psychology. He is irresistibly drawn to speculate on the place of mind in the scheme of things and on the nature of mind itself. Such speculations are provoked by what we have now learnt about the fundamental strangeness of the physical world, and by the conflicting messages arising from the new physics. On the one hand man seems totally insignificant in the immensities of space and time, and doomed to extinction without trace; on the other hand mind seems implicated in the very texture of the physical universe. Indeed some writers on physics go so far as to state that 'physics is the study of the structure of consciousness'.[29] It is widely agreed among both philosophers and scientists that the revolution in physical thought has moved the mind 'to the centre of the inquiry about the ultimate nature of things'.[30] So where does mind come in?

Looked at fundamentally, a primary function, perhaps *the* primary function, of mind is the mastery of time. Heraclitus was the first western thinker to grasp the full import of the flux of time. It was he who said, according to Plato, 'that all things move and nothing remains still, and he likened the universe to the current of a river, saying that you cannot step twice into the same stream.'[31] But though the water changed the river remained. Behind the flux there was a κόσμος (order), and mind through a joint sharing in the λόγος (reason) of the universe could break free from its mutable privacy into the common world.[32] 'The central insight of Heraclitus', wrote a recent commentator, was 'this identity of structure between the inner personal world of the psyche and the larger natural order of the universe.'[33] Immersed as it was in the flux of time, mind by right ordering could transcend the flux.

Time always has been, and still is, 'a rich source of philosophical perplexity', and 'perhaps the most puzzling aspect of time is the relation between time and consciousness.'[34] Existential thinkers, like Merleau-Ponty, regard time not as a real process at all, but as a function of consciousness; and there certainly is a 'lived time' with distinctive characteristics of its own. But as Hamlyn observes in his outline of descriptive metaphysics, 'the explanation of why we see events as past, present and future cannot be entirely in facts about us. It must have something to do with time itself.'[35] We are immersed in a stream of history larger than ourselves; our societies have their histories; the biological world, and indeed the physical universe have their evolutionary histories. All things have a beginning and an end, including, it would seem, time itself. For us in our mortal lives time is all too real.

Within this universal flux, as Spinoza saw in his doctrine of '*conatus*', 'everything endeavours to persevere in its being.'[36] Certainly at the level of the organic this '*conatus*' must be regarded as an ultimate postulate, as basic as the force of gravity in the world of physics. It shows itself in the will to live and to replicate, in the strategies of 'the selfish gene', and at the level of the third world, in the urge to perpetuate ideas, causes, and institutions, and in the hope of immortality. It is in the service of this basic '*conatus*' that mind would seem to have evolved. Mind begins when information is retained; it is retained to make anticipation possible and thus to enhance the chances of survival. As mind evolves, temporal integration, to use Lashley's expression,[37] increases in scope. 'An animal's awareness', wrote

Langer, 'is always of things in its own place and life. In human awareness the present actual situation is often the least part. We have not only memories and expectations; we have a *past* in which we locate our memories, and a *future* that vastly overreaches our own imagination.'[38] It is this faculty of mind which makes language and human culture possible and which gives mankind entry into the third world and greatly increases his powers of foresight and control. 'It is this self-transcendence', according to Popper, 'which is the most important fact of all life and evolution.'[39] Perhaps Spinoza was right in supposing that all the complex emotional life of man, his joys, his fears, his anxieties, his hatreds, as well as his intellectual and creative drives, derive from the basic '*conatus*', the endeavour to persist within the infinite ambit of nature. It seems to support the view that the basic function of mind is the mastery of time. Within this general framework the endless permutations of genetic factors, the particular circumstantial features of the physical, social and historical environments, and the element of chance, all ensure the lush growth of individuality in its rich profusion. No science can capture the details of this profusion; all that psychology can do is to search for general principles underlying the growth and functioning of personality, and the general causes of the various disorders and aberrations to which personality is prone.

The main task confronting psychology is, therefore, to explore these general principles at every level and by every available method, taking into account relevant advances in other disciplines. Two and a half thousand years of history have laid the foundations. Enormous advances in biology have provided a mass of data on the physical basis of behaviour, mind and personality; psychology itself has adopted the powerful concepts of information processing and acquired revolutionary new technological facilities; while the social sciences have begun to explore the pervading influence of cultural and social factors. Over and above these scientific and technical advances the newer and sharper philosophies of mind have increased critical awareness of conceptual problems. What the future holds we cannot tell; but what we can affirm is that psychology has not only become of central theoretical importance in the intellectual cosmos, but also, in the rapidly changing and turbulent circumstances of the contemporary world, of great practical relevance. The unsolved problems are, of course, many; there are strange fringes, like the area dealt with by parapsychology, which cannot be dismissed dogmatically even if, at present, it offers no firm findings and is often vitiated by credulity and fraud. Psychology is still an immature discipline, still searching for the way forward. Perhaps there are inherent limits to what we can find out; and perhaps, in the end, we shall have to agree with the verdict of our father figure, Heraclitus, the great thinker who gave us 'for the first time a psychology worthy of the name',[40] when he concluded, 'ψυχῆς πείρατα ἰὼν οὐκ ἂν ἐξεύροιο πᾶσαν ἐπιπορευόμενος ὁδόν · οὕτω βαθὺν λόγον ἔχει. (You will not find out the limits of the soul by going, even if you travel over every way, so deep is its report).[41]

Notes

Chapter 1 Introduction

1 Coleridge, S.T., *Treatise on Method*. Originally published in *Encyclopedia Metropolitana*, 1818. Reprinted, edited by Snyder, A.D., 1976.

2 Bacon, F., *Tempus Partus Masculus*, 1603. Translated by Farrington, B., in *The Philosophy of Francis Bacon*, 1970, as *The Masculine Birth of Time*, p.69. Bacon frequently expressed similar views. C.f. *Novum Organum*, I.31.

3 Wundt, W., *Grundzüge der Physiologischen Psychologie*, 1st edn, 1874, 6th edn, 3 vols, 1908-11.

4 See, for example, Watson, J.B., *Behaviourism*, 1924, ch.1, and Skinner, B.F., *Beyond Freedom and Dignity*, 1971, ch.1.

5 Fodor, J., *The Modularity of Mind: An Essay on Faculty Psychology*, 1983.

6 Kuhn, T.S., 'Reflections on my critics', p. 244 in Lakatos, I. and Musgrave, A.(eds), *Criticism and the Growth of Knowledge*, 1970.

7 Sir Karl Popper, born in Vienna, but resident in England since the Second World War, has been described as 'incomparably the greatest philosopher of science that has ever been' (Sir Peter Medawar, quoted by Magee, B., *Popper* (Fontana Modern Masters), 1973, p.9). His principal works on the philosophy of science include: *The Logic of Scientific Discovery*, English trans. 1959 (German original, 1934); *Conjectures and Refutations: The Growth of Scientific Knowledge*, 1963; *Objective Knowledge: An Evolutionary Approach*, 1972.

8 T.S. Kuhn, Director of the Program in History and Philosophy of Science at Princeton, is the author of the influential *The Structure of Scientific Revolutions* (International Encyclopedia of Unified Science, vol. II. 2, 1962. Revised with postscript, 1970). Some of Kuhn's more recent papers have been collected in *The Essential Tension*, 1977.

9 The quotations are from Feyerabend, P., *Against Method: Outline of an Anarchistic Theory of Knowledge*, 1975. See particularly pp. 299-303.
Feyerabend, who was educated in Vienna, and subsequently moved to America, earlier made some valuable contributions to the philosophy of science.

10 Popper, K.R., *The Logic of Scientific Discovery*, 1959, p.111.

11 Bacon, F., *Novum Organum*, 1620, LXXIII.

12 For example, see Habermas, J., *Knowledge and Human Interests*, 1972. The arguments are well reviewed in Mary Hesse's *Revolutions and Reconstructions in the Philosophy of Science*, 1980.

13 Feyerabend, P., *Against Method*, 1975, p.21.

14 Polanyi, M., *Personal Knowledge*, 1955, provides the fullest statement of

his views. Briefer accounts may be found in his *The Study of Man*, 1959, and The *Tacit Dimension*, 1967. Polanyi, born in Hungary, was an able physical chemist, who settled in Manchester and became a Fellow of the Royal Society. He devoted himself to the philosophy of science from the 1950s onwards.

15 Popper, K.R., *Objective Knowledge: An Evolutionary Approach*, 1972.
16 Popper, K.R., *Conjectures and Refutations*, 1963, p.215.
17 Kuhn, T.S., *The Structure of Scientific Revolutions*, 1970, p.151.
18 Popper, K.R. and Eccles, J.C., *The Self and its Brain*, 1977, p.140.
19 Hooykaas, R., *Religion and the Rise of Modern Science*, 1972, p.xi.
20 See Chapter 13 for amplification.
21 Gergen, K.J., *Towards Transformation in Social Knowledge*, 1982. See particularly p.190.
22 Ibid., pp.17, 34, 79 and 200-7.
23 Harré, R. and Secord, P.T., *The Explanation of Social Behaviour*, 1972. Harré, R., *Social Being: A Theory for Social Psychology*, 1979, and, *Personal Being: A Theory for Individual Psychology*, 1983.
24 Moscovici, S., 'Perspectives d'avenir en psychologie sociale'. in Fraisse, P. (ed.), *Psychologie de demain*, 1982, p.141.
25 Robinson, D.N., *An Intellectual History of Psychology*, 1976 (2nd edn 1981), p.28, maintains that 'Histories will always contain a prophetic element'. Popper, K.R., in *The Poverty of Historicism*, 1957, has convincingly shown that history does not enable us to predict the future.
26 Stern, W., *General Psychology from the Personalistic Standpoint*, 1938 (German original, 1935), p.9.
27 Bruner, J.S., 'Psychology and the Image of Man' (Herbert Spencer lecture, Oxford, 1976). *Times Literary Supplement*, 17 December 1976.

Chapter 2 Animistic beginnings

1 Bacon, Francis, *De Sapientia Veterum* (The Wisdom of the Ancients), 1609, Preface.
2 Richard Leakey and Roger Lewin in *People of the Lake* (1979) have reconstructed man's early history and mode of life over the three million or so years of prehistory from archaeological, anthropological and ethological findings. See also Read, C., *The Origin of Man and his Superstitions* (1920).
3 The quotations from Jung are taken from volume 9 of his *Collected Works, The Archetypes and the Collective Unconscious*, viz. from 'The psychology of the child archetype' (1940) and 'Psychological aspects of the mother archetype' (1938/1954).
4 This is argued by Popper in *The Self and its Brain*, 1977, 2nd edn 1983, by Popper K.R. and Eccles J.C., ch.4, 'Some remarks on the Self'.
5 Köhler, W., *The Mentality of Apes*, 1925, p.267.
6 I have taken my anthropological examples from Australia and New Zealand as I have travelled extensively in both these countries and have some acquaintance with their indigenous peoples. For the Australian aborigines see in particular: Elkin, A.D., *The Australian Aborigines*, rev. edn 1979; Berndt, R.M. and Phillips, E.S. (eds), *The Australian Aboriginal Inheritance*, 1973; and the classic work, Spencer B. and Gillen F.J., *The Native Tribes of Central Australia*, 1899.
7 Lévy-Bruhl, L., *The 'Soul' of the Primitive*, 1928. English trans., p. 16.
8 For the 'Mana' concept see Codrington, R.H., *The Melanesians*, 1891.

9 Brett, G.H., article 'Psychology', *Encyclopedia Britannica*, 14th edn, 1929.

10 Jung, C.G., *Collected Works*, vol. 11, *Psychology and Religion: East and West*. From 'Psychological commentaries on the Tibetan Book of the Dead' (1935/1953).

11 James, W., *The Varieties of Religious Experience*, 1902 (1937 reprint, p.122).

12 Frazer, J.G., *The Golden Bough*, abridged edn 1922, p.2.

13 Tylor, E.B., *Primitive Culture*, 1871.

14 Crawley, A.E., *The Idea of the Soul*, 1909.

15 A phrase employed by F.C. Bartlett to explain results of his experiments on perception and memory. See Bartlett, F.C., *Remembering*, 1932, p.44.

16 Cassirer, E., *An Essay on Man*, 1944, ch.2, 'A clue to the nature of Man: the Symbol'. See also Cassirer, E., *The Philosophy of Symbolic Forms*, 3 vols, English trans. 1953-7, and Langer, Suzanne, *Philosophy in a New Key*, 1942.

17 The classic works on the New Zealand Maori are by Elsdon Best: Best, E., *The Maori*, 2 vols, 1924 and *The Maori as He Was*, 1934; and his two specialized monographs, Best, E., *Some Aspects of Maori Myth and Religion*, 1922, and *Spiritual and Mental Concepts of the Maori*, 1922, published by the Dominion Museum, Wellington, New Zealand.

18 For psychological and religious ideas of the civilizations of the Middle East see Frankfort, H. *et al.*, *Before Philosophy* (Penguin, 1949), originally published as *The Intellectual Adventure of Ancient Man*, 1946.

19 Onians, R.B., *The Origins of European Thought*, 1954, is a detailed analysis of the evidence of the origin of psychological terms and the basic concepts of early European psychology. It also contains appendices on Jewish, Hindu and Chinese conceptions of the soul.

20 Gustav Jahoda in *The Psychology of Superstition*, 1969, deals with both primitive and contemporary superstitions.

21 Hebb, D.O., *The Organization of Behavior*, 1949, p.xviii.

22 Popper, K. and Eccles, J.C., *The Self and its Brain*, 1977, p.158 (2nd edn 1983).

Chapter 3 Greek philosophers

General references

Guthrie, W.K.C., *The Greek Philosophers: From Thales to Aristotle*, 1950.
Armstrong, A.H., *Introduction to Greek Philosophy*, 1957.
Armstrong covers the whole period to the end of the ancient world, and is particularly valuable on the transition from the pagan to the Christian world.
For reference: Guthrie, W.K.C., *A History of Greek Philosophy*, various dates, 6 vols, for the period up to and including Aristotle.

1 For the general background: Murray, O., *Early Greece*, 1980, in the Fontana History of the Ancient World, is useful.

2 See Frankfurter, H. *et al.*, *Before Philosophy*, Penguin, 1949, particularly ch.8.

3 Hallpike, C.R., *The Foundations of Primitive Thought*, 1979 – a discussion by an anthropologist of the differences between primitive and

scientific thought in terms of Piaget's developmental psychology. He notes that 'Primitive thought is unable to grasp the notion of mind as a mediating factor between the external world and the experiencing subject; correspondingly there seems to be no awareness of the body as an organised system distinct from mind', p.487.

4   Goody, J., *The Domestication of the Savage Mind*, 1977, p.37.
5   Thomson, G., *The First Philosophers*, 1977, p.241.
6   Dodds, E.R., *The Greeks and the Irrational*, 1951, p.49.
7   There is a large literature on the Pre-Socratics. Kirk, G.S. and Raven, J.E., *The Presocratic Philosophers*. 1957, contains the surviving fragments of their works and translations. Barnes, J., *The Presocratic Philosophers*, 2 vols, 1979, discusses their doctrines. Popper, K.R., 'Back to the Presocratics', *Proc. Aristot. Soc.* LIX, 1958-9, is a lively re-evaluation of them. Reprinted in *Conjectures and Refutations*, ch.5, 1963. See also Lloyd, G.E.R., *Magic, Reason and Experience*, 1979, for an interesting discussion of the transition from 'traditional' to 'scientific' thought.
8   Russell, B., *A History of Western Philosophy*, 1946, p.47.
9   Dodds, C.R., op.cit., ch.7.
10 Aristotle, *De Anima*, 411a, 20.
11 Plato, *Laws*, X, 891C.
12 Ibid., 892A.
13 Cornford, F.M., 'Mystery religious and Pre-Socratic philosophy', in *Cambridge Ancient History*, vol.4, ch.15, 1926, p.533.
14 Snell, B., *The Discovery of the Mind*, English trans. 1953.
15 Ibid., p.111.
16 Onians, R.B., *The Origins of European Thought*, 1954, p.116.
17 Barnes, J., op.cit., p.170.
18 Theophrastus, *De Sensibus*, 25. The text of Theophrastus with a translation, commentary, and introduction was produced by the American psychologist G.M. Stratton in 1917, under the title *Theophrastus and the Greek Physiological Psychology before Aristotle*.
19 Burnet, J., 'The Socratic Doctrine of the Soul', *Proc. Brit. Acad.* 1915-16, pp.235-59.
20 Kahn, C.H., *The Art and Thought of Heraclitus*, 1979: 'Heraclitus is the first to have given serious thought to, and had something to say about, the soul in man.'
21 Kahn, C.H., op.cit., contains the text and translations of the surviving fragments of Heraclitus. Fragments 28 and 31.
22 Ibid.
23 Cicero, M.T., *Tusculan Disputations*, V.10.
24 Guthrie, W.K.C., *A History of Greek Philosophy*, vol.3, part 1, 1969, deals with the Sophists.
25 For Socrates see Guthrie, W.K.C., part 2 of the above.
26 Aristotle, *Metaphysics*, 1078b.
27 For brief introductions to Plato see: Guthrie, W.K.C., *The Greek Philosophers*, chs 5 and 6, 1950, and Field, G.C., *The Philosophy of Plato*, 1949. For reference: Guthrie, W.K.C., *A History of Greek Philosophy*, vol.4, 1975, and vol.5, 1978. Crombie, I.M., *An Examination of Plato's Doctrines*, 2 vols, 1962. The Greek text with an English translation in 12 volumes is available in the Loeb Classical Library. There are translations of some of the more important dialogues in Penguin Classics.
28 For a full discussion of Plato's psychology see: Robinson, T.M., *Plato's*

Psychology, Toronto, 1970. See also Simon, B., *Mind and Madness in Ancient Greece*, 1978, pp.157-212, for comparisons between Plato and Freud.

29 Plato, *Phaedo*, 96A-99D.
30 Ibid., 66C.
31 Plato, *Republic*, 553C.
32 Plato, *Philebus*, 33C-34A.
33 Plato, *Timaeus*, 69D-70E.
34 Plato, *Laws*, X, 897A.
35 Plato, *Republic*, IV, 435A ff.
36 Ibid., VIII and IX.
37 Ibid.
38 Plato, *Republic*, 437B-439B.
39 Ibid., 572B.
40 There are numerous references to pleasure and pain scattered in Plato's dialogues. Among the more important are *Republic*, 580D-587B, *Timaeus*, 64A-65B, and *Philebus*.
41 Plato, *Philebus*. 33C.
42 Plato, *Charmides*, 168-9.
43 Plato, *Timaeus*, 65C-68E.
44 Plato, *Theaetetus*.
45 Plato, *Phaedrus*, 249B.
46 Kenny, A., *The Anatomy of the Soul*, 1973, p.1.
47 Plato, *Timaeus*, 87C.
48 Plato, *Republic*, 444B.
49 Plato, *Timaeus*, 89C.
50 Plato, *Republic*, 377-410, 522-37.
51 Plato, *Laws*, 716C.
52 Plato, *Republic*, 415A.
53 Plato, *Theaetetus*, 194C.
54 For the influence of Plato from the time of his death up to the present day an extremely valuable source translated from the Czech is: Novotny, F., *The Posthumous Life of Plato*, The Hague, 1977. Also valuable are: Klibansky, R., *The Continuity of the Platonic Tradition during the Middle Ages*, 1939, Muirhead, J.H., *The Platonic Tradition in Anglo-Saxon Philosophy*, 1931, and Inge, W.R., *The Platonic Tradition in English Religious Thought*, 1926.
55 Jaeger, W., *Aristotle*, 1934, p.3. For general introductions to Aristotle see: Ross, W.D., *Aristotle*, 1923, and Allan, D.J., *The Philosophy of Aristotle*, 1952. For Aristotle's psychology extremely useful is Barnes, J., Schofield, M. and Sorabji, R. (eds), *Articles on Aristotle*, vol.4, *Psychology and Aesthetics*, 1979. It contains an extensive bibliography of works on Aristotle's psychology. The Oxford translation of Aristotle by Smith, J.A. and Ross, W.D. (eds) contains his complete works in 12 volumes, recently reprinted in 2 volumes. There is an *Index to Aristotle* by Organ, T.W., Princeton, 1949. See also Hicks, R.D., Translation and commentary on *De Anima*, 1907. Hammond, W.A., *Aristotle's Psychology*, 1902 contains translations of the *De Anima* and *Parva Naturalia* with a long introduction.
56 Jaeger, W., op.cit. p.336.
57 Lefèvre, C., *Sur l'Evolution d'Aristote en psychologie*, Louvain, 1972.
58 Aristotle, *De Anima*, 402a, 12-16.
59 Aristotle, *Metaphysics*, 981b, 28.
60 Guthrie, W.K.C., *The Greek Philosophers*, 1950, p.125.

61 Jaeger, W., op.cit., ch.3.
62 Aristotle, *Historia Animalium*, VIII, 1.
63 Barnes, J., 'Aristotle's concept of Mind', *Proc. Arist. Soc.* LXXII, 1971-2, p.114. Reprinted in *Articles on Aristotle*, vol.4.
64 Aristotle, *De Anima*, 412a, 12, 20.
65 Skinner, B.F., *Beyond Freedom and Dignity*, 1971.
66 Aristotle, *De Anima*, 408b, 13.
67 Aristotle, *Historia Animalium*, 508b, 12.
68 Aristotle, *Metaphysics*, 980b.
69 Theophrastus, *De Sensibus*; see note 18 *supra*.
70 Aristotle, *De Anima*, 424b-427a.
71 Ibid., 427b, 15.
72 Sorabji, R., *Aristotle on Memory*, 1972, contains a translation of the *De Memoria* and a commentary.
73 Aristotle, *De Memoria*, 451b, 19-20.
74 Aristotle wrote two short treatises on dreams, *De Insomnis* and *De Divinatione*. The quotation is from *De Divinatione*, 463a.
75 Aristotle, *De Anima*, 427b.
76 Aristotle wrote several treatises on logic. The *Sophistic Elenchi* deals with fallacies in reasoning. As C.L. Hamblin points out in his *Fallacies*, 1970, 'The division of fallacies found in the modern books is, in the main, a development of that of Aristotle', p.50.
77 Ando, T., *Aristotle's Theory of Practical Cognition*, 1965.
78 Aristotle, *Nichomachean Ethics*, 1107a.
79 Hammond, W.A., *Aristotle's Psychology*, 1902, p.lxxxv, summarizing several passages in the *De Anima*.
80 Aristotle, *De Anima*, 431b.
81 Aristotle, *De Insomnis*, 454a, 2-3.
82 Aristotle, *Nichomachean Ethics*, 1170a, 29-34.
83 Aristotle, *De Anima*, 433a.
84 Ibid., 434b.
85 Ibid., 433b.
86 Aristotle, *Nichomachean Ethics*, 1111a.
87 Ibid., 1111b.4-1112a.17.
88 Ibid., 1145a.15-1152a.36.
89 Fortenbough, W.W., *Aristotle on Emotion*, 1975.
90 Aristotle, *De Anima*, 403a.17.
91 Aristotle, *Rhetoric*, 1182a.20.
92 Ibid., 1137a.20-2.
93 Aristotle, *Poetics*, 1419b.24.
94 Van Steenberghen, F., *Aristotle in the West*, Louvain, 1970, gives an account of the incursion of Aristotle into medieval Europe.
95 Brentano, F., *Psychology from an Empirical Standpoint*, 1874, English trans. 1973. Brentano wrote an earlier book on the psychology of Aristotle in 1867. For the influence of Catholics in recent psychology see Misiak, H. and Staudt, V.M., *Catholics in Psychology*, 1954.
96 Farrington, B., *Greek Science*, vol.2, Penguin, 1949. Jones, W.H.S. and Heath, T.L., 'Hellenistic science and mathematics'. in *Cambridge Ancient History*, vol.7, pp.284-311.
97 Long, A.A., *Hellenistic Philosophy: Stoics, Epicureans and Sceptics*.
98 Lucretius, *De Rerum Natura*, English trans. *On the Nature of the Universe*, Penguin classics.

99   Strachan-Davidson, J.L., *Cicero and the Fall of the Roman Republic*, 1925, p.369.
100 Cicero, *Tusculan Disputations*, text and English trans., Loeb Classical Library, 1927.
     Brett, G.S., *A History of Psychology*, vol.1, 1912, p.197.
101 Cicero, *Tusculan Disputations*, III.1.
102 Ibid., III.67.
103 Ibid., IV.65.
104 Ibid., V.41.
105 Ibid., V.68.
106 Marcus Aurelius, *Meditations*, II.17, trans. Farquharson, A.S.L., 1944.
107 Plotinus, *The Enneads*. Text and translation by A.H. Armstrong. Loeb Classical Library, 6 vols. For the general background to Plotinus see: Armstrong, A.H., *The Cambridge History of Later Greek and Early Medieval Philosophy*, 1967. On the question of the possible influence of Indian thought on Plotinus see Wolters, A.M., 'A Survey of Scholarly Opinion on Plotinus and Indian Thought', in Harris, R.B. (ed), *Neoplatonism and Indian Thought*, 1982. Wolters inclines to those who reject a direct influence on Plotinus, though there are remarkable parallels between the teachings of Plotinus and the Upanishads. I have used the earlier English translation of Plotinus by Thomas Taylor, first published in 1817.
108 Armstrong, A.H., *An Introduction to Ancient Philosophy*, 1957. 'Plotinus alone of the Greeks makes the first Principle something more than the supreme Intellect,' p.182.
109 Plotinus, *Enneads*, V.iii.13.
110 Ibid., VI.ix.3.
111 Ibid., IV.iii.8.
112 Ibid., II.ix.2.
113 Blumenthal, H.J., *Plotinus' Psychology: His Doctrines of the Embodied Soul*, The Hague, 1971.
114 Plotinus, *Enneads*, II.ix.18.
115 Ibid., IV.vii.1.
116 Ibid., IV.vii.6.
117 Ibid., III.vi.3.
118 Brett, G.S., *A History of Psychology*, vol.1, 1912, p.302. Brett would seem to exaggerate the emphasis on consciousness. Plotinus certainly refers to consciousness, but it does not occupy a systematic place in his doctrines.
119 Plotinus, *Enneads*, II.ix.1.
120 Blumenthal, H.J., 'Plotinus' psychology: Aristotle in the service of Platonism', *Internat. Philosoph. Quarterly*, vol.12, 1972, pp.340-64.
121 Plotinus, *Enneads*, IV.iii.8.
122 Ibid., VI.ix.
123 St Augustine, *Confessions*, VII.20.

Chapter 4 Christian theologians

General References

Knowles, D., *The Evolution of Medieval Thought*, 1962.

Coplestone, F., *A History of Philosophy*, vol.2, *Mediaeval Philosophy – Augustine to Scotus*, 1965.

Gilson, E., *The Spirit of Mediaeval Philosophy*, English trans. 1936.

Brett, G.S., *A History of Psychology*, vol.1, part 2, *Patristic*, 1912, vol.2, parts 1 and 2, *Mediaeval*, 1921.

McKeon, R. (ed.), *Selections from Medieval Philosophers*, vol.1, *Augustine to Albert the Great*, 1930, vol.2, *Roger Bacon to William of Ockham*, 1931.

There is a very full list of references to medieval thought and psychology in Mora, G., 'Mind-body concepts in the Middle Ages', *J. Hist. Behav. Sci.*, vol.14, pp.344-61 (1978) and vol.16, pp.58-72 (1980).

1 Carlyle, T., *Past and Present*, 1909 (first published 1843), II.ii.
2 Hooykaas, R., *Religion and the Rise of Modern Science*, 1972.
3 St Mark, VIII. 36.
4 St Matthew, X.30.
5 Cook, S. *The Rebirth of Christianity*, 1942, p.186.
6 Niebuhr, R., *The Nature and Destiny of Man*, 1941.
7 Tacitus, *Historiarum Libri*, V.8. For a brief general account of the Jews see Epstein, I., *Judaism*, 1959.
8 Cicero, *Pro Flacco*, 28.
9 Milman, H.H., *A History of the Jews*, 1909 (first published 1863).
10 Brett, G.S., *A History of Psychology*, 1912, vol.1, p.240. See also Isaiah, LVII.15 and LXVI.2.
11 Brett, G.S., op.cit., vol.1, p.261.
12 Barclay, W., *The Mind of St Paul*, 1958.
13 St Paul, *Epistle to the Romans*, I.14.
14 Ibid., VII.22.
15 St Paul, *First Epistle to the Corinthians*, II.11.
16 St Paul, *Epistle to the Romans*, VIII.22-3.
17 St Paul, *Epistle to the Ephesians*, IV.25.
18 Niebuhr, R., *The Nature and Destiny of Man*, 1941, I.193.
19 Russell, R.P., Introduction to Henry, P., *St Augustine on Personality*, New York, Macmillan, 1960.

General references to St Augustine

St Augustine, *Confessions*. Latin text and English translation by W.W. Watts, 1631. Loeb Classical Library.

Brown, P.R.L., *St Augustine of Hippo*, 1967.

Bourke, V.J., *The Essential Augustine*, 1978 (a useful anthology of translated extracts).

Markus, R.A. (ed.), *Augustine: A Collection of Critical Essays*, 1972.

Morgan, T., *The Psychological Teaching of St Augustine*, 1928.

Marrou, H., *St Augustine and his Influence through the Ages*, 1957.

Keyes, G.L., *Christian Faith and the Interpretation of History: A Study of St Augustine's Philosophy of History*, 1966.

Henry, P., *St Augustine on Personality*, 1960.

Clark, M.T., *Augustine: Philosopher of Freedom*, 1955.

20 Russell, B., *A History of Western Philosophy*, 1946, p.374.
21 St Augustine, *De Civitate Dei*, XXII.22.
22 St Augustine, *De Trinitate*.
23 St Augustine, *De Vera Religione*, 39.72.
24 St Augustine, *De Libero Arbitrio*, II.iii.
25 E.g. *De Civitate Dei*, XI.26, *De Libero Arbitrio*, II.3.7.

26   St Augustine, *De Trinitate*, X.10.
27   St Augustine, *Confessions*, I.6.
28   Ibid., I.8.
29   St Augustine, *De Vera Religione*, XXIV.45.
30   St Augustine, *De Perfectione Justitiae*, XXI.44.
31   St Augustine, *De Bono Viduitatis*, XX.26 (Brown's translation, see Brown, P., op.cit., p.351).
32   St Augustine, *De Trinitate*, III.8.
33   St Augustine, *De Civitate Dei*, XXI.10.
34   St Augustine, *Epistles*, IX.3.
35   St Augustine, *De Genesi ad litteram*, XII.11.
36   St Augustine, *De Civitate Dei*, XI. 5-6. *De Genesi ad litteram*, VIII. 20-6.
37   St Augustine, *Confessions*, XI.17.
38   Ibid., XI. 11-31.
39   Ibid., XI.36.
40   St Augustine, *De Musica*.
41   St Augustine, *Confessions*, XI.28 (Watts's translation).
42   Ibid., X.8-25.
43   Ibid., X.14.
44   Ibid., X.17.
45   Ibid., X.8.
46   Ibid., x.16.
47   Keyes, G.L., *Christian Faith and the Interpretation of History*, 1966.
48   St Augustine, *De Trinitate*, IV.16.
49   St Augustine, *De Civitate Dei*, XIX.6.
50   St Augustine, *Confessions*, VII.3.
51   St Augustine, *De Trinitate*, XI.
52   St Augustine, *Confessions*, VIII.5 (Brown's translation).
53   Ibid., VIII.9.
54   Ibid., VIII.10.
55   Henry, P., *St Augustine on Personality*, 1960.
56   St Augustine, *De Civitate Dei*, XIII.24.
57   *Encyclopedia Britannica*, 11th edn 1910, vol.14, p.871.
58   Russell, B., *A History of Western Philosophy*, 1946, p.456.
59   Whitehead, A.N., *Science and the Modern World*, 1926, pp.14-15.
60   There are various translations of the works of St Thomas Aquinas. The *Summa Theologiae* has recently been translated in 60 volumes in the Blackfriars edition. It contains the Latin text, translations and valuable introductions and notes. For the psychologist vols 11-22 are of particular relevance.
     Brief introductions to the doctrines of Aquinas may be found in Copplestone, F., *Aquinas* (Penguin, 1955) and Kenny, A., *Aquinas* (Past Masters, 1980).
61   Kenny, A., *Aquinas*, 1980, p.31.
62   Aquinas, *Summa Theologiae*, I.76.iii.
63   Ibid., I.82.iii.
64   Ibid., I. 76.v.
65   Spearman, C.F., '"General Intelligence": objectively determined and measured', *Am. J. Psychol.*, vol.15, 1904, pp.201-92.
66   Aquinas, *Summa Theologiae*, I.84.vii.
67   Ibid., I.84.i.
68   Ibid., I.79.iii.
69   Brentano, F., *Psychology from an Empirical Standpoint*, 1874. English trans. 1973, p.88.

70 Kenny, A., *Aquinas*, 1980, p.80.
71 Aquinas, *Summa Theologiae*, I.87.i.
72 Ibid., Ia.IIae.6.ii.
73 Ibid., Ia.IIae. 6-17 (vol.17 in the Blackfriars edition, trans. by F. Gilby).
74 Gilby, F., vol.17 of Blackfriars trans., 1970, Introduction, p.xvi.
75 Aquinas, *Summa Theologiae*, Ia.IIae.24.iii.
76 Ibid., Ia.IIae.46.i.
77 Ibid., Ia.IIae.51.i.
78 Kenny, A., vol.22 of the Blackfriars translation, 1964, p.xxxi.
79 Aquinas, *Summa Theologiae*, Ia.IIae,50.iii.
80 Duns Scotus, *Opus Oxoniense*, II.xvi.15.
81 Harris, C.R.S., *Duns Scotus*, vol.2, *Philosophical Doctrines*, 1927. p.276.
82 Harris, C.R.S., op.cit., p.309.
83 Duns Scotus, *Quaestiones Quodlibetales*, q.xviii.n.9.
84 Aquinas, *Summa Theologiae*, I.82.i.
85 Harris, C.R.S., *Duns Scotus*, vol.2, p.303.
86 Siebeck, H., 'Die Anfänge der neueren Psychologie in der Scholastik: 2. Der Scotismus', *Z.f. Philosophie*. 95.258, 1883.
87 Bacon, F., *The Advancement of Learning*, 1605, vol.1 of *The Philosophical Works of Francis Bacon*, p.55. Bacon's principal philosophical works were collected by Robertson, J.M., in one volume, *The Philosophical Works of Francis Bacon*, 1905, from the texts and translations of Ellis and Spedding. Referred to henceforth as E & S.
88 Knowles, D., *The Evolution of Medieval Thought*, 1962, p.339.
89 Brentano, F., op.cit. (see note 69). Mercier, C., *Psychologie*, 1892.
90 Misiak, H. and Staudt, V.M., *Catholics in Psychology*, 1954.
91 Lecky, W.E.H., *History of European Morals from Augustus to Charlemagne*, 2 vols, 1911 (first published 1869).
92 Ibid., vol.2, p.79.

Chapter 5 The scientific revolution

1 Watson, R.I., *The Great Psychologists*, 1962
2 Butterfield, H., *The Origins of Modern Science, 1300-1800*, 1949, p.1.
3 The phrase is taken from Koyré, A., *From the Closed World to the Infinite Universe*, 1957. The date, 1687, is, of course, the date of the publication of Newton's *Principia*.
4 The estimate is given by Randall, J.H. in *The Making of the Modern Mind*, 1926, p.119. This book was re-issued in 1976, and is still one of the most stimulating surveys of the intellectual background of the present age.
5 Bacon, F., *Novum Organum*, 1620, I.128.
6 For an account of Ockham's teachings see Copleston, F., *A History of Philosophy*, vol.3, 1953, chs 3-9.
7 Nicod, H., in Cassirer, E., Kristeller, P.O. and Randall, J.H. (eds), *The Renaissance Philosophy of Man*, 1948, p.23. This valuable book contains introductions and selected texts from the writings of Petrarch, Valla, Ficino, Pico della Mirandola, Pomponazzi and Vives. See also Kristeller, P.O., *Renaissance Concepts of Man*, 1972.
8 Petrarch, F., *De sui ipsius et multorum ignorantia*, 1368, in Cassirer *et al.*, op.cit., p.107.
9 This was the thesis that P. Ramus (1515-1572) defended in taking up his degree in 1536. He followed it up by the publication of *Aristotelicae Animadversiones* in 1543. Ramus had a considerable influence both on the

continent and in Great Britain in the sixteenth and seventeenth centuries. Milton wrote a short treatise on the logic of Ramus in 1672.

10 Pomponazzi, P., *De Immortalitate Animae*, 1516, in Cassirer *et al.*, op.cit., ch.9.

11 Pico della Mirandola, *On the Dignity of Man*, 1486. Extracts in Cassirer *et al.*, op.cit. and in Davies, S., *Renaissance Views of Man*, 1978.

12 Pico della Mirandola, in Davies, S., op.cit., p.67.

13 Luther, M., *De Servo Arbitrio*, 1525, in Davies, S., op.cit., p.112.

14 Ibid.

15 Erasmus, D., *De Libero Arbitrio*, 1524, extract in Davies, S., op.cit.

16 Erasmus, D., *Praise of Folly*, 1511, trans. by Betty Radice, Penguin, 1971.

17 Ibid., p.152.

18 Ibid., p.135.

19 Ibid., p.87.

20 Ibid., p.106.

21 Ibid., p.207.

22 Needham, J., *The Shorter Science and Civilization in China*, ed. Ronan, C.A., vol.1, 1978. See p.168.

23 Sorokin, P., *The Crisis of our Age*, 1941, p.65.

24 St Augustine, *De Fide*, 413.xvi.

25 Huizinga, J., *The Waning of the Middle Ages*, 1924 (Penguin, 1965, pp.218 and 225).

26 Whitehead, A.N., *Science and the Modern World*, 1926, p.19.

27 Ibid., p.3.

28 Butterfield, H., *The Origin of Modern Science, 1300-1800*, 1949, p.79.

29 Westfall, R.S., *Never at Rest: A Biography of Isaac Newton*, 1980.

30 Leonardo da Vinci, Selections from the Notebooks, ed. Richter, I.A., World's Classics, 1952, p.5.

31 Ibid., pp.7-8.

32 Ibid., pp.110-11.

33 Kline, M., *Mathematics in Western Culture*, 1953 (Penguin, 1972), p.122.

34 Ibid., p.115.

35 Burtt, E.A., *The Metaphysical Foundations of Modern Physical Science*, 1925, p.44.

36 Kepler, J., *Opera*, 8 vols, ed. Frisch, C., 1858 ff., vol.5, p.224, quoted in Burtt, E.A., op.cit.

37 Bacon, F., *Novum Organum*, 1620. I.129. E & S p.300 (see note 87 to ch.4, this volume).

38 Quinton, A., *Francis Bacon* (Past Masters, 1980), p.84. See also Whitehead, A.N., *Science and the Modern World*, 1926, p.54 and Webster, C.K., *The Great Instauration*, 1975, p.514, for similar judgments.

39 Brett, G.S., *A History of Psychology*, vol.2, 1921, pp.183-4.

40 Jardine, L., *Francis Bacon: Discovery and the Art of Discourse*, 1974, has a valuable chapter on dialectic in sixteenth century education, also a useful chapter on Bacon's general psychology.

41 Bacon, F., *The Great Instauration*, 1620, E & S p.247.

42 Bacon, F., *The Advancement of Learning*, 1605, E & S p.53.

43 Bacon, F., *The Great Instauration*, E & S p.241.

44 Bacon, F., *Novum Organum*, I.116, E & S p.294.

45 Bacon, F., *The Advancement of Learning*, E & S p.93.

46 Bacon, F., *Da Sapientia Veterum*, 1609, E & S pp.815-58.

47 Bacon, F., *Novum Organum*, 1620, E & S pp.256-287. Rossi, P., *Francis Bacon: From Magic to Science*, English trans. by Rabinovich, S., 1968, documents the changes in Bacon's attitudes towards myths and fables.

48 Bacon, F., *De Dignitate et Augmentis Scientarum*, 1623.
49 Bacon, F., *The Advancement of Learning*, E & S p.59.
50 Ibid., E & S p.92.
51 Bacon, F., *Parasceve*, vii, 1620, E & S p.406.
52 Bacon, F., *Valerius Terminus*, 1603, E & S pp.196-9.
53 Bacon, F., *Novum Organum*, I.46, E & S p.266. Von Wright, G.H., *Treatise on Probability and Induction*, 1951, p.152, quoted by Quinton, A., *Francis Bacon*, op.cit., p.56.
54 Bacon, F., *New Atlantis*, 1627.
55 Ibid., E & S p.731.
56 Bacon, F., *The Advancement of Learning*, 1605 and *De Dignitate et Augmentis Scientarum*, 1623.
57 Bacon, F., *The Advancement of Learning*, E & S p.101.
58 The term 'psychology' appears to have been first employed by Goclenius of Marburg who wrote a book entitled *Psychologia* in 1590. The book, on scholastic lines, went through several editions, and the term was adopted by his pupil Cosmann, but did not immediately pass into general use. It was reintroduced by Christian Wolff in the eighteenth century in his two books, *Psychologia Empirica*, 1732, and *Psychologia Rationalis*, 1734.
59 Bacon, F., *The Advancement of Learning*, E & S pp.101-48; *De Augmentis*, Books 4 and 7.
60 Bacon, F., *The Advancement of Learning*, E & S p.109.
61 Ibid., p.103.
62 Ibid., p.102.
63 Ibid., p.103.
64 Bacon, F., *Novum Organum*, I.127, E & S p.299.
65 Ibid.
66 Bacon, F., *The Advancement of Learning*, E & S p.142.
67 Ibid., p.131.
68 Ibid., p.142.
69 Ibid., p.143.
70 Ibid., p.155.
71 Ibid., p.158.
72 Bacon, F., *De Augmentis*, VII.3, E & S p.572.
73 Bacon, F., *The Advancement of Learning*, E & S p.144. Ibid., p.162.
74 Bacon, F., *De Augmentis*, VII.3, E & S p.574.
75 Ibid., p.575.
76 Bacon, F., *Novum Organum*, I.41, E & S p.264.
77 Bacon, F., *Cogitata et Visa*, 1607, xiv, p.89. This work, and two other brief works not included by Robertson in *The Philosophical Works of Francis Bacon*, were translated with introductory comments by Farrington, B., in *The Philosophy of Francis Bacon* (Liverpool University Press, 1970), p.89.
78 Ibid., p.81.
79 Bacon, F., *Temporis Partus Masculus*, 1603, translated in Farrington, op.cit., as *The Masculine Birth of Time*, p.62.
80 Bacon, F., *Redargutio Philosophiarum*, 1608, translated in Farrington, op.cit., as *The Refutation of Philosophies*, p.118.
81 Bacon, F., *New Atlantis*, E & S p.731.
82 Quinton, A., *Francis Bacon*, 1980, p.79.
83 Bacon, F., *Novum Organum*, Preface, E & S p.257.
84 Galileo, *Il Saggiatore*, 1623, quoted by Copleston, F., *A History of Philosophy*, vol.3, p.287.

85 Galileo, *Dialogues and Mathematical Demonstrations on two New Sciences* (Third Day). Short extracts from Galileo are contained in Heisenberg, W., *The Physicist's Conception of Nature*, 1958, see p.106.

86 Butterfield, H., *The Origins of Modern Science, 1300-1800*, 1949. Chapter 1 provides valuable and not too technical account of the Aristotelian theory of motion and its overthrow by Galileo.

87 Galileo, *Il Saggiatore*, vol.6, Milan, 1811.

88 Boas, M., *Robert Boyle and Seventeenth Century Chemistry*, 1958.

89 Cranston, M., *John Locke: A Biography*, 1957, p.75.

90 Westfall, R.S., *Never at Rest: A Biography of Isaac Newton*, 1980.

91 Newton, I., *Philosophiae Naturalis Principia Mathematica*, 1687, book 3, rule 1.

92 Ibid., rule 3. Heisenberg, W., op.cit. contains short extracts from book 3 of Newton's *Principia*, pp.115-20.

93 Newton, I., *Principia*, book 3, rule 5, Heisenberg, op.cit., p.119.

94 Burtt, E.A., *The Metaphysical Foundations of Modern Physical Science*, 1925, pp.236-7. Burtt's book remains one of the most brilliant studies of the philosophical foundations and implications of the scientific revolution.

Additional and general references

The Renaissance

Debus, A.G., *Man and Nature in the Renaissance*, 1978.
Mandrou, R., *From Humanism to Science, 1480-1700*, Pelican History of European Thought, vol.3, 1978.
Burkhardt, J., *The Civilization of the Renaissance in Italy*, 1860. English trans. 1878.

Science

Singer, C.J., *A Short History of Scientific Ideas to 1900*, 1959.
Bernal, J.D., *Science in History*, vol.2, 1954 (Pelican, 1969).
Westfall, R.S., *The Construction of Modern Science*, 1971 (contains a particularly useful annotated bibliography).
Kuhn, T.S., *The Copernican Revolution*, 1957.
Yates, F., *Giordano Bruno and the Hermetic Tradition*, 1964.

Seventeenth Century

Willey, B., *The Seventeenth Century Background*, 1934.

Chapter 6 The philosophical renaissance

1 Brandt, F., *Thomas Hobbes' Mechanical Concept of Nature*, 1928, p.151. 'An indispensable classic for all serious students of Hobbes' (Peters). Peters, R.S., *Hobbes* (Penguin, 1956) is a good general introduction. Also Watkins, J.W.N., *Hobbes's System of Ideas*, 1965. There are a good many editions of Hobbes's *Leviathan*. For the other works of Hobbes it is necessary to consult William Molesworth's edition, English works, 1839; Latin works, 1845.

2 Brandt, F., op.cit., Introduction.

3 Hobbes, T., *De Corpore*, Dedication.

4 Ibid., I.vi.6.

5 Hobbes, T., *Latin Works*, vol.1, p.xc, quoted in Brandt, op.cit., ch.5.

6 Hobbes, T., *English Works*, vol.4, p.309.

7 Hobbes, T., *Leviathan*, p.207 (pagination of the first edition).

8 Ibid., Introduction.
9 Hobbes, T., *De Corpore*, xxv.1, p.389.
10 Ibid.
11 Ibid., p.391.
12 Hobbes, T., *Leviathan*, I.i.3.
13 Ibid., I.iv.
14 Ibid.
15 Hobbes, T., *De Corpore*, II.x.9, p.132.
16 Hobbes, T., *Leviathan*, VI.28.
17 Hobbes, T., *Human Nature*, IV.ix.53.
18 Hobbes, T., *Leviathan*, XI.47.
19 Ibid., XIII.62.
20 Ibid., III.10.
21 Ibid., IX.
22 Ryle, G., *The Concept of Mind*, 1949, p.323.
23 Descartes. For brief introductions to Descartes's philosophy see Keeling, S.V., *Descartes*, 1934, and Rée, J., *Descartes*, 1974. Rée gives a select bibliography of additional works. My reference to Descartes are to *The Method, Meditations and Selections from the Principles of Descartes*, ed. Veitch, J., 1925. The quotation is from Descartes, R., *Discourse on Method*, II, p.14.
24 Descartes, R., *Meditations*, IV, p.33.
25 Ibid., Synopsis, p.94.
26 Ibid., VI.
27 Ibid., IV, p.132.
28 Ibid., VI, p.164.
29 Ibid., VI, p.165.
30 Descartes, R., *Reply to the Second Objections*, in Veitch, ed., op.cit., p.273.
31 Descartes, R., *Discourse on Method*, V, p.57.
32 Ibid., IV. p.33.
33 Descartes, R., *Meditations*, II, p.109.
34 Descartes, R., *Reply to the Second Objections*, p.267.
35 Descartes, R., *Principles of Philosophy*, II.i, p.232.
36 Descartes, R., *Meditations*, II, p.113.
37 Descartes, R., *Rules for the Direction of the Mind*, ed. Joachim, H.H., 1957, p.19 (an early work probably written by Descartes between 1628-29).
38 Descartes, R., *Principles of Philosophy*, I. 48, p.214.
39 Descartes, R., *Dioptrique*. Also *Les Passions de l'âme*, I, sections 19-25.
40 Pastore, N., *Selective History of Theories of Visual Perception, 1650-1950*, 1971, p.19. Ch.2 deals with Descartes.
41 Descartes, R., *Dioptrique*, Discourse VI.
42 Descartes, R., *L'Homme*, IV, pp.349-63.
43 Descartes, R., *Les Passions de l'âme*, I.38.
44 Ibid., Prefatory letters.
45 Ibid., III.211.
46 Ibid., II.52.
47 Descartes, R., *Principles of Philosophy*, IV, p.265.
48 Ibid., I, p.216.
49 Spinoza, B. de, *Ethic*, V, Preface. For general introductions to Spinoza see: Hampshire, S., *Spinoza*, 1951, and Hallett, H.F., *Spinoza: Elements of his Philosophy*, 1957. For a more detailed study of his psychology, see Bidney, D., *The Psychology and Ethics of Spinoza*, 1940.

More recent studies are: Kashap, S.P. (ed.), *Studies in Spinoza*, 1972 (papers from various dates), and Hessing, S. (ed.), *Speculum Spinozanum*, 1977.

50 Hume, D., *A Treatise of Human Nature*, 1740, IV.v.
51 Pollock, F., *Spinoza: His Life and Philosophy*, 1880. Elwes, R.H.M., *The Chief Works of Spinoza*, 1883.
52 Murphy, G., *An Historical Introduction to Modern Psychology*, 1929, p.11. Bernard, W., 'Spinoza's Influence on the rise of scientific psychology', *J. Hist. Behav. Sci.*, vol.8, 1972.
53 This was noted by Leibniz in his *Théodicée*.
54 Russell, B., *History of Western Philosophy*, 1946, p.592.
55 Spinoza, *Ethic*, II.vii.
56 Ibid., II.xiii, Schol.
57 Spinoza, B. de, *Improvement of the Understanding*.
58 Spinoza, B.de, *Ethic*, II.xiii. Lemm. vii.
59 Ibid., II.xi.
60 Ibid., II.vii.
61 Ibid., II.xvii.
62 Ibid., II.xviii.
63 Ibid., II.xiii. Schol.
64 Ibid., III.ii.
65 Armstrong, D.M., *A Materialist Theory of the Mind*, 1968.
66 Spinoza, B. de, *Ethic*, I.xxix.
67 Ibid., III. Preface.
68 Ibid.
69 Ibid., I. Appendix.
70 Ibid.
71 Ibid., I.xxxii. Coroll.2.
72 Spinoza, B. de, *Ethic*. V.xiii, Schol.
73 Ibid., II.vi.
74 Ibid., III.vii.
75 Ibid., V.xxxiii.
76 Ibid., II. Def. iii.
77 Ibid., II.xlix. Coroll.
78 Ibid., V.xlii.
79 Ibid., II. Preface.
80 Ibid., III.xi.
81 Ibid., III.xiii.
82 Ibid., III.lvi.
83 Ibid., III.lix, Schol.
84 Ibid., III.li.
85 Ibid., III.xiv,xv,xviii,xvi.
86 Ibid., IV.xlv, Schol.
87 Ibid., IV.xxiii,xxiv.
88 Ibid., IV.vii.
89 Ibid., V.ii.
90 Ibid., V.iii.
91 Ibid., V.x.
92 Ibid., V, Preface.
93 Hamblin Smith, M., 'Spinoza's anticipation of recent psychological developments', *Brit. J. Med. Psychol.*, vol.5, 1925, pp.257-78. Hampshire, S., *Spinoza*, 1951. Andreas-Salome, L., *Freud Journal*, 1961, pp.75 6.
94 Bidney, D., *The Psychology and Ethics of Spinoza*, 1940, p.386.
95 Hessing, S., 'Freud's relation with Spinoza', in *Speculum Spinozanum*,

ed. Hessing, S., 1977, p.227.

96 Ibid.

97 Hampshire, S., 'Spinoza and the idea of freedom', in Kashap, S.P., ed., *Studies in Spinoza*, 1972, pp.310-31 (originally in the *Proc. of the Brit. Acad.*, 1960), quotation on pp.327-8. Seel also Neu, J., *Emotion, Thought and Therapy*, 1977 (a study of Hume and Spinoza and the relationship of philosophical theories of the emotions to psychological theories of therapy).

98 Alexander, S., 'Spinoza and time', in Kashap, S.P., op.cit., pp.68-85.

99 Russell, B., *History of Western Philosophy*, 1946, p.624. Tipton, I.C., ed., *Locke on Human Understanding*, 1977, contains a collection of papers on Locke and a useful bibliography. For studies of Locke's philosophy see: Aaron, R.I., *John Locke* 1937, and O'Connor, D.J., *John Locke* (Penguin), 1952. And for his life: Cranston, M., *John Locke: A Biography*, 1957. Locke's *Essay Concerning Human Understanding*, ed. Nidditch, P.H., 1975 is the most recent edition of Locke's major work. My page references are to Locke, *Selections*, ed. Lamprecht, S.P., 1928.

100 Locke, J., Letter, 1693, *Selections*, p.348.

101 Locke, J., *Essay*, IV.xii.12, *Selections*, p.296.

102 Ibid., IV.xii.12, *Selections*, p.295.

103 Cranston, M., *John Locke: A Biography*, 157, p.117.

104 Locke, J., *Essay*, IV.xii.12, *Selections*, p.295.

105 Ibid., II.i.2, *Selections*, p.111.

106 Locke, J., *Some Thoughts Concerning Education*, *Selections*, p.3.

107 Reported by Lady Masham; quoted in Cranston, M., op.cit., p.100.

108 Locke, J., *Essay*, I.i.1, *Selections*, p.96.

109 Locke, J., *Some Thoughts Concerning Education*, *Selections*, pp.14-15.

110 Locke, J., *Treatise of Civil Government*, *Selections*, p.62.

111 Locke, J., *Essay*, IV.iii.28, *Selections, p.249.*

112 *Locke, J., Letter, Selections*, p.334.

113 Locke, J., *Some Thoughts Concerning Education*, *Selections*, p.11.

114 Locke, J., *Essay*, II.xxvii.9, *Selections*, p.198.

115 Ibid., Introduction, I.2, *Selections*, p.20.

116 Ibid., Introduction, I.i.8, *Selections*, p.95.

117 Ibid., II.ii.2, *Selections*, p.116.

118 Ibid., II.i.24, *Selections* p.115.

119 Ibid., II.xxxiii, *Selections*, p.221.

120 Piaget, J., *Introduction à l'Epistemologie Génétique*, 1950 (*Genetic Epistemology*, 1970).

121 Allison, H.E., 'Locke's theory of personal identity', *J. Hist. of Ideas*, vol.27, 1966, pp.41-58 (reprinted in Tipton, I.C., *Locke on Human Understanding*, pp.77-104).

122 Kretzmann, N., 'The main thesis of Locke's semantic theory', *Phil.Rev.*, vol.77, 1968, pp.175-96 (reprinted in Tipton, I.C., op.cit., pp.123-40).

123 Locke, J., *Essay*, IV.iii.21, *Selections*, 243.

124 Ibid., IV.ix.3, *Selections*, p.258.

125 Ibid., III.iii.15 and III.v.3, *Selections*, pp.275 and 277.

126 Ibid., II.xx.

127 Russell, B., *History of Western Philosophy*, 1946, p.609. The most convenient compendium of Leibniz's works in English is Loemker, L.E., *Leibniz: Philosophical Papers and Letters*, 2 vols, 1956. The earlier collection of Latta, R., *Leibniz: The Monadology and other Philosophical Writings*, 1898, is still useful. Both works contain long and valuable

introductions. Among general works on Leibniz are: Russell, B., *A Critical Exposition of the Philosophy of Leibniz*, 1900; Broad, C.D., *Leibniz: An Introduction*, ed. Lewy, C., 1975; Rescher, N., *Leibniz: An Introduction to his Philosophy*, 1979. For Leibniz's psychology the main work is: Leibniz, G.W., *New Essays on Human Understanding*, trans. and ed. Remnant, P. and Bennett, J., 1981. The commentary by Dewey, J., *Leibniz's New Essay concerning Human Understanding*, 1888, is still worth consulting. Also McRae, R., *Leibniz: Perception, Apperception and Thought*, 1976.

128 Dewey, J., op.cit., p.272.
129 Quoted in Latta, R., op.cit., p.199.
130 Leibniz, G.W., *New Essays*, p.431.
131 Leibniz, G.W., *Discourse on Metaphysics*, section ii, in Loemker, op.cit., pp.474-5.
132 Yates, F., *The Art of Memory*, 1966, ch.17.
133 Dewey, J., op.cit., p.21.
134 Leibniz, G.W., *New Essays*, p.372.
135 Russell, B., *A Critical Exposition of the Philosophy of Leibniz*, Introduction, p.vii.
136 Couturat, L., *La Logique de Leibniz*, 1901.
137 See Rescher, N., *Leibniz: An Introduction to his Philosophy*, ch.9.
138 Leibniz, G.W., *Elements of Natural Law*, in Loemker, op.cit., p.204.
139 Loemker, L.E., *Struggle for Synthesis: The Seventeenth Century Background of Leibniz's Synthesis of Order and Freedom*, ch.10, 1972.
140 Leibniz, G.W., *New Essays*, p.392.
141 Ibid., p.111.
142 Leibniz, G.W., 'Letter to the Queen of Prussia', in Loemker, op.cit., p.895 (quoted by McRae, R., *Leibniz: Perception, Apperception and Thought*, 1976, p.117).
143 Leibniz, G.W., *New Essays*, p.55.
144 Ibid., pp.91-2.
145 Ibid., pp.203 and 511.
146 Leibniz, G.W., *Discourse on Metaphysics*, in Loemker, op.cit., pp.492-3.
147 Locke, J., *Essay*, I.ii.5.
148 Leibniz, G.W., *New Essays*, p.53.
149 Ibid., p.56.
150 Leibniz, G.W., 'Letter to Arnauld', in Loemker, op.cit., p.521.
151 Leibniz, G.W., *Monadology*, section 60.
152 Ibid., section 19.
153 Whyte, L.L., *The Unconscious before Freud*, 1960, ch.5.
154 Leibniz, G.W., *New Essays*, p.115.
155 Ibid., p.165.
156 Ibid., p.189.
157 Russell, B., *A Critical Exposition of the Philosophy of Leibniz*, p.156.
158 Whyte, L.L., op.cit., ch.3.
159 Rescher, N., *Leibniz: An Introduction to his Philosophy*, p.86.
160 Leibniz, G.W., *Monadology*, section 71.
161 Ibid., section 15.
162 Leibniz, G.W., *The Monadology and other Philosophical Writings*, ed. Latta, R., Introduction, p.138.
163 Leibniz, G.W., *New Essays*, p.317.
164 Leibniz, G.W., *New System of the Nature of Substances and of Communication Between Them*, section 12, in Latta, op.cit., p.311.
165 Leibniz, G.W, *New Essays*, pp.67 and 217.

166   See Adler, M., *What Man has made of Man*, 1937, Lecture 3.

Chapter 7 Eighteenth century developments

For general background to the eighteenth century see: Berlin, I., *The Age of Enlightenment*, 1979; Brown, S.C. (ed.), *Philosophers of the Enlightenment*, 1974; Coppleston, F., *A History of Philosophy*, vol.6, Wolff-Kant, 1960; Engell, J., *The Creative Imagination*, 1981; Hazard, P., *European Thought in the Eighteenth Century*, 1946 (Penguin, 1965); Willey, B., *The Eighteenth Century Background*, 1940.

 1   Berlin, I., Preface to Schenk, H.G., *The Mind of the European Romantics*, 1966, pp.xiii,xiv.
 2   Marx, K. and Engels, F., *The Communist Manifesto*, 1848, section I.
 3   Warren, H.C., *A History of Association Psychology*, 1921.
 4   Hartley, D., *Observations on Man*, 1749, I. Introduction.
 5   Newton, I., University Library, Cambridge, Add. Ms. 3970 f.479 (quoted by Rogers, G.A.J. in Brown, S.C. (ed.), op.cit., p.23).
 6   Höffding, H., *A History of Modern Philosophy*, 1955 (quoted by Pastore, N. *Selective History of Theories of Visual Perception*, p.71).
 7   Berkeley, G., *Alciphron*, IV. 'Divine visual language', 1732, section 8.
 8   Berkeley, G., *A New Theory of Vision*, 1709, section 2.
 9   Ibid., section 12.
10   Molyneux, W., *Dioptrika Nova*, 1692.
11   Chesselden, W., *Phil. Trans. Roy. Soc.*, 1728 (reproduced in Pastore, N. op.cit., Appendix A).
12   Ibid.
13   Pastore, N., op.cit., p.99.
14   See Senden, M. von, *Space and Sight*, English trans. 1960, and Gregory, R.L., *Eye and Brain*, 1966, ch.11.
15   Held, R. *et al*, *Proc. Nat. Acad. of Sci.*, vol.77, 1980, p.5572.
16   Piaget, J., *The Child's Conception of Space*, 1948, English trans. 1956.
17   Berkeley, G., *Treatise on the Principles of Human Knowledge*, 1710, section 65.
18   Pavlov, I.P., 'Natural sciences and the brain', 1909, reprinted in *Lectures on Conditioned Reflexes*, 1929, p.127.
19   Hume, D., *An Enquiry concerning Human Understanding*, 1748, section 12.
20   Hume, D., *A Treatise of Human Nature*, 1740, IV. Conclusion.
21   Ibid., III. section 16.
22   Ibid., IV, section 6.
23   Michotte, A., *The Perception of Causality*, 1946, English trans. 1963. Piaget, J., *The Child's Conception of Physical Causality*, English trans. 1930.
24   James, W., *The Principles of Psychology*, 1890, ch.10.
25   Hartley, D., *Observations on Man*, 1749, Preface, p.iv.
26   Wolff's *Psychologia Empirica* (1732) was earlier, but was essentially philosophical in its approach.
27   Hartley, D., op.cit., vol.1, prop.10.
28   Priestley, J., *Hartley's Theory of the Human Mind on the Principles of the Association of Ideas*, 1775.
29   Mill, J.S., 'Essay on Bentham', *Dissertations and Discussions*, 1859, vol.1, pp.330-92.

30 Condillac, E., *Traité des sensations*, 1754. La Mettrie, J., *L'Homme Machine*, 1748. Cabanis, P., *Rapports du physique et du moral de l'homme*, 1799. Helvetius, C., *De L'Esprit*, 1758. *De l'homme, de ses facultés et de son éducation*. 1772.
31 Reid, T., *Inquiry into the Human Mind*, 1764, p.127 (all page references are to Hamilton's edition of Reid's works, 1846).
32 Reid, T., *Essays on the Intellectual Powers of Man*, 1785, p.249. (The abridged edition edited by A.A. Woozley, 1941, is the most readable version of *Intellectual Powers*.)
33 Ibid., I.ch.5.
34 Ibid., p.350.
35 Reid, T., *Inquiry*, p.165.
36 Ibid., p.172.
37 Reid, T., *Essays on the Active Powers of Man*, 1788, p.545.
38 Reid, T., *Inquiry*, p.130.
39 Reid, T., *Intellectual Powers*, p.221.
40 Reid, T., *Active Powers*, p.548.
41 Ibid., p.595.
42 Reid, T., *Intellectual Powers*, I. ch.8.
43 Brown, T., *Lectures on the Philosophy of the Human Mind*, 1820, lecture 37.
44 Wellek, R., *Immanuel Kant in England, 1793-1838*, 1931.
45 Roback, A.A., *History of American Psychology*, 1964, ch.4.
46 Hoeveler, D., *James McCosh and the Scottish Intellectual Tradition*, 1980.
47 Norris, J., *Essay Towards the Theory of the Ideal or Intelligible World*, 1701; see also Muirhead, J.H., *The Platonic Tradition in Anglo-Saxon Philosophy*, 1931.
48 Butler, J., *Sermons*, 1726, Preface.
49 Smith, A., *Theory of Moral Sentiments*, 1759, II.i.5; see Drever, J., *Instinct in Man*, 1921.
50 Smith, A., *Theory of Moral Sentiments*, III.i.
51 Ibid., III.i.
52 See Woodworth, R.S., *Contemporary Schools of Psychology*, rev. edn 1964, ch.11.
53 Wolff, C., *Gesammelte Schriften*, 51 vols, 1965-
54 Lepointe, F.H., 'The origin and evolution of the term "psychology"', *Am. Psychol*, vol.25, 1970, pp.640-6.
    Lepointe, F.H., 'Who originated the term "psychology"?', *J. Hist. Behav. Sci.*, vol.8, 1972, pp.328-35.
55 Rand, B., *The Classical Psychologists*, 1912. Contains extracts from Wolff's *Psychologia Rationalis*.
56 Engell, J., *The Creative Imagination*, 1981.
57 Tetens, J., *Philosophische Versuche über die menschliche Natur und ihre Entwicklung*, 1776.
58 Hamilton, W., *Lectures on Metaphysics and Logic*, 1858-60, vol.2, p.416, discusses the question of Tetens's priority in the tripartite division.
59 Brentano, F., *Psychology from the Empirical Standpoint*, 1874. English trans. 1973. Book 2, ch.5 surveys the principal attempts to classify mental phenomena. See also Stout, G.F., *Analytical Psychology*, 1896, ch.1.
60 Essentially because Kant had argued that mind could not be studied by scientific and quantitative methods.
61 Gouaux, C., 'Kant's view on the nature of empirical psychology', *J. Hist. Behav. Sci.*, vol.8, 1972, pp.237-42.

324 / Notes to pages 98-103

62 Leary, D.E., 'The philosophical developments of the conception of psychology in Germany, 1780-1850', *J. Hist. Behav. Sci.*, vol.14, 1978, pp.113-21.

63 Kant, I., *Metaphysical Foundations of Natural Science*, 1786. English trans. 1970, p.8.

64 Kant, I., *Introduction to Logic*, 1800. English trans. 1974, pp.1-2.

65 Kant, I., *Critique of Pure Reason*, 1781, p.283. (Page references are to Max Müller's edition, Macmillan, 1933.)

66 Kant, I., *Critique of Pure Reason*, 1781, 2nd. edn 1787; Kant, I., *Critique of Practical Reason*, 1788; Kant, I., *Critique of Judgment*, 1790.

67 Kant, I., *Critique of Pure Reason*, p.40.

68 Ibid., p.221.

69 Ibid., p.309.

70 Ibid., p.88.

71 Kemp Smith, N., *A Commentary to Kant's Critique of Pure Reason*, 1918, p.254.

72 Kant, I., *Critique of Pure Reason*, preface to 2nd edn, p.700.

73 Lorenz, K., 'Kant's doctrine of the a priori in the light of contemporary biology', *General Systems Yearbook* 1962. VII, p.23-30 (reprinted in Averill, J.R., *Patterns of Psychological Thought*, 1976, pp.466-80).

74 Leary, D.E., 'The philosophical development of the conception of psychology in Germany, 1780-1850', *J. Hist. Behav. Sci.*, vol.14, 1978, pp.113-21.

75 Herbart, J.F., *Textbook in Psychology*, English trans. by Smith, M.K., 1891. Extracts in Rand, B., *The Classical Psychologists*, 1912, pp.395-415.

76 Boring, E.G., *A History of Experimental Psychology*, 2nd edn 1950, p.252.

77 Herbart, J.F., *Textbook*, vol.3, section 152.

78 Adams, J., *The Herbartian Psychology Applied to Education*, 1897. For a general account of Herbart's psychology see the articles by Stout, G.F. in *Mind*, 1888, 1889 and 1891.

79 Jones, E., *Sigmund Freud: Life and Work*. vol.1, 1953, p.407.

80 Berlin, I., *Vico and Herder*, 1976.

81 Vico, G., *Scienza Nuova*, 1725. English trans. by Bergin, T.G. and Fisch, M.H. 1948.

82 Berlin, I., *Vico and Herder*, p.67.

83 Voltaire, *Essai sur les Moeurs*, 1754.

84 Berlin, I., *Vico and Herder*, p.140.

85 Toulmin, S. and Goodfield, J., *The Discovery of Time*, 1965, particularly ch.6.

86 Saintsbury, G., article on Montesquieu, *Encyl. Brit.*, 11th edn 1911.

87 Berlin, I., *Vico and Herder*, p.67.

88 Burke, E., *Reflections on the French Revolution*, 1790.

89 Addison, J., 'The pleasures of imagination', *Spectator*, 1712; Akenside, M., *The Pleasures of Imagination*, 1744. There is a large literature on the Romantic movement. The following may be specially mentioned: Schenk, H.G., *The Mind of the European Romantics*, 1966; Thorlby, A., *The Romantic Movement*, 1966; Furst, L.R., *Romanticism in Perspective*, 1969; Engell, J., *The Creative Imagination*, 1981; Honour, H., *Romanticism*, 1981.

90 See Engell, J., op.cit., ch.2.

91 Blake, W., 'Milton' and 'London' in *Songs of Innocence and Experience*, 1794.

92 Goethe, J.W. von, quoted by Thorlby, A., op.cit., p.59.
93 Novalis, F., quoted by Furst, L.R., op.cit., p.219.
94 Shelley, P.B., *Defence of Poetry*, 1821.
95 Gerard, A., *An Essay on Genius*, 1774. This work had a great influence on German Romantic thought. See Engell, J., op.cit., ch.10.
96 Rousseau, J.-J., *Émile*, 1762. Everyman edition 1905, p.320.
97 Ibid., p.5.
98 Ibid., p.26.
99 Ibid., p.213.
100 Ibid., p.172.
101 Ibid., p.292.
102 Rousseau, J.-J., *The Social Contract*, 1762, I.8.
103 Ibid., I.9.
104 Rousseau, J.-J., *Émile*, op.cit., p.162.
105 Mill, J.S., *System of Logic*, 1843, book 6.

Chapter 8 The impact of the life sciences on psychology

For general references see the bibliographies in the following: Hall. T.S., *History of General Physiology*, 2 vols, 1969; Coleman, W., *Biology in the Nineteenth Century*, 1971; Allen, G., *Life Science in the Twentieth Century*, 1978; Oldroyd, D.R., *Darwinian Impacts*, 1980; Young, J.Z., *An Introduction to the Study of Man*, 1971.

1 Brett, G.S., *A History of Psychology*, vol.1, 1912, p.24.
2 Hartley, D., *Observations on Man*, 1749. See book I, props.4 and 5.
3 Galen's complete works in twenty-two volumes, edited by D.C.G. Kühn, were published in Leipzig between 1821 and 1833. The Loeb library contains the Greek text of 'On the natural faculties', translated by A.J. Brock (1916). The best guide to Galen's work is the three-volume account by R.E. Siegal, *Galen's System of Physiology and Medicine*, published in Basel. Part II (1970) deals with Galen's writings on the sensory organs and pain; part III (1973) deals with his works on psychology, psychopathology, and the functions and diseases of the nervous system.
4 For the debate between vitalism and mechanism see: Hall, T.S., *History of General Physiology*, chs 25-35; Merz, J.T., *A History of European Thought in the Nineteenth Century*, vol.2, 1903, ch.10. A classic statement of the vitalist case was contained in the Gifford lectures by Hans Driesch, *The Science and Philosophy of the Organism*, 1908; and of the mechanistic case in J. Loeb, *The Mechanistic Conception of Life*, 1912.
5 Medawar, P.B. and Medawar, J.S., *The Life Science*, 1977, ch.22.
6 Hooke, R., *Micrographia*, 1665.
7 Bacon, F., *The Advancement of Learning*, 1605, p.57 in Ellis and Spedding (see note 87 to ch.4, this volume); *The Philosophical Works of Francis Bacon*, ed. J.M. Robertson, 1905.
8 Helmholtz, H.L.F. von, *Über die Erhaltung der Kraft*, 1847.
9 Kant, I., *General History of Nature and Theory of the Heavens*, 1755; Monboddo, J.B., Lord, *The Origins and Progress of Language*, 1773.
10 Paley, W., *Natural Theology*, 1802.
11 Toulmin, S. and Goodfield, J., *The Discovery of Time*, 1965, ch.7.
12 Gruber, H.E., *Darwin on Man*, 1974.
13 Darwin, C., 'A biographical sketch on an infant', *Mind*, vol.2, 1877 (this sketch was actually written in 1840, but not published until 1877).

14   Darwin, C., *The Descent of Man*, 1871, p.226.
15   Spencer, H., *The Principles of Psychology*, 2nd edn 1870, p.129.
16   Mendel, G., 'Experiments in plant hybridisation', *Proc. Nat. Hist. Soc.*, *Brunn* vol.4, 1865. The article was translated and published in the *Journal of The Royal Horticultural Society* in 1901, and reprinted in Bateson, W., *Mendel's Principles of Heredity*, 1909.
17   Morgan, T.H., Sturtevant, A.H., Muller H.J. and Bridges, C.B., *The Mechanism of Mendelian Heredity*,1915.
18   Fisher, R.A., 'The correlation between relatives on the supposition of Mendelian inheritance', *Trans. Roy. Soc. Edin.*, vol.52, 1918, pp.399-433; *The Genetical Theory of Natural Selection*, 1930; Haldane, J.B.S., *The Causes of Evolution*, 1932.
19   For a short account of the current (1982) account of Darwinian theory see Cherfas, J., ed., 'Darwin up to date', *New Scientist*, 1982. Also *Journal of the History of the Behavioral Sciences*, vol.19, no.1, January 1983, Special Issue: 'Charles Darwin and the Human Sciences'.
20   Monod, J., *Chance and Necessity*, 1971, ch.5.
21   Popper, K., 'Evolution and the Tree of Knowledge', in *Objective Knowledge*, 1972, ch.7.
22   Jacob, F., *The Logic of Living Systems*, English trans. 1974, ch.3, 'Time'. Jacob's book is a brilliant survey of the development of the life sciences during the modern period, and should be regarded as essential reading for psychologists.
23   For the history of the understanding of the human brain and spinal cord, the collection of source material by Clarke, E. and O'Malley, C.D., *The Human Brain and Spinal Cord* (a historical study illustrated by writings from antiquity to the twentieth century), 1968, is invaluable. For recent material Pribram, K.H., *Brain and Behaviour*, 4 vols, Penguin, 1969, is a useful anthology. The quotation is from Willis, T., *Cerebri Anatome*, 1664 (quoted by Hall, T.S., op.cit., vol.1, p.317).
24   Haller, A. von, *Primae Lineae Physiologae*, 1747 (quoted by Hall, T.S., op.cit., vol.1, p.401).
25   Bell, C., *Idea of a New Anatomy of the Brain*, 1811 (reprinted in Dennis, W., *Readings in the History of Psychology*, 1948, pp.113-24).
26   Flourens, P.J.M., *Recherches expérimentales sur les propriétés et les fonctions du système nerveux dans les animaux vertébrés*, 1824.
27   Müller, J., *Handbuch der Physiologie der Menschen*, 1833-40. English trans., *Handbook of Human Physiology*, 1837-42.
28   For fuller details consult Clarke, E., and O'Malley, C.D., op.cit.; and *The History and Philosophy of Knowledge of the Brain and its Functions*, an Anglo-American symposium sponsored by the Wellcome Historical Medical Library, Blackwell, 1958.
29   Katz, B., *Nerve, Muscle and Synapse*, 1966, gives a popular account of knowledge of the nerve signal, and process of intercellular communication, up to the middle 1960s.
30   Walter, W.G., *The Living Brain*, 1953.
      Brazier, M.A.B., *The Electrical Activity of the Nervous System*, 1960.
31   Canguilhem, G., *La Formation du concept de réflexe aux XVIIe et XVIIIe siècles*, 1955; Liddell, E.G.T., *The Discovery of Reflexes*, 1960.
32   Hall, M., 'On the reflex function of the medulla oblongata and the medulla spinalis', *Phil. Trans. Roy. Soc.*, vol.123, 1833, pp.635-65. Extracts from Hall's later writings are contained in Herrnstein, R. and Boring, E.G., *A Source Book in the History of Psychology*, 1965, pp.299-308.

33 Laycock, T. *Mind and Brain*, 1859. His paper on the reflex action of the brain was published in the *British and Foreign Medical Review* in January 1845. It was read before the British Association in 1844.
34 Cannon, W.B., *The Wisdom of the Body*, 1932. For early work on the autonomic nervous system see Langley, J.N., *The Autonomic Nervous System*, 1921.
35 *Scientific American*, vol.241, no.3, September 1979.
36 Jackson, J.H., *Selected Writings*, ed. Taylor, J., 2 vols, 1931. Vol. 1 deals with epilepsy, vol. 2 with the evolution and dissolution of the nervous system, aphasia, etc. A biographical memoir by J. Taylor is prefaced to *Neurological Fragments* (1925), a collection of short articles published by Hughlings Jackson in *The Lancet* between 1891 and 1909.
37 Zangwill, O., *Cerebral Dominance and its Relation to Psychological Function*, 1961.
38 Luria, A.R., *The Working Brain*, 1973.
39 Ryle, G., *The Concept of Mind*, 1949, p.11.
40 Hall, T.S., op.cit., vol.2, p.125.
41 Bain, A., *The Senses and the Intellect*, 1855, Preface.
42 See Barcroft, J., *The Brain and its Environment*, 1938, ch.3.
43 Holland, H., *Chapters on Mental Physiology*, 1852, ch.2; Tuke, D.H., *Illustrations of the Influence of the Mind upon the Body in Health and Disease*, 2 vols, 1884.
44 Huxley, T.H., *Collected Essays*, 1893-4, vol.6, p.94.
45 Hebb, D.O., *The Organization of Behavior*, 1949. Introduction, p.xiii.
46 Sherrington, C.S., *Man on his Nature*, 1940, p.347.
47 Eccles, J.C., *The Neurophysiological Basis of Mind*, 1953, ch.8.
48 Popper, K. and Eccles, J.C., *The Self and its Brain*, 1977, p.81.
49 Green, T.H., *Prolegomena to Ethics*, 1883, book I, chs 2 and 3.
50 Bain, A., *Body and mind*, 1878; Wundt, W., *Outlines of Psychology*, 1897; Koffka, K., *Principles of Gestalt Psychology*, 1936, pp.57-67. (The doctrine of isomorphism was originally propounded by Max Wertheimer.)
51 See Rescher, N., *Leibniz: An Introduction to his Philosophy*, 1979, ch.11, 'Monadic hierarchies'.
52 Mills, J.S., *System of Logic*, 1843, book 3, ch.6; Bergson, H., *L'Évolution créatrice*, 1907; Alexander, S., *Space, Time and Deity*, 1920; Morgan, C.L., *Emergent Evolution*, 1923.
53 Rubinshtein, S.L., *Printsipy i Puti Razviti Psychologii* (Principles and Paths of the Development of Psychology), Moscow, 1959 (in Russian).
54 Woodger, J.H., *Biological Principles*, 1929. Beckner, M., *The Biological Way of Thought*, 1959.
55 Wolman, B.B., *Scientific Psychology*, 1965, ch.30.
56 Medawar, P.B. and Medawar, J.S., op.cit., p.165.

Chapter 9 The beginnings of scientific psychology

1 Bryce, J., Preface to the English translation of Conrad's *The German Universities*, 1885.
2 Flexner, A., *Universities: American, English, German*, 1930, p.327.
3 Ross, D., *G. Stanley Hall*, 1972.
4 Weber, E.H., 'Der Tastsinn und das Gemeinsgefühl' in Wagner, R., *Handwörterbuch der Physiologie*, 1846, pp.481-588.
5 Boring, E.G., *A History of Experimental Psychology*, 2nd edn 1950,

ch.14; Boring, E.G., 'Fechner: inadvertent founder of psychophysics', *Psychometrika*, vol.26, 1961, pp.3-8.

6   Fechner, G.T., Elements of Psychophysics, vol.1, trans. by Adler, H.E., 1966.
7   Gregory, R.L., *Mind in Science*, 1981, p.501.
8   Fechner, G.T., *Elements of Psychophysics*, Preface, p.xxvi.
9   Ibid., p.57.
10 Ibid., Preface, p.xxix.
11 See for example: Muntz, A., 'An eighteenth century attempt at an experimental psychology', *J. gen. Psychol.*, vol.50, 1954, pp.63-77; Zapan, M.L., 'The conceptual development of quantification in experimental psychology', *J. His. Behav. Sci.*, vol.12, 1976, pp.145-58.; Pièron, H., *The Sensations*, English trans. 1956, pp.314-15, for the work of P. Bougier at the beginning of the eighteenth century which anticipated Weber's law.
12 Fechner, G.T., *Elements of Psychophysics*, p.47.
13 Fechner, G.T., *Vorschule der Aesthetik*, 1876.
14 Hacking, I., *The Emergence of Probability*, 1975.
15 Corso, J.F., 'A theoretico-historical review of the threshold concept', *Psychol. Bull.*, vol.60, 1963, pp.356-70.
16 Ekman, G., 'Weber's law and related functions', *J. Psychol.*, vol.47, 1959, pp.343-52.
17 James, W., *The Principles of Psychology*, 1890, vol.1, p.540.
18 See the symposia in *Brit. J. Psychol.*, vol.6, 1913, pp.137-89, 'Are the intensity differences of sensation quantitative?', and British Association for the Advancement of Science, *Proceedings*, 1940, vol.2, pp.331-49. Also Savage, C.W., *The Measurement of Sensation*, 1970; Stevens, S.S., *Psychophysics*, 1975.
19 Adrian, E.D. and Matthews, R., 'The action of light on the eye', I-III, *J. Physiol.*, vol.63, p.378, vol.64, p.279, vol.65, p.273, 1927-8.
20 Stevens, S.S., 'On the brightness of lights and the loudness of sounds', *Science*. vol.118, 1953, p.576; Stevens, S.S., 'On the psychophysical law', *Psychol. Rev.*, vol.64, 1957, pp.153-81.
21 Ekman, G. and Sjöberg, L., 'Scaling', *Ann. Rev. Psychol.*, vol.16, 1965, pp.451-74.
22 v.Békésy, G., 'Über das Fechner'sche Gesetz und seine Bedeutung für die Theorie der akustischen Beobachtungsfehler und die Theorie des Hörens', *Ann. der Physik*, vol.7, 1930, pp.329-54.
23 Tanner, W.P. and Swets, J.A., 'A decision-making theory of visual detection', *Psychol. Rev.*, vol.61, pp.401-9.
24 Luce, R.D., Bush, R.R. and Galanter, E. (eds), *Handbook of Mathematical Psychology*, 2 vols, 1963. Among the journals may be mentioned *Psychometrika*; *J. Math. Psychol.*, and *Brit. J. Math. and Statistical Psychol.*
25 Luce, R.D., 'A mathematician as psychologist', in Krawiec, T.S., *The Psychologists*, vol.3, 1978, p.157.
26 Campbell, N.R., *The Foundations of Science*, 1957; Churchman, C.W. and Ratook, P. (eds), *Measurement: Definition and Theories*, 1957 (includes an article by Stevens, S.S., on 'Measurement and Psychophysics', pp.18-64); Stevens, S.S., 'Mathematics, measurement and psychophysics', in Stevens, S.S. (ed.), *Handbook of Experimental Psychology*, 1951, pp.1-49.
27 Stern, W., *General Psychology*, 1935. English trans. 1938, p.180.

28   Koenigsberger, L., *Hermann von Helmholtz*, 1906 (Dover edn 1965), a valuable life of Helmholtz by one closely associated with him. For the address to the Academy of Berlin, 1893, see Koenigsberger, op.cit., p.212. Also Helmholtz, H., *Sensations of Tone*, 1863, English trans. 1875, p.1.
29   Brett, G.S., *A History of Psychology*, vol.3, 1921, p.123.
30   Helmholtz, H., *Über der Erhaltung der Kraft*, 1847; also 'On the conservation of force', in *Popular Lectures on Scientific Subjects*, first series, English trans. 1873 (a lecture given in Karlsruhe in 1862).
31   Bernal, J.D., *Science in History*, vol.2, 1954, p.555 (Penguin, 1969).
32   Boring, E.G., *A History of Experimental Psychology*, 2nd edn 1950, ch.8, 'The personal equation'.
33   Helmholtz, H., 'On methods of measuring very small intervals of time', trans. in *Phil Mag.*, vol.6, 1850.
34   Helmholtz, H., *Treatise on Physiological Optics*, vol.1, 1856, vol.2, 1860, vol.3, 1867. English trans. 1924, from 3rd German edn of 1909-11 (Dover edition, 1962).
35   James, W., *Principles of Psychology*, 1890, vol.2, p.273.
36   Helmholtz, H., *Sensations of Tone*, 1863, English trans. 1875.
37   Helmholtz, H., *Popular Lectures on Scientific Subjects*, vol.1, p.176.
38   Helmholtz, H., *Physiological Optics*, vol.1, part 1.
39   Koenigsberger, L., *Hermann von Helmholtz*, p.160.
40   Ibid., p.129.
     Helmholtz, H., *Popular Lectures*, vol.1, p.321.
41   Koenigsberger, op.cit., p.284. Quoted from Helmholtz's preface to Tyndall's *Fragments of Science*, 1874.
42   Helmholtz, H., *Popular Lectures*, vol.1, p.171.
43   Ibid., vol.1, p.18.
44   Ibid., vol.1, p.278.
45   Koenigsberger, op.cit., p.305.
46   In addition to the *Physiological Optics* and *Sensations of Tone* see Helmholtz's *Popular Lectures*, vol.2. On the relation of optics to painting, see pp.73-138.
47   James, W., *Principles of Psychology*, 1890, vol.1, p.285.
48   Helmholtz, H., *Sensations of Tone*, English trans. part 1, p.5.
49   Ibid., part 1, p.65.
50   Koenigsberger, op.cit., p.305.
51   Helmholtz, H., *Physiological Optics*, vol.2, part 3, Dover edn p.29.
52   Helmholtz, H., 'The origin of the current interpretation of our sensory impressions', *Z.für Psych u. Physiol. der Sinnesorgane*, vol.7, 1894, pp.81-96. Trans. in Warren, R.M. and Warren, R.D., *Helmholtz on Perception: Its Physiology and Development*, 1968, p.250.
53   Gregory, R.L., *Mind in Science*, 1981, p.395.
54   Mill, J., *Analysis of the Phenomena of the Human Mind*, 1829.
55   Bain, A., *The Senses and the Intellect*, 1855, 3rd edn 1868, p.220.
56   Mill, J.S., *A System of Logic*, 1843, book 6, iii.2.
57   The separation, consolidation and institutionalization of psychology can be regarded as the *result* of Wundt's work, in spite of the fact that he himself remained something of a philosopher and that his Institute was attached to the department of philosophy.
58   Wundt, W., *Beiträge zur Theorie des Sinneswahrnehmung*, 1862: 'a book that has some claim to be the beginning of experimental psychology' (Boring). The quotation is from the translation in Shipley, T. (ed.),

Classics in Psychology, 1961, p.70.
59 Wundt, W., *Grundzüge der physiologischen Psychologie*, 1st edn 1874, Preface.
60 Boring, E.G., *A History of Experimental Psychology*, 2nd edn 1950, p.316.
61 Wundt, W., *Vorlesungen über die Menschen und Thierseele*, 1st edn 1863, 2nd edn 1892. English trans. *Lectures on Human and Animal Psychology*, 1894.
62 Boring, E.G., 'On the subjectivity of important historical data', Leipzig, 1879. *J. Hist. Behav. Sci.*, vol.1, 1965, pp.5-9.
63 Wundt, W., *Völkerpsychologie*, 10 vols, 1900–20; *Elemente der Völkerpsychologie*, 1912, English trans. *Elements of Folk Psychology*, 1916.
64 Titchener, E.B., *Wilhelm Wundt, Am. J. Psychol*, 2nd edn, ch.16.
65 Mischel, T., 'Wundt and the conceptual foundations of psychology', *J. Phil & Phenom. Res.*, vol.31, 1970, pp.1-26.
Blumenthal, A.L., 'A reappraisal of Wilhelm Wundt', *Am. Psychol.*, vol.30, 'Wilhelm Wundt: psychology as a propaedeutic science', in Buxton, C. (ed.) *Points of View in the History of Modern Psychology*, 1985; Danziger, K., 'The positivist repudiation of Wundt', *J. Hist Behav. Sci.*, vol.15, 1979, pp.205-30; Rieber, R.W. (ed.), *Wilhelm Wundt and the Making of Scientific Psychology*, 1980; Bringmann, W. and Tweney, R. (eds), *Wundt Studies*,1980.
66 Wundt, W., *Lectures on Human and Animal Psychology*, 1892, p.1.
67 Wundt, W., *Einführung in die Psychologie*, 1911, English trans. *An Introduction to Psychology*, 1912, p.153.
68 Wundt, W., *Grundzüge der Physiologischen Psychologie* 6th edn, vol.1, 1908, p.25.
69 Wundt, W., *Grundriss der Psychologie*, 1896. English trans. *An Outline of Psychology*, 1897.
70 Wundt, W., *An Introduction to Psychology*, p.44.
71 Rieber, R.W. (ed.), op.cit., Preface, p.viii.
72 Wundt, W., *Grundzüge der Psychologie*, 6th edn, vol.1, pp.398-679; vol.2, pp.1-383.
73 Wundt, W., *Logik*, 1908, vol.3, p.162.
74 Wundt, W., *An Introduction to Psychology*, p.63.
75 Ibid., p.75.
76 Diamond, S., 'Wundt before Leipzig', in Rieber, R.W. (ed.), op.cit., p.3.
77 Wundt, W., *An Outline of Psychology*, English trans. 1897. 'There must be an elementary process on the physical side, corresponding to every such process on the psychical side. This general principle is known as the principle of psycho-physical parallelism', p.318.
78 Sexton, V.S. and Misiak, H. (eds), *Psychology Around the World*, 1976.
79 Hearst, E. (ed.), *The First Century of Experimental Psychology*, 1979.
80 Stern, W., *General Psychology*, 1935. English trans. 1938, p.9.
81 Boring, E.G., *A History of Experimental Psychology*, 2nd edn, chs 17-19, pp.351-456. Establishment of modern psychology in Germany.
82 Müller-Freienfels, R., *The Evolution of Modern Psychology*, English trans. 1935, p.80.
83 Külpe, O., *Grundriss der Psychologie*, 1893. English trans. 1895.
84 Titchener, E.B., *Lectures on the Experimental Psychology of the Thought Processes*, 1909.
Humphrey, G., *Thinking*, 1951, chs 2-4.

85 Ebbinghaus, H., *Uber das Gedächtnis*, 1885. English trans. *Memory*, 1913.
86 Sanford, E.C., *A Course in Experimental Psychology*, 1897, rev.edn 1902; Titchener, E.B., *Experimental Psychology: A Manual of Laboratory Practice*, I.Qualitative, 1901, II.Quantitative, 1905.
87 Watson, J.B., 'Psychology as the behaviorist views it', *Psychol. Rev.*, vol.20, 1913, pp.158-77.
88 Wundt, W., *Lectures on Human and Animal Psychology*, English trans., p.10.
89 Myers, C.S., *A Textbook of Experimental Psychology*, 3rd edn 1925; Woodworth, R.S., *Experimental Psychology*, 1938; Stevens, S.S. (ed.), *Handbook of Experimental Psychology*, 1951.
90 Hick, W.E., 'On the rate of gain of information', *Q.J.Expt. Psychol.*, vol.4, 1952, pp.11-26; Welford, A.T. (ed.), *Reaction Times*, 1980, p.18.
91 Hebb, D.O., *The Organization of Behavior*, 1949; Broadbent, D.E., *Perception and Communication*, 1958; Sokolov, E.N., 'The orienting reflex and the problems of higher nervous activity' (in Russian), *Voprosy Psikhologii*. vol.1, 1958, pp.58-65; Sokolov, E.N., 'Neuronal models and the orienting reflex', in Brazier, M.A.B. (ed.), *The Central Nervous System and Behavior*, 1960, pp.187-239.
92 Hearst, E. (ed.), *The First Century of Experimental Psychology*, 1979.
93 Ribot, T., in *De la méthode dans les sciences*, 1909, quoted in Fraisse, P. and Piaget, J., *Experimental Psychology: Its Scope and Method*, vol.1, History and method, English trans. 1968, p.36.
94 For further details see Hearnshaw, L.S., *A Short History of British Psychology, 1840-1940*, 1964, chs 1-6.
95 Boring, E.G., *A History of Experimental Psychology*, 2nd edn, 1950, devotes less than a page to Lloyd Morgan. Watson, R.I., *The Great Psychologists*, 1963, devotes two pages to him. Murchison, C. (ed.), *A History of Psychology in Autobiography*, vol.2, 1932, contains an autobiography by Lloyd Morgan.
96 Wundt, W., *Lectures on Human and Animal Psychology*, English trans., p.350. Wundt invokes the *lex parsimoniae* 'which allows recourse to be had to complex principles of explanation when the simplest ones have proved inadequate'. He concludes that 'it seems that the entire life of animals can be accounted for on the simple laws of association'.
97 Morgan, C.L., *Introduction to Comparative Psychology*, 1894, p.53.
98 Ibid., p.359.
99 Thorpe, W.H., *The Origins and Rise of Ethology*, 1979, p.26.
100 This commonly receives inadequate recognition; for example, see Day, W.F., 'The historical antecedents of contemporary behaviorism', in Rieber, R.W. and Salzinger, K. (eds), *Psychology: Theoretical-historical Perspectives*, 1980.
101 Thorndike, E.L. 'Animal intelligence: an experimental study of the associative processes in animals', *Psychol. Rev. Monogr. Suppl*, vol.8, 1898, reprinted in *Animal Intelligence*, 1911.
102 Morgan, C.L., *Animal Behaviour*, 1900, p.2.
103 Morgan, C.L., *An Introduction to Comparative Psychology*, 1894, p.338. Morgan does not employ the term learning; he speaks instead of habit.
104 Morgan, C.L., *Animal Behaviour*, p.296.
105 Morgan, C.L., *Introduction to Comparative Psychology*, pp.338-9.
106 Morgan, C.L., *Habit and Instinct*, 1896.
107 Thorpe, W.H., *The Origins and Rise of Ethology*, p.26.

108 Morgan, C.L., *Introduction to Comparative Psychology*, p.191.
109 Morgan, C.L., *Animal Life and Intelligence*, 1890, p.327.
110 Ibid., p.327.
111 Morgan, C.L., *Emergent Evolution*, 1923.
112 Perry, W.B., *The Thought and Character of William James*, 2 vols, 1935, vol.1, p.274.
113 Ibid., vol.1, p.540.
114 James, H., *The Letters of William James*, 2 vols, 1920, vol.1, p.118.
115 For details see Perry, R.B., op.cit., vol.1, part 1.
116 Perry, R.B., op.cit., vol.2, chs 90 and 91.
117 James, H., op.cit., vol.1, p.84.
118 James, W., *The Varieties of Religious Experience*, 1937, p.157. See Knight, M., *William James*, 1950, p.29.
119 Perry, R.B., op.cit., vol.1, p.541.
120 James, H., op.cit.
Perry, R.B., op.cit., contains some five hundred letters written by William James and not included in H. James's collection.
121 Perry, R.B., op.cit., vol.1, p.228.
122 Ibid., vol.2, pp.1-204, 'Psychology', gives details of James's taking up of psychology, and the origin of the *Principles*.
123 James, W., *Principles of Psychology*, 2 vols, 1890. A new edition in three volumes was issued by Harvard University Press in 1981. Vol. 1 contains essays on 'The intellectual context' by Myers, G.E. and on 'The historical context' by Evans, R.B. Vol.3 contains notes on the text, appendices, and a 'History of the text of the *Principles*'.
124 James, W., *Principles of Psychology*, vol.1, p.350.
125 Ibid., vol.1, p.553.
126 James, W., 'Reflex action and theism', 1881, in *The Will to Believe and Other Essays*, 1896, p.129.
127 James, W., *Principles of Psychology*, vol.1, p.543.
128 James, W. *The Will to Believe*, p.114.
129 James, W., *Principles of Psychology*, vol.1, ch.16.
130 Ibid., vol.2, ch.25.
131 Ibid., vol.2, p.661.
132 Ibid., vol.2, ch.26.
133 James, W., 'The energies of men', Presidential address to the American Philosophical Association, *Phil. Rev.*, vol.17, 1907.
134 James, W., *Principles of Psychology*, vol.1, p.134; James, W., 'Does consciousness exist?', *Essays in Radical Empiricism*, 1912, pp.1-28.
135 James, W., *Principles of Psychology*, vol.1, p.185.
136 Ibid., vol.1, ch.9.
137 Ibid., vol.1, p.243.
138 Ibid., vol.1, p.254.
139 Ibid., vol.1, p.225.
140 Ibid., vol.1, ch.10, p.294.
141 Ibid., vol.1, ch.10, p.297.
142 Perry, R.B., op.cit., vol.2, p.142.
143 Ibid., vol.2, p.195.
144 James, W., *Principles of Psychology*, vol.1, p.534.
145 Perry, R.B., op.cit., vol.2, p.68. A letter to Stumpf, 1887.
146 James, W., *Psychology: A Briefer Course*, 1892, pp.467-81.
147 Ibid., p.468.
148 James, W., 'The energies of men', *Phil. Rev.*, vol.16, 1907, quoted by Perry, R.B., op.cit., vol.2, p.51.

149 James, W., *The Varieties of Religious Experience*, p.228.
James was thinking of the investigation by E. Gurney into automatic writing, Janet's *L'Automatisme psychologique*, 1889, and Binet's *L'altération de la personnalité*, 1891, English trans. *Alterations of Personality*, 1896.
150 Perry, R.B., op.cit., vol.2, p.121.
Janet, P., *L'état mental des hystériques*, 1892, English trans. 1920.
151 James, W., Lowell lectures on psychopathology, 1896. See Perry, R.B., op.cit., vol.2, p.123.
152 James, H., op.cit., vol.2, pp.327-8.
Perry, R.B., op.cit., vol.2, p.122.
153 James, W., *The Varieties of Religious Experience*, p.107.
154 James, W., *Pragmatism*, 1907; James, W., *The Meaning of Truth*, 1909; James, W., *A Pluralistic Universe*, 1909; James, W., *Some Problems of Philosophy*, 1911; James, W., *Essays in Radical Empiricism*, 1912.
155 James, W., *A Pluralistic Universe*, p.212.

Chapter 10 Medical influences

1 Foucault, M., *Madness and Civilization: A History of Insanity in the Age of Reason*, English trans. 1967.
Ellenberger, H.F., *The Discovery of the Unconscious: The History and Evolution of Dynamic Psychiatry*, 1970. See particularly ch.4, 'The background of dynamic psychiatry'. The whole book is a masterly account of the rise and development of dynamic psychiatry.
2 Battie, W., *A Treatise on Madness*, 1758, p.1.
3 Hunter, R. and Macalpine, Ida, *Three Hundred Years of Psychiatry, 1535-1860: A History Presented in Selected English Texts*, 1963, p.404. An admirable and full collection of material on psychiatric history with excellent commentaries.
4 Jones, Kathleen, *Lunacy, Law and Conscience, 1744-1845*, 1955.
5 Whyte, L.L., *The Unconscious before Freud*, 1960, p.63.
6 Mesmer, F., *Mémoire sur la découverte du magnétisme animal*, 1779. English trans. *Mesmerism*, 1948. The 'Propositions asserted' summarize Mesmer's main contentions, pp.54-7.
7 Hippocrates. The most convenient version of the works of Hippocrates and the Hippocratic school is the Loeb edition in four volumes, 1923-31, with Greek texts and English translations. 'The nature of man' is in vol.4. For the four humours see ch.9 sections 38-40.
8 Hippocrates, 'Humours'. Loeb edn, vol.4, ch.9.
9 For an account of Galen's doctrine of temperaments see Siegel, R.E., *Galen on Psychology, Psychopathology and Function and Disease of the Nervous System* (Part 3 of *Galen's System of Physiology and Medicine*, 1973), ch.3. The temperaments: normal and psychopathic types in relation to somatic features.
10 Roback, A.A., *The Psychology of Character*, 1927, contains a long historical section on the doctrine of temperaments from ancient times to the 1920s. See particularly chs 3-5.
11 Kant, I., *Anthropologie*, 1800, II.2; Wundt, W., *Grundzuge der physiologischen Psychologie*, vol.3, 1911, pp.612-13.
12 Pavlov, I.P., 'A psychological study of the types of nervous system, i.e. temperaments', 1927, in *Lectures on Conditioned Reflexes*. English trans. 1928.
13 Jung, C.G., *Psychological Types*, 1924; Kretschmer, E., *Physique and*

    Character, 1925; Sheldon, W.H. and Stevens, S.S., *The Varieties of Temperament*, 1942.

14 Eysenck, H.J. and Eysenck, S.B.G., *Personality Structure and Measurement*. 1969.

15 Hunter, R. and Macalpine, Ida, *Three Hundred Years of Psychiatry*, 1963. p.641.

16 Stewart, D., *Elements of the Philosophy of the Human Mind*. vol.3, 1827. Quoted in Hunter and Macalpine, op.cit., p.641.

17 Hamilton, W., *Lectures on Metaphysics and Logic*, 1870, vol.I. Lecture 18, p.340. Hamilton died in 1856, and his lectures were published posthumously in 1870.

18 Elliotson was editor of *The Zooist*, 'a journal of cerebral physiology and Mesmerism', which appeared between 1843 and 1856. It was the first psychological periodical in English, and exerted a considerable influence. Braid's views were set out in *Neurypnology*, 1843.

19 W.B. Carpenter was Professor of Physiology at the Royal Institution, London. The fourth edition of his *Principles of Human Physiology*, 1852, contained a large section on physiological psychology, which was expanded into a separate book, *Principles of Mental Physiology*, in 1874. T. Laycock's main work was *Mind and Brain*, 1860. For further details of this school of physiological psychologists see Hearnshaw, L.S., *A Short History of British Psychology*, 1964, ch.2, 'Physiological and abnormal psychology to 1875'.

20 Carpenter, W.B., *Principles of Mental Physiology*, 1874, ch.9.

21 Maudsley, H., *The Physiology and Pathology of Mind*, 1867, Preface.

22 See Hearnshaw, L.S., op.cit., ch.8, 'Changes in philosophical climate'.

23 Lotze, R.H., *Medizinische Psychologie*, 1852, part 3.

24 Wundt, W., *Grundzüge der physiologischen Psychologie*, vol.3, 1911, section 5; and 'Hypnotismus und Suggestion', in *Philosophische Studien*, vol.8.

25 Ellenberger, H.F., *The Discovery of the Unconscious*, 1970. Ch.2 in particular gives a good account of these developments, including the criticisms to which Charcot was subjected. See also Veith, Ilza, *Hysteria: The History of a Disease*, 1965, which deals with hysteria from antiquity to modern times.

26 Taine, H.A., *De l'Intelligence*, 1870, English trans. *On Intelligence*, 1871.

27 Ribot, T., *La Psychologie anglaise contemporaine*, 1870. English trans. *English Psychology*, 1889.

28 Ribot, T., *Les Maladies de la personnalité*, 1885. English trans. *Diseases of Personality*, 1891, p.35.

29 Ribot, T., *Diseases of Personality*, p.55.

30 Ibid., p.114.

31 Ribot's other main works were: *Hérédité, étude psychologique*, 1882; *La Psychologie allemande contemporaine*, 1879; *Les Maladies de la volonté*, 1883; *La Psychologie de l'attention*, 1888; *La Psychologie des sentiments*, 1896; *L'Evolution des idées genérales*, 1897; *Essai sur l'imagination créatrice*, 1900; *La Logique des sentiments*, 1904; *Essai sur les passions*, 1906.

32 Wood, T.H., *Alfred Binet*, 1973. An admirable account of Binet's life and work.

33 Binet, A. and Féré, C., *Le Magnétisme animal*, 1887, English trans. *Animal Magnetism*, 1887.

34 Binet, A., *La Psychologie du Raisonnement*, 1886, English trans. *The Psychology of Reasoning*, 1889: 'the first work in psychology founded on

experimental researches by hypnotism' (P. Janet).

35 Binet, A. and Féré, C., *Le Magnétisme animal*. Quoted by Wood, T.H., op.cit., p.68.

36 Claparède, E., *Arch. de Psychologie*, 1911, vol.11, pp.37-88. Quoted by Wood, T.H., op.cit., p.332.

37 Ellenberger, H.F., *The Discovery of the Unconscious*, 1970, p.406.

38 Janet, P.M.F., *Les Médications psychologiques*, 1919. English trans. *Psychological Healing*, 1925, p.1213.

39 Ibid., p.16.

40 Ibid., p.1214.

41 Ibid., p.639.

42 Freud, S., *An Autobiographical Study*, 1925, Standard Edition (SE), vol.20, p.54.

43 *Five Lectures on Psychoanalysis*, 1910. Lecture 2, SE, vol.11.

44 Ibid.

45 Medawar, P.B., 'Victims of psychiatry', *New York Review of Books*, 23 January 1975, p.17.

46 Popper, K.R., 'Philosophy of science', in Mace, C.A., *British Philosophy in Mid-century*, 1955.

47 Eysenck, H.J., *Uses and Abuses of Psychology*, 1953, ch.12, 'What is wrong with psychoanalysis?', pp.221-41.

48 Reiff, P., *Freud: The Mind of the Moralist*, 1960, Preface, p.x.

49 Lee, S.G. and Herbert, M., *Freud and Psychology*, Penguin Readings, 1970, Introduction, p.9.

50 Terence, *Hauton timorumenos* (The Self Tormentor), I.i.25, c.160 BC.

51 Freud, S., *The Interpretation of Dreams*, 1900, SE, vol.5, p.514.

52 Freud, S., *New Introductory Lectures on Psychoanalysis*, 1933, SE, vol.22, p.15.

53 Freud, S., *An Autobiographical Study*, Postscript, 1935, SE, vol.20, pp.71-4.

54 Sulloway, F.J., *Freud, Biologist of the Mind*, 1979, emphasizes Freud's debt to Darwin.

55 Freud, S., *Outline of Psychoanalysis*, 1940, SE, vol.23, p.196.

56 Ellenberger, H.F., *The Discovery of the Unconscious*, 1970; Sulloway, F.J., *Freud, Biologist of the Mind*, 1979.

57 Freud, S., 'Project for a scientific psychology', in *The Origins of Psychoanalysis*, ed. Bonaparte, M., Freud, A. and Kris, E., 1954.

58 Freud, S., 'On narcissism', 1914, SE, vol.14, p.78.

59 Freud, S., *An Autobiographical Study*, 1925, SE, vol.20, p.8.

60 Sulloway, F.J., *Freud, Biologist of the Mind*, 1979.

61 Darwin, C., *The Origin of Species*, 1859, ch.8, 6th edn, 1872, p.321.

62 Binet, A., 'Le fétichisme dans l'amour', *Rev. philosophique*, vol.24, 1887, pp.143-67, 252-74.

63 Freud, S., Letter to W. Fliess, 1 February 1900. Quoted by E. Jones, *Sigmund Freud: Life and Work*, vol.1, 1953, p.382.

64 Freud, S., *An Autobiographical Study*, 1925, SE, vol.20, p.59.

65 Sulloway, F.J., *Freud, Biologist of the Mind*, 1979. Fontana edn, p.49.

66 Jones, E., *Sigmund Freud: Life and Work*, vol.1, 1953, p.62.

67 See chapter 7, section 3, p.75.

68 Sulloway, F.J., op.cit., p.468. See also Ellenberger, H.F., *The Discovery of the Unconscious*, 1970, p.277.

69 Jones, E., op.cit., vol.1, p.406.

70 Ibid., p.410.

71 Freud, S., *An Autobiographical Study*, 1925, SE, vol.20, p.59.

72 Freud, S., 'Project for a scientific psychology', op.cit.
73 Jones, E., *Sigmund Freud: Life and Work*, vol.1, 1953, p.269.
74 Ibid., p.270.
75 Galton, F., 'Psychometric experiments', in *Inquiries into Human Faculty and its Development*, 1883. Everyman edn 1906, p.134.
76 Ibid., p.145.
77 Freud, S., *New Introductory Lectures on Psychoanalysis*, 1933, SE, vol.20, p.151.
78 Freud, S., 'Analysis terminable and interminable', 1937, SE, vol.23, pp.211-53.
79 Freud, S., *New Introductory Lectures on Psychoanalysis*, 1933, SE, vol.20, p.7.
80 Freud, S., *The Interpretation of Dreams*, Foreword to the 3rd English edition, 1931, SE, vol.4, p.xxxii.
81 Sulloway, F.J., *Freud: Biologist of the Mind*, 1979, ch.9.
82 Freud, S., 'Thoughts for the times on war and death', 1915, SE, vol.14, p.286.
83 Freud, S., *The Interpretation of Dreams*, 1900, SE, vol.4, ch.5, p.182.
84 Hall, C.S., 'A cognitive theory of dreams', *J. Gen. Psychol.*, vol.49, 1953, pp.273-82.
85 Jung, C.G., 'On the nature of dreams', *Collected Works*, vol.8, p.550.
86 Kimmins, C.W., 'Children's dreams', in Murchison, C. (ed., *A Handbook of Child Psychology*, 1931, pp.527-54.
87 Lee, S.G., 'Social influences in Zulu dreaming', *J. Soc. Psychol.*, vol.47, 1958, pp.265-83.
88 Farber, L.H. and Farber, C., 'An experimental approach to dream psychology through the use of hypnosis', *Psychoanalytic Quart.*, vol.12, 1943, pp.202-16. Reprinted in Moss, C.S., *The Hypnotic Investigation of Dreams*, 1967.
89 Piaget, J., *Play, Dreams and Imitation*, English trans. 1951, ch.7.
90 Freud, S., *The Interpretation of Dreams*, 1900, SE, vol.4, p.60.
91 Aserinsky, E. and Kleitman, N., 'Regularly occurring periods of eye motility and concomitant phenomena during sleep', *Science*, vol.118, 1953, p.273.
92 Snyder, F., 'Towards an evolutionary theory of dreaming', *Am. J. of Psychiatry*, vol.123, 1966, pp.121-42.
93 Freud, S., *Introductory Lectures on Psychoanalysis*, 1917, Lecture 10, SE, vol.15, p.150.
94 Freud, S., 'The antithetical sense of primal words', 1910, SE, vol.11, p.155.
95 Freud, S., *The Interpretation of Dreams*, 1900, SE, vol.5, p.620.
96 Freud, S., *An Autobiographical Study*, 1925, SE, vol.20, p.57.
97 Freud, S., 'On the grounds for detaching a particular syndrome from neurasthenia under the description "anxiety neurosis"', 1895, SE, vol.3, pp.87-115.
98 Freud, S., *Group Psychology and the Analysis of the Ego*, 1921, SE, vol.18, p.90.
99 Freud, S., *Three Essays on the Theory of Sexuality*, 1905, SE, vol.7, pp.125-243.
100 Freud, S., *Five Lectures of Psychoanalysis*, 1910, SE, vol.11, Lecture 4, p.47.
101 Money, J., 'The developments of sexuality and eroticism in humankind', *Quart. Rev. Biology*, vol.256, 1981, pp.379-404.
102 Flugel, J.C., 'The death instinct, homeostasis and allied concepts', in

Studies in Feeling and Desire, 1955, pp.96-154.

103 Sulloway, F.J., Freud, Biologist of the Mind, 1979, p.413.

104 Freud, S., New Introductory Lectures on Psychoanalysis, Lecture 32, 1933, SE, vol.22, p.105.

105 Jung, C.G., 'In memory of Sigmund Freud', Collected Works, vol.15, p.69.

106 Freud, S., New Introductory Lectures on Psychoanalysis, Lecture 32, SE, vol.22, p.95.

107 Freud, S., Group Psychology and the Analysis of the Ego, 1921, SE, vol.18, pp.67-143; The Ego and the Id, 1923, SE, vol.19, pp.3-59.

108 Freud, S., The Ego and the Id, p.25.

109 Freud, S., New Introductory Lectures on Psychoanalysis, Lecture 31, 1933, SE, vol.22, p.77.

110 Freud, S., The Ego and the Id, SE, vol.19, p.23.

111 Freud, S., New Introductory Lectures on Psychoanalysis, Lecture 31, SE, vol.22, p.73.

112 Freud, S., The Interpretation of Dreams, 1900, SE, vol.5, p.612.

113 This is the view of the so-called 'ego-psychologists', e.g. N. Hartmann. See Hartmann, H., Essays on Ego Psychology, 1964.

114 Freud, S., 'The neuro-psychoses of defense', 1894, SE, vol.3, pp.43-61.

115 Freud, S., Inhibition, Symptoms and Anxiety, 1926, SE, vol.20, p.163.

116 Sears, R.R., 'Survey of objective studies of psychoanalytic concepts', Soc. Sci. Res. Council. Bulletin, vol.51, 1943. Kline, P., Fact and Fantasy in Freudian Theory, 1972. Fisher, S. and Greenberg, R.P., The Scientific Credibility of Freud's Theories and Therapy, 1977. Farrell, B.A., The Standing of Psychoanalysis, 1981.

117 Freud, S., Leonardo da Vinci and a Memory of his Childhood, 1910, SE, vol.11, pp.59-137; Totem and Taboo, 1912, SE, vol.13, pp.1-161; The Future of an Illusion, 1927, SE, vol.21, pp.3-56; Civilization and its Discontents, 1930, SE, vol.21, pp.59-145; Moses and Monotheism, 1939, SE, vol.23, pp.3-137.

118 Rieff, P., Freud: The Mind of the Moralist, 1960, p.255.

119 Freud, S., Group Psychology and the Analysis of the Ego, 1921, SE, vol.18, p.69.

120 Freud, S., New Introductory Lectures on Psychoanalysis, Lecture 34, SE, vol.22, pp.150-1.

121 Freud, S., Civilization and its Discontents, 1930, SE, vol.21, pp.59-145.

122 Freud, S., The Future of an Illusion, 1927, SE, vol.21, pp.31-2.

123 Freud, S., New Introductory Lectures on Psychoanalysis, Lecture 35, SE, vol.22, p.159.

124 Ibid., p.174.

125 Freud, S., An Outline of Psychoanalysis, 1940, SE, vol.23, p.196.

126 Farrell, B.A., The Standing of Psychoanalysis, 1981, p.45.

127 Freud, S., Introductory Lectures on Psychoanalysis, 1917, Lecture 1, SE, vol.15, p.17.

128 Voloshinov, V.N., Freudianism: A Marxist Critique, 1927. English trans. 1976.

129 Ricoeur, P., 'The questions of proof in Freud's psychoanalytic writings', in Hermeneutics and the Human Sciences, ch.10. English trans. 1981, p.247.

130 Freud, S., New Introductory Lectures on Psychoanalysis, Lecture 34, 1933, SE, vol.22, p.138.

131 Ansbacher, H.L. and Ansbacher, R.R., The Individual Psychology of Alfred Adler, 1956, is a convenient source of material about Adler. It

contains a systematic selection from his writings together with an introduction and commentaries.

132   Adler, A., *The Science of Living*, 1929, p.103.
133   Ellenberger, H.F., *The Discovery of the Unconscious*, 1970, p.644. Ch.8 surveys Adler's life and work.
134   Jung, C.G., *The Psychology of Dementia Praecox*, 1907; *Studies in Word Association*, 1919.
135   McGuire, W.J. (ed.), *The Freud-Jung Letters*, 1974.
136   Jung, C.G., 'On the limits of the exact sciences', 1896; 'On the psychology and pathology of so-called occult phenomena', 1902, *Collected Works*, vol.1, pp.3-88.
137   Jung, C.G., *Man and his Symbols*, 1964, p.102.
138   Ibid.
139   Jung, C.G., 'On the psychology of the unconscious', *Collected Works*, vol.7, p.111.
140   Fine, R., *A History of Psychoanalysis* 1979; Hale, N.G., *Freud and the Americans*, vol.1, 1971.
141   Fine, R., op.cit., p.3.
142   Szasz, T., *The Myth of Mental Illness*, 1961, p.296.
143   Woodworth, R.S., *Psychology: The Study of Mental Life*, 1st edn, 1921, p.569.
144   Woodworth, R.S., *Dynamic Psychology*, 1918, p.153.
145   Jung, C.G., *Two Essays on Analytical Psychology*, 1917. English trans. 1928, pp.2-3.

Chapter 11 The social dimension

1   Aristotle, *Politics*, I. 1253a, c.330 BC.
2   Niebuhr, R., *The Nature and Destiny of Man*, vol.1, 1941, pp.57-8. Ch.3, 'Individuality in modern culture', is a valuable discussion of the subject. See also J.H. Randall's *The Making of the Modern Mind*, 1926 (reprinted 1976) and Talcott Parsons's *The Structure of Social Action*, 1937, chs 2 and 3.
3   Locke, J., *Treatise of Civil Government*, II.ii, 1690.
4   Mill, J.S., *Considerations on Representative Government*, 1861, p.15.
5   Mill, J.S., *A System of Logic*, 1843, VI.7.
6   Hobbes, T., *Leviathan*, 1651, I.xiii.
7   Shaftesbury, Lord, *An Enquiry concerning Virtue*, 1699. I, iii,3; Butler, J., *Sermon I*, 'Upon the social nature of man', 1726; Smith, Adam, *Theory of Moral Sentiments*, 1759, ch.1; Hume, D., *An Enquiry Concerning the Principles of Morals*, 1751, II.ii.
8   Hume, D., op.cit., III.ii.
9   McDougall, W., *An Introduction to Social Psychology*, 1908, p.18.
10   Hearnshaw, F.J.C., *A Survey of Socialism*, 1928. Chapter 1 Section 1 discusses the origin of the terms 'socialism' and 'socialist'.
11   For example by Robinson, D.N. in *An Intellectual History of Psychology*, revised edn, 1981, p.352.
12   Engels, F., *Speech at the Graveside of Karl Marx*, 1883. Translated from the printed German version in *Der Sozialdemokrat*, 22 March, 1882, and included in *The Portable Karl Marx*, ed. Kamenka, E. (Penguin, 1983). For the psychologist who does not want to wade through the whole corpus of Marx's writings this is a very useful anthology of his key works, with an excellent introduction and bibliographies.
13   Berlin, I., *Karl Marx*, 4th edn, 1978, p.208.

14 Brett, G.S., *A History of Psychology*, vol.3, 1921, p.38.
15 Taylor, C., *Hegel*, 1975, p.571.
16 The exaggeration is stressed by Plamenatz, J., in *Karl Marx's Philosophy of Man*, 1975, pp.447-9.
17 Marx, K., *Theses on Feuerbach*, 1847, Thesis 11, Kamenka, op.cit., p.158.
18 Marx, K., *Critique of Political Economy*, 1859, Kamenka, op.cit., p.169.
19 Marx, K., *Theses on Feuerbach*, 1847, Thesis 6, Kamenka, op.cit., p.157.
20 Marx, K., 'Alienated labour', from *Economico-Philosophical Manuscripts of 1844*, Kamenka, op.cit., pp.131-46.
21 Marx, K. and Engels, F., *Manifesto of the Communist Party*, 1848, Kamenka, op.cit., p.241.
22 Plato, *Parmenides*, 132.B, c.367 BC.
23 Popper, K., *Objective Knowledge*, 1972, p.154.
24 Hegel, G.W.F., *Philosophy of Mind*, 1830, II.c, Section 544.
25 Marx, K., *Critique of Political Economy*, 1859, Kamenka, op.cit., p.169.
26 Marx, K. and Engels, F., *Manifesto of the Communist Party*, 1848, Kamenka, op.cit., pp.218-28, Section 2.
27 Freud, S., *New Introductory Lectures in Psychoanalysis*, 1933, Lecture 35, Standard Edition, vol.22, p.178 ff.
28 Marx, K., *Capital*, vol.1, 1867, p.25.
29 Popper, K., *The Open Society and its Enemies*, vol.2, 1945, ch.23, 'The sociology of knowledge'.
30 Among the first books in the west to give an adequate account of Marx's view of human nature was that by Venables, V., *Human Nature: The Marxian View*, 1946.
31 Yaroshevsky, M.F., *Psychologia v. XX. Stoletii* (Psychology in the Twentieth Century), Moscow, 1971 (in Russian). Ch.4 deals with Lenin's analysis of scientific method, and its significance for psychology.
32 McLeish, J., *Soviet Psychology: History, Theory, Content*, 1975, pp.149-50.
33 Ananiev, B.G., *Uspekhi Sovetskoi Psychologii* (The Achievements of Soviet Psychology), Leningrad, 1948 (in Russian), summarized in McLeish, J., op.cit., pp.169-70.
34 Vygotsky, L.S., *Thought and Language*, 1934, English trans. by Hanfmann, E. and Vakar, G. 1962. For a survey of Vygotsky's work see 'The psychological ideas of L.S. Vygotskii', by Leontiev, A.N. and Luria, A.R., in Wolman, B.B. (ed.), *Historical Roots of Contemporary Psychology*, 1968, pp.338-67.
35 Vygotsky, L.S., *Mind in Society: The Development of the Higher Psychological Processes*, ed. Cole, M. *et al*, 1978, p.6.
36 Ibid., p.57.
37 Luria, A.R., *Cognitive Development: Its Cultural and Social Foundations*, English trans. 1976. There is also a shorter account in Luria, A.R., *The Making of Mind: A Personal Account of Soviet Psychology*, ed. Cole, M. and Cole, S., 1979, ch.4, 'Cultural differences in thinking'. See also Luria, A.R., 'Towards the problem of the historical nature of psychological processes', *Internat. J. Psychol.*, vol.6, 1971, pp.259-72.
38 Frazer, J.G., 'The scope of social anthropology', a lecture delivered before the University of Liverpool, 14 May 1908. Reprinted in *Psyche's Task: The Devil's Advocate: A Plea for Superstition*, 2nd edn, 1913.
39 Penniman, T.K., *A Hundred Years of Anthropology*, 1935, ch.2, 'The formulary period: anthropology before 1835'.
40 Amongst the earliest literary references was Montaigne's essay 'On

cannibals', *Essays*, 1580. For further references see Penniman, op.cit.

41 See Radcliffe-Brown, A.R., 'Five chapters on social anthropology', in *Method in Social Anthropology: Collected Essays*, 1958.

42 The Ethnological Society soon after merged into what became The Royal Anthropological Institute.

43 Tylor, E.B., *Primitive Culture*, 1871, vol.1, p.1.

44 Frazer, J.G. *The Golden Bough*, 12 vols, 1890-1915. Abridged edn in one vol., 1922. This classic work had a profound influence on psychologists, including Freud, in the first quarter of the century.

45 Spencer, W.B. and Gillen, F.J., *The Native Tribes of Central Australia*, 1899. Also, *The Northern Tribes of Central Australia*, 1904, and *The Arunta: A Stone Age People*, 1927.

46 Boas, F., *The Kwakiutl of Vancouver Island*, Am. Mus. Nat. Hist. Memm., VIII.ii, 1908.

47 For an account of British field work see Kuper, A., *Anthropologists and Anthropology: The British School, 1922-72*, 1973.

48 For an account of American work see Honigman, J.J. (ed.), *Handbook of Social and Cultural Anthropology*, 1973.

49 See Kuper, A., op.cit.

50 Rivers, W.H.R., *Psychology and Ethnology*, 1926. Rivers was a member of the Cambridge Anthropological Expedition to the Torres Straits under A.C. Haddon, in 1898. Also included were the psychologists W. McDougall and C.S. Myers. It was the first major collaboration between anthropologists and psychologists. See *Reports of the Cambridge Anthropological Expedition to Torres Straits*, 1901, 1903. For a recent account of Rivers's work see Slobodin, R., *W.H.R. Rivers*, 1978.

51 Jahoda, G., *Psychology and Anthropology: A Psychological Perspective*, 1982, p.273.

52 Spencer, H., *The Study of Sociology*, 1873, p.386.

53 For a brief account of Lévi-Strauss's work see Leach, E., *Lévi-Strauss*, Fontana Modern Masters, 1970.

54 Lévi-Strauss, C., *Tristes Tropiques*, 1955, English trans. 1976, p.513.

55 Tylor, E.B., *Primitive Culture*, 1871, vol.1, p.1.

56 Benedict, R., *Patterns of Culture*, 1935, p.33.

57 Among Malinowski's most influential works were: *Argonauts of the Western Pacific*, 1922; *Crime and Custom in Savage Society*, 1926; *Sex and Repression in Savage Society*, 1926; *The Sexual Life of Savages*, 1929. For an appreciation of his work see Firth, R. (ed.), *Man and Culture: An Evaluation of the work of Bronislaw Malinowski*, 1957.

58 For an account of the influence of Mead, Malinowski and others on social psychology, see Kardiner, A., *The Individual and Society*, 1939, and Young, K., *Handbook of Social Psychology*, 1946, Part 1.

59 Mead, M., *Sex and Temperament in Three Primitive Societies*, 1935, p.280.

60 Ibid., p.311.

61 Mead, M., *Coming of Age in Samoa*, 1928. Mead's work in Samoa has recently been heavily criticized by Freeman, D., in *Margaret Mead and Samoa: The Making and Unmaking of an Anthropological Myth*, 1982.

62 Segall, M.H., Campbell, D.T. and Herskovits, M.J., *The Influence of Culture on Visual Perception*, 1966.

63 Bartlett, F.C., *Remembering*, 1932, Part 2, 'Remembering as a study in social psychology'. See also Wagner, D., 'Culture and memory development', in Triandis, H., Lamber, W., Berry, J., Lonner, W. and Heron, A., *A Handbook of Cross-Cultural Psychology*, 6 vols, 1980-81.

64 Cole, M., Gay, J., Glick, J.A. and Sharp, D.W., *The Cultural Context of Learning and Thinking*, 1971.
65 Triandis, H., *et al*, op.cit. See also the summary reviews of work in cross-cultural psychology in *Annual Review of Psychology*, vol.24, 1973, vol.30, 1979, vol.34, 1983, and Price-Williams, D.R. (ed.), *Cross-Cultural Studies*, Penguin Readings, 1969.
66 Mead, M., *Growing-up in New Guinea*, 1930, p.276.
67 Tylor, E.B., *Researches into the Early History of Mankind*, 1865, p.53.
68 Tylor, E.B., *Primitive Culture*, 1871, vol.1, pp.425-6.
69 Frazer, J.G., *The Golden Bough*, abridged edn, 1922, p.2.
70 Bastian, P.W.A., *Der Mensch in der Geschichte: Zur Begründung einer psychologischen Weltanschauung*, 1860. See Penniman, T.K., *A Hundred Years of Anthropology*, 1935, pp.147-52, for a brief account of Bastian's work.
71 Lévi-Strauss, C., *Tristes Tropiques*, 1955, English trans. 1976.
72 Lévi-Strauss, C., *Structural Anthropology*, 1958, English trans. 1963, p.315.
73 Ibid., p.301.
74 Lévi-Strauss, C., *Mythologiques*, vol.1, 1964, vol.2, 1966, vol.3, 1968, vol.4, 1971.
75 Leach, E., *Lévi-Strauss*, 1970, p.113.
76 Lévi-Strauss, C., *Structural Anthropology*, English trans. 1963, p.21.
77 Ibid., p.3.
78 Lévi-Strauss, C., *Tristes Tropiques*, English trans. 1976, p.501.
79 Lévi-Strauss, C., *Structural Anthropology*, English trans. p.102.
80 Boas, F., *The Mind of Primitive Man*, 1911, p.v.
81 Ibid., P.136.
82 Evans-Pritchard, E.E., *Witchcraft, Oracles and Magic among the Azande*, 1937.
83 Frazer, J.G., *The Golden Bough*, abridged edn, 1922, p.711.
84 Lévy-Bruhl, L., *Primitive Mentality*, English trans. 1923; *How Natives Think*, English trans. 1926.
85 Cole, M., Gay, J., Glick, J.A and Sharp, D.W., *The Cultural Context of Learning and Thinking*, 1971.
86 Ibid., p.225.
87 Werner, H., *Comparative Psychology of Mental Development*, 2nd edn, 1948.
88 Hallpike, C.R., *The Foundations of Primitive Thought*, 1979.
89 Cole, M. *et al.*, op.cit., p.215.
90 Lewes, G.H., *Comte's Philosophy of the Sciences*, 1853, Preface.
91 Spencer, H., *Autobiography*, vol. II, Appendix B. Letter to G.H. Lewes, written in 1864.
92 Spencer, H., *The Principles of Sociology*, vol.1, 1876, Section 6.
93 Ibid., Section 10.
94 For example, Peel, J.D.Y., *Herbert Spencer: The Evolution of a Sociologist*, 1971.
95 Abraham, J.H., *The Origins and Growth of Sociology*, Penguin, 1973, p.95.
96 Durkheim, E., *The Rules of Sociological Method*, 1895, English trans. 1938, p.110.
97 Durkheim, E., *Suicide: A Study in Sociology*, 1897, English trans. 1952, p.208. For a commentary on Durkheim's work, which has been criticized by several recent writers, see Pope, W. *Durkheim's Suicide: A Classic Analysed*, 1976.

98 Durkheim, E., *The Elementary Forms of the Religious Life*, 1912, English trans. 1915, p.211.
99 Piaget, J., *The Moral Judgment of the Child*, 1932.
100 Runciman, W.G., *Weber: Selections in Translation*, 1978, Preface, p.vii. For a brief introduction to Weber see Parkin, M., *Max Weber*, 1982.
101 Weber, M., *Wirtschaft und Gesellschaft*, 1922, English trans. *The Theory of Social and Economic Organization*, 1947, trans. Parsons, T., and quoted in *The Structure of Social Action*, 1937, pp.640-1.
102 Ibid.
103 Weber, M., 'Methodological introduction for the survey of the Society for Social Policy concerning selection and adaptation for the workers in major industrial enterprises', in *Gesammelte Aufsatze zur Sociologie und Socialpolitik*, trans. by Hijtch, D., in Eldridge, J.E.T., *Max Weber: The Interpretation of Social Reality*, 1970, pp.103-55.
104 Hughes, H.S., *Consciousness and Society: The Reorientation of European Social Thought, 1890-1930*, 1974, p.335.
105 Hobhouse, L.T., *Development and Purpose*, 1913 (revised edn, 1927) was probably his most important work. See also *Sociology and Philosophy*, 1966, a collection of essays and articles with an introduction by M. Ginsberg. Ginsberg, M., *Sociology*, 1931, contains a brief reference to Weber. Ginsberg was the only contributor to *The Study of Society*, ed. Bartlett, F.C., Ginsberg, M., Lindgren, E.J. and Thouless, R.H., to show any awareness of the continentals, and even he made no mention of Weber in his article 'The problems and methods of sociology'.
106 Mannheim, K., *Man and Society in an Age of Reconstruction*, German edn, 1935, English trans. revised and enlarged, 1940. Also *Ideology and Utopia*, 1929, English trans. 1936.
107 For an appreciation of Mannheim's work see 'Thinking things out', a review of Mannheim's *Essays on the Sociology of Knowledge*, 1952, *Times Lit. Supp.*, 9 January 1953, and the leading article in the same issue.
108 For example: Giddings, F.H., *Principles of Sociology*, 1898; Ward, L.F., *Outlines of Sociology*, 1898; Small, A.W., *General Sociology*, 1905; Ross, E.A., *Foundations of Society*, 1905.
109 Sumner, W.G., *Folkways*, 1906, quoted in Abraham, J.F., *The Origins and Growth of Sociology*, 1973, p.336.
110 Cooley, C.H., *Human Nature and the Social Order*, 1902, quoted in Abraham, J.F., op.cit., p.358.
111 Thomas, W.I. and Znaniecki, F., *The Polish Peasant in Europe and America*, 2nd edn, 2 vols, 1927; Park, R.E. *et al.*, *The City*, 1925; Lynd, R.S. and Lynd, H.M., *Middletown*, 1929, *Middletown in Transition*, 1937.
112 Peel, J.D.Y., *Herbert Spencer: The Evolution of a Sociologist*, 1971, p.249.
113 Parsons, T., *The Structure of Social Action*, 1937, Introduction to paperback edition, 1968.
114 Hamilton, P., *Talcott Parsons*, 1983, gives a clear analysis of the stages of Parsons's development, and a ten-page bibliography of Parsons's principal writings. See also Savage, S.P., *The Theories of Talcott Parsons*, 1981.
115 Mills, C.W., *The Sociological Imagination*, 1959, ch.2.
116 Hamilton, P., *Talcott Parsons*, 1983, p.131.
117 Lockwood, P., 'Some remarks on the "Social System"', *Brit. J. Sociol.*, vol.7, 1956, pp.134-43; Giddens, A., 'Power in the recent writings of

Talcott Parsons', *Sociology*, vol.2, 1968, pp.257-70.
118 See Brenner, M. (ed.), *The Structure of Action*, 1980.
119 University Commission to advise on the Future of Psychology at Harvard, *The Place of Psychology in an Ideal University*, 1947.
120 Reprinted in Parsons, T., *Social Structure and Personality*, 1964; 'The superego and the theory of social systems', *Psychiatry*, vol.15, 1952, pp.15-25; 'Social structure and the development of personality: Freud's contribution to the integration of psychology and sociology', *Psychiatry*, vol.21, 1958, pp.321-40.
121 King, G., *Natural and Political Observations and Conclusions upon the State and Condition of England*, 1696.
122 *Census of England and Wales for the Year 1871*, vol.4, General Report, 1873, Section 4, The Blind, Deaf and Dumb, Idiots or Imbeciles, Lunatics and Inmates of Hospitals, Workhouses and Prisons, pp.liv-lxxi and Tables 161-8.
123 Kay-Shuttleworth, J.P., *The Moral and Physical Conditions of the Working-class employed in the Cotton Manufacture in Manchester*, 1832; Engels, F., *The Condition of the Working Class in England*, 1845. American trans. 1887; English trans. 1892.
124 Engels, F., op.cit., Panther edn, 1969, p.98.
125 Booth, C., *The Life and Labour of the People of London*, 9 vols, 1892-97. Booth estimated that 30 per cent of the population of central London were living in poverty.
126 Rowntree, B.S., *Poverty: A Study of Town Life*, 1922.
127 Park, R.E., Introduction to Bogardus, E.S., *The New Social Research*, p.14, quoted by Sutherland, E.H., in Rice, S.A. (ed.), *Methods in Social Science*, 1931, p.540.
128 The Charity Organization Society was renamed the Family Welfare Association in 1944.
129 Klein, P., 'Mary Richmond's formulation of a new science', in Rice, S.A. (ed.), *Methods in Social Science*, 1931, pp.95-108.
130 James, W., *Principles of Psychology*, 1890, vol.1, pp.293-4.
131 Ross, E.A., *Social Psychology*, 1908, (22nd reprint, 1925).
     McDougall, W., *An Introduction to Social Psychology*, 1908 (23rd edn, 1936. Reissued in paperback, 1960).
132 Ross, E.A., op.cit., p.1.
133 McDougall, W., op.cit., 1st edn, p.16, 21st edn, p.14.
134 The development of social psychology can be traced in : Murchison, C. (ed.), *Handbook of Social Psychology*, 1935; Lindzey, G., (ed.), *The Handbook of Social Psychology*, 1st edn, 1954; Lindzey, G. and Aronson, E., *The Handbook of Social Psychology*, 2nd edn, 5 vols, 1969. Useful for the early history up to 1940 is G.W. Allport's chapter 'The historical background of modern social psychology', in Lindzey and Aronson, op.cit., pp.1-80.
135 Allport, F.H., *Social Psychology*, 1924.
136 Ibid., p.3.
137 Ibid., p.11.
138 Murphy, G., and Murphy, L.B., *Experimental Social Psychology*, 1931. Revised edn with Newcomb, T.M., 1937.
139 Higbee, K.L. and Wells, M.C., 'Some research trends in social psychology during the 1960's', *Amer. Psychologist*, vol.27, 1977, pp.963-6.
140 Mead, G.H., *Mind, Self and Society: From the Standpoint of a Social Behaviorist*, 1934, Phoenix edn 1967, p.133.

141 For an account of some of the theories consult Lindzey, G. and Aronson, E., *The Handbook of Social Psychology*, 2nd edn, 1969, vol.1, 'Systematic Positions'. Evans, R.I., *The Making of Social Psychology*, 1960, is a fairly popular, but useful, account of contemporary theories based on discussions with creative contributors.

142 These are Tajfel's descriptions. See Tajfel, H.J., *Human Groups and Social Categories*, 1981, p.149.

143 Harré, R. and Secord, P.F., *The Explanation of Social Behaviour*, 1972, p.293.

144 See, for example, Milgram's *Obedience to Authority*, 1974.

145 Lindzey, G. and Aronson, E., *The Handbook of Social Psychology*, 2nd edn, 1969, vol.2, 'Research Methods'.

146 Allport, G.W., 'The historical background of modern social psychology', in Lindzey and Aronson, op.cit., vol.1, p.69.

147 Gergen, K.J., *Towards Transformation in Social Knowledge*, 1982. Also, Harré, R., *Social Being: A Theory for Social Psychology*, 1979.

148 Moscovici, S., 'Perspectives d'avenir en psychologie sociale', in Fraisse, P. (ed.), *Psychologie de demain*, 1982, pp.137-47.

149 Triplett, N. 'The dynamogenic factors in pacemaking and competition', *Amer. J. Psychol.*, vol.9, 1897, pp.507-33.

150 Hinde, R.A. (ed.), *Non-verbal Communication*, 1972.

151 Scientific American, *Human Communication: Language and its Psycho-biological Basis*, 1982.

152 Argyle, M., *The Psychology of Interpersonal Behaviour*, 1967, p.181.

153 Lewin, K., *A Dynamic Theory of Personality*, 1935; *Principles of Topological Psychology*, 1936.

154 Lindzey G. and Aronson, E., *The Handbook of Social Psychology*, 2nd edn, 1969, vol.4, 'Group Psychology and Phenomena of Interaction'.

155 Sherif, M., *The Psychology of Social Norms*, 1966.

156 Le Bon, G., *Psychologie des foules*, 1895, English trans. *The Crowd: A Study of the Popular Mind*, 1920.

157 Goffman, E., *The Presentation of Self in Everyday Life*, 1959.

158 The phrase is Harré's. Harré, R., *Social Being*, 1979, p.26.

159 Tajfel, H.J., *Human Groups and Social Categories*, 1981, is a particularly valuable discussion of the broader problems of social psychology.

160 Ibid., p.7.

161 Lashley, K.S., 'The problem of serial order in behavior', in Jeffress, L.A. (ed.), *Cerebral Mechanisms in Behavior: The Hixon Symposium*, 1951.

162 Dawkins, R., *The Selfish Gene*, 1976 (Granada edition, 1978, p.206).

163 See Zigler, E. and Child, I.L., 'Socialization', in Lindzey and Aronson, op.cit., vol.2, ch.24.

164 Graham, D., *Moral Learning and Development*, 1972.

165 Vygotsky, L.S., *Thought and Language*, 1934, English trans. 1962, ch.6. Luria, A.R., *Cognitive Development: its Cultural and Social Foundations*, 1974, English trans. 1976.

166 Tinbergen, N., 'Functional ethology and the human sciences', *Proc. of Royal Soc.*, vol.182, 1972, pp.385-410, abridged reprint in Hollander, E.P. and Hunt, R.G., *Current Perspectives in Social Psychology*, 4th edn, 1976; Milgram, S., 'The experience of living in cities', *Science*, vol.167, 1970, pp.1461-8.

167 Lindzey, G. and Aronson, E., *The Handbook of Social Psychology*, 2nd edn, 1969, vol.5, 'Applied Social Psychology'.

Chapter 12 Application, specialization and fragmentation

1 Ryle, G., *The Concept of Mind*, 1949, p.323.
2 Beloff, J., *Psychological Sciences: A Review of Modern Psychology*, 1973.
3 Grasha, A.F., *Practical Applications of Psychology*, 1978.
4 Spencer, H., *Education, Intellectual, Moral and Physical*, 1861; Bain, A., *Education as a Science*, 1879.
   Ward, J., delivered a series of lectures on 'Psychology applied to Education' from 1880 onwards. They were not published in book form until 1926: *Psychology Applied to Education*, 1926. Sully, J., *The Teachers' Handbook of Psychology*, 1886. For Stanley Hall, whose early work was published in journals, see Ross, D., *G. Stanley Hall: The Psychologist as Prophet*, 1972; Meumann, E., *Experimentelle Pädagogik*, 2 vols, 1905, 2nd edn, 3 vols, 1911-14.
   Thorndike, E., *Educational Psychology*, 3 vols, 1913-14, did much to establish the subject in the United States.
5 Goodenough, F.L., *Mental Testing: Its History, Principles and Applications*, 1949, Part 1, 'Historical orientation', deals with the historical background of the testing movement.
6 See Thorndike, E., op.cit., and Rusk, R.R., *Experimental Education*, 1919.
7 Bruner, J.S., *Towards a Theory of Instruction*, 1966; Resnick, L.B., 'Instructional psychology', *Ann. Rev. Psychol.*, vol.32, 1981, pp.659-704.
8 Münsterberg, H., *Psychologie und Wirtschaftsleben: Ein Beitrag zur angewandten Experimentel-Psychologie*, 1912. An English version (not a translation) was published in 1913 under the title *Psychology and Industrial Efficiency*.
9 Münsterberg, H., *Psychology and Industrial Efficiency*, p.10.
10 For the early history of industrial psychology see Viteles, M.S., *Industrial Psychology*, 1933. In the same year Elton Mayo's *Human Problems of an Industrial Civilization* appeared, a book which did much to change the direction of industrial psychology towards the social aspects of work.
11 The Ergonomics Research Society is now named 'The Ergonomics Society'. It publishes several journals, *The Ergonomist, Ergonomics*, and *Applied Ergonomics*. A standard work is Murrell, K.F.H., *Ergonomics: Man in his Working Environment*, 1965. See also Fitts, P.M., 'Engineering psychology and equipment design', ch.15, in Stevens, S.S., *Handbook of Experimental Psychology*, 1951.
12 Lomov, B.F., *Chelovek i Technika: Ocherky Inzhenernoi Psychologii*, 1963 (in Russian) (Man and Technics: Contributions to Engineering Psychology) – a standard Soviet work.
13 Kraepelin, E., 'Der psychologische Versuch in der Psychiatrie', *Psychol. Arbeiten*, vol.1, 1895, pp.1-91.
14 Stevenson, G.S., *Child Guidance Clinics*, 1934.
15 Reavley, W., 'Clinical psychology in practice', ch.2, in Canter, S. and Canter, D., *Psychology in Practice*, 1982.
16 For details see Sexton, V.S. and Misiak, H., *Psychology around the World*, 1976. For Great Britain see Department of Health and Social Security, *The Role of Psychologists in the Health Services*, 1977 (The Trethowen Report).
17 Haward, L., 'Forensic psychology', ch.5 of Canter, S. and Canter, D., *Psychology in Practice*, 1982.

18 Stern, W., *Beiträge Zur Psychologie der Aussage*, 1902; Münsterberg, H., *On the Witness Stand*, 1908; Blau, G. and Müller Luckmann, E. (eds), *Gerichtliche Psychologie*, 1962.
19 Tapp, J.L., 'Psychology and law: an overture', *Ann. Rev. Psychol.*, vol.27, 1976, pp.359-404; Monakan, J. and Loftus, E.F., 'The psychology of law', *Ann. Rev. Psychol.*, vol.33, 1982, pp.441-75.
20 Home Office Prison Department, *Review of the Prison Psychological Service*, 1980; Marcus, B., 'Psychologists in the Prison Department', ch.6 of Canter, S. and Canter, D., *Psychology in Practice*, 1980.
21 Clifford, B.C. and Bull, R., *The Psychology of Person Identification*, 1978.
22 Benussi, V., 'Die Atmungssymptome der Lüge', *Arch. gesam. Psychol.*, vol.31, 1914, pp.244-73. The experiments are described in Woodworth, R.S., *Experimental Psychology*, 1st edn, 1938, pp.264-5, which also describes Marston's experiments using blood pressure on p.273 (Marston, W.M., 'Systolic blood-pressure symptoms of deception', *J. Exp. Psychol.*, vol.2, 1917, pp.117-65).
23 Yerkes, R.M. (ed.), 'Psychological examining in the United States Army', *Memoirs Nat. Acad. Sci.*, vol.15, 1921, p.890; Myers, C.S., *Shell Shock in France, 1914-18*, 1940; War Office, *Report of the Committee of Enquiry into Shell Shock*, 1922; Ministry of Munitions, *Final Report of the Health of Munition Workers Committee*, 1918. For further details of experimental work see Hearnshaw, L.S., *A Short History of British Psychology, 1840-1940*, 1964, p.248.
24 In Great Britain applied psychology was continued by the Industrial Fatigue Research Board (later Industrial Health Research Board), which issued nearly a hundred reports before being disbanded at the end of the Second World War, and by the National Institute of Industrial Psychology, founded in 1921 by C.S. Myers, and continuing to work until 1973. See the Jubilee Volume of *Occupational Psychology*, vol.44, 1970. In the USA a Division of Applied Psychology under W.V. Bingham was established at the Carnegie Institute of Technology in 1915, and the Psychological Corporation for 'the promotion of useful applications of psychology' set up in New York in 1921.
25 Privy Council Office, *Report of an Expert Committee on the work of Psychologists and Psychiatrists in the Services*, 1947; Office of Strategic Services (OSS) *Assessment of Men*, 1948; Vernon, P.E. and Parry, J.B., *Personnel Selection in the British Forces*, 1949.
26 Air Ministry, *Psychological Disorders in Flying Personnel of the Royal Air Force*, 1947.
    Eysenck, H.J., *Dimensions of Personality*, 1947.
27 Stouffer, S.A. *et al.*, *The American Soldier*, 2 vols, 1949.
28 Particularly important were the work of the Applied Psychology Unit in Cambridge and the stimulating contributions of K.J.W. Craik. See Craik, K.J.W., *The Nature of Explanation*, 1943. Notable among the early work emanating from Cambridge were various government reports: Davis, D.R., *Pilot Error*, 1948; Mackworth, N.H., *Researches on the Measurement of Human Performance*, 1950; Bartlett, F.C. and Mackworth, N.H., *Planned Seeing*, 1950.
    For American work see Fitts, P.M., 'Engineering psychology and equipment design', in Stevens, S.S., *Handbook of Experimental Psychology*, 1951, pp.1287-340.
29 Canter, S. and Canter, D., *Psychology in Practice*, 1982, p.4.
30 The International Association of Applied Psychology was until 1955

named The International Association of Psychotechnics. Its twentieth congress was held in 1982. It publishes a journal in French and English, *International Review of Applied Psychology* (*Revue internationale de Psychologie appliquée*). For historical background, see Hearnshaw, L.S., 'Homage to the past', *Proceedings of the XVIIth Congress*, pp.29-33.

31 Cronbach, L.J., 'The two disciplines of scientific psychology', *American Psychologist*, vol.12, 1957, pp.671-84.

32 Galton, F., 'Co-relations and their measurement', *Proc. Roy. Soc*, vol.45, 1885; Pearson, K., 'Notes on the history of correlation', *Biometrika*, vol.13, 1920, pp.25-45.

33 The χ^2 test was worked out by K. Pearson in 1900, the 't' test by W.S. Gossett (student) in 1908; R.A. Fisher expounded the analysis of variance in *Statistical Methods for Research Workers*, 1925, and followed it by *The Design of Experiments*, 1935. Factor analysis began with C.E. Spearman's article, '"General intelligence" objectively determined and measured', *Amer. J. Psychol.*, vol.15, 1904, pp.201-92, and was developed by various workers, particularly L.L. Thurstone, in *Multiple Factor Analysis*, 1947.

34 Miller, N.E., 'Behavioral medicine: symbiosis between laboratory and clinic', *Ann. Rev. Psychol.*, vol.34, 1983, p.1.

35 Binet, A. and Henri, V., 'La psychologie individuelle', *L'Année Psychologique*, vol.2, 1895, pp.411-65.

36 Cicero, M.T., *De Inventione*, II.53, c.82 BC.

37 See Chapter 6.

38 Herbart, J.F., *Lehrbuch zur Psychologie*, vol.3, 1816, p.152.

39 Stout, G.F., *Analytical Psychology*, vol.1, 1896, p.18.

40 Stout, G.F., *A Manual of Psychology*, 1st edn, 1899.

41 Sully, J., *Outlines of Psychology*, 1884, p.32.

42 Hearnshaw, L.S., 'The concepts of aptitude and capacity', *Proceedings of the XIIth Congrès International d'Histoire des Sciences*, Paris, 1968, pp.345-54.

43 Galton, F., *Natural Inheritance*, 1889.

44 Wechsler, D., *The Range of Human Capacities*, 1952.

45 Spearman, C.E., '"General intelligence" objectively determined and measured', *Ameri. J. Psychol.*, vol.15, 1904, pp.201-94.

46 Jensen, A.R., *Bias in Mental Testing*, 1981, ch.6.

47 Spearman, C.E., *The Nature of Intelligence and the Principles of Cognition*, 1923.

48 According to Binet, 'comprehension, invention, direction, and censorship; intelligence lies in these four words'. Binet, A., *Les idées modernes sur les enfants*, 1909, quoted by Spearman, op.cit., 1923, p.9.

49 See: Carol, J.B. and Maxwell, S.E., 'Individual differences in cognitive abilities', *Ann. Rev. Psychol.*, vol.30, 1979, pp.603-40; Resnick, L.B. (ed.), *The Nature of Intelligence*, 1976; Sternberg, R.J. (ed.), *Handbook of Human Intelligence*, 1982.

50 Sternberg, R.J. (ed.), op.cit., various chapters.

51 Kausler, D.H., *Experimental Psychology and Human Aging*, 1982.

52 Theophrastus, 'Ηθικὰ Χαρακτῆρες (The Characters), c.300 BC.

53 Roback, A.A., *The Psychology of Character*, 1927.

54 Mill, J.S., *A System of Logic*, 1843, VI. v.2.

55 Ibid., VI. v. 6.

56 Shand, A.Γ., *The Foundations of Character*, 1914.

57 Janet, P., *L'état mental des hystériques*, 1892, English trans. 'The mental state of hystericals', in Series C, vol.2, *Significant Contributions to the*

348 / Notes to pages 204-7

History of Psychology, 1978, p.35, quoted by Robinson, D.N., *An Intellectual History of Psychology*, 2nd edn, 1981, p.384.

58 Prince, M., *The Dissociation of a Personality*, 1906 (the case of Sally Beauchamp).
59 Gordon, R.G., *Personality*, 1926.
60 Ibid., Preface, p.xiii.
61 Allport, G.W., *Personality: A Psychological Interpretation*, 1937, p.48.
62 Murray, H.A., *Explorations in Personality*, 1938, p.3.
63 Ibid., pp.530-45, and Murray, H.A., *Thematic Apperception Test Manual*, 1943.
64 Privy Council Office, *Report of an Expert Committee on the Work of Psychologists and Psychiatrists in the Services*, 1947; Vernon, P.E. and Parry, J.B., *Personnel Selection in the British Forces*, 1949.
65 Office of Strategic Services, *Assessment of Men*, 1948.
66 Spearman, C.E., *Psychology down the Ages*, vol.2, 1937, ch.42.
67 Burt, C.L., *The Factors of the Mind*, 1940, Part 3, 'The distribution of temperamental types'.
68 Eysenck, H.J., *Dimensions of Personality*, 1947.
69 Cattell, R.B., *The Scientific Analysis of Personality*, 1965.
70 Bromley, D.B., *Personality Description in Ordinary Language*, 1977, Preface, p.ix. C.f. Rogers, C.R., 'Some observations on the organization of personality', *Amer. Psychologist*, vol.2, 1947, pp.358-68.
71 Murphy, G., *Personality*, 1947, p.927.
72 Broadbent, D.E., *Perception and Communication*, 1958, p.109.
73 James, W., *Principles of Psychology*, vol.1, 1890, p.402.
74 For Wundt, see Leahey, T.H., 'Something old, something new: attention in Wundt and modern cognitive psychology', *J. Hist. Behav. Sci.*, vol.15, 1979, pp.242-52; Ward, J., *Psychological Principles*, 1920, ch.3 (based on an article in the *Encyclopedia Britannica*, 9th edn, 1885); Stout, G.F., *Analytical Psychology*, vol.1, 1896, Book 2, chs 2 and 3.
75 Titchener, E.B., *An Outline of Psychology*, 1897, ch.6; *The Psychology of Feeling and Attention*, 1909.
76 Boring, E.G., Langfeld, H.S. and Weld, H.P., *Foundations of Psychology*, 1948.
77 Wyatt, S. and Langdon, J.N., *Inspection Processes in Industry: A Preliminary Report*, Industrial Health Research Board, Report 63, 1932.
78 Head, H., *Aphasia and Kindred Disorders of Speech*, vol.2, 1926, Part 4.
79 Mackworth, N.F., 'Vigilance', *The Advancement of Science*, vol.53, 1957, p.389; *Researches on the Measurement of Human Performance*, Medical Research Council Special Report no.268, 1950.
80 Cherry, E.C., 'Some experiments on the recognition of speech with one and two ears', *J. Acoust. Soc. Amer.*, vol.25, 1953, pp.975-9; Broadbent, D.E., *Perception and Communication*, 1958.
81 For a short summary see the two books by Mackworth, J.F. in the Penguin Science of Behaviour Series: *Vigilance and Habituation: A Neuropsychological Approach*, 1969, and *Vigilance and Attention: A Signal Detection Approach*, 1970. The first Attention and Performance Symposium was held in the Netherlands in 1966. The fifth report, *Attention and Performance, V*, edited by Rabbitt, P.M.A. and Dornic, S., was published in 1975.
82 Moruzzi, G. and Magoun, H.W., 'Brain stem reticular formation and activation of the EEG', *Electroenceph. Clin. Neurophysiol.*, vol.1, 1949, pp.455-73.
83 Sokolov, E.N., *Vospriyatie i. uslovne reflex*, 1958, English trans.

Perception of the Conditioned Reflex, 1963; (ed.) *Neironnie mechanismi orienterovochnogo refleksa* (in Russian), 1970.

84 Tanner, W.P. and Swets, J., 'A decision-making theory of visual detection', *Psychol. Rev.*, vol.61, 1954, pp.401-9.

85 Aristotle, *Nichomachean Ethics*, Book 3, iii. 1113a. c.340 BC.

86 Ibid., Book 6, ii. 1138b.

87 Aquinas, T., *Summa Theologiae*, I 2ae. 6-17, 1266-71.

88 James, W., *Principles of Psychology*, vol.2, 1890, pp.531-5.

89 Waddington, C.H., *Operational Research in World War II*, 1973.

90 Bernouilli, J., *Ars Conjectandi*, 1713; Bayes, T., 'An essay towards solving a problem in the doctrine of chances', *Phil. Trans. of the Roy. Soc.*, vol.53, 1763, pp.370-418.

91 Tanner, W.P. and Swets, J., op.cit.; Edwards, W., 'The theory of decision-making', *Psychol. Bull.* vol.51, 1954, pp.380-417; Savage, L.J., *The Foundations of Statistics*, 1954.

92 See Edwards, W. and Tversky, A., *Decision-making. Selected Readings*, Penguin Modern Psychology, 1967. Also chapters in the *Annual Review of Psychology* for additional references: Edwards, W., 'Behavioral decision theory', vol.12, 1961, pp.473-98; Rapoport, A. and Wallsten, T.S., 'Individual decision behavior', vol.23, 1972, pp.131-76; Slovic, P., Fischoff, B. and Lichenstern, S., 'Behavioral decision theory', vol.27, 1977, pp.1-39; Einhorn, H.T. and Hogarth, R.M., 'Behavioral decision theory: processes of judgement and choice', vol.32, 1981, pp.53-88.

93 Bryan, W.L. and Harter, N., 'Studies in the psychology and physiology of the telegraphic language', *Psych. Rev.*, vol.4, 1895, pp.27-55, and *Psych. Rev.*, vol.6, 1899, pp.345-75; Book, W.F., *The Psychology of Skill*, 1908; Lahy, J.M., *La Selection psychophysiologique des travailleurs: conducteurs de tramways et d'autobus*, 1927; Viteles, M.S., 'Research in the selection of motormen', *J. Pers. Res.*, vol.4, 1925, pp.173-99.

94 Pear, T.H., *Skill in Work and Play*, 1924; Cox, J.W., *Manual Skill: Its Organization and Development*, 1934 (an analysis based on Spearman's noegenetic principles); Blackburn, J.M., *The Acquisition of Skill: An Analysis of Learning Curves*, Ind. Health Res. Board, Report no. 73, 1936.

95 Bartlett, F.C., 'Fatigue following highly skilled work', *Proc. Roy. Soc. B*, vol.131, 1943, pp.248-57.

96 Craik, K.J.W., 'Theory of the human operator in control systems': I. 'The operator as an engineering system', *Brit. J. Psychol.*, vol.38, 1947, pp.51-61; II 'Man as an element in a control system', ibid., pp.142-8.

97 Wiener, N., *Cybernetics*, 1948.
    Shannon, C.E. and Weaver, W., *The Mathematical Theory of Communication*, 1949.

98 Bartlett, F.C., *Thinking: An Experimental and Social Study*, 1958, ch.1.

99 Welford, A.T., *Fundamentals of Skill*, 1968.

100 Broadbent, D.E., *Perception and Communication*, 1958, p.295.

101 Mosso, A., *La Fatica*, 1891, English trans. *Fatigue*, 1904; Kraepelin, E., 'Die Arbeitskurve', *Phil. Stud.*, vol.19, 1902, pp.459-507. Other researches are summarized in Viteles, M.S., *Industrial Psychology*, 1933, ch.21.

102 See Reports of the Health of Munitions Workers Committee, and the Industrial Fatigue (later Health) Research Board.

103 Selye, H., 'A syndrome produced by diverse nervous agents', *Nature*, vol.138, 1936, p.32; *Stress*, 1950; *The Stress of Life*, 1956. Some of the issues treated under the term 'stress' were dealt with in more general

terms by nineteenth century psychiatrists. See Tuke, D.H., *Illustrations of the Influence of the Mind upon the Body in Health and Disease*, 2 vols, 1872, (2nd edn, 1884).

104 Mackworth, N.F., *Researches on the Measurement of Human Performance*, Medical Research Council Special Report no.268, 1950, Part 2.
105 Davis, D.R., *Pilot Error*, Air Ministry, 1948.
106 Air Ministry, *Psychological Disorders in Flying Personnel of the Royal Air Force*, 1947.
107 Everly, G.S. and Rosenfeld, R., *The Nature and Treatment of Stress*, 1981.
108 Broadbent, D.E., *Decision and Stress*, 1971.
109 See Stokols, D., 'Environmental psychology', *Ann. Rev. Psychol.*, vol.29, 1978, pp.253-95, and Eron, L.D. and Peterson, R.A., 'Abnormal behavior: social approaches', *Ann. Rev. Psychol.*, vol.33, 1982, pp.247-52, 'Social class, stress, coping and abnormality'.
110 *Annual Review of Psychology*, vol.21, 1970, Preface, p.v.
111 Thomas, G.H., 'Vision', *Ann. Rev. Psychol.*, vol.6, 1955, p.63.
112 Pieron, H., *Aux Sources de la Connaissance: La Sensation, Guide de Vie*, 1945, English trans. 1951.
113 Geldard, F.A., *The Human Senses*, 1st edn, 1953, 2nd edn, 1972. Preface to 1st edn.
114 Wundt, W., *Beiträge zur Theorie der Sinneswahrnehmung*, 1862. (Wundt was primarily concerned with tactile perception.)
115 Wundt, W., *Grundzüge der physiologischen Psychologie*, 6th edn, 3 vols, 1908-11. More than half of vol.2 is devoted to visual sensation and perception.
116 Boring, E.G., *Sensation and Perception in the History of Experimental Psychology*, 1942, Preface.
117 Helmholtz, H.L.F., *Handbuch der physiologischen Optik*, 2nd edn, edited by König, A., 1896 (cited by Boring, E.G., op. cit., p.120).
118 Autrum, H. *et al.*, *Handbook of Sensory Physiology*, 1971-8, 24 vols. Series 7 (9 vols) is devoted to vision.
119 Davson, H., *The Eye*, 1969-74, 6 vols.
120 Marr, D., *Vision*, 1982. David Marr (1945-80) was a brilliant theoretical psychologist, educated at Cambridge, who spent the last four years of his brief life at the Artificial Intelligence Laboratory at the Massachusetts Institute of Technology. He completed his book just before his death from leukaemia.
121 Marr, D., op.cit., p.19.
122 Barlow, H.B., 'Single units and sensation: a neuron doctrine for perception psychology?', *Perception*, vol.1, 1972, pp.371-94, quoted in Marr, D., op.cit., p.13. See also Barlow, H.B. and Mollon, J.D., *The Senses*, 1982.
123 Sully, J., *Studies of Childhood*, 1896. G.S. Hall wrote voluminously on childhood and adolescence from 1883 onwards. In 1891 he founded the *Pedagogical Seminary*. For details see Ross, D., *G. Stanley Hall*, 1972.
124 Murchison, C. (ed.), *A Handbook of Child Psychology*, 1st edn, 1931, 2nd edn, 1933.
125 Ibid., 2nd edn, Preface.
126 Carmichael, L. (ed.), *Manual of Child Psychology*, 1st edn, 1946, 2nd edn, 1954.
127 Mussen, P.H. (ed.), *Carmichael's Manual of Child Psychology*, 3rd edn, 2 vols, 1970; Mussen, P.H. (ed.), *Handbook of Child Psychology*, 4 vols, 1983; vol.1, 'History, Theory and Methods', ed. Kessen, W.; vol.2,

'Infancy and Developmental Psychology', ed. Haith, M.M. and Campes, J.J.; vol.3, 'Cognitive Development', ed. Flavell, J.H. and Markham, E.M.; vol.4, 'Socialization, Personality and Social Development', ed. Hetherington, E.M.

128 Mussen, P.H., Conger, J.J. and Kagan, J., *Child Development and Personality*, 5th edn, 1979 (1st edn, 1956).

129 Ibid., 5th edn, pp.ix and x.

130 Murchison, C. (ed.), *Psychologies of 1925*, 1926; *Psychologies of 1930*, 1930; Woodworth, R.S., *Contemporary Schools of Psychology*, 1931, 3rd edn with Sheehan, M.R., 1964; Heibredder, E., *Seven Psychologies*, 1933.

131 Griffiths, C.R., *Principles of Systematic Psychology*, 1943, p.116.

132 Wolman, B.B., *Contemporary Theories and Systems in Psychology*, 1960.

133 Coan, R.W., 'Dimensions of psychological theory', *Amer. Psychologist*, vol.23, 1968, pp.715-22. See also Coan, R.W., *Psychologists: Personal and Theoretical Pathways*, 1979.

134 Marx, M.H. and Hillix, W.A., *Systems and Theories in Psychology*, 1963, 2nd edn, 1973; Smith, F.V., *Explanation of Human Behaviour*, 2nd edn, 1960; Krantz, D.L., (ed.), *Schools of Psychology: A Symposium*, 1969; Neel, A., *Theories of Psychology: A Handbook*, revised edn, 1977. See also notes 130 and 132, and Koch, S. (ed.), *Psychology: A Study of a Science*, 6 vols, 1959-63, and Hilgard, E.R., *Theories of Learning*, 1st edn, 1950, 4th edn, with Bower, G.A., 1975.

135 Boring, E.G., *A History of Experimental Psychology*, 2nd edn, pp.410-21.

136 Titchener's most important work was his four-volume *Experimental Psychology* (1901-5), a classic handbook of old-fashioned introspective experimental psychology. His system is more briefly discussed in *An Outline of Psychology*, 1896, and *A Textbook of Psychology*, 1909. For a full bibliographical sketch, see Boring, E.G., *Amer. J. Psychol.*, vol.38, 1927, pp.489-506.

137 Leahey, T.H., 'The mistaken mirror: on Wundt's and Titchener's psychologies', *J. Hist. Behav. Sci.*, vol.17, 1981, p.273-82.

138 Titchener, E.B., 'The postulates of structural psychology', *Phil. Rev.*, vol.7, 1898, p.450.

139 Boring, E.G., *The Physical Dimensions of Consciousness*, 1953, revised with a new preface, 1963.

140 Spearman, C.E., *The Abilities of Man*, 1927.

141 Burt, C.L., *The Factors of the Mind*, 1940; Eysenck, H.J., *Dimensions of Personality*, 1947; Eysenck, H.J., *The Scientific Study of Personality*, 1952; Eysenck, H.J., *The Structure of Personality*, 1953.

142 Thurstone, L.L., *Multiple Factor Analysis*, 1947; Guilford, J.P., *The Nature of Human Intelligence*, 1967; Stephenson, W., *The Study of Behavior: Q-technique and its Methodology*, 1953; Cattell, R.B., *Personality and Motivation Structure and Measurement*, 1957.

143 Spearman, C.E., *The Nature of Intelligence and the Principles of Cognition*, 1923; *Psychology down the Ages*, 2 vols, 1937.

144 Wertheimer, M., 'Experimentelle Studien uber das Sehen von Bewegung', *Zeitschrift für Psychologie*, vol.61, 1912, pp.161-265 (brief translated extracts are contained in Herrnstein, R.U. and Boring, E.G., *A Source Book in the History of Psychology*, pp.163-8).

145 Koffka, K., *Principles of Gestalt Psychology*, 1936, Ellis, W.D. (ed.), *A Source Book of Gestalt Psychology*, 1938, contains translations of a number of the original papers of the Gestalt school.

146 Wertheimer, M., *Über Gestalttheorie*, 1925 (translation in Ellis, W.D. op.cit., p.2).

147 Köhler, W., *The Mentality of Apes*, 1925, revised edn, 1927; Koffka, K., *Principles of Gestalt Psychology*, 1936; Wertheimer, M., *Productive Thinking*, 1945; Lewin, K., *A Dynamic Theory of Personality*, 1935; Lewin, K., *Field Theory in Social Science* (papers 1935-46, ed. Lewin, G.W.), 1957.

148 Köhler, W., 'Psychology and evolution', *Acta Psychologica*, vol.7, 1950 (reprinted in Henle, M., *Documents of Gestalt Psychology*, 1961, pp.69-75.

149 Dewey, J., 'The reflex arc concept in psychology', *Psychol. Rev.*, vol.3, 1896, pp.357-70; Angell, J.R., 'The province of functional psychology', *Psychol. Rev.*, vol.14, 1907, pp.61-91.

150 McDougall, W., *An Introduction to Social Psychology*, 1st edn, 1908, 30th edn, 1950.

151 Ibid., 20th edn, p.407.

152 McDougall, W., *An Outline of Psychology*, 1923, ch.1, p.17.

153 Tinbergen, N., *The Study of Instinct*, 1951; Thorpe, W.H., *Purpose in a World of Chance*, 1978; Thorpe, W.H., *The Origins and Rise of Ethology*, 1979.

154 Washburn, M., *The Animal Mind*, 1908, 3rd edn, 1926. Washburn was a pupil of the introspective structuralist psychologist Titchener, and devoted her book largely to sensory and perceptual processes in animals.

155 Watson, J.B., 'Psychology as a behaviorist views it', *Psychol. Rev.*, vol.20, 1913, pp.158-77.

156 Watson, J.B., *Psychology from the Standpoint of a Behaviorist*, 3rd edn, 1929, p.3.

157 Watson, J.B., *Behaviorism*, 1924, p.74.

158 Ibid., ch.10.

159 Watson, J.B., 'The place of the conditioned reflex in psychology', *Psychol. Rev.*, vol.23, 1916, pp.89-117.

160 Pavlov, I.P., 'Experimental psychology and psycho-pathology in animals', paper read before the International Congress of Medicine, Madrid, April 1903. Reprinted in translation in *Lectures on Conditioned Reflexes*, trans. Gantt, W.A., 1928.

161 Pavlov, I.P., *Lectures on Conditioned Reflexes*, chs 27 and 28.

162 Pavlov, I.P., *Pavlovian Wednesdays: Protocols and Stenographic Notes of Physiological Conversations*, vol.2, 1949.

163 Watson, J.B., 'The place of the conditioned reflex in psychology', *Psychol. Rev.*, vol.23, 1916, pp.89-117.

164 Pavlov, I.P., *Conditioned Reflexes: An Investigation of the Physiological Activity of the Cerebral Cortex*, English trans. 1927; *Lectures on Conditioned Reflexes*, English trans. 1928. A second volume, *Conditioned Reflexes and Psychiatry*, was translated in 1941.

165 Hull, C.L., *Principles of Behavior*, 1943, p.3.

166 The final account of his system was published in the year of Hull's death in *A Behavior System*, 1952.

167 Koch, S., 'Clark L. Hull', in Estes, W.K. (ed.), *Modern Learning Theory*, 1954, pp.1-176.

168 Tolman's final statement of his system was given in Koch, S. (ed.), *Psychology: A Study of a Science*, vol.2, 1959, pp.92-157.

169 Tolman, E.C., 'The determiners of behavior at a choice point', *Psychol. Rev.*, vol.45, 1938, pp.1-41.

170 Skinner, B.F., *Science and Human Behavior*, 1953, p.91.

171 Ibid., p.107.
172 Ibid., p.79.
173 Skinner, B.F., *Beyond Freedom and Dignity*, 1971, p.18.
174 Ibid.
175 Kazdin, A.E., *History of Behavior Modification*, 1978, p.x.
176 Skinner, B.F., *Verbal Behavior*, 1957; Chomsky, N., 'Review of verbal behavior', *Language*, vol.35, 1959, pp.26-58; MacCorquodale, K., 'On Chomsky's review of Skinner's verbal behavior', *J. Expt. Anal. Behav.*, vol.13, 1970, pp.83-99.
177 Skinner, B.F., *Science and Human Behavior*, 1953; *Beyond Freedom and Dignity*, 1971.
178 Skinner, B.F., *Walden Two*, 1948.
179 Skinner, B.F., 'The experimental analysis of operant behavior: a history', ch.10 of Rieber, R.W. and Salzinger, K., *Psychology: Theoretical-Historical Perspectives*, 1980, p.199.
180 Carnap, R., 'Psychology in physical language', *Erkenntnis*, vol.3, quoted by Malcolm, N. 'Behaviorism as philosophy of psychology', in Wann, T.W. (ed.), *Behaviorism and Phenomenology: Contrasting Bases for Modern Psychology*, 1964, p.144. See also Hearnshaw, L.S., 'Psychology and operationism', *Austral. J. of Psychol. and Phil.*, vol.19, 1941, pp.44-57 and references.
181 Chapman, A.J. and Jones, D.M., *Models of Man*, Brit. Psychol. Soc., 1980.
182 Woodworth, R.S. and Sheehan, M.R., *Contemporary Schools of Psychology*, revised edn, 1964, ch.8.
183 Ibid., p.254.
184 For example, Munn, N.L., *Psychology: The Fundamentals of Human Adjustment* (1st edn, 1946) was a widely adopted text. For Munn anything that contributed to an understanding of any aspect of human nature regardless of its origin was grist for psychology, and his text included material from every main school in a very loose framework.
185 Dashiell, J.F., 'Some rapprochements in contemporary psychology', *Psychol. Bull.*, 1939, pp.1-24.
186 Woodworth, R.S., op.cit., revised edn, p.254.
187 Beloff, J., *Psychological Sciences: A Review of Modern Psychology*, 1973, Preface, p.ix.
188 Koch, S. (ed.), *Psychology: A Study of a Science*, vol.1, 1959, pp.1-8.
189 Brunswik, E., *The Conceptual Framework of Psychology*, vol.1, 1952, no.10 of the *International Encyclopedia of Unified Science*, ed. Neurath, O.
190 Brunswik, E., op.cit., p.29.
191 Zener, K. and Gaffron, M., 'Perceptual experience: an analysis of its relations to the external world through internal processes', in Koch, S. (ed.), *Psychology: A Study of a Science*, vol.4, 1962, p.541.
192 Koch, S., 'Psychology and emerging conceptions of knowledge as unitary', in Wann, T.W. (ed.), *Behaviorism and Phenomenology*, 1964, p.20.
193 Razran, G., *Mind in Evolution*, 1971, p.2.
194 Ibid., p.309.
195 Ibid., p.284.
196 Ibid., pp.326-7.
197 Stern, W., *Allgemeine Psychologie auf personalistischer Grundlage*, 1st edn, 1935, 2nd edn, 1950, English trans. *General Psychology from the Personalistic Standpoint*, 1938.
198 Ibid., Preface, p.vii.

199 Stern, W., *Psychologie der Veränderungsauffassung*, 1898, 2nd edn, 1906.
200 The best short account of Stern's life and work is his own autobiography in Murchison, C. (ed.), *A History of Psychology in Autobiography*, vol.1, 1930, pp.335-88.
201 Stern, W., *Über Psychologie der individuellen Differenzen*, 1900; *Beiträge Zur Psychologie der Aussage*, 1902; *Angewandte Psychologie*, 1903; *Die Kindersprache* (with Stern, C.), 1907; *Errinerung, Aussage und Lüge in der ersten Kindheit*, 1908; *Psychologische Methoden der Intelligenzprüfung*, 1912, English trans. *Psychological Methods of Testing Intelligence*, 1914; *Psychologie der frühen Kindheit bis zum sechsten Lebensjahre*, English trans. *The Psychology of Early Childhood up to the Sixth Year of Life*, 1924, 3rd edn, 1930.
202 Stern, W., *Person und Sache*, 3 vols, 1906-24.
203 Allport, G.W., 'William Stern, 1871-1938', obituary notice, *Amer. J. Psychol.*, vol.51, 1938, pp.770-3; 'The personalistic psychology of William Stern', *Character and Personality*, vol.5, 1937, pp.231-46. See also Allport's *Personality*, 1937, passim and particularly pp.550-6.
204 Stern, W., *General Psychology*, 1938, p.20.
205 Ibid., p.70.
206 Ibid., p.89.
207 Ibid., p.89.
208 Ibid., p.72.
209 Ibid., ch.4, pp.68-100.

Chapter 13 Philosophical critiques

1 Croom Robertson, G. (ed.), *Mind*, vol.1, January 1876. Quotations from the Introduction, pp.3-5.
2 Frege, G., *Begriffschrift*, 1879. This work was followed by *Grundlagen der Arithmetik* in 1884 (English trans. 1950). For a brief account of Frege's work, see Nidditch, P.H. *The Development of Mathematical Logic*, 1962, ch.6.
3 Bradley, F.H., *The Principles of Logic*, 1883 (2nd edn, revised, 1922); Husserl, E., *Logische Untersuchungen*, 1900, English trans. 1965; Husserl, E., *Ideas: General Introduction to Pure Phenomenology*, English trans. 1962. J.S. Mill was a classical exponent of the 'psychologistic' view of logic.
4 Ward, J. and Rivers, W.H.R. (eds), *British Journal of Psychology*, vol.1, January 1904, editorial, p.1.
5 Ziehen, T., *Introduction to Physiological Psychology*, 1895, p.1, quoted by Robinson, D.N., *An Intellectual History of Psychology*, 2nd edn, 1981, p.403.
6 Polkinghorne, J.C., *The Quantum World*, 1984, p.5. J.C. Polkinghorne was Professor of Mathematical Physics at the University of Cambridge from 1968 to 1979. For further comments on the implications of quantum theory see the contribution by Wheeler, J.A. in Elvee, R.Q. (ed.), *Mind in Nature*, Nobel Conference, XVII, 1982, 'Bohr, Einstein and the strange lesson of the quantum'.
7 Polkinghorne, J.C., op.cit., Preface, p.ix.
8 Ibid., p.10.
9 Weinberg, S., *The Discovery of Subatomic Particles*, 1983. An excellent popular account of the subatomic world by a Nobel prize-winner.
10 Jones, H. Spencer., *General Astronomy*, 1922.

11   Shu, F.H., *The Physical Universe: An Introduction to Astronomy*, 1982.
12   Tillich, P., *The Shaking of the Foundations*, 1949.
13   Dilthey, W., 'Ideen über eine beschreibende und zergliedernde Psychologie', 1895, in *Gesammelte Schriften*, vol.5, p.180, quoted in Hodges, H.A., *Wilhelm Dilthey: An Introduction*, 1944, p.45.
14   Bergson, H., *An Introduction to Metaphysics*, 1903, English trans. 1913, pp.31 and 63.
15   Collingwood, R.G., *An Autobiography*, Penguin, 1944, p.66.
16   Wittgenstein, L., *Philosophical Investigations*, 1953, p.232.
17   Peters, R.S., *The Concept of Motivation*, 1958, ch.4.
18   In addition to the book by Peters mentioned above, other notable books in the 'Studies of philosophical psychology' series were *Mental Acts* by Geach, P.T., and *The Idea of a Social Science* by Winch, P., 1958.
19   Jaspers, K., 'Zu Nietzsche's Bedeutung in der Geschichte der Philosophie' (English trans. *Hibbert Journal*, April 1951), quoted in Kaufmann, W., *From Shakespeare to Existentialism*, 1959, p.302. For a general introduction to *Nietzsche*, see Hollingdale, R.J., *Nietzsche*, 1973. Also Hollingdale, R.J. (ed.), *A Nietzsche Reader*, Penguin, 1977, which contains a bibliography of English translations of Nietzsche's works.
20   Jones, E., *Sigmund Freud: Life and Work*, vol.3, 1955, p.385.
21   For a brief sketch of the historical development of logic see Stebbing, L.S., *A Modern Introduction to Logic*, 2nd edn, 1933, ch.25.
22   Short accounts of the logical positivist movement by A.J. Ayer, who popularized the movement in *Language, Truth and Logic*, (1936), are contained in *The Revolution in Philosophy* (1956) by Ryle, G., and others, and in Ayer's *Philosophy in the Twentieth Century* (1982). A rather longer account is given in chapter 14 of Passmore, J., *A Hundred Years of Philosophy* (2nd edn, 1966). Chapters 15, 17 and 18 are also relevant.
23   Carnap, R., *The Logical Syntax of Language*, 1937, p.xiii.
24   Neurath, O., Carnap, R. and Morris, C. (eds), *International Encyclopedia of Unified Science*. Of special interest to psychology were Brunswick, E. *The Conceptual Framework of Psychology*, vol.1, no.10, 1952, and Hempel, C.G., *Fundamentals of Concept Formation in Empirical Science*, vol.2, no.7, 1952.
25   Stevens, S.S. 'Psychology and the science of science', *Psychol. Bull.*, vol.36, 1939, pp.221-63.
26   Ibid., p.222.
27   Bridgman, P.W., *The Logic of Modern Physics*, 1927, p.5.
28   Skinner, B.F., 'The operational analysis of psychological terms', *Psychol. Rev*, vol.52, 1945, pp.270-7 and 291-4.
29   I pointed out some of these objections in an early article. See Hearnshaw, L.S., 'Psychology and operationism', *Aust. J. Psychol and Phil.*, vol.19, 1941, pp.44-57. A rather less restrictive view of concept formation in science by a member of the Vienna school was given in Hempel, C.G., op.cit. Pp.39-50 discuss operationism.
30   Popper, K.R., *The Logic of Scientific Discovery*, English trans. 1959, revised edn, 1972, p.27.
31   Pratt, C.C., *The Logic of Modern Psychology*, 1939, p.89.
32   Eysenck, H.J., *The Scientific Study of Personality*, 1952, p.16.
33   Fisher, R A *The Design of Experiments*, 1935, p.19.
34   Stevens, S.S., 'Mathematics, measurement and psychophysics', in Stevens, S.S. (ed.), *Handbook of Experimental Psychology*, 1951, pp.1-49.

35   Feigl, H., *The 'Mental' and the 'Physical'*, 2nd edn with Postscript, 1967.
36   Koch, S., 'Psychology and emerging conceptions of knowledge as unitary', in Wann, T.W. (ed.), *Behaviorism and Phenomenology: Contrasting Bases for Modern Psychology*, 1964, pp.21-34, quotation on p.30. See also Mancias, P.T. and Secord, P.F., 'Implications for psychology of the new philosophy of science', *Amer. Psychologist*, 1983, pp.399-413.
37   Lowrie, W., *Kierkegaard* (1938), was one of the first full accounts of Kierkegaard in English. For a short, more recent, introduction with good bibliography, see Grimsley, R., *Soren Kierkegaard: A Biographical Introduction*, 1973. Princeton University Paperbacks have produced a new English translation of Kierkegaard's principal works. For a general account of the existentialist movement see Macquarrie, J., *Existentialism*, 1973.
38   Kierkegaard, S., *Either/Or: A Fragment of Life*, 1943, English trans. 1944.
39   Quotations from Kierkegaard, S., *The Concept of Anxiety*, Princeton edition, 1980, pp.61 and 159.
40   Brentano, F., *Psychology from an Empirical Standpoint*, 1874, English trans. 1973.
41   Ibid., p.12.
42   Ibid., p.77.
43   Ibid., p.89.
44   Lauer, Q. in Husserl, E., *Phenomenology and the Crisis in Philosophy*, Introduction to English translation, 1965. The two lectures of Husserl's contained in this book, together with Lauer's introduction, plus Husserl's *Paris Lectures* delivered in 1929, translated with an Introductory Essay by P. Koestenbaum, 1975, are the best short accounts of Husserl's philosophy. See also McKenna, W.K., *Husserl's Introductions to Phenomenology*, 1982. Husserl's two principal early works (see note 3) are extremely difficult.
45   For an account of C. Stumpf (1848-1936) see Boring, E.G., *A History of Experimental Psychology*, 2nd edn, 1950, pp.362-71. His extensive correspondence with Willaim James is illuminating. See ch.9, note 120.
46   Husserl, E., *The Paris Lectures*, 1975, p.4.
47   Ibid., p.10.
48   Husserl, E., 'Philosophy and the crisis of European man', 1935, in *Phenomenology and the Crisis of Philosophy*, 1965.
49   This is well expounded in Woodruff Smith, D. and McIntyre, R., *Husserl and Intentionality*, 1982.
50   Husserl, E., 'Philosophy and the crisis of European man', in *Phenomenology and the Crisis of Philosophy*, p.187.
51   Merleau-Ponty, M., *Phenomenology of Perception*, 1945, English transl. 1964. See also Sullis, J. (ed.), *Merleau-Ponty: Perception, Structure and Language*, 1981.
52   Steiner, G. *Heidegger*, Fontana Modern Masters, 1978, p.11. This is a useful short introduction to Heidegger's thought. As few English readers are likely to venture into the 'impenetrable thicket' of Heidegger's works the selection of *Basic Writings* ed. by Krell, D.F., containing nine key essays, plus the Introduction to Heidegger's principal work, *Sein und Zeit* (*Being and Time*), 1927, can be recommended to those who want to read him in translation.
53   Carnap, R., 'The overcoming of metaphysics through logical analysis of language', *Erkenntnis*, vol.2, 1931. Translated in Murray, M. (ed.),

Heidegger and Modern Philosophy, 1978.
54 Ryle, G., Review of Heidegger's *Sein und Zeit*, *Mind*, vol.38, 1929, p.370.
55 Arendt, H., 'Heidegger at eighty', *New York Review of Books*, 1971.
56 Heidegger, M., 'Letter on humanism', 1947, in Krell, op.cit., p.129.
57 Heidegger, M., 'What is metaphysics?', Inaugural Lecture, 1929, in Krell, op.cit., p.107.
58 Heidegger, M., 'On the essence of truth', 1967, in Krell, op.cit., p.129.
59 Heidegger, M., *Sein und Zeit*, Introduction, 1927, in Krell, op.cit., pp.41-89.
60 Heidegger, M., 'Letter on humanism', in Krell, op.cit., p.210.
61 Ibid., p.193.
62 Ibid., p.210.
63 Heidegger, M., 'What is metaphysics?', in Krell, op.cit., p.105.
64 Heidegger, M., 'Building, dwelling, thinking', 1954, in Krell, op.cit., p.327.
65 This is a statement by the Gestalt psychologist Koffka. The Gestaltists were pupils of Stumpf, who was himself a pupil of Brentano. See Koffka, K., *Principles of Gestalt Psychology*, 1936, p.73.
66 See: Katz, D., *The World of Colour*, 1911, English trans. 1935; Michotte, A., *The Perception of Causality*, 1946, English trans. 1964; Merleau-Ponty, M., *Phenomenology of Perception*, English trans. 1964.
67 For accounts of the influence of phenomenology and existentialism on psychology see: May, R. (ed.), *Existential Psychology*, 1967; Thinès, G., *Phenomenology and the Science of Behaviour*, 1977; Valle, R.S. and King, M., *Existential-Phenomenological Alternatives for Psychology*, 1978.
68 For accounts of its influence on psychiatry see: May, R. *et al* (eds), *Existence*, 1958; Keen, E., *Three Faces of Being: Toward an Existential Clinical Psychology*, 1970.
69 Gergen, K.J., *Towards a Transformation in Social Knowledge*, 1982, p.ix.
70 For an autobiography by Ryle, a chronological list of his publications 1927-68, and a set of critical comments, see Wood, O.P. and Pitcher, G. (eds), *Ryle*, Modern Studies in Philosophy, 1970. For Ryle's review of Heidegger see note 54.
71 Ryle, G., *The Concept of Mind*, 1949, p.25.
72 Ibid., p.328.
73 Ibid., p.7.
74 Ibid., p.247.
75 The literature on Wittgenstein is huge. There are several recent short introductions: Pears, D., *Wittgenstein*, Fontana Modern Masters, 1971; Kenny, A., *Wittgenstein*, Penguin, 1973; Von Wright, G.H., *Wittgenstein*, 1983. The references to St Augustine and Kierkegaard are in the last mentioned. Among Wittgenstein's posthumous publications are *Remarks on the Philosophy of Psychology*, 2 vols, Anscombe, G.E.M., Von Wright, G.H. and Nyman, H. (eds), 1980.
76 Pears, D., op.cit., p.16.
77 Wittgenstein, L., *Philosophical Investigations*, 1953, p.26.
78 Quoted by Malcolm, N., 'Wittgenstein on the nature of the mind', in *Studies in the Theory of Knowledge*, 1970, p.9-29.
79 Wittgenstein, L., *Philosophical Investigations*, 599, p.156.
80 Ibid., 126, p.50.
81 Ibid., 571, p.151.

82 Ibid., II.xiv, p.232.
83 Ibid., 363, pp.114 and 412, p.124.
84 Malcolm, N., loc.cit., p.18.
85 Murray, M. (ed.), *Heidegger and Modern Philosophy*, 1978.
86 Wittgenstein, L., *Tractatus Logico-Philosophicus*, 1922, 6.57.
87 Heidegger, M., 'The end of philosophy and the task of thinking', in Krell, D.F., *Martin Heidegger: Basic Writings*, 1978, pp.369-92.
88 Feigl, H., *The 'Mental' and the 'Physical'*, 1967; Armstrong, D.M., *A Materialist Theory of Mind*, 1968; Smart, J.J.C., *Philosophy and Scientific Realism*, 1963; Popper, K.R. and Eccles, J.C., *The Self and its Brain*, 1977.
89 Davidson, D., *Essays on Actions and Events*, 1980, p.xi.
90 Wittgenstein, L., *Tractatus Logico-Philosophicus*, 5.631.
91 Strawson, P.F. 'Persons', in Feigl, H., Scriven, M. and Maxwell, G. (eds), *Minnesota Studies in the Philosophy of Science. II.Concepts, Theories and the Mind-Body Problem*. 1958, p.390. See also Strawson, P.F., *Individuals*, 1959.
92 Davidson, D., 'Psychology as philosophy', in Brown, S.C. (ed.), *Philosophy of Psychology*, 1974, p.41.
93 Searle, J.R., *Intentionality: An Essay in the Philosophy of Mind*, 1983.
94 Ibid., p.1.
95 Ibid., p.100.
96 Ibid., p.141.
97 Ibid., pp.143 and 154.
98 Ibid., p.264.
99 Ibid., p.15.
100 Ibid., p.265.
101 Borger, R., 'Human action and psychological research', in Brown, S.C. (ed.), *Philosophy of Psychology*, 1974, p.102.
102 For the scholastic theory of action see vol.17 of the Blackfriars edition of St Thomas Aquinas, *Summa Theologiae*, 1a 2ae. 6-17. Also the outline of the theory in Appendix I, pp.211-17, by T. Gibley.
103 See Chapter 12 section 4.
104 There is now a large literature on the philosophy of mind and theories of action. See: Block, N. (ed.), *Readings in the Philosophy of Psychology*, 2 vols, 1980; Winch, P., *The Idea of a Social Science, and its Relations to Philosophy*, 1958.
Brenner, M. (ed.), *The Structure of Action*, 1980.
105 Plato, *Theaetetus*, 209 A.
106 Aristotle, *De Interpretatione (On Interpretation)*, Loeb Classical Library, vol.1, 1938.
107 Ricoeur, P., *Hermeneutics and the Human Sciences*, English trans. 1981, p.43.
108 Schleiermacher, F., *Hermeneutik und Kritik, Sammtliche Werke*, vol.7, 1928. See references in Ricoeur, op.cit.
109 Dilthey, W., 'Die Entstehung der Hermeneutik', 1900, *Gesammelte Schriften*, vol.5, pp.317-31. There is a translated extract in Hodges, H.A., *Wilhelm Dilthey: An Introduction*, 1944, pp.124-28. Also in full in Rickman, H.P., *Dilthey: Selected Writings*, 1976, pp.246-63.
110 Holt, R.R., 'Individuality and generalization in the psychology of personality', *J. Personality*, vol.30, 1962, pp.377-404.
111 Ricoeur, P., *Hermeneutics and the Human Sciences*, English trans. 1981; Gadamer, H.G., *Truth and Method*, English trans. 1975; Hirsch, E.D., *Validity in Interpretation*, 1967; Palmer, R., *Hermeneutics: Interpretation*

Theory in Schleiermacher, Dilthey, Heidegger and Gadamer, 1969; Thompson, J.B., *Critical Hermeneutics: A Study in the Thought of Paul Ricoeur and Jürgen Habermas*, 1981.

112 Ricoeur, P., op.cit., p.36.
113 Gergen, K.J., *Towards a Transformation in Social Knowledge*, 1982, pp.62-8 and 192-5.
114 Hayek, F., *The Sensory Order*, 1952, pp.185 and 194.
115 Some of these problems are entertainingly discussed in Hoffstadter, D.R. and Dennett, D.C., *The Mind's I: Fantasies and Reflections on Self and Soul*, 1982.
116 Piaget, J., *Insights and Illusions of Philosophy*, 1965, English trans. 1971.
117 Wittgenstein, L., *Philosophical Investigations*, 126, p.50.
118 Quine, W.V.O., 'Two dogmas of empiricism', *Phil. Rev.*, 1951, reprinted in *From a Logical Point of View*, 1953. For a brief account of Quine's philosophy see Orenstein, A., *Willard Van Orman Quine*, Twayne's World Leader Series, 1977.
119 Piaget, J., op.cit., Postscript.
120 Darwin, C.R., 'N' Notebook, 3 October 1838, quoted in Gruber, H.E., *Darwin on Man*, 1974.
121 Quine, W.V.O., loc.cit. See Orenstein, op.cit., p.61.
122 Rychlak, J.F., *The Psychology of Rigorous Humanism*, 1977, p.3.
123 Bronowski, J., 'The ascent of man', *The Listener*, 2 August 1973, p.147.

Chapter 14 New Vistas I

1 *Annual Review of Psychology*, vol.1, 1950 to vol.35, 1984, continuing.
2 Tulving, E. and Madison, S.A., 'Memory and verbal learning', *Ann. Rev. Psychol.*, vol.21, 1970, p.442.
3 See Chapter 12, Section 5.
4 Melzack, R. and Wall, P.D., 'Pain mechanisms: a new theory', *Science*, vol.150, 1965, p.971.
5 Hughes, J. *et al.*, 'Identification of two related pentapeptides from the brain with potent opiate agonist activity', *Nature*, vol.158, 1975, pp.577-9. See also Bolles, R.C., 'Endorphins and behavior', *Ann. Rev. Psychol.*, vol.33, 1982, pp.87-101.
6 Hubel, D.H. and Wiesel, T.N. 'Receptive fields, binocular interaction and functional architecture in the cat's visual cortex', *J. Physiol.*, vol.160, 1962, pp.106-54, and 'Receptive fields and functional architecture of monkey striate cortex', *J. Physiol.*, vol.195, 1968, pp.215-43.
For a brief and more recent account of Hubel and Wiesel's work see their article 'Brain mechanisms of vision', *Sci. American*, vol.241, 1979, pp.130-44.
7 Gibson, J.J., *The Perception of the Visual World*, 1950, and *The Senses Considered as Perceptual Systems*, 1966.
8 Gregory, R.L., *Mind in Science: A History of Explanations in Psychology and Physics*, 1981.
9 Weintraub, D.J., 'Perception', *Ann. Rev. Psychol.*, vol.26, 1975, p.281.
10 Among recent books on memory are: Anderson, J.R., *Language, Memory and Thought*, 1976; Baddeley, A.D., *The Psychology of Memory*, 1976; Crowder, R.G., *Principles of Learning and Memory*, 1976; Eysenck, M.W., *Human Memory: Theory, Research and Individual Differences*, 1977; Neisser, U., *Memory Observed: Remembering in Natural Contexts*, 1982; Martinez, J.L. *et al.*, *Endogenous Peptides and*

360 / Notes to pages 248-52

Learning and Memory Processes, 1981; Tulving, E., *Elements of Episodic Memory*, 1983.
11 Baddeley, A.D., op.cit., pp.372 and 374.
12 Craik, F.I.M. and Lockhart, R.S., 'A framework for memory research', *J. Verb. Learn. Verb. Behav.*, vol.11, 1972, pp.671-84.
13 Tulving, E., op.cit.
14 Lashley, K.S., 'In search of the engram', *Symposium of the Society of Experimental Biology*, vol.4, 1950, pp.451-82. The term 'engram' was originally used by the German R. Semon, in his book *Die Mneme*, 1904, English trans. 1921.
15 See Eccles, J.C., *The Human Mystery*, 1979, ch.9, 'Learning and memory', for a summary of the evidence.
16 Jones, M.R. and Arnold, W.J. (eds), *Nebraska Symposia on Motivation*, vol.1, 1953, onwards.
17 Madsen, K.B., *Theories of Motivation*, 4th edn, 1968. A useful brief summary is contained in Madsen, K.B., 'Theories of motivation', ch.33 in Wolman, B.B. (ed.), *Handbook of General Psychology*, 1973.
18 Pfaff, D.W. (ed.), *The Physiological Mechanisms of Motivation*, 1982.
19 Olds J. and Milner, B., 'Positive reinforcement produced by electrical stimulation of septal area and other regions of the rat's brain', *J. Comp. Physiol. Psychol.*, vol.47, 1954, pp.419-27.
20 See Vernon, M.D., *Human Motivation*, 1969.
21 Grether, W.F., 'Psychology and the space frontier', *Am. Psychologist*, vol.17, 1962, pp.92-101.
22 Cloudsley-Thompson, J.L., *Rhythmic Activity in Animal Physiology and Behaviour*, 1961; Colquhoun, W.P. (ed.), *Biological Rhythms and Human Performance*, 1971; Moore-Ede, M.C. *et al.*, *The Clocks That Time Us*, 1982.
23 Attneave, F., *Applications of Information Theory to Psychology*, 1959; Underwood, G. (ed.), *Strategies in Information Processing*, 1978.
24 See Roberts, D.F. and Bachen, C.M., 'Mass communication effects', *Ann. Rev. Psychol.*, vol.32, 1981, pp.307-56.
25 Boden, M. *Artificial Intelligence and Natural Man*, 1977.
26 Hebb, D.O., *The Organization of Behavior*, 1949, p.xvi.
27 Miller, G.A., Galanter, E. and Pribram, K.H., *Plans and the Structure of Behavior*, 1960.
28 Maslow, A.H., *Towards a Psychology of Being*, 1962.
29 Kelly, G.A., *The Psychology of Personal Constructs*, 1955.
30 Rorer, L.G. and Widiger, T.A., 'Personality structure and assessment', *Ann. Rev. Psychol.*, vol.34, 1983, p.442.
31 Meehl, P.E., 'Theoretical risks and tabular asterisks. Sir Karl, Sir Ronald, and the slow progress of soft psychology', *J. Consult. Clin. Psychol.*, vol.46, 1978, p.817.
32 Eccles, J.C., *The Human Mystery*, 1979, p.160.
33 Hubel, D.H., 'The brain', *Sci. American*, vol.241, 3, 1979, p.46.
34 Rose, S., *The Chemistry of Life*, Penguin, 2nd edn, 1979 is a useful introduction to biochemistry. See also Young, J.Z., *An Introduction to the Study of Man*, 1971.
35 Thudichum, J.W.L., *A Treatise on the Chemical Composition of the Brain*, 1884.
36 Barcroft, J., *The Brain and its Environment*, 1938.
37 Brožek, J. and Fabrykant, M., *Psychodietetics*, 1962. See also Brožek, J., 'Nutrition, malnutrition and behavior', *Ann. Rev. Psychol.*, vol.29, 1978, pp.157-77.

38 Barnes, J.M., 'Effects of some poisonous substances on the central nervous system', in Steinberg, H. (ed.), *Animal Behaviour and Drug Action*, 1964, pp.163-74.

39 See Penrose, L.S., *The Biology of Mental Defect*, 1949, pp.142-8, revised edn 1963. A Norwegian biochemist, A. Fölling, first described the abnormality in 1934. The disability was then termed phenylpyruvic oligophrenia.

40 See Katz, B., *Nerve, Muscle and Synapse*, 1966, and Eccles, J.C., *The Neurophysiological Basis of Mind*, 1953.

41 Dale, H.H., Feldberg, W. and Vogt, M., 'Release of acetylcoholine at voluntary motor nerve endings', *J. Physiol.*, vol.86, 1936, pp.353-80.

42 Iversen, L.L. 'The chemistry of the brain', *Sci. American*, vol.241, 3, 1979, pp.118-29.

43 Friedhoff, A.J. (ed.), *Catecholamines and Behavior*, 2 vols, 1975; Iversen, S.D. and Iversen, L.L. 'Central neurotransmitters and the regulation of behaviour', in Gazzaniga, M.S. and Blakemore, C. (eds), *Handbook of Psychobiology*, 1975, pp.153-200.

44 Croyden Smith, A., *Schizophrenia and Madness*, 1982, pp.96-100.

45 Cobb, I.G., *The Glands of Destiny*, 1927.

46 Cannon, W.B., *Bodily Changes in Pain, Hunger, Fear and Rage*, 2nd edn, 1929.

47 Reiss, M., *Psychoneuroendocrinology*, 1958. More recent accounts may be found in: Levine, S. (ed.), *Hormones and Behavior*, 1972; Lissak, K. (ed.), *Hormones and Brain Function*, 1973.

48 McGaugh, J.L., 'Hormonal influences on memory', *Ann. Rev. Psychol.*, vol.34, 1983, pp.297-323.

49 McGeer, P.L. and McGeer, E.G., 'Chemistry of mood and emotion', *Ann. Rev. Psychol.*, vol.31, 1980, pp.273-307; Feder, H.H., 'Hormones and sexual behavior', *Ann. Rev. Psychol.*, vol.35, 1984, pp.165-200.

50 Burn, H., *Drugs, Medicine and Man*, 1962.

51 *Drug Addiction: Reports of the Interdepartmental Committee*, First Report, HMSO, 1961, Second Report, HMSO, 1965; *Proceedings of the White House Conference on Narcotics and Drug Abuse*, Government Printing Office, Washington, 1963; Wells, B., *Psychedelic Drugs: Psychological, Medical and Social Issues*, 1973.

52 Kumer, R., Stolerman, I.P. and Steinberg, H., 'Psychopharmacology', *Ann. Rev. Psychol.*, vol.21, 1970, pp.595-628; Groves, P.M. and Rebec, G.V., 'Biochemistry and behavior: some central actions of amphetamine and antipsychotic drugs', *Ann. Rev. Psychol.*, vol.27, 1976, pp.91-127.

53 Eleftheriou, B.E. (ed.), *Psychopharmacogenetics*, 1975.

54 Steinberg, H. (ed.), *Animal Behaviour and Drug Action*, 1964.

55 See 'The brain', *Sci. American*, vol.241, 3, 1979, p.46.

56 Moruzzi, G. and Magoun, H.W., 'Brain stem reticular formation activation of the E.E.G.', *Electroenceph. Clin. Neurophysiol.*, vol.1, 1949, p.455.

57 Oswald, I., *Sleep and Waking*, 1962, p.3.

58 Luria, A.R., *The Working Brain*, 1973, p.290.

59 Sperry, R.W., 'Experiments on perceptual integration in animals', *Psychiatr. Res. Rep.*, vol.6, 1956, pp.151-60.

60 For a brief summary see Gazzaniga, M.S., 'Brain mechanisms and behavior', in Gazzaniga, M.S. and Blakemore, C. (eds), *Handbook of Psychobiology*, 1975, ch.19.

61 Beaumont, J.G., *Introduction to Neuropsychology*, 1983, Part III, 'Experimental studies'.

62 Young, J.Z., *Programs of the Brain*, 1978.
63 Chapter 8, Section 3.
64 See Judson, H.F., *The Eighth Day of Creation: Makers of the Revolution in Biology*, 1979 for a fascinating and not too technical account.
65 Hall, C.S., 'The genetics of behavior', in Stevens, S.S. (ed.), *Handbook of Experimental Psychology*, 1951, ch.9, pp.304-29. Quotation from p.314.
66 Ibid., p.328.
67 Fuller, J.L. and Thompson, W.R., *Behavior Genetics*, 1960. 2nd edn 1978.
68 *Annual Review of Psychology*, vols 12, 1960; 17, 1966; 23, 1971; 25, 1974; 29, 1978; 33, 1982. Quotation from Lindzey, G., Loehlin, J., Manosevitz, M. and Thiessen, D., 'Behavioral genetics', *Ann. Rev. Psych.*, vol.23, 1971, p.79.
69 See Fuller and Thompson, op.cit., ch.3.
70 Newman, H.H., Freeman, F.N. and Holzinger, K.J., *Twins: A Study of Heredity and Environment*, 1937; Burks, B.S., 'The relative influence of nature and nurture upon mental development: a comparative study of foster parent-foster child resemblance and true parent-true child resemblance', *27th Yearbook Nat. Soc. Stud. Educ.*, 1928, Part 1, pp.219-316.
71 See *Heredity in Nervous and Mental Disease*, Assoc. for Res. in Nervous and Mental Disease, 1923; *The Report of the Royal Commission on the Feeble-minded*, 1908. vol.8, ch.27 held that the great majority of cases of amentia were hereditary.
72 Burt, C.L. and Howard, M., 'The multifactorial theory of inheritance and its application to intelligence', *Brit. J. Stat. Psychol.*, vol.9, 1956, pp.95-131; Jensen, A.R., 'Kinship correlations reported by Sir Cyril Burt', *Behav. Genetics*, vol.4, 1974, pp.1-28.
73 Tijo, J.H. and Levan, A.', 'The chromosome number in man', *Hereditas*, vol.42, 1956, pp.1-6.
74 McLearn, G.E. and Meredith, W., 'Behavioral genetics', *Ann. Rev. Psychol.*, vol.17, 1966, pp.516-21, for references.
75 Jinks, J.L. and Fulker, D.W., 'Comparison of the biometrical, genetical MAVA and classical approaches to the analysis of human behavior', *Psychol. Bull.*, vol.73, 1970, pp.311-49.
76 Eysenck, H.J., *The Inequality of Man*, 1973.
77 Numerous references are given in the successive surveys in the *Annual Review of Psychology*, 1960-82. See note 68.
78 Jensen, A.R., 'How much can we boost I.Q. and scholastic achievement?', *Harvard Educ. Rev.*, vol.39, 1969, pp.1-123.
79 Jensen, A.R., *Educability and Group Differences*, 1973, ch.7, 'Race differences in intelligence', pp.158-201; Jensen, A.R., 'Race and mental ability', in Ebbing, F.J. (ed.), *Racial Variations in Man*, 1975, reprinted in Halsey, A.H. (ed.), *Heredity and Environment*, 1973, pp.215-61.
80 Smith, G. and James, T., 'The effects of preschool education: some American and British evidence', *Oxford Rev. of Educ.*, vol.1, 1975, pp.223-40, reprinted in Halsey, A.H. (ed.), op.cit., pp.288-311.
81 A useful collection of material on the question of early learning and its effects is: Sluckin, W. (ed.), *Early Learning and Early Experience*, Penguin Modern Psychology Readings, 1971.
82 Henderson, N.D., 'Human behavior genetics', *Ann. Rev. Psychol.*, vol.33, 1982, pp.404-5.
83 Tinbergen, N., 'Functional ethology and the human sciences', *Proc. Roy.*

Soc. B, vol.182, 1972, pp.397-408. reprinted in Halsey, A.H. (ed.), op.cit., pp.72-86, quotations from pp.75 and 76.

84 Wilson, E.O., *Sociobiology: The New Synthesis*, 1975; Wilson, E.O., *On Human Nature*, 1978 (see ch.2, 'Heredity').
Rather earlier Desmond Morris had popularized somewhat similar views in *The Naked Ape*, 1967, 'an attempt to discuss the fundamental biological nature of our species as a whole'. A useful collection of material on the developments behind sociobiology is Clutton-Brock, T.H. and Harvey, P.H. (eds), *Readings in Sociobiology*, 1978.

85 Wilson, E.O., *On Human Nature*, 1978, pp.1 and 167.

86 Dawkins, R., *The Selfish Gene*, 1976, Granada edn, 1978, p.x.

87 Ibid., pp.203 and 215.

88 Dawkins, R., *The Extended Phenotype*, 1982.

89 For details on phenylketonuria see Penrose, L.S., *The Biology of Mental Defect*, revised edn, 1963, and Lyman, F.L. (ed.), *Phenylketonuria*, 1963. The correction of genetic 'mistakes' must be distinguished from 'positive genetic engineering', which raises serious moral problems. See Glover, J., *What Sort of People Should There Be?*, Penguin, 1984.

90 Thorpe, W.H., *The Origins and Rise of Ethology*, 1979, p.ix.

91 Huxley, J.S., Preface to Lorenz, K., *On Aggression*, 1966, p.vii.

92 Thorpe, W.H., op.cit., Part 1, 'The origins of ethology'.

93 Ibid., p.67.

94 Lorenz, K., *King Solomon's Ring*, 1952.
Tinbergen, N., *The Study of Instinct*, 1951.

95 *Zeitschrift für Tierpsychologie*, 1937; *Bulletin of Animal Behaviour*, 1938; *Behaviour*, 1948.

96 See Hinde, R.A., *Ethology*, 1982, ch.5, for details.

97 See Thorpe, W.H., *Learning and Instinct in Animals*, 1956.

98 Lorenz, K., 'Der Kumpan in der Unwelt des Vogels' (The companion in the bird's world), *J.f. Ornith*, vol.83, 1935, pp.137 and 289-413.

99 Thorpe, W.H., *Bird Song*, 1961.

100 Skinner, for example, asserted that species differences could be ignored when dealing with schedules of reinforcement. Similar performances could be demonstrated with diverse species. See Ferster, C.B. and Skinner, B.F., *Schedules of Reinforcement*, 1957, p.4. Also Skinner, B.F., 'The experimental analysis of behavior', *Am. Scientist*, vol.45, 1957, pp.343-7. On the other hand Breland, K. and Breland, M. present contrary evidence in 'The misbehavior of organisms', *Am. Psychologist*, vol.16, 1961, pp.681-4.

101 See Hinde, R.A., *Ethology*, 1982, ch.10.

102 Stone, C.P. (ed.), *Comparative Psychology*, 3rd edn, 1951.

103 Mason, W.A. and Lott, D.F., 'Ethology and comparative psychology', *Ann. Rev. Psychol.*, vol.27, 1976, p.150.

104 Thorpe, W.H., *Learning and Instinct in Animals*, 1956, p.v.

105 Hinde, R.A., *Animal Behaviour: A Synthesis of Ethology and Comparative Psychology*, 1966, 2nd edn, 1970.

106 Von Frisch, K., *The Dancing Bees*, 1954.

107 Barlow, F.W., 'Modal action patterns', in Sebeok, R.A. (ed.), *How Animals Communicate*, 1977, quoted in Hinde, R.A., *Ethology*, 1982, p.44.

108 Hinde, R.A., op.cit. Much earlier the ornithologist David Lack, in his *The Life of the Robin* (1953), had suggested that 'the term instinct should be abandoned'. See ch.15.

109 Hinde, R.A., op.cit., ch.9.

110 Hinde, R.A. (ed.), *Non-Verbal Communication*, 1972.
111 Mason, W.A. and Riopelle, A.J., 'Comparative psychology', *Ann. Rev. Psychol.*, vol.15, 1964, p.143.
112 Ladygina-Kots, N.N. and Dembovskii, Y.N., 'The psychology of primates', in Cole, M. and Maltzman, I., *A Handbook of Contemporary Soviet Psychology*, 1969.
113 Yerkes, R.M. and Yerkes, A., *The Great Apes*, 1929; Nissen, H.W., 'A field study of chimpanzees', *Comp. Psychol. Monog.*, vol.8, 1931; Bingham, H.C., 'Gorillas in a native habitat', *Carnegie Inst. Washington, Pub. 426*, 1932; Carpenter, C.R., *Naturalistic Behavior of Nonhuman Primates*, 1934; Zuckerman, S., *The Social Life of Monkeys and Apes*, 1932.
114 Köhler, W., *The Mentality of Apes*, 1925.
115 Goodall, J., 'Chimpanzees of the Gombe Stream Reserve', in De Vore I. (ed.), *Primate Behavior*, 1965, pp.425-72; Goodall, J., *In the Shadow of Man*, 1971; Fossey, D., *Gorillas in the Mist*, 1983.
116 Gardner, R.A. and Gardner, B.T., 'Teaching sign language to a chimpanzee', *Science*, vol.165, 1964, pp.664-72; Premack, D., 'A functional analysis of language', *J. Exp. Anal. Behav.*, vol.14, 1970, pp.107-25.
117 Locke, J., *Essay concerning Human Understanding*, 1690, II.i.1.
118 Harré, R., *Social Being*, 1979, ch.1.
119 Midgley, M., *Beast and Man: The Roots of Human Nature*, 1978, p.xiii.
120 Lorenz, K., *On Aggression*, English trans. 1966, particularly chs 12-14.
121 Tinbergen, N., *The Study of Instinct*, 1951, pp.205-8.
122 Hinde, R.A., *Ethology*, 1982, Part 3, quotations from p.201.
123 Hinde, R.A. (ed.), *Non-Verbal Communication*, 1972.
124 Crook, J.H., *The Evolution of Human Consciousness*, 1980.
125 In *Sociobiology*, 1975, E.O. Wilson claimed that eventually sociobiology would engulf ethology and comparative psychology. Both Thorpe (1979) and Hinde (1982) dispute this claim.

Chapter 15 New Vistas II

1 Wiener, N., *Cybernetics: Or Control and Communication in the Animal and the Machine*, 1948;, Shannon, C.E. and Weaver, W., *The Mathematical Theory of Communication*, 1949.
2 Newell, A. and Simon, H.A., *Human Problem Solving*, 1972, p.873. The 'Historical addendum' (pp.873-89) in this book gives a fuller account of information-processing developments, particularly up to 1958, than is possible in my own brief section.
3 Craik, K.J.W., *The Nature of Explanation*, 1943, ch.5.
4 Ibid., p.57.
5 These were touched on in Wiener's *Cybernetics*, and also developed in his *The Human Use of Human Beings*, 1950.
See also Rose, J. (ed.), *Survey of Cybernetics*, 1969.
6 Monod, J., *Chance and Necessity*, 1970, English trans. 1972; Jacob, F., *The Logic of Living Systems*, 1970, English trans. 1974; Jacob, F., *The Possible and the Actual*, 1982; Piaget, J., *Biology and Knowledge*, 1967, English trans. 1971.
See also Boden, M., *Piaget*, 1979, ch.7, 'Piaget and cybernetics'; Parsons, T., *Social Systems and the Evolution of Action Theory*, 1977.
7 Fairbanks, G. and Jaeger, R., 'Delayed feed-back of speech and disruption of speech', *J. Speech and Hearing Disorders*, vol.16, 1951,

pp.162-4; Yates, A.J., 'Delayed auditory feed-back', *Psychol. Bull.*, vol.50, 1963, pp.213-51.

8   Ashby, W.R., *Design for a Brain*, 1952, 2nd edn, 1960.
9   Ashby, W.R., *Introduction to Cybernetics*, 1956, p.4.
10 von Bertalanffy, L., *General Systems Theory: Foundations, Development, Applications*, 1968. See also Emery, F.E. (ed.), *Systems Thinking: Selected Readings*, Penguin, 1969; and Koestler, A. and Smythies, J.R. (eds), *Beyond Reductionism: The Alpach Symposium*, 1969.
11 Walter, W.G., *The Living Brain*, 1953.
12 Newell, A. and Simon, H.A., *Human Problem Solving*, 1972.
13 Aleksander, I. and Burnett, P., *Reinventing Man: The Robot Becomes Reality*, 1984.
14 Shannon, C.E. and Weaver, W., *The Mathematical Theory of Communication*, 1949.
15 Hartley, R.V.L., 'Transmission of information', *Bell System Tech. J.*, vol.7, 1928, p.535. Discussed in Cherry, C., *On Human Communication*, 1957, ch.2. See also Parry, J., *The Psychology of Human Communication*, 1967.
16 Miller, G.A. and Frick, F.C., 'Statistical behavioristics and sequences of response', *Psychol. Rev.*, vol.56, 1949, pp.311-29.
17 Miller, G.A., 'What is information measurement?', *Amer. Psychologist*, vol.8, 1953, pp.3-11. 'The magical number seven, plus or minus two: some limits on our capacity for processing information', *Psychol. Rev.*, vol.63, 1956, pp.81-96, reprinted in Miller, G.A. *The Psychology of Communication*, Penguin, 1970.
18 Hick, W.E., 'On the rate of gain of information', *Q.J. Exp. Psychol.*, vol.4, 1952, pp.11-26.
19 Attneave, F., *Applications of Information Theory to Psychology*, 1959.
20 Newell, A., Shaw, J.C. and Simon, H.A., 'Elements of a theory of human problem solving', *Psychol. Rev.*, vol.65, 1958, pp.151-66. The claim is made on p.885 of Newell and Simon's book *Human Problem Solving*, 1972.
21 See Simon, H.A., 'Information processing models of cognition', *Ann. Rev. Psychol.*, vol.30, 1979, pp.363-96. A good many textbooks of psychology are now based on information processing, e.g. Lindsay, P.H. and Norman, D.A., *Human Information Processing: An Introduction to Psychology*, 2nd edn, 1977.
22 Walter, W.G., *The Living Brain*, 1953, ch.7, p.108.
23 Searle, J., *Minds, Brains and Science*, the Reith Lectures, BBC, 1984, Lecture 3.
24 Nisbett, R.E. and Wilson, T.D., 'Telling more than we can know: verbal reports on mental processes', *Psychol. Rev.*, vol.84, 1977, pp.231-59; Ericsson, K.A. and Simon, H.A., 'Verbal reports as data', *Psychol. Rev.*, vol.87, 1980. pp.215-52.
25 Wiener, N., *Cybernetics*, 1948, p.155.
26 MacKay, D.M., 'Quantal aspects of scientific information', *Phil. Mag.*, vol.41, 1950, pp.289-311.
27 See Miller, G.A. and Selfridge, J.A., 'Verbal context and the recall of meaningful material', *Am. J. Psychol.*, vol.63, 1950, pp.176-86; Marks, M.R. and Jack, O., 'Verbal context and memory span for meaningful material', *Am. J. Psychol.*, vol.65, 1952, pp.298-300. Also, Osgood, C.E., *Method and Theory in Experimental Psychology*, 1953, ch.16, 'Language behavior'.
28 Marr, D., *Vision*, 1982, p.3.

29   Michie, D., *On Machine Intelligence*, 1974, p.199.
30   Hyman, A., *Charles Babbage: Pioneer of the Computer*, 1982.
31   For details see Evans, C., *The Making of the Micro: A History of the Computer*, 1981.
32   Turing, A.M., 'On computable numbers, with an application to the Entscheidungs-problem', *Proc. London. Math. Soc.*, Series 2, vol.42, 1936, pp.230-65.
33   Turing, A.M. 'Computing machinery and intelligence', *Mind*, vol.59, 1950, pp.433-60. For further information about Turing's life and work see Hodges, A., *Alan Turing: the Enigma*, 1983.
34   Berkeley, E.C., *Giant Brains, or Machines that Think*, 1949.
35   Shannon, C.E., 'A symbolic analysis of relay and switching circuits', *Trans. Am. Inst. of Elect. Engineers.*, vol.57, 1938, pp.713-23.
36   Burton, A.M., 'Computer use in British university departments of psychology', *Bull. Brit. Psychol. Soc.*, vol.38, 1985, pp.1-5. This article gives references to earlier reports.
37   Apter, M.J. and Westby, G. (eds), *The Computer in Psychology*, 1973.
38   Longuet-Higgins, H.C., 'Comment', in *Artificial Intelligence: A Paper Symposium*, Science Res. Council, 1973, p.36.
39   Boden, M.A., *Artificial Intelligence and Natural Man*, 1977, p.401.
40   For Hebb, see Rochester, N. *et al.*, 'Test on a cell assembly theory of action of the brain, using a large digital computer', *I.R.E. Transactions on Information Theory*, IT-2, 3, 1956, pp.80-93. For Piaget, see Roden, M.A., *Minds and Mechanisms: Philosophical Psychology and Computational Models*, 1981, ch.11, 'Artificial intelligence and Piagetian theory'.
41   See: Corcoran, D.W.J., *Pattern Recognition*, 1971; Boden, M.A., *Artificial Intelligence and Natural Man*, 1977, Part 4, 'The visual world'; Marr, D., *Vision*, 1982.
42   Michie, D., *On Machine Intelligence*, 1974, p.145.
43   For example the WISARD recognition device constructed by I. Aleksander at Brunel University. See Aleksander, I. and Burnett, P., *Reinventing Man: The Robot becomes Reality*, 1984.
44   Samuel, A.L., 'Some studies in machine learning using the game of checkers', *I.B.M.J. of Res. and Develop.*, vol.3, 1959, pp.211-29 (reprinted in Feigenbaum, E.A. and Feldman, J., *Computers and Thought*, 1963, discussed in Michie, D., op.cit., pp.38-43).
45   Newell, A. and Simon, H.A., *Human Problem Solving*, 1972, Part 4, 'Chess'. The first attempt was that of Shannon. See Shannon, C.E., *Programming a Computer for Playing Chess*, 1948.
46   Newell, A. and Simon, H.A., op.cit.
47   Boden, M.A., *Artifical Intelligence and Natural Man*, 1977, ch.7, 'Sense and semantics'.
48   Discussed in some detail in Boden, M.A., op.cit., ch.6, 'Intelligence in understanding'. For the original work see Winograd, T., *Understanding Natural Language*, 1972.
49   See Boden, M.A., op.cit., chs 2-5.
50   Von Neumann, J., *The Computer and the Brain*, 1958.
     See also Hunt, E., 'Computer simulation: artificial intelligence studies and the relevance to psychology', *An. Rev. Psychol.*, vol.19, 1968, pp.135-68.
51   Lighthill, J., *Artificial Intelligence*, Sci. Res. Council, 1973.
52   Ayer, A.J., Foreword to Bolter, J.D., *Turing's Man: Western Culture in the Computer Age*, 1984, pp.xii-xiii.

53   Searle, J.R., *Minds, Brains and Science*, the Reith Lectures, BBC, 1984. Lecture 2.

54   So described by Hofstadter, D.R., in *Gödel, Escher, Bach: An Eternal Golden Braid*, 1979, bibliography, p.747. Hofstadter's book is an entertaining and stimulating 'fugue' on the theme of minds and machines.

55   Boden, M.A., *Artificial Intelligence and Natural Man*, 1977, p.473.

56   Turing, A.M., 'Computing machines and intelligence', *Mind*, vol.59, 1950, pp.446-60.

57   Bolter, J.D., *Turing's Man: Western Culture in the Computer Age*, 1984, pp.220 and 221.

58   Aquinas, T., *Summa Theologiae*, 1266, I. 77.4.

59   Watson, J.B., *Behaviorism*, 1924, p.191.

60   Bruner, J.S., *In Search of Mind: Essays in Autobiography*,1983, p.105.

61   Missiak, H. and Staudt, V.M., *Catholics in Psychology*, 1954.

62   For an account of the Würzburg psychologists see Humphrey, G., *Thinking*, 1951, chs 2-4.

63   Köhler, W., *The Mentality of Apes*, 1925; Koffka, K., *The Growth of the Mind: An Introduction to Child Psychology*, 1924.
     See also Duncker, K., 'On problem solving', *Psychol. Mon.*, vol.58, 1945, no.270, and Wertheimer, M., *Productive Thinking*, 1945.

64   For a summary of this work see Woodworth, R.S., *Experimental Psychology*, 1938, ch.30. The account in the second edition (1954) is less full.

65   Humphrey, G., *Thinking*, 1951, p.308.

66   Leeper, R., 'Cognitive processes', in Stevens, S.S. (ed.), *Handbook of Experimental Psychology*, 1951, ch.19, pp.730-57; Vinacke, W.E., *The Psychology of Thinking*, 1952; Rapaport, D., *The Organization and Pathology of Thought*, 1951.

67   Woodworth, R.S. and Schlosberg, R., *Experimental Psychology*, 2nd edn, 1954, ch.26.

68   Hebb, D.O., 'The American revolution', *Amer. Psychologist*, vol.15, 1960, pp.735-45, quotation from p.745.

69   Bruner, J.S., *In Search of Mind*, 1983, p.63.

70   Ibid., ch.7.

71   *Annual Review of Psychology*, vol.4, 1953, p.53.

72   Taylor, D.W. and McNemar, O.W., 'Problem solving and thinking', *Ann. Rev. Psychol.*, vol.6, 1955, p.455.

73   Gagné, R., 'Problem solving and thinking', *Ann. Rev. Psychol.*, vol.10, 1959, p.147.

74   Kendler, T.S., 'Concept formation', *Ann. Rev. Psychol.*, vol.12, 1961, p.467.

75   Van de Geer, J.P. and Jaspers, J.F.M. 'Cognitive functions', *Ann. Rev. Psychol.*, vol.17, 1966, pp.145-76.

76   Bourne, L.E. and Dominowski, R.L., 'Thinking', *Ann. Rev. Psychol.*, vol.23, 1972, p.105.

77   Neimark, E.D. and Santa, J.L, 'Thinking and concept attainment', *Ann. Rev. Psychol.*, vol.26, 1975, p.173.

78   For further details see: Wason, P.C. and Johnson-Laird, P.N., *Thinking and Reasoning: Selected Readings*, Penguin, 1968; Bolton, N., *The Psychology of Thinking*, 1972.

79   Bartlett, F.C., *Thinking: An Experimental and Social Study*, 1958.

80   De Groot, A.D., *Thought and Choice in Chess*, 1965.

81   Pylyshyn, Z.W., 'What the mind's eye tells the mind's brain. A critique of mental imagery', *Psychol. Bull.*, vol.80, 1973, pp.1-24.

82   Bruner, J.S., Goodnow, J.J. and Austin, G.A., *A Study of Thinking*, 1956.
83   Bruner, J.S., *In Search of Mind*, 1983, pp.63-4 and 122-6.
84   Hunt, E.B., *Concept Learning: An Information Processing Problem*, 1962.
85   Hovland, C.I., 'A communication analysis of concept learning', *Psychol. Rev.*, vol.59, 1952, pp.461-72.
86   Hunt, E.B., op.cit., p.276.
87   Neisser, U., 'The multiplicity of thought', *Brit. J. Psychol.*, vol.54, 1963, pp.1-14, reprinted in a slightly shortened form in Wason, P.C. and Johnson-Laird, P.N., op.cit.
88   Neisser, U., in Wason and Johnson-Laird, op.cit., p.316.
89   Neisser, U., *Cognitive Psychology*, 1967, p.289.
90   Neisser, U., *Cognition and Reality: Principles and Implications of Cognitive Psychology*, 1976. The book was dedicated to J.J. and Eleanor Gibson.
91   Newell, A., Shaw, J.C. and Simon, J.A., 'Elements of a theory of human problem solving', *Psychol. Rev.*, vol.65, 1958, pp.151-66. For further references see bibliography in Newell, A. and Simon, H.A., *Human Problem Solving*, 1972.
92   Fodor, J.A., *The Modularity of Mind: An Essay on Faculty Psychology*, 1983, p.129.
93   Ibid., p.107.
94   Johnson-Laird, P.N., *Mental Models*, 1983. Chapters 4 and 5 deal with syllogistic reasoning. See also Johnson-Laird, P.N. and Bara, B.G., 'Syllogistic inference', *Cognition*, vol.16, 1984, pp.1-61, and the earlier book by Johnson-Laird, P.N. and Wason, P.C., *The Psychology of Reasoning*, 1972.
95   Johnson-Laird, P.N., *Mental Models*, p.1.
96   Ibid., p.8.
97   Ibid., p.448. See also Johnson-Laird, P.N., 'A computational analysis of consciousness', *Cognition and Brain Theory*, vol.6, 1983, pp.499-508.
98   Johnson-Laird, P.N., *Mental Models*, p.40.
99   Anderson, J.R., *The Architecture of Cognition*, 1983, ch.1, 'Production systems and ACT'.
100 Neisser, U., *Cognitive Psychology*, 1967, p.281.
101 Ibid., p.305.
102 Peel, E.A., *The Pupil's Thinking*, 1960; Lovell, K., 'A follow-up of some aspects of the work of Piaget and Inhelder on *The Child's Conception of Space*', *Brit. J. Educ. Psychol.*, vol.29, 1959, pp.104-17; Lovell, K., 'A follow-up study of Inhelder and Piaget's *The Growth of Logical Thinking*', *Brit. J. Psychol.*, vol.52, 1961, pp.143-53; Flavell, J.H., *The Developmental Psychology of Jean Piaget*, 1963.
103 Several of the symposia of the Piaget Society have been published. See Sigel, I.E., Brodzinsky, D.M. and Golinkopf, R.M. (eds), *New Directions in Piagetian Theory and Practice*, 1981, and Liben, L.S. (ed.), *Piaget and the Foundations of Knowledge*, 1983.
104 Modgil, S. and Modgil, C., *Piagetian Research*, 8 vols, 1976. This was preceded by *Piagetian Research: A Handbook of Recent Studies*, 1974.
105 Piaget, J., 'Autobiography', in Murchison, C. (ed.), *A History of Psychology in Autobiography*, vol.4, 1952, pp.237-56.
106 Piaget, J., *The Language and Thought of the Child*, 1923, English trans. 1926; *Judgment and Reasoning in the Child*, 1924, English trans. 1928; *The Child's Conception of the World*, 1926, English trans. 1929; *The*

Child's Conception of Physical Causality, 1927, English trans. 1930; *The Moral Judgment of the Child*, 1932, English trans. 1932.

107 Piaget, J., *The Origins of Intelligence in the Child*, 1936, English trans. 1952; *The Child's Construction of Reality*, 1936, English trans. 1955; *Play, Dreams and Imitation in Childhood*, 1946, English trans. 1951.

108 Piaget, J., *The Child's Conception of Number*, 1941, English trans. 1952; *The Child's Conception of Time*, 1946, English trans. 1969; *The Child's Conception of Movement and Speed*, 1946, English trans. 1970; (with B. Inhelder) *The Child's Conception of Space*, 1948, English trans. 1956; (with B. Inhelder and A. Szemanka) *The Child's Conception of Geometry*, 1948, English trans. 1960; (with B. Inhelder) *The Growth of Logical Thinking*, 1955, English trans. 1958; *The Mechanisms of Perception*, 1961, English trans. 1969.

109 Piaget, J., (with E.W. Beth) *Mathematical Epistemology and Psychology*, 1965, English trans. 1966; *Insights and Illusions of Philosophy*, 1965, English trans. 1971; *Biology and Knowledge*, 1967, English trans. 1971; *Structuralism*, 1968, English trans. 1971; *Principles of Genetic Epistemology*, 1970, English trans. 1972; *The Grasp of Consciousness*, 1974, English trans. 1976; *The Development of Thought: Equilibrium and Cognitive Structures*, 1975, English trans. 1978; *Experiments in Contradiction*, English trans. 1980.

110 Piaget, J., 'Psychology, interdisciplinary relations and the system of sciences', *18th Int. Congress Psychol.*, Moscow, 1966.

111 A translation of 'The mission of the idea', together with extracts from other early biological writings of Piaget, is contained in Gruber, H.E. and Vonèche, J.J. (eds), *The Essential Piaget*, 1977. This compendium, which contains long extracts from Piaget's writings from the beginning up to 1975 together with editorial comments, is a valuable introduction to Piaget.

112 Piaget, J., *Psychology and Epistemology: Towards a Theory of Knowledge*, 1970, English trans. 1972, ch.4, 'The myth of the sensory origin of scientific knowledge'.

113 Piaget, J., 'Autobiography', 1952. Murchison, op.cit., p.239.

114 Spencer, H., *First Principles*, 1862, ch.22, 'Equilibration'. Spencer regarded evolution as 'progress towards equilibrium' and wrote of 'A gradual advance towards harmony between man's mental nature and the conditions of his existence'.

115 Russell, J., *The Acquisition of Knowledge*, 1978.

116 Piaget, J., *The Child's Construction of Reality*, English trans. 1955, p.3.

117 Piaget, J., *Genetic Epistemology*, 1970, p.15.

118 Piaget, J., *Traité de logique*, 1942. Revised in 1972 under the title *Essai de logique opératoire*. Neither of these works has been translated into English. For a brief account in English see his Manchester lectures, *Logic and Psychology*, 1953.

119 Boden, M.A., *Piaget*, 1979, p.11. A very useful brief introduction to Piaget's theories.

120 Isaacs, S., *The Intellectual Growth of Young Children*, 1930; Valentine, C.W., *The Psychology of Early Childhood*, 1942; Bryant, P., *Perception and Understanding in Young Children*, 1974; Donaldson, M., *Children's Minds*, 1979.

121 Donaldson, M., op.cit., p.121.

122 Gruber, H.E. and Vonèche, J.J. (eds), *The Essential Piaget*, 1977, Introduction, p.xxv.

123 For a philosophical critique see Hamlyn, D.W., *Experience and the*

Growth of Knowledge, 1978. For comments by a logician see Parsons, C., 'Inhelder and Piaget's *The Growth of Logical Thinking from Childhood to Adolescence*: a logician's viewpoint', *Brit. J. Psychol.*, vol.51, 1960, pp.75-84. 'Surplus baggage' is a phrase used by J. Bruner in '*The Growth of Logical Thinking*: a psychologist's view', *Brit. J. Psychol.*, loc.cit., pp.363-70. Boden, M.A., in her *Piaget* complains that his theory of cognitive development 'lacks specification of detailed procedural mechanisms' (p.23).

124 Russell, J., 'Piaget's theory of sensorimotor development', ch.1, p.16, in Butterworth, G. (ed.), *Infancy and Epistemology: An Evaluation of Piaget's Theory*, 1981. See also Russell's *The Acquisition of Knowledge*, 1978.

125 Piaget, J., *Biology and Knowledge: An Essay on the Relations between Organic Regulations and Cognitive Processes*, 1967, English trans. 1971, p.367.

126 Piaget, J., 'Psychology, interdisciplinary relations and the system of sciences', *18th Int. Congress Psychol.*, Moscow, 1966, p.25.

127 Piaget, J., *Psychology and Epistemology*, 1972, p.93.

128 Piaget, J., *Biology and Knowledge*, 1971, p.359.

129 Piaget, J., *The Psychology of Intelligence*, 1947, English trans. 1950, ch.6.

130 Beilin, H., 'Language and thought', ch.8, p.125, in Sigal, I.E., Brodzinsky, D.M. and Golinkopf, R.M. (eds), *New Directions in Piagetian Theory and Practice*, 1981.

131 Sinclair-de Zwart, H., 'Developmental psycholinguistics', p.315 in Elkind, D. and Flavell, J.H. (eds), *Studies in Cognitive Development: Essays in Honor of Jean Piaget*, 1969, pp.315-36.

132 Piaget, J., *The Psychology of Intelligence*, 1947, p.5.

133 Berlyne, D.E., 'Emotional aspects of learning', *Ann. Rev. Psychol.*, vol.15, 1964, p.219.

134 Russell, J., *The Acquisition of Knowledge*, 1978, p.268.

135 Baldwin, J.M., *Elements of Psychology*, 1893, ch.19, 'Interest, reality and belief'.

136 Hunt, J. McV., 'The impact and limitations of the giant of developmental psychology', p.56 in Elkind D. and Flavell, J.H., op.cit.

137 Miller, G.A., *Language and Speech*, 1981, p.2.

138 On grammarians and rhetoricians see Bacon, F., *De Augmentis Scientarum* 1623, Book 6. For the important part these disciplines played in medieval times see Jardine, L., *Francis Bacon: Discovery and the Art of Discourse*, 1974.

139 Descartes, R., *Meditations*, V, 1641.

140 Locke, J., *Essay concerning Human Understanding*, 1690, III.ix.21. The whole of Book III is devoted to the question of language.

141 Reid, T., *Essays on the Intellectual Powers of Man*, 1785, Bk.1, ch.1.

142 Vico, G., *De Nostri Temporis Studiorum Ratione*, 1708, quoted in Berlin, I., *Vico and Herder*, 1976, p.42.

143 Berlin, I., op.cit., p.51.

144 Langer, S., *Philosophy in a New Key*, 1942; Cassirer, E., *The Philosophy of Symbolic Forms*, vol.1, *Language*, 1923, English trans. 1953; Polanyi, M. and Prosch, H., *Meaning*, 1975.

145 Cassirer, E., *An Essay on Man*, 1944, pp.25 and 26.

146 For brief sketches of the development of linguistics see: Dixon, R.M.W., *What is Language?*, 1965; Potter, S., *Language in the Modern World*, 1960.

147 Potter, S., op.cit., p.9.
148 Bloomfield, L., *Language.*, 1933.
149 Blumenthal, A.L., *Language and Psychology*, 1970, ch.5.
150 For a list of Bühler's extensive writings on language, see Blumenthal, A.L., op.cit., p.55, footnote. Part of chapter 2 discusses Bühler's work.
151 Blumenthal, A.L., op.cit., ch.3.
152 Darwin, C., *The Descent of Man*, 1874, ch.3; Meumann, E., *Die Sprache des Kindes*, 1899; Sully, J., *Studies of Childhood*, 1896, ch.5; Stern, C. and Stern, W., *Die Kindersprache*, 1907 (translated extracts in Blumenthal, A.L., op.cit., pp.86-100).
153 Blumenthal, A.L., op.cit., p.67.
154 Guttenplan, S. (ed.), *Mind and Language*, 1975; Passmore, J., *A Hundred Years of Philosophy*, 2nd edn, 1966, ch.18. For a criticism of linguistic philosophy see Gellner, E., *Words and Things*, 1959 (Penguin 1968).
155 Wang, W.S.Y. (ed.), *Human Communication: Language and its Psychobiological Bases*, 1982.
Fiske, J., *Introduction to Communication Studies*, 1982.
156 Pavlov, I.P., *Psychopathology and Psychiatry: Selected Works*, 1961, vol.2, p.262.
157 Vygotsky, L.S., *Thought and Language* (1934), English trans. 1962; Luria, A.R., *The Making of Mind*, 1979. Ch.6 relates Luria's 'The verbal regulation of behaviour' which dates from 1927.
158 Lashley, K.S., 'The problem of serial order in behavior', in Jeffress, L.A., *Cerebral Mechanisms in Behavior*, 1951 (reprinted in Pribram, K.H. (ed.), *Brain and Behaviour*, 1969, vol.2, pp.515-40. References are to this reprint. Quotations from pp.516 and 525).
159 Osgood, C.E., *Method and Theory in Experimental Psychology*, 1953, ch.16.
160 Morris, C.W., *Signs, Language and Behavior*, 1946.
161 Osgood, C.E., op.cit., p.696. The mediation hypothesis was cogently attacked by J.A. Fodor in 'Could meaning be an r_m?', *J. Verb. Learn. Verb. Behav,*, vol.4, 1965, pp.73-81.
162 Mowrer, O.H., *Learning Theory and Symbolic Processes*, 1960, was a sequel to *Learning Theory and Behavior*, 1960.
163 Chomsky, N., *Syntactic Structures*, 1957; *Aspects of the Theory of Syntax*, 1965; *Topics in the Theory of Generative Grammar*, 1966. For a brief introduction to Chomsky's work see Lyons, J., *Chomsky*, Fontana Modern Masters, 1970.
164 Beloff, J., *Psychological Sciences*, 1973, p.175.
165 Chomsky, N., *Cartesian Linguistics*, 1966.
166 Chomsky, N., *Language and Mind*, 1972, p.64.
167 Greenberg, J.H. (ed.), *Universals of Language* quoted in Slobin, D.I., *Psycholinguistics*, 2nd edn, 1979, p.63.
168 Miller, G.A., 'The psycholinguists', *Encounter*, vol.13, pp.29-47 (reprinted in Miller, G.A., *The Psychology of Communication*, 1970, pp.74-94).
169 Lashley, K.S., *loc.cit.* (see note 158), pp.518-20.
170 Miller, G.A., *Language and Speech*, 1981, p.77.
171 See the contributions of Chomsky and Miller in Luce, R.D., Bush, R.R. and Galanter, E. (eds), *Handbook of Mathematical Psychology*, vol.2, 1963, ch.11, Chomsky, N. and Miller, G.A., 'Introduction to the formal analysis of natural languages', pp.269-322; ch.13, Chomsky, N., 'Formal properties of grammar', pp.323-418; ch.13, Miller, G.A. and Chomsky, N.,

'Finitary models of language users', pp.419-92.

172 Chomsky, N., *Language and Mind*, 1968, Preface.

173 Ibid., p.114.

174 Ibid., p.62.

175 Ibid., p.77.

176 Lennenberg, E.H., *Biological Foundations of Language*, 1967.

177 See Miller, G.A., *Language and Speech*, 1981; also articles by various authors reprinted in Oldfield, R.C. and Marshall, J.C. (eds), *Language: Selected Readings*, 1968. For more recent material see the articles in the *Annual Review of Psychology* on 'Experimental psycholinguistics': Johnson-Laird, P.N., vol.25, 1974, pp.135-60; Danks, J.H. and Gluckberg, S., vol.31, 1980, pp.391-417.

178 De Villiers, J.G. and De Villiers, P.A., *Language Acquisition*, 1978.

179 Hinde, R.A. (ed.), *Non-Verbal Communication*, 1972; Weitz, R. (ed.), *Non-Verbal Communication: Readings with a Commentary*, 1974.

180 See Thorpe, W.H., 'The comparison of vocal communication in animals and men', in Hinde, R.A. (ed.), op.cit., ch.2. Also references in ch.14, section 5, of the present work.

181 See Fillenbaum, S., 'Psycholinguistics', *Ann. Rev. Psychol.*, vol.22, 1971, p.301, for references.

182 Cain, A.J., *Animal Species and their Evolution*, 1954.

183 Popper, K.R., 'Of clocks and clouds', section 14, *Objective Knowledge*, 1972, ch.6.

184 Campbell, R. and Wales, R., 'The study of language acquisition', in Lyons, J. (ed.) *New Horizons in Linguistics*, 1970, p.248 (a valuable collection of papers on many aspects of linguistics).

185 Fodor, J.A., *The Modularity of Mind*, 1983.

186 See Miller, G.A., *Language and Speech*, 1981, ch.4.

187 Plato, *Cratylus*, 438 E.

188 See Malinowski, B., 'The problem of meaning in primitive languages', in Ogden, C.K. and Richards, I.A., *The Meaning of Meaning*, 1923, 10th edn, 1949, Appendix pp.296-336: 'Language is essentially rooted in the reality of a culture, the tribal life and the customs of a people, and it cannot be explained without constant reference to the broader contexts of verbal utterance' (p.305).

189 Hebb, D.O., *The Organization of Behavior*, 1949, p.xviii.

190 Delafresnaye, J.F. (ed.), *Brain Mechanisms and Consciousness: A Symposium*, 1954. The phrase 'the great sphynx' is in a contribution by Wilder Penfield, p.489.

191 Moruzzi, G. and Magoun, J.W., 'Brain stem reticular formation and the activation of the E.E.G.', *Electroenceph. Clin. Neurophysiol.*, vol.1, 1949, pp.455-73. See also the contributions by Moruzzi and Magoun to Delafresnaye, op.cit.

192 Heron, W., Bexton, W.H. and Hebb, D.O., 'Cognitive effects of decreased variation to sensory environment', *Amer. Psychologist*, vol.8, 1953, p.366 (abstract). For a fuller account see Zubek, J.P. (ed.), *Sensory Deprivation: Fifteen Years of Research*, 1969.

193 Schaefer, K.E. (ed.), *Environmental Effects on Consciousness*, 1962.

194 Globus, C.G., Maxwell, G. and Savodnik, I. (eds), *Consciousness and the Brain*, 1976; Schwartz, G.E., Shapiro, D. and Davidson, R.J. (eds), *Consciousness and Self-Regulation*, vol.1, 1976, vol.2, 1978, vol.3, 1983; Pope, K.S. and Singer, J.L. (eds), *The Stream of Consciousness*, 1978; Underwood, G. (ed.), *Aspects of Consciousness*, 3 vols, 1981-2.

195 Hilgard, E.R., 'Consciousness in contemporary psychology', *Ann. Rev.*

Psychol., vol.31, 1980, pp.1-26.

196 Descartes, R., *The Principles of Philosophy*, 1644, I.ix and xi.

197 Reid, T., *Essays on the Intellectual Powers of Man*, 1785, I.i.7.

198 James, W., 'Does consciousness exist?', *J. Phil. Psychol. and Sci. Meth.*, vol.1, 1904, reprinted in *Essays in Radical Empiricism*, 1912, ch.1.

199 Moore, G.E., 'The refutation of idealism', *Mind*, NS, vol.12, 1903, reprinted in *Philosophical Studies*, ch.1, 1922.

200 Brunswik, E., 'The conceptual framework of psychology', *Int. Encycl. of Unified Science*, vol.1, no.10, 1952, pp.13 and 14.

201 Hilgard, E.R., 'Hypnosis', *Ann. Rev. Psychol.*, vol.26, 1980, pp.19-44; Tart, C.T. (ed.), *Transpersonal Psychologies*, 1975 (contains an extensive bibliography).

202 Miller, G.A., Gallanter, E. and Pribram, K.H., *Plans and the Structure of Behavior*, 1960, ch.1, 'Images and plans'.

203 Holt, R.R., 'Imagery: the return of the ostracized', *Amer. Psychologist*, vol.19, 1964, pp.254-64; Paivio, A., *Imagery and Verbal Processes*, 1971; Kosslyn, S.M., *Image and Mind*, 1980 (includes historical material); Richardson, J.T.E., *Mental Imagery and Human Memory*, 1980. Rather older books are McKeller, P., *Imagination and Thinking*, 1957 and Richardson, A., *Mental Imagery*, 1969, both by Australasian psychologists.

204 Ornstein also edited a useful book of readings: Ornstein, R.E. (ed.), *The Nature of Human Consciousness*, 1973.

205 Quoted by Hilgard, E.R., *Ann. Rev. Psychol.*, vol.31, 1980, p.9.

206 Churchland, P.M., *Matter and Consciousness*, 1984, p.160.

207 Harris, R.B. (ed.), *Neoplatonism and Indian Thought*, 1982.

208 For the mystical element in St Augustine, see *Confessions*, Book 7, particularly chapters 10 and 17. The Psuedo-Dionysius posed as Dionysius the Areopagite (Acts xvii.34). He probably lived in the fifth century AD, and his writings on mystical matters exerted an enormous influence on Christian theology and art in the medieval world.

209 Schopenhauer, A., *The World as Will and Idea*, 1818, selections in Parker, D.H. (ed.), *Schopenhauer, Selections*, 1928.

210 Max Müller, F. (ed.), *The Sacred Books of the East*, 51 vols, 1875-1900.

211 Brett, G.S., *A History of Psychology*, vol.1, 1912, Part 1, ch.18.

212 Keyserling, H., *The Travel Diary of a Philosopher*, English trans. 1925.

213 Tagore, R., *Sadhana: The Realisation of Life*, 1921; Tagore, R., *The Religion of Man*, 1931; Radhakrishnan, S., *Eastern Religions and Western Thought*, 1939.

214 Jung, G.C., Commentary on 'The Tibetan Book of the Great Liberation', *Collected Works*, vol.11, p.802. Vol.11 contains most of Jung's writings on eastern religions. The commentary on 'The Secret of the Golden Flower' (Chinese) is in vol.13 dealing with alchemical studies.

215 Suzuki, D.T., *Zen Buddhism*, 1956.

216 See Tart, C.T. (ed.), *Transpersonal Psychologies*, 1975. For a balanced account of eastern philosophical thought see Copleston, F.C., *Philosophies and Cultures*, 1980, which contains a useful bibliography of works on Indian, Chinese and Islamic philosophy.

217 For a comparison between the assumptions of western and eastern psychologies see Tart, C.T. in Tart C.T. (ed.), op.cit., ch.2.

218 Patanjali, *Yoga Sutras*, III.12 (2nd century AD) in Coster, G., *Yoga and Western Psychology*, 1934, p.123.

219 Suzuki, D.T., 'Lectures on Zen Buddhism', in Fromm, E., Suzuki, D.T. and De Martino, R., *Zen Buddhism and Psychoanalysis*, 1960, p.25.

220 Ibid., p.10.

221 *Bhagavad-Gita: The Song of God*, trans. by Swami Prabhavananda and C. Isherwood, with an Introduction by Aldous Huxley, 1947.
222 Lashley, K.S., 'Dynamic processes in perception', in Delafesnaye, J.F. (ed.), *Brain Mechanisms and Consciusness*, 1954, p.430.
223 James, W., *Principles of Psychology*, 1890, vol.1, p.144.
224 Lashley, K.S., 'The problem of serial order in behavior' (see note 158).
225 Sperry, R.W., 'Mental phenomena as causal determinants in brain function', in Globus, G.G., Maxwell, G. and Savodnik, I., *Consciousness and the Brain*, 1976, p.165.
226 Freud, S., *The Ego and the Id*, 1923, Standard Edition, vol.19, p.25.
227 Jaynes, J., *The Origins of Consciousness in the Breakdown of the Bicameral Mind*, 1976.
228 Crook, J.H., *The Evolution of Human Consciousness*, 1980, particularly chs 7-9.
229 Piaget, J., *The Grasp of Consciousness*, 1974, English trans. 1976; Vygotsky, L.S., *Thought and Language*, 1934, English trans. 1962.
230 Nagel, T., 'What is it like to be a bat?', *Phil. Rev.*, 1974 (reprinted in Hofstadter, D.R. and Dennett, D.C., *The Mind's I*, 1981, Penguin edn, 1982, pp.391-403).
231 Berkeley, G., *New Theory of Vision*, 1709, sections 140-7.
232 Berkeley, G., *Visual Language Vindicated*, 1733, section 43.
233 Wittgenstein, L., *Philosophical Investigations*, 1953, section 293.
234 Bartlett, F.C., *Remembering*, 1932, p.206.
235 Hoffstadter, D.R., in Hofstadter, D.R. and Dennett, D.C., op.cit., p.281.
236 James, W., *Principles of Psychology*, 1890, vol.1, ch.10, 'The consciousness of self'.
237 Bolter, J.D., *Turing's Man*, 1984.
238 Plato, *Phaedrus*, 246A and 253C.
239 Aristotle, *Nichomachean Ethics*, VI. 1139a.
240 Nietzsche, F., *The Birth of Tragedy*, 1872.
241 Stern, W., *General Psychology from the Personalistic Standpoint*, 1938, ch.4.
242 Eccles, J.C., *The Human Mystery*, 1979, p.118.
243 Sperry, R., *Science and Moral Priority*, 1983, p.10.
244 Thorpe, W.H., *Purpose in a World of Chance*, 1978; Young, J.Z., *Programs of the Brain*, 1978.
245 Langer, S., *Mind: An Essay on Human Feeling*, 3 vols, 1967, vol.1, p.32.
246 Ibid., p.65.
247 For examples of psychological work see: Vernon, P.E. and Allport, G.W., 'A test for personal values', *J. Abn. Soc. Psychol.*, vol.26, 1931, pp.233-48; Greene, J.G., *Elementary Theoretical Psychology*, 1968, ch.2, 'Choice and preference' (a useful summary of work in the area of decision theory); Piaget, J., *The Moral Judgment of the Child*, 1932; Kohlberg, L., 'Education for justice: a modern statment of the Platonic view', Gustafson, J.M. (ed.), *Moral Education*, 1970; Rokeach, M., *The Nature of Human Values*, 1973. Mention must also be made of Köhler, W., *The Place of Value in a World of Fact*, a gestalt attempt at treating values as 'tertiary qualities'.
248 Stern, W., 'Wertphilosophie', vol.3 of *Person und Sache*, 1924.
249 Popper, K.R., 'Autobiography', in Schlipp, P.A. (ed.), *The Philosophy of Karl Popper*, vol.1, 1974, p.154.
250 Spinoza, B., *Ethic*, 1677, III. vi and xi.
251 Ibid., III. xxxix. Schol.

252 Ibid., V. xlii.
253 Popper, K.R., 'Autobiography', loc.cit., p.155.
254 See Sperry, R., *Science and Moral Priority*, 1983, Addendum.
255 Ibid., ch.1.
256 Maslow, A.H., *Toward a Psychology of Being*, 1962, p.192.
257 Infeld, L., *Quest: The Evolution of a Scientist*, 1941, p.240.

Chapter 16 Metapsychology

1 Strawson, P.F., *Individuals: An Essay in Descriptive Metaphysics*, 1959, p.10.
2 See ch. 12, note 188.
3 Krech, D., 'Epilogue', in Royce, J.R. (ed.), *Toward Unification in Psychology*, First Banff Conference on Theoretical Psychology, 1970, p.300.
4 Wittgenstein, L., *Philosophical Investigations*, 1953, II.xiv, p.232.
5 Heraclitus, 'The fragments', VII, in Kahn, C.H., *The Art and Thought of Heraclitus*, 1979.
6 Ibid., Fragment XVII.
7 Bacon, F., *The Advancement of Learning*, 1605, I.v.5.
8 Popper, K.R., *The Logic of Scientific Discovery*, English trans. 1959, p.280.
9 Freud, S., 'Analysis terminable and interminable', 1937, Standard Edition (SE), vol.23, p.225.
10 Freud, S., *The Origins of Psychoanalysis*, 1954, Letter 41, p.157; *The Psychopathology of Everyday Life*, 1901, SE, vol.6, p.259;
11 'The unconscious', 1915, SE, vol.14, p.181.
12 Stern, W., *General Psychology from the Personalistic Standpoint*, English trans. 1938 (see ch.12, section 7 above).
13 Jacob, F., *The Logic of Living Systems*, 1974, Conclusion: 'The Integron', pp.299-324.
14 Popper, K.R., *Objective Knowledge: An Evolutionary Approach*, 1972, p.106.
15 Ibid., p.149.
16 Stern, W., op.cit., p.73.
17 Hegel, G.W.F., *Introduction to the Philosophy of History*, 1837. Bohn edn, 1857, p.82.
18 Alexander, S., *Space, Time and Deity*, 1920, vol.2, p.46; Lloyd Morgan, C., *Emergent Evolution*, 1923; Bergson, H., *L'Evolution Créatrice*, 1907.
19 Piaget, J., *The Psychology of Intelligence*, English trans. 1950, p.49; Broad, C.D., *The Mind and its Place in Nature*, 1925 (particularly ch.14); Popper, K.R., in Popper, K.R. and Eccles J.R., *The Self and its Brain*, 1977, ch.P.1, 'Materialism transcends itself'; Woodger, J.H., *Biological Principles*, 1929; Beckner, W.M., *The Biological Way of Thought*, 1959; 'Medawar, P.B. and Medawar, J.S., *The Life Science*, 1977, p.165.
20 Nagel, E., *The Structure of Science*, 1961, p.445.
21 Beveridge, W.I.B., *The Art of Scientific Investigation*, 1950, p.7.
22 James, W., *Principles of Psychology*, 1890, vol.1, p.6.
23 Moscovici, S., 'Perspectives d'avenir en psychologie sociale', in Fraisse, P. (ed.), *Psychologie de demain*, 1982, p.141.
24 Darwin, C., 'Autobiography', in Darwin, F. (ed.), *Charles Darwin*, 1892, p.52.
25 Dennett, D.C., *Elbow Room*, 1984.

26 Gergen, K.J., *Towards a Transformation in Social Knowledge*, 1982, p.17.
27 Hume, D., *An Enquiry Concerning Human Understanding*, 1748, VI.1.
28 Bacon, F., *De Augmentis*, 1623. (See ch.5, this volume, notes 74 and 75.)
29 Zukav, G., *The Dancing Wu Li Masters: An Overview of the New Physics*, 1979, p.56.
30 Elvee, R.Q. (ed.), *Mind in Nature*, Nobel Conference no.17, 1982, p.xi.
31 Plato, *Cratylus*, 402A.
32 Kahn, C.H., *The Art and Thought of Heraclitus*, 1979, Fragments III, XXXI and XXXVI.
33 Ibid., p.21.
34 Newton-Smith, W.H., *The Structure of Time*, 1980, pp.3, 7, 242.
35 Hamlyn, D.W., *Metaphysics*, 1984, p.149.
36 Spinoza, B., *Ethic*, 1677, III. vi.
37 Lashley, K.S., 'The problem of serial order in behaviour', in Jeffress, L.A., *Cerebral Mechanisms in Behavior*, 1951, reprinted in Pribram, K.H. (ed.), *Brain and Behaviour*, 1969.
38 Langer, S., 'Man and animal: the city and the hive', in *Philosophical Sketches*, 1962, Mentor Books, 1964, p.98.
39 Popper, K.R., *Objective Knowledge*, 1972, p.147.
40 Reinhardt, K., *Parmenides*, 1916, p.201, quoted in Kahn, C.H., op.cit., p.127.
41 Heraclitus, 'The Fragments', Fragment XXXV (Kahn's translation) in Kahn, C.H., op.cit., p.45, and commentary pp.126-30.

Bibliography

Aaron, R.I. (1937), *John Locke* (Oxford University Press).

Abraham J.H. (1973), *The Origins and Growth of Sociology* (Harmondsworth: Penguin).

Adams, J. (1897), *The Herbartian Psychology Applied to Education* (London: Isbister).

Adler, A. (1929), *The Science of Living* (London: Allen & Unwin).

Adler, M. (1937), *What Man has Made of Man* (New York: Longmans Green).

Air Ministry (1947), *Psychological Disorders in Flying Personnel of the Royal Air Force* (London: HMSO).

Akenside, M. (1744), *The Pleasures of Imagination* (London).

Akhilananda, S. (1947), *Hindu Psychology: Its Meaning for the West* (London: Routledge).

Aleksander, I. and Burnett, P. (1984), *Reinventing Man: The Robot Becomes Reality* (London: Kogan Page).

Alexander, S. (1920), *Space, Time and Deity*, 2 vols (London: Macmillan).

Allan, D.J. (1952), *The Philosophy of Aristotle* (Oxford University Press).

Allen, G. (1978), *Life Science in the Twentieth Century* (Cambridge University Press).

Allport, F.H. (1924), *Social Psychology* (Boston: Houghton Mifflin)

Allport, G.W. (1937), *Personality: A Psychological Interpretation* (London: Constable).

Ananiev, B.G. (1948), *Uspekhi Sovetskoi Psikhologii* (in Russian) (Leningrad: Lenizdat).

Anderson, J.R. (1976), *Language, Memory and Thought* (Hillside: Erlbaum).

Anderson, J.R. (1983), *The Architecture of Cognition* (Harvard University Press).

Ando, T. (1965), *Aristotle's Theory of Practical Cognition* (The Hague: Nijhoff).

Andreas-Salome, L. (1964), *Freud Journal* (London: Hogarth Press).

Annual Review of Psychology (1950–), Annual Volumes (Stanford: Annual Reviews).

Ansbacher, H.L. and Ansbacher, R.R. (1956), *The Individual Psychology of Alfred Adler* (London: Allen & Unwin).

Anscombe, G.E.M., Von Wright, G.H. and Nyman, H. (1980), *Ludwig Wittgenstein: Remarks on the Philosophy of Psychology*, 2 vols (Oxford: Blackwell).

Apter, M.J. and Westby, G. (eds) (1973), *The Computer in Psychology* (London: Wiley).

Aquinas, T. (1924), *Summa Contra Gentiles* (London: Burns Oates).
Aquinas, T. (1963-75), *Summa Theologiae*, 60 vols (London: Eyre & Spottiswoode).
Argyle, M. (1967), *The Psychology of Interpersonal Behaviour* (Harmondsworth: Penguin).
Aristotle (1984), *The Works of Aristotle Translated into English*, revised edn 2 vols (Princeton University Press).
Armstrong, A.H. (1957), *An Introduction to Ancient Philosophy* (London: Methuen).
Armstrong, A.H. (ed.) (1967), *The Cambridge History of Later Greek and Early Medieval Philosophy* (Cambridge University Press).
Armstrong, D.M. (1968), *A Materialist Theory of the Mind* (London: Routledge & Kegan Paul).
Ashby, W.R. (1956), *Introduction to Cybernetics* (London: Chapman & Hall).
Ashby, W.R. (1960), *Design for a Brain*, 2nd end (London: Chapman & Hall).
Attneave, F. (1959), *Applications of Information Theory to Psychology* (New York: Holt, Rinehart & Winston).
Augustine, A. (1871-76), *The Works of Aurelius Augustinus*, 15 vols (Edinburgh: Clark).
Augustine, A. (1948), *Basic Writings of St Augustine*, 2 vols (New York: Random House).
Augustine, A. (1912), *Confessions*, 2 vols (London: Heinemann. Loeb Classical Library).
Aurelius, M. (1944), *Meditations*, edited with translation and commentary by A.S.L. Farquharson, 2 vols (Oxford: Clarendon Press).
Autrum, H. *et al.* (eds) (1971-8), *Handbook of Sensory Physiology*, 24 vols (Berlin: Springer).
Averill, J.R. (1976), *Patterns of Psychological Thought* (New York: Wiley).
Ayer, A.J. (1936), *Language, Truth and Logic* (London: Gollancz).
Ayer, A.J. (1982), *Philosophy in the Twentieth Century* (London: Weidenfeld & Nicolson).
Bacon, F. (1905), *The Philosophical Works of Francis Bacon*, edited by Ellis, R.L. and Spedding, J. (London: Routledge).
Bacon, F. (1970), *Tempus Partus Masculus*, translated by B. Farrington in *The Philosophy of Francis Bacon* (Liverpool University Press).
Baddeley, A.D. (1976), *The Psychology of Memory* (New York: Harper & Row).
Bain, A. (1855), *The Senses and the Intellect* (London: Longmans Green).
Bain, A. (1878), *Body and Mind* (London: Kegan Paul).
Baldwin J.M. (1893), *Elements of Psychology* (New York: Holt).
Barclay, W. (1958), *The Mind of St Paul* (Glasgow: Collins).
Barcroft, J. (1938), *The Brain and its Environment* (Yale University Press).
Barlow, H.B. and Mollon, J.D. (1982), *The Senses* (Cambridge University Press).
Barnes, J. (1979), *The Presocratic Philosophers*, 2 vols (London: Routledge & Kegan Paul).
Barnes, J., Schofield, M. and Sorabji, R. (eds) (1979), *Articles on Aristotle*, vol.4, *Psychology and Aesthetics* (London: Duckworth).
Bartlett, F.C. (1932), *Remembering* (Cambridge University Press).
Bartlett, F.C. (1958), *Thinking: An Experimental and Social Study* (London: Allen & Unwin).
Bartlett, F.C. and Mackworth, NH. (1950), *Planned Seeing* (London: HMSO).
Bartlett, F.C., Ginsberg, M., Lindgren, E.S. and Thouless, R.H. (eds) (1939), *The Study of Society* (London: Kegan Paul, Trench & Trubner).
Bastian, A. (1860), *Der Mensch in der Geschichte: Zur Bergründung einer psychologischen Weltanschauung* (Leipzig).

Bateson, W. (1909), *Mendel's Principles of Heredity* (Cambridge University Press).

Battie, W. (1758), *A Treatise on Madness* (London: Whiston & White).

Beach, F.A. (1948), *Hormones and Behavior* (New York: Harper).

Beaumont, J.G. (1983), *Introduction to Neuropsychology* (Oxford: Blackwell).

Beckner, W.K. (1959), *The Biological Way of Thought* (University of Columbia Press).

Bell, C. (1811), *Idea of a New Anatomy of the Brain* (London: Strahan and Preston).

Beloff, J. (1973), *Psychological Sciences* (London: Crosby, Lockwood, Staples).

Benedict, R. (1935), *Patterns of Culture* (London: Routledge).

Bergson, H. (1907), *L'Évolution Créatrice* (Paris: Alcan).

Bergson, H. (1910), *Time and Free Will* (London: Sonnenschein).

Bergson, H. (1913), *An Introduction to Metaphysics* (London: Macmillan).

Berkeley, E.C. (1949), *Giant Brains, or Machines that Think* (New York: Wiley).

Berkeley, G. (1948-57), *The Works of George Berkeley*, 9 vols, ed. A.A. Luce and T.E. Jessop (London: Nelson).

Berlin, I. (1976), *Vico and Herder* (London: Chatto & Windus).

Berlin, I. (1978), *Karl Marx*, 4th edn (Oxford University Press).

Berlin, I. (ed.) (1979), *The Age of Enlightenment: The Eighteenth Century Philosophy* (Oxford University Press).

Bernal, J.D. (1969), *Science in History*, 4 vols (Harmondsworth: Penguin).

Berndt, R.M. and Phillips, E.S. (eds) (1973), *The Australian Aboriginal Inheritance* (Sydney: Ure Smith).

Bernouilli, J. (1713), *Ars Conjectandi* (Basle).

Best, E. (1922), *Some Aspects of Maori Myth and Religion* (Wellington: Dominion Museum).

Best, E. (1922), *Spiritual and Mental Concepts of the Maori* (Wellington: Dominion Museum).

Best, E. (1924), *The Maori* 2 vols (Wellington: Polynesian Society).

Best, E. (1934), *The Maori As He Was* (Wellington: Dominion Museum).

Beveridge, W.I.B. (1950), *The Art of Scientific Investigation* (London: Heinemann).

Bhagavad-Gita: The Song of God (1947), translated by Swami Prabhavananda and C. Isherwood, with an Introduction by A. Huxley (London: Phoenix House).

Bidney, D. (1940), *The Psychology and Ethics of Spinoza* (Yale University Press).

Binet, A. (1899), *The Psychology of Reasoning* (London: Kegan Paul).

Binet, A. (1896), *Alterations of Personality* (London: Chapman & Hall).

Binet, A. (1909), *Les Idées modernes sur les Énfants* (Paris: Flammarion).

Binet, A. and Féré, C. (1887), *Animal Magnetism* (London: Kegan Paul).

Bingham, H.C. (1932), *Gorillas in a Native Habitat* (Washington: Carnegie Institute).

Blackburn J.M. (1936), *The Acquisition of Skill: An Analysis of Learning Curves*, IHRB Report 73 (London: HMSO).

Blake, W. (1977), *Complete Poems* (Harmondsworth: Penguin).

Bloomfield, L. (1933), *Language* (New York: Holt, Rinehart & Winston).

Blumenthal, A.L. (1970), *Language and Psychology: Historical Aspects of Psycholinguistics*. (New York: Wiley).

Blumenthal, H.J. (1971), *Plotinus' Psychology: His Doctrines of the Embodied Soul* (The Hague: Nijhoff).

Boas, F. (1963), *The Mind of Primitive Man*, revised edn (New York: Collier) (first published 1911).
Boas, M. (1958), *Robert Boyle and Seventeenth Century Chemistry* (Cambridge University Press).
Boden, M.A. (1977), *Artificial Intelligence and Natural Man* (Brighton: Harvester).
Boden, M.A. (1979), *Piaget* (London: Fontana).
Boden, M.A. (1981), *Minds and Mechanisms: Philosophical Psychology and Computational Models* (Brighton: Harvester).
Bolton, N. (1972), *The Psychology of Thinking* (London: Methuen).
Book, W.F. (1925), *The Psychology of Skill* (New York: Gregg).
Booth, C. (1892-7), *The Life and Labour of the People of London*, 9 vols (London: Macmillan).
Boring, E.G. (1933), *The Physical Dimensions of Consciousness* (London: Constable).
Boring, E.G. (1942), *Sensation and Perception in the History of Experimental Psychology* (New York: Appleton, Century, Crofts).
Boring, E.G. (1950), *A History of Experimental Psychology*, revised edn (New York: Appleton, Century, Crofts).
Boring, E.G., Langfeld, H.S. and Weld, H.P. (1948), *Foundations of Psychology* (New York: Wiley).
Boulding, K.E. (1956), *The Image* (University of Michigan Press).
Bourke, V.J. (1978), *The Essential Augustine* (Indianapolis: Hackett).
Boyle, R. (1666), *The Origin of Forms and Qualities* (Oxford).
Boyle R. (1964), *The Sceptical Chymist* (London: Dent).
Bradley F.H. (1922), *The Principles of Logic*, 2nd edn (Oxford University Press).
Braid, J. (1843), *Neurypnology* (Edinburgh: Black).
Brandt, F. (1928), *Thomas Hobbes' Mechanical Concept of Nature* (Copenhagen: Munksgaard).
Brazier, M.A.B. (1960), *The Electrical Activity of the Nervous System* 2nd edn (London: Pitman).
Brazier, M.A.B. (1960), *The Central Nervous System and Behaviour* (New York: Macy Foundation).
Brenner, M. (ed.) (1980), *The Structure of Action* (Oxford: Blackwell).
Brentano, F. (1973), *Psychology from an Empirical Standpoint* (London: Routledge & Kegan Paul) (first published 1874).
Brett, G.S. (1912-21), *A History of Psychology*, 3 vols (London: Macmillan).
Bridgman, P.W. (1927), *The Logic of Modern Physics* (New York: Macmillan).
Broad, C.D. (1925), *The Mind and its Place in Nature* (London: Kegan Paul, Trench & Trubner).
Broad, C.D. (1975), *Leibniz: An Introduction*, ed. Lewy, C. (Cambridge University Press).
Broadbent, D.E. (1958), *Perception and Communication* (London: Pergamon).
Broadbent, D.E. (1971), *Decision and Stress* (London: Academic Press).
Bromley, D.B. (1977), *Personality Description in Ordinary Language* (London: Wiley).
Brown, P.R.L. (1967), *St Augustine of Hippo* (London: Faber & Faber).
Brown, S.C. (ed.) (1974), *Philosophers of the Enlightenment* (Brighton: Harvester).
Brown, T. (1820), *Lectures on the Philosophy of the Human Mind*, 4 vols (Edinburgh: Tait).

Brožek, J. and Fabrykant, M. (1962), *Psychodietetics* (Springfield, Ill.: Thomas).

Bruner, J.S. (1966), *Towards a Theory of Instruction* (Harvard University Press).

Bruner, J.S. (1983), *In Search of Mind: Essays in Autobiography* (New York: Harper & Row).

Bruner, J.S., Goodnow, J.J. and Austin, G.A. (1956), *A Study of Thinking* (New York: Wiley).

Brunswick, E. (1952), *The Conceptual Framework of Psychology*, International Encyclopedia of Unified Science, vol.1, no.10 (University of Chicago Press).

Burckhardt, J. (1878), *The Civilization of the Renaissance in Italy* (London: Kegan Paul).

Burke, E. (1910), *Reflections on the French Revolution* (London: Dent) (first published 1790).

Burn, H. (1962), *Drugs, Medicine and Man* (London: Allen & Unwin).

Burt, C.L. (1940), *The Factors of the Mind* (University of London Press).

Burtt, E.A. (1925), *The Metaphysical Foundations of Modern Physical Science* (London: Kegan Paul, Trench & Trubner).

Bury, J.B., Cook, S.A., Adcock, F.E. and Charlesworth, M.D. (eds) (1923-39), *The Cambridge Ancient History* 12 vols (Cambridge University Press).

Butler, J. (1949), *Sermons* (London: Bell) (first published 1726).

Butterfield, H. (1949), *The Origins of Modern Science 1300-1800* (London: Bell).

Butterworth, G. (ed.) (1981), *Infancy and Epistemology: An Evaluation of Piaget's Theory* (Brighton: Harvester).

Buxton, C. (ed.) (1985), *Points of View in the History of Modern Psychology*. (New York: Academic Press).

Cabanis, P. (1799), *Rapports du physique et du morale de l'homme* (Paris).

Cain, A.J. (1954), *Animal Species and their Evolution* (London: Hutchinson).

Campbell, N.R. (1957), *The Foundations of Science* (New York: Dover).

Canguilhem, G. (1955), *La Formation du concept de réflexe aux XVIIE et XVIIIE siècles* (Paris: Presses Universitaires de France).

Cannon, W.B. (1929), *Bodily Changes in Pain, Hunger, Fear and Rage*, 2nd edn (New York: Appleton).

Cannon, W.B. (1932), *The Wisdom of the Body* (London: Kegan Paul).

Canter, S. and Canter, D. (eds) (1982), *Psychology in Practice* (New York: Wiley).

Cardano, G. (1968), *Ars Magna* (Cambridge, Mass., MIT Press).

Carlyle, T. (1909), *Past and Present* (Oxford University Press).

Carmichael, L. (ed.) (1954), *Manual of Child Psychology* 2nd edn (New York: Wiley).

Carnap, R. (1937), *The Logical Syntax of Language* (New York: Harcourt Brace).

Carpenter, C.R. (1934), *Naturalistic Behavior of Nonhuman Primates* (Pennsylvania State University Press).

Carpenter, W.B. (1852), *Principles of Human Physiology*, 4th edn (London: Churchill).

Carpenter, W.B. (1874), *Principles of Mental Physiology* (London: King).

Cassirer, E. (1944), *An Essay on Man* (Yale University Press).

Cassirer, E. (1953-7), *The Philosophy of Symbolic Forms* 3 vols (Yale University Press).

Cassirer, E., Kristeller, P.O. and Randall, J.H. (eds) (1948), *The Renaissance*

Philosophy of Man (Chicago University Press).

Cattell, R.B. (1957), *Personality and Motivation Structure and Measurement* (New York: Harcourt Brace).

Cattell, R.B. (1965), *The Scientific Analysis of Personality* (Harmondsworth: Penguin).

Chapman, A.J. and Jones, D.M. (eds) (1980), *Models of Man* (Leicester: British Psychological Society).

Chateaubriand, F.R. (1802), *Génie du Christianisme, ou Beautés de la Religion Chrétienne* (Paris).

Cherry, C. (1957), *On Human Communication: A Review, a Survey and a Criticism* (London: Chapman & Hall).

Chomsky, N. (1957), *Syntactic Structures* (The Hague: Mouton).

Chomsky, N. (1965), *Aspects of the Theory of Syntax* (Cambridge, Mass.: MIT Press).

Chomsky, N. (1966), *Topics in the Theory of Generative Grammar* (The Hague: Mouton).

Chomsky, N. (1966), *Cartesian Linguistics: A Chapter in the History of Rationalist Thought* (New York: Harper & Row).

Chomsky, N. (1968), *Language and Mind* (New York: Harcourt, Brace).

Churchland, P.M. (1984), *Matter and Consciousness* (Cambridge, Mass.: MIT Press).

Churchman, C.W. and Ratook, P. (eds) (1959), *Measurement: Definition and Theories* (American Association for the Advancement of Science).

Cicero, M.T. (1927), *Tusculan Disputations*, Loeb Classical Library, vol.17 (London: Heinemann).

Cicero, M.T. (1937), *Pro Flacco*, Loeb Classical Library, vol.10 (London: Heinemann).

Cicero, M.T. (1949), *De Inventione*, Loeb Classical Library, vol.2 (London: Heinemann).

Clark, M.T. (1955), *Augustine: Philosopher of Freedom* (New York: Desclée).

Clarke, E. and O'Malley, C.D. (1968), *The Human Brain and Spinal Cord* (Berkeley: University of California Press).

Clifford, B.R. and Bull, R. (1978), *The Psychology of Person Identification* (London: Routledge & Kegan Paul).

Cloudsley-Thompson, J.L. (1961), *Rhythmic Activity in Animal Physiology and Behaviour* (New York: Academic Press).

Clutton-Brock, T.H. and Harvey P.H. (eds) (1978), *Readings in Sociobiology* (San Francisco: Freeman).

Coan, R.W. (1979), *Psychologists: Personal and Theoretical Pathways* (New York: Irvington).

Cobb, I.G. (1927), *The Glands of Destiny* (London: Heinemann).

Codrington, R.H. (1891), *The Melanesians* (Oxford University Press).

Cole, M. and Maltzman, I. (1969), *A Handbook of Contemporary Soviet Psychology* (New York: Basic Books).

Cole, M., Gay, J., Glick, J.A. and Sharp, D.W. (1971), *The Cultural Context of Learning and Thinking* (London: Methuen).

Coleman, W. (1971), *Biology in the Nineteenth Century* (Cambridge University Press).

Coleridge, S.T. (1976), *Treatise on Method*, ed. Snyder, A.D. (Norwood, Pennsylvania: Norwood Editions).

Collingwood, R.G. (1944), *An Autobiography* (Harmondsworth: Penguin).

Colquhoun, W.P. (ed.) (1971), *Biological Rhythms and Human Performance* (New York: Academic Press).

Comte, A. (1896), *Comte's Philosophy of the Sciences* (an exposition of the

Cours de Philosophie Positive, by G.H. Lewes) (London: Bell).
Condillac, E. (1754), *Traité des sensations* (Paris).
Conrad, T. (1885), *The German Universities* (Glasgow: Bryce).
Cook, S. (1942), *The Rebirth of Christianity* (Harmondsworth: Penguin).
Cooley, C.H. (1902), *Human Nature and the Social Order* (New York: Scribners).
Copplestone, F.C. (1947-75), *A History of Philosophy*, 9 vols (London: Burns, Oates & Washbourne).
Coplestone, F.C. (1955), *Aquinas* (Harmondsworth: Penguin).
Coplestone, F.C. (1980), *Philosophies and Cultures* (Oxford University Press).
Corcoran, D.W.J. (1971), *Pattern Recognition* (Harmondsworth: Penguin).
Coster, G. (1934), *Yoga and Western Psychology* (Oxford University Press).
Couturat, L. (1901), *La Logique de Leibniz* (Paris).
Cox, J.W. (1934), *Manual Skill: Its Organization and Development* (Cambridge University Press).
Craik, K.J.W. (1943), *The Nature of Explanation* (Cambridge University Press).
Cranston, M. (1957), *John Locke: A Biography* (London: Longmans).
Crawley, A.E. (1909), *The Idea of the Soul* (London: Black).
Crombie, I.M. (1962), *An Examination of Plato's Doctrines* (London: Routledge & Kegan Paul).
Crook, J.H. (1980), *The Evolution of Human Consciousness* (Oxford: Clarendon Press).
Crowder, R.G. (1976), *Principles of Learning and Memory* (Hillside: Erlbaum).
Darwin, C. (1872), *The Origin of Species*, 6th edn (London: Murray).
Darwin, C. (1874), *The Descent of Man*, 2nd edn (London: Murray).
Darwin, C. (1889), *The Expression of the Emotions in Man and Animals*, 2nd edn (London: Murray).
Darwin, E. (1794), *Zoonomia* (London: Johnson).
Darwin, F. (ed.) (1892), *Charles Darwin* (London: Murray).
Davidson, D. (1980), *Essays on Actions and Events* (Oxford: Clarendon Press).
Davies, S. (1978), *Renaissance Views of Man* (Manchester University Press).
Da Vinci, L. (1952), *Selections from the Notebooks*, ed. Richter, I.A. (Oxford University Press).
Davis, D.R. (1948), *Pilot Error* (London: HMSO).
Davson, H. (1969-74), *The Eye* 6 vols, (London: Academic Press).
Dawkins, R. (1976), *The Selfish Gene* (Oxford University Press).
Dawkins, R. (1982), *The Extended Phenotype* (Oxford University Press).
Debus, A.G. (1978), *Man and Nature in the Renaissance* (Cambridge University Press).
De Groot, A.D. (1965), *Thought and Choice in Chess* (The Hague: Mouton).
Delafresnaye, J.F. (ed.) (1954), *Brain Mechanisms and Consciousness: A Symposium* (Oxford: Blackwell).
Dennett, D.C. (1984), *Elbow Room: The Varieties of Free Will Worth Wanting* (Oxford: Clarendon Press).
Dennis, W. (ed.) (1948), *Readings in the History of Psychology* (New York: Appleton, Century, Crofts).
Department of Health and Social Security (1977), *The Role of Psychologists in the Health Services* (London: HMSO).
Descartes, R. (1931), *Philosophical Works*, ed. Haldane, E.S and Ross, G.R.T. (Cambridge University Press).
Descartes, R. (1957), *Rules for the Direction of the Mind*, ed. Joachim, H.H.

(London: Allen & Unwin).

Descartes, R. (1925), *The Method, Meditations and Selections from the Principles of Descartes*, ed. Veitch, J. (Edinburgh: Blackwood).

De Villiers J.G. and De Villiers, P.A. (1978), *Language Acquisition* (Cambridge, Mass.: Harvard University Press).

De Vore, I. (1965), *Primate Behavior* (New York: Holt).

Dewey, J. (1888), *Leibniz's New Essay concerning Human Understanding* (Chicago: Griggs).

Dicey, A.V. (1905), *Lectures on the Relation between Law and Opinion in England during the Nineteenth Century* (London: Macmillan).

Dilthey, W. (1914-58), *Gesammelte Schriften*, 12 vols (Leipzig).

Dilthey, W. (1976), *Selected Writings* ed. Rickman, H.P. (Cambridge University Press).

Dixon, R.M.W. (1965), *What is Language? A New Approach to Linguistic Description* (London: Longmans).

Dodds, E.R. (1951), *The Greeks and the Irrational* (University of California Press).

Donaldson, M. (1979), *Children's Minds* (Glasgow: Fontana).

Drever, J. (1921), *Instinct in Man* (Cambridge University Press).

Driesch, H. (1908), *The Science and Philosophy of the Organism* (London: Black).

Du Bois Reymond, R. (1848), *Tierische Elektricität* (Berlin).

Duns Scotus (1506), *Opus Oxoneiensis* (Venice).

Durkheim, E. (1915), *The Elementary Forms of the Religious Life* (London: Allen & Unwin).

Durkheim, E. (1952), *Suicide: A Study in Sociology* (London: Routledge & Kegan Paul).

Durkheim, E. (1938), *The Rules of Sociological Method* (University of Chicago Press).

Ebbing, F.J. (ed.) (1975), *Racial Variations in Man* (Institute of Biology. Symposium 22).

Ebbinghaus, H. (1913), *Memory* (New York: Teachers College Press, Columbia University).

Eccles, J.C. (1953), *The Neurophysiological Basis of Mind* (Oxford: Clarendon Press).

Eccles, J.C. (1979), *The Human Mystery* (Berlin: Springer).

Edwards, W. and Tversky, A. (eds) (1967), *Decision-Making: Selected Readings* (Harmondsworth: Penguin).

Eldridge, J.E.T. (1971), *Max Weber: The Interpretation of Social Reality* (London: Nelson).

Eleftheriou, B.E. (ed.) (1975), *Psychopharmacogenetics* (New York: Plenum).

Elkin, A.D. (1979), *The Australian Aborigines*, revised edn (Sydney: Angus & Robertson).

Elkind, D. and Flavell, J.H. (1969), *Studies in Cognitive Development: Essays in Honor of Jean Piaget* (New York: Oxford University Press).

Ellenberger, H.F. (1970), *The Discovery of the Unconscious* (London: Lane).

Ellis, H. (1936), *Studies in the Psychology of Sex*, 2 vols (New York: Random House).

Ellis, W.D. (ed.) (1938), *A Source Book of Gestalt Psychology* (London: Routledge & Kegan Paul).

Elvee, R.Q. (ed.) (1982), *Mind in Nature* (Nobel Conference no.17) (San Fransisco: Harper & Row).

Elwes, R.H.M. (1883), *The Chief Works of Spinoza* (London: Bohn).

Emery, F.E. (ed.) (1969), *Systems Thinking: Selected Readings* (Harmondsworth: Penguin).

Engell, J. (1981), *The Creative Imagination: Enlightenment to Romanticism* (Harvard University Press).

Engels, F. (1972), *The Condition of the Working Class in England* (St Albans: Panther((first published 1845).

Epstein, I. (1959), *Judaism* (Harmondsworth: Penguin).

Erasmus, D. (1969), *De Libero Arbitrio*, in *Luther and Erasmus: Free Will and Salvation* (London: SCM Press).

Erasmus, D. (1971), *In Praise of Folly* (Harmondsworth: Penguin).

Estes, W.K. (1954), *Modern Learning Theory* (New York: Appleton, Century, Crofts).

Evans, C. (1981), *The Making of the Micro: A History of the Computer* (London: Gollancz).

Evans, R.I. (1980), *The Making of Social Psychology* (New York: Gardner).

Evans-Pritchard, E.E. (1937), *Witchcraft, Oracles and Magic among the Azande* (Oxford: Clarendon Press).

Everly, O.S. and Rosenfeld, R. (1981), *The Nature and Treatment of Stress* (New York: Plenum).

Eysenck, H.J. (1947), *Dimensions of Personality* (London: Kegan Paul, Trench & Trubner).

Eysenck, H.J. (1952), *The Scientific Study of Personality* (London: Routledge & Kegan Paul).

Eysenck, H.J. (1953a), *The Structure of Personality* (London: Methuen).

Eysenck, H.J. (1953b), *Uses and Abuses of Psychology* (Harmondsworth: Penguin).

Eysenck, H.J. (1973), *The Inequality of Man* (London: Temple Smith).

Eysenck H.J. and Eysenck, S.B.G. (1969), *Personality Structure and Measurement* (London: Routledge & Kegan Paul).

Eysenck, M.W. (1977), *Human Memory: Theory, Research and Individual Differences* (Oxford: Pergamon).

Farrell, B.A. (1981), *The Standing of Psychoanalysis* (Oxford University Press).

Farrington, B. (1944, 1949), *Greek Science*, 2 vols (Harmondsworth: Penguin).

Fechner, G.T. (1966), *Elements of Psychophysics* (New York: Holt, Rinehart & Winston).

Fechner, G.T. (1876), *Vorschule der Aesthetik* (Leipzig).

Feigenbaum, E.A. and Feldman, J. (eds) (1963), *Computers and Thought* (New York: McGraw-Hill).

Feigl, H. (1967), *The 'mental' and the 'physical'*, 2nd edn with postscript (University of Minnesota Press).

Feigl, H., Scriven, M. and Maxwell, G. (1958), *Minnesota Studies in the Philosophy of Science. II. Concepts, Theories and the Mind-Body Problem* (University of Minnesota Press).

Ferster, C.B. and Skinner, B.F. (1957), *Schedules of Reinforcement* (New York: Appleton, Century, Crofts).

Feuerbach, L.A. (1935), *Kritik des 'anti-Hegel's'* (Ansbach).

Feyerabend, P. (1975), *Against Method* (London: NLB).

Field, G.C. (1949), *The Philosophy of Plato* (London: Butterworth).

Fine, R. (1979), *A History of Psychoanalysis* (Columbia University Press).

Firth, R. (ed.) (1957), *Man and Culture: An Evaluation of the Work of Bronislaw Malinowski* (London: Routledge & Kegan Paul).

Fisher, R.A. (1925), *Statistical Methods for Research Workers* (Edinburgh: Oliver & Boyd).

Fisher, R.A. (1930), *The Genetical Theory of Natural Selection* (Oxford: Clarendon Press).

Fisher, R.A. (1935), *The Design of Experiments* (Edinburgh: Oliver & Boyd).

Fisher, S. and Greenberg, R.P. (1977), *The Scientific Credibility of Freud's Theory and Therapy* (Brighton: Harvester).

Fiske, J. (1982), *Introduction to Communication Studies* (London: Methuen).

Flavell, J.H. (1963), *The Developmental Psychology of Jean Piaget* (Princeton: Van Nostrand).

Flexner, A. (1930), *Universities: American, English, German* (New York: Oxford University Press).

Flourens, P.J.M. (1824), *Reserches expérimentales sur les propriétés et les fonctions du système nerveux dans les animaux vertébrés* (Paris).

Flugel, J.C. (1955), *Studies in Feeling and Desire* (London: Duckworth).

Fortenbough, W.W. (1975), *Aristotle on Emotion* (London: Duckworth).

Fossey, D. (1983), *Gorillas in the Mist* (London: Hodder & Stoughton).

Foucault, M. (1967), *Madness and Civilization: A History of Insanity in the Age of Reason* (London: Tavistock).

Fraisse, P. (ed.) (1982), *Psychologie de demain* (Paris: Presses Universitaires de France).

Fraisse, P. and Piaget, J. (eds) (1968), *Experimental Psychology: Its Scope and Method*, vol.1, 'History and Method' (London: Routledge & Kegan Paul).

Frankfort, H., Wilson, J.A. and Jacobsen, T. (1949), *Before Philosophy* (Harmondsworth: Penguin).

Frazer, J.G. (1922), *The Golden Bough*, abridged edn (London: Macmillan).

Frazer, J.G. (1913), *Psyche's Task: The Devil's Advocate: A Plea for Superstition* (London: Macmillan).

Freeman, D. (1982), *Margaret Mead and Samoa: The Making and Unmaking of an Anthropological Myth* (Harvard University Press).

Frege, G. (1879), *Begriffschrift* (Halle).

Frege, G. (1950), *Foundations of Arithmetic* (Oxford: Blackwell).

Freud, S. (1953-74), *Complete Works* Standard Edition, 24 vols (London: Hogarth Press).

Freud, S. (1954), *The Origins of Psychoanalysis: Letters to Wilhelm Fliess, Drafts and Notes* ed. Bonaparte, M., Freud, A. and Kris, E. (London: Methuen).

Fuller, J.L. and Thompson, W.R. (1978), *Behavior Genetics*, 2nd edn (New York: Wiley).

Furst, L.R. (1969), *Romanticism in Perspective* (London: Macmillan).

Gadamer, H.G. (1975), *Truth and Method* (London: Sheed & Ward).

Galen, C. (1821-33), *Complete Works*, 22 vols (Leipzig).

Galen, C. (1916), *On the Natural Faculties*, vol. 71, Loeb Classical Library (London: Heinemann).

Galileo, G. (1623), *Il Saggiatore* (Rome: Lincei).

Galileo, G. (1953), *Dialogue concerning the Two Chief World Systems* (Chicago University Press).

Galileo, G. (1963), *Dialogues and Mathematical Demonstrations on Two New Sciences* (New York: McGraw-Hill).

Gall, F.J. (1819), *Anatomie et physiologie du système nerveux en général, et du cerveau en particulier* (Paris).

Galton, F. (1889), *Natural Inheritance* (London: Macmillan).

Galton, F. (1906), *Inquiries into Human Faculty and its Development* (London: Dent).

Gazzaniga, M.S. and Blakemore, C. (eds) (1975), *Handbook of Psychobiology* (New York: Academic Press).

Geldard, F.A. (1953), *The Human Senses* (London: Chapman & Hall).

Gellner, E. (1968), *Words and Things* (Harmondsworth: Penguin).

Gerard, A. (1774), *An Essay on Genius* (London).

Gergen, K.J. (1982), *Towards a Transformation in Social Knowledge* (New York: Springer).

Gibson, J.J. (1950), *The Perception of the Visual World* (Boston: Houghton Mifflin).

Gibson, J.J. (1966), *The Senses Considered as Perceptual Systems* (Boston: Houghton Mifflin).

Giddings, F.H. (1898), *Principles of Sociology* (New York: Macmillan).

Gilson, E. (1936), *The Spirit of Medieval Philosophy* (London: Sheed & Ward).

Ginsberg, M. (1931), *Sociology* (London: Thornton Butterworth).

Globus, C.G., Maxwell, G. and Savodnik, I. (eds) (1976), *Consciousness and the Brain* (New York: Plenum).

Glover, J. (1984), *What Sort of People Should There Be?* (Harmondsworth: Penguin).

Goffman, E. (1969), *The Presentation of Self in Everyday Life* (Harmondsworth: Penguin) (first published 1959).

Goodall, J. van L. (1971), *In the Shadow of Man* (New York: Dell).

Goodenough, F.L. (1949), *Mental Testing: Its History, Principles and Applications* (London: Staples).

Goody, J. (1977), *The Domestication of the Savage Mind* (Cambridge University Press).

Gordon, R.G. (1926), *Personality* (London, Kegan Paul, Trench & Trubner).

Graham, D. (1972), *Moral Learning and Development* (London: Batsford).

Grasher, A.F. (1978), *Practical Applications of Psychology* (Cambridge, Mass.: Winthrop).

Green, T.H. (1883), *Prolegomena to Ethics* (Oxford: Clarendon Press).

Greenberg, J.H. (ed.) (1978), *Universals of Human Language* (Stanford University Press).

Gregory, R.L. (1966), *Eye and Brain* (London: Weidenfield & Nicolson).

Gregory, R.L. (1981), *Mind in Science: A History of Explanations in Psychology and Physics* (London: Weidenfeld & Nicolson).

Griffiths, C.R. (1943), *Principles of Systematic Psychology* (University of Illinois Press).

Grimsley, R. (1973), *Søren Kierkegaard: A Biographical Introduction* (London: Studio Vista).

Gruber, H.E. (1974), *Darwin on Man* (London: Wildwood House).

Gruber, H.E. and Vonèche, J.J. (1977), *The Essential Piaget* (London: Routledge & Kegan Paul).

Guilford, J.P. (1967), *The Nature of Human Intelligence* (New York: McGraw-Hill).

Gustafson, J.M. (ed.) (1970), *Moral Education* (Harvard University Press).

Guthrie, W.K.C. (1950), *The Greek Philosophers: From Thales to Aristotle* (London: Methuen).

Guthrie, W.K.C. (1962-81), *A History of Greek Philosophy*, 6 vols (Cambridge University Press).

Guttenplan, S. (ed.) (1975), *Mind and Language* (Oxford: Clarendon Press).

Habermas, J. (1972), *Knowledge and Human Interests* (London: Heinemann).

Hacking, I. (1975), *The Emergence of Probability* (Cambridge University Press)

Hall, T.S. (1969), *History of General Physiology*, 2 vols (University of Chicago Press).

Haldane, J.B.S. (1932), *The Causes of Evolution* (London: Longmans Green).

Hale, N.G. (1971), *Freud and the Americans* (New York: Oxford University Press).

Haller, A.von (1765), *Primae Lineae Physiologae* (Edinburgh: Drummond).

Hallett, H.F. (1957), *Spinoza: Elements of his Philosophy* (London: Athlone Press).

Hallpike, C.R. (1979), *The Foundations of Primitive Thought* (Oxford: Clarendon Press).

Halsey, A.H. (ed.) (1977), *Heredity and Environment* (London: Methuen).

Hamblin, C.L. (1970), *Fallacies* (London: Methuen).

Hamilton, P. (1983), *Talcott Parsons* (London: Tavistock).

Hamilton, W. (1870), *Lectures on Metaphysics and Logic*, 2 vols (Edinburgh: Blackwood).

Hamlyn, D.W. (1984), *Metaphysics* (Cambridge University Press).

Hammond, W.A. (1902), *Aristotle's Psychology* (London: Swan Sonnenschein).

Hampshire, S. (1951), *Spinoza* (Harmondsworth: Penguin).

Harré, R. (1979), *Social Being: A Theory for Social Psychology* (Oxford: Blackwell).

Harré, R. (1983), *Personal Being: A Theory for Individual Psychology* (Oxford: Blackwell).

Harré, R. and Secord, P.T. (1972), *The Explanation of Social Behaviour* (Oxford: Blackwell).

Harris, C.R.S. (1927), *Duns Scotus*, 2 vols (Oxford University Press).

Harris, G.W. (1955), *Neural Control of the Pituitary Gland* (London: Arnold).

Harris, R.B. (ed.) (1982), *Neoplatonism and Indian Thought* (Albany: State University of New York Press).

Hartley, D. (1834), *Observations on Man* (London: Tegg) (first published 1749).

Hartmann, H. (1964), *Essays on Ego Psychology* (London: Hogarth Press).

Hayek, F. (1952), *The Sensory Order* (London: Routledge & Kegan Paul).

Hazard, P. (1965), *European Thought in the Eighteenth Century* (Harmondsworth: Penguin).

Head, H. (1926), *Aphasia and Kindred Disorders of Speech* (Cambridge University Press).

Hearnshaw, F.J.C. (1928), *A Survey of Socialism* (London: Macmillan).

Hearnshaw, L.S. (1964), *A Short History of British Psychology, 1840-1940* (London: Methuen).

Hearst, E. (ed.) (1979), *The First Century of Experimental Psychology* (Hillside: Erlbaum).

Hebb, D.O. (1949), *The Organization of Behavior: A Neuropsychological Theory* (New York: Wiley).

Hegel, G.W.F. (1857), *Lectures on the Philosophy of History* (London: Bohn).

Hegel, G.W.F. (1971), *Philosophy of Mind* (Oxford: Clarendon Press).

Heidbredder, E. (1933), *Seven Psychologies* (New York: Century).

Heidegger, M. (1978), *Basic Writings* ed. Krell, D.F. (London: Routledge & Kegan Paul).

Heisenberg, W. (1958), *The Physicist's Conception of Nature* (London: Hutchinson).

Helmholtz, H. (1875), *Sensations of Tone* (London : Longmans).

Helmholtz, H. (1889), *Über die Erhaltung der Kraft* (Leipzig) (first published 1847).

Helmholtz, H. (1893), *Popular Lectures on Scientific Subjects*, 2 vols (London: Longmans).

Helmholtz, H. (1924), *Treatise on Physiological Optics*, 3 vols (New York:

Optical Society of America).
Helvetius, C.A. (1758), *De l'Esprit* (Paris).
Helvetius, C.A. (1773), *De l'Homme: de ses facultés et de son education* (London).
Henle, M. (ed.) (1961), *Documents of Gestalt Psychology* (University of California Press).
Henry, P. (1960), *St Augustine on Personality* (New York: Macmillan).
Herbart, J.F. (1824-5), *Psychologie als Wissenschaft* (Königsburg).
Herbart, J.F. (1891), *Textbook of Psychology* (New York: Appleton).
Herder, J.G. (1968), *Ideas towards a Philosophy of History* (University of Chicago Press).
Herrnstein, R.J. and Boring, E.G. (eds) (1965), *A Source Book in the History of Psychology* (Harvard University Press).
Hesse, M. (1980), *Revolutions and Reconstructions in the Philosophy of Science* (Brighton: Harvester).
Hessing, S. (ed.) (1977), *Speculum Spinozanum* (London: Routledge & Kegan Paul).
Hinde, R.A. (1970), *Animal Behaviour: A Synthesis of Ethology and Comparative Psychology*, 2nd edn (New York: McGraw-Hill).
Hinde, R.A. (1982), *Ethology* (Oxford University Press).
Hinde, R.A. (ed.) (1972), *Non-Verbal Communication* (Cambridge University Press).
Hippocrates (1923-31), *Works*, 4 vols, Loeb Classical Library, vols 147-50 (London: Heinemann).
Hirsch, E.D. (1967), *Validity in Interpretation* (Yale University Press).
Hobbes, T. (1839-45), *Works* (London, William Molesworth).
Hobhouse, L.T. (1913), *Development and Purpose* (London: Macmillan).
Hobhouse, L.T. (1915), *Mind in Evolution*, 2nd edn (London: Macmillan).
Hobhouse, L.T. (1966), *Sociology and Philosophy* (London: Bell).
Hodges, A. (1983), *Alan Turing: The Enigma* (London: Burnett Books).
Hodges, H.A. (1944), *Wilhelm Dilthey: An Introduction* (London: Kegan Paul, Trench, Trubner).
Hoeveler, D. (1980), *James McCosh and the Scottish Intellectual Tradition* (Princeton University Press).
Höffding, H. (1900), *History of Modern Philosophy* (New York: Macmillan).
Hofstadter, D.R. (1979), *Gödel, Escher, Bach: An Eternal Golden Braid* (Brighton: Harvester).
Hofstadter, D.R. and Dennett, D.C. (1982), *The Mind's I: Fantasies and Reflections on Self and Soul* (Harmondsworth: Penguin).
Holland, H. (1852), *Chapters on Mental Physiology* (London: Longmans Green).
Hollingdale, R.J. (1973), *Nietzsche* (London: Routledge & Kegan Paul).
Hollingdale, R.J. (1977), *A Nietzsche Reader* (Harmondsworth: Penguin).
Home Office (1980), *Review of the Prison Psychological Service* (London: HMSO).
Honigman, J.J. (ed.) (1973), *Handbook of Social and Cultural Anthropology* (Chicago: Rand McNally).
Honour, H. (1981), *Romanticism* (Harmondsworth. Penguin).
Hooke, R. (1938), *Micrographia* (Oxford University Press) (first published 1665).
Hooykaas, R. (1972), *Religion and the Rise of Modern Science* (Edinburgh: Scottish Academic Press).
Hughes, H.S. (1959), *Consciousness and Society: The Reorientation of European Social Thought, 1890-1930* (London: MacGibbon & Kee).

Huizinga, J. (1965), *The Waning of the Middle Ages* (Harmondsworth: Penguin).

Hull, C.L. (1943), *Principles of Behavior: An Introduction to Behavior Theory* (New York: Appleton, Century, Crofts).

Hull, C.L. (1952), *A Behavior System* (Yale University Press).

Hume, D. (1957), *An Enquiry Concerning the Principles of Morals* (Oxford: Clarendon Press) (first published 1751).

Hume, D. (1975), *An Enquiry Concerning Human Understanding* (Oxford: Clarendon Press).

Hume, D. (1978), *A Treatise of Human Nature* (Oxford: Clarendon Press) (first published 1740).

Humphrey, G. (1951), *Thinking: An Introduction to its Experimental Psychology* (London: Methuen).

Hunt, E.B. (1962), *Concept Learning: An Information Processing Problem* (New York: Wiley).

Hunter, R. and Macalpine, I. (1963), *Three Hundred Years of Psychiatry, 1535-1860* (Oxford University Press).

Husserl, E. (1962), *Ideas: General Introduction to Pure Phenomenology* (New York: Collier).

Husserl, E. (1965a), *Phenomenology and the Crisis of Philosophy* (New York: Harper & Row).

Husserl, E. (1965b), *Logical Investigations* (London: Routledge & Kegan Paul).

Husserl, E. (1975), *The Paris Lectures* (The Hague: Nijhoff).

Huxley, T.H. (1893-4), *Collected Essays*, 9 vols (London: Macmillan).

Hyman, A. (1982), *Charles Babbage: Pioneer of the Computer* (Oxford University Press).

Infeld, L. (1941), *Quest: The Evolution of a Scientist* (London: Gollancz).

Inge, W.R. (1926), *The Platonic Tradition in English Religious Thought* (London: Longmans Green).

Isaacs, S. (1930), *The Intellectual Growth of Young Children* (London: Routledge).

Jackson, J.H. (1931), *Selected Writings* (London: Hodder & Stoughton).

Jacob, F. (1974), *The Logic of Living Systems* (London: Lane).

Jacob, F. (1982), *The Possible and the Actual* (New York: Random House).

Jaeger, W. (1934), *Aristotle* (Oxford: Clarendon Press).

Jahoda, G. (1969), *The Psychology of Superstition* (London: Lane).

Jahoda, G. (1982), *Psychology and Anthropology* (New York: Academic Press).

James, H. (ed.) (1920), *The Letters of William James*, 2 vols (London: Longmans, Green).

James, W. (1890), *Principles of Psychology* 2 vols (London: Macmillan).

James, W. (1892), *Psychology: A Briefer Course* (London: Macmillan).

James, W. (1896), *The Will to Believe and Other Essays* (New York: (Longmans Green).

James, W. (1907), *Pragmatism* (New York: Longmans Green).

James, W. (1909), *The Meaning of Truth* (New York: Longmans Green).

James, W. (1909), *A Pluralistic Universe* (New York: Longmans Green).

James, W. (1911), *Some Problems of Philosophy* (New York: Longmans Green).

James, W. (1912), *Essays in Radical Empiricism* (New York: Longmans Green).

James, W. (1937), *The Varieties of Religious Experience* (London: Longmans Green) (first published 1902).

Janet, P.M.F. (1889), *L'Automatisme psychologique* (Paris: Evreux).

Janet, P.M.F. (1920), *The Mental State of Hysterics* (New York: Putnam).
Janet, P.M.F. (1925), *Psychological Healing*, 2 vols (London: Allen & Unwin).
Jardine, L. (1974), *Francis Bacon: Discovery and the Art of Discourse* (Cambridge University Press).
Jaynes, J. (1976), *The Origins of Consciousness in the Breakdown of the Bicameral Mind* (Boston: Houghton Mifflin).
Jeffress, L.A. (ed.) (1951), *Cerebral Mechanisms in Behavior: The Hixon Symposium* (New York: Wiley).
Jensen, A.R. (1973), *Educability and Group Differences* (London: Methuen).
Jensen, A.R. (1981), *Bias in Mental Testing* (London: Methuen).
Johnson-Laird, P.N. (1983), *Mental Models: Towards a Cognitive Science of Language, Inference and Consciousness* (Cambridge University Press).
Johnson-Laird, P.N. and Wason, P.C. (1972), *The Psychology of Reasoning: Structure and Content* (London: Batsford).
Jones, E. (1953-7), *Sigmund Freud: Life and Work*, 3 vols (London: Hogarth Press).
Jones, H.S. (1922), *General Astronomy* (London: Arnold).
Jones, K. (1955), *Lunacy, Law and Conscience, 1744-1845* (London: Routledge & Kegan Paul).
Jones, M.R. and Arnold, W.J. (eds) (1953-), *Nebraska Symposia on Motivation* (Nebraska University Press).
Judson, H.F. (1979), *The Eighth Day of Creation: Makers of the Revolution in Biology* (London: Cape).
Jung, C.G. (1953-77), *Collected Works*, 19 vols (London: Routledge & Kegan Paul).
Kahn, C.H. (1979), *The Art and Thought of Heraclitus* (Cambridge University Press).
Kamenka, E. (ed.; (1983), *The Portable Karl Marx* (Harmondsworth: Penguin).
Kant, I. (1755), *General History of Nature and Theory of the Heavens* (Zeitz).
Kant, I. (1914), *Critique of Judgment* (London: Macmillan).
Kant, I. (1933), *Critique of Pure Reason* (London: Macmillan).
Kant, I. (1949), *Critique of Practical Reason* (Chicago University Press).
Kant, I. (1970), *Metaphysical Foundations of Natural Science* (Indianapolis: Liberal Arts).
Kant, I. (1974a), *Introduction to Logic* (Indianapolis: Liberal Arts).
Kant, I. (1974b), *Anthropology from a Pragmatic Point of View* (The Hague: Nijhoff).
Kardiner, A. (1939), *The Individual and Society* (Columbia University Press).
Kashap, S.P. (ed.) (1972), *Studies in Spinoza* (University of Californai Press).
Katz, B. (1966), *Nerve, Muscle and Synapse* (New York: McGraw-Hill).
Katz, D. (1935), *The World of Colour* (London: Kegan Paul, Trench & Trubner).
Kaufmann, W. (1959), *From Shakespeare to Existentialism* (Princeton University Press).
Kausler, D.H. (1982), *Experimental Psychology and Human Aging* (New York: Wlley).
Kay-Shuttleworth, J.P. (1932), *The Moral and Physical Conditions of the Working-class Employed in the Cotton Manufacture in Manchester* (London: Ridgway).
Kazdin, A.E. (1978), *History of Behavior Modification* (Baltimore: University Park Press).
Keeling, S.V. (1934), *Descartes* (London: Benn).

Keen, E. (1970), *Three Faces of Being: Toward an Existential Clinical Psychology* (New York: Appleton, Century, Crofts).

Kelly, G.A. (1955), *The Psychology of Personal Constructs* (New York: Norton).

Kemp Smith, N. (1918), *A Commentary to Kant's Critique of Pure Reason* (London: Macmillan).

Kenny, A. (1973a), *The Anatomy of the Soul* (Oxford: Blackwell).

Kenny, A. (1973b), *Wittgenstein* (Harmondsworth: Penguin).

Kenny, A. (1980), *Aquinas* (Oxford University Press).

Kepler, J. (1858-71), *Opera* 8 vols (Stuttgart).

Keyes, G.L. (1966), *Christian Faith and the Interpretation of History: A Study of St Augustine's Philosophy of History* (University of Nebraska Press).

Keyserling, H. (1925), *The Travel Diary of a Philosopher* (London: Cape).

Kierkegaard, S. (1944), *Either/Or: A Fragment of Life* (Princeton University Press).

Kierkegaard, S. (1980), *The Concept of Anxiety* (Princeton University Press).

King, G. (1810), *Natural and Political Observations and Conclusions upon the State and Condition of England* (London).

Kirk, G.S. and Raven, J.E. (1957), *The Pre-Socratic Philosophers* (Cambridge University Press).

Klibansky, R. (1939), *The Continuity of the Platonic Tradition during the Middle Ages* (London: Warburg Institute).

Kline, M. (1972), *Mathematics in Western Culture* (Harmondsworth: Penguin).

Kline, P. (1972), *Fact and Fantasy in Freudian Theory* (London: Methuen).

Knowles, D. (1962), *The Evolution of Medieval Thought* (London: Longmans).

Koch, S. (ed.) (1959-63), *Psychology: A Study of a Science*, 6 vols (New York: McGraw-Hill).

Koenigsberger, L. (1965), *Hermann von Helmholtz* (New York: Dover Books).

Koestler, A. and Smythies, J.R. (eds) (1969), *Beyond Reductionism: The Alpach Symposium* (London: Hutchinson).

Koffka, K. (1924), *The Growth of the Mind: An Introduction to Child Psychology* (London: Kegan Paul, Trench & Trubner).

Koffka, K. (1936), *Principles of Gestalt Psychology* (London: Kegan Paul, Trench & Trubner).

Köhler, W. (1925), *The Mentality of Apes* (London: Kegan Paul, Trench & Trubner).

Köhler, W. (1938), *The Place of Value in a World of Fact* (New York: Liveright).

Kosslyn, S.M. (1980), *Image and Mind* (Harvard University Press).

Koyré, A. (1957), *From the Closed World to the Infinite Universe* (Johns Hopkins University Press).

Kraepelin, E. (1895-1927), *Psychologisches Arbeiten*, 9 vols (Leipzig).

Kraft-Ebbing, R. (1965), *Psychopathia Sexualis* (London: Staples).

Krantz, D.L. (ed.) (1969), *Schools of Psychology: A Symposium* (New York: Appleton, Century, Crofts).

Krawiec, T.S. (ed.) (1978), *The Psychologists*, vol.3 (Brandon: Clinical Psychology Publishing Co.).

Kretschmer, E. (1925), *Physique and Character* (London: Kegan Paul, Trench & Trubner).

Kristeller, P.O. (1972), *Renaissance Concepts of Man* (New York: Harper & Row).

Kuhn, T.S. (1957), *The Copernican Revolution* (Cambridge, Mass: MIT Press).

Kuhn, T.S. (1970), *The Structure of Scientific Revolutions* (University of Chicago Press) (originally published 1962).

Kuhn, T.S. (1977), *The Essential Tension* (University of Chicago Press).

Külpe, O. (1895), *Outlines of Psychology* (London: Allen & Unwin).

Lack, D. (1953), *The Life of the Robin* (Harmondsworth: Penguin)

Lahy, J.M. (1927), *La Selection psychophysiologique des travailleurs: conducteurs de tramways et d'autobus* (Paris).

Lakatos, I. and Musgrave, A. (eds) (1970), *Criticism and the Growth of Knowledge* (Cambridge University Press).

La Mettrie, J. (1748), *L'Homme Machine* (Paris).

Langer, S. (1942), *Philosophy in a New Key: A Study in the Symbolism of Reason, Rite and Art* (Harvard University Press).

Langer, S. (1964), *Philosophical Sketches* (New York: Mentor Books).

Langer, S. (1967), *Mind: An Essay on Human Feeling*, 3 vols (Baltimore: Johns Hopkins University Press).

Langley, J.N. (1921), *The Autonomic Nervous System* (Cambridge: Heffer).

Lavoisier, A.L. (1790), *Elements of Chemistry* (Edinburgh: Creech).

Laycock, T. (1860), *Mind and Brain* (Edinburgh: Sutherland & Knox).

Leach, E. (1970), *Lévi-Strauss* (Glasgow: Fontana).

Leakey, R. and Lewin, R. (1979), *People of the Lake* (London: Collins).

Le Bon, G. (1920), *The Crowd: A Study of the Popular Mind* (London: Unwin) (first published 1895).

Lecky, W.E.H. (1911), *History of European Morals from Augustus to Charlemagne* (London: Longmans Green).

Lee, S.G. and Herbert, M. (1970), *Freud and Psychology* (Harmondsworth: Penguin).

Lefèvre, C. (1972), *Sur l'evolution d' Aristote en psychologie* (Louvain: Wulf-Mansion).

Leibniz, G.W. (1898), *The Monadology and other Philosophical Writings* ed. Latta, R. (Oxford: Clarendon Press).

Leibniz, G.W. (1952), *Theodicée* (London: Routledge & Kegan Paul).

Leibniz, G.W. (1956), *Philosophical Papers and Letters*, 2 vols, ed. Loemker, L.S. (Chicago University Press).

Leibniz, G.W. (1981), *New Essays on Human Understanding* ed. Remnant, P. and Bennett, J. (Cambridge University Press).

Lenin, V.I. (1947), *Materialism and Empirio-Criticism* (Moscow: Foreign Languages Publishing House).

Lenneberg, E.H. (1967), *Biological Foundations of Language* (New York: Wiley).

Leonardo da Vinci (1953), *Notebooks*, Selections, ed. Richter, I.A. (Oxford University Press).

Levine, S. (ed.) (1972), *Hormones and Behavior* (New York: Academic Press).

Lévi-Strauss, C. (1963), *Structural Anthropology* (Harmondsworth: Penguin).

Lévi-Strauss, C. (1964-71), *Mythologiques*, 4 vols (Paris: Plon).

Lévi-Strauss, C. (1976), *Tristes Tropiques* (Harmondsworth: Penguin).

Levy-Bruhl, L. (1923), *Primitive Mentality* (London: Allen & Unwin).

Levy-Bruhl, L. (1926), *How Natives Think* (London: Allen & Unwin).

Levy-Bruhl, L. (1928), *The 'Soul' of the Primitive* (London: Allen & Unwin).

Lewes, G.H. (1853), *Comte's Philosophy of the Sciences* (London: Bohn).

Lewin, K. (1935), *A Dynamic Theory of Personality* (New York: McGraw-Hill).

Lewin, K. (1936), *Principles of Topological Psychology* (New York: McGraw-Hill).

Lewin, K. (1957), *Field Theory in Social Science: Selected Theoretical Papers* (New York: Harper).

Lewis, C.I. (1929), *Mind and the World Order* (London: Scribners).

Liben, L.S. (1983), *Piaget and the Foundations of Knowledge* (Hillside: Erlbaum).

Liddell, E.G.T. (1960), *The Discovery of Reflexes* (Oxford: Clarendon Press).

Lindsay, P.H. and Norman, D.A. (1977), *Human Information Processing: An Introduction to Psychology* (New York: Academic Press).

Lindzey, G. and Aronson, E. (eds), *The Handbook of Social Psychology* 2nd edn 1969, 5 vols (Reading: Addison-Wesley).

Lissak, K. (ed.) (1973), *Hormones and Brain Function* (New York: Plenum).

Lloyd, G.E.R. (1979), *Magic, Reason and Experience* (Cambridge University Press).

Locke, J. (1928), *Selections*, ed. Lamprecht, S.P. (New York: Scribners).

Locke, J. (1975), *Essay Concerning Human Understanding*, ed. Nidditch, P.H. (Oxford: Clarendon Press).

Loeb, J. (1912), *The Mechanistic Conception of Life* (Chicago University Press).

Loemker, L.E. (1972), *Struggle for Synthesis: The Seventeenth Century Background of Leibniz's Synthesis of Order and Freedom* (Harvard University Press).

Lomov, B.F. (1963), *Chelovek i Technika: Ocherky Inzhenernoi Psychologii* (in Russian) (Leningrad University Press).

Long, A.A. (1974), *Hellenistic Philosophy: Stoics, Epicureans, Sceptics* (London: Duckworth).

Lorenz, K. (1952), *King Solomon's Ring* (London: Methuen).

Lorenz, K. (1966), *On Aggression* (London: Methuen).

Lotze, R.H. (1852), *Medizinsche Psychologie, oder Physiologie der Seele* (Leipzig).

Lowrie, W. (1938), *Kierkegaard* (Oxford University Press).

Luce, R.D., Bush, R.R. and Galanter, E. (eds) (1963), *Handbook of Mathematical Psychology*, 2 vols (New York: Wiley).

Lucretius. (1951), *On the Nature of the Universe* (Harmondsworth: Penguin).

Luria, A.R. (1973), *The Working Brain: An Introduction to Neuropsychology* (Harmondsworth: Penguin).

Luria, A.R. (1976), *Cognitive Development: Its Cultural and Social Foundations* (Harvard University Press).

Luria, A.R. (1979), *The Making of Mind: A Personal Account of Soviet Psychology*, ed. Cole, M. and Cole, S. (Harvard University Press).

Luther, M. (1969), *De Servo Arbitrio*, in *Luther and Erasmus* (London: SCM Press).

Lyell, C. (1830-3), *Principles of Geology* (London: Murray).

Lyman, F.L. (ed.) (1963), *Phenylketonuria* (Springfield, Ill.: Thomas).

Lynd, R.S. and Lynd, H.M. (1929), *Middletown* (London: Constable).

Lynd, R.S. and Lynd, H.M. (1937), *Middletown in Transition* (London: Constable).

McCosh, J. (1860), *The Intuitions of the Mind* (London: Murray).

McCosh, J. (1880), *The Emotions* (London: Macmillan).

McCosh, J. (1886), *Psychology: The Cognitive Powers* (New York: Scribners).

McCosh, J. (1887), *Psychology: The Motive Powers, Emotions, Conscience and Will* (New York: Scribners).

McDougall, W. (1908), *An Introdcution to Social Psychology* (London: Methuen).

McDougall, W. (1923), *An Outline of Psychology* (London: Methuen).

McGuire, W.J. (ed.) (1974), *The Freud-Jung Letters* (London: Hogarth Press).
Mackay, D.M. (1969), *Information, Mechanism and Meaning* (Cambridge, Mass.: MIT Press).
McKeller, P. (1957), *Imagination and Thinking* (London: Cohen & West).
McKenna, W.R. (1982), *Husserl's Introductions to Phenomenology* (The Hague: Nijhoff).
McKeon, R. (ed.) (1930-1), *Selections from Medieval Philosophers*, 2 vols (New York: Scribners).
Mackworth, J.F. (1969), *Vigilance and Habituation: A Neuropsychological Approach* (Harmondsworth: Penguin).
Mackworth, J.F. (1970), *Vigilance and Attention: A Signal Detection Approach* (Harmondsworth: Penguin).
Mackworth, N.H. (1950), *Researches on the Measurement of Human Performance* (London: HMSO).
McLeish, J. (1975), *Soviet Psychology: History, Theory, Content* (London: Methuen).
Macquarrie, J. (1973), *Existentialism* (Harmondsworth: Penguin).
McRae, R. (1976), *Leibniz: Perception, Apperception and Thought* (Toronto University Press).
Madsen, K.B. (1968), *Theories of Motivation*, 4th edn (Copenhagen: Munskgaard).
Magee, B. (1973), *Popper* (London: Fontana-Collins).
Malcolm, N. (1970), *Studies in the Theory of Knowledge* (Oxford: Blackwell).
Malinowski, B. (1922), *Argonauts of the Western Pacific* (London: Routledge).
Malinowski, B. (1926), *Crime and Custom in Savage Society* (London: Kegan Paul).
Malinowski, B. (1927), *Sex and Repression in Savage Society* (London: Routledge).
Malinowski, B. (1929), *The Sexual Life of Savages* (London: Routledge).
Mandrou, R. (1978), *From Humanism to Science, 1480-1700*, Pelican History of European Thought, vol.3 (Harmondsworth: Penguin).
Mannheim, K. (1936), *Ideology and Utopia* (London: Kegan Paul, Trench & Trubner).
Mannheim, K. (1940), *Man and Society in an Age of Reconstruction* (London: Kegan Paul, Trench & Trubner).
Mannheim, K. (1952), *Essays on the Sociology of Knowledge* (London: Routledge & Kegan Paul).
Markus, R.A. (ed.) (1972), *Augustine: A Collection of Critical Essays* (New York: Doubleday).
Marr, D. (1982), *Vision* (San Fransisco: Freeman).
Marrou, H. (1957), *St Augustine and His Influence through the Ages* (New York: Harper).
Martinez, J.L. *et al.* (1981), *Endogenous Peptides and Learning and Memory Processes* (New York: Academic Press).
Marx, K. (1981), *The Portable Karl Marx* ed. Kamenka, E. (Harmondsworth: Penguin).
Marx, K. and Engels, F (1948), *The Communist Manifesto* (London: Allen & Unwin).
Marx, M.H. and Hillix, W.A. (1973), *Systems and Theories in Psychology* 2nd edn (New York: Macmillan).
Maslow, A.H. (1962), *Toward a Psychology of Being* (Princeton: Van Nostrand).
Maudsley, H. (1867), *The Physiology and Pathology of Mind* (London: Macmillan).

Max Müller, F. (ed.) (1875-1900), *The Sacred Books of the East*, 51 vols (Oxford University Press).

May, R. *et al.* (eds) (1958), *Existence* (New York: Basic Books).

May, R. (ed.) (1967), *Existential Psychology* (New York: Random House).

Mayo, E. (1933), *Human Problems of an Industrial Civilization* (New York: Macmillan).

Mead, G.H. (1971), *Mind, Self and Society: From the Standpoint of a Social Behaviorist* (Chicago University Press).

Mead, M. (1935), *Sex and Temperament in Three Primitive Societies* (New York: Morrow).

Mead, M. (1928), *Coming of Age in Samoa* (New York: Morrow).

Mead, M. (1930), *Growing up in New Guinea* (New York: Morrow).

Medawar, P.B. and Medawar, J.S. (1977), *The Life Science* (London: Wildwood House).

Melzack, R. (1973), *The Puzzle of Pain* (Harmondsworth: Penguin).

Mercier, D.F.F.J. (1892), *Psychologie* 2 vols (Louvain: Bibliothèque de Philosophie).

Merleau-Ponty, M. (1964), *Phenomenology of Perception* (London: Routledge & Kegan Paul).

Merz, J.T. (1896-1904), *A History of European Thought in the Nineteenth Century*, 4 vols (Edinburgh: Blackwood).

Mesmer, F. (1948), *Mesmerism* (London: Macdonald).

Meumann, E. (1899), *Die Sprache des Kindes* (Zurich).

Meumann, E. (1905), *Experimentelle Pädagogik*, 2 vols (Leipzig: Engelmann).

Michie, D. (1974), *On Machine Intelligence* (Edinburgh University Press).

Michotte, A. (1963), *The Perception of Causality* (London: Methuen).

Midgley, M. (1978), *Beast and Man* (Brighton: Harvester).

Milgram, S. (1974), *Obedience to Authority* (New York: Harper & Row).

Mill, J. (1829), *Analysis of the Phenomena of the Human Mind* (London: Baldwin & Craddock).

Mill, J.S. (1859-75), *Dissertations and Discussions: Political, Philosophical and Historical*, 4 vols (London: J.W. Parker).

Mill, J.S. (1906), *A System of Logic* (London: Longmans) (first published 1843).

Miller, G.A. (1907), *The Psychology of Communication* (Harmondsworth: Penguin).

Miller, G.A. (1981), *Language and Speech* (San Fransisco: Freeman).

Miller, G.A., Gallanter, E. and Pribram, K.H. (1960), *Plans and the Structure of Behavior* (New York: Holt).

Mills, C.W. (1959), *The Sociological Imagination* (New York: Oxford University Press).

Milman, H.H. (1909), *A History of the Jews*, 2 vols (London: Dent).

Ministry of Munitions (1918), *Final Report of the Health of Munition Workers Committee* (London: HMSO).

Mirandola, P.della (1978), *On the Dignity of Man*, in Davies, S. (ed.), *Renaissance Views of Man* (Manchester University Press).

Misiak, H. and Staudt, V.M. (1954), *Catholics in Psychology* (New York: McGraw-Hill).

Modgil, S. and Modgil, C. (1974), *Piagetian Research: A Handbook of Recent Studies* (Windsor: NFER).

Modgil, S. and Midgil, C. (1976), *Piagetian Research*, 8 vols (Windsor: NFER).

Moll, A. (1891), *Die Conträre Sexualempfindung* (Perversions of the Sex Instinct) (Berlin).

Molyneux, W. (1692), *Dioptrika Nova* (London).

Monod, J. (1972), *Chance and Necessity* (London: Collins).

Montaigne, M. de (1928), *Essays* (London: Dent).

Montesquieu, C.L. (1743), *Esprit des Lois* (Paris).

Moore, G.E. (1922), *Philosophical Studies* (London: Routledge & Kegan Paul).

Moore-Ede, M.C. *et al.* (1982), *The Clocks that Time Us* (Harvard University Press).

Morgan, C.L. (1890), *Animal Life and Intelligence* (London: Arnold).

Morgan, C.L. (1894), *Introduction to Comparative Psychology* (London: Scott).

Morgan, C.L. (1896), *Habit and Instinct* (London: Arnold).

Morgan, C.L. (1900), *Animal Behaviour* (London: Arnold).

Morgan, C.L. (1923), *Emergent Evolution* (London: Williams & Norgate).

Morgan, T.H. *et al.* (1915), *The Mechanism of Mendelian Heredity* (London: Constable).

Morris, C.W. (1946), *Signs, Language and Behavior* (New York: Prentice-Hall).

Mosso, A. (1904), *Fatigue* (London: Allen & Unwin).

Mowrer, O.H. (1960), *Learning Theory and Behavior* (New York: Wiley).

Mowrer, O.H. (1960), *Learning Theory and Symbolic Processes* (New York: Wiley).

Muirhead, J.H. (1931), *The Platonic Tradition in Anglo-Saxon Philosophy* (London: Allen & Unwin).

Müller, J. (1837-42), *Handbook of Human Physiology* (London: Taylor & Walker).

Müller-Frienfels, R. (1935), *The Evolution of Modern Psychology* (Yale University Press).

Munn, N.L. (1946), *Psychology: The Fundamentals of Human Adjustment* (Boston: Houghton Mifflin).

Münsterberg, H. (1908), *On the Witness Stand* (New York: Clark, Boardman).

Münsterberg, H. (1913), *Psychology and Industrial Efficiency* (London: Constable).

Murchison, C. (ed.) (1926), *Psychologies of 1925* (Clark University Press).

Murchison, C. (ed.) (1930), *Psychologies of 1930* (Clark University Press).

Murchison, C. (ed.) (1931), *A Handbook of Child Psychology* (Clark University Press).

Murchison, C. (ed.) (1935), *Handbook of Social Psychology* (Clark University Press).

Murchison, C. (ed.) (1930-52), *A History of Psychology in Autobiography*, 4 vols (Clark University Press).

Murphy, G. (1929), *An Historical Introduction to Modern Psychology* (London: Kegan Paul, Trench & Trubner).

Murphy, G. (1947), *Personality: A Biosocial Approach to its Origins and Structure* (New York: Harper).

Murphy, G., Murphy, L.B. and Newcomb, T.M. (1937), *Experimental Social Psychology*, 2nd edn (New York: Harper).

Murray, H.A. (1938), *Explorations in Personality* (New York: Oxford University Press).

Murray, H.A. (1943), *Thematic Apperception Test Manual* (Harvard University Press).

Murray, O. (1980), *Early Greece* (London: Fontana).

Murrell, K.F.H. (1965), *Ergonomics: Man in his Working Environment* (London: Chapman & Hall).

Mussen, P.H. (ed.) (1970), *Carmichael's Manual of Child Psychology*, 2 vols (New York: Wiley).

Mussen, P.H. (ed.) (1983), *Handbook of Child Psychology*, 4 vols (New York: Wiley).

Mussen, P.H., Conger, J.J. and Kagan, J. (1979), *Child Development and Personality* 5th edn (New York: Harper & Row).

Myers, C.S. (1925), *A Textbook of Experimental Psychology*, 3rd edn, (Cambridge University Press).

Myers, C.S. (1940), *Shell Shock in France, 1914-18* (Cambridge University Press).

Myers, F.W.H. (1906), *Human Personality and its Survival of Bodily Death* (London: Longmans, Green).

Nagel, E. (1961), *The Structure of Science* (London: Routledge & Kegan Paul).

Needham, J. (1978), *The Shorter Science and Civilization in China*, ed. Ronan, C.A., vol.1 (Cambridge University Press).

Neel, A. (1977), *Theories of Psychology: A Handbook*, revised edn (Cambridge, Mass: Schenkman).

Neisser, U. (1967), *Cognitive Psychology* (New York: Appleton, Century, Crofts).

Neisser, U. (1976), *Cognition and Reality: Principles and Implications of Cognitive Psychology* (San Fransisco: Freeman).

Neisser, U. (1982), *Memory Observed: Remembering in Natural Contexts* (San Fransisco: Freeman).

Neu, J. (1977), *Emotion, Thought and Therapy* (London: Routledge & Kegan Paul).

Neurath, O. *et al.* (eds) (1938-55), *International Encyclopedia of Unified Science* (Chicago University Press).

Newell, A. and Simon, H.A. (1972), *Human Problem Solving* (New York: Prentice-Hall).

Newton, I. (1931), *Opticks* (London: Bell).

Newton, I. (1969), *Philosophia Naturalis Principia Mathematica* (London: Dawsons).

Newton-Smith, W.H. (1980), *The Structure of Time* (London: Routledge & Kegan Paul).

Nidditch, P.H. (1962), *The Development of Mathematical Logic* (London: Routledge & Kegan Paul).

Niebuhr, R. (1941), *The Nature and Destiny of Man*, 2 vols (New York: Scribners).

Nietzsche, F. (1968), *Basic Writings*, ed. Kaufmann, W. (New York: Modern Library).

Norris, J. (1701), *Essay towards the Theory of the Ideal or Intelligible World* (London).

Novotny, F. (1977), *The Posthumous Life of Plato* (The Hague: Nijhoff).

O'Connor, D.J. (1952), *John Locke* (Harmondsworth: Penguin).

Office of Strategic Services (1948), *Assessment of Men* (New York: Rinehart).

Oldfield, R.C. and Marshall, J.C. (eds) (1968), *Language: Selected Readings* (Harmondsworth: Penguin).

Oldroyd, D.R. (1980), *Darwinian Impacts* (Milton Keynes: Open University Press).

Onians, R.B. (1954), *The Origins of European Thought* (Cambridge University Press).

Orenstein, A. (1977), *Willard van Orman Quine* (Boston: Twayne).

Ornstein, R.E. (1972), *The Psychology of Consciousness* (San Fransisco: Freeman).

Ornstein, R.E. (ed.) (1973), *The Nature of Human Consciousness: A Book of*

Readings (San Fransisco: Freeman).

Organ, T.W. (1949), *Index to Aristotle* (Princeton University Press).

Osgood, C.E. (1953), *Method and Theory in Experimental Psychology* (New York: Oxford University Press).

Oswald, I. (1962), *Sleep and Waking: Physiology and Psychology* (Amsterdam: Elsevier).

Paivio, A. (1971), *Imagery and Verbal Processes* (New York: Holt, Rinehart & Winston).

Paley, W. (1802), *Natural Theology* (London: Wilks & Taylor).

Palmer, R. (1969), *Hermeneutics: Interpretation Theory in Schleiermacher, Dilthey, Heidegger and Gadamer* (Evanston, Ill.: Northwestern University Press).

Park, R.E. *et al.* (1925), *The City* (Chicago University Press).

Parry, T. (1967), *The Psychology of Human Communication* (University of London Press).

Parsons, T. (1937), *The Structure of Social Action* (New York: McGraw-Hill).

Parsons, T. (1951), *The Social System* (New York: Free Press).

Parsons, T. (1977), *Social Systems and the Evolution of Action Theory* (New York: Free Press).

Passmore, J. (1966), *A Hundred Years of Philosophy* (London: Duckworth).

Pastore, N. (1971), *Selective History of Theories of Visual Perception, 1650-1950* (Oxford University Press).

Pavlov, I.P. (1927), *Conditioned Reflexes: An Investigation of the Physiological Activity of the Cerebral Cortex* (Oxford University Press).

Pavlov, I.P. (1928), *Lectures on Conditioned Reflexes* (London: Lawrence).

Pavlov, I.P. (1961), *Psychopathology and Psychiatry: Selected Works* (Moscow: Foreign Languages Publishing House).

Pears, D. (1971), *Wittgenstein* (London: Fontana/Collins).

Peel, E.A. (1960), *The Pupil's Thinking* (London: Oldbourne).

Peel, J.D.Y. (1971), *Herbert Spencer: The Evolution of a Sociologist* (London: Heinemann).

Penniman, T.K. (1935), *A Hundred Years of Anthropology* (London: Duckworth).

Penrose, L.S. (1963), *The Biology of Mental Defect*, revised edn (London: Sidgwick & Jackson).

Perry, W.B. (1935), *The Thought and Character of William James*, 2 vols (London: Longmans Green).

Peters, R.S. (1956), *Hobbes* (Harmondsworth: Penguin).

Peters, R.S. (1958), *The Concept of Motivation* (London: Routledge & Kegan Paul).

Petrarch, F. (1958), *De sui ipsius et multorum Ignorantia* (Venice: Grimaldo).

Pfaff, D.W. (ed.) (1982), *The Physiological Mechanisms of Motivation* (New York: Springer).

Piaget, J. (1926), *The Language and Thought of the Child* (London: Kegan Paul, Trench & Trubner).

Piaget, J. (1927), *Judgment and Reasoning in the Child* (London: Kegan Paul, Trench & Trubner)

Piaget, J. (1930), *The Child's Conception of Physical Causality* (London: Kegan Paul, Trench & Trubner).

Piaget, J. (1932), *The Moral Judgment of the Child* (London: Kegan Paul, Trench & Trubner).

Piaget, J. (1942), *Traité de Logique* (Paris: Vrin).

Piaget, J. (1951), *Play, Dreams and Imitation in Childhood* (London: Heinemann).

Piaget, J. (1953), *Logic and Psychology* (Manchester University Press).
Piaget, J. (1955), *The Child's Construction of Reality* (London: Routledge & Kegan Paul).
Piaget, J. (1956), *The Child's Conception of Space* (with B. Inhelder) (London: Routledge & Kegan Paul).
Piaget, J. (1958), *The Growth of Logical Thinking: From Childhood to Adolescence* (with B. Inhelder) (London: Routledge & Kegan Paul).
Piaget, J. (1969), *The Child's Conception of Time* (London: Routledge & Kegan Paul).
Piaget, J. (1970), *Genetic Epistemology* (Columbia University Press).
Piaget, J. (1971a), *Biology and Knowledge* (Edinburgh University Press).
Piaget, J. (1971b), *Structuralism* (London: Routledge & Kegan Paul).
Piaget, J. (1971c), *Insights and Illusions of Philosophy* (London: Routledge & Kegan Paul).
Piaget, J. (1972a), *Essai de Logique Operatoire* (Paris: Dunod).
Piaget, J. (1972b), *Psychology and Epistemology: Towards a Theory of Knowledge* (Harmondsworth: Penguin).
Pièron, H. (1956), *The Sensations: Their Functions, Processes and Mechanisms* (London: Garnett Miller).
Plamenatz, J. (1975), *Karl Marx's Philosophy of Man* (Oxford: Clarendon Press).
Plato. (1914-29), *Dialogues*, 12 vols, Loeb Classical Library (London: Heinemann).
Plotinus, (1929), *Select Works* (London: Bell).
Plotinus (1966-84), *The Enneads*, 6 vols, Loeb Classical Library (London: Heinemann).
Polanyi, M. (1955), *Personal Knowledge* (London: Routledge & Kegan Paul).
Polanyi, M. (1959), *The Study of Man* (London: Routledge & Kegan Paul).
Polanyi, M. (1967), *The Tacit Dimension* (London: Routledge & Kegan Paul).
Polanyi, M. and Prosch, H. (1975), *Meaning* (University of Chicago Press).
Polkinghorne, J.C. (1984), *The Quantum World* (London: Longman).
Pollock, F. (1880), *Spinoza: His Life and Philosophy* (London: Kegan Paul).
Pomponazzi, P. (1954), *De Immortalitate Animae* (Bologna).
Pope, K.S. and Singer, J.L. (eds) (1978), *The Stream of Consciousness* (New York: Wiley).
Pope, W. (1976), *Durkheim's Suicide: A Classic Analysed* (Chicago University Press).
Popper, K.R. (1945), *The Open Society and its Enemies*, 2 vols (London: Routledge & Kegan Paul).
Popper, K.R. (1957), *The Poverty of Historicism* (London: Routledge & Kegan Paul).
Popper, K.R. (1959), *The Logic of Scientific Discovery* (London: Hutchinson).
Popper, K.R. (1963), *Conjectures and Refutations: The Growth of Scientific Knowledge* (London: Routledge & Kegan Paul).
Popper, K.R. (1972), *Objective Knowledge: An Evolutionary Approach* (Oxford: Clarendon Press).
Popper, K.S. and Eccles, J.C. (1983), *The Self and its Brain* (London: Routledge & Kegan Paul).
Potter, S. (1960), *Language in the Modern World* (Harmondsworth: Penguin).
Pratt, C.C. (1939), *The Logic of Modern Psychology* (New York: Macmillan).
Preyer, W.T. (1893), *The Mind of the Child* (New York: Appleton).
Pribram, K.H. (ed.) (1969), *Brain and Behaviour* 4 vols (Harmondsworth: Penguin).

Price-Williams, D.R. (ed.) (1969), *Cross-Cultural Studies* (Harmondsworth: Penguin).

Priestley, J. (1775), *Hartley's Theory of the Human Mind on the Principle of the Association of Ideas* (London).

Prince, M. (1906), *The Dissociation of a Personality* (New York: Longmans Green).

Privy Council Office (1947), *Report of an Expert Committee on the Work of Psychologists and Psychiatrists in the Services* (London: HMSO).

Ptolemy, C. (1515), *Almagest* (Venice).

Quine, W.V.O. (1953), *From a Logical Point of View* (Harvard University Press).

Quinton, A. (1980), *Francis Bacon* (Oxford University Press).

Rabbitt, P.M.A. and Dornie, S. (eds) (1975), *Attention and Performance, V* (London: Academic Press).

Radcliffe-Brown, A.R. (1958), *Method in Social Anthropology: Collected Essays* (Chicago University Press).

Radhakrishnan, S. (1939), *Eastern Religions and Western Thought* (Oxford University Press).

Rand, B. (ed.) (1912), *The Classical Psychologists* (New York: Houghton Mifflin).

Randall, J.H. (1976), *The Making of the Modern Mind* (Columbia University Press) (first published 1926).

Rapaport, D. (1951), *The Organization and Pathology of Thought* (Columbia University Press).

Razran, G. (1971), *Mind in Evolution* (Boston: Houghton Mifflin).

Rée, J. (1974), *Descartes* (London: Lane).

Reid, T. (1895), *The Works of Thomas Reid*, ed. Hamilton, W., 8th edn (Edinburgh: Thin).

Reid, T. (1941), *Intellectual Powers*, abridged edn, ed. Woozley, A.A. (London: Macmillan).

Reinhardt, K. (1916), *Parmenides und die Geschichte der Greschischen Philosophie* (Bonn).

Reiss, M. (1958), *Psychoneuroendocrinology* (New York: Grune & Stratton).

Rescher, N. (1979), *Leibniz: An Introduction to his Philosophy* (Oxford: Blackwell).

Resnick, L.B. (ed.) (1976), *The Nature of Intelligence* (Hillsdale: Erlbaum).

Ribot, T. (1882), *Heredité: étude psychologique* (Paris).

Ribot, T. (1883), *Les Maladies de la volonté* (Paris).

Ribot, T. (1885), *Les Maladies de la Personnalité* (Paris: Alcan).

Ribot, T. (1886), *German Psychology* (New York: Scribners).

Ribot, T. (1889), *English Psychology* (London: Kegan Paul, Trench).

Ribot, T. (1890), *The Psychology of Attention* (Chicago: Open Court).

Ribot, T. (1896), *La Psychologie des sentiments* (Paris).

Ribot, T. (1899), *The Evolution of General Ideas* (London: Kegan Paul, Trench).

Ribot, T. (1900), *Creative Imagination* (London: Kegan Paul, Trench).

Ribot, T. (1906), *Essai sur les passions* (Paris).

Ribot, T. (1912), *The Psychology of the Emotions* (New York: Scribners).

Richardson, A. (1969), *Mental Imagery* (London: Routledge & Kegan Paul).

Richardson, J.T.E. (1980), *Mental Imagery and Human Memory* (New York: St Martin's).

Richmond, M. (1917), *Social Diagnosis* (New York: Russell Sage Foundation).

Ricoeur, P. (1981), *Hermeneutics and the Human Sciences* (Cambridge University Press).

Rieber, R.W. (ed.) (1980), *Wilhelm Wundt and the Making of Scientific*

Psychology (New York: Plenum).

Rieber, R.W. and Salzinger, K. (eds) (1980), *Psychology: Theoretical-Historical Perspectives* (New York: Academic Press).

Rieff, D. (1960), *Freud: The Mind of the Moralist* (London: Gollancz).

Rivers, W.H.R. (1926), *Psychology and Ethnology* (London: Kegan Paul, Trench & Trubner).

Roback, A.A. (1927), *The Psychology of Character* (London: Kegan Paul, Trench & Trubner).

Roback, A.A. (1964), *History of American Psychology* (New York: Collier).

Robinson, D.N. (ed.) (1978), *Significant Contributions to the History of Psychology*, 7 vols (Washington: University Publications of America).

Robinson, D.N. (1981), *An Intellectual History of Psychology* (New York: Macmillan).

Robinson, T.M. (1970), *Plato's Psychology* (Toronto University Press).

Rokeach, M. (1973), *The Nature of Human Values* (New York: Free Press).

Rose, J. (ed.) (1969), *Survey of Cybernetics: A Tribute to Dr Norbert Wiener* (London: Iliffe).

Rose, S. (1979), *The Chemistry of Life* (Harmondsworth: Penguin).

Ross, D. (1972), *G. Stanley Hall: The Psychologist as Prophet* (Chicago University Press).

Ross, E.A. (1908), *Social Psychology* (New York: Macmillan).

Ross, W.D. (1923), *Aristotle* (London: Methuen).

Rossi, P. (1968), *Francis Bacon: From Magic to Science* (London: Routledge & Kegan Paul).

Rousseau, J.J. (1905), *Emile* (London: Dent).

Rousseau, J.J. (1953), *Confessions* (Harmondsworth: Penguin).

Rousseau, J.J. (1968), *The Social Contract* (Harmondsworth: Penguin).

Rousseau, J.J. (1984), *Discourse on Inequality* (Harmondsworth: Penguin).

Rowntree, B.S. (1922), *Poverty: A Study of Town Life* (London: Macmillan).

Royce, J.R. (ed.) (1970), *Toward Unification in Psychology*, First Banff Conference on Theoretical Psychology (University of Toronto Press).

Rubinshtein, S.L. (1959), *Printsipy i Puti Razviti Psychologii* (Moscow: Izd. Akad. Nauk. SSSR).

Rusk, R.R. (1919), *Experimental Education* (London: Longmans).

Russell, B.A.W. (1900), *A Critical Exposition of the Philosophy of Leibniz* (Cambridge University Press).

Russell, B.A.W. (1921), *The Analysis of Mind* (London: Allen & Unwin).

Russell, B.A.W. (1946), *A History of Western Philosophy* (London: Allen & Unwin).

Russell, J. (1978), *The Acquisition of Knowledge* (London: Macmillan).

Rychlak, J.F. (1977), *The Psychology of Rigorous Humanism* (New York: Wiley).

Ryle, G. (1949), *The Concept of Mind* (London: Hutchinson).

Ryle, G. *et al.* (1956), *The Revolution in Philosophy* (London: Macmillan).

Sallis, J. (ed.) (1981), *Merleau-Ponty: Perception, Structure and Language* (Atlantic Highlands: Humanities Press).

Sanford, E.C. (1897), *A Course in Experimental Psychology* (Boston: Heath).

Savage, C.W. (1970), *The Measurement of Sensation* (University of California Press).

Savage, L.J. (1954), *The Foundations of Statistics* (London: Chapman & Hall).

Schaefer, K.E. (ed.) (1962), *Environmental Effects on Consciousness* (New York: Macmillan).

Schenk, H.G. (1966), *The Mind of the European Romantics* (London: Constable).

Schleiermacher, F. (1928), *Hermeneutik und Kritik* (Berlin: Reimer).
Schlipp, P.A. (ed.) (1974), *The Philosophy of Karl Popper*, 2 vols (La Salle: Open Court).
Schopenhauer, A. (1928), *Selections*, ed. Parker, D.H. (New York: Scribners).
Schwartz, G.E., Shapiro, D. and Davidson, R.J. (eds) (1976-83), *Consciousness and Self-Regulation*, 3 vols (New York: Plenum).
Science Research Council (1973), *Artificial Intelligence: A Paper Symposium* (London: Science Research Council).
Scientific American (1982), *Human Communication: Language and its Psychobiological Basis* (San Fransisco: Freeman).
Searle, J.R. (1979), *Expression and Meaning* (Cambridge University Press).
Searle, J.R. (1983), *Intentionality: An Essay in the Philosophy of Mind* (Cambridge University Press).
Searle, J.R. (1984), *Minds, Brains and Science*, The Reith Lectures (London: BBC).
Sebeok, T.A. (ed.) (1977), *How Animals Communicate* (Indiana University Press).
Sechenov, I. (1965), *Reflexes of the Brain* (Cambridge, Mass: MIT Press).
Segall, M.H., Campbell, D.T. and Herskovits, M.T. (1966), *The Influence of Culture on Visual Perception* (Indianapolis: Bobbs-Merrill).
Selye, H. (1950), *Stress* (Montreal: Acta).
Selye, H. (1956), *The Stress of Life* (New York: McGraw-Hill).
Semon, R. (1921), *Mneme* (London: Macmillan).
Senden, M.von (1960), *Space and Sight* (London: Methuen).
Sexton, V.S. and Misiak, H. (eds) (1976), *Psychology Around the World* (Monterey: Brooks-Cole).
Shaftesbury, A.A.C. (1699), *An Enquiry concerning Virtue* (London).
Shand, A.F. (1914), *The Foundations of Character* (London: Macmillan).
Shannon, C.E. (1948), *Programming a Computer for Playing Chess* (Bell Telephone Laboratory).
Sheldon, W.H. and Stevens, S.S. (1942), *The Varieties of Temperament* (New York: Harper).
Shelley, P.B. (1919), *The Defence of Poetry* (London: Macmillan).
Sheriff, M. (1966), *The Psychology of Social Norms* (New York: Harper).
Sherrington, C.S. (1940), *Man on His Nature* (Cambridge University Press).
Sherrington, C.S. (1947), *The Integrative Action of the Nervous System* (Cambridge University Press).
Shipley, T. (ed.) (1961), *Classics in Psychology* (New York: Philosophical Library).
Shu, F.H. (1982), *The Physical Universe: An Introduction to Astronomy* (Mill Vale, California: University Science Books).
Siegal, R.E. (1968-73), *Galen's System of Physiology and Medicine*, 3 vols (Basel: Karger).
Sigal, I.E., Brodzinsky, D.M. and Golinkopf, R.M. (eds) (1981), *New Directions in Piagetian Theory and Practice* (Hillsdale, New Jersey: Erlbaum).
Simon, B. (1978), *Mind and Madness in Ancient Greece* (Cornell University Press).
Singer, C.J. (1959), *A Short History of Scientific Ideas to 1900* (Oxford: Clarendon Press).
Skinner, D.F. (1938), *The Behavior of Organisms* (New York: Appleton-Century).
Skinner, B.F. (1948), *Walden Two* (New York: Macmillan).
Skinner, B.F. (1953), *Science and Human Behavior* (New York: Macmillan).

Skinner, B.F. (1957), *Verbal Behavior* (New York: Appleton, Century, Crofts).

Skinner, B.F. (1971), *Beyond Freedom and Dignity* (London: Cape).

Slobin, D.I. (1979), *Psycholinguistics* (Glenview: Scott, Foresman).

Slobodin, R. (1978), *W.H.R. Rivers* (Columbia University Press).

Sluckin, W. (ed.) (1971), *Early Learning and Early Experience* (Harmondsworth: Penguin).

Small, A.W. (1905), *General Sociology* (Chicago University Press).

Smart, J.J.C. (1963), *Philosophy and Scientific Realism* (London: Routledge & Kegan Paul).

Smith, A. (1759), *Theory of Moral Sentiments* (London) (first published 1751).

Smith, F.V. (1960), *Explanation of Human Behaviour* (London: Constable).

Snell, B. (1953), *The Discovery of the Mind* (Oxford: Blackwell).

Sokolov, E.N. (1963), *Perception and the Conditioned Reflex* (New York: Pergamon).

Sokolov, E.N. (1970), *Nervnie Mechanismi Orienternochnogo Refleksa* (Moscow: Akad. Pedagog. Nauk).

Sorabji, R. (1972), *Aristotle on Memory* (London: Duckworth).

Sorokin, P. (1941), *The Crisis of our Age* (Sydney: Angus & Robertson).

Spearman, C.E. (1923), *The Nature of Intelligence and the Principles of Cognition* (London: Macmillan).

Spearman, C.E. (1927), *The Abilities of Man* (London: Macmillan).

Spearman, C.E. (1937), *Psychology down the Ages*, 2 vols (London: Macmillan).

Spencer, B. and Gillen, F.J. (1899), *The Native Tribes of Central Australia* (London: Macmillan).

Spencer, B. and Gillen, F.J. (1904), *The Northern Tribes of Central Australia* (London: Macmillan).

Spencer, B. and Gillen, F.J. (1927), *The Arunta: A Stone-Age People* (London: Macmillan).

Spencer, H. (1870), *The Principles of Psychology*, 2 vols (London: Williams & Norgate).

Spencer, H. (1873), *The Study of Sociology* (London: Williams & Norgate).

Spencer, H. (1876), *The Principles of Sociology*, 2 vols (London, Williams & Norgate).

Spencer, H. (1892), *Social Statics* (London: Williams & Norgate).

Spencer, H. (1904), *Autobiography*, 2 vols (London: Williams & Norgate).

Spencer, H. (1911), *Education, Intellectual, Moral and Physical* (London: Williams & Norgate).

Sperry, R. (1983), *Science and Moral Priority* (Oxford: Blackwell).

Spinoza, B. (1930), *Selections*, ed. Wild, J. (New York: Scribners).

Stebbing, L.S. (1933), *A Modern Introduction to Logic* (London: Methuen).

Steinberg, H. (ed.) (1964), *Animal Behaviour and Drug Action* (London: Churchill).

Stephenson, W. (1953), *The Study of Behavior: Q-technique and its Methodology* (University of Chicago Press).

Stern, C. and Stern, W. (1907), *Die Kindersprache* (Leipzig: Barth).

Stern, W. (1900), *Über Psychologie der individuellen Differenzen* (Leipzig: Barth).

Stern, W. (1902), *Beiträge zur Psychologie der Aussage* (Leipzig: Barth).

Stern, W. (1906), *Psychologie der Veränderungsauffassung* (Breslau: Preuss u Jünger).

Stern, W. (1906-24), *Person und Sache*, 3 vols (Leipzig: Barth).

Stern, W. (1914), *Psychological Methods of Testing Intelligence* (Baltimore: Warwick & York).

Stern, W. (1930), *The Psychology of Early Childhood up to the Sixth Year of Life* (London: Allen & Unwin).

Stern, W. (1938), *General Psychology from the Personalistic Standpoint* (New York: Macmillan).

Stevens, S.S. (ed.) (1951), *Handbook of Experimental Psychology* (New York: Wiley).

Stevens, S.S. (1975), *Psychophysics* (New York: Wiley).

Stevenson, G.S. (1934), *Child Guidance Clinics* (New York: Commonwealth Fund).

Stewart, D. (1827), *Elements of the Philosophy of the Human Mind*, 2 vols (Edinburgh: Constable).

Stone, C.P. (ed.) (1951), *Comparative Psychology* (New York: Prentice-Hall).

Stouffer, S.A. *et al.* (1949), *The American Soldier*, 2 vols (Princeton University Press).

Stout, G.F. (1896), *Analytical Psychology*, 2 vols (London: Sonnenschein).

Stout, G.F. (1899), *A Manual of Psychology* (London: University Tutorial Press).

Strachan-Davidson, J.L. (1925), *Cicero and the Fall of the Roman Republic* (London: Putnam).

Stratton, G.M. (1917), *Theophrastus and the Greek Physiological Psychology before Aristotle* (London: Allen & Unwin).

Strawson, P.F. (1959), *Individuals* (London: Methuen).

Sulloway, F.J. (1979), *Freud: Biologist of the Mind* (New York: Basic Books).

Sully, J. (1884), *Outlines of Psychology* (London: Longmans Green).

Sully, J. (1886), *The Teacher's Handbook of Psychology* (London: Longmans Green).

Sully, J. (1892), *The Human Mind: A Textbook of Psychology*, 2 vols (London: Longmans Green).

Sully, J. (1896), *Studies of Childhood* (London: Longmans Green).

Sumner, W.G. (1906), *Folkways* (Boston: Ginn).

Szasz, T. (1961), *The Myth of Mental Illness* (London: Secker & Warburg).

Tacitus (1931), *Histories* vol.3, Loeb Classical Library, vol.249 (London: Heinemann).

Tagore, R. (1921), *Sadhana: The Realisation of Life* (London: Macmillan).

Tagore, R. (1931), *The Religion of Man* (London: Allen & Unwin).

Taine, H.A. (1871), *On Intelligence* (London: Reeve).

Tajfel, H.J. (1981), *Human Groups and Social Categories* (Cambridge University Press).

Tart, C.T. (1975), *States of Consciousness* (New York: Dalton).

Tart, C.T. (ed.) (1975), *Transpersonal Psychologies* (London: Routledge & Kegan Paul).

Taylor, C. (1964), *The Explanation of Behaviour* (London: Routledge & Kegan Paul).

Taylor, C. (1975), *Hegel* (Cambridge University Press).

Tetens, J.N. (1776), *Philosophische Versuche über die menschliche Natur und Ihre Entwicklung* (Leipzig)

Theophrastus (1929), *Characters*, Loeb Classical Library, vol.225 (London: Heinemann).

Thinès, G. (1977), *Phenomenology and the Science of Behaviour* (London: Allen & Unwin).

Thomas, W.I. and Snaniecki, F. (1927), *The Polish Peasant in Europe and America* (New York: Knopf).

Thompson, J.B. (1981), *Critical Hermeneutics: A Study in the Thought of Paul Ricoeur and Jürgen Habermas* (Cambridge University Press).

Thomson, G. (1977), *The First Philosophers* (London: Lawrence & Wishart).

Thorlby, A. (1966), *The Romantic Movement* (London: Longmans).

Thorndike, E. (1913-14), *Educational Psychology*, 3 vols (Columbia University Press).

Thorpe, W.H. (1961), *Bird Song* (Cambridge University Press).

Thorpe, W.H. (1956), *Learning and Instinct in Animals* (London: Methuen).

Thorpe, W.H. (1978), *Purpose in a World of Chance: A Biologist's View* (Oxford University Press).

Thorpe, W.H. (1979), *The Origins and Rise of Ethology* (London: Heinemann).

Thudichum, J.W.L. (1884), *A Treatise on the Chemical Composition of the Brain* (London: Tindall & Cox).

Thurstone, L.L. (1947), *Multiple Factor Analysis* (Chicago University Press).

Tinbergen, N. (1951), *The Study of Instinct* (Oxford: Clarendon Press).

Tipton, I.C. (ed.) (1977), *Locke on Human Understanding* (Oxford University Press).

Titchener, E.B. (1896), *An Outline of Psychology* (New York: Macmillan).

Titchener, E.B. (1901-5), *Experimental Psychology: A Manual of Laboratory Practice*, 4 vols (New York: Macmillan).

Titchener, E.B. (1908), *Lectures on the Elementary Psychology of Feeling and Attention* (New York: Macmillan).

Titchener, E.B. (1909a), *Lectures on the Experimental Psychology of the Thought Processes* (New York: Macmillan).

Titchener, E.B. (1909b), *A Textbook of Psychology* (New York: Macmillan).

Tolman, E.C. (1932), *Purposive Behavior in Animals and Man* (New York: Appleton, Century, Crofts).

Toulmin, S. and Goodfield, J. (1965), *The Discovery of Time* (London: Hutchinson).

Triandis, H., Lamberg, W., Berry, J., Lonner, W. and Heron, A. (eds) (1980-1), *A Handbook of Cross-Cultural Psychology*, 6 vols (Boston: Allyn & Bacon).

Tuke, D.H. (1884), *Illustrations of the Influence of the Mind upon the Body in Health and Disease*, 2 vols (London: Churchill).

Tulving, E. (1983), *Elements of Episodic Memory* (New York: Oxford University Press).

Tylor, E.B. (1865), *Researches into the Early History of Mankind* (London: Murray).

Tylor, E.B. (1871), *Primitive Culture*, 2 vols (London: Murray).

Underwood, G. (ed.) (1978), *Strategies in Information Processing* (New York: Academic Press).

Underwood, G. (ed.) (1981-2), *Aspects of Consciousness*, 3 vols (London: Academic Press).

University Commission to Advise on the Future of Psychology at Harvard (1947), *The Place of Psychology in an Ideal University* (Harvard University Press).

Valentine, C.W. (1942), *The Psychology of Early Childhood* (London: Methuen).

Valle, R.S. and King, M. (1978), *Existential-Phenomenological Alternatives for Psychology* (New York: Oxford University Press).

Van Steenberghen, F. (1970), *Aristotle in the West* (Louvain).

Veith, I. (1965), *Hysteria: The History of a Disease* (Chicago University Press).

Venables, V. (1946), *Human Nature: The Marxian View* (London: Dobson).

Vernon, M.D. (1969), *Human Motivation* (Cambridge University Press).

Vernon, P.E. and Parry, J.B. (1949), *Personnel Selection in the British Forces* (University of London Press).

Vesalius, A. (1952), *De Humani Corporis Fabrica* (Oxford University Press).
Vico, G. (1948), *The New Science of Giambattista Vico* (Cornell University Press).
Vigo, G. (1965), *On the Study Methods of our Time* (New York: Bobbs-Merrill).
Vinacke, W.E. (1952), *The Psychology of Thinking* (New York: McGraw-Hill).
Viteles, M.S. (1933), *Industrial Psychology* (London: Cape).
Voloshinov, V.N. (1976), *Freudianism: A Marxist Critique* (New York: Academic Press).
Voltaire, F.M.A. (1758), *Essai sur les Moeurs* (Edinburgh: Donaldson).
Von Bertalanffy, L. (1968), *General System Theory: Foundations, Development, Applications* (New York: Braziller).
Von Neumann, J. and Morgenstern, O. (1947), *The Theory of Games and Economic Behavior* (Princeton University Press).
Von Neumann, J. (1958), *The Computer and the Brain* (Yale University Press).
Von Wright, G.H. (1951), *Treatise on Probability and Induction* (London: Routledge & Kegan Paul).
Von Wright, GH. (1983), *Wittgenstein* (Oxford: Blackwell).
Vygotsky, L.S. (1962), *Thought and Language* (Cambridge, Mass: MIT Press).
Vygotsky, L.S. (1978), *Mind in Society: The Development of the Higher Psychological Processes* ed. Cole, M. *et al.* (Harvard University Press).
Waddington, C.H. (1973), *Operational Research in World War II* (London: Elek).
Wagner, R. (1846), *Handwörterbuch der Physiologie* (Brunswick: Venag).
Walter, W.G. (1953), *The Living Brain* (London: Chapman & Hall).
Wang, W.S.Y. (ed.) (1982), *Human Communication: Language and its Psychological Bases* (San Francisco: Freeman).
Wann, T.W. (ed.) (1964), *Behaviorism and Phenomenology: Contrasting Bases for Modern Psychology* (Chicago University Press).
Ward, J. (1920), *Psychological Principles* (Cambridge University Press).
Ward, J. (1926), *Psychology Applied to Education* (Cambridge University Press).
Ward, L.F. (1898), *Outlines of Sociology* (New York: Macmillan).
War Office (1922), *Report of the Committee of Enquiry into Shell Shock* (London: HMSO).
Warren, H.C. (1921), *A History of Association Psychology* (London: Constable).
Warren, R.M. and Warren, R.D. (1968), *Helmholtz on Perception* (New York: Wiley).
Washburn, M. (1926), *The Animal Mind* (New York: Macmillan).
Wason, P.C. and Johnson-Laird, P.N. (eds) (1968), *Thinking and Reasoning* (Harmondsworth: Penguin).
Watkins, J.W.N. (1965), *Hobbes's System of Ideas* (London: Hutchinson).
Watson, J.B. (1924), *Behaviorism* (London: Kegan, Paul, Trench & Trubner).
Watson, J.B. (1929), *Psychology from the Standpoint of a Behaviorist* (Philadelphia: Lipincott)
Watson, R.I. (1963), *The Great Psychologists* (Philadelphia: Lipincott).
Weber, M. (1948), *The Protestant Ethic and the Spirit of Capitalism* (London: Allen & Unwin).
Weber, M. (1978), *Selections in Translation*, ed. Runciman, W.G. (Cambridge University Press).
Webster, C.K. (1975), *The Great Instauration* (London: Duckworth)
Wechsler, D. (1952), *The Range of Human Capacities* (London: Ballière).

Weinberg, S. (1983), *The Discovery of Subatomic Particles* (New York: Scientific American Books).

Weitz, R. (ed.) (1974), *Non-Verbal Communication: Readings with a Commetary* (New York: Oxford University Press).

Welford, A.T. (1968), *Fundamentals of Skill* (London: Methuen).

Welford, A.T. (ed.) (1980), *Reaction Times* (London: Academic Press).

Wellek, R. (1931), *Immanuel Kant in England, 1793-1838* (Princeton University Press).

Wells, B. (1973), *Psychedelic Drugs: Psychological, Medical and Social Issues* (Harmondsworth: Penguin).

Werner, H. (1948), *Comparative Psychology of Mental Development* (Chicago: Follett).

Wertheimer, M. (1925), *Über Gestalttheorie* (Erlangen).

Wertheimer, M. (1945), *Productive Thinking* (London: Tavistock).

Westfall, R.S. (1971), *The Construction of Modern Science* (Cambridge University Press).

Westfall, R.S. (1980), *Never at Rest: a Biography of Isaac Newton* (Cambridge University Press).

Whitehead, A.N. (1926), *Science and the Modern World* (Cambridge University Press).

White House (1962), *Proceedings of the White House Conference on Narcotics and Drug Abuse* (Washington: Government Printing Office).

Whyte, L.L. (1960), *The Unconscious before Freud* (New York: Basic Books).

Whyte, L.L. (1965), *Internal Factors in Evolution* (New York: Braziller).

Wiener, N. (1948), *Cybernetics: Or Control and Communication in the Animal and the Machine* (New York: Wiley).

Wiener, N. (1950), *The Human Use of Human Beings* (Boston: Houghton Mifflin).

Willey, B. (1934), *The Seventeenth Century Background* (London: Chatto & Windus).

Willey, B. (1940), *The Eighteenth Century Background* (London: Chatto & Windus).

Willis, T. (1664), *Anatomy of the Brain* (London).

Willis, T. (1683), *The Soul of Brutes* (London: Dring).

Wilson, E.O. (1975), *Sociobiology: The New Synthesis* (Harvard University Press).

Wilson, E.O. (1978), *On Human Nature* (Harvard University Press).

Winograd, T. (1972), *Understanding Natural Language* (Edinburgh University Press).

Wittgenstein, L. (1922), *Tractatus Logico-Philosophicus* (London: Kegan Paul, Trench & Trubner).

Wittgenstein, L. (1953), *Philosophical Investigations* (Oxford: Blackwell).

Wolff, C. (1965-), *Gesammelte Schriften*, 51 vols (Hildesheim: Olms).

Wolman, B.B. (ed.) (1965), *Scientific Psychology* (New York: Basic Books).

Wolman, B.B. (1968), *Historical Roots of Contemporary Psychology* (New York: Harper & Row).

Wolman, B.B. (ed.) (1973), *Handbook of General Psychology* (Englewood Cliffs: Prentice-Hall).

Wood, O.P. and Pitcher, G. (eds), *Ryle* (London: Macmillan).

Wood, T.H. (1973), *Alfred Binet* (Chicago University Press).

Woodger, J.H. (1929), *Biological Principles* (London: Kegan Paul, Trench & Trubner).

Woodruff Smith, D. and McIntyre, R. (1982), *Husserl and Intentionality* (Dorderecht: Reidel).

Woodworth, R.S. (1918), *Dynamic Psychology* (Columbia University Press).
Woodworth, R.S. (1921), *Psychology: The Study of Mental Life* (London: Methuen).
Woodworth, R.S. (1938), *Experimental Psychology* (New York: Holt).
Woodworth, R.S. and Sheehan, M.R. (1964), *Contemporary Schools of Psychology* (London: Methuen).
Woodworth, R.S. and Marquis, D.G. (1949), *Psychology*, 20th edn (London: Methuen).
Woodworth, R.S. and Schlosberg, R. (1954), *Experimental Psychology*, 2nd edn (New York: Holt).
Wooton, B. (ed.) (1961, 1965), *Reports of the Interdepartmental Committee on Drug Addiction* (London: HMSO).
Wundt, W. (1862), *Beiträge zur Theorie des Sinneswahrnehmung* (Leipzig: Winter).
Wundt, W. (1894), *Lectures on Human and Animal Psychology* (London: Macmillan).
Wundt, W. (1897), *An Outline of Psychology* (New York: Stechert).
Wundt, W. (1906-8), *Logik*, 3 vols (Stuttgart: Enke).
Wundt, W. (1908-11), *Grundzüge der physiologischen Psychologie*, 3 vols, 6th edn (Leipzig: Englemann).
Wundt, W. (1912), *An Introduction to Psychology* (London: Allen & Unwin).
Wundt, W. (1900-20), *Völkerpsychologie*, 10 vols (Leipzig: Engelmann).
Wundt, W. (1916), *Elements of Folk Psychology* (London: Allen & Unwin).
Wyatt, S. and Langdon, J.N. (1932), *Inspection Processes in Industry: A Preliminary Report*, Industrial Health Research Board, Report 63 (London: HMSO).
Yaroshevsky, M.F. (1971), *Psychologia v XX Stoletii* (Moscow: Political Literature Publishing House).
Yates, F. (1964), *Giordano Bruno and the Hermetic Tradition* (Bari: Latzera).
Yates, F. (1966), *The Art of Memory* (London: Routledge & Kegan Paul).
Yerkes, R.M. and Yerkes, A. (1929), *The Great Apes* (Yale University Press).
Young, J.Z. (1971), *An Introduction to the Study of Man* (Oxford University Press).
Young, J.Z. (1978), *Programs of the Brain* (Oxford University Press).
Young, K. (1946), *Handbook of Social Psychology* (London: Kegan Paul, Trench & Trubner).
Zangwill, O. (1961), *Cerebral Dominance and its Relation to Psychological Function* (Edinburgh: Oliver & Boyd).
Ziehen, T. (1895), *Introduction to Physiological Psychology* (London: Sonnenschein).
Zubek, J.P. (ed.) (1969), *Sensory Deprivation: Fifteen Years of Research* (New York: Appleton, Century, Crofts).
Zuckerman, S. (1932), *The Social Life of Monkeys and Apes* (London: Kegan Paul, Trench & Trubner).
Zukav, O. (1979), *The Dancing Wu Li Masters: An Overview of the New Physics* (London: Rider-Hutchinson).

Name index

Subject index

Laila, age 9

'Your book was so good it made me
stop fighting with my sister'

Adam, age 8

'This story was the first ever one that made me and my dad
cry and laugh at the exact same time!'

Cerys, age 7

'The story made me care about things I hadn't
thought of before and want to help people'

Musa, age 7

because

...this is no ...acts

...rage and friendship'

AWARDS FOR ONJALI Q. RAÚF'S BOOKS

Winner of the Blue Peter Book Award for Best Story 2019

Winner of the Waterstone's Children's Book Prize 2019

Shortlisted for the Branford Boase Award 2019

Shortlisted for the Independent Bookshop Week Award
for Children's Book 2019 and 2021

Shortlisted for the Jhalak Prize Book of the Year 2019

Carnegie Award 2019 Nominee

Shortlisted for Children's Fiction Book of the Year 2020
at the British Book Awards

Winner of Diverse Book Award's Best Children's Book 2020

Winner of Concorde Book Award 2020

Winner of the Golden Cowbell Book Award,
Switzerland 2020

ORION CHILDREN'S BOOKS

First published in Great Britain in 2021
by Hodder & Stoughton

1 3 5 7 9 10 8 6 4 2

A CIP catalogue record for this book is available from the British Library.

Typeset in Sabon by Avon DataSet Ltd, Arden Court, Alcester, Warwickshire

ISBN 978 1 51010 675 8
WTS ISBN 978 1 510 11061 8

Printed and bound in Great Britain by Clays Ltd, Elcograf, S.p.A.

The paper and board used in this book are made
from wood from responsible sources.

MIX
Paper from
responsible sources
FSC
www.fsc.org   FSC® C104740

Orion Children's Books
An imprint of Hachette Children's Group
Part of Hodder & Stoughton Limited
Carmelite House
50 Victoria Embankment
London EC4Y 0DZ

An Hachette UK Company

www.hachette.co.uk
www.hachettechildrens.co.uk

THE
LION above the DOOR

ONJALI Q. RAUF
অঞ্জলি ক. রাউফ

Orion

Dedicated to the bravery of:

Tan Kay Hai
Elizabeth Choy
Birendra Nath Mazumdar
Noor Inayat Khan
Manta Singh and Assa Singh
Jaston Khosa
John Henry Clavell Smythe
Adelaide Hall
and the millions of men and women whose names and
stories deserve to be known and honoured by those
they fought, saved and died for.

And for Mum, Zak, and our foremothers and fathers.
Always.

When wasteful war shall statues overturn
And broils roots out the work of masonry,
Nor mars his sword nor war's quick fire shall burn
The living record of your memory.
– William Shakespeare

আজি সেই চির-দিবসের প্রেম অবসান লভিয়াছে
রাশি রাশি হয়ে তোমার পায়ের কাছে।
– রবীন্দ্রনাথ ঠাকুর

Today it is heaped at your feet, it has found its end in you
The love of all man's days, both past and forever . . .
– Rabindranath Tagore

CONTENTS

THE SCHOOL TRIP

'Yesssss! School trip tomorrow – did you get your form signed? I hope there's cool things to buy in the gift shop. I hate it when they only have a few tiny rubbers and rulers and then everything else is super sad grown-up stuff – like tea towels and biscuits. Apparently people *collect* tea towels. I wonder why. Maybe they hang them up on a wall like pictures in a gallery. Some people are so *strange* . . .'

Sangeeta looked over at me to make sure I was still listening, and then carried on talking. If I decided to never ever speak again, I'm pretty sure she could go on talking all by herself for the rest of both our lives. My dad says she could talk the hind legs off a donkey or any animal with four legs. Maybe that's why her mum and dad have only ever given her fish for pets. Even though what she's always wanted is a cat.

'Hey, you know Katie? And Sarah? And Tom with no teeth in Mrs Thompson's class? Well, apparently they've already been to the cathedral – for like a concert or something. And they said there's a naughty word on one of the slabs on the floor, right by the front of the church. I wonder what it says – and if the vicar knows about it. They *must* do if it's right at the front. I hope we see it tomorrow – Oooooh! Bell! Come on. Race ya!'

Sangeeta sprinted towards the school doors, her bright yellow wellies flashing at everyone like muddy thunderbolts, and her two long plaits of shiny black hair zigzagging through the air.

Sangeeta loves racing. Even more than she loves talking. And she doesn't just race with her legs but with her brain too. Like in class when we're reading, she always has to be the first to finish her book and when we get asked a question, she always has to be the first to answer. I think she even races against herself when there's no one around. Sometimes I think it's strange that we're friends because we're so different. But we're

2

the only ones who look like us in the whole school, so somehow the differences don't matter.

I ran after her at full speed too, when someone suddenly stuck a foot out and tripped me over. Luckily I was used to it, so instead of falling straight down, I caught myself by crashing into a wall instead.

'Watch it, chopstick head,' hissed Toby, quiet enough so that no one else could hear. Looking around to make sure no one was watching, he gave me a push and ran off. Right behind him was Harry, who pretended that I didn't exist and never looked at me, and Catherine, who always giggled because she thought whatever Toby did was funny.

Ignoring them like I always do, I made my way into class.

'Right! Bottoms on seats! Settle down, please. NOW,' shouted Mr Scott, thumping his desk loudly to make everyone quiet. Mr Scott loves thumping his desk. It's why his hands are always the colour of squashed raspberries.

As everyone fell quiet and stopped shuffling and whispering, Mr Scott leaned against his desk and picked up a clipboard. It was time to find out the most important answer to the most important question we had all had been asking ourselves the whole day long: who was going on the school trip tomorrow, and who wasn't because their parents clearly hated them and wanted to ruin the rest of their lives by not signing the form.

'Right,' said Mr Scott, holding up a clipboard of names. We all squinted and tried to make out the names, as if we were taking an eye test together, but the letters were way too small to make out.

As Mr Scott turned the clipboard around so that only he could see it, I crossed my fingers under the table extra-hard. Mum and Dad had promised me that I could go and said that they had sent all the forms in, but you could never be too sure with parents. Especially not ones who forgot which one of them was meant to pick you up from school and always arrived late.

'David, Catherine and Toby . . .' read out Mr Scott. 'None of your parents have sent the forms back, and this morning was the final cut-off. So I'm afraid you'll all be staying behind tomorrow.'

The whole class turned to look at the sad victims of parental cruelty who were going to be left behind with the worst form of torture our school had: Mr Denby. The only teacher in the world who thought reading Shakespeare all day beat even going to Disneyland. We know because he always wore a T-shirt that said: *To Disneyland, say Nay! To reading Shakespeare all day? Yay!*

'Sir, how come Leo and Sangeeta are allowed to go and I'm not?' shouted Toby. 'They're probably not even allowed inside a church! AND my great-grandparents lived through the war and things – theirs didn't. So *I* should get to go more than them!'

'Yeah!' added Catherine, her eyes all wet and pink.

The whole class turned to look at me and Sangeeta. We stared straight ahead at Mr Scott, just like we always do when everyone looks at us. That's the problem with being the only ones who look different to everyone else. There's always someone who doesn't like you, and then doesn't like you *even more* when you can do something that they can't.

'Because their parents said they could go, and yours didn't,' said Mr Scott, throwing the clipboard onto his desk loudly. 'Anything else?'

Toby gave me and Sangeeta a look that told us his

life wasn't fair and that it was somehow our fault. Then he shook his head and growled at his hands. David gave a sniffle and Catherine crossed her arms, glaring angrily at everyone and everything. Even the ceiling.

'Right, now that's settled, ground rules for tomorrow . . .'

Mr Scott walked up to the whiteboard and, picking up a bright red pen, began to write out words that looked as loud and as angry as the ones he was now shouting out at us.

'NO pushing, shoving, or fighting! NO being a smart-aleck to anyone at the RAF museum OR the cathedral. NO losing your partner on purpose OR pretending you've forgotten who your partner is. Adam and Evelyn – I'm looking at you both. NO running off and trying to join another school group – Kerry and Christina, I'll be watching you. NO bringing in extra spending money. And NO impertinent questions . . . Quick, someone tell me what "impertinent" means!'

I watched as the usual three hands catapulted themselves into the air.

'Yes, Gary?' asked Mr Scott.

Gary took his hand down, turned bright red, and

said, 'Something that doesn't . . . last a long time?'

Sangeeta tutted and continued waving her hand in the air.

'No . . . you're thinking of im*permanent* there,' replied Mr Scott. 'Sangeeta?'

'Being rude and disrespectful to people who are older than you,' said Sangeeta. She gave me a grin because we both knew why she knew the meaning of that word so well. It was because her parents and aunts and uncles and grandparents were always telling her not to be it.

'Exactly,' said Mr Scott. 'So long as none of you are *impertinent* and you all follow those rules, maybe we can have just one day of the year where I'm not shouting at you. And maybe Mrs Fitzgerald will trust us to have another school trip soon.'

'Yeah!' muttered Toby loudly. 'Probably to the stupid fruit farm again!'

Everyone giggled, because that's where most of our school's class trips took place. Going to a school in a village in the middle of nowhere meant taking a trip to see the local farmers was considered a 'thrilling learning experience'. That's what all the teachers promised those trips would be. Except they weren't ever thrilling and no one really learned anything except that farms really smell of poo.

That was why everyone was so excited about the school trip tomorrow. It was the first time ever that we were going to get on a real coach and travel into a *real* town with a *real* museum and, hopefully, some *real*, proper sweet shops too. The kind of shops that didn't sell vegetables and double up as a post office.

'Come on now, kids. I know Whot isn't exactly London, but we should be proud of all our farms and businesses,' said Mr Scott, seriously. 'Most of your parents make a living from them, remember? Now, books open, and let's have a recap of what tomorrow is all about.'

Mr Scott began talking about some of the World War Two stories we were going to learn more about at the museum the next day. We had already learned about how the war had started when Germany had invaded Poland, and how Hitler had blitzed France and lots of other countries across Europe. Now it was time for the 'Battle of Britain'.

I opened up my workbook and looked down at the

black-and-white pictures staring back at me. They were all photos of RAF pilots, smiling and wearing scarves and leather jackets, or coats with medals made out of extra-large coins. They looked like actors from an action movie and had names like 'Arthur' and 'William' and 'George' – as if they were members of the Royal family. Maybe you needed to look like an actor and have a royal-family sounding name to fight in wars and get medals and make it into history books.

I looked over at Sangeeta who was racing to finish reading the worksheet Mr Scott had given us. I could tell she was racing because her face was less than a centimetre away from her piece of paper, and her lips were moving up and down quickly. She looked like a fish that was talking to itself.

When she had finished, she looked over at me and frowned.

'What?' she asked.

I shrugged. 'Do you know what your great-grandad's name was?' I asked.

Sangeeta frowned at me. 'My *great*-grandad? Er . . . no,' she replied. 'But it was probably Something Singh. *Everyone* in my family is called Singh. It's well boring.'

I spent the rest of the day wondering about what my great-grandad's name might have been. It definitely wasn't 'Arthur' or 'William' or 'George' like the soldiers in the booklet.

'Right! Eight-thirty *sharp* in front of the school gates,' announced Mr Scott at the end of the day. 'Not eight thirty-*one*! Not eight thirty-one and thirty-seconds! Eight-thirty! And remember to tell your parents ALL spending money needs to be in an envelope with your name AND the amount written on the front of it, and handed to ME! The maximum you can bring is five pounds. If I catch anyone bringing in extra, you won't be spending any of it!'

'That's so stupid,' whispered Sangeeta, as she shoved her workbook into her rucksack quickly, hoping to beat the whole class again. 'What can we buy with five pounds? Sometimes a pencil's two-pound-fifty! This school doesn't know anything about the rates of inflation in gift shops.'

I could tell everyone else was grumbling about the same thing, and I knew for a fact most of them – including me and Sangeeta – were going to try and sneak in at least a few extra coins somehow. I had heard

Kerry say she was going to tape everything she had to her belly. And I was pretty sure Adam would be limping again tomorrow. Adam always limped when he had something hidden in his sock. One time Mr Scott had found three marbles and a packet of chewing gum in one. But only because the marbles kept clanking together and Andrew's feet had started to smell like fruit. I was going to keep it simple and hide all my saved-up birthday money in my pencil case. That way if Mr Scott saw me opening it, he would just think I was working extra-hard.

'I'm going to keep my secret stash up my sleeve,' said Sangeeta, as we headed out to the playground to meet her parents. Sangeeta's parents were always early, and they knew mine were always late, so they let me sit in the back of their car with her and gave me snacks until my mum or dad arrived. Usually they gave me a huge samosa that was the size of my face or a crispy onion bhaji that looked like an orange UFO with squashed up tentacles, but sometimes I got lucky and would get a big bar of chocolate too.

'How will that work?' I asked, as her mum beeped at us from her car.

'Shhh!' whispered Sangeeta. Then, turning around so that her mum couldn't see us from the car, she pulled up her school jumper sleeve. A single crisp, five-pound note was fixed to her shirt sleeve with a huge silver paperclip. 'I tested it out today. See? And it worked! No one noticed. Not even when I had to wash my hands in the sink right in front of Mr Scott.'

'Clever.' I grinned, wondering if I should do the same.

'You should do the same,' suggested Sangeeta, as she turned back around and began running towards a shiny black car. 'Come on! Race ya!'

I ran after her and *nearly* beat her too. Sangeeta smiled and stuck her tongue out at me as she reached the door handle first, and then opened it for us both to pile in.

'Hello, Leo! Would you like one?' asked Mrs Singh, in her musical voice. 'It's veggie as usual.' She shoved a plastic container lined with tissue and filled with two giant triangle samosas in front of us.

'Thanks, Mrs Singh,' I said, as I grabbed one and Sangeeta grabbed the other. We both sank our faces into them at the exact same time.

'Are you excited for the school trip tomorrow?' asked Mrs Singh, as she handed us each a tissue.

We nodded, too busy munching through big chunks of bright yellow potato and half-mushy peas to speak.

'Good,' said Mrs Singh. 'Mr Singh and I have never been to the museum you're going to. So I will be looking forward to hearing all about it when you come back tomorrow!'

As I gulped down a giant mouthful of spicy potato, a question popped into my head and then out of my mouth.

'Mrs Singh – have *you* ever met anyone who was in the Second World War?'

Mrs Singh turned around from her driver's seat and looked at me with a frown. 'Hmmm . . .' she murmured. 'As a matter of fact, yes, I have! Before Sangeeta was born I met a man—'

'Ew! Mum!'

Mrs Singh rolled her eyes. 'Stop being impertinent, Sangeeta!' She shook her head before continuing. 'As I was saying, before you were born, I lived next door to a very, very old man who had fought in Italy, and then in India, and then in Burma. We had lots of interesting discussions. But sadly he died a long time ago.'

'What was his name?' asked Sangeeta.

'George . . . George something . . . Marshwall?' replied Mrs Singh.

Another George. I knew it! 'Do you think he might have been related to the royal family?' I asked, wondering if my secret suspicion was true.

Sangeeta frowned at me as her mum laughed and said, 'No. I don't think members of the royal family live in council flats in Birmingham. Ah! Look, here is your dad!'

Giving a short beep, Mrs Singh rolled down the window and waved to my dad.

'See you tomorrow – at eight-thirty sharp!' said Sangeeta, as I shoved the rest of the samosa into my mouth and jumped out of the car. 'And don't forget the paperclip!' she added in a whisper.

I grinned as I slammed the door shut. I ran over to my dad and grabbed his hand.

'Sorry I'm late, son,' he said, his face red and sweaty as if he had just run a marathon. 'Got stuck at work. And your mum's somewhere up in Bristol.'

'That's OK, Dad.' We began heading home, my

hand swinging in his. As we walked through town, I could feel people staring out of the corner of their eyes, and talking more quietly as they watched us pass by. I was used to it, so I tried not care. Besides, I had more important things to worry about. Like how to change all my birthday coins into a five-pound note, and where to find a giant paperclip.

THE INVISIBLE BRUISE

'Ready, Leo?'

I nodded. Mum was shoving a large lunch box into my rucksack. By her feet, my baby sister Jingyi was trying to stick a whole teddy bear's head into her mouth. Mum grabbed an extra apple, a banana and a plum from the fridge, and placed them on top of the lunch box.

'Mum! I don't need that much food! I'm not leaving the country!' I complained. I needed room in my bag for all the sweets I wanted to buy! Plus I could already smell the kecap manis chicken wraps wafting from my bag, and knew immediately they would stink up the whole coach. They were my favourite, but sometimes I wished Mum and Dad would just give me a simple cheese sandwich like everyone else had.

It was a good thing Toby and Catherine weren't coming today – they would have made fun of me for sure. One time Sangeeta's dad had packed her a bright green broccoli bhaji for lunch, and Toby and Catherine had told the class she was eating luminous bogies. It had taken us two whole days to convince the school it was only broccoli.

'You'll be thanking your mum later when you're starving,' said Dad as he passed the kitchen door. He stopped in front of the mirror in the hallway, just like he did every morning. He was always trying to style his straight black hair in a new way. But it never made any difference. No matter which way he tried to scrunch it and pull it, it still fell into the exact same place. He had the same kind of hair I did: the kind that never listened.

'DAD! OUT OF THE WAY! I'M LATE!' shrieked my brother Bo, as he came plummeting down the stairs like a human boulder. Dad jumped backwards with his hands up in the air as Bo ran out of the door and slammed it shut behind him.

'That boy!' Mum tutted, as she ran into the corridor. I followed her, watching as she grabbed her coat and bag in one arm and picked up Jingyi, who had crawled after her, with the other. She turned and gave me a kiss on the top of my head. 'Just like his Uncle Tai. Always a pain in the ear.'

'Mum, it's pain in the *neck*,' I corrected. 'Not ear.'

Even though Mum had lived in England since before even Bo was born and was a super-brainy scientist, she still always got things wrong. Even spellings!

'Er, no. He is a pain in my ear, so I will say "ear",' replied Mum, tutting at me. She pushed Jingyi out towards me with her hip so that I could kiss her goodbye. Jingyi stared at me and made her eyes bulge out, as if she was warning me not to even think about it. For a ten-month-old baby who couldn't speak yet, she sure knew how to get a message across.

I kissed her anyway, so Jingyi slapped me in the face. With both hands.

Satisfied, Mum turned to Dad and gave him a kiss too. Then, even though I was standing right next to her, she shouted, 'I'll be picking you up today, Leo! So see you later!' Running out of the door with Jingyi gurgling loudly, she slammed it in exactly the same way Bo had.

'Like mother, like son, huh?' Dad smiled. 'Got everything?'

I nervously touched my jumper sleeve. Underneath it lay my secret five-pound note, clipped with two clothes pegs from the washing line. I wasn't taking any chances. If I had been a normal kid in a normal family and got pocket money every week, I would have easily been able to get my hands on a five-pound note. But no grown-up in the history of my family had ever given their kids money for not doing anything, so I had counted every bit of change I had from my leftover birthday and lunch monies, and given Bo all the chicken dumplings from my dinner plate too, for this one single note. Making sure it was extra safe and sound, I nodded.

Dad swung open the door and waved me through it and out onto the street. It was exactly eight-o-three am. Which meant there was no way we could be late for Mr Scott and the coach.

Feeling excited, I hurried after Dad as he turned right, and headed up towards the centre of the tiny village we lived in.

Like all tiny villages that are built in the middle

of nowhere for reasons I don't think anyone really knows, our village centre has a baker's shop, a mini-supermarket, a chemist, a newsagents, and a pub. The pub is called The Wandering Swan, even though no one has ever seen a swan around the village. I think it must have been named after a swan that had been wandering, got lost, ended up here, couldn't believe how boring it was, and wandered right back off again. And then told all the other swans not to bother coming this way too.

There was also a bank that was never open with a cashpoint that never worked, a tiny train station, and a bus stop that always seemed to have three people standing next to it, no matter what time of the day or night it was. Even though the bus only came twice every hour, and didn't run past nine o'clock at night. My school was right on the other end of the village from our house, past lots of fields with crops that were taller than me, and on the very last bit of the main road before it turned and became a motorway.

Walking past the shops and the station and the bus stop, I did what I always did: I looked straight down at the floor and tried to ignore all the people glancing at me and Dad as we passed. But even though I couldn't see them, I could feel them, because when people look at you, they send their energy out through their eyes – just like Superman's heat lasers. That's what Sangeeta says anyway. She gets looked at all the time too, so she knows what it's like.

Dad is always telling me that people look at me because I'm 'special' and 'so handsome that people can't take it'. Which must make him 'special' and 'so handsome they can't take it' as well, because people like to look at him a lot too. Not in a bad way. Just as if they're making sure he's real, and that I'm real, and that Mum and Jingyi and Bo are real too. It happens everywhere and all the time too. It doesn't matter if we're in a restaurant or in the park or at the seaside, we always get stared at and spoken to differently. Sometimes people speak very loudly and slowly to us, because they think we can't speak English. That's why we always have to be on our best behaviour – just in case we scare people. Even when other people don't seem to worry about being on *their* best behaviour or scaring us at all.

'Baba?'

'Hmmm?'

'Did *you* ever meet anyone who fought in World War Two – like, from our country and in our family and things?' I asked, as we reached the long stretch of fields that lined the road to school. Up ahead, I could see Kerry with her nan and older sister, and, in front of them, Toby, walking on his own, bouncing a tennis ball against the pavement.

Dad shook his head. 'No. Not really. I know that some of our family worked in factories and did things to aid the war effort from inside Singapore. But none of them fought or died on the battlefields – not that I'm aware of anyway. Most of them died before I was even born so I never got to meet them. Why?'

'Oh,' I said, my heart sinking. Maybe Toby was right, and me and Sangeeta didn't deserve to go on the trip. Not when no one in our families had been war heroes like his great-grandparents had. 'No reason.'

As we reached the gates of the school, I forgot all about my question to Dad, because there it was. A real, proper coach! The kind with curtains and everything. It looked super-grand – like a moving hotel – and much more comfortable than the small white minibuses we always took for our farm trips.

Mr Scott and Mrs Whittaker were by the big front doors, along with all the volunteering parents dressed in bright yellow vests. They were holding clipboards and throwing out waves to everyone, as if they were superstars. My whole year seemed to have already arrived, and were standing in pairs in a long line. Kids from other years were staring enviously as they passed by and a boy from Year Six yelled, 'Gary! Oi! Gary! Yeah, you! I'm your brother's mate, remember? Bring us back some chocolate bars, yeah?'

As Dad approached Mr Scott to give him my legal spending money envelope, I spotted Sangeeta, dressed in her favourite bright blue wellies, and ran to join her. It didn't matter how hot or cold it was, Sangeeta always had wellies on. She had at least thirteen different pairs, and said she liked wearing them all the time because then she was always ready to splash in puddles and kick a football. I was just about to show her my hidden five-pound note when, suddenly, something hit me in the leg, hard, like a tiny, bright missile.

'OWWWWW!' I cried out, as my hands immediately

went to rub the hurt place. I watched as the bright yellow tennis ball that had hit me bounced straight back into Toby's hands.

Toby gave a smirk and threw the ball at me extra-hard again. I tried to dodge it, but I was too slow – it hit me in the arm. Before it could bounce away from me, I leaped forwards and caught it quickly.

'SIR, SIR! HE'S GOT MY BALL!' cried Toby. 'LEO'S STOLEN MY BALL!'

Mr Scott and my dad both turned to look at us, as everyone around us fell quiet.

'What's going on here then?' asked Mr Scott, giving a huge sigh as if he was already tired.

'LEO'S taken MY ball!' shouted Toby again, pointing at me as if to make sure Mr Scott knew who I was.

'He hit me with it FIRST,' I shouted back.

'Is that true?' asked Mr Scott, looking at Toby with a frown.

Toby shook his head, but Sangeeta shouted, 'YES! It IS true! Toby threw it at Leo – twice! And it nearly hit me too!'

'It was an ACCIDENT,' lied Toby.

Mr Scott held out his hand to me and I handed him the ball.

'The exact same accident can't happen *twice*, Toby,' said Mr Scott, shaking his head. 'Off you go – to Mr Denby's classroom! And I'm confiscating this,' he added, holding up the tennis ball. 'Off you go. NOW.'

I stared at Mr Scott and then at Sangeeta. Toby had hit me with a ball – twicc! – on purpose, and he wasn't getting a detention or even being told off properly! I looked over at Dad. I wanted him to do something, to say something. Maybe tell Toby off for hurting me! But Dad just stood there, quietly watching everything happen. Like he always did.

As soon as Mr Scott turned his back, Toby gave me a grin, telling me that he had won. Then he ran off through the school gates and disappeared into the playground.

I looked at the empty space he had left behind, feeling my eyes begin to burn and my cheeks heat up and my throat close as if I had been stung by a gang of angry wasps.

'Sorry about that, Mr Lim. Toby's one of our . . . more spirited lads,' explained Mr Scott, putting the ball in his bag. 'Needs a talking-to every now and then.'

My dad said, 'No matter. These things happen.' Then, with a wink and a, 'Have fun, kids', he quickly walked off, heading back down towards the village to catch his train to work.

Within seconds, everything went back to normal, and after a few minutes, we were allowed to board the coach and take our seats. I wanted to be as excited about the trip as I had been yesterday. But the bruises on my leg and arm were hurting and felt like they were spreading to my chest too, and instead of feeling excited, I felt sore. Now that Toby knew no one really cared if I had balls chucked at me, he would probably do it all the time! Why did Dad think it was 'no matter' if people threw things at me and didn't even get detention? Why did he *never* say anything to anyone who wasn't nice to me? Why was he always super-quiet and super-friendly to horrible people? Didn't he care that it hurt?

The more I thought about it, the more I could feel the bruise inside me getting bigger and bigger and sorer and sorer. Not even the fact that we were going to a real museum to see a real plane and to a cathedral surrounded by sweet shops could make it go away.

26

Because some bruises can't be healed in a day. Especially not ones that are old and keep getting hit over and over.

As everyone around me talked and buzzed and whispered excitedly, I stared down at the floor. It felt like the bruise inside me was going to be there for ever, and would only go away if something big and unexpected and brilliant happened. Something that could make me completely forget it even existed.

But the chances of something like that happening to someone like me – or Sangeeta – was zero. In fact, it was less than zero. We were too different for brilliant things to ever happen to us. And the bruise knew it.

THE LION THAT ROARED

'We're here! Race you off the coach!' cried Sangeeta, punching me on the arm and probably giving me my third bruise of the day.

Before anyone else had even begun to move, Sangeeta quickly undid her seatbelt and jumped up excitedly. But she had forgotten about the low ceiling and banged straight into it, then fell right back down again. I looked at her and tried not to laugh.

'Shut up,' she muttered, grinning and rubbing the top of her head.

'Everyone, stay seated!' shouted Mr Scott, shaking his head at Sangeeta. 'And ONLY get up when I tell you to . . . Front three rows, let's go,' he ordered, as Mrs Whittaker waved at the first lucky batch to follow her outside.

I looked out of the window at the large white sign that said '**RAF PLANES OF WWII MUSEUM**' and felt something with wings begin to shake itself awake inside me. I love planes. The first – and last – time Mum and Dad took me on a plane was when I was four. They had taken me 'home' to Singapore to meet people who talked about me every day but who had never seen me. The only thing I can really remember from it is looking out of the window and seeing the town and cities and lights and clouds all float away beneath us like brightly coloured dreams.

But now – now we were about to see Hurricane and Spitfire planes. Planes that been flown by heroes and won wars! They were the *real* deal! The thought of seeing them in real life made the bruise inside me feel a bit smaller, and as Mr Scott finally called mine and Sangeeta's row, I jumped up as quickly as she did – without banging my head.

Everyone was talking as we followed Mr Scott and Mrs Whittaker into the museum, sounding like a huge flock of squawking birds. They led us into a large room with nothing in it but a desk with a tall woman with short, shiny brown hair and large blue eyes standing in front of it. She clapped her hands, and everyone instantly went quiet.

'Good morning, everyone! Welcome to the RAF Planes of World War Two Museum. My name is Ms Fletcher, and I'll be your guide for today. Now, before I take you inside, just a few ground rules . . .'

As Ms Fletcher talked about fire alarms and toilets and something about not flushing any crayons down them, I looked past her bright blue dress to the double doors behind her. Through them, I could see the tip of a plane's red nose, and giant propellers, all grey and shiny and huge. I wondered what it sounded like with its engines on and if we would be allowed to touch it – or maybe even sit inside it, just like the real heroes used to do.

'One for you too, here you go.'

I looked up, confused. Katie's mum, who was famous for wearing so much hairspray that her hair never moved, was holding out a worksheet to me. Everyone else was getting one too. I took it with a small smile, and Katie's mum and her stiff hair nodded at me.

Sangeeta was already racing with herself to fill it out,

and had put her name on it in extra-large handwriting. Behind her, Tom and Jerry were doing the same.

'Follow me, as we head into the first room of the museum, the Hurricane Gallery,' called Ms Fletcher. As we walked through the doors clutching our worksheets, I heard Nancy whisper, 'Cool' and Drew cry out, 'Woah! A real plane!' Someone in Mrs Whittaker's class shouted excitedly, 'My grandad's got pictures like these in his house! I told Mum he belongs in a museum!'

We made our way around the giant hall and the plane that stood in the middle of it, and I gazed up at the huge glass cabinets and framed photographs that decorated the room's brick walls. There were black-and-white pictures of men in uniforms with medals, shaking hands with other men, who were also wearing lots of medals. Photos of pilots in leather jackets and goggles, smiling and posing near planes that looked exactly like the one we were walking around. There were newspaper clippings about all the heroes who had helped win the war. And sad stories about men who had died because they were so brave and fearless. They all looked like movie stars, just like everyone in the history books at school.

Ms Fletcher finished speaking about the Hurricane plane and how over fourteen thousand just like it had helped win the war. Then she waved us through a door with a big sign hanging above it, which said 'THE SPITFIRE GALLERY'.

The plane in this room was much smaller, and the people in the photos looked even more royal than the ones before. There was a picture of Princess Mary in a glass cabinet, which made me wonder again if my theories were true, and everyone in all the pictures *was* secretly related to someone royal.

'This is stupid,' whispered Sangeeta, glaring at her finished worksheet.

'What is?' I asked, hurriedly trying to copy some of her answers. She never minded, because she knew I would never get as good a mark as her, even with her help.

'There's nothing on here about any women in the air force,' said Sangeeta, frowning. 'And I know there were loads, because my Uncle Ramjit bought me a book about it last year for my birthday – about women from all over the world who helped during the war. They broke codes and helped fix the planes. And Hazel

Hill should be here too! She helped do all the calculations and things. It's not fair. She's not in our textbooks at school either.'

I shrugged. 'Maybe it's because they didn't actually fly the machines and go and fight.'

Sangeeta frowned. 'I guess. But they still *helped*, didn't they? And they were super-clever too.'

I shrugged again. Sangeeta was always getting upset about things. Things that Mr Scott never seemed to know or care about and which museums and history books seemed not to care too much about either.

As we followed Mrs Fletcher around the final part of the hall and stopped in front of a leather jacket that had belonged to a real World War Two pilot, I thought about all the faces and names I had seen and heard. Katie and Tom and Drew and Nancy had found people who had the same last names as them. Even quiet Dennis pointed out a soldier he said looked like his dad. There weren't any names or faces me and Sangeeta could say that about. It was as if people who looked like us hadn't existed on the planet at the time or had been invisible.

But then, maybe it was also because nobody who

33

looked like us had done anything that mattered enough to have their photos and stories put inside glass cages. Maybe they were all like Dad and had been so busy being nice to people that they hadn't been brave enough to fight all the bullies and Nazis. Newspaper stories and medals and leather jackets were only for people who were brave enough to take action. There wasn't anyone who looked like me and my family, or Sangeeta and her family, in the museum, because they had probably never done anything to deserve a place inside it.

After Mrs Fletcher had said goodbye, Mr Scott let us loose in the gift shop. I bought three chocolate-shaped planes for me, Bo and Jingyi, a small ruler with silver Spitfires on it and a cardboard RAF plane I could hang above my bed with invisible string – all with my envelope money. It made me feel instantly better. Especially as I still had nearly a whole pound left over *and* my secret five-pound note for the cathedral and the sweet shops.

'Hope Mr Scott gives us more time in the shops at the cathedral,' said Sangeeta, as we all climbed back on the coach after quickly gulping down our packed lunches.

'Yeah,' said Nancy from behind us. She was gripping

34

a RAF pencil with a Spitfire-shaped rubber on its end like it was the most important thing in the world. 'I've got two extra pounds taped to the bottom of my shoe for it! That's why I'm walking funny.'

'Remind me to buy the new Super-Flying-Ninja chocolate bar,' said Drew from in front of us. 'Or my brother will kill me.'

'Don't worry, I will,' Sangeeta promised. 'I have to get one for my dad too.'

As the coach swished its way past huge patches of green fields and sped down the motorway, I listened to Sangeeta talk about all her favourite bits from the RAF museum – mostly the gift shop, and the flight simulation machine that none of us had been allowed to go on. 'We need to go back one day and try it out,' she declared, before finally moving on to the list of sweets she was going to buy because our village was too tiny and boring to have them yet. I was beginning to feel sleepy, but just as I was about to close my eyes, we came to a stop.

'Right, here we are! Rochester Cathedral. No one get up until I say you can,' shouted Mr Scott, as everyone unclicked their belts again.

'Woah! It's like one of the ancient temples I saw in India last year,' whispered Sangeeta, as we climbed down from the coach and lined up in front of the cathedral doors. 'With all the statues everywhere. Ooh, there's the Queen of Sheba. She looks like she's melted, just like Mr Scott said. And I can see the ox and the lion above the door! How cool is that?'

But I wasn't looking at the melted queen or the lion or anything else Mr Scott had told us to keep an eye out for in our lessons yesterday. I was too busy looking for the sweet shops. But there weren't any. There was only a stone castle on a hill across the road, a huge tree that had a gate around it for some reason, and a small café near an old archway.

'Where's the sweet shops?' asked Drew, with a look of disbelief in his eyes. Like me, he was probably wondering if the row of sweet shops in Rochester had been a lie – a legend made up by people to torture us.

'On the other side!' said Sangeeta. 'We're on the west side, remember? All the shops are on the other side.'

Drew sighed with relief. 'Better be, or I'm going to make an official complaint.'

'Follow me,' shouted Mr Scott, as he pushed his way past us to the front of the line. 'Stay in pairs, and listen RESPECTFULLY and QUIETLY to what we're about to be told.'

We all followed him through the large glass doors of the cathedral and found ourselves inside a giant hall. It was echoey and cold compared to outside, and smelled earthy and rich – like the inside of an ancient tree which had seen more history take place than the human mind could even imagine.

Everyone hushed, as if they instantly knew they were in a place that was sacred and precious and should be respected. I peered around, seeing rows of white stone arches, and long lights dangling down from the ceiling in circles like solar systems. Right at the very end of the hall, where the priest probably stood on Sundays, was a wall with a row of statues carved into it: eight men with beards, all holding what looked like tall swords. It was like the inside of a castle I had seen in a film about King Arthur and his knights. All magical and impossible and huge. As if anything could happen inside it, and as if kings and queens and knights and heroes of the past had met and talked and made plans for their kingdoms here.

'Well, hello, everyone! My name is Mr Young, and I'll be your guide today,' said a man who had appeared in front of us without anyone noticing.

His words broke the spell of silence and someone in front of me laughed out loud. We all knew why: Mr Young didn't look as if he had *ever* been young. He had stark white hair and bushy white eyebrows, and his face had so many wrinkles it was like a piece of paper someone had scrunched up and then tried to flatten out again.

Ignoring the laugh, Mr Young smiled at us, and waved everyone over to him. 'Before I take you down to the crypt and out to our war memorials, how about you all come over here, and take a look at the wall behind you? The best view is from where I'm standing.'

We all shuffled as close to Mr Young as we could without knocking him over, and looked up in the direction he was pointing.

'Rochester Cathedral dedicated commemorations to lots of wars, including of course, World War Two,' began Mr Young.

'Sir! Were you in it – in World War Two?' cried

Steve from Mrs Whittaker's class.

Mr Scott gave Steve a glare.

'No,' chuckled Mr Young. 'I'm not as old as you might think. Nor as brave!'

Someone whacked Steve loudly on the arm and whispered 'Idiot!' before everyone fell quiet again.

'Now, as you can see, the cathedral has marked lots of wars, and named soldiers who came not just from Britain, but other parts of the Empire too. See?'

We all looked up at a giant arch filled with words like 'The Royal Engineers' and 'RAF' and 'Campaigns'. But next to them were words I had never read before. Like 'Bengal Sappers' and 'Waziri' and 'Kaffir Zvlv'. And, on both sides of the arch, were lists of hundreds of names carved into the church wall.

'Hey, Leo! Look!' cried Drew, pointing up. 'Under that golden lion – right there! There's YOU!'

I followed the direction of Drew's finger to a golden lion above the door.

Carved into a slab of cream marble, right beneath the shining golden shape of a winged lion, was the name:

LEO KAI LIM, DFC

Drew was right . . . it *was* my name!

It was *exactly* my name! Not just the Leo part but all of it – *Leo Kai Lim*! But what was it doing inside a cathedral? On part of an old wall that remembered soldiers? And why did it have a golden lion above it, when none of the other names did? And what did 'DFC' mean?

I stared and stared at the three names – *my* three names – as all around me, everyone nudged and poked each other and repeated my name, until the sound of it echoed around the cathedral and came back to me like a roar.

THE PROMISE

'Man! That is WAY cool,' said Drew, swinging his arm around my neck and plonking it on my shoulder. 'You can tell people you're famous!'

'Oi! Leo! You look well young for a *dead* person!' shouted Terry, throwing his hands up in the air as if he had just scored a goal and making everyone giggle.

'Shhh! Quiet!' warned Mrs Whittaker, tutting and bringing Terry's hands down for him. 'We are in a place of worship!' She turned to a family who had just walked in and apologised.

'Quiet down, everyone,' ordered Mr Scott sternly. 'So sorry, Mr Young. Excitable bunch this lot. Please do start the tour.'

But instead of leading us away, Mr Young walked

past everyone and came to stand right next to me. He looked up at the wall and then back to me, giving me a smile that made his wrinkly face crinkle up even more.

'So, that's your name up there is it, son?' he asked, his voice diving deeper and becoming more echoey.

Everyone fell quiet and even Terry stopped laughing.

I opened my mouth, but nothing came out except a nod.

'Well now, that *is* interesting,' said Mr Young. 'Do you know if he was a relation of yours?'

I shook my head. I had never heard of another Leo in my family. I was the only one. At least, as far as I knew . . .

'Ah, well. We get people coming here from all over the world you know. The great-grandsons and daughters – and the great-*great* ones too – of heroes, looking for names they couldn't find anywhere else. I don't think we've ever had anyone come in to ask about a "Lim". His family might not even know his name is honoured here. A huge shame, especially with him being so decorated and all.'

'Decorated?' I asked, frowning up at Mr Young.

I wondered if he was talking about the golden lion.

Mr Young pointed up. 'See those letters, "DFC"?'

I nodded and could feel everyone else doing the same behind me.

'That stands for "Distinguished Flying Cross". It's a medal given by the Royal Air Force. He must have done something extraordinarily brave to get one of those. And to get a golden lion next to his name too. It's all a mystery. Especially as the RAF's symbol was—'

'An eagle!' shouted Nancy from behind me.

'Exactly!' cried out Mr Young.

'Good girl!' whispered Mrs Whittaker, proudly.

'Anyway . . .' Giving me a pat on my shoulder, Mr Young turned around and walked back to his place in front of the class. 'Follow me, if you please,' he said cheerily, leading the class straight down the middle of the hall.

Everyone rushed off. I tried to move. But my feet didn't want to budge. It looked as if Sangeeta's feet couldn't either. She was standing straight and staring up at the wall too, her mouth wide open.

For a few seconds, we had the wall of names and the golden lion all to ourselves.

'Look. There's an "R Singh" up there,' she said, quietly. 'Right under your name. And another "Singh" over there!'

I tore my eyes away from my name to read some of the other names around it. Sangeeta was right. There were lots of Singhs up there. And there were other names too. Names that were different to all the ones I had ever seen on war memorials or read about in the history books at school. Names Like 'Sooltan Ali' and 'Mahomed Khan' and 'Ram Lall' and 'Cheng Nu'. I opened my mouth to say something back to Sangeeta, but my brain couldn't find the words for what I wanted to say.

'Sanjeeta and Leo, come on!' called out Katie's mum, from the front of the hall.

Sangeeta sighed and rolled her eyes at me. She always rolled her eyes when people said her name wrong, even though it was so easy to say.

'We better go,' I said, even though that was the last thing I wanted to do.

'Yeah, guess so . . .' said Sangeeta. We both turned around and ran down the hall to join the rest of our year. When we reached them, we could hear Mr Scott telling everyone off for finding the naughty word on the slab on the floor.

As Mr Young led everyone out of the hall, I looked over my shoulder at the memorial wall one more time, and made the strangest promise I had ever made. It was strange because I had never made a promise to someone who wasn't alive before. And especially not someone who had died before I was even born! But I made it because I wanted to know – I *had* to know.

It was a promise to Leo – the Leo whose name had been carved onto a wall and who had been so brave that he had been given a medal and a golden lion too. I made him a promise that I would find out everything I could about him and make sure everyone knew about him too. After all, he was a hero and deserved to have someone come and say hello to him sometimes.

And, since we had the same name, I thought maybe that someone could be me.

* * *

On the journey home, with everyone's rucksacks filled with so many sweets that the whole coach seemed to be rustling, I listened to Drew explaining the order he was going to eat everything in, and how much he was going to sell half his stash for back at school.

Now that the trip was over and we were on our way back, Mr Scott had let everyone switch seats with whoever they wanted to, so me and Nancy had swapped right away. I could hear her and Sangeeta in the seats in front of me, talking so fast it was as if they were in a race to see who could speak the most and listen the least.

While Drew added up how much money he was going to make, I stared through the window on the other side of him, watching the roads and trees go by in a blur. I wasn't really listening to him or to anything else, because all I could think about was the real Leo, and who he was, and where his family might be.

He made me start to wonder, for the first time ever, where *my* name came from too. I was pretty sure I was the only one in my whole family called Leo, so I couldn't be related to the cathedral Leo. Plus, if he was part of our family, there was no way I wouldn't have heard about him already. My great-great-grandad's cousin had once won an award for his pickle factory, and everyone still talked about him as if he had changed the world. So I would definitely have heard about a *real* hero in the family if there had been any.

But it made me think – maybe Mum and Dad could still help me find out who he was. They knew nearly everyone in Singapore – and Malaysia and Indonesia too – so there was bound to be *someone* they knew who knew *something* about him . . .

'Hey, how much do you think a Galactic Lights pogo stick costs? Do you think I could afford one if I sold the Fizzing Wombats for two pounds each instead of just a pound? I've got like seven of them . . . which would be fourteen pounds . . . and then, if I sold the Super-Flying Ninja bars for two-pound fifty instead of just one-pound fifty . . .' Drew scratched the tip of his freckly nose and then, counting on his fingers, began to check his maths.

Just when Drew was coming to the conclusion that he would have to sell all of his sweets, his RAF pencil and probably half the things in his house too if he really wanted the newest pogo stick, the coach came to a stop. Mr Scott clapped his hands to make everyone quiet down and listen. We were home again, in boring old Whot.

Leaning past Drew, I looked out of the window to see if Mum and Jingyi were nearby. But I couldn't see any black, shiny hair in the bobbing sea of blonde and brown and red heads that were now standing by the gates.

'Right, everyone! Remember to complete your homework tonight! Mrs Whittaker and I want one WHOLE page on everything you learned today, handed in FIRST thing tomorrow,' ordered Mr Scott. Everyone gave a groan. 'With a drawing too – just ONE drawing.'

'Olivia – did you hear what Mr Scott said? *One* drawing only,' ordered Mrs Whittaker.

Everyone turned around to the back of the coach where Olivia Morris was sitting. She was famous in school for handing in her homework *covered* in drawings. She even drew stuff on her arms and knees too, and, if she liked you – really, really liked you – she would draw on you.

Everyone secretly wanted to be drawn on by Olivia – even Sangeeta, though she would never admit it – because Olivia was one of the most popular girls in school. She always wore the newest trainers and was really good at dodging people when she played tag in the playground. But Olivia was too cool for most of the school. So she was definitely too cool for me and Sangeeta and Drew and Nancy. We would never get drawn on by her.

Olivia flicked her shiny dark brown fringe away from her face and shrugging, stared back at everyone. No one wanted to be caught out by her greenish-brown eyes, so we all instantly looked away.

The moment Mr Scott ordered the coach doors to open, we all clambered out and instantly felt like superstars as our parents shouted out our names and stretched out their arms to grab us like they hadn't seen any of us in ten years. I heard my name being called out too. But it wasn't Mum's voice. It was Bo's!

I ran up to him, feeling proud and happy that he had come to get me. Bo was kind of like Olivia. He was popular at college and was usually too cool to be seen with me. He never let me inside his room, and when his friends came round, he always warned me to stay away and pretend I didn't exist. He almost never came to school to pick me up, so when he did, it felt super special.

'Hi, Bo! Where's Mum?' I asked, turning to give Drew and Sangeeta and Nancy and everyone else who might see me a wave. But they were all being hugged tightly by their parents, like mice being squeezed by cobras.

'She's busy. Come on, walk faster. I've got things to do,' ordered Bo. He put his hands in his pockets and began hurrying up the road.

Skip-running beside him, I told Bo all about the trip and the planes and the gift shop and the sweet shop and the cathedral too. I couldn't wait to tell him about my name being on the wall, but I wanted him to have all the details first.

'Bo, have you ever been to the cathedral – the one I went to today? You know, in Rochester?'

'No. Why would I go to a boring cathedral in Rochester?' answered Bo.

I hurried along beside him.

'Didn't you go even once? With school?' I asked.

Bo grunted a 'no' and then asked, 'Why? What's so special about it?'

'Because it . . . it had *my name* . . . on a wall! With a golden lion above it!'

'Wait a minute,' said Bo, coming to a stop outside the newsagents.

I looked up at Bo, surprised. Maybe he *was* as excited as I was! But it turned out he wasn't at all. Because all he said was, 'Stay there and DON'T follow me in!' and disappeared behind the big, buzzing door of the newsagent's shop. After a minute, he came back out with two packets of crisps and two cans of lemonade.

'Here, eat that,' he said, shoving a packet of crisps and a can at my chest.

I looked down at the snacks. I hated salt and vinegar crisps *and* lemonade too.

'Mum and Dad are both going to be late for dinner,' he explained. 'So Mum said to get you a snack.' He pulled open his crisps and shoved a handful into his mouth. 'Come on.'

With that, Bo walked off ahead of me. I stood still, wondering if Bo even knew me at all. Or if he had ever seen his name anywhere except on his own exercise books. He probably hadn't, which was why he didn't care that I had just seen mine on a real wall next to the names of lots of heroes.

'Come ON, Leo!' he yelled, looking back at me.

Running after him with my rucksack and stash of sweets bouncing up and down against my back, I made another promise. Except this one was just to myself. And it was that I would *make* Bo listen. In fact, I would make *everyone* listen. Not just to Leo's story when I found out all about him. But about other things too. Like what *I* wanted, so that they could stop giving me things that I *didn't* want. Like tangy lemonade, and even tangier salt-and-vinegar crisps and being secretly stared at all the time, but never being heard.

THE BOARDS OF HONOUR

'Homework in, everyone seated, and all eyes on me!' shouted Mr Scott the next morning, as the whole class rushed in to beat the bell before it stopped ringing. We all threw our homework down onto his desk before scrambling to our chairs.

I slam-dunked my sheet down, hoping Mr Scott wouldn't notice that I had made my handwriting bigger than normal so that I could fill up the page without having to write too much. My drawing of the cathedral was rubbish, but I had been thinking about the real Leo so much that I hadn't really cared what it looked like.

When Mum and Dad had finally got home last night, I had rushed downstairs to tell them all about the trip and to ask about my name and where it had come from, but by the time I reached them, Dad was ordering a pizza on the phone. Takeaway pizza nights only happened when Mum and Dad were too tired to cook or talk, so I knew they wouldn't have the energy to listen to me properly. I would have to wait for the right moment, so I was going to try again after school instead.

'Hey, did you see?' asked Sangeeta, giving my elbow three taps with hers. 'Olivia drew two planes on her knees today – just like the ones from the museum! I drew one for my report, but I couldn't get the nose right so it looks like a plane with a really bad cold. What'd you draw?'

'Just the cathedral – the outside of it,' I answered.

'What? With all the statues and things?' asked Sangeeta, looking impressed. 'That sounds amazing.'

I grinned to myself, wondering what she was going to say when she saw the blob I had drawn which made the cathedral look like a sandcastle that had just been stepped on.

'Settle down! Quickly! I have some VERY exciting news to share,' hollered Mr Scott, thumping his desk so hard that the floor seemed to shake. Crossing his arms until we had all become quiet, he continued. 'Good. Now. It seems Mrs Fitzgerald was so impressed by the way everyone behaved on the trip yesterday, and by all the work you've been doing on World War Two, that she's going to give OUR class the main display board in reception AND the assembly to do for Remembrance week!'

Everyone immediately began squealing and bouncing up and down in their chairs. Sangeeta grabbed my arm, shaking it like a glowstick she was trying to light up.

'AND! That's not all,' added Mr Scott, giving a loud clap, as if thumping his desk wasn't enough any more. 'She has also told me . . .'

Everyone leaned in, waiting and holding their breaths, as Mr Scott made his pause even longer – just like the judges do on the singing contests on the telly before the winner is announced.

'Come on, sir!' cried Drew, unable to bear it any longer.

Mr Scott smiled. 'She has also told me that OUR school has been chosen to take part in the *Real Kidz Rule* Remembrance Day competition!'

'The REAL *Real Kidz Rule* – the one on TV?'
gasped Kerry.

'The exact one,' said Mr Scott, nodding proudly.

'NO WAY!' shouted Toby.

'Yes, *way*,' replied Mr Scott.

Sangeeta shook my arm again so hard I was sure it was about to come off.

But I didn't shake her arm back, because I suddenly had a thought. Maybe *this* was it! Maybe this was how I could keep my promise to the real Leo! *Real Kidz Rule* was the best programme on the planet, and everyone – even superstars and singers and footballers and Olympic gold medal winners – watched it and came on it to be interviewed and do all kinds of fun things. It held the best competitions and its Remembrance Day competition was one of the most serious and famous competitions of the year. Every school wished they could be in it, even though only ten classes from ten different schools across the whole country got picked to compete. And of those ten classes, the class with the best World War Two display board and assembly got to be interviewed about their projects on TV by Ben and Lily, the show's super-famous presenters!

Which meant that if our class won, then I might get to speak about Leo on TV to the whole world. And that would make him so super-famous that everyone would hear about him – maybe even his family too – no matter where they were!

In that one instant, I think everyone in class imagined themselves being on telly and winning the competition and being interviewed by Ben and Lily, because we all went quiet for exactly three seconds.

'And one more thing,' added Mr Scott over the chattering that had started up again. 'Because our school is the *only* school in Kent to have been selected by the show's judges, the *Whot Gazette* will be doing a piece on us. How about that?'

This time, everyone fell so silent we could hear the wind whistling outside the windows. It was as if our brains had received too much information and needed a Time Out. Then, one by one, as we all understood we were about to become famous, everyone began to whisper and grab each other and hold their faces in their hands and squeal as loudly as a group of mice holding megaphones.

'Mrs Fitzgerald must have forgotten about our last

assembly,' whispered Sangeeta, giving me a grin. 'Or she would never have picked us!'

I nodded, because the truth was, our class hadn't been allowed to do an assembly in ages. Mainly because in our last one, Christine had fallen off the stage, and Harry and Drew had got into a silent fight and accidentally pulled down one of the curtains, and Nancy got the hiccups so bad she was sick in a bucket. I hadn't done anything except pretend to be a rock like I was supposed to, but I still got told off along with the rest of the class. And now suddenly, here we were, about to do the Remembrance Day assembly – the biggest, grandest assembly of the whole year – not just for the whole school, but for the *Real Kidz Rule* show too!

'Now, this is a *huge*, monumental honour,' said Mr Scott, his hands hovering above his desk, ready to thump out the words that mattered. 'And we are going to have to work *very* (THUMP!) hard if we're going to be ready in just three weeks for both the assembly, *and* (THUMP!) the display board! So I want each and every one of you to give it one thousand and one percent. Understand? (Extra-loud THUMP!)'

Everyone nodded solemnly, as if we were all silently swearing allegiance to each other and the board and assembly we had to create together too.

'I want you all to make me proud, make yourselves proud and make Whot proud,' said Mr Scott. 'The whole county will be looking to us to give everyone a memorial project they won't forget. So, are we ready?'

Everyone mumbled a quiet, serious 'yes'.

'I can't hear you,' said Mr Scott.

'YES, SIR!' cried the whole class together.

'Good. Now I'm going to need two teams of volunteers. The first team will help organise the assembly, and the second team will organise the content and design of the display board. The rest of the class will help, of course, but you'll all be guided by the team leaders. So, first, let's *assemble* the assembly team!'

We all stared at Mr Scott in pity as he chuckled at his own joke. But as soon as he asked who wanted to be a part of the assembly team, nearly everyone's hands shot up into the air like arrows getting ready to be released. Even Toby put his hand up, and he *never* put his hand up for anything.

Next to me, Sangeeta was desperately trying to

stretch her arrow of an arm higher than everyone else's.

I kept mine down. I never got good parts in assemblies. In our last assembly where everything had fallen apart, I hadn't wanted to play a silly rock at all. What I had *really* wanted to do was play one of the pirates and get dressed up with an eye patch and a sword. But I didn't get picked because even in make-believe stories, pirates who look like me don't exist.

It didn't matter anyway. Because I wanted to be on the display-board team and put Leo's story on it and make it so big and interesting, that Ben and Lily would have no choice but to interview me and want to find out all about him.

'Kerry, Harry, Tracey and . . .' Mr Scott looked around. 'Toby? Really? You want to volunteer for this?'

We all turned to watch as Toby nodded, his cheeks flushing bright red.

'You sure?' asked Mr Scott again, now frowning and tapping his finger against his chin.

Toby nodded even harder.

'You're going to treat this seriously, and stay behind during lunch breaks and after school to help your team out?'

Toby's head became a blur as his nods sped up. 'Yeah, I promise, sir,' he answered. 'Pleeeeeeeease, sir! I want to do it for my great-grandad.'

Mr Scott paused, and then nodded. 'OK. Let's see how it goes.'

Toby punched the air and whispered 'Yessssss!' As he did so, he looked straight at me, and raising his eyebrows, gave me a sneer.

Ignoring him, I looked back up at Mr Scott.

'Right, now who would like to take the lead for the display board?'

Everyone except the four chosen to lead the assembly threw their hands back into the air again. Sangeeta was biting her lip as she reached as high up into the air as she could. This time, I put my hand up too. I even cheated a bit and sat on my legs so my arm would be higher than Sangeeta's.

'Laura, Gary, Evelyn and . . .'

Mr Scott was looking at the other side of the classroom and not my way at all! I had to do something, so without even thinking, I lifted myself up off my chair and whispered, 'Pleeeeeeeeeeeeeeeeeeeease!'

Mr Scott instantly looked my way. He looked at

me, as if he was surprised to see my hand in the air, and after a few seconds, announced, 'Leo!'

Sangeeta dropped her arm and looked at me in surprise.

'How come you volunteered? You never volunteer for anything!' she whispered, as Mr Scott stuck a huge piece of chart paper up on the wall.

I shrugged, and answered, 'I just felt like it.'

Sangeeta raised her eyebrows and then went back to listening to Mr Scott, who was asking everyone to write down ideas for the topics we wanted our Remembrance Day project to be about.

I already had my idea, so I picked up my pencil and, writing it out quickly, waited for the rest of the class to finish.

'Right, pencils down,' Mr Scott said at last. 'Let's hear what you've got then. Oscar?'

Oscar jumped as if he had just then been bitten on the bottom by an invisible crocodile. Holding his piece of paper out in front of him, he announced, 'I think we should do the bit in the war where everyone goes to France – to Dundee.'

'Dun*kirk*,' corrected Mr Scott.

'Yeah, there,' said Oscar. 'But instead of everyone fighting with guns and grenades and things, we could, like, fight with baguettes and cheese and tomatoes!'

The whole class giggled and Mr Scott bit his lip. Mr Scott was always biting his lip when Oscar said something, because it was usually something that was half-silly and half-clever.

'Interesting idea, Oscar,' he said, writing DUNKIRK out on the big piece of chart paper. 'Next? Nancy, what's your idea?'

Nancy went bright red and shouted, 'Spitfires!'

Mr Scott nodded, writing it down. 'Good. So something about the planes we saw yesterday. Right. Next – Toby?'

We all watched as Toby scratched the tip of his nose with his pencil and then said, 'My great-great-grandfather fought in the war – we should do stories about people like him. You know, people who we're all related to.'

'Ah! I like that idea, Toby,' said Mr Scott, grabbing his red marker and scribbling 'FAMILY HEROES', next to 'SPITFIRES' and 'DUNKIRK'.

Toby gave a silent, proud 'hmph!' as he crossed his

arms and smiled like his idea had already won.

'Yes, Leo?'

Even though I had been raising my hand, I jumped when Mr Scott said my name, and the whole class turned to stare at me. Mr Scott was holding his pen ready in the air, as if it couldn't wait to write out the words I was going to say.

Dropping my hand, I gripped my pencil tight.

'Yes?' prodded Mr Scott.

'I think – I think maybe . . . maybe we could do stories about people who were in the war that no one else knows about – like those people on the wall in the cathedral,' I said, trying to speak as loudly as I could. But my voice came out tiny and muffled, like an echo that was trying to travel through a large, thick cloud.

After a few seconds, my words seemed to reach Mr Scott's ears and finally make their way up into his mind. 'Ah!' he said. 'I see – you mean, forgotten heroes of the Second World War. I like that, Leo! And that might even include people from our own families who haven't been remembered, mightn't it?' Mr Scott tapped Toby's idea with his pen. 'Well! We are on good form today!'

And writing out 'FORGOTTEN HEROES' underneath Toby's idea, Mr Scott drew a star – right next to my idea!

I didn't know what the star meant, but it felt like my small idea and the promise that lay behind it, had just become more real.

By the end of second period, the class had come up with so many ideas that Mr Scott had used two more sheets of chart paper to get everything down. When the bell for first break began to ring, he clapped his hands and said, 'That's an excellent start to our mission. Well done everyone. Right. Now, a lot of the ideas overlap. So . . . let's group them into five key areas, shall we?'

Picking up a large green marker, Mr Scott began circling the five groups of words he thought all the others could fit into.

'He'd better circle mine!' muttered Sangeeta, watching with her eyes narrowed as Mr Scott circled Toby's idea of 'FAMILY HISTORIES', Oscar's 'DUNKIRK' and Kerry's 'BATTLES OF THE SKIES'.

Mr Scott paused, and stepped back to look at the whole list. After a long moment, he went back to the board and first circled my 'FORGOTTEN HEROES' and then, after another pause, Sangeeta's 'WOMEN OF THE WAR'. My heart sprang up like a pogo stick while Sangeeta looked over at me proudly.

'We'll have a vote after lunch, shall we? For the one idea we want to focus all our work for the competition on.'

The whole class nodded excitedly. Everyone in our class loves voting for things. Last week we had voted on whether or not to have a vote on what books we wanted to read for reading time.

'Off you go – tables one, two and three first, please – QUIETLY!' ordered Mr Scott.

As we all left the classroom, I looked back at the five ideas circled in green pen. It was the first time I had ever thought of anything that was special enough to make it up onto the board. And it was the first idea I really cared about. There was no way I could let Mr Scott rub it out or put a cross through it. Not if I wanted to share Leo's story and prove to everyone that people like him had been real war heroes who deserved to be remembered too.

All I had to do was convince everyone in my class

to vote for it. And I had exactly one lunch hour to do it in.

THE LUNCHTIME CAMPAIGN

'Will you vote for me then?' I asked Sangeeta and Nancy and Drew, as we landed at our lunch tables with our trays. I was running out of time – it had already taken fifteen minutes to explain to them why I needed them to vote for my idea. I hadn't even spoken to anyone else yet!

'Hold on,' said Drew, stuffing a huge fork piled high with mashed potato into his mouth. We all waited as he gulped loudly three times. 'You made a promise – to the *dead* guy who's got your name – that you would get him on the *Real Kidz Rule* show? But how did you know we were going to be in the competition? We only found out today!'

Nancy rolled her eyes at him. 'No, silly! He

68

made the promise first, and then the competition came after. It's like Indiana Jones. Indiana always makes the promise first, and then lots of things happen to help him keep his promise. Even though he didn't plan for them. Leo didn't plan the competition. It just came along.'

'Huh? Indiana *who*?' asked Drew, looking even more confused.

'Jones!' answered Nancy. 'Have you never watched an Indiana Jones movie? My dad makes us watch them every Christmas. He's like this hero guy who finds famous lost things from history and gets them for museums and librariers and all sorts of places.'

'He sounds well boring,' muttered Drew, shaking his head back at Nancy.

'Look, will you just vote for me?' I asked, wondering what the point of having friends was if they asked so many questions all the time. 'Here, I'll give you my chocolate pudding if you do.'

'Deal,' Drew said immediately, grabbing the pudding.

'Wait! You can't do that!' said Sangeeta. 'You can't go around BUYING votes. That's like . . .

indoctrination or something. Anyway, it's against the law and you could . . .' Sangeeta looked around and finished in a whisper, '. . . go to JAIL for it!'

I shook my head. 'Kids aren't allowed to be put in jail!'

'Well, maybe you'll go to a detention centre then! My Aunty Vayla says there's one next to her house in Liverpool, and it looks like a prison,' warned Sangeeta.

'Woah . . . a whole centre just for detentions,' said Drew, his mouth hanging open. 'I'm definitely never going there!' And with a shake of his head, he pushed the pudding bowl back over to my side of the table.

'Don't be silly. No one will find out if you don't tell them.' I pushed it back to Drew. He stared at me for a few seconds, his face all scrunched up, before finally picking it back up.

'Fine! Well, *I'm* not voting for yours. I want my idea to win,' said Sangeeta. 'It's every bit as good as yours. You'll vote for it, won't you Nancy? All the girls should, you know!'

Nancy stared at Sangeeta for a second, and then at me, and then quickly stuck a huge chunk of broccoli into her mouth. She must have been desperate to not say anything because we all knew she hated broccoli.

'I'll vote for yours, if you vote for mine,' I said to Sangeeta, looking over at her. Her idea was good too, even if I really needed mine to win. 'We're not allowed to vote for our own ideas anyway.'

Sangeeta raised her eyebrows at me. 'All right. But you'd better.'

'Yeah, of course,' I promised. 'Your idea goes with my idea anyway – because they were kind of forgotten too. The women I mean. Just like you were saying at the museum – that there should have been more about them because they helped the RAF too.'

'Yeah, that's right,' said Sangeeta, looking impressed.

'So, if you think about it,' I went on, 'if MY idea wins, then you get to do your idea too. We could find out about some forgotten *women* heroes too. It could be half-women, half-men.'

'Oh yeah!' said Sangeeta, her eyes lighting up. 'That'd be cool! OK. I'm definitely voting for you then – Nancy, you should too. Let's get everyone to vote for Leo!'

Nancy plonked the half-chewed broccoli back onto

her plate and nodded, looking happier.

I stared up at the dinner hall clock that stood above the big entrance doors. It had taken nearly half an hour to get just three votes. No wonder politicians on the news looked so tired all the time – it was hard work getting people to vote for you. And they probably didn't even have any chocolate puddings to give out!

Gobbling down my pizza in under ten seconds flat, I jumped up from the bench.

'I'm going to go and ask the others,' I said, trying to act braver than I felt. I never really spoke to anyone in class except for Sangeeta and Drew and Nancy. But now I had to – if I really wanted to win.

'I'll come with you,' said Sangeeta, quickly finishing her pudding. I wanted to tell her she didn't have to, but I was secretly glad it wouldn't be just me on my own.

We hurried over to Kerry and Liam and Will and Tracey at the next table. Just behind them were Toby and Catherine. I could tell they were watching me but I ignored them and cleared my throat loudly instead.

'Eh–he–he–HUM!'

Kerry and Tracey both looked up at me and Sangeeta, their eyes all shiny and full of questions.

But Will and Liam kept on eating. So I 'Eh–he–he-HUMMM'd' again, until they looked up too.

'Erm . . . I was wondering. Would you all vote for my idea after lunch. Please?'

'Huh? What did you say?' asked Liam, frowning.

Sangeeta nudged me in the arm. I was being too quiet.

I took a deep breath and tried again. 'I was – I was wondering if you would all vote for my idea – in class. You know, after lunch? My idea about doing things on forgotten heroes.'

They all stared at me. Tracey's mouth fell open, showing me mashed up fish fingers and potato and even peas. It was gross.

'I'm voting for it,' added Sangeeta, her voice a little bit quieter than usual. 'It's important we remember people who've been forgotten. That could include people in our own families too.'

'Can't,' said Liam, quickly looking over his shoulder and then back again at me as if he was scared. 'I promised Toby and Catherine already.'

'Yeah, me too,' said Kerry, half-whispering.

'My great-uncle fought in the war, and Toby said

I'd get to play him in the assembly,' said Will, loudly, as if he wanted Toby to know he wasn't a traitor. 'So, I'm voting for his idea as well.'

Tracey didn't say anything but she nodded in agreement.

I said, 'Oh.'

Then, with a nearly silent 'thanks' that even I couldn't hear, I walked away, heading back to Drew and Nancy. From behind me, I could feel Toby and Catherine laughing at me.

'Wait! Where are you going? We've got like, five more tables left,' said Sangeeta, grabbing my arm and pulling me to a stop.

'There's no point, is there?' I asked, feeling my face burning. 'Toby's already got everyone to vote for him. He's going to win. And anyway, everyone else has got people in their families they can play and talk about to the *Real Kidz Rule* people. Not like us! So of course they're going to vote for his idea. Let's just leave it.'

Snatching my arm away from Sangeeta, I plonked myself back down at our table, and began stuffing my face with mashed potato. I didn't want to look at Sangeeta or anyone else. If I hadn't had to spend so long trying to get them to understand what I meant earlier, maybe I could have tried to convince more people. But now it was too late!

After a few seconds, Sangeeta came and sat down next to me, and began pushing things around loudly on her plate. Even her mashed potato began to screech, which meant she was super-angry at me. But I didn't care, so I didn't bother looking over at her. Not even once.

We all ate our lunch in silence and afterwards, Drew forced us all to play a short game of tennis-ball rounders to help us try and be friends again. When the school bell finally rang again, we rushed back to class. Mr Scott had taken down all the sheets of paper, and had written out the top five ideas in giant green lettering on the whiteboard instead.

Seeing my idea in even bigger letters than before made my insides jump up for a second, before falling right back down again. There was no chance I was going to win. Not when Toby had spoken to everyone already and had probably threatened to throw bigger things than just tennis balls at them if he didn't win.

'Right, everyone, hop to it,' said Mr Scott, closing

the door loudly. 'Remind yourselves of the top five ideas, any one of which will be brilliant for us to explore and bring to life in the coming weeks. And then write down your favourite one – just ONE – on a piece of paper.'

Mr Scott walked around the class, giving a small strip of paper to each of us. 'After you're done, fold it up, and put it in this mug.'

Mr Scott held up the giant mug he always used for votes, as if we had never seen it before. It was a *Lord of the Rings* one, which showed Frodo and Sam, both looking dirty and half-crying – as if they were both so exhausted by the number of voting papers they had to hold for us every week, that they couldn't be bothered to finish their quest.

There was silence as everyone furiously grabbed their pencils. Sangeeta gave me a nudge, to make sure I was going to honour my promise. I gave her a nod and began writing out 'Women of the War' on my sheet. I wondered if Nancy and Drew were keeping their promises. Maybe they would, or maybe they secretly wanted to talk about all the heroes in their families and would vote for Toby too.

Slowly, one by one, everyone walked up to the front of the class to drop their piece of paper into the tops of Frodo's and Sam's heads. Mr Scott was sitting in his chair with his feet up on his desk, and his eyes closed, looking like a big cat basking in the sun.

I watched as Toby got up to hand his paper in, and wondered if he remembered he couldn't vote for himself. Probably not. I even hoped he *wouldn't* remember, so that Mr Scott could catch him and disqualify him.

After everyone had given their votes in, Mr Scott told us to get our maths books out and do all the equations on page sixty-seven in silence. We all opened our books, but I could tell that no one cared about doing any of the equations correctly. We were too busy watching Mr Scott count the votes and make marks for each one on a piece of paper.

Trying to ignore the ticking of the clock, which felt as if it was ticking inside my brain, I managed to copy three of Sangeeta's sums and do a few on my own, before Mr Scott finally got up, and told us to close our books.

It was time!

Crossing my fingers under the table again, I watched as Mr Scott went over to the whiteboard with his bright green super-spongey eraser.

'Right, here we go then! Drum roll, please . . .'

Everyone in class made a drum roll by banging their hands on their tables or stomping on the floor.

'In last place . . . Battles of the Skies,' announced Mr Scott as he wiped it off the board.

There were giggles as Kerry booed.

'In fourth place . . . Women of the War.' Another swipe and Sangeeta's idea vanished too.

Next to me, Sangeeta gave a wolf-like growl and looked over her shoulder to growl at everyone else too.

I put my head in my hands and looked through my fingers, feeling slightly sick. The next idea to be voted out was going to be mine . . . I just knew it.

'In third place . . . Dunkirk!' With a third swish of the eraser, Oscar's idea disappeared.

'Ah, maaaaaaaaaaaaaaaaaaan!' cried Oscar, as he jumped up and put his hands on his hips. 'We could have thrown tomato bombs – tomato bombs!'

As the class laughed, Sangeeta seemed to forget she was angry and rattled my arm. 'You're still in!' she whispered, as if I didn't know already. I peeked through my fingers at the two remaining ideas on the board: there was just mine and Toby's left now . . .

The whole class fell quiet, watching Mr Scott as he looked down at his results sheet.

'And now . . .'

'YESSSSSSSSSSSSSSSSSS!' hissed Toby, as if he had won already.

'TIED for first place . . . with an equal number of votes exactly, are Family Histories AND Forgotten Heroes!'

'WHAT!' cried out Toby, jumping up in protest.

'It's a tie, Leo – you've tied with Toby!' said Sangeeta, shaking me so hard I almost fell off my chair. 'You won – kind of!'

I took my hands away from my face and stared at the board. The words for my idea were still up there. Somehow enough people in my class had voted for it to be joint first – even though my lunchtime campaign had failed and I hadn't even had a chance to speak to most of them! I looked around at everyone as they began banging their desks and stomping their feet at the results, wondering who had voted for me and why.

'RECOUNT,' yelled Toby.

'Yeah!' shouted Catherine. 'I don't want to do Forgotten Heroes – they were probably forgotten for a reason!'

'QUIET! And Toby, sit back down, NOW,' said Mr Scott, his eyes bulging out. 'There will be no recount; it was a tie. And as the ideas work nicely together, this shouldn't be a problem, now, SHOULD it? We can easily cover both themes with our project.'

Toby sat down reluctantly and scowled at me. But I didn't care. Not even a little bit! I gazed up at my two words, FORGOTTEN HEROES, as they glowed out at me with a bright green shimmer. They were words everyone had liked enough to keep up. Words that were going to help me find out about the real Leo, and maybe even make everyone in school and on TV know that someone with a name like mine could be special and important after all.

DOUBLE LIVES

'The library? But it's Friday!' protested Drew. 'We can't go to the library on a *Friday night* – what will people say?'

'Yeah,' agreed Nancy. 'Plus I've got recorder practice. So I can't come anyway.'

'And I've got a life that's *not* sad, so I'm definitely not going,' said Drew. 'Just imagine if Toby or Catherine saw us in there? They'd *demolish* us. No thanks.'

'Fine, you guys go then! I'll see you on Monday,' I said, speeding up and leaving Drew and Nancy behind in the corridor.

Sangeeta had left already. She had rushed off the second the bell had rung to meet her dad; her grandmother was coming for the weekend and she had to go and try and look human. 'Human' to Sangeeta's grandmother meant extra-neat hair and lots of bangles and clothes that looked as if they were made for a princess – a princess in India that is. Not in Whot. I don't think any real princesses have ever been to Whot. Not even an English one.

Running up the corridor, I headed up the stairs and past the upper floor hall to where the school library was. It wasn't very big, but it was the only one in the whole of Whot. If anyone who wasn't at school wanted to borrow books or go to a bookshop, they had to travel to a real town somewhere else in Kent.

As I reached the library doors, I could see Mr Davies, the assistant librarian, helping someone out with something. The rest of the place looked empty, so I made my way inside and hurried past the counter to where the shelves marked 'History' were. But when I turned the corner, there was someone there already, leaning against the shelves with a big book in their hands.

It was Olivia! I froze.

She looked down at me with a frown. I stared back – mainly at her knees. She had drawn an ice cream on her left knee and a helicopter on the right one, and had even coloured them in.

I pulled my eyes up to her face. Without saying a single word, her eyes told me to get lost, so I ran straight out of the library into the playground without looking back even once. I knew right away that she didn't want anyone else to know I had seen her and looked directly into her eyes – even if it was by accident. But I couldn't help wondering why the coolest girl in school was in the library on a Friday night holding a book about World War Two. And why, just seconds before she had seen me, she had grabbed the corner of a page as if she was about to rip it right out.

* * *

'Come on, Leo, gǎnkuài, gǎnkuài! We haven't got all day! And Bo! Your room *better* be tidy – don't make me go in there, please!'

Bo muttered, 'As if they're going to see my room!'

He rushed past me into the kitchen, where Dad was cooking and making a thousand smells mingle in the air. Clouds of steam and hissing noises were coming from the direction of the stove, along with the sound of Dad singing his favourite Malay song, like a bird that was being strangled. Dad sang songs in all the languages we could speak but never spoke outside the house – like Tamil and Chinese and Malay. He loved singing The Beatles too. But he always sang in Malay when he had to do lots of cooking.

'Oh no . . . they'll be here any minute!' squealed Mum, as she finished polishing the big wooden dining table and began to polish Jingyi too.

I quickly finished dusting the books and the million trinkets on our bookshelves, and held the brush out to Mum, ready for my next task. Mum frowned at me, instantly suspicious.

'Are you feeling OK, Leo?' she asked, as Jingyi crawled over to me and slapped me on the leg.

'Yeah,' I shrugged. 'Why?'

'Nothing . . .' Mum's frown became even deeper. 'It's just not like you to be so . . . helpful.'

I shrugged and tried not to grin. Usually I hated Saturdays when we were having guests over – which was nearly every Saturday! It seemed that just because we lived in the countryside and had a big garden, everyone on the planet who we were related to – and lots of people we weren't related to – wanted to come for lunch and dinner and sometimes even stay the whole weekend. I didn't really mind the actual lunch or dinner bits. Or the tea and everyone laughing and talking and playing games. They were fun and often meant I was allowed to stay up extra-late too.

The bit I hated was the bit that came *before* all those bits. The bit that made Mum turn into a wild-eyed monster who roared at us to clean up the whole house all morning, while Dad cooked a million dishes, and Bo grunted louder and louder, like an angry bear, with each passing hour. It was like getting the house ready for a Christmas party every week – but without a tree or any cool presents. So of course I hated most Saturday mornings.

But this Saturday was different.

This Saturday I had a question that I needed to ask my Aunty Leia and Uncle Hilaal and whoever else was coming with them – and Mum and Dad too. I had been waiting days to find the perfect moment to ask them my questions, and this was going to be it! Because Mum and Dad always listened to me in front of guests. They never told me they were too busy to talk, or pretended they hadn't heard me. Plus Dad always said Aunty Leia and Uncle Hilaal were world-class gossips and knew everything about everyone dead or alive, so I figured having them there would help too.

I planned to ask them about my name and why I had been given it *and* see what they knew about the real Leo too. All I had to do was make sure everyone was in the best mood ever. So I had brushed my hair and teeth until they were extra-shiny and had put on my smartest blue teluk belanga shirt without putting up a fight, and as soon as the guests came, I was going to smile extra hard and bring everyone so many cups of green tea that they would have no choice but to answer my questions.

After another hour of scrubbing and shining and plumping and hoovering, everything in the house was finally sparkling, just like the houses in adverts for cleaning products. Bo had helped Mum lay the table with our best plates and glasses, and everyone was so dressed up we all looked like we were in a film. Mum was in her favourite blue laced baju kurung – a long, lacy top with a silk skirt – and wearing a long string of pearls and beads that Jingyi was trying to eat. Bo and

Dad were dressed in the same kind of shirt as me but in different colours. If anyone from school or from Mum and Dad's workplaces had looked through our windows just then, I don't think they would have recognised us even a bit. It was as if we were living double lives – with different foods and smells and music and clothes that no one could know about unless they were invited. I was sure no one else in my class had to do any of this every weekend – except Sangeeta. She had to live a double life too. Except she was a princess in hers, while I was an unpaid servant.

DING DONG.

'They're here!' screamed Mum, as if the arrival of our guests was a surprise and we hadn't been cleaning up for them all morning. She ran out onto the corridor with Jingyi crawl-running behind her.

Dad gave us a pat on our backs and whispered, 'Best behaviour, boys. And usual drill. If anyone gives you any money, you are NOT to take it. Got that?'

Bo grunted, but shook his head at me as soon as Dad had looked away. It was the one thing we both agreed on: not being able to take money from people trying to give you some was definitely a crime against humanity. Which is why we never, ever listened to Dad about it.

'Ohhhhhhh! Look at the boys!' screamed Aunt Leia, as she dived straight for my cheeks. Before I could even take a breath, her huge hands had grabbed my face and was pulling it in three different directions, as her nose squished itself up against mine.

As she moved on to do the same to Bo and Dad, Uncle Hilaal grabbed me by the hand and pulled me into his wall of a chest three times for a three-time hug. On the last one, he whispered, 'Don't tell your dad!' and slipped something into my hand.

I looked down and grinned: stuffed into my palm was a ten-pound note. Score! I quickly hid it in my shirt pocket, just as an old man I was sure I had seen before but couldn't remember the name of, came to give me a three-time hug too. He was tall and had extra-shiny eyes and extra-wrinkly hands and cheeks, so it was like being hugged by a turtle. I waited for him to give me something too, but he just patted me on the head and smiled.

Once everyone had greeted everyone else, I tried to look as sweet and as cute as possible by helping to get all of Dad's hot dishes out of the kitchen, and showing people where to sit and smiling so much that I was sure my cheeks were going to fall off. I knew I had to find the perfect moment to ask my question, so all through dinner, I listened and looked for it. Then, just as Aunt Leia had finished telling yet another story about her neighbour back in Singapore, I found it: the prefect moment.

Mum and Dad were busy serving some more rice to everyone, Jingyi had fallen asleep in her high chair, and Aunt Leia and Uncle Hilaal and the old turtle man, whose name seemed to be Grand-Elder, were nodding at one another as if they were having a secret silent conversation. This was it! I had to ask it now!

'Why am I called Leo?' I asked the table, as loudly as I could.

Everyone stopped and stared at me. In the silence, a big dollop of rice fell off Dad's serving spoon and splashed into his lobster soup.

I looked back at everyone, and waited for an answer.

'Why are you asking, son?' asked Dad. I could see Mum shaking her head and heard her whisper, 'Funny boy!'

'Just – I want to know,' I said, telling my cheeks to not even think about turning any redder.

My Aunt Leia looked over at Mum and raised her long, pencilled-over eyebrows. She and Mum looked too different to be related at all, but, sometimes, flashes of them being cousins shone out – like now. When they were standing close and looking at each other, everyone could see they had the same-shaped nose and lips too.

'Yes, I have always wondered about that too,' said Aunt Leia.

'Well, it's no secret,' said Dad, sitting down and looking at me. 'My father, your yeye – asked us to.'

'Really?' I asked, feeling confused. 'But wasn't Grandad's name Tan?'

Dad nodded. 'Yes. That's right. But when we told him we were expecting you, he said we had to name you Leo – that it was his wish.'

'He never explained why,' said Mum. 'He was going to tell us when he came to visit. He had booked his plane ticket to come and see you, but just a few days before he was due to fly, he died. So he never got to see you, and we never found out.'

'Why are you asking, Leo? Has someone at school

said something?' asked Dad, looking both stern and worried at the same time.

I shook my head. I wanted to tell Mum and Dad about the Leo from the cathedral wall and the *Real Kidz Rule* competition, but the perfect moment for doing that hadn't come yet. I didn't want to say something that might sound silly in front of Aunt Leia or Uncle Hilaal – or the old turtle man.

'I just – I just wanted to know,' I said, shrugging to make it seem as if I didn't care and sticking a huge piece of prata bread into my mouth.

'Well, we've always thought that someone who your grandfather loved very much must have been named Leo,' said Dad. 'Someone in his family. Or maybe a friend. So we honoured him by following his last wish. But we didn't have anyone else to ask who this Leo might have been. Your grandmother might have known, but she didn't even live to see Bo, and everyone else – like your uncles and aunts – knew even less than we did.'

Everyone went quiet again – especially Dad. He always went extra-quiet when he thought about his mum and dad and remembered that they weren't alive any more. We had lots of photos of them in Singapore – mainly of them smiling and waving from different chairs or from their garden. In every single one of them, my grandmother had a flower in her hair, and my grandad had his topi hat on. I wished they were still alive. It would have been nice to pick up the phone and hear their voices or even have got to meet them. They looked like they had been nice people – the kind of people who would have spoiled their grandkids.

'*Leo* . . .' whispered the old turtle man. '*Leo*. Kai. Lim . . . it is a good name.'

I sat up straight and waited, willing him to say something else. Maybe he had been friends with my grandad before my dad or my uncles and aunts had even been born! He definitely looked old enough. Maybe he knew my grandad and knew that he actually had a *secret* life where maybe he'd been a spy called Leo! Or maybe there was another Leo hidden away in the family that no one knew of, who might have been linked to the Leo from the cathedral, and who only my grandad knew about. Maybe that was why he had wanted to fly to come and see me – so he could tell my mum and dad about the secret in person!

I waited, as the old man smiled at me with his large, droopy eyes. Reaching out, he gave me another pat on the head and went straight back to eating his plate of rice-and-prawn curry.

An invisible boulder sank to the bottom of my stomach.

He didn't know. He didn't know anything at all. And the only person who did had died before I had even been born, in a house and in a country on the other side of the planet.

— — — •—•• —••

MISSING PAGES

'Well, that sucks.'

Sangeeta looked over at me as we waited in line for the tuck shop. It was a bad idea to get in line for the tuck shop on a Monday in first break – it was always super-long. But for some reason, every week, Sangeeta just had to, which meant I had to as well.

Shaking her head in pity at me as if I was a stray puppy no one wanted, Sangeeta gave me a light thump on the arm. 'Maybe your grandad wanted to name you "Leo" so you'd get good jobs and no one would know where you really came from. That's why my cousins Amardeep and Jasleen are really called Andrew and Laura in their passports and things – although their last names are still Singh, so I don't think my aunt and uncle thought it through. But it doesn't matter. The cool thing is, your idea won – which means, *my* idea also kind of won! So what if your parents don't know why you're called Leo? The main thing is finding out about the other Leo from the cathedral. He's more important, isn't he?'

I nodded. Sangeeta was right. The Leo in the cathedral *was* more important than me and whoever it was I had been named after.

'Well then. I'll find out about soldiers named Singh who have been forgotten, and women from India too, and you'll find out about the Leo from the cathedral, and it'll all be awesome,' finished Sangeeta, looking proud of her mini lecture.

'Yeah . . . It would still be nice to know, though. Are *you* named after anyone?' I asked, as I glanced around the playground. I could see Drew having some kind of wrestling match in the corner of the playground with Gary. Kerry and Nancy and Stuart were playing tag. Catherine and Toby and Daniel and Adam were staring at everyone in the tuck shop queue – as if we were bits of candy that they were going to feast on later. I bet all of them had been named after someone they knew – or at least for a reason their parents knew about.

'Yeah – I'm named after my nani on my mum's side. Although I hope I don't end up as crazy as she is. Look at what she did! Even though I told her not to . . .' Sangeeta showed me the palms of her hands, which were covered in giant swirls of orange flowers. 'Who wants mehndi on in the middle of school! It's going to be orange for days, and then it'll look I've got some weird disease. It's not even Diwali or Baba Nanak's birthday or anything!'

Sangeeta shoved her hands in her pockets. 'Sometimes I really hate being Indian.'

I knew what she meant. Leading a secret double life at home only worked if that life didn't ever spill out into school. But no matter how hard Sangeeta and I tried to blend in, something always went wrong. Like our parents' accents being heard by everyone on parents' evenings. Or having to take extra days off from school to celebrate days that were just as big as Christmas, but which no one else knew or really cared about. Or eating things at the packed-lunch table that made everyone stare.

The only good thing about having a double life was that we both had families in places no one else in school had heard of – not even the teachers – which meant we got sent all kinds of presents and gifts and foods that no one else could buy, *especially* not in Whot. And we got to go on holiday to cool places too, although the last time I had been to Singapore I was so little that I couldn't really remember anything about it.

Sometimes I looked at the big fat photo albums that were all as thick as dictionaries, that Mum and Dad kept in a special cabinet. They contained memories that didn't seem real. Memories of homes that looked like summer hotels, surrounded by lakes and mango trees and giant birds, and filled with cousins and aunts and uncles who I had never seen again, but who, in the photos, seemed to be hugging me as if one day I might.

'Anyway,' said Sangeeta, standing up on her tiptoes to try and see how many people were still in front of us in the queue, 'did you find out anything about the other Leo in the library?'

With a jolt, I suddenly remembered Olivia, and told Sangeeta what I had seen.

'No WAY!' she gasped. 'She was going to rip a page out of a library book? That's illegal!'

I rolled my eyes at her. 'That's not what's important. What's important is, what was *on* the page that she was going to rip out?'

'Maybe it was something for homework? The whole school's doing World War Two right now.'

'Maybe, but then, why wouldn't she just borrow the book?' I asked, as from up ahead, Mrs Harris shouted, 'NEXT!'

I didn't say anything else to Sangeeta, but I couldn't get rid of the feeling that I had seen something more important than Olivia just doing homework. She had looked like she had been upset at something in the book. And it had upset her so much that she had wanted to rip a part of it out.

After morning lessons were finally over and the lunch bell rang, I decided to run back to the library and begin my research properly. Mr Scott had told us the volunteer leaders for the board and the assembly were going to have their first planning meeting the very next day – so I had to work fast and hard now if I wanted the real Leo to be included in them.

'I'll see you at lunch,' I told Sangeeta, as I ran out of class. 'I need to do some research.'

'Oooh! Hold on!' shouted Sangeeta, as she ran after me. 'I'll come too – I need to find things out as well, remember.'

We sprinted up the stairs leading to the library doors. It was much busier than it had been on Friday – it looked as if everyone was trying to get books returned or doing last-minute homework.

Along the back wall, I spotted two computers that were free, and made a dash for them. We were only allowed fifteen minutes on the computers during lunch break, and that wasn't going to be enough time, but I could at least make a start. I wished I had my own computer at home, but Mum and Dad told me I couldn't have my own one until I turned eleven – which was still two whole years away. Bo was meant to share his computer and tablet with me, but he never did, and Mum and Dad were always on the home one, so it was like having no computer at all.

As Sangeeta sat down with a thud next to me, I quickly typed in my school username and logged in, and then tapped the internet icon. It was the rule that if an internet search wasn't linked to a school subject, it would get blocked. So as the bar popped out in front of me, I typed in the words, 'World War 2 Leo Kai Lim DFC', and waited for all the results to appear. There had to be results – lots and lots of them. There just had to be.

But instead of pages and pages of search results, an empty page popped up, with the words:

No results found. Did you mean **Leo Kay Hai?**

I clicked on the name being offered – only to find out it was the name of a famous actor.

I tried again, this time taking away the letters 'D F C'. But again, there was nothing on the whole of the internet to be found.

I tried a third time, deleting the words 'World War 2'. But a big box appeared on the screen and flashed red, warning me that 'NO UNAUTHORISED SEARCHES ARE PERMITTED.' The computer had locked me out!

'Well, what do we have here?'

I jumped in my seat and looked over my shoulder.

Mr Davies was standing behind me with his arms crossed.

Sangeeta blinked at me like an owl while everyone else in the library fell quiet.

'You do know you can't do personal searches, right?' asked Mr Davies, as if the big red box still flashing at me from the computer screen hadn't made that clear enough already. 'Can you tell me what you were searching for?'

I opened my mouth and wanted to tell him I was searching for a war hero who had the same name as me, which was emblazoned on a cathedral wall. But instead, all that came out a hiccup, followed by the words, 'My name.'

'You're googling your own name?' asked Mr Davies, frowning. 'Done something to change the world already, have you?'

I shook my head, as Sangeeta jumped in.

'It's for our class project, sir,' she explained. 'Leo found a name – his exact name – above the door of the cathedral we went to for our school trip last week. We wanted to find out about *that* Leo.'

'Ah,' said Mr Davies, his face immediately less

frowny. 'You won't be able to search just names on here, I'm afraid,' he said, leaning over me and typing fast. 'Best you try the history section instead – we've got lots of books there that might have the information you're searching for. And maybe ask your teacher to come authorise your search or help you do one in class. OK?'

As the red box disappeared and a new login screen appeared, I nodded. Everyone else in the library went back to what they had been doing, disappointed that nothing more had happened. Mr Davies was famous for never, ever getting angry. Not even when someone put bubble-gum in between the pages of all the copies of *Great Expectations*. It was a secret mission of lots of kids to make him so angry that he burst. It hadn't happened yet though, so everyone was always on the lookout, just in case.

Mr Davies went back to join Ms Fields at the big desk.

'Can I use that now then?' asked a small kid standing next to me, carrying so many books he looked like he might fall over.

I got up and gave him my chair.

'I'm staying here,' said Sangeeta. 'I've still got ten minutes.'

'OK,' I said. 'I'm going to the history section.'

Sangeeta nodded absent-mindedly, as she quickly scribbled something down in her pad. It looked as if she had found enough stories about women in the war to fill the whole board already!

Heading over to the same shelves I had tried to search on Friday, I was glad to see that this time there was no one around. With my fingers, I scanned the shelves for the section I needed. Ancient Romans . . . The Vikings . . . Ancient Greece . . . The Tudors . . . The Victorians . . . The British Empire . . . and finally, World War Two.

I picked up the biggest book I could find there, a book filled with photographs of heroes just like the ones we had seen at the RAF museum. Flicking through it, I searched for a face that might be a Leo Kai Lim, but didn't see any. I turned to 'L' in the index, just in case our surname was there. It wasn't. There was a section labelled 'RAF' but everyone in it looked the same as all the pictures in the museum.

I opened another book, and then another and

another, but none of them had anything about soldiers who weren't from Britain or America or Europe. I opened one book about the people who had been hurt by the Nazis and put in horrible camps. It was filled with terrible pictures of people starving and looking scared, so I quickly put it back onto the shelf again and grabbed the next one. This one was heavier than all the rest, and as soon as I pulled it out, I knew it was the book Olivia had been holding. I recognised the faces on the cover right away.

Right away, it fell open to a space where some pages were missing. The jagged edges of paper that had been ripped away stuck out like the sharp teeth of a saw. I touched them and counted the layers . . . four saws. Meaning four whole pages had been ripped out.

'What's that?'

I looked up to see Sangeeta standing in front of me, holding a sheet of paper filled with scribbles and arrows.

'YOU didn't do that, did you?' she asked in a whisper.

'No!' I whispered back. 'But this is the book I saw Olivia with – I think she did it!'

Sangeeta pointed to the number at the bottom of the open page.

'Sixty-two,' she said. 'The first missing page is sixty-three. Look in the contents page to see what was on it.'

I flipped to the contents page. We both scrolled down the list of page numbers on the right until our fingers hit 'Pages 63–68'. The heading to the left of it read: *The Role of Africa & Asia in World War Two*.

'Why would Olivia tear out these pages?' asked Sangeeta.

I shook my head. It didn't make any sense for Olivia to tear the pages out. But what made even less sense was that the pages that had been torn out, were pages I had never even known existed. No-one had ever said anything about Africa and Asia being a part of World War Two in class or in assembly – or even in our school textbooks. And as I stared down at the torn out pages, I began to ask myself why.

DEAD ENDS

All that afternoon, as Mr Scott talked about multiple division and, for some reason, threw marbles into a jam jar, I thought about the missing pages of the library book and why Olivia would want to rip them out.

Was it so that no one else could ever read them? But why would those pages matter to her? It didn't make sense. Just like it didn't make sense that in all our lessons about the war, and in all those glass cabinets at the RAF museum, there were no pictures or newspapers about people from those continents being part of the war too.

Ding-ding-ding-ding-ding!

The school bell shook me awake. I had been thinking so much about the ripped pages and Olivia that I hadn't even realised it was home-time.

'Everyone, stay seated!' said Mr Scott, as the class started packing their pencil cases and grabbing their rucksacks. 'I have something to give you all.' He began handing out a sheet of paper to each of us.

'These are permission slips. If your parents are happy for you to be included in the filming for the *Real Kidz Rule* show, they HAVE to sign them by this Friday morning at the latest. Got that?'

We all nodded as the precious pieces of paper landed in our eagerly stretched out hands.

'No signature means no filming. No exceptions,' said Mr Scott. 'The film crew may be coming as early as next week. Tonight, I want you all to think of one story from your family history, or one forgotten hero, who you want to talk about for this project. First thing tomorrow, leaders of the board and assembly teams, you'll be getting together to listen to all the stories and decide how you want to have them be acted out or displayed. Then you'll be presenting your ideas back to the rest of the class. Remember, I want *everyone's* stories to be included both on the board and in the assembly. Understood?'

Everything suddenly sounded so big and important that the whole class was quiet. Mr Scott must have felt the change in the air, because after he gave out the last sheet of paper to the back row, he headed to the door and, instead of opening it up to let us go, turned around to look at us. We all waited, our permission slips glued to our hands.

'Now, you lot, before you leave, I want you to understand this,' said Mr Scott, his voice suddenly deep and echoey. 'If we're going to have even a chance of winning this competition for the school, you are going to have to work extra-hard *together* and really help each other. I want you to remember that you are all on the same side, working to complete the same mission. Understood?'

'Kind of like an army?' asked Nancy, shyly.

Mr Scott smiled. 'That's an excellent way of putting it, Nancy. Yes! Just like an army. Because each of you will have different roles that you will need to complete to the best of your ability so that everyone in the class wins. You'll need to listen to your leaders. Think of them like generals, making a call to arms. Can anyone remember what a "call to arms" is?'

Sangeeta thrust her hand into the air, and as soon as she was picked, explained, 'An appeal for help! And, like, an order for everyone to take action.'

'Exactly! So everyone needs to be ready to help and get stuck in, until our mission is complete. Understood?'

The whole class nodded in silence.

'Good. Off you go then.'

Mr Scott threw the door wide open, and we left the classroom in a hurricane of excited whispers. Even though we weren't doing anything even a bit as serious as going into a real war, being told we were like an army made us feel as serious as if we were.

'Out of my way, LOSER,' hissed Toby, pushing me aside and running on ahead.

Ignoring Toby, Drew shook his head at me. 'All this extra homework – and we don't even get paid,' he said, tutting.

Walking home with Dad that afternoon, I decided I had to tell him and Mum and Bo that I was a leader-general now. Making the call to the arms of my class wasn't going to be enough if I really wanted to find out about the real Leo's story. I was going to have to call on all my family's arms too.

Waiting for Mum and Dad and Bo and even Jingyi to be in the same room and be quiet at the exact same time is never easy. That kind of quiet only ever happened at dinner-time. And even then, it didn't *always* happen. But I waited anyway, right up until we had all sat down and finished our first bowls of soup, and then I did it: I told them all about it! About the competition and how my idea had been chosen and how I might get to be on the *Real Kidz Rule* show if my part of the project was really good. Bo grunted at me, Mum told me she was really proud of me, and Jingyi threw a dumpling at my face, which I think was her way of celebrating too. But Dad gave my hair a ruffle which he only ever did when he was really happy with me, and said I could have whatever I wanted for dessert, so I chose three scoops of chocolate ice cream with nuts on top.

I wanted so much to tell Mum and Dad all about the Leo on the church wall and his DFC, but I decided I didn't want to do it in front of Bo again – not when I had tried already and he hadn't really cared. So I had to wait until I could be alone with them, properly.

Straight after dinner, Bo ran up to his room like a prisoner released from jail, and Jingyi went to sleep in her downstairs cot. Mum and Dad sat down to watch their favourite Chinese drama, which always had people staring dramatically at each other whilst the camera zoomed in on them as if looking for zits.

'Dad?'

'Hm?'

Dad was munching on a pack of spicy crackers, his eyes fixed on the TV.

'What time is it in Singapore right now?'

My question made Dad look over at me right away. Mum carried on watching the telly, bursting out laughing as one of the characters went flying into a bush.

'Well, let's see . . .' Dad looked up at our giant living-room clock. 'It's nearly eight o'clock here, so it would be . . .' Dad counted the hours out on his fingers. 'Four in the morning over there. Why?'

'Oh,' I said, realising that my plan wasn't going to work even a little bit.

'Why do you want to know, Leo?' Dad tried again.

'I – I . . .' I could feel my voice starting to disappear, so I forced it out. 'I wanted to ask if . . . if maybe I could call someone – over there.'

'Like who?' asked Mum, now looking over at me too.

'Grand-aunty Lin,' I answered, without even thinking about it. Grand-aunty Lin was Dad's oldest living aunt. She lived in Indonesia, but whenever she came to visit us – which was at least once a year, she always told everyone all kinds of family stories.

'I – I wanted to see if maybe *she* knows why Grandad called me Leo. And maybe if she knew a famous soldier from history who had my name – like, from her school books.'

Mum reached out and paused the telly with the remote control. 'Why this interest in your name all of a sudden?' she asked.

'You're *sure* no one is making fun of you at school, Leo?' asked Dad, sitting up straighter.

I shook my head, thinking that even if they were, Dad would never do anything about it. 'No – it's for the display board,' I replied. 'For the Second World War project I'm a leader of. I have to find out about real heroes who have been forgotten. Like the hero on the church wall – in Rochester. The one with the exact same name as me.'

Mum and Dad stared at me with their crackers only half-munched as I told them all about the Leo carved into stone and his golden lion, and why I had to find out about him and put him on the board so that everyone else in the world could know about him too. When I finished, Dad said, 'Ah! That explains it.'

But Mum was shaking her head.

'Sweetheart, it's *wonderful* that there's a soldier who had the same name as you. But I doubt your Grand-aunty Lin or anyone in the family would know anything about him. Lots of people from all across Asia fought in the Second World War. But we don't have all their names in our history books,' said Mum, pulling me towards her. 'So many of them came back and never spoke about what happened to them.'

'So you *knew* that people from our country fought in the Second World War?' I asked, wondering why they had never said anything to me before. Was I the only one who didn't know?

'Of course,' said Dad. 'It's called a *world* war for a reason, Leo. There was barely a country in the world that wasn't involved somehow.'

'Did we – so did we have anyone in our family who

went abroad to fight in it too, then – and, who like, died?' I asked, my words tripping over one another to get out. I pulled my mum's arms closer around me.

'Maybe,' said Mum. 'The thing is, we don't really know. I'm not sure if anyone in our immediate family went *abroad* to fight in the war. They had to protect their own homes too, you see.'

'Oh,' I said, feeling my insides drown like a freshly hit battleship. After a few seconds of thinking hard about what to ask next, I decided to try and ask something completely different instead.

'Well, do you think Grand-aunty Lin would remember why Grandad named me Leo then?' I asked, crossing my fingers secretly.

Dad shook his head. 'I doubt it. If she did, she would have told us.'

'What about Su?' asked Mum, looking at Dad. 'She might know something. She spent the most time with your baba before he left us.'

Suddenly the battleship inside me bobbed back up to the surface of the water again. Of course – Aunt Su – Dad's sister! She had only ever visited us once, but she was always writing things down and I knew she had been living in my grandparents' old house since they had died. She would *definitely* know.

'Oh! Can we call her?' I asked. 'Pleeeeeeeeeeeeeeeee-eeeeeeeease!'

Dad sighed. 'Leo, she doesn't know. I asked her too – when you were first born. Nobody knows. Maybe it's meant to stay that way – a mystery.'

'Well, maybe they just didn't remember before – and might remember now?' I tried.

Mum gave me a tight squeeze. 'That's unlikely, darling. Now. No more questions. It's getting late. Time to go get ready for bed, please.' With a kiss, she released me and pressed play on the remote control.

I slowly climbed the stairs and got ready for bed like I had been told to. But instead of going to sleep, I decided I had to do whatever I could to stay awake. Because if Mum and Dad weren't going to help me make the calls and get my family to remember things they might not have remembered before, then I would just need to make the calls all by myself. I knew where the huge family phone book with the millions of numbers in it was. And even though it was late here, Singapore was hours ahead of us, so everyone there would be waking up by the time Mum and Dad had gone to bed.

To keep my eyes from closing, I decided to draw out my ideas for the display board. I did a much better drawing of the cathedral than the one I had done for my homework report, and then added a huge lion above the door, and the real Leo's name. Then I tried to draw one of the RAF badges I had seen in the museum, but the eagle came out looking like a huge, bald ostrich. Just as I was trying to fix it, Dad shouted at me to turn off the lights.

So I got out my mini glow-in-the-dark alien figures and, sitting up under my duvet so that it covered me like a tent, I pretended that they were soldiers and I was the real Leo, flying a plane with a golden lion on it, right into the heat of battle. I put-put-putted my way through all my other glow-in-the-dark enemies, and swerved and ducked and steered right and left and freed all the captured lands. I was just about to fly out to sea when, suddenly, I heard my bedroom door creaking open!

I immediately dropped dead like an Egyptian mummy that was wrapped up in bedsheets instead of bandages and held my breath. I could hear Dad whispering my name to check I was asleep, before closing the door, and heading down the corridor to shout at Bo to go to sleep.

Mum and Dad were finally going to bed.

Pulling the duvet off, I crept up to my door and listened. Mum and Dad's bedroom door and then the bathroom door kept opening and shutting. Finally, after I felt like I had aged by three whole years and turned twelve, everything fell silent. Even Jingyi.

This was it . . . my chance.

Grabbing a handful of my alien figures, I tiptoed out of my room and started making my way down the stairs. I threw an alien ahead of me every few steps so they could help me through the dark with their luminous green light . . .

Creeeeeeeeeeeeaaaaaak.

My foot had accidentally landed on one of the bad steps! I froze.

The darkness of the house stayed silent and unbroken. Luckily, nobody seemed to have heard me.

Feeling the rest of the stairs with the tips of my toes, I made it into the dining room, and across to the large wooden cabinet behind the dinner table. It was locked, but the key was in the hole. I twisted it around and pulled down the door.

Two shelves squashed with books and papers and half-opened envelopes appeared. Reaching into it, I pulled out the biggest, fattest book from the top shelf: Mum and Dad's telephone book. Stuffed with extra pages and Post-it notes of numbers and names of family from all around the world, it was as big as a school textbook – and a lot heavier too.

Lugging it to the telephone table next to the big sofa, I switched on the lamp, and looked for the letter 'L'. I didn't care what Mum and Dad said – Grand-aunty Lin might not have known my grandad that well, but she seemed to know everyone in Singapore and Malaysia – and Indonesia too. So she might know *someone* who knew *something* about the real Leo, and if she didn't, then she might know something about my name.

My fingers and eyes hunted through the long list of names, until I finally found Grand-aunty Lin's. The number underneath it looked like the longest number I had ever seen. I knew it was going to be expensive calling her, because the longer a number is, the more energy it takes to call. But Mum and Dad were always ringing people all over the planet, so I was sure they wouldn't notice one more extra call on the phone bill.

Picking up the house phone, I pressed in the numbers and watched as they flashed up, one by one, on the small green screen. Finally, I typed in the last digit and, turning off the lamp, waited in the dark, trying my best not to shiver.

I waited and waited, but instead of ringing, a noise that sounded like a heart machine when someone's heart had stopped working, hummed in my ear. And then a few seconds later, a woman's voice said: 'We're sorry, but the number you have dialled has not been recognised.'

I quickly switched the light on, and carefully dialled the number in the phone book again. But again, there was no ringing – only that dead heart machine noise and that annoying voice!

Giving up, I flipped the phone book over to the letter 'S'. There were lots of Su's, but I finally found my Aunt Su's name, with a large star drawn next to it and the Chinese word for 'sister' written in brackets too:

*Su (姐姐 – *District 26, Tagore*).

I dialled in her number – which was even longer than Aunty Lin's – and, turning off the lamp again, waited with my fingers and toes crossed.

'Please ring, please ring,' I whispered to the crackling phone.

Brrrrrrrrrrring-brrrrrrrrrrrrrrrrrrring!

It was working!

Brrrrrrrrrrrrring-brrrrrrrrrrrrrrrrrrrrrring!

Brrrrrrrrrrrrrrrrring-brrrrrrrrrrrrrrrrrrrrrrrrrrring!

'Please be there . . .' I begged.

Brrrrrrrrrrr – 'Ni hao?'

'Aunt Su?' I whispered, as my voice and fingers started to shake. 'Is that you?'

'Huh? Who is this?' shouted Aunt Su, her voice coming through the phone so loudly I was sure she was going to wake up the whole house!

'Shhhhhh! Aunt Su, it's me, Leo! Your nephew Leo – from Whot! In England!'

'Leo? From England? What are you doing ringing me at this time of the day? Oh no! Omo! Is it your dad? Has something happened? Is he dead? I told him

120

not to live somewhere so cold and wet!'

'No, no!' I whispered back, gripping the phone even tighter and trying to muffle her voice with my cheek. 'Aunty Su, everything is fine. Mama and Baba and everyone are fine! I just need to ask you some things.'

'Ask me what?' asked Aunty Su, even louder.

'I – I just want to ask if you've ever heard about a soldier – a hero from World War Two called Leo? Someone who died here – in England. In Rochester? And who had the exact same name as me?'

The other end of the phone fell silent.

'Hello? Hello? Aunty Su?' I stared at the phone.

'You woke me up *and* nearly murdered me in my bed, just to ask me a silly question like this?' shouted Aunty Su. I couldn't see her, but I knew she was shaking her head of silvery-black hair at me.

Not knowing what to say, I stayed quiet, and waited.

A sigh flooded through the holes of the phone and made the air next to my ear feel hot and sweaty. 'No, Leo, I have never heard of any man from World War Two with your name and who died in Ro-lobster. Why are you asking this?'

'For – for school . . . For a project,' I answered.

'Ah, well, the answer is still no,' replied Aunty Su.

I felt my fingers loosen on the phone from disappointment. 'Oh . . . Well, do you know why Grandad asked Mum and Dad to name me 'Leo'?'

There was a moment's silence, before Aunty Su's voice came back again. This time, it was gentler and sounded sad too. 'I'm sorry, Leo. Your grandad never told anyone. The only thing he said was that it was to do with an old neighbour. He told us he would explain later, once he met you. But that later, it never came.'

'A neighbour?' I asked, my heart thumping. 'You mean, a neighbour called Leo with the same surname as us?'

'LEO? WHAT ARE YOU DOING?!' thundered an angry voice, and in a flash, the living room lights came to life.

My whole body jumped up, terrified, as the shouting of my name and the sudden flicking on of a light blinded me. The giant phone book fell from the table with a CRASH onto the floor, and my hands dropped the phone with a loud THUD.

Standing in his vest and shorts, with Bo behind him,

was Dad – holding a tennis racket in one hand, and a not-so-luminous alien in the other. We all stood like statues, as from the other side of the world and through the phone, Aunt Su's voice cried out, 'LEO? WHAT IS HAPPENING? OMO! ARE YOU DEAD?'

A CALL TO ARMS

'Woah, you're LUCKY you didn't get *killed*,' said Sangeeta. 'If my mum or dad caught me with their telephone book, I don't even know what would happen! One time they thought they'd lost it and Mum nearly phoned the police – she didn't even do that when she lost me in a shopping centre that one time! I can't believe you didn't get punished!'

The truth was, I couldn't believe it either. After I had been caught, Dad had spoken to Aunt Su and apologised, and Bo had shaken his head at me as if I was the thickest person on the planet. And then, nothing had happened.

Dad had said he would think about what my punishment for not listening to him and Mum would be and told me to go to bed. But at breakfast and on the way to school, he hadn't said anything about it – not a single word. Which, in lots of ways, was way worse.

'Hey, Kerry's got the new ankle-skipper! Let's go have a look before school starts!' shouted Sangeeta, as she raced over to where Kerry was showing off the latest gadget to half the school.

But I didn't care about the ankle-skipper – even if it did go faster and faster every time it spun around your ankle and was so cool that every top footballer in the world was using it. Maybe I was ill.

With my head bowed down low, I followed Sangeeta slowly through the playground, wondering what to do next. Because if no one in Singapore knew who the real Leo was – even though he most likely came from there – then what chance did I have of finding anything out about him here?

'Hey! Look where you're going, dumbo!'

It was Catherine, and standing right next to her were Toby and Harry. I had walked right into their group without noticing.

Toby stepped forward and gave my shoulders a

shove. 'Get lost, loser! Or we'll send you right back home to your smelly, loser country.'

I stood still and looked at them all. I wanted to be brave and tell them to get lost and shove them right back! But then Toby raised a fist and lurched forwards as if he was going to hit me, and I automatically covered my head with my arms.

'Ha ha! Scaredy-cat!' teased Toby. 'I bet where you come from they're all scaredy-cats, just like you!'

'Yeah,' sneered Catherine. 'Scaredy-cats that probably wet themselves all the time.'

'Ha ha!' laughed Toby. 'Yeah! Hey, loser! Why don't you do your *stupid* board about *losers* who wet themselves? Because that's all anyone from your stinky country ever does. Ha ha! Come on, let's leave the baby alone before he goes crying to his stinky mum!'

Toby ran off with Catherine and Harry, but he left his laughter behind, swirling around me like a mini hurricane and poking at the old bruise inside my chest. The one I had hoped had gone away, but was now telling me that I *was* a scaredy-cat. Just like Dad. And maybe like everyone who ever came from where I came from too.

I turned and ran to the doors of the school. I wanted them to be open so that I could get swallowed up by the building. But they were locked shut. I was trying to pull them open when, suddenly, the bell started to ring and the metal doors swung right into me.

'All right there, Leo?' asked Mr Wickers, who always opened the doors in the morning. There was no one behind me yet, but I could hear a thousand footsteps heading my way.

I rubbed my nose where the door had hit me and without replying, rushed past Mr Wickers and sprinted all the way to class. The room was nice and empty – except for Mr Scott.

'Ah! First in, Leo, good, good!'

Mr Scott smiled at me, but I didn't want to look at him. I threw my bag under my table and without even bothering to take my coat off, sat down in my chair and stared down at the table.

'Something wrong, Leo?' asked Mr Scott.

I shook my head and continued staring at the table.

'You know, I think it's brilliant you volunteered to help lead the display-board team. I'm really looking forward to seeing what you add to it.'

I looked up, surprised that Mr Scott was talking to me at all. He was usually too busy wiping boards or tidying his desk to talk to anyone before the register had been taken.

Mr Scott came and stood in front of my table, as Evelyn and Kerry giggled their way into the classroom. Not taking any notice of them, Mr Scott kneeled down and asked, 'Have you come up with an idea then, for your team?'

I nodded and, still not looking at him, took out my drawings from the previous night from my rucksack. I wanted him to see them before anyone else came in.

Mr Scott pulled the piece of paper towards himself. 'Ah, the cathedral and the golden lion – and the soldier with your name on the wall. Yes . . . I thought that might be what you wanted to base your project on. That's an *excellent* idea, Leo.' He handed it back to me. 'I can't wait to see what you find out about this other Leo. You'll have to think about how to bring him to life for us on the board – and the assembly too.'

Before I could look up at him, Mr Scott had jumped back to his feet and was telling Oscar off for dropping chewing-gum balls everywhere. I stared down at my ideas and Leo's name and the RAF badge with the ostrich-eagle on it. Mr Scott didn't think my idea was stupid at all. And if I found out enough about him, I might even get to play the real Leo in assembly! I hadn't even thought about that. The bruise inside me began to shrink a little.

'Hey Leo, where did you get to?' asked Drew, plonking himself into his chair. 'Sangeeta's been looking for you.'

'Yeah,' said Nancy. Her cheeks were flushed pink as if she had just done a cross-country race. 'You missed out on having a go on Kerry's ankle-spinner! It's wicked!'

A second later, Sangeeta appeared. 'Hey! Where did you go? I was looking for you.'

'I was . . . er, cold,' I lied, as a huge beam of sunlight shone through the window and lit up our table.

Sangeeta opened her mouth to say something, but, luckily, Mr Scott interrupted her.

'Right, listen up, everyone,' called out Mr Scott, putting the register away in a drawer. 'We've got a lot to get through today. Anyone with their permission slips signed already, come put them on my desk, please.'

Nearly half the class rushed over with their signed sheets. Luckily Mum had signed mine, even though I was in trouble. As I hurried after Sangeeta to hand mine in, I noticed that Toby and Catherine had put their sheets down too.

'Brilliant job, guys. The rest of you, remember – no later than Friday! Now. All assembly leaders on table one, over here,' he said pointing to the left side of the classroom. 'And board leaders over here.' Mr Scott pointed at mine and Sangeeta's table. 'Anyone sitting on those tables who are NOT leading those groups, find another seat. Quick! And get your homework out whilst you're at it. It's time to get presenting!'

Half the class got onto its feet and shuffled around hurriedly, bumping and skidding to sit down at the right tables. Gary and Evelyn and Laura came and sat with me, putting their homework books down seriously in front of them.

'Right, group leaders.' Mr Scott smiled. 'It's a listening morning for you. I want you to be thinking really hard about how you're going to show off all the stories we're about to hear in a fair *and* exciting way. And everyone else, it's your chance to really make the story you want to tell us come alive – to really honour the people you're talking about! Who wants to go first?'

Oscar and Sangeeta's hands rose immediately, but Mr Scott picked Nancy instead, even though she hadn't put her hand up at all. Clasping her piece of paper just like I did when I was nervous, Nancy got up and began telling us about her great-grand-aunt who had worked in a factory making food tins to go out to millions of soldiers. Her voice was quiet at first, but the more she talked, the stronger her voice got, and by the time she was finished, she looked happy and proud.

Next it was Kerry, and then Drew, and then Toby and then Laura, until, one by one, almost the whole class had presented their ideas to us. Nearly everyone had talked about someone in their family who had fought or lived in the war, and who they wanted the whole world to remember. As Oscar jumped up and talked about his idea of showing his great-grandfather in a big battle scene and using ketchup as blood, I could feel myself getting more and more nervous about having to share my idea with everyone. Especially since I didn't really have anything out about the real

Leo to share just yet.

'And Leo?'

I jumped to my feet at Mr Scott's question and quickly said, 'My story's going to be about the man with the same name as me – the one in the cathedral with the golden lion.' I sat back down again, my ears burning red.

'Good, we look forward to it,' said Mr Scott. 'Now that we've heard everyone's stories, leaders, I'm going to give you a poster sheet, and I want you to discuss how to display and present it all on our board and in our assembly. Think about what the title of the project will be – your call to arms as it were. Everyone else, go get your workbooks from your trays and complete chapter seven quietly!'

I stared down at the huge, blank poster sheet Mr Scott put in front of me, and then up at Evelyn and Laura and Gary who were each reaching for a different coloured pen.

'Right, so we have to decide how to display everyone's stories,' said Evelyn. 'That's so many! Anyone have any ideas?'

'I do!' I said, before my mouth could stop me.

But then my brain froze and wouldn't let me say anything else.

'Go on then,' said Gary, waiting.

'Leo, why don't you show the team your idea – like you showed me earlier?' asked Mr Scott, who had come over to us to see how we were getting on.

Mr Scott's words instantly unfroze my brain and made my hands start working too. I picked up my homework book and opened it up to my drawings. 'I thought . . . maybe we could have a huge drawing of the cathedral we went to,' I said. 'We could put the names of all the forgotten heroes and people we want to remember on its bricks. And then, stories and drawings about them could be placed next to their names. Like I could do the soldier with my name on it who got the special RAF award,' I added, pointing to my eagle that didn't really look like an eagle at all. 'And everyone else could do stories about the people they just talked about . . . and it would be like a wall of stories.'

Evelyn and Gary both said 'Cool'.

Laura said, 'So what would the title be then?"

I thought about it for one whole second, and then,

pulling the poster paper towards me, picked up a big black felt-tip pen and wrote out in giant letters:

OUR FORGOTTEN HEROES

A NEW RECRUIT

For the next two and a half days, right up until the bell for lunch rang on Friday afternoon, everyone in class worked harder than we had ever worked on anything in our entire lives.

Mr Scott had split the class into two armies: the display-board army, and the assembly army, headed by the teams of generals. Each had the same mission: to beat all the other schools and make our project so brilliant that the *Real Kidz Rule* show would have no choice but to make us the winners.

Us winning clearly mattered to the rest of the school too, because after Mrs Fitzgerald announced in assembly that the *Real Kidz Rule* show was coming to the school – and that our class was the reason why – everything changed. Suddenly, instead of being asked to swap sweets or play tag at breaktime by the other classes, we were being offered tips on what to do in front of the cameras. Tips like, 'Make sure you wear extra deodorant so you don't smell', and 'Iron everything at least three times – even your underpants because the camera makes everything look extra-wrinkly', and 'Drink three glasses of milk the night before so your teeth get whiter'.

I wanted to be just as excited as everyone else in school, but I was beginning to get worried. Because no matter how hard I worked or where I looked, I couldn't find any information about the real Leo.

Mr Scott wanted us to hand in our first drafts of each project by the end of Friday, but by Friday lunchtime, I still hadn't found out a single thing about him. Sangeeta was struggling too. She had found some pictures of men and even some women fighters from India and parts of Africa in old photos on the internet, but most of them weren't named. And she couldn't find anything about the soldier named R Singh who she had picked out from the cathedral wall to research. It was almost as if the wall was lying to us, and the people being remembered on it hadn't really existed at all. Mr Scott had even tried to help and had searched for things on his own computer. But he couldn't find anything either.

'I give up,' said Sangeeta, slamming a book we had both double-checked already shut again. She pushed it back onto the library shelf. 'It's no use. Ben and Lily are never going to interview us for the show – not when everyone else has got a story ready and we haven't.'

My stomach gave an angry growl. It was the end of Friday lunchtime, and we had gone through every book in the library from the World War Two shelf at least twice. Sangeeta was right. Ben and Lily and the *Real Kidz Rule* show weren't going to care about us or the real Leo or R Singh. None of the books cared, so why should they? The school library books about the war hardly mentioned any countries outside Europe and America. Even the ones that did only ever said things like 'parts of the Commonwealth' or 'the Far East' or 'Africa' – as if those words were just a single thing and weren't made up lots of huge countries with millions of people who might have been heroes too. Except for the book Olivia had torn out all the pages from . . .

The worst thing was that now I knew all these people from all these countries were missing, I couldn't see anything else. They haunted the pages like invisible ghost-words, hiding between the actual printed ones, waiting to be found and made real again.

'Come on, let's see if the dinner hall's still open,' said Sangeeta. 'Maybe we can ask for something to eat before the bell goes.'

I followed Sangeeta down to the dinner hall. It had been tidied already, and the silver shutters to the kitchen had been locked. My nose could still catch the smell of chips and fish fingers wafting through the air like extra-delicious perfume, and it made my stomach give another growl. This time Sangeeta's growled right back.

'Shall we go out or go back to class?' asked Sangeeta. 'We've only got—'

'Pssssssssssst! Guys. Where have you been? We've been waiting for you!'

We looked up as Nancy and Drew's heads popped out from around a corner. Checking there were no teachers around, they half-ran and half-skipped over to us. They were both wearing the hoods of their coats on their heads, and looked like superheroes.

'Here,' said Nancy, her cheeks red with excitement. She held something out to us.

Wrapped in a tissue was a small pile of chips and two slices of cake.

'We saved them,' whispered Drew. 'Thought you might miss lunch again.'

'No, *I* saved them,' said Nancy, shaking her head free from the lie. 'These are my slices. You didn't save anything!'

'Well, it's my tissue,' said Drew, defensively.

'Oh, wicked!' I cried, snatching a handful of chips and cake and pushing the whole lot into my mouth. 'I'm HARVING! FANK OO.'

Sangeeta grabbed a single chip and, chewing on it like a fast-eating camel, made it disappear too, before getting to work on the rest.

'Want to go play a quick game before the bell goes?' asked Drew, glancing towards the playground doors.

'Let's go and see the display board in reception instead!' suggested Sangeeta. 'So we can imagine how our project will look on it.' She grabbed mine and Nancy's arms. 'Maybe looking at it will help us come up with new ideas about how to find Leo and Mr R Singh and everyone.'

'Still no luck in the library?' asked Nancy, looking sad for us.

Sangeeta shook her head. 'But it might be because we're not thinking outside the box. Dad always stares at things when he gets stuck. So maybe staring at the board might help us.'

'OK,' I said, even though I wasn't sure how staring at something was going to help us find anyone.

The main display board hung in the reception area, which was the fanciest entrance to school, and led to the special corridor where Mrs Fitzgerald's office was. We weren't allowed to go in that way unless our parents had to tell the teachers something, or we were sick and had to be taken home. But from the back doors of the dining hall, you could squash your face up against the windows and see right inside it.

So that's exactly what we did.

'It's *humongous* . . .' whispered Nancy, as Drew dragged his nose down the glass, making it squeak.

Nancy was right. The board was huge. For this month, one of the upper classes had done a display on it about climate change, so there were plastic bottles and squashed drink cans and sweet wrappers swimming all across it in an ocean of junk, along with frowning tortoises and a sad-looking whale.

'We can put *loads* of stuff on there,' whispered Sangeeta.

'Yeah, you could put ME up there – like with staples – and still have room!' said Drew, excitedly.

While Sangeeta was guessing how many centimetres tall the cathedral should be, Nancy and Drew began arguing about whether or not to use glitter for all the sides. But all I could think about was that I had so much space for the real Leo's story – and didn't have anything to fill it with yet.

'Hey, are you Leo?'

We all jumped at the unexpected voice. And as we turned to see who it belonged to, our mouths fell open one by one.

It was Olivia. She was standing in front of us with her arms crossed, a tractor drawn on her left knee and a double decker bus on her right.

But more importantly, she had said my name. Which meant . . . which meant she *knew* my name!

'Yeah. I'm – I'm Leo,' I answered.

Olivia blew a bright blue balloon of bubble gum out of her mouth and popped it back in again.

'Can I speak to you. Like, on your own,' she asked, even though she wasn't really asking at all, but giving an order.

Drew immediately half-ran out of the hall without saying a word. Sangeeta whispered, 'We'll wait outside' and left, pulling Nancy by the arm behind her.

Olivia waited for the dinner hall to be completely empty, and then walked up to the doors behind me. She looked through the glass panes and up at the display board.

I wanted to ask her why she wanted to see me – and why she had stolen those pages from the library book – but I knew if I did, she might never speak to me again. Cool kids always had to speak first. That was the rule. So I waited.

'Is it true that it was your idea to find out about forgotten heroes?' she asked.

I nodded.

'That's cool,' she said. Then, turning away from the board, she narrowed her eyes and looked at me, up and down and side to side, like a robot with lasers for eyes. She blew out another blue balloon and popped it again. And then finally, she spoke.

'I think I want to help you. But only if you help me first.'

This time my mouth fell open. '*You* want to help me? But w–why?'

Olivia rubbed the side of her nose. 'Because I know someone who should go on your board and be on the *Real Kidz Rule* show too. Someone who's been forgotten and who shouldn't have been, because he was a hero too.'

'Who?' I asked, before I could stop myself.

Olivia shook her head. 'First you promise to help and add my story to your display board, and then I'll tell you who it is. Deal?'

She held out her hand.

I looked over my shoulder at the display board and wondered if there was enough space or time for yet another forgotten story that needed to be found out about. I decided that there was – because that's what the real Leo would want. He would want him *and* everyone like him to be found out about and not stay forgotten. And me and Sangeeta had to help, even if that meant working even harder and trying to squeeze even more things onto the board.

Turning back around, I took Olivia's hand.

'Good,' said Olivia. 'This means I'm on your team now – but only in secret. OK?'

I looked down at my hand, wondering if anyone would ever believe that Olivia, one of the coolest girls on the planet, had actually shaken hands with me.

'Come and meet me behind the tuck shop at home-time,' ordered Olivia. 'Make sure no one sees you. And bring that weird girl with you – the one in the wellies who never stops talking. She can help too, because we're kind of all the same. You know – different.'

And, blowing one last bubble-gum balloon, Olivia turned and walked out, leaving me and the dinner hall behind in a state of shocked silence.

CLASSIFIED INFORMATION

'Before you all rush off for the weekend, a couple of things!' called out Mr Scott.

The bell had just rung – it was finally home-time! Which meant it was finally time to go and find Olivia! I willed Mr Scott to hurry up and finish whatever it was he wanted to say.

'First off, well done on making a miracle happen and getting all your permission slips in on time. Secondly, we've received confirmation that, next week, the *Real Kidz Rule* team will be coming in for a day or two to film us working on our projects, and hopefully to speak with some of you too. So I want everyone on their ULTIMATE best behaviour. Understood?'

'Sir, which days?' prodded Evelyn.

Mr Scott shrugged. 'They haven't told us. It might be any days of the week.'

Sangeeta asked, 'Sir! Will Ben and Lily be coming?'

Everyone groaned as Mr Scott shook his head. 'They will only come and see our work the week after – IF we win.'

'Aw, MAN,' cried Toby.

'Aw, man indeed,' agreed Mr Scott. 'But one more reason to keep working hard. Now, off you all go, and make sure to get as much done on your projects as you can over the weekend!'

Jumping up so fast that her plaits hit me in the face, Sangeeta shoved her stuff in her rucksack, and then stood impatiently, jumping from foot to foot as I packed my pencil case and books. Drew and Nancy each gave us a thumbs up as me and Sangeeta hurried out the door. They knew where we were going and why, and that Olivia was too cool for them to come join us when they hadn't been invited.

Running out to the playground, I headed towards the narrow gap of grass between the back wall of the tuck shop and the school gates, with Sangeeta following me so closely that she kept bumping into me.

Olivia was already there – along with two of her friends. They looked up as the squeaking of Sangeeta's bright yellow wellies announced our arrival. As soon as Olivia saw us, she nodded at her friends, who turned to go. They walked off, frowning at us. It was a fact that if you wanted to be friends with Olivia, you had to be able to frown for five minutes straight without saying a word.

'Hi,' said Olivia.

Sangeeta gave a nervous wave. I had never seen her so quiet before.

'Thanks for saying you'll help me get this on the board,' said Olivia, looking around to make sure we were alone. 'Remember. You can't tell anyone about this. OK? Not even my friends know. They think I'm trying to get some information out of you about when Ben and Lily from the *Real Kidz Rule* show are coming.'

Olivia pulled something out of her bright white socks: it was a folded-up piece of paper.

She handed it to me.

Carefully, I opened it up. It was an old photocopy. On it was a picture of a man with a thin, fluffy black moustache and large eyes. He was smiling and wearing a soldier's uniform and a cap, just like the soldiers we had seen at the museum. The jacket and his cap had a badge with RAF wings on it, and underneath his picture were the words:

RICHARD 'KOJO' MORRIS

1917–1944

"Nobody willingly walks to his own death."

Except to save his fellow man.

MEMORIAL SERVICE

FOR FALLEN SOLDIERS OF THE

WEST AFRICAN NATIONS

Commencing 5th June, 1945

11am, Saint Matthew's Church, Brixton

ALL WELCOME

'Woah,' I whispered.

'Where did you get this?' asked Sangeeta, more quietly than I had ever heard her ask anything before.

Olivia held out her hand and waited until I gave the precious paper back to her.

'I found it, in one of my dad's old photo albums. Richard Morris was my great-granddad.'

'WOAH!' I shouted, making Sangeeta kick me in the ankle.

Olivia put the piece of paper back into her socks. 'The thing is . . . I don't know much about him. Except that he died in the war. And that he was in the RAF. Just like the man with your name.' Olivia nodded at me. 'I need your help to find out more about him and to get his story onto your board and onto the telly and everything.'

Sangeeta looked over at me, but didn't say anything. I knew she was thinking the same thing as me: that we might not be able to help Olivia as much as she thought we could. Not when we had already failed in our own missions.

'There's nothing about him anywhere,' Oliva went on. 'Not online, or in the history books. He wasn't on that cathedral wall or any of the memorials there either. I've asked my mum and dad too. They don't know anything. All they know is he died fighting out in Europe and never even got to see my gran when she was born. But I want to find out, so everyone can know about him.' Olivia stood up straighter, and seemed to grow by two more feet.

'So that's why you ripped the pages from the library book,' I whispered. I clamped my hands over my mouth as soon as I had said the words.

'I was only borrowing them,' said Olivia, her cheeks flushing red. 'I'm going to tape them back in on Monday. I just wanted time to read them properly without anyone seeing me take a big fat history book home. There wasn't much on them anyway. Just some photos.'

I sighed. It sounded like the pages were just as useless as the others we had seen in the library.

'But – but if . . . that man in the picture is your great-grandad, then doesn't that mean you're . . . that your mum and dad are . . .' Sangeeta bit her lip, not knowing how to ask the question.

I didn't know how to ask it either. I remembered what Olivia had said – that the three of us were the same, because we were different. Was this what she had meant?

'I'm mixed,' Olivia confirmed, whispering, her eyes looking left and right as if she was afraid someone would hear her. 'My mum's from Wales, and my dad's family are from Ghana. But my dad was born here!' she added, as if it made things better.

'But you don't *look* . . .' whispered Sangeeta, scanning Olivia's face and arms and hair and light brown freckles for any signs she had missed.

'I look more like my mum than my dad,' explained Olivia. 'I'm lucky because no one can tell really. Not unless they see my dad, and he works overseas a lot and travels all the time when he's here too. No one knows what I am really. Not even my best friends. It's super-top-secret classified information. And if you tell *anyone*, you'll regret it. So you better not.'

Me and Sangeeta nodded and shook our heads all at once.

'Promise,' I said, secretly wishing I was mixed too. Olivia really was lucky. She could hide all the parts of herself that would have got her bullied and called names. And she got to be cool and secretive and mysterious. But I couldn't help wondering if her dad knew that he was being kept a secret, and if maybe that was why he travelled so much. As hard as it was being stared at and pointed at and bullied, I didn't think I would ever want to go home and not find my dad there.

'So, will you help me?' Olivia asked.

Sangeeta looked at me, worried. I knew right away what she was thinking, so I took a step forward.

'The problem is,' I said, feeling braver now that I knew Olivia lived a double life too, 'we haven't managed to find anything out about the people we've been researching yet.'

'Not even Mr Scott has found anything and he's been looking for days too,' added Sangeeta, quietly.

Olivia rubbed the side of her nose again. 'Oh. I thought you might know where to go to get more information and things.'

Sangeeta shook her head, but I didn't shake mine. I could feel something happening inside it, and I didn't want to disturb it.

'Can I look at the piece of paper again?' I asked, looking at Olivia.

Olivia took it out of her secret filing sock and gave it back to me.

I opened it back up and looked down at Richard Morris's face. Slowly, I started to feel them – all the pieces whirling around inside me beginning to fit and make sense. Maybe there *was* another way of getting more information – a way that we hadn't tried.

'I think I've got an idea,' I said, quietly. 'I think I know how we can find out about all of them. The Leo in the church, and Mr R Singh too – and your great-grandad. And about women in the RAF too. But we'd have to make them believe us . . .'

'Make who believe what?' asked Olivia.

I signalled to Sangeeta and Olivia to come into a huddle, and whispered my idea to them. Saying the words out loud made them seem even more unreal and dangerous than they had felt in my head.

'You're crazy,' said Sangeeta when I had finished, shaking her head. 'It'll never work.'

'It might work!' I argued.

Sangeeta continued shaking her head. I looked over at Olivia. She was biting her lip and staring at the floor.

'I think – I think we have to at least try it!' I said. 'The real Leo and your great-grandad and R Singh and all the RAF women – *they* would have done it!'

Olivia finally looked up.

'OK. Let's do it,' she declared. 'Tomorrow!'

Sangeeta gasped. 'It'll never work. They'll know it's us!'

'We'll *make* it work,' I promised.

'And – and I can't tomorrow!' Sangeeta went on. 'I've got a family wedding at five. *And* I'm the bridesmaid.'

'We can do it well before you have to go,' said Olivia. 'It probably won't take more than hour. If you come to mine, I can get the phone from my parents' room, and steal my sister's tablet for a bit. I live on the street behind the bank in the village – at number eleven.'

'You want us to come to your house?' asked Sangeeta. 'To . . . to your *actual* house?'

Olivia gave a single nod. 'Yeah. Why?'

'Nothing,' replied Sangeeta, even though it was much more than nothing. As far as we knew, no one had ever been to Olivia's house – not even her best friends. And now suddenly, here we were, being invited like it was the most normal thing in the world!

I tried to remember if Mum and Dad had said anything about any family events at the weekend. Then I decided that it didn't matter. Mum and Dad were always telling me that school was the most important place on the planet, and that if I didn't do my best at it, I would be killing their dreams and all the dreams of everyone who knew us too. So all I had to do was use their own words against them and *make* them let me go.

I could tell Sangeeta was thinking exactly the same thing, because we both nodded at the same time.

'Cool,' said Olivia, making sure her great-grandad's details were safely stored away in her sock again. 'I'll get the phone and everything ready. Come to mine for exactly two o'clock, OK? My mum and dad are usually out by then. And remember: nobody at school can *ever* know we've spoken about any of this. Ever.'

And, giving us a nod that bound us together like spies on a top-secret super-classified mission, Olivia ran back out into the playground and disappeared into the crowd.

MMI — THE IMITATION GAMES

'Leo, what's wrong with you? Why are you so jumpy today? It's like shopping with a frog!'

Dad shook his head at me as he took over the shopping trolley. My hands were rattling and shaking the trolley which had made Jingyi, who was sitting in the seat in the front, rattle and shake too.

'Go, grab two packets of biscuits,' ordered Dad, as he came to a standstill by the crisps section. 'One for you, one for Bo – I just need to go down this aisle first.'

I ran off. Mum and Dad had both decided that as punishment for me ringing my Aunt Su and nearly making her die, I had to do a full day of extra chores. And if I did them really well, they promised they would consider letting me go to Olivia's house.

So I had spent the whole morning cleaning Mum's car and hoovering the stairs, and then doing the most disgusting job in the world: changing Jingyi's nappy after she had done a number two! It was so lethal I nearly went blind, but I pretended I was a soldier and wrapped a towel around my head like a gas mask. Afterwards, Dad inspected my cleaning and sealing skills and said I had done a good job, so my chances of going to Olivia's house were looking hopeful.

My final punishment of the day – apart for doing the dishes at night – was to help Dad do the weekly shop. We all hated shopping with Dad because he never let anyone buy anything that wasn't on his list, and went up and down every single aisle – even when he didn't need anything from that section. Mum said it was more painful than giving birth to us, so she never came, and Bo hadn't been shopping with Dad since he turned twelve and learned he had human rights. Only Jingyi still went, and that was because she was a baby and didn't know how to say 'no' yet.

Skipping and leaping and jumping down the aisle, I got mine and Bo's favourite biscuits and slam-dunked them into the trolley, making Jingyi giggle.

'List complete,' said Dad, as we finally reached the last row of the store. 'Let's go.'

Waiting in line at one of the checkout stations, I could feel people in the other queues staring at me and Dad and Jingyi. Dad noticed too and put on his plastic grin – the one that tried to tell people he was normal, just like them.

Ignoring all the eyes, I gazed up at the magazine and news rack next to our counter. The magazines all looked the same – filled with pictures of famous people whose glossy hair and faces and smiles were only meant for other people who looked like them. I was about to go back to playing with Jingyi again, when I noticed the headline in the *Whot Gazette*.

Usually the *Whot Gazette* only ever featured stories about the weather and the latest jumble sales, and had headlines like 'URGENT APPEAL FOR GRANDMOTHER'S LOST DOG', and 'GRANDMOTHER'S LOST DOG FOUND!'

But today was different. Today's headline was actually important, because it read:

REAL KIDZ RULE SHOW COMING TO TOWN:
WHOT SCHOOL IN NATIONAL COMPETITION

As Dad began to unload the trolley, I ran and picked up a copy of the *Whot Gazette*. It was a whole £1.50 and I hadn't brought any of my leftover money from the school trip. Which meant . . .

'Dad?'

'Hm?' asked Dad, placing a single courgette onto the conveyer belt.

'Dad, can I please get this?'

Dad frowned. 'What for?'

'Because look – it's about the competition – the one my class are in. Pleeeeeeeeeeease.'

I put on my best begging face and waited. Dad leaned forward and shouted, loud enough for the whole store to hear, 'One pound fifty! And it's not on the list!' before doing a mouth fart. His lips always farted when something was so expensive his mouth couldn't believe it.

'Pleeeeeeeeeeeeeeease, Dad,' I tried again. 'I can put my biscuits back. And my chocolates too! Or I can do extra chores tomorrow? Pleeeeeeeeeeeeeeease?'

'Awww! Let him have the paper, son,' said a woman who was standing behind us. Jingyi cried out 'ba-ba' and clapped her hands as if she was cheering me on too.

'OK!' said Dad, shaking his head. 'It's not on the list . . . but OK. Just this one time!'

I looked back at the woman and her bright pink lips, wondering if she would be scared of me if I gave her a smile. But she was already smiling at me, so I gave her one back, and put the paper on the conveyor belt, feeling even jumpier inside than ever.

As soon as we got home, I grabbed the newspaper and stood to attention in front of Mum and Dad. It was nearly one o'clock already and I had to know!

'Mum,' I said breathlessly. 'Can I go?'

'Yes, OK. You can go,' said Mum, with a smile. 'Just for an hour or two!'

Dad nodded. 'Eat lunch, and then go and get ready. I'll get Bo to walk you over to your new friend's house.'

Hugging them both so hard that I nearly crumpled up the newspaper, I raced through my lunch and ran upstairs. Before I got ready, I quickly read the article first. On the front page, there was a picture of Ben and Lily from *Real Kidz Rule*, and a whole paragraph from

Mrs Fitzgerald talking about how proud the school was to represent Kent and how she was looking forward to seeing our projects come to life.

Then, on the next page, was a huge picture of school, and a list of all the other competing schools – there was one from Scotland and two from Wales and one from Northern Ireland and four from England, including a school in London. I wished the article had listed what all their projects were too – but it said everything was going to be revealed on the *Real Kidz Rule* Remembrance Day special in two Fridays' time.

Two Fridays' time. It was so soon . . . and I still had nothing on the real Leo!

'LEO! ARE YOU READY?' shouted Dad. 'IT'S TIME TO GO! BO! COME AND TAKE YOUR BROTHER!'

I shouted back 'COMING!', then I jumped off the bed and, stuffing the newspaper into my already packed rucksack, ran downstairs, ready for the first major mission ahead.

* * *

'You sure it's number eleven?' asked Bo, as we reached the street behind the bank.

'That's what she said.'

Turning the corner, Bo asked. '*She*? Whose house are you going to again?'

'Olivia's – Olivia Morris.' Then I added proudly, 'She's the coolest girl in school.'

'Wait a minute,' said Bo, slowing down. 'You mean – *Jules* Morris's sister?'

I shrugged. 'Maybe. Look! We're here!'

Pointing to the blue door with a shining number eleven on it, I opened the garden gate and walked in. But Bo wasn't behind me. He had stopped on the pavement and was licking his hand and stroking his hair as fast as he could – like a giant cat.

'What are you doing?' I asked.

'Nothing!' he snarled, coming through the gate.

I rang the doorbell, trying to imagine what the house of the coolest girl in school might look like. Maybe it had a cinema – and a swimming pool. And a room just for games. Olivia probably had the newest gadgets in her room too!

After a few seconds, the door swung open and a

tall girl with long, dark-brown curly hair and large greyish-brown eyes stood in front of us. She stared at us blankly, music blaring out from the earphones looped around her neck.

'Yeah?' she asked, raising her eyebrows.

I was going to say I was here to see Olivia, when Bo suddenly squeaked, 'H-hey, Jules! I'm Bo!'

I looked back at Bo, wondering why his face had gone as red as a bowl of strawberry jelly.

'Oh yeah, from college,' said Jules, her eyebrows rising. 'Hey.'

'Hey,' said Bo. He went to lean against the doorframe, but missed the bit of wall he had been aiming for and slipped to the side. It made his face turn even redder.

'I'm Leo,' I announced. 'I'm here to do homework with Olivia.' Turning to Bo, I added, 'You can go now!'

'Nah, nah, it's OK,' said Bo, putting his hands on my shoulders and speaking in a weird, deep voice. 'I've got to watch out for my little brother, don't I?'

'That's sweet,' remarked Jules, blowing out a bright pink bubble at us.

'Yeah, that's me – sweet! Like ice cream,' said Bo.

Then he laughed as if he had said something funny. And Jules giggled as if *she* thought he had said something funny too.

From inside the house came the noise of someone thundering down the stairs. It was Olivia, dressed in some dungarees and a bright purple T-shirt. I shoved Bo's hands away quickly.

'Hi, Leo,' said Olivia. 'Jules, this is Leo! We're doing homework in my room.'

'Eh-huh,' said Jules, not really listening. She was still giggling at Bo's stupid joke.

'What's wrong with them?' whispered Olivia, as we both headed inside.

I shrugged. 'They think ice cream's funny for some reason.'

'*Sad,*' whispered Olivia, shaking her head. 'But Mum says my sister's got hormones. Apparently you get millions of them when you get older. Like invisible zits. And they make you go all weird. I hope I never get them. Come on! Sangeeta's here already.'

As Olivia led me upstairs and into her room, I quickly took a look around. It was nothing like I had imagined it would be – there wasn't a single cool gadget in it – not even a computer! But one wall had a giant world map plastered across it, which was cool. And, above her desk, dangling down from some invisible strings, was the exact same cardboard RAF plane I had bought from the gift shop.

Sangeeta looked up at me and gave me a wave. She was sitting in the middle of a purple rug, wearing a long, bright-blue skirt and a matching top, covered in sequins and beads and embroidery. I knew the skirt was called a lehenga and the top was called a choli, because some of Mum's friends wore them at our parties. She was wearing lots of blue and silver bangles and had flowers in her plait too.

'I'm the bridesmaid, remember?' explained Sangeeta, looking miserable. 'Mum and Dad said I had to get ready before coming here because I wouldn't have time later.'

'I think you look awesome,' said Olivia, sitting down on the rug where a glistening white house phone and a large tablet was waiting. 'Like a Hollywood actress – only shinier!'

Sangeeta looked down at her clothes and gave the skirt a pat, as if she was suddenly proud of it.

'Anyway, look,' said Olivia, as I sat down next to her. She picked up the tablet, swiped the screen and showed me the website for Rochester Cathedral. 'I've got everything ready. I'll dial, and then, Leo, you do the talking. And try to be quick, OK? If my sister sees her tablet missing, I won't be able to go to school on Monday because I'll be dead.'

'Hold on – you want *me* to do the talking?' I asked, my throat immediately beginning to shrink. 'I thought Sangeeta was going to do it.'

'I can't – I tried, but I sound weird,' answered Sangeeta. 'Listen.' Then squashing her face into her neck and making her voice go funny, she moaned, 'Halooooo, my name is Mrs HENderson!'

I clutched my hands together, wishing she was wrong. But she wasn't. She did sound weird – like a shouty, melting marshmallow.

'It'll be easier for you to sound like a grown-up because your voice is deeper,' said Sangeeta.

'Go on, Leo,' urged Olivia. 'Just say all the things you said yesterday – we'll help!'

Before I could shake my head or say another word, Olivia had grabbed the phone and punched in the number. 'Go!' she whispered, throwing the phone at me as if it was a hot potato. 'And make your voice go deep-deep, OK?'

'And don't forget to ask about R Singh too!' warned Sangeeta. 'And sound posh!'

I held the phone to my ear and gulped, hard, as the other end of the line began to ring. Once . . . twice . . . thr—

'Hello, Rochester Cathedral visitor information. Rachel speaking. How may I help?'

'It's a WOMAN!' I whispered, holding the phone away from me. 'Not Mr Young!'

'So? Just ask her instead!' whispered Sangeeta, shoving the phone back towards me.

'Hello?' called out the lady from inside the phone.

Making my voice go as deep as it could and telling myself to sound posh, I answered, 'Yes! Well, hellooo there . . . this is er – the Mayor of Wester . . . bury . . . hampshireland!'

Sangeeta slapped her hands into her face as Olivia stared at me, her mouth half–open.

There was a pause on the other end of the line, before the voice came back – this time sounding as if it might be laughing at me. 'Well – eh-hum! Thank you for calling, Mr . . . *Mayor*. And how may I help you?'

'I er . . . I was er . . . wondering . . .' For an instant my mind went blank, before an image of the golden lion flashed up at me. 'I er – I came to visit yooou a few weeks agoooo. For my constitutional rights. AW-fully nice trip! And Mr Young – he showed me some VEH-ry interesting names on a wall. Er – names of soldiers from abrooooad – what ho!'

The woman on the other end of the line fell so silent, that I wondered if she was pushing a secret police alert button – like they did in the movies. Worried, Sangeeta and Olivia both pressed their ears to the phone too. But then, finally, Rachel said, sounding curious, 'You mean our World War Two plaques for overseas soldiers?'

I let out a sigh of relief.

'Yes! That's it! Jolly good – Miss – Rachel! Well, you see – one of them was called Leo Kai Lim – and he belonged to the RAF . . . And another one – Mr R Singh – is on your wall too . . .' I paused to stop my voice from shaking. 'And I was wondering if you had . . .' I had forgotten the word I wanted. I looked over to Sangeeta and Olivia for help.

'DOCUMENTS!' whispered Sangeeta. 'FILES!'

'TOP SECRET FOLDERS!' added Olivia.

'Er – top secret document folder files – about those soldiers at your church – that I could see?' I finished.

We all waited, holding our breaths, until finally Rachel answered slowly, 'No. I'm afraid we don't hold any records about the actual soldiers themselves.'

My insides took a nosedive at the thought of yet another dead end, and Sangeeta and Olivia sighed.

'But we would have the date the memorial was commissioned, and the name of the organisation responsible,' she went on. 'In this case, most likely a department of RAF-Kent.'

'That won't help,' whispered Olivia, shaking her head.

'So if you would like to give me your number Mr . . . ah . . . Mayor, I can let Mr Young know you called and—'

'Er – NO THANK YOU!' I shouted, before slamming the phone back down.

We all stared at each other in silence for a few seconds, before Sangeeta asked, 'The Mayor of *Westburyhampshireland*?'

I shrugged and grinned at the same time, because even though we didn't get the information we wanted, I had done it! I had done a whole phone call and talked to a stranger and I hadn't choked or had a heart attack. I had actually completed the first major mission!

'It was all I could think of,' I said.

'Come on. Let's try the museum next then,' said Olivia, picking up the phone again. 'They're the RAF *and* they're in Kent. Maybe they're the ones who did the plaques.'

Using the tablet, Sangeeta found the website for the museum, and Olivia tapped in the number.

'This time, try to pretend you're a *normal* adult human,' suggested Sangeeta.

'Yeah – not a mayor of somewhere weird . . . it's ringing! Quick!' whispered Olivia.

She pushed the phone into my hands again, then we joined our heads together and waited.

Brrrrrrrrrrrring-brrrrrrrrrrrrrrrrrrrrrring. Brrrrrrrrrr—

'Good afternoon, this is Philip of the RAF World War Two Museum. How may I be of assistance?'

'Hellooo, Mr Phillip! My name is – is, er – Mr – Scott!'

Olivia shook her head as Sangeeta mouthed 'WHAT?' at me. I hadn't meant to give Mr Scott's name at all! But now that I had, it gave me an idea about how I could get the information we needed.

'Yes, er, Mr . . . Scott? How can I help?' asked Philip.

'I'm a teacher – and my class, we, er . . . we wanted to know if the museum has – er, records of RAF pilots from World War Two. Especially those who are from abroad. Like from Singapore or, or India – or Ghana maybe?'

'Do you know if the soldiers flew Spitfires or Hurricanes?' asked Philip.

Olivia and Sangeeta both frowned at me, as if the question was somehow my fault.

'I don't know,' I said, struggling to keep my voice deep.

'Well, we have a logbook of all RAF pilots who flew Spitfires and Hurricanes from 1939 to 1945. No matter where they were recruited from. If the pilots you are looking for flew those planes and are in the logbook, then there's a chance we may have more details about them on our wider database too.'

'Really?' I cried out, forgetting to use my deep voice.

Olivia and Sangeeta froze.

'I – mean, er, how wonderful!' I quickly added, making my voice go so deep that even I didn't recognise it. 'Where are those logbooks kept perchance-ly very much? And how much is it to look at them? Do you sell tickets?'

There was a pause. 'The logbooks are kept in our main offices upstairs, here in the museum,' said Philip, starting to sound suspicious. 'There is no charge, but there is an application process which takes about a week, after which we would arrange a time for you to come in and take a look through them at your leisure.'

'Oh,' I said, not knowing what to say next. All I knew was that waiting a whole week was way too long.

'Ask *him* to look for us!' whispered Olivia, her eyes wide. 'Say you're – you're too ill!'

I nodded and continued. 'Er! Righty – ho . . . The problem is, Mr Philips, sir, I – I, er . . .' Panicking and not knowing what illness to pretend I had, I blurted out, 'I'm – I'm blind!'

The voice on the line went silent whilst both

Sangeeta and Olivia squeezed their eyes shut like they were trying to block out the sounds of an accident.

I forced myself to go on with the stupidest lie that had ever been told in all of history. 'So I can't see the book . . . you see? Could you look for us – I mean, me – and find out if the pilots I need are there – like right now? Please and kindly thank you.'

'I'm sorry, Mr – er, Scott,' said Philip slowly. 'Which school did you say you were ringing on behalf of?'

'No thank you!' I cried, slamming the phone down.

For a few seconds, we all sat in silence, staring down at the phone like it was a dead body we had just discovered.

Finally, Sangeeta spoke. 'So er . . . *that* was interesting. What do we do now?' she asked.

'Well,' said Olivia, starting to smile. 'We still need to find out what names are in the logbook – don't you knooooow, tally-hoooo . . .' She trailed off, and started to giggle.

Sangeeta covered her mouth and started giggling too, and within a few seconds, they were rolling and bursting with laughter. At first I just felt silly, but then I couldn't help laughing too.

'You stupid ninny!' cried Olivia. 'Why did you say you were *blind*?'

'That Philip man is going to be so confused!' said Sangeeta, as she wiped her eyes.

It felt good to laugh about it. As if the pressure of everything we were trying to do was being let off and released into the air like steam from a rice cooker.

After we all calmed down and the laughter turned into thoughts, we became quiet and serious again.

'I guess we could fill in the application form,' said Olivia.

'If it takes a week to apply, it'll be too late for us,' I said. 'We won't get the information in time for the board.' I began to feel hopeless again. It was starting to seem as if people with names like mine and Sangeeta's and Olivia's great-grandad just weren't ever meant to be found.

'Shall we call again?' suggested Sangeeta. 'Olivia or I could try?'

Both Olivia and I shook our heads.

'We can't do that – two different people asking about the exact same thing in one day will be too suspicious,' said Olivia.

'Yeah,' I agreed. 'He might, like, think we're pranksters and call the police or something.'

We all fell quiet again, thinking.

'Maybe we've done this all wrong,' said Olivia. 'Maybe if we just tell him the truth, he might help us. We could just . . .' Olivia picked up the phone, but after staring at it for a few seconds, put it down again. 'No. That won't work, he won't believe us after our first call . . .' Olivia trailed off, but a moment later she leaped up, looking excited. 'Why don't we just *go* there – like right now? And explain everything to him and everyone at the museum?' Olivia grabbed mine and Sangeeta's arms excitedly. 'If we went in person, I could show them my great-grandad's picture – and Leo, you could show them the news about the competition! That way they'd know we weren't lying any more, and we wouldn't have to apply, and they could just find the names for us and look in the database thing *today*.'

'We can't go to the museum,' said Sangeeta. 'It's like, a million miles away! How would we even get there? The train would be way too expensive.'

As Sangeeta finished asking her question, Bo and Jules' giggles floated up to us again. Olivia looked over at me and I could tell right away she was thinking the same thing as me – hormones!

'I think I know a way,' I said, slowly.

'Me too,' said Olivia, excitedly. 'But do you think they would . . . ?'

'Maybe!' I said.

'What are you guys talking about?' asked Sangeeta, confused.

'A way to get to the museum,' I said. 'And it won't cost us a thing.'

MM 11: OPERATION BROOM CUPBOARD

'Are you sure this will work?' asked Sangeeta, as I grabbed my rucksack and Olivia stashed her globe-shaped money jar into it. 'Mum's coming to pick me up at four.'

'It's only two-twenty now, Sangeeta,' said Olivia. 'We'll be back way before then. Look.' Olivia quickly typed something into the tablet and showed us a map. 'It's not *that* far. Not with a car.'

'But I – I can't go to a museum dressed like this! What if someone from school sees me?' cried Sangeeta.

'Here, borrow this,' said Olivia, pulling a bright red cardigan from a drawer. 'Maybe the museum will think you're super-rich and like royal or something – that can't hurt. Come on. Ready?'

Sangeeta pulled on the cardigan, and we followed Olivia down the stairs to where Bo and Jules were. Their hormones had obviously made their legs stop working because they hadn't even moved away from the front door and were still giggling.

We silently watched them for a few seconds before I said, 'Hi, Bo! Didn't realise you were still here.'

They both jumped.

'What are you guys doing down here?' said Jules, turning red. 'I thought you were meant to be doing homework.'

'We are,' said Olivia. 'But we need to go back to the RAF museum for some research. And Mum and Dad said I should ask you if I needed help with anything, remember?'

'We have to interview someone there – and take pictures,' I added.

'And look, it's only forty minutes away,' said Olivia, holding up the tablet with the map on it.

'What are you doing with MY tablet?' asked Jules, snatching it out of Olivia's hands.

'Can you take us?' asked Sangeeta, stepping forward. 'Olivia said you have a *really* cool car.'

'Hang on,' said Bo, placing an arm high up against the doorframe as if he was in charge. 'Mum and Dad didn't say anything about you going to no museum!'

'It's for the *Real Kidz Rule* show project,' I said. 'I'm a leader, remember? And they said I could do whatever I needed to for it if Olivia and Sangeeta were with me.'

Bo opened his mouth, but before he could say anything, I added, 'And if you came too, Bo, you could keep Jules company. That way, while *we're* in the museum doing our homework, she won't be all alone and get bored . . .'

I stared at Bo and tried to hypnotise him with my eyes so he would do all the things we needed him to do.

'Oh,' said Bo, dropping his arm and looking confused. 'I guess . . . if it's for the school project . . . and, er . . . you don't mind . . . Jules?'

'No,' said Jules, smiling at Bo. 'I don't mind. My car's just there. I could drive us all.'

My eyes flicked over to Olivia and then to Sangeeta. The plan was working. Teenagers were so dumb!

'Which one's your car?' asked Bo.

Jules pointed. 'It's just there – the blue hatchback one.'

'Cool,' said Bo. 'Mine's a black Kiandra Jazz.'

I let out a snort and immediately tried to cover it up with a cough. The only way Bo's car could ever be called black, was if the name for 'dark blue' got changed.

Turning to Bo and making her eyelashes look like they were trying to fly away, Jules added, 'Are you coming too, then?'

'Yeah – yeah – that'd be nice,' said Bo, running his hands through his hair.

From behind me, Olivia and Sangeeta pretended they were about to be sick, as Bo and Jules grinned at each other for absolutely no reason at all.

As we all bundled ourselves into Jules' tiny blue car, Sangeeta whispered, 'I can't *believe* it worked.'

'I know!' I whispered. I'd had no idea that older brothers could be so nice and helpful if you asked them for things in front of someone they wanted to impress. I was learning so much!

As the car swished up the motorway and the same sights from that very first coach trip went rushing past us again, I wondered if I was finally going to learn about the real Leo. Maybe, in less than half an hour, I was going to know what kind of plane he had fought his battles in and what he had done to get a medal. And maybe, just maybe, the RAF folders would have a picture of him in them, and I wouldn't have to wonder what he looked like any more – or wonder if he might have looked – even a little bit – like me.

'Is this it?' asked Jules, as the car came screeching to a halt in front of the museum. I looked up at the glass doors and bright white letters, hoping everything I needed to find the real Leo lay behind them.

'Yup! Thanks, Jules!' cried out Olivia.

'We'll wait here – don't be too long,' ordered Bo, pretending to be a grown–up.

'Yeah, OK,' I replied, doing my best not to stick my tongue out at him as I jumped out of the car and ran into the museum with Olivia and Sangeeta.

As soon as we were in the reception area, we slowed down to an extra-straight walk – just like we did at school whenever a teacher was watching us – and headed to the desk. A tall man was standing behind it. From his name tag, we could see right away it was the

Philip I had spoken to on the phone.

'Well, hello,' he said. He had shiny curly hair that bounced up and down as he moved. 'And how may I help you?'

'Hello,' said Olivia, whilst Sangeeta and me stared at him with our mouths hanging open. Now that we were here, everything suddenly felt impossible.

'Are you all here to see the museum?' Glancing at the doors, Philip added, 'On your own?'

'No,' I said, making my voice go as high as possible so that I didn't sound like Mr Scott from the phone. 'My older brother's waiting outside in the car for us.'

'We're here – for a special assignment,' added Sangeeta, finally becoming her normal self again.

'Oh, yes? And what assignment is that?' asked Philip. The clock above his head told us it was three o'clock exactly and that we didn't have much time.

'We need to look in your special folder – the one with all the soldiers' names in it who fought in the RAF,' I announced. 'Our teacher, Mr Scott, sent us!'

'Yeah. He rang you earlier,' added Olivia. 'It's for our Remembrance Day project.'

'Mr Scott?' asked Philip, narrowing his eyes at us. 'As

I told him over the phone, there's an application process. You can't just come in and look at them, I'm afraid.'

'That's OK. Couldn't you do it for us?' asked Olivia, hopefully. 'We can pay you.'

Olivia took out her money jar from my rucksack and poured all the coins it had out onto the counter.

'We just need to know about three RAF soldiers – that's all. It's for our homework.'

Philip looked down at the money. 'I'm afraid even I can't look at the logbook without prior approval,' he said gently. 'I'm sorry, but those are the rules. It's best you tell your . . . *Mr Scott* that when you see him next.'

Next to me, I could feel Sangeeta and Olivia's shoulders slump. We knew there wasn't any point in showing Philip the *Whot Gazette* or telling him about the competition when he wasn't allowed to look at the logbook either.

'Now, if you would like to see the museum today, we're still open for another hour. And it's free entry. Would you like to go in?' asked Philip.

Olivia and Sangeeta were about to shake their heads when I shouted out, 'YES! We would!'

'We would?' whispered Sangeeta.

'Good idea,' said Philip. 'You have until four o'clock. I'm afraid you've just missed the last tour of the day and of course, the flight simulation sessions are closed too, but there's plenty to see that might help you in your – er – special assignment.'

Without waiting a second more, I ran off towards the large entrance doors to the first hall, Olivia and Sangeeta hurrying after me. I could feel Philip's eyes watching us, so I didn't look back.

Inside, the museum was nearly empty. There was only us and a very old couple looking at some pictures at the end of the hall. In front of us was the familiar shimmering old Hurricane plane which had greeted us the first time.

'Why are we wasting our time by coming in here?' asked Olivia, as we all came to a standstill beside it.

'Listen,' I said. 'We need to get upstairs and see the records! Maybe – maybe we can create a distraction . . .'

'You mean, like an undercover operation?' asked Olivia, looking around. 'Where we pretend we're just tourists but then secretly break in!'

'Yes!' I said. 'Exactly.'

'Have you both gone *mad*?' asked Sangeeta, her

eyes huge. 'We can't break in! We'd go to jail! And then after we were allowed out we'd have to go into hiding for the rest of our whole lives because our parents would DEFINITELY kill us!'

'Hiding! That's it! Sangeeta – we just need a place to *hide* . . . until anyone who's upstairs has left!' I gave Sangeeta's shoulders a happy shake and looked around the hall. Immediately, my eyes fell on the old Hawker Hurricane.

'The flight simulator!' I said, grabbing Olivia's and Sangeeta's arms. 'It's closed – so what if we just go and hide inside it until the museum shuts, and then run upstairs? Easy!'

'Easy? What about your brother and Jules – they'll get worried and probably come in! And that Philip man will see if we don't leave the museum when it's closing,' whispered Sangeeta. 'Plus, my parents are coming to get me at four, remember? I'm not dressed like this for fun, you know.'

'Oh yeah . . .' I said, telling my brain to try harder.

'I know!' said Olivia, clicking her fingers. 'What if instead of using the simulator to hide in, we use it to create a distraction instead! One of us could go inside and turn it on and it'll make loads of noise . . . and then as soon as everyone runs over to see what's happened, we give them the slip and meet upstairs, and go look for the logbook together!'

'That's an even better idea!' I cried, louder than I meant to. I saw the old couple look over at us from across the room and I went on in a whisper. 'Let's do *that*.'

'No, let's *not*. It's mad!' said Sangeeta, twisting her hands and making her bangles jangle.

'Come on, Sangeeta! Think about all the things actual soldiers like Leo had to do – like in their real operations and missions,' I urged. 'This might be our last chance to find out something.'

'Yeah,' agreed Olivia. 'Something *real*. It's not like we've got loads of other places to go and try!'

Sangeeta sighed. 'OK. Fine . . . but we'd better not get caught!'

Grinning, I nodded. 'Let's find a place to hide. Like the toilets or something. And then I'll go and make the distraction.'

'Wait! We can't hide in the toilets – they're right next to the reception. We'll have to hide in *this* room,' said Sangeeta thoughtfully. 'When you make the distraction, everyone will go through the Spitfire room to investigate what's happening so we can't hide in there. It has to be in here! It's close enough to the stimulator that you'll be able to run here and hide before anyone comes to investigate the noises and then we can run *back* through reception and upstairs without anyone seeing us.'

'She's right,' said Olivia, looking around the room and its row of gleaming glass cabinets.

I spun around, trying to look for somewhere safe and big enough for the three of us to hide in too. But there was nothing. Everything was see-through. Wondering what to do, my eyes followed the old couple leaving through the double doors to the next room, and suddenly, I saw it – a small white door that I hadn't noticed before.

Running past all the shimmering heroes in their glass frames and cages, I made my way over to the door and tried the handle, expecting it to be locked. But to my surprise, the door flew open, and out fell . . . the long wooden handle of a mop!

It was an old broom cupboard, filled with shelves of

cleaning products and a bucket and mop and an old hoover. It was smelly and a bit small – and absolutely perfect for our new mission!

'Guys! Over here! Quick!' I called out, waving.

Olivia and Sangeeta came running over. When she saw what I had found, Olivia whispered, 'Awesome!' but Sangeeta took a step back.

'I can't go in there – my dress! It'll get stinky and dirty,' she whispered. 'And—'

'Quick! Someone's coming!' hissed Olivia. From outside the hall, footsteps and voices began to echo towards us. Leaping into the cupboard, Olivia pulled Sangeeta in. I jumped into the remaining tiny space, and pulled the door shut behind me, instantly plunging us all into a thick and smelly darkness.

NOT-SO-FRIENDLY FIRE

'Ouch!'

'Shhh!'

'How long has it been? I think my foot's stuck inside a hoover pipe!'

'There's something crawling on my neck! Oh no! I think it's a spider!

'Sorry, that was my hair!'

'Shhhhhhhhh! Guys! Stop moving!'

We all fell silent again, our breaths bouncing around the small space like volleyballs of hot air. I was sweating so much that there was salty water trickling into my eyes and making them sting.

'We're all going to need to take about five showers when we get out of here,' whispered Sangeeta.

'I'm going to look again – so be quiet,' I ordered, and, ever so slowly, I pushed the handle down and opened the door by barely a millimetre, listening. For a few seconds, all I could hear was my heartbeat, but then it calmed down, and I realised there wasn't anyone in the hall. Everyone had left.

'Thank God!' exclaimed Olivia, as I opened the door a little wider so we could all get some fresh air. 'Now I know what chickens getting roasted in an oven feel like! I think I might become vegetarian.'

'Me too,' said Sangeeta, gulping at the air as if she was eating it. 'How long has it been? It's not four already, is it?'

'Don't worry – we still have plenty of time!' I promised, even though I wasn't sure what time it was at all. But we couldn't stop now. 'I'll run to the simulator and create the distraction – so make sure you let me back in after I set it off. Easy!'

Olivia and Sangeeta nodded at me, even though I think we all knew it wasn't going to be easy at all.

Taking two deep breaths and reminding myself that the real Leo had done far braver things, I slipped out of the broom cupboard, and silently made my way into the next hall.

The old couple had gone, but a family were now looking at the flight simulation pod, right by the exit doors. I pretended to look at a display cabinet filled with medals, and waited, wishing they would leave. After a few minutes, the family left too. I was finally alone.

Quickly, I made my way over to the flight simulator. It was shaped like a giant, shiny white pebble and was standing on a large black base. The door of the pod was open so everyone could see inside. But a red rope had been chained to two poles to keep people out, along with a sign that said: CLOSED. BOOK A FLIGHT WITH US ONLINE!

I hurried up to the sign, and crawling under the rope, stepped inside. I half-expected an alarm to start ringing or something to start moving, but nothing did, so I went over to where the two large pilot chairs were waiting. One day, when I wasn't breaking at least fifty rules, maybe I could sit in one of those chairs and take a flight – just like the real Leo might have done to train for the RAF.

Looking at all the buttons and dials and levers, I tried to find one that might turn something on and draw everyone's attention. But I couldn't see anything, so I decided to do what Jingyi did when she got annoyed with a toy – which was press every single button one at a time until she found the one she wanted.

First I pressed a large red button, which didn't seem to do anything except make the screens brighter. Then I tapped a smaller button and another and another and another, until I had pressed a whole row of tiny square buttons and lit them all up.

There was *still* nothing happening, so I flicked a switch with lots of numbers on it all the way up to one hundred and waited a few more seconds. Just as I began to wonder if it was broken, the pod suddenly began to vibrate and shake and move side to side like a small boat riding a huge and horrible stormy wave. The screen in front of me came alive with the moving picture of a runway. From all around me, a woman's voice loudly announced: 'Flight simulation activated. Doors closing. Please prepare for take-off. High altitude terrain.'

I lunged forwards to the controls, hoping I could find a button to make it stop, but the ground beneath me grunted and jerked backwards, flinging me to the back of the pod like a small fish. I tried to crawl over to the door, but it was too late! The door was closing! I was trapped!

'Full throttle capacity activated,' announced the woman, as the machine shook and rattled around. It felt like I was inside a washing machine on its highest spin. The runway image began to swirl and circle and lots of bright golden-orange rays surrounded the screen. 'Enemy aircraft detected. Incoming. Awaiting flight navigation.'

'No!' I cried out. The machine lunged forward and shuddered as if something had hit its side, slamming me forwards and right into the controls. Feeling like I was about three seconds from throwing up, I staggered over to one of the pilot chairs and managed to click the seatbelt around me.

'Off switch!' I moaned, hoping the controls were voice activated somehow and begging the machine lady to understand me. The pod rolled and rocked and it felt like my head and eyes were both spinning in separate directions. 'OFF SWITCH! PLEASE! OFF SWITCH! OFF SWITCH!!!'

And then, all at once, everything stopped.

The floor stopped rocking and my head stopped

swimming and all the lights on the control board and screen stopped flashing. It was as if someone had pulled the plug on it all.

From behind me, the swishing noise of a door opening cut through the air. Followed by a voice.

'What in heavens . . .'

I froze in my pilot's chair, too afraid to turn around. Instead, I pulled my legs quickly up onto the seat, and curled myself into a ball. Maybe, somehow, whoever had opened the flight simulator would think there was no one in the seats and that the machine had malfunctioned. Maybe they wouldn't come and check.

The sound of footsteps began to make their way towards me. I squeezed my eyes shut, wishing and hoping this was all a nightmare and that Saturday hadn't even begun yet and that I was actually still in bed. But then a hand grabbed the top of my seat and spun me around.

'What on earth do we have here?'

One after the other, I opened my eyes and looked up. It was Mrs Fletcher – the lady who had taken our class around on that first visit. Except, now, she wasn't looking kind and friendly and smiley. She was looking confused and red and angry.

'Hold on,' she said. 'I remember your face. You were here before – for a school trip, weren't you?'

I nodded silently at the ground, as a huge, invisible boulder seemed to place itself on my chest. I had failed our mission and broken my promise to the real Leo and now, because of me, his story and Olivia's great-grandad's story and R Singh's story weren't ever going to be told. Mum and Dad would probably never talk to me again and, since I had probably broken the flight simulator, I would have to go to jail and work for the rest of my life to pay for all the damages.

The thought of it all made me want to lie down and never get up again.

'Now, young man, what's your name?' asked Mrs Fletcher, her voice sounding kinder.

I opened my mouth to tell her, but nothing came out.

'OK, you can tell me that later. For now, I think we had better reunite you with your accomplices, so you can all tell me what is going on.'

Accomplices? Did that mean Olivia and Sangeeta had been caught too?

Undoing my seatbelt, Mrs Fletcher helped me gently out of the pod. Leading me out to the reception area, she directed me to the very same stairs I had been hoping to climb with Olivia and Sangeeta, and on reaching the top, took me to a small office with huge windows.

'Leo!' gasped Sangeeta, from a seat on the other side of a wide metal table. I looked up, and felt the bottom half of my jaw fall open.

Sangeeta and Olivia both looked as if they had been on something much worse than a flight simulator. They had dust and dirt *everywhere* – all over their faces and clothes and hands. Bits of fluffy yellow washing-up sponge lay tangled in Olivia's hair, like bright flies caught in a spider's web. But the very worst were the splashes of bright white paint streaking across Sangeeta's once sparkling blue lehenga skirt.

I wanted to ask what had happened, but instead I sat down quietly next to Olivia, and shut my eyes. But when I opened them again, everyone was still there.

'Right, children,' said Mrs Fletcher, sitting on the other side of the table from us, as Philip and another much shorter woman came and stood at the doorway. 'First thing first. Where have you all come from?'

'Whot,' answered Olivia.

Mrs Fletcher tried again. 'I said, where have you kids travelled in from – where do you live?'

'Whot,' answered Sangeeta.

'Now, this is rude! It's a simple question,' said Mrs Fletcher, frowning. 'Where do you—'

'No! We mean – we come from the village of Whot,' interrupted Olivia.

We all nodded. Living in Whot meant people always thought we were rude or too stupid to understand questions about where we lived.

'Ah. I see,' said Mrs Fletcher. 'My apologies. Of course! Whot. Now, second thing. We're going to need your parents' telephone numbers.'

'Please, miss, my sister is downstairs – in the car park – with Leo's brother,' said Olivia. 'In a blue car. Maybe you can just tell them and . . . not call our parents?'

We all looked up in hope.

'I'm afraid that won't quite do,' answered Mrs Fletcher. 'Philip – would you go down, please, and retrieve their siblings?'

Philip hurried out of the room. Olivia gave a whine like a puppy who had found out it was being taken away from its owners, and put her head in her hands. Sangeeta stared so hard at everyone that I was sure she had forgotten how to blink.

'Now, thirdly and most importantly. Why don't you tell me what this is all about? Leo, how about we start with you?'

RAISING THE DEAD

'We are so dead,' whispered Olivia, fiddling with the straps of her dungarees.

'You're not as dead as me,' said Sangeeta, peeling bits of paint off her face. 'We were meant to be at my mum's second cousin's sister-in-law's nephew's wedding by now.'

We all looked back at the closed door to Mrs Fletcher's office. Inside, everything seemed deathly silent. All our parents were now behind it, and it was never a good sign when parents were so quiet that a whole group of them couldn't be heard.

'Do you think Mr Scott's going to find out about everything?' Sangeeta asked me quietly. 'What if he bans us from the project?'

I didn't reply. All I could do was sit as stiff as a piece of cardboard, and wait for everything to be over.

Suddenly, the door to Mrs Fletcher's office clicked open. We instantly sat up straighter.

First, Sangeeta's mum and dad and grandmother came out. Mr Singh shook his head at Sangeeta, which made his beard and moustache shake too. Mrs Singh was red in the face, and looked like she had just climbed fifty flights of stairs. She had clearly been getting ready for the wedding when Mrs Fletcher called, because she was wearing a long bejewelled green dress. The sleeves had tiny golden bells at the end, and she had flowers in her hair. Sangeeta's nani was wearing a salwar kameez, which was pink and far less sparkly. She was the only one of the three who didn't look angry. Putting her hands around Sangeeta's face, she gave it a pat.

'Sangeeta. Car. Now,' ordered Mrs Singh. With her bangles jangling and her ruined lehenga skirt rustling, Sangeeta followed them, her eyes glued to the floor.

Olivia's mum was the next to come out. She left Mrs Fletcher's room quietly, shutting the door behind her. I had never seen her before, so I didn't know what she normally looked like or what her angry face might be. She came over to stand in front of us. Her light brown hair was tied high in a bun and she had bright brown eyes. She raised one eyebrow and gave us a small smile.

'What are you kids like, eh?' she said. 'Mad, the whole lot of you. Come on, Olivia. Lots of explaining to do to your dad and sister, I think – but not before a long shower. What a mess!'

Then, looking at me, she said, 'So you're Leo, huh?'

I nodded.

'Interesting.' Olivia's mum began heading towards the stairs. 'Come on then, I haven't got all night,' she called back to Olivia.

'Good luck, Leo!' whispered Olivia, as she jumped up and ran after her mum. 'See you Monday.'

I nodded again, wondering when my turn would come. I waited. And waited. And waited. But the office door remained closed.

Finally, just when I was starting to wonder if everyone had secretly left me, the office door clicked open again, and I could hear Mum and Dad's footsteps approaching. The heavy silence made the click of their shoes sound like thunder echoing around a cave.

I stared at the wall in front of me, wishing it would open up and suck me into it, as Mum and Dad's shoes came to a stop in front of me.

'Leo, up,' ordered Dad, in his extra-quiet, extra-disappointed voice.

Mum stayed silent. My head still bowed, I followed them down the stairs and out to the car where Bo was waiting with Jingyi, who was fast asleep.

'Idiot,' whispered Bo, as I got in.

'Not a word, please. Anyone,' said Mum, signalling left to head out of the car park. 'When we get home, Leo, bath first, and then straight to your room. Bo, not a word out of you, please. Leo needs to think about everything he's done today. We will speak all about it tomorrow.'

'But—'

'I said not a WORD, Leo, and that was a word,' warned Mum.

Wiping away an angry tear, I stared out of the window, and made a wish that the road would never end and that we could just stay on it for ever. It wasn't fair – any of it. If people had helped us like they were supposed to, and grown-ups hadn't made everything so hard and complicated and stupid, then Olivia and Sangeeta and I would never have had to come back to the museum in the first place! All we had wanted was some information. Why did there have to be silly application forms and so many rules just to look for some names? If Philip had gone and checked for us like we'd asked, then that would have been it! Or if all the soldiers and pilots and everyone's names were on the internet or in the history books, then we would never have had to think of new ways to find them!

That night, Mum and Dad and Bo were extra-quiet around me. Dad cancelled our trip to London for an uncle's dinner party, Mum stayed on the phone all evening in her office, and Bo growled whenever he saw me. Even Jingyi seemed to be ignoring me – as if she knew that playing with me would somehow land her in trouble.

Sunday was even worse. I didn't have to do any extra chores or change any more nappies, but I wasn't allowed to watch TV or play computer games, and I had to spend the whole day writing apology letters.

The first one was to the museum for nearly breaking their flight simulator, and the second one was to Mr

Scott for pretending to be him on the phone. They weren't long letters, but they took the whole day because every time I thought I had written one perfectly, Dad would come and check, and shaking his head, tell me to write a better one. So I did. Again, and again and again, until my hand began to hurt. Finally, just before dinner-time, Dad read my latest attempts, nodded and gave me two envelopes to put them in.

'I'll give this one to Mrs Fletcher,' said Dad, taking the envelope with her name on it. 'And this one, you will give to Mr Scott before school. We'll go early tomorrow, so that we can speak with him and your head teacher privately.'

As Dad turned to leave, I knew I had to say something. He had to know why the real Leo was so important. And how finding out about someone like him and making everyone know about him could stop me from being bullied and ignored and treated like I was different and stupid all the time. And not just me, but him and Bo and Mum and Jingyi too.

I blurted out, 'Dad – I'm sorry. I just wanted to find . . .' But the rest of the words got caught by the large boulder in my throat.

Dad turned to look at me. His eyes looked watery and sad.

'I know, Leo, I know,' he whispered, before turning away, and closing my bedroom door behind him.

* * *

'What did the flight machine feel like? Oh, man! I wish I'd been there!'

'Do Mr Scott's voice for us – the one you did on the phone! Go on!'

'Do you think you'll get expelled?'

'Why was Olivia helping you – did you pay her? Was it expensive?'

I nodded and shrugged and shook my head, as Sangeeta spoke a thousand words a minute to tell everyone everything that had happened at the weekend. Even though we had been sworn to secrecy and no one except me and Sangeeta and Olivia – and now Mr Scott and Mrs Fitzgerald – knew what we had done, somehow the whole school had found out by first break. It was as if there was a secret version of the *Whot Gazette* made just for school, floating around the hallways and classrooms.

'Make way, make way!' cried Drew, as he and Nancy pushed their way through the crowd to where me and Sangeeta were standing. 'Best friends to the criminals coming through!'

Everyone giggled as Drew swung his arms over both me and Sangeeta.

'Now, if you want to hear the story in full, from the actual real-life witnesses, it'll cost you one bar of chocolate,' announced Drew.

'That's not fair,' protested Kerry.

Drew shrugged. 'Only way. Meet us in the tag corner at lunchtime if you want to hear any more! *With* your chocolate bars.'

Suddenly everyone went quiet, as the sound of a bouncing ball ricocheted around us. Like birds sensing a giant cat approaching, the crowd scattered and Toby and Catherine came walking up to us, each of them holding a bright yellow tennis ball. Drew instantly dropped his arms from our shoulders, and we all stood still, waiting.

Toby stood for a few seconds in front me, bouncing his tennis ball up and down, up and down. My body stiffened, waiting to be hit.

'Funny you haven't both been arrested yet,' said Toby, as his ball hit the tarmac again. 'Stinky criminals like you should be sent right back home!' Then, quickly looking around to make sure there weren't any teachers close by, he threw the tennis ball straight at my face whilst Catherine threw hers at Sangeeta's legs.

'Owwwwwww!' cried Sangeeta.

I was in too much pain to make a noise. My eyes were watering.

'Hey, Catherine, look – cry-baby is CRYING!'

Catherine smirked. 'Good!' she yelled. Raising her hand to throw the ball again, she lunged forwards.

'Stop it!' yelled Nancy, jumping in front of us and spreading out her hands.

'Yeah. I *would* stop it if I were you.'

I looked up because it couldn't be – but it was! It was Olivia, standing behind Toby and Catherine, with her hands on her hips and a bear and an elephant drawn on her knees. Her best friends were with her too, although they didn't seem too happy about it.

'Go get lost. Before I get my sister to come down with HER friends and sort you out!'

Slowly, everyone who had run away tiptoed back again to watch what would happen next. The whole playground fell silent, as Olivia stared down at Toby and Catherine, and they looked back at her, their eyes narrowed and their hands nervously holding on to their tennis balls. Then suddenly, Olivia tilted her head to the side and took a step forward. The move made Toby and Catherine jump and, like two wounded cats, run off.

'Everyone, get lost,' ordered Olivia, turning her eyes to the crowd. 'Except you two,' she added, looking at me and Sangeeta.

'Are you OK?' asked Olivia, once the crowds had all hurried away.

Sangeeta bent down to rub her leg. My face was hurting and throbbing, as if my heart had climbed right up to the surface of it.

We still both nodded, even though we weren't OK at all.

'I hate Toby. He's always been horrible. We'll have to get him back one day – you know, when we're not in so much trouble already. So what did your parents say?' she asked. 'I got grounded – and so did Jules.

But only for the rest of the weekend. My dad actually found it funny.' Olivia smiled. 'We spoke over the phone last night and he said my great-grandad would be proud of me for trying to find out more about him.'

'Wish my parents were like yours,' said Sangeeta. 'Mum isn't speaking to me because she thinks I got paint on myself and destroyed my dress *on purpose*. And Dad said I'm grounded "for the foreseeable future", which basically means I'm never leaving Whot again.'

'Aw, man! That sucks. What about you, Leo?' asked Olivia.

'Just letters to say sorry to the museum and Mr Scott, and no TV or games and things,' I said.

'That's not too bad,' said Olivia.

I shrugged. I hadn't told Sangeeta or Olivia that after I had given in my letter to Mr Scott and explained what had happened, he had said he was incredibly disappointed and that he would be thinking about what punishments he was going to give the three of us. Maybe that *would* mean banning Sangeeta and me from the project. Even though we had tried so hard to make it the best project ever and help it win the competition.

Before anyone could say anything else, the bell rang

and we all headed silently back to our classrooms.

For the rest of the day, it almost felt as if everything was back to normal. No one mentioned what had happened on Saturday – not even Mr Scott. After breaktime, we did maths and had lunch, and in the afternoon, we all worked on our bits of the board and assembly. I drew a huge brick for the cathedral display and coloured in Leo's name and the lion, even though I still didn't have a story to go with it yet, and Sangeeta helped make costume helmets for the assembly out of old colanders and plastic leaves.

But then, at the very end of the day, Mr Scott clapped his hands and told everyone to stay seated.

We all waited. Sangeeta was tapping her foot so hard it was making the table shake.

'It's been confirmed that the *Real Kidz Rule* film crew are coming in to visit our school . . . *tomorrow*,' announced Mr Scott.

'Yesssssss!' shouted Gary, as the whole class erupted into squeals.

'I want you all to be on your absolute best behaviour. No messing around, no breaking the rules. And NO ONE is permitted to speak to the *Real Kidz Rule* people about the incidents that took place this past weekend – if I even hear a whisper of it, you'll be taken off the project.'

Instantly, everyone's eyeballs swivelled towards me and Sangeeta.

'But, Sir!' yelled Toby. 'How come Sangeeta and Leo haven't been taken off the project yet?'

'Because Mrs Fitzgerald and I say so,' answered Mr Scott firmly, as Toby scowled. 'Right, everyone. Off you go – everyone except for Leo and Sangeeta.'

The room emptied as quickly as a tub of water being poured down a sinkhole. For a few seconds, Mr Scott waited in silence, as if he was expecting me or Sangeeta to say something first. But then the classroom door opened and Olivia and her teacher, Mrs Malcolm, and behind them, Mrs Fitzgerald, came in. And behind Mrs Fitzgerald were a man and a woman we had never seen before, wearing 'Visitor' badges.

Sangeeta made a small whimpering sound. I wanted to make one too. This was it. Those visitors were probably the police, and this was our last day in school. I knew the sorry letters Dad had made me write had been a waste of time!

Everyone sat down. Then Mrs Fitzgerald cleared her throat, and began to speak.

'Leo, Sangeeta and Olivia, this is Ms Smol and Mr Verne. They're producers for the *Real Kidz Rule* Show.'

Sangeeta gasped and Olivia looked over at me with at least three questions on her face. I gave her an invisible shrug back.

'They're here because we thought it only right that we inform them – prior to their official visit tomorrow – of the trouble caused at the museum at the weekend,' continued Mrs Fitzgerald. 'And they would like to hear about it in more detail – from you.'

'But – but – miss!'

'Yes, Sangeeta?' asked Mrs Fitzgerald.

'Miss – I – we don't want to be taken off the project – we didn't mean to cause so many problems. We just wanted to find some information.'

'Nobody is taking anyone off the project,' said Mrs Fitzgerald, calmly.

'That's right,' said the lady called Ms Smol. 'We just want to hear your version of events. That's all.' She flicked her blondish-red fringe out of her eyes and smiled at us in a friendly way.

'What do you think? Can you tell us *your* side of the story?' asked Mr Verne. He had the longest rivers of black dreadlocks I had ever seen and the latest Cool-Skool trainers. I stared at them, thinking that Mr Verne was definitely the coolest man I had ever seen on the planet, let alone in the whole of Whot.

Sangeeta and me and Olivia all looked at each other, and gave a united nod.

'Good,' said Mrs Fitzgerald. 'We've already rung ahead and asked your parents to pick you up a bit later. So you can take your time. Now, who should we start with?'

Olivia pointed at me and said, 'Leo. It's him and the other Leo that started everything, really.'

'There's another Leo?' asked Mr Verne, as Ms Smol got out a notepad and started scribbling.

'Yeah,' said Sangeeta, before I could speak. 'Except he's dead.'

'Sangeeta, why don't we hear Leo tell it?' asked Mr Scott, gently.

'Oh yeah, sorry,' said Sangeeta, looking over at me with a sorry-grin.

Everyone now stared at me, waiting.

I took a deep breath. 'It's like Olivia said – it all started because of the real Leo.' My voice wobbled a little bit, but I took a deep breath to make it stronger, and went on. 'He flew for the RAF in the Second World War and he won a medal for it, and his name is on the cathedral wall – the one in Rochester. Right next to a golden lion . . .'

PAPER CHAINS

'So? You been expelled yet?' asked Bo, as I ran up to him. He was waiting by the school gates and kicking pebbles down the pavement.

'No,' I said, wishing it was Dad who had come to pick me up. Bo hadn't really spoken to me since Saturday. Probably because he had been told off by Mum and Dad for taking us to the museum.

'Shame,' muttered Bo.

As we began walking towards the village, I looked back over my shoulder. Sangeeta had jumped into her mum's car and was probably already halfway through her second samosa, and Olivia had sprinted up the road so fast all I had seen was the bottom of her shoes. I wished they were both with me now so that Bo would pretend to be all nice again.

We came to a stop outside the newsagents. But instead of saying 'Stay here,' like he usually did, Bo asked, 'So? You want anything then?'

I stared up at him, wondering if my ears needed cleaning.

'Hurry up,' ordered Bo. 'What drink and crisps do you want?' I couldn't believe it. Bo was *asking* me what I wanted! Which meant . . . I had done it! I had made one of my own promises come true. I was so surprised I shouted out, 'YES!'

'Huh?'

'I mean – can I have an apple-pop and er – er – cheese-and-onion crisps?' And then deciding to use all my luck up whilst I still had it, I added, 'AND a Wild Beasts chocolate bar?'

Bo narrowed his eyes at me. 'We'll see,' he said, before tinkling open the shop door and vanishing behind it.

Maybe this was the only time Bo was ever going to ask me what I wanted instead of giving me what *he* wanted. But it *had* happened – and the real Leo had helped make it happen, and I was never ever going to forget it. I began to jump up and down on the spot, like a kangaroo with nowhere to go.

'Here,' said Bo, dropping down all the things I had asked for like a tall tree shedding crispy, shimmering packets of crisps and sweets instead of leaves. I walked alongside him, slurping my drink every time he slurped his and eating a crisp every time he did too.

'So . . .' said Bo, as we waited to cross the road. 'Did er, Olivia say anything to you – about me – from her sister?'

I shook my head, one half of my mouth stuffed with the Wild Beasts bar and the other with crisps.

'Ba – O-hivia – hinks ha – hih–ter – hikes – oo,' I tried.

'What did you say?'

I swallowed the biggest chocolate-crisps ball ever. 'I said, Olivia thinks her sister likes you,' I repeated.

Bo's cheeks flushed bright pink and his mouth did something funny. 'Cool. Come on,' he ordered, as the green man flashed at us and allowed us to cross the road.

'Do you like *her*?' I asked, feeling a bit weird. It was strange to be having a conversation with Bo about something as icky as liking someone.

Bo shrugged. 'She's all right.'

I told my brain to remember to let Olivia know that Bo had got the hormones too, so we could both make 'Ew!' faces together.

'So did you find anything out about that Leo dude then?' asked Bo. 'The one from the cathedral?'

'No,' I said. 'But we told the *Real Kidz Rule* show people all about him, so maybe they'll find something.'

'Thought as much . . .'

Bo took out something from his pocket. 'Here,' he said, holding out a square of folded-up paper. 'Found this for you. At college.'

I unfolded the sheet of paper. It was a photocopied page, taken from what looked like a history book. On the top half was a title about the bombing of Pearl Harbour. I remembered Mr Scott telling us about it, and how Japan hurting Pearl Harbour had made America come and join the fight to beat the Nazis. Japan seemed to be the only country near to Singapore that had made it into the history books. None of the other countries that weren't Europe or America seemed to have mattered.

But they did matter. And this piece of paper was proof. Because on the bottom half of the page was a map of Singapore. And, right next to it, a heading that read:

THE ALLIED FORCES & THE BATTLE FOR SINGAPORE: CHURCHILL DEMANDS EVERY MAN FIGHT ON.

'There was a *whole battle*? In Singapore?' I cried. 'I just thought some of the soldiers *came* from there. I didn't know they had to fight *in* Singapore too!'

'Yup,' said Bo.

'And – and even Winston Churchill knew about it?'

'Well, d'oh!' said Bo, rolling his eyes.

'Did *you* know we had a battle?' I asked.

Bo shook his head. 'Not until now. We never got taught about any of it at school. I guess only the people who were there know all about it – and most of them have died. I only started looking after you nearly got us grounded for life on Saturday.'

I fell silent because there were too many questions inside my head. Questions like: why had none of the history books at school mentioned a battle in Singapore?

What other battles had they missed out? And was this battle the reason Leo had ended up in a cathedral – because he had been trying to stop the Nazis from destroying Singapore?

For the first time ever, I wished I was a grown-up with my very own computer and no school work or chores to do, so that I could find everything out.

'Come on,' said Bo, pushing me on in a friendly way. 'Read it at home. Mum and Dad will be wondering where we are.'

I folded the piece of paper away and, holding it tightly in my hands, hurried home with Bo.

That night, over dinner, Mum and Bo asked me lots of questions about the *Real Kidz Rule* people. Dad was still quiet, but I could tell he was listening because he nodded a lot. Then, just as I was in the middle of showing everyone what Bo had given me and getting ready to ask them what they knew about the Battle of Singapore, the phone rang.

Dad jumped up and grabbing the phone, hurried into Mum's office with it. He didn't come back out the rest of the evening. Not even for dessert. Or to help clear up the table. Or to put Jingyi to bed. Or even to say goodnight to us.

'He's just busy with something,' explained Mum. 'Go to bed. And don't worry about anything.'

But I *was* worried. I was worried that maybe it was the police who had rung and that Dad was begging them not to arrest me. Or maybe he was selling the house to pay for the broken flight machine. I couldn't sleep, or stop the squirming feeling in the bottom of my belly.

Not until I heard Dad climbing the stairs. I waited for him to check on me like usual, but he didn't. He just went into his bedroom and shut the door.

* * *

'Leo? Wake up, Leo. Time to get ready for school.'

I rubbed my eyes open and saw Mum standing above me.

I glanced at my alarm clock with one eye closed. It was a whole half hour earlier than I was meant to get up.

'I'm afraid I have to drop you off a little early today. I've got a big meeting at nine. OK?'

As Mum headed to the door, I sat up and asked, 'But, Mum – why isn't Dad taking me?'

Mum turned to look at me, and I could tell right away she was hiding something. 'He's had to leave early for work. Now, come on. Up you get.'

As she left and shut my bedroom door behind her, I dragged my feet out of bed and plonked them onto the floor. Dad was so mad at me that he didn't even want to take me to school any more. Not even having proof that my country had fought in World War Two and had been important enough for Winston Churchill to care about it, was enough to make me feel any better.

After Mum dropped me off at the school gates, I started to forget all about Dad. Because nearly everyone at school had arrived early too. Even Toby – who was hanging around by the tuck shop wearing a brand-new jacket and a face so shiny it looked as if someone had smeared Vaseline all over it.

'Hey, Leo!' cried out Sangeeta, running over to me. 'Everyone is early! Just wait until they find out the *Real Kidz Rule* people have already talked to us. Hey. Is it just me, or does everyone look . . . a bit strange today?'

I stared back at Sangeeta, not really knowing what to say. Mainly because she had put at least one hundred different coloured hair clips in her hair, all with animals and flowers on them, and transformed her long plaits into two rivers of metal.

But she was right. Everyone *did* look different. Like themselves, except . . . shinier, somehow. The playground was a sea of hair that was silkier than usual, and smiles that were brighter and whiter, and uniforms that had been ironed crisp for the first time in perhaps ever, and glossy shoes. It was as if everyone had been lifted out from real life and transported into the middle of one of Mum and Dad's TV dramas.

'By the way, I like how you've done *your* hair today,' said Sangeeta.

'Really?' I asked, as I carefully patted the top of the single spike I had managed to create, right at the front of my head. It had only taken half a tub of Bo's hair gel and five whole minutes in front of the mirror. I just had to make sure I didn't move my head too much.

'Oh my holy . . .' gasped Sangeeta, poking me in the arm and pointing to the middle of the playground. 'Look at Drew!'

I turned in the direction that Sangeeta was pointing, and felt my mouth drop open. Drew was making his way towards us like a superstar, parting the playground as everyone stopped and turned to stare at him. His uniform wasn't wrinkled or muddy like it usually was, and his hair had been rolled into exactly seven dagger-shaped spikes.

But no one was really looking at any of those things. What everyone was really staring at were the two huge streaks of bright pink and silver glitter that had been painted across his eyes like sparkling jam. Even Nancy was staring at him as she walked beside him. She looked just like her normal self – except for the gigantic purple bow in her hair, which was bigger than her whole face.

'Hey. You all look . . . nice,' said Olivia, as she came to stand next to us like it was a normal thing for her to do. She had covered her knees in glittery stickers, which Drew and Nancy were staring at whilst pretending not to.

'Hey, you can use this – for the board,' said Olivia, holding out what I knew right away was her great-grandad's piece of paper. 'I want you to put it up there and let everyone know that I gave it to you. OK?'

'But – isn't it supposed to be . . .' Sangeeta leaned in and whispered, '*a secret?*'

Olivia shook her head. 'I don't want it to be any more. I want everyone to know he was my great-grandad and not just someone you found out about by accident. Leo, promise you'll put it up?'

I nodded a promise and took the precious piece of paper from her.

From across the air, the bell began to ring and the doors to the school were flung open. From behind them, Mrs Fitzgerald stepped out in shoes so high that she looked like a human skyscraper, and began shouting at everyone to walk in sensibly.

As we all headed into our classes, I soon realised that it wasn't only the kids in school who had specially prepared for the *Real Kidz Rule* show. Mr Scott's beard was in on the act too – it looked extra-shiny and extra-puffy and round, like a hairy football that had attached itself to his chin. He had also put gel in his hair and was wearing a red bow tie. The classroom was straighter and tidier and neater than it had ever been before.

Whilst Mr Scott took the register, I pulled out Bo's piece of paper and showed it to Sangeeta.

Sangeeta read it and gave me a whispered 'WOW'. Then she pulled out her homework book and added, 'Look what my dad helped me find last night too!'

She opened up her book to show me two printed-out pieces of paper stored inside it. One page had a map of a country that looked like a squashed diamond with the words 'British India' stamped across it, and, next to it, a photo of lots of women in saris and military jackets, being inspected by an English general.

Underneath it, in tiny letters, were the words, 'Field Marshal Sir Claude inspecting members of the Women's Auxiliary Corps (India), 1944'.

'Cool!' I whispered. I was glad that Sangeeta had found out so much for her part of the project, but sad that I had failed to find anything about the real Leo yet. Trying to forget that fact, I watched as Sangeeta turned the page to show me a picture of a man in a turban with a big beard and a curly moustache. He looked exactly like Sangeeta's dad – except he was wearing a brown military uniform. And right next to him, were the words:

Assa Singh fought in both the British
Army's North Africa campaigns and in
the Battle of Monte Cassino, Italy,
during World War II. He is the son of
the legendary Manta Singh, who fought
and died during World War I, after
being shot in the leg whilst trying
to rescue his friend, Captain George
Henderson.

Sangeeta leaned over and whispered, 'And my dad found lots more stories too, Leo – on a website made by people in India. Way too many for our board or the assembly – or for even a whole museum! Can you believe it?'

I looked down at all the pieces of papers – mine and Sangeeta's and Olivia's. We were getting closer – I could feel it! Maybe *this* was what the real Leo wanted – for us to find *lots* of stories, not just his. Because, on their own, each story seemed small. But, together, they were like the paper chains we put up in class at Christmas – the ones made out of different pieces of paper all linked together. One led to the next, and next and next, and when they had been hung up above our heads across the classroom ceiling, they looked as strong and as unbreakable as the chains of a ship's anchor.

A KNOCK AT THE DOOR

All morning, the whole class worked hard practising their lines for the assembly. It was going to be the most exciting assembly our school had ever had. The first half was going to show a huge battle scene, and the second half was going to show the Blitz in London, and all the way through, we were all going to freeze, and one by one, tell stories about the person we were pretending to be and what they had done to help win the war. And then, at the very end, the whole class was going to get into one long line and shout out the names of the people they had just played so that no one forgot them.

I was playing a pretend version of the real Leo, and Sangeeta was now playing Assa Singh – with a beard and everything. I only had two lines to say about Leo, but I was going to get dressed in a RAF uniform I was making by sticking the RAF bird to my school uniform, and shout his name out louder than anyone else's at the end.

The whole class was running around looking busy, but nobody was really concentrating. We kept getting distracted by the thought that the *Real Kidz Rule* cameras were about to show up, which made us all jittery and jumpy. Even Mr Scott kept looking over his shoulder at the door.

But it wasn't until after lunch, when I was in the middle of trying to stick a moustache on my face – because I thought that the real Leo might have had one – that the knock on the door finally came.

'Hi, everyone. Don't mind us,' said Ms Smol as she walked in, flicking her fringe. Instantly, everyone sat up straight and froze – including Mr Scott. Behind Ms Smol came Mr Verne, carrying a camera on his shoulder, and behind *him*, was a lady with purple hair and a ring through her nose, carrying what looked like a dead, hairy grey dog stuck to the end of a long black pole.

'I'm Annie,' said Ms Smol. 'And this is Lenny and

Katharina. We're here from *Real Kidz Rule*.'

Mr Scott stood up. 'Purple class – what do we say to our guests?'

Immediately, everyone shouted out, 'Welcome to Purple class!'

Annie smiled and Jo gave everyone a thumbs up.

'Now, don't mind us – just pretend we're not here, and go on as you were,' said Annie, probably knowing that none of us were going to do that. 'We'll be filming some shots of you all working, and then we'll be chatting to a few of you separately in the next room.'

Mr Scott nodded and tapped his bow tie. 'Absolutely – they've all got their permission slips in, so we're good to go.'

'Brilliant,' said Annie. 'Thank you. So . . . as you were, then, everyone.'

'You heard our guest,' said Mr Scott. 'Back to work! NOW.'

Right away, everyone fell to work, buzzing and crackling like electricity. The assembly army went back to practising their lines and had their colander hats on. And the board army went back to finishing painting the cathedral and gathering everyone's stories and pictures.

Annie and Lenny and Katharina filmed the assembly groups first. I tried not to care, but it was hard when I could hear Toby shouting, 'That was MY idea you know!' every few seconds. Then, after a short while, Annie picked Toby and Kerry to leave the room and be interviewed separately – which meant they were definitely going to be shown on the show.

'That's not fair,' grumbled Sangeeta, as she stuck her cut-out picture of the Indian women officers onto a piece of bright golden card. 'I bet they believe everything Toby says too.'

I shrugged and kept on colouring in the long pointy roof of the cathedral. I could see Evelyn and Laura finishing off the black swirly gates and Gary and Oscar making a macaroni pasta tank. Everyone in class had given in their stories and drawings and photos, and now it was up to us to decorate them before we stuck them up on the board for real. I wanted to make it all look as amazing as possible, so that no matter how much Toby lied about how brilliant he was and everything he'd done, the board and all the stories on it would show the truth and beat all his words.

Toby and Kerry were gone for so long that, when

last break began, all anyone tried to do was find out what they'd been asked.

'Apparently, Toby got asked if he's the director of the whole project – and he said yes!' reported Drew, accidentally rubbing his eyes and making his eye-glitter streak down his face.

'And Kerry got asked if she wants to be an actress!' said Nancy, shaking her head in awe.

'They're going be the stars of the show – and Mrs Fitzgerald is going to present Toby with a special certificate,' whispered Laura. 'I heard it from Evelyn who heard it from Joseph who heard it from Mrs Fitzgerald herself!'

'Kerry said they're DEFINITELY going to meet Ben and Lily!' shouted Gary, as he ran past.

'Knew it,' said Sangeeta, as we leaned against the wall, watching the crowd of people surrounding Toby and Kerry. From the back of the playground, I could see Olivia and her gang watching them too, all chewing and blowing out bubbles together.

After break, anyone with a speaking part in the Blitz half of the assembly had to leave for their first major rehearsal in hall. That meant that when Annie and

Lenny and Katharina came back to the class to film their piece about the display board, it was only me, Sangeeta, Evelyn and three others who had been left behind in class, watched over by Mr Denby and his Shakespeare T-shirt.

I waited to see if Annie and Lenny would say anything to me or Sangeeta about having met us before, but they didn't. In fact, they acted like they didn't even know us and, after telling us all to just carry on as normal, hovered above our tables like human mosquitoes looking for a place to land.

After Jo's camera zoomed in and out at us drawing and painting and glittering things for at least ten minutes, Annie asked Evelyn, 'Can you tell us what your piece is about?'

Evelyn immediately sat up like a meerkat and began talking about her great-grand-uncle and all his medals. I listened and concentrated on my drawing of the real Leo's imaginary face, focusing on his eyes, which I decided to make look just like Dad's. I hated that I still didn't even know what he actually looked like and was having to make things up. Next to me, Sangeeta was colouring over the picture of Assa Singh, making his moustache darker and his turban bright red. She had done a whole piece about all the women from India who had helped make weapons and uniforms too. Even though she hadn't found out about R Singh, she had found out about so many other people. And I couldn't find out anything about just one. I had failed in every way. I didn't deserve to be a leader of the board. No wonder Annie and Lenny didn't want to interview me or film me.

'Thank you, all,' said Annie, after Evelyn had finished talking. Then, with a wave, she and Lenny and Katharina left the class.

'Is that it?' asked Nelson.

'Shush now, please,' said Mr Denby, looking at us over his gigantic copy of *Henry IV*, which had Shakespeare's face on the front, staring out at us as if he was watching us too.

Disappointed, we all went on working, until there was a knock on the door and Annie stuck her head round.

'Sangeeta and Laura, can you both come with me?' she asked, giving us all a smile. 'And bring your work, please.'

Sangeeta glanced over at me as she gathered up all her bits of paper. I didn't want her to feel bad about being chosen, so I gave her a smile to show her I was happy for her, and then looked down again until they had left the classroom.

I didn't blink until the door shut behind them. I was glad I hadn't, because, as soon as I did, a single drop of water plonked down onto the Leo of my imagination, and smudged one of his eyes too.

* * *

'Leo, can you switch the telly off and go lay the table, please?'

Sighing, I hit the power button on the remote control, and began to get out our usual bamboo placemats.

'No, not those,' said Mum. 'Get out the nice ones we use for guests – your dad is bringing someone home today. So lay an extra setting, OK?'

Sighing even harder, I put the usual placemats back and got out the larger, posher ones, which each had a single bright pink orchid painted on them. Mum left to go and give Jingyi a bath and I got out the plates and glasses and our special chopsticks, wondering why Dad was bringing home a guest on a school night. He usually never did that because he knew how tired everyone would be.

I set down the plates extra-hard. I didn't want to get dressed up and smile and pretend I was in a good mood tonight. Not after I had failed to keep my promise to the real Leo, and Annie and Lenny hadn't even bothered asking me to talk to them about his story.

I had tried super-hard to be happy for Sangeeta and Laura after they had come back from their interviews and had smiled so much my cheeks still hurt. But now I just couldn't pretend to be happy any more. My insides weren't letting me. Instead, they kept reminding me that I didn't even deserve to share the real Leo's name. That *everyone* else's stories would be going up on the board except his. Even Olivia's great-grandad's story – and she wasn't even in our class!

Outside, a crack of thunder whipped the air, and within minutes, streams of rain were running down our windows. The world outside looked exactly like how I felt on the inside, so after I finished laying the table, I went and laid back down on the couch, wishing I didn't ever have to move from it again.

'Here, look after Jingyi while I get dinner on,' ordered Mum, as she plonked Jingyi on top of my chest. 'Your dad's on his way home already and I have NO time!'

Mum rushed back into the kitchen and the sound of pots and pans filled the air. I stared up at Jingyi and she stared down at me. Suddenly, giggling, she raised her hand and slapped me.

'OWWWWWW!' I cried, rubbing my cheek, but that only made her giggle harder and then roll forward, squishing her whole face into mine. I was just blowing raspberries into her neck, when, through the sound of the rain and her giggles, I heard a knock on the front door.

'MUM! THERE'S SOMEONE AT THE DOOR!' I shouted, holding Jingyi's hands away from my face.

'SEE WHO IT IS THEN!' shouted back Mum. 'THE DOORBELL MUST NOT BE WORKING!'

Groaning, I picked Jingyi up and headed to the front door, swinging it open.

Standing in the rain outside our door, underneath a large green brolly, was an old man dressed in a long black coat. As I peered through the raindrops at him, wondering if he was lost and had come to the wrong house by mistake, I realised with a jolt that I knew him. It wasn't just any old man – it was the old turtle man! The one who had come to our house weeks ago and who had whispered Leo's name back at me as if he had heard it before. And right behind him, poking his head out at me, was Dad, all wet and shiny. He gave me a smile and said, 'Hello, son. Want to let us in?'

REPORTING FOR DUTY

I quickly shuffled backwards and held the door open.

'Thank you, young Leo,' whispered the old man, folding his umbrella and shaking a large plastic bag dry.

'CHEN! CHEN! OUR GUEST IS HERE!' called out Dad, taking off his coat and the old man's too and hanging them up in the hallway. From behind me the kitchen door slid open, and Mum came running into the corridor.

'Uncle Heng, welcome, welcome,' said Mum, looking like a completely different person to the one that I had seen a few minutes ago. Her office clothes and ponytail had been exchanged for a long dress and a bun. It was like she had accessed a secret wardrobe hidden in the kitchen.

'Please come and sit down,' said my dad, leading the way to the biggest sofa in the living room. 'Leo, give me Jingyi, and go and make us some tea. Then come and join us. We have some important things to talk about.'

For a flash of a moment, as Dad took Jingyi and gave her a kiss, I suddenly felt afraid. What if, as a part of my punishment for my illegal trip to the RAF museum and breaking the flight machine, Mum and Dad were going to make me do never-ending chores at the old man's house? Or what if they were getting ready to tell me that he was going to come and live with us and that I had to have to give up my bedroom? I had lots of cousins who lived with elders in their homes, and most of them looked like they hadn't slept in years. Probably because of all the snoring. I suddenly wished Bo was at home instead of football practice, so that he could protest against the changes and make Mum and Dad listen to us.

'The water is already boiled,' said Mum. 'So be careful pouring it out.'

In the kitchen, I found that Mum had already put

everything out on our best tea tray. There were bright green, coconut-covered Ondeh-ondeh balls piled high on a platter, a plate of mini curry puffs and a bowl of spicy masala peanuts. And, laid out next to them, was the extra-*extra*-super-special tea set, the one which was bright blue and had hand-painted white cherry blossoms on it. I had only ever seen Mum and Dad use it once in my whole life – and that was for a guest who was actually *related* to one of the kings of Malaysia. Maybe the old turtle man was a secret royal too? But, if he was, why did he need me to do his chores and move in with us?

Carefully pouring the hot water, I filled the cups and then carried everything into the living room, the heavy tray tinkling and shaking.

'Thank you, Leo,' said Dad, looking at me properly for the first time since Saturday's events. I sat down and watched Mum and Dad pour the tea and offer the snacks, willing them to hurry up so I could find out what was going on.

'Leo, do you remember Uncle Heng?' asked Dad.

I nodded, as the old man took the loudest, slurpiest sip I had ever heard.

'And do you remember speaking to him about your name – and asking why you were called Leo?'

I nodded again, but this time I pushed myself to the edge of the seat. My pulse began to throb inside me, faster. 'He – he said my name was a good name.'

'That I did, that I did,' said Uncle Heng.

'Well, after your er . . . antics on Saturday, it got me thinking, and I made some calls and . . .' Dad stopped and looking at the old man. 'Uncle Heng, why don't you tell him?'

Uncle Heng shook his head. 'I think it wiser if I *show* him.'

Putting down his cup, Uncle Heng reached down for the large plastic bag he had been carrying. As he did so, I looked over at Dad. I had been wrong. He hadn't been so angry with me that he couldn't look at me any more – he had been trying to help me. Even though I had embarrassed him and gone behind his back and nearly killed my Aunt Su and broken a flight machine that was more expensive than our whole house . . .

'Young man, I believe this is yours to open.'

Uncle Heng was leaning towards me, holding out a big envelope, covered in brightly coloured stamps and about twenty 'Special Delivery' and 'Air Mail' stickers. I took it from him. My fingers were cold. I reached in and pulled out . . . an old book.

It had a brown cover that was as cracked and wrinkly as Uncle Heng's hands. Across the front, written out in black marker, were the words:

WWII ARTICLES FROM THE MALAYA TRIBUNE: 1941

'This was sent to me by the son of an old friend,' explained Uncle Heng. 'Luckily for us, he is a hoarder, much like his father was, and has a memory longer than any elephant. After I heard your wise question, I contacted him, and he found and sent me this.

'You see, my friend used to cut out stories from the newspaper, stories he thought mattered, and make books out of them. And now his son does the same. An invaluable service to us all. Now, turn to the page marked with the yellow sticker – carefully. Very, very carefully. This is history you are holding in your hands.'

'Here, I'll help,' said Dad, seeing my hands tremble. Handing Jingyi over to my mum, he came and sat beside me, and carefully held the book steady for me.

I took hold of the small yellow tab marked with a star and pulled open the book to a page with a single newspaper article glued to its centre. In the middle of the article was a small black-and-white photo of a man in a white shirt and stripey tie, looking out at us. His flat black hair was parted neatly in a super-straight line, just off to the side of his head, and his large eyes seemed to be smiling along with his mouth. The headline above him read:

LEO KAI LIM BECOMES FIRST MALAYAN
CHINESE RAF PILOT
TO LEAVE SINGAPORE FOR ALLIED FORCE COMBAT

I stared and stared at the picture and the headline without daring to blink. It was him! It was Leo . . . the *real Leo* – with a face and clothes and hair and a tie and words written about him!

I quickly read the article, my eyes gobbling up the words. It said that Leo used to be a car salesman and had first learned to fly at the Royal Singapore Flying Club because it was the only airspace in the city that he could learn to fly in. It didn't tell me all the other things

I wanted to know – like why Leo had been buried at the cathedral in Rochester. Or what battles he had fought in. But it was enough – enough to prove to everyone that people who looked like me, and lived where my parents and grandparents and great-grandparents came from, had also fought in the war.

I finished reading the article and looked back at the real Leo's picture. A rush of tickling water gushed up and out of my nose and eyes – as if an invisible bruise had been burst open and everything inside it had been released. And without even knowing what it was doing, my throat opened up and my own voice cried out, 'Dad! He looks like you! Like you – and Bo!'

Dad wrapped an arm around me and whispered, 'He does – a bit! He definitely looks a lot like your Uncle Tan – and you too, actually.'

Mum laughed and said, 'Well, maybe the hair!'

Wiping my face with my sleeves, I looked at Uncle Heng. A question had begun to bubble away inside me, so I cleared my throat and asked it – much more loudly than I expected to. 'Do you think this Leo – do you think he was the reason I was named Leo? Do you think my great-grandad might have known him?'

I waited, hoping someone would answer 'yes' straight away. But Uncle Heng shook his head.

'I'm afraid that I don't know, young man,' he said. 'I think, as this Leo died here in the UK . . . it's unlikely. But one can never say never. Maybe they did meet. They certainly would have been around the same age. Your father has lots of people searching, here and back home, for more information about this Leo. Your aunts and uncles – and my friend's son too.'

Dad gave my shoulder a squeeze. 'That's right. Your Aunt Su is leading the charge and has been messaging and emailing and writing letters to everyone she knows. And now that we have some dates and background, information should be easier to find.'

'Aunt Su? Even though I . . . nearly gave her a heart attack?'

Uncle Heng gave a long, wheezy chuckle that made him sound like he might be having a heart attack right at that very moment! 'Ah, yes! Your dawn call – now famous across Singapore. And half of Malaysia too. Along with your trip to the museum on Saturday. Quite the news story of the decade.'

I looked back down at the paper and at Leo's face,

and told him that I didn't really mind if everyone was talking about me or laughing about me in every country in the world. Not now that I knew what he looked like and knew a part of his story.

From the other side of the wall, the sound of the front door slamming shut made us all jump. Bo came thundering into the room, back from rugby practice. He flung his wet rucksack in the corner, then noticed the old man sitting on our couch.

'Oh!' he said loudly.

'Bo, do you remember Uncle Heng?'

Bo immediately gave a respectful hello, even though he was covered in wet mud. Then, noticing me bent over the old newspaper book, he asked, 'What's going on?'

'We found him, Bo – the Leo from the cathedral. Look!' I held the book high, so that Bo could see the real Leo without having to come too close. He was way too muddy and smelly.

'That's cool,' said Bo. 'So, are we like, related to him or something? He looks like Uncle Tan.'

'That's what Dad said!' I exclaimed.

Uncle Heng smiled. 'It is not likely, my son, and I do

not believe in raising hopes where there may be none. But if there is a connection, we shall find it. And if there is not, well, then we can be happy in the knowledge that *our* Leo, sitting right here, has created a connection of his very own, to a Leo we might never have known about – and one who will not be forgotten now. Isn't that so, Leo?' Uncle Heng looked over at me and gave me a smile that made me feel as if I could do anything in the world.

'In the meantime, Bo, perhaps you should go and connect with a hot shower,' hinted Dad.

'Yes, before poor Mr Heng decides to flee and Jingyi starts crying,' added Mum, showing us all Jingyi's face. It was crumpled up and red, as if she was trying to figure out why the room was smelling so bad when she hadn't done anything yet.

'All right, all right,' muttered Bo, picking up his bag. 'Leo, save me a photocopy of that, yeah? I need it for something.' And, without waiting for a reply, Bo ran out and thundered up the stairs.

'So, Leo, do you think this is enough information for your board project – for now?' asked Dad, as he joined me in looking back down at the real Leo.

I opened my mouth to say that it wasn't just enough. It was *more* – much, much more! It was everything. Because now I could fulfil my promise, and get Leo's picture and his story up on the board and have him be seen by the whole class and the *Real Kidz Rule* show and Toby and Catherine and anyone else who thought my country didn't help win the war too. And not just that, but because it also meant that I had family – everywhere! Family who had helped me find the real Leo, even though I lived so far away and had nearly given some of them heart attacks and broken a flight simulation machine. Even when I had thought they hated me.

None of those words came out, but I knew Mum and Dad and Uncle Heng understood. I knew because, after Bo went to shower, Mum got up and made about a million photocopies of the real Leo's newspaper article in her office, just for me and Bo. And Uncle Heng picked up his teacup and holding it up to me, said 'To you, my child', before taking a sip. And on the couch next to me, with eyes as watery as mine, Dad ruffled my hair and whispered, 'Good . . .'

THE MISSING BRANCH

'Leo! Look! Look what Mum gave me last night,' shouted Sangeeta across the playground.

Everyone had come to school extra-early again and they were looking as clean and bright as they had yesterday – just in case the *Real Kidz Rule* team came back to film us again. Flying towards me and Drew, her bright green wellies a blur, Sangeeta threw a book into my hands. On the cover was a picture of an Indian woman with large round eyes, wearing a uniform.

'Er – you do know we have loads of those things in the library, right?' asked Drew, grinning at his own joke. This morning he had come into school with bright green glitter on his eyes instead of silvery-pink, and his hair gelled into a single, high tidal wave, instead of lots of spikes.

'Not *this* book,' said Sangeeta. 'It's the real-life story of an Indian spy – a *woman* Indian spy! Can you believe it? A friend of Mum's loaned it to her for me to read! I'm going to put her on my part of the board too – right next to the bit about all the women in the RAF.'

'What – you mean a *spy*-spy? Like James Bond?' asked Drew, looking at the book with new interest.

'Yes, look!' Sangeeta turned the book over and pointed to the back cover. 'Her name was Noor Inayat Khan – and she was the bravest person I've ever read about. When she was a spy she was captured but didn't give a *single* secret away to the enemies, even though it might have saved her life if she had. She was so awesome that Winston Churchill put her on his special force.'

'If she was so special, how come we don't know about her?' asked Drew, as Nancy came running up to join us with three humungous bows in her hair.

'Know about who?' asked Nancy, leaning in to see the book in my hands.

'Noor Yat Can,' answered Drew.

'No, Noor Inayat KHAN,' stressed Sangeeta. 'She was a famous British spy. Oh! I wish I hadn't been interviewed yesterday and could have been interviewed *today* instead. I could have told Annie and Lenny all about her! I've decided I'm going to dress up as her for the assembly instead of Assa Singh – even though I was looking forward to wearing a beard! And I'm going to say her name at the end too! The assembly team can't stop me – not when she was an undercover spy for Britain.'

'She sounds awesome,' I said to Sangeeta, who was jumping up and down like a rubber ball. 'I found out something too!'

'Really? About the other Leo?' cried Sangeeta, as Drew and Nancy came closer.

I pulled out the photocopy of Leo's article and laid it out flat on top of Sangeeta's book.

I was in the middle of explaining what the article said when Nancy glanced over my shoulder and whispered, 'Look out!'

'What you all got there then?' came Toby's voice.

I turned around, ready to tell him to get lost and leave us all alone, but before I could open my mouth,

Toby snatched Sangeeta's new book *and* Leo's article out of my hands.

'Hey, give that back!' I shouted, looking around desperately for a teacher. But I couldn't see one anywhere. Just lots of kids quietly standing by and looking at us.

'Look – Nugget Ingot Can-Can,' laughed Toby, showing the book to Catherine, who sniggered at the picture. 'And another stupid loser too!' he said, looking at the real Leo's article. 'Who are they then? Illegal criminals?'

'No!' cried out Sangeeta. 'They were heroes – and they DIED for this country!'

'As if!' sneered Toby. And suddenly, before we even knew what was happening, he had grabbed the cover of Sangeeta's book and ripped it clean away before tearing the real Leo's article in two.

Our faces frozen into silent screams, we watched, horrified, as Toby lifted the book and pieces of paper high into the air, ready to throw them away. But, just before his fingers let go, a hand appeared out of nowhere and caught his wrist, stopping him.

I followed the hand to an arm, and the arm to a

body, and saw that it was Olivia. Toby realised it at the exact same moment, and instantly seemed to shrink by two whole inches.

'What do you think you're doing to my friends?' she asked, calmly.

Before he could respond, she snatched Sangeeta's book and my article out of Toby's hands and, grabbing the basketball too, catapulted it as far as she could.

'Go and fetch then!' she ordered him, glaring at Catherine too.

'I'll – I'll –' stammered Toby.

'You'll WHAT?' asked Olivia, jutting forwards like a headbutting and super-angry bull.

Toby shrunk even smaller. 'I'll get you back!' he promised, running off after his ball, with Catherine hurrying behind him.

After a few seconds of none of us being able to speak, Olivia handed me the remains of the book and the ripped-up pages of the real Leo's face. Drew picked up the book cover from the ground where it had fallen and handed it back to Sangeeta looking sorry.

'Thanks,' said Sangeeta, quietly. 'Mum's going to kill me. She only borrowed the book from her friend.

Why does he have to be so horrible all the time?'

'Because he's an idiot,' said Nancy.

'And jealous. Or afraid,' added Olivia.

'Afraid?' I asked, wondering what Toby and Catherine could ever be jealous or afraid of. Except Oliva, obviously.

'I don't know. Mum always says it whenever anyone is horrible to Dad,' answered Olivia. 'Or any of my aunts and uncles on that side of the family.'

'From what side of the family?' asked Nancy, looking terrified at her own question.

Olivia narrowed her eyes and looked Nancy up and down. 'The side that's from Ghana,' she said, her eyebrows raised. 'Got a problem with that?'

Nancy shook her head. 'No. Isn't that where chocolate comes from? My uncle flies there all the time for his chocolate company.'

'You didn't tell me you've got an uncle with a chocolate company!' said Drew, accusingly.

'He doesn't own it, dumbo – he just tests the seeds or something,' explained Nancy. 'Anyway, he loves Ghana. He said he wants to take me one day because the food there is the best.'

'Your uncle sounds cool,' said Olivia, smiling. 'Anyway. Leo, Sangeeta – I've still not had any luck finding out about my great-grandad. My mum and dad and even Jules have been phoning my family everywhere, but it seems there's no one left who knew him. He died too early. My nan was only a baby when he died, so she never met him. And we even tried to see if he was on one of those ancestry website things, but we couldn't find anything. Not about him, or any of us. Dad says it's because our ancestors had all their records destroyed by people taking our lands and stealing people for slavery. So there's nothing to find.'

'That's horrible,' I said, feeling sorry for her and wondering if I had ancestors from a really long time ago that had been stolen from me too. 'But we've decorated his piece of paper – for the board – so he'll be on it.'

'And I talked about him on the camera to the *Real Kidz Rule* show people,' said Sangeeta. 'And I talked about the other Leo too. So if my bit gets on the TV next week, everyone will know about them.'

'You did?' I asked, surprised. I had been so caught up in my own worries about the real Leo, I hadn't even asked Sangeeta about her interview. 'Thanks, Sangeeta.'

Sangeeta gave a shrug, as if what she had done was no big deal.

Before Olivia could say her thanks too, the bell began to ring. 'Well . . . if you find out anything else, let me know, won't you?' she asked, rushing off.

'Woah,' exclaimed Drew, as we began to make our way into school. 'Wonders will never get creased. Who'd have thought it, eh?'

'Thought what?' I asked, wondering if Drew meant Olivia's dad and half of her family being from Ghana.

'That Olivia Morris would call *us* her friends,' said Drew. And, patting his eyelids to check his eye glitter was still in place, he followed me and Sangeeta and Nancy through the school doors with a proud grin on his face.

* * *

Despite everyone hoping they would, the *Real Kidz Rule* team didn't come back to film us that morning. Or that afternoon. Or the next day either. And by first break on Monday morning, lots of rumours that had been thought up over the weekend had begun to crackle and fly across the playground like lightning.

The first was that our school had been disqualified because of mine and Sangeeta's and Olivia's criminal actions at the RAF museum.

The second was that the board and assembly ideas had been so rubbish that the mayor had had declared a state of emergency, and would soon be announcing that no school in Kent would ever be allowed to enter a competition again – not unless she died, and someone climbed over her dead body to destroy her new law.

And the third was that Mr Scott's beard had scared the TV producers away as much as our rubbish work.

The rumours made everyone stare and whisper and point at me and Sangeeta and Olivia – even more than usual. Nancy and Drew stared and pointed and whispered right back, because they knew the rumours weren't true and didn't like how they made us feel. And after a while of watching us from across the playground like we were a reality TV show, Olivia's friends started to tell people to back off and leave us alone too. At first I thought they were only doing it because Olivia had told them to, but then I realised it was because they thought we were funny enough to kind of be Olivia's friends too. I knew, because they kept calling us 'the funny ones' and saying 'we'll allow it' whenever Olivia walked over to us. The fact that not just Olivia but now her friends were protecting us too, made us all feel cooler and even taller somehow, and made what everyone was saying about us matter less.

But even though the rumours changed everything in the playground, they didn't stop things proceeding at full speed in class. Or stop Mr Scott from sounding more and more like a real general in a real army.

'FOUR days to go, Purple class – FOUR (THUMP!)!' he shouted as we all came in from our lunch breaks, banging on the table so hard his pen was knocked to the floor. 'FOUR days until ALL our work is assessed by the judges of the competition. So, assembly team – full hour rehearsals in the halls, every day, starting from tomorrow! I suggest you all make sure everyone has their lines AB-SO-LUTELY SPOT (THUMP!) ON (THUMP!)! We haven't got a single second to waste.

'And board team, the display has to go up TONIGHT! Any last bits that need to be done, get them done NOW – and map out where each story is going to go. Move four tables together so you can lay it all out for me. GO (THUMP!)!'

The whole class jumped up and got to work. All the stories and mini-projects for the board were finished – from tanks made out of macaroni cheese, to shining medals made out of coins, to family photos and swirly, written biographies. The huge cut-out of the cathedral spire Mr Scott had helped us draw and paint was done, along with our wall of names too.

It felt the best kind of strange seeing my idea of the wall come to life in paper and pen and glitter. Each brick had been drawn by a member of the class, just like I had imagined, and the name of the person they were remembering written on it. My brick had the real Leo and his golden lion on it, and Sangeeta had done four bricks – one for R Singh, because he had started her on her journey to finding so many stories, one for Assa Singh, one for Noor Inayat Khan, and the last one for 'All the women whose names we don't know' written on it.

'Leo, where do you think we should put the other Leo?' asked Evelyn, as the whole group stood around the four tables and tried out different places for all the stories.

I pointed to the top right-hand corner. That was the corner that was closest to the top of the painted cathedral doors, where I had first seen the real Leo's name. Picking up my portrait of him, which had taken me thirteen attempts to get perfect at the weekend, along with my newspaper clip and a map of Singapore, I placed them all neatly in my chosen spot.

'I want to place mine here,' said Sangeeta, grabbing her paintings of Noor Inayat Khan and Assa Singh and the photo of the Indian women officers, all of which were glued inside a map of India, and placing them right next to Leo's section.

'Oh, wait,' I added, grabbing the extra drawing Sangeeta had done of Olivia's great-grandad Richard Morris, the slightly wonky map of Ghana I had drawn, and a brightly coloured-in photocopy of the memorial invitation. 'These need to go . . . here.' I put them next to Sangeeta's drawings, so that all three of our projects were in a straight line. Nobody except Nancy and Drew knew that Richard was Olivia's great-grandad – yet! It was fun having him on the board as a secret addition.

Even Mr Scott didn't know. He had been so interested in his story, that he hadn't asked a single question about how we had found out about him.

As I watched everyone squeeze and position and push and pull their stories to fit on our make-believe board, I realised that the whole thing looked like a giant family tree. Except, this wasn't a normal family tree where everyone was related to each other. This one was made up of people belonging to families who had never met and who all came from different parts of the world, but who became a family because they had all been through the same thing and fought the same enemy. With every name, the branches grew and grew and would never end, so long as everyone remembered their stories.

'Brilliant!' clapped Mr Scott, coming over to help us squeeze in the last two stories. 'That is definitely one of the BEST World War Two boards I have ever seen! We'll be able to get it up before we finish for the day.'

Hearing the bell for last break begin to ring, Mr Scott clapped his hands and, congratulating us all on our hard work, told us to go out and enjoy our break.

'Enjoy our break?' asked Drew, as we headed down towards the assembly hall instead of the playground. 'Has he looked out of the window?'

We all immediately looked out of the window. The day had become so grey and heavy and wet that there was no way anyone was going to be allowed outside.

'Man! I'm so sleepy,' groaned Drew. 'I wish schools had beds you could go take naps in – like in Mum's hospital.'

'Just have a nap on the table,' said Nancy, as Sangeeta pointed to a free one at the back of the hall. We rushed towards it before anyone else could take it.

'Yeah, good idea,' said Drew, plonking himself down and immediately wrapping his arm around his head.

'I might join you,' I said. I felt tired too. So while Sangeeta and Nancy talked about some new TV drama and Olivia and her friends came and listened and popped bubbles at us, I closed my eyes just for a few seconds . . .

'Leo, wake up! Come on!' said Sangeeta, shaking my arm. 'We need to go!'

I jumped up and saw that the hall was nearly empty. Everyone else had gone, and Mr Henderson was tapping his watch at us. Hurrying to my feet, I followed Sangeeta and ran to class.

We rushed inside, hoping Mr Scott wouldn't notice us being late. But instead of being busy and noisy like usual, the room was completely silent.

The whole class was standing in a circle around the display-board table, just like they would have around a fight or an accident in the playground. As I ran in behind Sangeeta, Mr Scott looked up at us both. His eyes looked the saddest I had ever seen them – even sadder than when England had lost the World Cup.

'Er – I'm sorry for being late, sir,' I muttered, wondering just how late I was anyway.

Mr Scott looked at me, and then back down at the display-board table.

Sangeeta followed his eyes. Then crying out 'Oh no!' she covered her mouth with her hands.

I reached the table and looking down too, realised why everyone had gone quiet and why Mr Scott had looked so sad. Because in place of our portraits of the real Leo and Noor Inayat Khan and Assa Singh and

Richard Morris, were four large round blobs of red paint. Each one shaped like a bleeding wound that had seeped out across our stories, and made the faces underneath disappear.

CRASH LANDINGS

'You're quiet. Everything OK?' asked Dad, as we walked back home from school that afternoon.

I shrugged and kicked a stone down the road. The bruise inside me was so big and sore, it wouldn't let me speak. All I wanted to do was kick things until they hurt as much as I did. I found another stone and kicked it even harder. It bounced down the wet road and dove into a big puddle. It wasn't raining any more, but I wished that it was. Then I could have cried and no one would have noticed a thing.

'How's your project going?' tried Dad again. 'Mum and I will be coming to the assembly on Friday, you know. We can't wait to see everything.'

I wondered what my dad would say when I told him

that Toby had destroyed everything I had done. I knew it was him – him and Catherine. I couldn't prove it, but I knew it was. They were the only ones in the whole school who hated me enough to do anything so mean. Mr Scott had shouted at the whole class and said everyone would be punished until someone confessed. But it hadn't worked. Instead, Toby seemed to enjoy it and whenever Mr Scott wasn't watching, he flashed hidden smiles at me.

'Leo?'

'Everything's FINE, Dad!' I yelled, pulling the hood of my jacket up and walking ahead of him so that he couldn't see my face. If he had been a normal dad who got angry and fixed things, I might have told him what had happened. But he wouldn't ever do that. He would just say, 'Oh! These things happen' – like he always did!

'LEO KAI LIM! You stop right there!' ordered Dad, catching up with me and grabbing me by the arm to make me stop. 'You do not walk away from your father like that! Do you understand?'

I looked down at the floor, my whole face as hot and as steamy as coals on a barbecue. I could tell people were staring at us but for the first time in my life, I didn't care.

'Did you hear me?' asked Dad, bending down to catch my eyes.

'Fine!' I said, trying to get free of him.

'No,' he said, holding on tight. 'We are not going anywhere until you tell me what's wrong.'

'Dad! You're embarrassing me!' I cried out. 'You're always embarrassing me!'

As the words lifted up into the air and landed on my dad's shocked face, I wished I hadn't opened my mouth. I wished I had never even learned to speak in the first place.

'I see,' said Dad, quietly, standing still.

'No,' I tried, desperately wanting to make things better. 'I mean – I mean . . .'

'Yes?' asked my dad, sternly.

He just didn't understand! He never understood! I could feel the bruise inside me beginning to throb and pulse and fizz like a lightbulb that was about to explode, and suddenly it all burst out of me in a huge rush of words. 'I mean, you never do anything to anyone who's horrible to us! You just – you just act like it's normal and you're always nice to everyone – even to people who are horrible to Mum and me and Bo because we don't look like them! But it doesn't make things better! It only makes things worse and I don't want to be like that! I want to fight back! Why don't you *ever* want to fight back?'

A dollop of cold, hard, grey rain landed on my nose, quickly followed by about twenty more. They instantly made the people around us hurry away.

'I see,' said Dad again, his eyes unblinking, acting as if it wasn't raining at all.

Wiping my nose with my sleeve, I stared down at the pavement. I had never shouted at my dad before. And now that I had, my insides felt empty and scared, like caves that were about to collapse.

I heard Dad take a step towards me and felt his hands grab mine, and then saw his face pop up underneath my own. He was kneeling on the wet ground.

'Look at me, Leo,' he ordered.

Dragging my eyes to his, I waited for him to tell me off for being disrespectful. But instead, he asked, 'What makes you think I do *not* want to fight back, Leo? Do you really think I like smiling and speaking back gently to those who do not deserve those things from me?'

I shrugged, because there wasn't a single answer I could think of.

'I do not – I do not like doing those things,' said Dad, his voice shaking now. 'But I *have* to. Because if I fight back, then they win. If I fight back, I turn into the very thing they want me to be – uneducated, ill-mannered, and rude. But I am *not* those things. *We* are not those things – *they* are. So I try to be nice and forgiving, even in the face of their rudeness and ignorance. I show them that I am bigger than them. That my world is not as small and as hateful and as unkind as theirs. And when I show them this, then Leo, they lose.'

'They do?' I asked, confused.

Dad smiled at me, making a giant raindrop run along his lips and jump off them like a professional diver. 'Yes, they lose. Maybe not straight away, but over time. Because it makes them start to think. It makes them start to wonder why they hate or want to hurt someone who does not hate or hurt them back. Do you understand? We do not stoop – we *never* stoop down to the level of those who hurt us. To do what they do, and act like they act, is to lose your dignity and the dignity of your family and your people. And to lose those things, is to lose at life. And as your father, I cannot lose. No matter how hard it might be.'

Letting go of my hands, Dad got back up onto his feet. 'Now, tell me what has happened today. Otherwise, we will be standing here in the rain for a very long time.'

I stared up at my dad, amazed at how different he looked all of a sudden. He was the same, but taller, and stronger. As if I had just discovered that he was a secret soldier.

Up above us, a deep rumble shook the belly of the sky.

'Leo?' asked Dad. He didn't add any more words to his question, but I knew what he was asking.

'Someone at school destroyed all our work – my painting of the real Leo and Sangeeta's drawings of Noor Inayat Khan and Assa Singh and Olivia's great-grandad Richard Morris,' I answered quickly, wanting to get it all out of me in one go.

'How did they do this?' Dad asked.

'They poured red paint on the pictures. They're all

ruined. And the board had to go up today because of the competition rules, so we don't have time to do them again . . . and . . .' I stopped. My voice was wobbling too much for it to go on, and the bruise in my chest was spreading to my throat and making it close up.

Dad took a deep breath. 'Who did this?' He had to shout so I could hear him over the rain, which had begun to pour down so hard that both of us were soaking wet.

I shook my head, because I knew if I said Toby's name, Dad would ask me for proof. He always needed evidence before he acted. Even when he shouldn't need it at all.

'Was it that boy – with the tennis ball? The one who hurt you?'

I looked up, surprised. 'Yes,' I answered, waiting for the usual shrug of the shoulders and Dad's usual 'Well, these things happen'. But this time, they didn't come.

'Go home,' he ordered, taking out his keys. 'Take these. You are old enough to let yourself in. I will see you later.'

'But Da—'

'Do not argue with me, Leo. Go.'

Frightened by the calm anger in my dad's voice, I took the keys and began to run home. After a few seconds, I looked over my shoulder, expecting him to be watching me. But like magic, Dad had gone – as if he had melted into the air.

After I got home, I washed and changed, and waited by the window for Dad. One hour passed and Mum and Jingyi came home.

'Mum, do you know where Dad is?' I asked. 'Or Bo?'

'Dad messaged to say he has a few things to take care of, and Bo is helping,' Mum said. 'We're going to have to have dinner without them I'm afraid.'

Two hours passed and we ate dinner. Three hours passed, and still Dad wasn't home. Neither was Bo. And all the while, the rain poured and poured and poured.

'Mum, where are they?' I asked. I didn't even care about Toby or the red paint any more. I just wanted them home.

'I told you already, Leo,' said Mum, humming as she rocked Jingyi to sleep. 'Now get to bed. You'll see them tomorrow.'

'Mum, please can I just stay awa—'

'No,' said Mum, sternly. 'Bed. Now.'

Running upstairs, I climbed into bed, and promised myself I would stay awake until I heard Dad and Bo come home. But the duvet was so warm, and my eyes were so sore, and my insides were aching so much, that, gradually, I fell into a deep sleep, where I dreamed of soldiers in planes, flying through the night sky, calling on their radios for help.

* * *

For three seconds after waking up the next morning, I didn't remember anything at all, and then it came back to me, like tiny paint bombs exploding in my mind. Leo's portrait. The red paint. Dad!

Throwing the covers off, I ran downstairs. Mum was singing in the kitchen and Jingyi was gurgling, but when I opened the kitchen door, I saw Dad wasn't there.

Guessing who I was looking for, Mum shook her head. 'He had to leave super-early, darling. And so did Bo. But they'll see you after school tonight, OK?

275

Go get ready, and I'll drop you off to school. Aren't the winners of your competition being announced today?'

I nodded, but I didn't care about the announcement any more. We had missed the deadline for putting up our display board so there was no chance of winning.

After Mum dropped me off at school, I spotted Olivia and Sangeeta standing huddled by the tuck shop. As I got closer to them, I could hear them talking.

'This means WAR,' Sangeeta was saying.

Olivia nodded. 'He's crossed too many lines.'

'I know!' said Sangeeta. 'Why don't we deflate all his stupid tennis balls and basketballs – just all the balls!'

'What do you think we should do, Leo?' asked Sangeeta, when I joined them. 'We're planning our revenge on Toby and Catherine and whoever else helped them ruin our board.'

'I'm telling you, we should sabotage the assembly,' declared Olivia. 'But only for Toby and Catherine. Not anyone else. It'll be easy. We can pour slugs into their costumes. I've got loads of slugs in the garden.'

'They're so gross they probably like slugs!' said Sangeeta. 'And even if they don't, they'll just take them out and do the assembly anyway. I know! Mum got a new bag of chillies from London – the proper red hot Indian ones! What if we put some in their lunches? Then they wouldn't be able to speak, let alone do a whole assembly. Trust me, I've seen them make grown-ups cry they're that hot! Toby and Catherine's hair would probably fly right off their heads.'

'Whose hair would fly right off their heads?' asked Nancy, joining us.

Sangeeta explained her plan.

'Oh, wicked? Can I be there?' asked Drew, who had come up behind her. But before we could all figure out how to sneak bright red chillies into a jacket potato without them being seen, the school bell rang and called us all inside.

As we headed into class, we stopped our chattering, and fell silent. Because standing at Mr Scott's desk, was Mrs Fitzgerald – and Annie from the *Real Kidz Rule* show. They were standing on either side of Mr Scott, who looked so nervous and sweaty he was glowing.

'Good morning, children,' said Mrs Fitzgerald, giving us a nod. 'Sit down quickly, please. I have something very serious to say to you all.'

Hurrying to our desks, the whole class sat down

extra-straight and waited. Nearly everyone had their hands clasped together, as if we were praying without words for something good to have happened. It must have done – especially if Annie was here.

'Now, I'm sure you all remember Annie from the *Real Kidz Rule* show?' asked Mrs Fitzgerald. Annie gave us a wave.

'She has joined me here this morning because of something quite unacceptable that took place in this very classroom yesterday,' continued Mrs Fitzgerald. 'I'm speaking of course, of the destruction of a very important part of the display board. Annie, over to you.'

The air in the room instantly changed from something hopeful to something scared.

Stepping forwards, Annie looked around at us. Then she began. 'Now, as you know, at Real Kidz Rule, we celebrate stories and people from all over the world. That means we will not tolerate anyone who tries to harm another person or destroy another person's works because of racism. Does everyone know what racism is?'

I turned back to look at the class, as everyone – even Toby – answered back, 'Yes, miss!'

'Good,' said Annie. 'And you will also know, since you have been studying it in detail, that the Second World War – a war fought by the *whole* world – was won by the Allies. And that those Allies worked together to stop *the* most terrible, racist people from being in power.'

I looked back over my shoulder again. Except for Toby and Catherine, who looked as if they had both turned into statues, everyone cried out, 'Yes, miss!' again.

'Good,' repeated Annie. 'I am glad to hear that. Because that means you will all understand why yesterday's destruction of Leo and Sangeeta's works, which featured the only stories on your board about people who were *not* white, is being treated as a racist attack. And one which is being thoroughly investigated. Isn't that right, Mr Scott and Mrs Fitzgerald?'

Mr Scott and Mrs Fitzgerald each gave a stern nod.

Annie went on. 'I am especially pained this happened, because you see, if their works *hadn't* been destroyed in such a horrible way, I can tell you right now, that your school had a high chance of *winning* this competition.'

Everyone gasped and broke out into a wave of exclamations.

'The *Real Kidz Rule* judges *loved* the video clips we sent them of your assembly rehearsal and your board, and thought your topic was different to anything any of the other schools had created,' continued Annie. 'But, of course, one act of vandalism destroyed that chance. Until . . .'

The class fell quiet, listening.

Opening a folder in front of her, Mrs Fitzgerald took out a painting. It was of Noor Inayat Khan. And then another one – of the real Leo. And another one of Richard Morris. Except the drawings were a million times better than ours had been!

I stared at the swirly, slanted writing of their names underneath their portraits, all thick in the circles and thin on the lines . . . I recognised the handwriting right away. It was Dad's handwriting! And the drawing of Leo looked exactly like the portraits Bo used to do for his art exams – all streaky and realistic and moody . . .

Was *that* what Dad and Bo had been doing last night? Had they been recreating our parts of the display board and making the stories come alive again?

'Thanks to Leo, Sangeeta and Olivia's families all helping Mr Scott create these last night, *ahead* of the midnight deadline, they will be going up on the board where they belong,' said Mrs Fitzgerald.

'That means we still have a chance,' said Mr Scott, giving me and Sangeeta a wink.

Sangeeta gave me a kick of joy under the table.

'Yes. However,' said Annie, 'that chance is *conditional*. Those guilty of committing the act of vandalism will need to be excluded from the competition, and we can't do that if we don't know who they are. So unless the culprit – or culprits – who destroyed the portraits make themselves known to Mr Scott and Mrs Fitzgerald by lunchtime today, I'm afraid we will *not* be able to consider your class's excellent works as a qualified entry. For the simple fact that we do not condone acts of racism.'

My heart dropped as fast as Sangeeta's foot. There was no way Toby and Catherine would ever confess.

'So, to whoever the culprits are,' piped up Mrs Fitzgerald, handing the paintings to Mr Scott. 'I want you to be brave – just like our soldiers and heroes would have been – and come and confess to me or Mr Scott.

You have until midday today. It will be up to YOU to decide for the class – and the whole school too – whether or not we can still win this competition. The judges and I will be waiting.'

And with a final nod, Mrs Fitzgerald and Annie exited the room, leaving us all behind in a state of shell-shocked silence.

FORCES ASSEMBLE

'So that's where Jules was last night!' said Olivia, after we had run to tell her everything that had happened at first break. 'I was wondering why Mum and Dad had let her stay out so late!'

'And my mum,' said Sangeeta. 'I didn't even know she could paint!'

'And my dad – and Bo,' I said, proudly. I knew that Bo wouldn't like it, but the second as I saw him and Dad, I was going to hug them just as hard as I could.

'So do you think they'll do it?' asked Olivia. 'Do you think Toby and Catherine and whoever else it was will actually have the guts to confess what they did?'

'Maybe they will,' said Nancy, hopefully.

I gave her a sad smile. Nancy always wanted to believe that even horrible people could be nice sometimes.

'Never,' I said. 'Not in a million years.'

Olivia blew out a bubble. 'If they don't and they ruin the chance of our stories winning, we need to come up with a proper plan to get them back,' she said, matter-of-factly.

Sangeeta and me and Drew and Nancy all agreed.

'Let's wait until home-time to hear if they've confessed,' said Sangeeta. 'If we don't hear by then, that means they've become traitors.'

That morning, we did our final rehearsal dressed up as soldiers. The whole school felt quiet, as if the entire building was holding its breath and waiting. But no news of a confession reached the class. And as the hours and minutes ticked by and it got closer and closer to lunchtime, everyone's eyes became glued to Toby and Catherine.

'What's wrong with them?' whispered Sangeeta, as Toby retold his great-grandad's story of bravery on stage for the third time. 'His great-grandad fought against Hitler and all the Nazis. And Catherine's great-grandmother went and nursed people out in

Europe! Maybe someone should remind them again what they were fighting for?'

'Maybe they don't care,' I whispered back, from under my colander helmet.

'Well, they should,' said Sangeeta, giving a small growl.

The lunchtime deadline came and went, and there was still no news. By last break the class had stopped talking to Toby and Catherine and was giving them angry stares instead. But instead of looking embarrassed or ashamed, they seemed to be enjoying the attention, and had even begun waving at the people who were glaring at them and giggling.

By home-time, we'd had enough.

'That's it! We need to take those cowards *down*!' declared Olivia. 'We have to make sure they're not in that assembly. Sangeeta, what were you saying before, about chillies?'

Listening as Sangeeta explained how we could sneak chillies onto a plate without anyone seeing, I started to think about all the soldiers who had gone behind enemy lines and carried out surprise attacks.

'Wait – I think I've got a better idea,' I said.

We didn't need to take Toby and Catherine *out* of the assembly at all. That would be doing exactly what Dad said we shouldn't – playing tricks and hurting them just like they had hurt us. Instead, we needed to go *in* and take over the assembly somehow!

I quickly told everyone my idea.

'It's crazy,' said Olivia. 'But I like it!'

'Me too,' said Drew, copying Olivia and folding his arms as well.

'We'll get into so much trouble,' warned Sangeeta. 'Like, we might even get expelled.'

'No, we won't!' I promised. 'This is our chance to tell the stories of who we are properly. And it'll only be for our bit! We're not taking anyone else's lines away or anything. We didn't win the competition because of what Toby and Catherine did. So none of our stories are getting shown on TV. And your interview won't be heard, Sangeeta – which means no one is going to know about Assa Singh or Noor or Leo or Olivia's great-grandad! We can fix that and make sure that at least everyone at our *school* knows about them. And our parents too. And maybe if the *Whot Gazette* come, then them too. They might even do a front-page story!

It's the only way to make it fair.'

Seeing they were all listening closely to my every word, I took a deep breath and carried on.

'All we have to do is make sure no one sees what we've got on underneath our uniforms. We can practice at breaktimes tomorrow, to make sure we've got it all perfect. And it'll only be for a few minutes, and then it'll be over, and the assembly can go back to normal. Come on, Sangeeta – this is worth getting into trouble for!'

Finishing the longest speech I had ever made, I waited for an answer.

'Woah, Leo,' exclaimed Drew. 'If Winston Churchill was Chinese-looking and nine years' old, I'd have thought you were him just then!'

We all giggled and shook our heads at Drew.

'But what about me?' asked Olivia. 'I'm not in your class, remember? Will one of you be my great-grandad? I've found something out about him that I want everyone to know.'

'You should do it,' I said immediately. 'All you have to do is sit near the front, then come join us at the exact right moment.'

Olivia smiled. 'OK. I'm in.'

'All right. Me too,' declared Sangeeta, twisting one of her plaits around her fingers nervously. 'Even if it means we get detention for the rest of our lives.'

'And we'll help,' said Nancy. 'We can be undercover operational lookout support.'

'Yeah, with like the signals and things,' promised Drew.

'OK,' I said. 'Let's meet super-early tomorrow before school. We only have one day to get it right.'

From over Nancy's shoulder, I saw Dad standing at the gates looking for me – he was on time! That had *never* happened before. I couldn't wait another second to hug him and ask him to tell me about everything he had done, so with a hurried goodbye, I ran over to him and wrapped my arms around his waist just as tight as I could.

That night, over dumplings and desserts, Dad told me how he had run back to the school to put in a formal complaint about what had happened to my work, and how Mrs Fitzgerald had promised to launch a proper investigation and contacted the *Real Kidz Rule* team to tell them all about it right away. Bo explained how *he* had come up with the idea of recreating our artwork, and how he had gone to Olivia's house and told Jules the plan, and how she had wanted to help too. And Mum told us how she had called Sangeeta's mum to tell them about what Bo and Dad were doing, which made Sangeeta's mum run to the school to help with the display. And Dad finished by telling me that Mr Scott had insisted on staying super-late to help repaint the faces.

While they were all speaking, I couldn't help jumping up and hugging them again and again and again – even though it made Bo screw up his face and roll his eyes. They had made what Toby and Catherine did not matter any more. It didn't even matter that we had been disqualified from the competition now. All that mattered was that they had helped make the real Leo and Noor and Richard come alive again. And even though they didn't know it yet, they were going to be a part of everything I had planned next.

* * *

'I'm so nervous I think I'm going to be sick,' whispered Sangeeta, as we hurried to school on Friday morning.

'Can you tell I'm wearing something underneath?' she added, nervously patting herself.

I shook my head, even though I could see sequins shimmering a little bit from underneath her school jumper. I was feeling sick too, and my legs felt shaky – like I was seasick, but on land.

Even though we had practised what we were calling our Top-Secret Assembly Takeover Mission with Olivia at least fifty times yesterday, I couldn't help thinking about everything that could go wrong. What would happen if my voice didn't work? Or if I lost my words? I had never stood up in an assembly and done proper lines before. And now here I was, planning to say a whole string of them!

Even though it was so early that the sky was still dark and sleepy, the school doors had been opened for our class so that we could get ready for what Mr Scott said was going to be the 'best assembly this century'.

Walking into our classroom, we found Mr Scott, Mr Davies from the library and Mrs Gill, the deputy head, helping everyone get ready. Faces were being painted with black and brown streaks, colander hats decorated with fake ivy were being arranged on heads, water guns placed in hands, and camouflage jackets and giant camping rucksacks hoisted onto backs. I stuck on my hand-drawn RAF wings and the cap Mr Scott had found for me, and tried not to speak to anyone because I was worried bits of my breakfast would come out. Everyone was serious and silent, and looking green too, as if we really were all getting ready to go into a battle.

'Your uniform's a bit tight, Leo,' said Mr Davies, as he helped us put on our oversized rucksacks, which had been stuffed with paper and boxes to make them look heavy. 'Yours too, Sangeeta. You might need to ask your parents for an upgrade soon!'

Sangeeta and I nodded and checked each other to make sure nothing was popping out from under our uniforms. Luckily, nothing was. All we had to do now was make it onto the stage without being sick.

'Right, looks like you're all about ready!' said Mr Scott, as the school bell rang and we all stood to attention, looking like miniature soldiers. 'Now, before we head out and start this assembly, I have a special announcement to make.'

We all stood to attention, wondering what it could be.

'Yesterday evening, one of the students who vandalised the display board came forward and, very bravely, confessed,' said Mr Scott.

Instantly, we all swivelled our heads to where Toby was standing, looking like a camouflaged soldier. He looked surprised, and then narrowed his eyes angrily to let us know it definitely wasn't him who had confessed.

We swivelled our heads back to the other side of the room, towards Catherine. She was staring at the floor and trying to avoid everyone's eyes – especially Toby's. He was glaring at her, as if he wished he could banish her from the assembly and then the planet.

'Which is why, this morning, the *Real Kidz Rule* team WILL be filming our assembly, along with all our competing schools,' finished Mr Scott.

I felt my jaw drop open and heard Sangeeta whimper an 'Oh noooooooooooo . . .', while everyone else erupted into cheers.

'Sir! Sir! Are we still in the competition then? Could we still win?' cried Gary.

'I don't know,' said Mr Scott. 'I guess we'll find out tonight when we get home and watch the show. But either way, I am VERY proud of the person who confessed, for thinking about the class and not just themselves. And I am also VERY proud of the hard work you've put into this competition. Whatever happens, you're all winners already. Understood?'

Everyone shouted out 'Yes, sir' at the top of their voices – everyone except me and Sangeeta. We looked over at each other, wondering the exact same thing: should we abort our mission? Or go ahead and risk our class losing the competition?

'Good. Follow me then, and remember – stay focused and have fun!' ordered Mr Scott, leading us into the corridor.

As we marched down to the hall, we could feel the rest of the school trying to get a peek of us through the classroom windows and doors. My head was pounding even louder than my heart, both asking me what I was going to do.

Inside the main hall, a sea of chairs had been laid out. In the very front row, I could see Sangeeta's mum and nan, in her brightly-coloured dress, and her dad too, who wore a deep navy-blue turban. Bo was sitting behind them, next to Jules, who was giggling and turning red at something he was saying to her. Mum and Dad were on Bo's other side, and then further along were Olivia's mum and someone who I guessed was Olivia's dad. Her dad looked almost exactly like the picture of Olivia's great-grandad, Richard – except without the thin moustache. All smart and smiling with deep brown eyes.

Our families waved and smiled and gave us all thumbs ups as we passed. The *Real Kidz Rule* team were already positioned and waving at us too. Annie was on one side of the stage with a new camera person, and on the other were Lenny and Katharina, whispering and pointing in different directions.

'Right, everyone,' whispered Mr Scott, as we all took up our positions behind the stage curtains. 'Just do everything you did yesterday. Ignore the cameras. Ignore the hall. And remember, no matter what happens, just keep going.'

The hall had been filling with the sound of footsteps and voices, but now it finally fell silent as Mrs Fitzgerald's voice began to ring out. I heard the words, 'Welcome' and 'remembering and honouring our dead' and 'our Year Fours in Purple Class!'

'Leo?' whispered Sangeeta. 'Are we doing it?'

'Yeah,' whispered Drew. 'Do you still want me to make the signals?'

'I don't know,' I whispered back. 'I don't know any more.'

Before I could say anything else, the stage curtains swished aside, and the action began.

Off went the explosion sounds, and the giant paper waves on the stage began to move and roll, signalling us all to dive and duck and run as though we were the real soldiers of Dunkirk. Then with a bang, we all froze to hear Gary's story, and then Kerry's, and then Toby's, and on and on and on, until, finally, it was time for Leo's!

Shouting out at the top of my voice, so that everyone could hear me, I yelled the words, 'I am Leo Kai Lim! I'm from Singapore, and I flew in the RAF. I was given the Distinguished Flying Cross for helping Britain!'

When I finished, I looked out and tried to see Mum and Dad and Bo, but the lights were too bright and I couldn't see anything but a bobbing ocean of dark heads.

Next it was Sangeeta's turn. She jumped into position in her black jacket and cap, and cried out, 'I'm

Noor Inayat Khan! I was an Indian princess who became a British spy! I died for my country because I refused to tell the enemy everything I knew.' Then, even though she was meant to finish there, Sangeeta quickly added, 'And I'm better than James Bond!'

There was laughter from the audience, as the light on Sangeeta moved over to Oscar.

Before we knew it, the assembly was coming to an end, and it was time for everyone to line up, and shout out the name of the person they were honouring one last time.

Sangeeta came and stood next to me at the very end of the line, her arms shaking so much they were making me shake too.

'Leo? Are we doing it?' she whispered urgently, as the names got closer and closer and closer to us.

I shut my eyes and tried to imagine what the real Leo would do. Right away, I knew the answer.

Kerry stepped forwards. 'Henry Worthington, my great-grand-uncle,' she cried out, then stepped back into line.

'Captain Harris, my mum's grandad,' shouted Tanya, quickly hopping forwards and then back again.

'Julia Miles, who broke codes at Bletchley,' yelled Nancy.

'My great-grand aunt, Louisa Potter, who made ammunitions,' declared Lindsey, loudly.

Next it was my turn. I stepped forwards.

'Leo Kai Lim!' I shouted out. But instead of stepping back like I was supposed to, I stayed exactly where I was, and pulled off my costume and school jumper and shirt to reveal the green teluk belanga shirt that I always wore when guests came to my house. 'His name is in Rochester Cathedral, and he was from Singapore – just like me. And he was the first person from my country to go and fight in the RAF with the Allied forces in World War Two. He died trying to help this country too – I think. I don't know because his history is missing, even though it shouldn't be. But he is buried near here, and everyone should know about him and go and visit him and respect him.'

Finishing my last line, I stepped back. Out of the corner of my eye, I saw Drew flapping his arms like a bird and crying out 'Ca-caw!' to give Olivia the signal.

It was Sangeeta's turn. She was the last in line and, giving me a grin, she stepped forwards.

'Noor Inayat Khan AND Assa Singh AND R Singh!' she cried out. Then, without a single second's hesitation, she pulled off her spy jacket and her school jumper and shirt to reveal a bright green Indian top covered in sequins and shining stones. Ignoring the gasps, she continued, 'And all the men and women of India who fought across the world and helped planes fly and made uniforms and machines in Indian factories, and who aren't in our history books even though they should be!'

Olivia had run up the stairs to join us and now stood squeezed up next to us. The moment Sangeeta finished, she shouted out, 'Richard "Kojo" Morris. My great-grandfather. Who was in the RAF like Leo. I'm proud to be his great-granddaughter, because he was a hero, and he was all the colours I am too!'

I watched, waiting for her to pull off her school jumper and show everyone a top from Ghana like we'd planned. But instead, she pulled down the long white socks she always wore.

The whole hall fell silent as everyone on stage broke ranks to try and see what was happening.

'Look at her legs!' whispered Nancy, her words

tumbling into all our ears.

Olivia smiled, as the whole hall did exactly that. Because in the place of where her shining white socks had been, were large patches of dark skin mixed in with large patches of white skin, making her legs look like rolled up black-and-white maps of the world.

THE FINAL ROAR

No one knew what to say or do.

That included the teachers too. Mr Scott's mouth had fallen so wide open his beard looked like it was growing a hole in the middle of it, and Mrs Fitzgerald's glasses had fallen off the end of her nose. Sangeeta was looking at Olivia's legs and knees so hard her head was almost upside down, and I was staring at Olivia's mum and dad to see if they were as shocked as everyone else was. But they were smiling and crying and hugging each other, as if they were watching the winner of *The X-Factor* being announced.

Then across the silence, Drew cried out, 'WOOOOOAH! THAT'S SO COOL!'

As if everyone had been waiting for those exact

words, a roar of applause broke out across the hall, deafening us all.

'Well, well,' said Mrs Fitzgerald, hurrying onto the stage. 'What a brilliant – and eye-opening – assembly! Take a bow, children! Take a bow!'

The audience clapped and whooped even louder and Olivia's mum and dad even stood up, which made everyone else stand up too. After what felt like for ever, the applause started to quiet down, and we all gave a final, proud bow before leaving the stage.

'That was awesome!' whispered Oscar, after Olivia ran back to join her class, and we had all got back to our classroom. 'I'm really glad I voted for your idea.'

'Me too,' said Kerry.

'Me three,' said Laura.

'Really?' I asked. 'You all voted for me? But I thought everyone voted for Toby.'

'No way,' said Evelyn. 'He's horrible. I think only the people who are really scared of him voted for him. Your idea was definitely the best. And besides, you're not mean like he is.'

I stared at everyone standing around me and Sangeeta, with their faces covered in war marks and with leaves popping out of their helmets and wished I was brave enough to hug all of them. I didn't know I had so many secret friends. I promised myself right away that I would be their friends right back – and that I would speak to them more, instead of thinking they didn't like me and Sangeeta because we were different to them. From the back corner of the room, I could see Toby staring at us angrily.

'Right, kids!' shouted Mr Scott, clapping his hands loudly as he made his way to the front of the room. 'Unexpected ending aside,' he said, looking at me and Sangeeta pointedly but with a smile too, 'you all did an EXCELLENT job! And I have it on good authority that even if we don't qualify or win this competition, the *Real Kidz Rule* team will be featuring our school on the show tonight. So give yourselves a massive round of applause!'

So we did, giving ourselves a round of applause so long and loud, that it made all our hands and throats happy and sore.

For the rest of the day in class, and in the playground too, everyone in school kept running up to me and Sangeeta and Olivia. They wanted to know where they could buy a top like Sangeeta's and if they could see Olivia's legs up close and ask me if I was named after the real Leo. I told them I probably wasn't, but I don't think anyone believed me. By the end of the day, everyone was sure I was secretly the real Leo's long-lost great-grandson; Sangeeta had begun planning a business to sell Indian clothes to everyone; and Olivia's legs had become so famous that Drew suggested she get them insured.

'I'm glad my grand-aunt rang from Jamaica last week to answer all my questions,' said Olivia, as we made our way to the school gates at home-time. 'She remembered my great-grandad had vitiligo on his hands, from when he played with her when she was a kid. She said she thought the sun had got trapped inside his skin and that he had superpowers because of it. Hearing that made me want to not hide mine any more.'

'That's so cool!' said Drew. 'Wish I could have the viti-thing too. I'd make so much money charging everyone to see it, it would be unreal!'

'Hey,' said Nancy. 'I just had a thought! What if they met – I mean, Leo and Noor and Mr Morris? And what if they were best friends too? They were all here in England during the war, so they might have been, you know!'

We all stopped walking as if an invisible giant boulder had suddenly crashed down in front of us.

'Woah!' cried out Drew, clasping the sides of his head. 'My brain can't handle it!'

We all stayed silent, and even after we started walking again, I knew we were wondering if Nancy's giant thought might have been a reality, and if friendships of the past had silently led to our own in some way.

After school that day, and all through the weekend, Mum and Dad and Bo and Jingyi and me watched and re-watched the *Real Kidz Rule* Remembrance Day Special again and again and again. In fact, I think we watched it at least forty times. Because even though Catherine's confession had come too late for us to win the competition, our assembly and the board had been so special, that the show had decided to do a whole ten minutes on just our class. Which meant Sangeeta's interview got shown, and while she was talking the real Leo's newspaper article and Olivia's great-grandad's church service memorial and pictures of Assam Singh and Noor Inayat Khan all took it in turns to fill up the screen.

And the more times I watched it, the more I realised: I had done it. I had kept my promise to the real Leo and had made him famous, which had made Olivia's story and Sangeeta's story and the stories of everyone in our whole class famous too. I could never have done of it without him. Leo being brave had made me become brave too.

* * *

Once the weekend was over, and the whole school had celebrated the fact that we had made it onto the show, even though we hadn't won, everything slowly started to go back to normal. But not quite the same normal it was before.

Toby and Catherine stopped being friends, and because he was alone and no one liked him for being a coward and not confessing, he went quiet and, after a while, left me alone.

Mr Scott went back to teaching us about World War Two – only now he was teaching us about countries and soldiers that weren't in our textbooks as well as the ones that were. Our parents all helped. My mum and dad worked with Mr Scott to put together a whole lesson about how Churchill had tried to save Singapore from being taken over. Sangeeta's mum and dad donated lots of books to the library about the Indian armies who had fought *and* some about women who had helped win the war too. And Olivia's dad had convinced her teacher and Mr Scott to do a special half-day lesson for both our classes about all the millions of soldiers who had come from lots of parts of Africa to help Europe win the war, but who hadn't been paid properly or given a medal or even a gravestone with their name on it for what they did.

I didn't expect anything else to happen after that, because all those things were like invisible gifts I had never even wished for. But then, just before the Christmas holidays, three whole weeks after we had finished studying World War Two, Mr Scott suddenly thumped his hands on his desk, and told us that our final lesson of the day was cancelled.

'Do you think it's something to do with the school Christmas tree?' asked Nancy, shoving things quickly into her tray. 'We're the only class in school who's *never* been allowed to help decorate it.'

I shrugged as we followed Mr Scott down to the assembly hall. Inside, I was surprised to see all of Olivia's class, sitting there on the floor, noisily waiting for something to happen.

'What's this for?' asked Drew nervously. 'Why are we having an assembly now? Do you think we're in trouble?'

'Children, quiet, please,' said Mrs Fitzgerald, as she came gliding into the hall, followed by two people I don't think any of us had expected to ever see again.

'Hey, look! Mr Young!' shouted Steve.

'And that lady from the RAF museum!' whispered Evelyn, so loudly that everyone, including Mrs Fletcher from the museum, could hear.

Clapping her hands three times to make us go silent, Mrs Fitzgerald said, 'Good afternoon, everyone,' in her assembly-voice.

'GOOD AFTERNOON, MISS-US FITZ-GERALD!' we replied.

'Now, hands up, who here remembers Mr Young from Rochester Cathedral?' asked Mrs Fitzgerald.

Every single one of us put our hands up, including Mr Scott.

'And Mrs Fletcher from the RAF museum?' continued Mrs Fitzgerald.

All our hands stayed up.

'Good, hands down,' ordered Mrs Fitzgerald. 'Now, both Mr Young and Mrs Fletcher have very kindly come to our school, to tell us something quite exciting, and I want you all to listen extra carefully. Over to you . . .'

Mrs Fitzgerald glided to the side of the hall, as Mrs Fletcher took her place. 'Hello, everyone! So lovely to see you all again.'

Both our classes waited, silent and unmoving. I could feel that Sangeeta was already bursting to ask at least twelve questions.

'Now, I think you've all heard how Leo, Sangeeta and Olivia came to look for help with something at the museum after your class visit.'

Everyone looked over their shoulders at us.

'Well, following that rather . . . *unconventional* visit,' Mrs Fletcher went on with a small smile at me, 'Mr Young and I joined forces, and began to research the stories of the soldiers they were each searching for.'

I stared at the two of them – Mrs Fletcher and Mr Young – wondering if what I was hearing could be real, and whether the real Leo was making more things happen than I could ever have imagined or hoped for.

'And,' continued Mrs Fletcher. 'Thanks to the help of the British embassies in Singapore, Ghana, and India, we have some information to gift you. Leo, would you like to come up first, please?'

Nancy and Sangeeta and Drew's hands pushed and poked my arms and legs to make me move. Feeling like I was in a strange dream, I got up, and made my way over to Mr Young and Mrs Fletcher.

'Leo, it is my deep honour to inform you that Leo Kai Lim DFC was an incredible, record-beating pilot, who was honoured with the Distinguished Flying Cross after shooting down *forty-two* enemy planes over France and Italy,' said Mrs Fletcher.

'Forty-two?' I gasped, my eyebrows rising so high that they hurt my head.

'At least!' whispered Mr Young.

'Sadly,' went on Mrs Fletcher, 'he later died in a prisoner-of-war camp after sustaining heavy injuries from his last mission.'

I clutched my hands together to stop them from shaking, still wondering how Leo's name had ended up in Rochester Cathedral.

As if reading my exact thoughts, Mr Young stepped in and explained, 'His body now rests in Singapore at the Commonwealth War Cemetery, but what he did for this country was so magnificent that the RAF felt he should be honoured here too. At one of the country's oldest cathedrals. Here . . .'

Mr Young handed me a folder he was carrying. It was navy blue and had a RAF symbol in the corner, and was super-light.

'Look inside,' he said.

I opened the folder. Inside was a photocopy of a form, filled in with lots of handwritten answers in Mandarin, and a picture of the real Leo – the same one that had been in his newspaper article. Paperclipped to it was a long strip of white paper, dotted with raised white dots that felt like tiny hills.

'What you have there, Leo, is a copy of his original application form to join the RAF,' explained Mrs Fletcher. 'Retrieved from RAF archives.' She pointed to the dotted piece of paper. 'And *this* is the last telegram he sent by morse code, to his best friend – a Mr Huang Kai Lim of Singapore district eleven. Who, records obtained by your Aunty Su prove, was your great-grandfather.'

I stared down at the real Leo's real handwriting, and the invisible last message he had sent to my great-grandad. 'So, I *am* named after the real Leo?' I asked.

I could feel every blood cell in my body rushing through me and everything in front of my eyes becoming blurred. I couldn't help wishing that my great-grandfather was alive so that he could tell me himself.

Mr Young smiled. 'It certainly seems possible. Once you decode what his last telegram says, you might know for sure!' Giving my shoulder a squeeze, which instantly made drops of water fall from my eyes, Mr Young stood back up straight again.

'Next, Olivia – please come and join us,' said Mrs Fletcher, as she took the other file from Mr Young's arms and handed it to Olivia. 'Richard "Kojo" Morris, was *also* an extraordinary pilot. He travelled from

Ghana to Sierra Leone, where he trained with the RAF to fly the Hurricane. He was so brilliant and so quick, that he was one of the few pilots brought from the African continent to fight on European soil. He went on to defend London against enemy fire, but sadly, was later shot down somewhere over Nazi Germany. I am sorry to say that his body was never recovered. But he was an extraordinary man – and I know he would have been very proud to have you as his great-granddaughter. As you have already found out, he had vitiligo. Which is why, according to his files, he was nicknamed Officer Patches.'

Through her giant tears, Olivia gave a giggle, and looked over at me with the biggest smile I had ever seen on her face.

'And, last but not least, Sangeeta.'

Sangeeta stepped forwards, hungry to hear the story that was waiting for her.

But Mrs Fletcher didn't give her a folder, because Mr Young didn't have any left.

'I'm sorry, Sangeeta – we haven't been able to locate the R Singh from the cathedral – but we are looking, I promise,' said Ms Fletcher, as Mr Young gave a nod.

'We all are. But we do have something very special that we want to tell you about.'

Mr Young held out a small white stone statue, sitting in the palms of his hands. It was a statue of what looked like an Indian temple, standing on a hill.

'What Mr Young has there is a miniature replica of the Chattri Memorial, which is here in the UK, in Brighton,' explained Ms Fletcher. 'It's where some of the Sikh and Hindu soldiers who fought in the *First* World War, and who died whilst being treated for their injuries in the hospitals here, are remembered. Some of them had sons and daughters in India, who would have gone on to fight in the *Second* World War.'

Sangeeta took the temple in her hands, and looked at it as if it was the world's largest and rarest diamond.

'How wonderful,' said Mrs Fitzgerald. 'Year Four, what do you think about making the Chattri Memorial your next class trip?'

Everyone agreed, even Mr Scott and Mrs Whittaker, and cheered and whooped and clapped right up until the assembly came to an end.

That night was one of the best nights I ever had in my whole life. Because as soon as I got home, Mum and

Dad and Bo and even Jingyi, helped me to find out what the real Leo's last message to my great-grandad had been, using a special website that helped us decode Morse code. Once we had found out what it said, we phoned Aunty Su to tell her all about it.

But instead, she ended up telling us about a box of letters she had found in an old suitcase which had once belonged to my grandad. Some of the letters had been written by my great-grandad to my great-grandmother, and spoke of a brave friend who had once saved his life when they were children and who had gone on to become his best friend. A best friend by the name of Leo, who had one day left to fight a great war, and had never come back. Which meant that Leo wasn't just a hero because he went to war. He was a hero who had helped make my family become the family it is today, by saving my great-grandfather's life.

And that's not all. In fact, I think it's only the beginning.

You see, now that I know about the real Leo, and Richard, and Noor and Assa too, I want everyone in the whole world to know about them. So do Olivia and Sangeeta and our parents and Bo and Jules. That's why we're all on a new mission now: to find out about all the other brave heroes whose names shouldn't be hidden away on old cathedral walls or in dusty folders, but who should be alive in all our school books and display boards and films and assemblies too. Ms Fletcher and Mr Young have said they're going to help us, and Ben and Lily and Annie and Lenny from the *Real Kidz Rule* show have all said they want to help too. Because after we were on the programme, it turned out lots of kids like me and Sangeeta and Olivia wanted help finding the heroes *they* might be related to as well.

Now every time I think about the other Leo, I can't help wondering about *all* the names and stories and histories that are waiting to be heard. Especially from places like Singapore and India and Ghana – the countries that me and Sangeeta and Olivia are lucky enough to belong to – as well as Britain. Mum and Dad feel the same and have said it's about time the whole family went to Singapore for a visit, which is exactly what we're going to do this summer! It will be our first trip since I was almost as small and as noisy as Jingyi.

My Aunt Su has promised that she's going to take me to visit the other Leo's resting place so that I can say thank you to him properly. She's still searching for the descendants from his family who survived the war, so that maybe, one day, I can meet them too. If I ever do, I'm going to invite them to come and visit me, so I can take them to say hello to their Leo in the cathedral. After all, people like him, who were as brave as lions and whose secret roars live on through every person they helped save, deserve to be known about and thanked for ever and ever and ever.

And, for as long as *I* can live and roar, I'm going to go on keeping my promise to him, to make sure none of us ever forget.

THEY GAVE THEIR LIVES
FOR COUNTRY
NOT FOR FAME
FOR LIBERTY
NOT THEIR NAME

– Inscription at the gates of Rochester Cathedral

ACTING AGAINST PREJUDICE AND RACISM

WHAT IS PREJUDICE?

Prejudice is treating someone (or a group of people) differently and unfairly simply because of their perceived differences. For example, treating someone differently because of:

- their skin colour (racism)
- where they come from (xenophobia)
- how they speak
- their religious belief/faith (religious intolerance)
- their culture
- what they wear
- their sex (sexism)

Leo and Sangeeta both learn a lot about the impacts of historical racism when they set out to uncover the stories of people of the past. Leo sadly also experiences racist bullying. Racism is an awful thing to experience – but knowing how to identify racism and take action *against* it is one of the bravest, most lion-like things you can do.

Sometimes it is obvious when someone is being racist. They may call someone names or cause physical hurt – just like Toby does to Leo. But at other times it can be almost invisible. Like when a person is not given a job or is paid less than someone else because of the colour of their skin.

Racism in all its forms is unacceptable, which is why it is up to all of us to help stop it.

Discussion point 1: If you saw someone being bullied or treated unequally because of their skin colour, what three actions might you take to stop it?

Discussion point 2: In this story, Olivia has vitiligo – which means that her skin is very special and is made up of different colours. Those colours are determined by something called 'melanin'. We all have melanin. Melanin affects our skin, hair and eye colour. What do you think we can do to celebrate people with different melanin content to ours?

If you, or someone you know, is being targeted by racist hate, talk to a parent, guardian or teacher. You can also call Stop Hate UK on 0800 138 1625 or visit www.stophateuk.org with an adult.

RACISM DURING WORLD WAR TWO

One of the ways we can help to combat racism in the present is by learning about racism in our shared histories. Sometimes these facts can be hard to read about or make us feel upset, so you may like to discuss them with a parent, guardian or teacher.

DID YOU KNOW?

At least 1.5 million soldiers from the European-ruled colonies of Africa fought in the Second World War. And the British Indian Army comprised over 2.5 million men by 1945.

But:

- they were paid up to three times *less* than white soldiers, despite having undertaken the same dangerous missions and even extra duties

- many were physically harmed by superiors and

treated as servants whilst in service, despite the army having outlawed such practices

- the number of deaths of African soldiers still remains unknown, whilst it is estimated that at least 80,000 soldiers from India were killed. They were rarely honoured with gravestones, despite records of names being available.* Their families were often not notified of their deaths

- many soldiers who survived weren't able to work when they went back to their homes, but never received the support or pensions they had been promised by their British and French colonial rulers

- in 2009, the BBC uncovered documents which revealed that West African soldiers were deliberately removed from the Free French Forces before they advanced into Paris. This was done so that the liberation would be seen to be a 'whites only' victory

*In 2020, the War Graves Commission apologised for the racism that led to Black and Asian soldiers not being memorialised in the same way as their white comrades.

THE S/HEROES OF THIS STORY

Some of the s/heroes that Leo, Sangeeta and Olivia discover
and learn about, are based on real-life men and women of
World War Two. They include . . .

TAN KAY HAI

The Straits Times © Singapore Press Holdings Limited

Born: 1914, Singapore

Died: 1991, aged 71, Singapore

What he did

After completing his training with the RAF in Singapore, Tan flew combat missions in North Africa and Italy, and undertook one of the most dangerous missions given to RAF pilots: to fly at low altitudes so that enemy aircraft would fire at his plane and give away their positions to military planners. But Tan went beyond the call of duty and, instead of flying away from the gunfire, would turn and attack!

In 1944, Tan was shot down and taken to a prisoner-of-war (POW) camp. He escaped in a daring jump from a transporter train and survived three days in the forests before being rescued by US troops. He went back to flying new missions until VE Day on 8th May 1945.

His legacy

Tan flew and survived 190 RAF missions. He was the first person from the British-controlled Straits settlements of Signapore, Penang and Malacca to be awarded the RAF's Distinguished Flying Cross (DFC) for courage. After the war, he gained a first-class degree at the London School of Economics, and returned to Singapore where he helped set up the Malayan Auxiliary Air Force and trained new pilots. He died many years later, with a bullet still lodged in his big toe.

The fictional Leo Kai Lim of this story is partly inspired by the accomplishments of hero Tan Kay Hai.

ELIZABETH CHOY

Courtesy of the National Archives of Singapore

Born: 1910, Malaysia
Died: 2006, aged 95, Singapore

What she did

During the Japanese invasion of Malaya in 1941, Elizabeth (nickname 'Gunner Choy'), served in the women's auxiliary arm of the Singapore Volunteer Corps, and also worked as a volunteer nurse. After the fall of Singapore in 1942, she and her husband started a regular ambulance service for British civilian internees.

But that's not all! Elizabeth also helped hundreds of prisoners of war receive cash, radio parts, fresh clothing, medicine and letters. When an informant told the Japanese military police of their secret works, Elizabeth and her husband were imprisoned and tortured, but luckily, both survived.

Her legacy

After the war, Elizabeth travelled to Britain and was awarded the Girl Guides' highest honour (the Bronze Cross), the Order of the Star of Sarawak and was made an Officer of the Order of the British Empire (OBE). She was also invited to a private audience with Queen Elizabeth.

NOOR INAYAT KHAN

Courtesy of Shrabani Basu

Born: 1914, Russia
Died: 1944, aged 30, Dachau

What she did

Despite being a pacifist, Noor joined the Women's Auxiliary Air Force in 1940 and became an Aircraftswoman. Renowned for her speed and accuracy in wireless communications, she was recruited as a British spy under the codename 'Madeleine' and became the first female wireless operator to be sent from the UK into occupied France to aid the resistance.

Even though her missions were exceptionally dangerous, she refused to abandon her post, and single-handedly ran a cell of spies across Paris. She was later betrayed and captured, and was killed at Dachau concentration camp.

Her legacy
After her death, Noor was awarded the George Cross (Britain's highest award for gallantry in the face of an enemy) and, in 2020, became the first woman of South Asian descent to be given a blue plaque in honour of her life in London. A statue of Noor can also now be found at Gordon Square in London, thanks to the incredible works of the Noor Inayat Khan Memorial Trust.

MANTA AND ASSA SINGH

Postcard of Muslin soldiers from the Punjab region of India, at the Pavilion Military Hospital in Brighton, released by the Brighton Corporation c.1915. Photograph by A M Fry.

Born: 1870, India and 1909, India

Died: 1915, Brighton and 2003, UK

What they did

Manta and Assa Singh are a father and son duo of heroes who each fought in a different world war.

Manta Singh

In 1915, Manta became a Subedar of the 15th Ludhiana Sikhs and was sent to fight in the Battle of Neuve Chapelle in France. In the middle of this battle, under heavy gunfire,

Manta rescued his comrade Captain George Henderson, who had been injured, and carried him to safety. As he did so, Manta was shot in the leg and severely wounded. He later died of his injuries in a hospital in Brighton (UK) and became one of the first Indian soldiers to be cremated on the South Downs, where the Chattri memorial now stands.

Assa Singh

Manta's son, Assa, went on to join the same British Indian Army regiment as his father. He became best friends with Captain Henderson's son Robert, and they fought together in France, Italy and North Africa during the Second World War. Both Assa and Robert survived the war, and remained best friends until their deaths.

In the story, Sangeeta finds out about the Chattri memorial. This is a real place where Manta Singh's name can be found.

JOHN HENRY CLAVELL SMYTHE

© Imperial War Museum

Born: 1915, Sierra Leone
Died: 1996, UK

What he did

John was one of the first West Africans to serve in the Royal Air Force (RAF) during the Second World War. Within six months of joining, he was promoted and sent to Britain on the first sailing of the troopship HMT *Empire Windrush*. He carried out twenty-six successful bombing missions and earned a reputation for being lucky for always returning home, even when his plane had been hit by enemy fire.

In 1943, however, he was shot down during a bombing mission over Nazi Germany and imprisoned in a prisoner-of-war (POW) camp for two years.

His legacy

After his liberation in 1945, John went on an official visit to the United States, where he met President John F. Kennedy. He later became the senior Colonial Office official responsible for West Indian communities arriving in England on the *Empire Windrush*, was appointed a Member of the Order of the British Empire (MBE) and served as Attorney General of Sierra Leone.

ADELAIDE HALL

WOUNDED SOLDIERS ENTERTAINED BY THE ROTARY CLUB

The soldiers watch a dancing display Inset: Adelaide Hall at the microphone.

Courtesy of *Leamington Courier*

Born: 1901, USA
Died: 1993, UK

What she did

Adelaide was a jazz singer who travelled to the UK for national tours before war broke out in 1939. Despite being offered a chance to go back to America, she stayed in London, risking her life during the Blitz to help people keep their spirits up through music. In 1940, there was a German air attack during her performance at the Lewisham

Hippodrome. Despite bombs and multiple fires trapping everyone inside, she kept people calm by singing songs until help could reach them.

Her legacy

Throughout the war, Adelaide's songs could be heard live on BBC radio stations. She also sang for the British Armed Forces and was one of the first entertainers in the world to join troops entering Germany. In 2003, she made it into the *Guinness World Records* book as the world's most enduring recording artist. In 2021, she was honoured by the Black Plaque Project. Her plaque can be found at the Abbey Road Studios in London, where she recorded some of her most famous songs.

HAZEL HILL

Indian Air Force squadron equipped with Hurricane fighters on the North West Frontier in November 1944. Image courtesy of the National Army Museum, London.

Born: 1920, UK
Died: 2010, UK

What she did

Hazel was just thirteen years old when her father asked her to help him calculate how many guns the new generation of Spitfires and Hurricanes would need to bring down an enemy plane. As well as being dyslexic, Hazel was a brilliant mathematician, and she and her father spent many nights calculating and adjusting theories at their kitchen table. They concluded that the experts had got their numbers wrong and went on to convince the designers and engineers to make crucial changes to aircraft guns. Thanks to those changes, the RAF went on to win the Battle of Britain six years later.

Her legacy

After finishing school, Hazel went on to study medicine and then joined the Royal Army Medical Corps. At the end of the war, she became a doctor. She died without receiving any formal recognition for her contributions to the Second World War.

THE HIDDEN WOMEN
OF WORLD WAR TWO

Indian women labourers, engaged in airfield construction work on an RAF base in Bengal, 1944. © Imperial War Museum.

Men have more often been celebrated for their contributions to the world wars than women – particularly women 'of colour', whose efforts often went undocumented.

For example, we know that in the UK, 80,000 women joined the Women's Land Army, and over 640,000 women joined the armed forces, including the Women's Royal Naval Service and the Women's Auxiliary Air and Territorial Services. Many more thousands of women flew unarmed aircrafts, drove ambulances, served as nurses and worked behind enemy lines as part of the European resistance. The true figures for these roles remain unknown.

In the USA, at least 640,000 women also joined the war effort, and in France, it is estimated that at least twenty percent of all resistance fighters were women. The true figures remain unknown.

Across India, China, Russia, Eastern Asia and countries across the continent of Africa, millions of women:

- worked in factories producing munitions and uniforms, building ships and aeroplanes

- took on crucial roles as air-raid wardens and fire and evacuation officers

- drove fire engines and trains

- lent their mathematical and navigation skills to official military units

- acted as secret message carriers

Many never received recognition, compensation or awards for their efforts. All deserve the world's love, respect and eternal gratitude.

BREAKING THE CODE

In this story, uncovering mysteries leads to Leo being given a Morse code message – one sent to his great-grandfather by the World War Two hero Leo Kai Lim. To find out what this message was, head to the beginning of each chapter, and use the Morse code alphabet below to decipher the letters and words.

DID YOU KNOW?

Morse code is a rhythm-based code. A short beat (the dot) is called 'dit'. The long beat (the dash) is called 'dah' and is three times as long as the dit. A pause is the same length as a dit. Try tapping out your name in Morse code and see if you can 'feel' the rhythm.

A	·—	B	—···	C	—·—·	D	—··
E	·	F	··—·	G	——·	H	····
I	··	J	·———	K	—·—	L	·—··
M	——	N	—·	O	———	P	·——·
Q	——·—	R	·—·	S	···	T	—
U	··—	V	···—	W	·——	X	—··—
Y	—·——	Z	——··	0	—————	1	·————
2	··———	3	···——	4	····—	5	·····
6	—····	7	——···	8	———··	9	————·
·	·—·—·—						

WHO'S THE LION
OF YOUR WORLD?

No matter who we are, every single one of us will be sure to know a real-life someone who was – or is – incredibly brave. They might be someone from long ago, buried deep in our family histories. Or someone you know right now, who you think deserves roaring about.

Here are three questions about the lions of your world, so we can all learn about them . . .

1. What is the name of your lion?

2. What did they do to make you proud of them?

3. Describe in three words how they make you feel.

(If you don't have a lion in your world just yet, don't worry! You are bound to come across one soon. In which case, come back to this page later, once you've done some digging like Leo!)

THE FACES OF S/HEROES PAST

Millions of Black and Asian men and women contributed to the efforts of World War Two. Sadly, many died without their faces or names ever being known by the wider world. Here are just some of their names and faces . . .

Second Officer Kalyani Sen of the Women's Royal Indian Naval Service (WRINS), the first Indian service woman to visit the UK, with Chief Officer Margaret L Cooper, Deputy Director of WRINS, 3rd June 1945. © Imperial War Museum.

A soldier of the 4th (Uganda) Battalion, The King's African Rifles, awaits inspection in front of his hand-made camp, 1945. Image courtesy of the National Army Museum, London.

An Indian infantry section of the 2nd Battalion, 7th Rajput Regiment, heading to the Arakan front, Burma, 1944. © Imperial War Museum.

A Sikh soldier receiving a garland of flowers form a nurse. c.1946. Image courtesy of the National Army Museum, London.

Members of the West Indies Auxiliary Territorial Service, c.1943. Image courtesy of the National Army Museum, London.

Women of the West Indies Auxiliary Territorial Service, c.1944. Image courtesy of the National Army Museum, London.

Admiral Lord Louis Mountbatten with Force 136 leaders, Singapore, 1946. Force 136 worked in collaboration with the Malayan Peoples' Anti-Japanese Army (MPAJA) to resist Japanese occupation in the Far East in World War Two. Image courtesy of the National Army Museum, London.

Field Marshal Sir Claude Auchinleck inspecting members of the Women's Auxiliary Corps, India, c.1947. Image courtesy of the National Army Museum, London.

A West Indian member of the Auxiliary Territorial Service, c.1943. Image courtesy of the National Army Museum, London..

A wounded British soldier being evacuated by Indian Army stretcher bearers, Burma, January 1944. Image courtesy of the National Army Museum, London.

Indian women training for Air Raid Precaution (ARP) duties in Bombay, India, 1942. © Imperial War Museum.

Private soldiers (sappers) Salmon, Lowe, Brown, Parker and Miller, all from Kingston, Jamaica, serving with the Royal Engineers in Clitheroe, Lancashire, c.1939–1945. © Imperial War Museum.

WAAF nursing orderlies set to fly on air-ambulance duties to France: Leading Aircraftwoman Myra Roberts, Corporal Lydia Alford and Leading Aircraftwoman Edna Birbeck, c.1943–1945. © Imperial War Museum.

Private Begum Pasha Shah in the Orderly Room of an RAF station in southern India, August 1943. Aged nineteen, she was 'The first Muhammedan [Muslim] girl to join the Women's Auxiliary Corps in India'. Speaking seven languages, she served as a clerk. © Illustrated London News/Mary Evans Picture Library

Tuskegee Airmen in Italy, World War II © Brettman Collection, Getty Images.

The Queen Mother on a visit to a rest camp for Indian ex-servicemen in Norfolk, 16th June 1945. © Popperfoto Collection, Getty Images.

WHAT'S IN A NAME?

In William Shakespeare's *Romeo and Juliet*, the character Juliet asks, 'What's in a name?'

For many people across the world, the answer would be, 'Quite a lot actually'. Especially as the names we are gifted at birth are often given to us for particular reasons or come with meanings attached, making each of us – as the holder of that name – incredibly special.

In this story, Leo's adventure all starts with a name – a name that is exactly the same as his, and which makes him realise just how special his name might be. So . . .

What's the history of *your* name?

What does it mean?

Who wanted you to have your name/chose it for you?

How do you feel every time someone calls out your name?

Do you know anyone famous who shares your name?

FROM A TO Z
THE ALLIED FORCES OF
WORLD WAR TWO

Sometimes it's easy to forget just how many countries were involved in the battles to win the Second World War, one of the biggest wars in history. The major countries listed below are those which were recognised for actively supporting the Allied forces. Many did so independently, many under orders of colonial rule. Either way, each harbours stories and names of heroes we may have yet to hear about. Maybe you could find out about some more of these stories!

Please note: This list does **not** include the names of countries whose leaders remained neutral, sided with the Axis powers or were invaded before their status could be declared.

Algeria
Australia
Bahrain
Belgium
Bangladesh (then 'British India')
Bolivia
Brazil
Cameroon (then

'French Equatorial Africa')
Caribbean Islands
Canada
Central African Republic (then 'French Equatorial Africa')
China

Colombia
Costa Rica
Cuba
Czechoslovakia
Dominican Republic
Ecuador
El Salvador
Ethiopia
Fiji

France
Gambia
Ghana (then the
Gold Coast)
Greece
Guatemala
Haiti
Honduras
India
Iran
Iraq
Kenya
Liberia
Luxemburg
Madagascar
Mali
Malawi (then
Nyasaland)
Malaysia (then
Malaya)
Malta
Mexico
Mongolia
Morocco

Myanmar (then
Burma)
Nepal
Netherlands
New Zealand
Nicaragua
Norway
Oman
Papa New Guinea
(then Papa and
New Guinea)
Pakistan (then
India)
Panama
Paraguay
Peru
Philippines
Poland
Russia (then the
Soviet Union)
Samoa
Singapore
South Africa
South Korea (then

Republic of Korea)
Sri Lanka (then
Ceylon)
Sudan
Trinidad & Tobago
(then the
Caribbean Islands)
Tunisia
Ukraine (then the
Soviet Union)
United Kingdom
Uruguay
USA
Uzbekistan (then
the Soviet Union)
Venezuela
Vietnam
Zambia (then
Northern
Rhodesia)
Zimbabwe (then
Southern
Rhodesia)

Do you know where all these countries are in the world? If not, there's a map on the next page which you can use to try and guess where they might be located. (TIP: Use a pencil.)

LION TRACKS: 1945 WORLD MAP*

GHANA

*This is what a map of the world looked like in 1945.
It looks a little different to one you'd see today!

This map shows the countries where Leo,
Sangeeta and Olivia found their s/heroes.
Where will you find yours?

AUTHOR'S NOTE

If you type 'Allies/soldiers of World War Two' into a search engine, chances are you will not see countries such as India, Indonesia, Singapore, Malaysia, Burma, Cameroon, Sri Lanka, the Central African Republic or even China listed. This is despite the fact that millions of hearts (over 15 million in China alone) from across these countries died in their efforts to help the official Allied forces (France, Great Britain, Russia and at a later stage, the USA) win the Second World War. Many did so unknown, uncounted, and even unnamed.

The exclusion of heroes 'of colour' from our wider histories and cultural narratives was always a source of bitter confusion to me as a child – just as it is to anyone whose ancestral legacies may have helped build the world we live in today. From the whitewashing of Cleopatra and the patron saint of England, St George, to non-white contributors to the history of art, science, fashion, politics, architecture, and culture being ignored by education curriculums at all levels – there is not just a mere lack of representation, but a glaring lack even of existence.

As a brown Muslim girl growing up in East London, it is no coincidence then that I was called names and told to 'go back home' more times than I can count. So much so that it became an expected part of life. And so much so that I became deeply embarrassed and ashamed of my ancestral, 'other' world. A world I could not defend to those who believed theirs mattered so much more than mine – and who were backed up by the 'facts' we were each taught at school.

That shame meant never listing the ability to speak, read and write in my mother tongue, Bengali, as a skill or achievement on my CV or job applications. At age eight, it meant secretly putting a clothes peg on my nose each night in the hopes it would straighten and become thin like the noses of my white friends at school. It also meant never wearing a traditional Indian outfit to school on non-uniform or school photo days, and even trying to hide when Mum came to pick me up wearing a salwar kameez that wasn't hidden by a big coat.

Fighting for the right to not be treated as an inferior human being because of race or a visibly religious faith is a daily reality – not a one-off happening. And it begins with that moment of self-awareness, often forced upon us at a young age, when something happens to make us realise that, for some unknown reason, the pigmentation of our beautiful skin, or the accent with which we speak, or the food, clothes, languages and different worlds we are of and from, are deemed 'different', 'exotic', and often inferior (except in the realm of travel documentaries and cookbooks).

How different might things have been if, for example, I and everyone around me had known that countries like India, inside which lay my mother's land, Bangladesh, helped forge one of the biggest 'voluntary' armies of both the First and Second World Wars?

Or if we were all aware that the reason why so many generations of Black, South and East Asian peoples forsook their staggeringly beautiful homelands to come and risk daily abuses, hostile cultures and even physical harm, was because they had been left impoverished by imperial and economic land grabs, politically enforced partitions (both geographical and race-based) and famines and droughts as a result of resources depleted by greedier nations, and weaponised wars? All of which led to the burning of ancestral records, the breaking up of families, lands and wealth, and the scattering, fleeing and deaths of millions trying to survive and end up on the 'right' side of imposed borders and poverty. This cruel, often ignored part of our histories is one of the reasons I refuse to use the word 'developing' when referring to countries beyond Europe: for that word ignores where the wealth and status of 'developed' nations came from in the first place.

The Second World War was a united effort, on a truly global scale, to bring an end to the very worst inhumanities born of racist political thinking. It remains a tragedy that despite this, the stories of men and women who contributed to that fight and who happened to be 'of colour' are not taught to us from a young age.

However, as the world awakens to the deep consequences of missing histories, long overdue, I hope more and more truths will continue to emerge. Not just from one group of peoples or one corner of the globe. But from all. Because only when those truths are confronted (no matter how painful), accepted, taught and honoured by everyone, will racism in all its forms finally be rooted out.

Here's hoping . . . And roaring.

* * *

A percentage of royalties received from this story will be going towards developments for a new scholarship programme for students of South and East Asian descent wishing to specialise in History at selected universities within the UK.

ACKNOWLEDGEMENTS

For families from countries colonised and/or ravaged by slavery in any form, oral stories of family heroes passed down from one generation to the next are really all we have. There are no ancestry.com or *Who Do You Think You Are?* teams capable of gifting us concrete evidence of the heroes contained within our DNA, so they live on, often as names without faces, to remind us of truths missing from the wider world.

In the forging of this particular story, there are many people and places which have led to its creation – not just in its actual writing, but from moments buried deep in the past too. So here it goes . . .

My first and foremost thanks goes to a man I was lucky enough to meet when he was 103, and I was barely ten: my maternal great-grandfather, my boro Nana, Mojid Ullah. It was thanks to your taking me on that unforgettable walk across the grounds of your beloved farmlands and mango groves in Bangladesh, and speaking to me like an equal about your life and past, that I realised 'history' went beyond mere pages in a book. That it was a living, breathing, precious thing, made up of voices and stories and happenings that existed beyond my school lessons and library shelves. You made a world I would never know come alive again for a single afternoon, and planted a hunger to know more that would eventually lead to this story. Every page of this is you.

Mum, thank you for landing in Newcastle all those decades ago, and being strong enough to battle the loneliness and painful slingshots thrown your way every day simply for being who you were. You have borne all the arrows of ignorance so beautifully and continue to do so with such grace that it bewilders me at times. Thank you for gifting Zak and me a path to take too when dealing with all of 'it'. And Zak, thank you for being my sounding board and keeping me watered and fed and laughing. Who and where would I be without you both? (Never answer that one!)

Silvia Molteni, Goddess Agent, thank you for battling away for my each and every story and creating new spaces for me to write in and for. Meeting you all those years ago, I could never have imagined that a fourth book – that *this* book – would have been a result of your never saying no to another madcap idea. Thank you for being one of the names in my world which gifts me perpetual hope and happiness.

Lena McCauley, Lioness Editor and fellow Audrey

Hepburn mega fan: first and foremost, thank you for not quitting and leaving Hachette and me, despite my no doubt pushing you to the brink of doing so! Once again, you have gently coaxed and waited for this story to be what it now is, and despite facing endless threats to our existences, have led us to the finishing line in one piece. Operation Broom Cupboard is forever in your debt, as am I. Thank you dear heart for getting absolutely where this story needed to go and why.

Pippa Curnick, Roarsome Illustrator Supreme (I could do this all day): I will never *ever* stop having a mini scream of utter joy in my head whenever I see your deeply epic cover for this book. It blows my mind anew every time my eyes fall on it. Thank you for every last touch of genius you have conjured up for this, our fourth book baby. And huge hugs to you Alison Padley for tweaking it all to perfection. You are both to blame if anyone ever catches me in public hugging the life out of my own book (weirdo)!

To Queen Genevieve for tightening up the story with your immense eagle-eyed copy-edits once more; Dominic Kingston, my forever maestro who helps keep me sane and joyous amidst all the dramas of life, and without whom I would be in a ditch of despair; Helen Hughes who fought so hard for this book to break the paper boundaries and include magical sheets of photo paper between the covers; James McParland (quiet wizard); Nazima Abdillahi (welcome to my worlds! And sorry!); Ruth Alltimes (Queen Bee); Becca Bryant (Step-in Saviour); Emily Thomas and all the Hachette family: thank you for your tireless support. You are the full package: deeds as well as words.

It may be strange to say thank you to a building, but in this case I must! Thank you, Rochester Cathedral, Kent (UK), for being the physical trigger which led to the creation of this story. Walking in through your doors over a decade ago to see the names of Bengal Sappers carved in stone filled me with a pride and joy I hadn't known I was looking for. It continues to do so, and always will. My eternal gratitude to Helen Bradshaw and Simon Lace for the chance to honour your sacred glory through Leo's story.

To Remona Aly, she of the village of Hoo (Whot?), whose friendship set my feet on the path to Rochester, its cathedral and those life-changing names, and who has never failed to lead me on new journeys of discovery: thank you for every atom that is you.

To the woman I met in The Story of King Sejong Exhibition Hall in Seoul, South Korea, and whose name (ironically and tragically) I cannot recall: thank you for gently enquiring where I came from as we stood beside an exhibit, and speaking to me of the legacy of Tan Kay Hai. Within a few sentences, you burst open my understanding of where heroes of the Second World War came from and who they could be, and led me to uncover a world of stories I didn't even know existed. This story would not have come to be without you. Wherever you are, I hope you go on always gently sparking truths.

My deep gratitude to Gayathri Gill of the National Archives of Singapore; Kong Yoke Mun of the Singapore Press Holdings; Shrabani Basu, lioness author, historian and founder of the Noor Inayat Khan Memorial Trust; Phil Hibble, wonderful editor of the *Leamington and Warwick Courier*; Andrew Bennett, Brighton and Hove archivist at The Keep; Lucinda Gosling of the Illustrated News Archive, Andrew Webb of the Imperial War Museum, Helen of the National Army Museum, and all at the Chattri Memorial Group, Wikimedia and Getty Images, for putting up with panicked emails about photos and copyrights and a million other hurdles I didn't know existed.

I also have to lay bare my unending thanks to Taylor Swift, for *Epiphany*: a song so aptly titled for the many epiphanies it gifted me. On a tough writing day, or in one of those many moments I just didn't know where to go with this story, the images conjured up of ancestors forgotten by the words of this one song, lit the way. In case you ever see this (unlikely, but this world is a strange and beautiful place), from my (tragically musically challenged) soul to yours: thank you.

Tan Kay Hai, Elizabeth Choy, Birendra Nath Mazumdar, Noor Inayat Khan, Manta and Assa Singh, Mahinder Singh Pujji, Jaston Khosa, John Henry Clavell Smythe, Karun Krishna Majumdar, Adelaide Hall . . . What can I say to those who will never see these words? How small it feels simply to type out 'Thank you'. But it's all I can gift really. And perhaps they grow heavier in weight when I add that it comes from all of 'us', the collective world. For leaving us your legacies and reminding us that there are so many more s/heroes waiting to be uncovered. I repeat your names both here and in coming years, in the hopes that every person who hears them will repeat and remember them too.

To all my beautiful nieces and nephews and godchildren (Kamilah, Zahir, Eshan, Inara, Rayyan, Tanni, Tanha and Luskhmi), and any child or adult fighting the everyday prodding reminders that the world has a long way to go yet: I hope this little offering helps you understand deeply that you are never alone. And that what went before is not an inevitable facet of our futures.

And last but never least, to the greatest preserver of every s/hero's story that ever was: to God. Thank you, dear possessor of 99 names, for helping me find pride (and the roar) in my own.

ONJALI Q. RAÚF

Onjali Q. Raúf is the founder of Making Herstory, an organisation which encourages men, women and children to work together to create a fairer and more equal world for women and girls everywhere; and O's Refugee Aid Team through which she delivers emergency aid and support for frontline refugee aid response teams in northern France and Greece. She can often be found with her head buried in a book at the local bookshop.

She is the author of *The Boy at the Back of the Class*, *The Star Outside My Window*, *The Day We Met The Queen* and *The Night Bus Hero*.